SOLUTIONS MANUAL

FINANCIAL ACCOUNTING

SOLUTIONS MANUAL

FINANCIAL ACCOUNTING

JAMIE PRATT

University of Washington

Prepared by

JAMES R. FREDERICKSON

HarperCollins*Publishers*

ISBN 0-673-17233-3

3 4 5 6-MAL-95 94 93 92 91

CONTENTS

TO THE INSTRUCTOR

This solutions manual is a teaching supplement of *Financial Accounting* by Jamie Pratt. Each text chapter (except Chapter 1) concludes with discussion questions, exercises, problems, and cases. This manual contains complete solutions to the exercises and problems and suggested answers to the cases. It is written to be used by students. Consequently, the solutions are self-explanatory, and answers to essay-type questions are geared toward a student's level of accounting knowledge. Further, care is taken to provide supporting calculations and/or explanations in those cases where the answer may not be obvious. Because Chapter 1 does not include exercises, problems, or cases, this manual begins with Chapter 2.

EXERCISES

The exercises illustrate a specific concept in a relatively simple manner. The exercises provide an initial test of a student's understanding of an accounting concept.

PROBLEMS

The problems generally are more complex than the exercises. They are designed to introduce some of the complexities faced by accountants and, in some cases, to integrate several accounting concepts into a single problem.

CASES

The cases are designed to provide real life examples of accounting issues, and often require students to exercise judgment in formulating an answer. The cases can be used as the basis for class discussion.

Suggested answers to the discussion questions are located in the *Instructor's Manual to Accompany Financial Accounting*. That manual also includes a **time and difficulty chart** for the exercises and problems. (Remember that the time estimates are averages and that on any given problem, a student may take longer than the indicated time because of mechanical error or misinterpretation of the information.) A **checklist of key figures** for the exercises, problems, and cases (when feasible) is also included in the instructor's manual. The checklist will aid students either in verifying answers or in discovering errors in their solutions.

Every effort has been made to make the solutions manual error free, including a panel of reviewers who worked all of the exercises and problems. However, should you find an error that escaped us, please send that information to Accounting Editor, Scott, Foresman/Little, Brown, 1900 East Lake Avenue, Glenview, IL 60025.

CHAPTER 2 The Four Financial Statements

E2–1

Transaction	Assets	=	Liabilities	+	Stockholders' Equity
(1)	+ 10,000				+10,000
(2)	(2,000)				
	+ 2,000				
(3)	+ 3,000		+3,000		
(4)	+ 4,000				+4,000
(5)	(4,500)				(4,500)
(6)	(500)				(500)

Note: Transactions (4), (5), and (6) are initially recorded in temporary accounts and are closed into stockholders' equity through the Retained Earnings account.

E2–2

	Assets			=	Liabilities	+	Stockholders' Equity	
Transaction	Cash	Accts Rec	Equipment	=	Notes Payable	+	Contributed Capital	Retained Earnings
(1)	+ 10,000						+ 10,000	
(2)	(2,000)		+ 2,000					
(3)	+ 3,000				+ 3,000			
(4)		+ 4,000						+ 4,000
(5)	(4,500)							(4,500)
(6)	(500)							(500)
TOTAL	6,000	4,000	2,000		3,000		10,000	(1,000)

Note: Transactions (4), (5), and (6) are initially recorded in temporary accounts and are closed into stockholders' equity through the Retained Earnings account.

E2–3

X Company
Income Statement
For the Year Ended________

Revenues	$4,000
Operating expenses	4,500
Net loss	$ 500

X Company
Statement of Retained Earnings
For the Year Ended ___________

Beginning retained earnings balance	$ 0
Less: Net loss	500
Dividends delivered	500
Ending retained earnings deficit	$1,000

X Company
Balance Sheet
[Date]

Assets		Liabilities & stockholders' equity	
Current assets			
Cash	$ 6,000	Notes payable	$ 3,000
Accounts receivable	4,000	Contributed capital	10,000
Total current assets	$10,000	Retained earnings deficit	1,000
Equipment	2,000	Total Liabilities &	
Total assets	$12,000	Stockholders' Equity	$12,000

X Company
Statement of Cash Flows
For the Year Ended ________

Cash flows from operating activities		
Cash Payments for Expenses		($4,500)
Cash flows from investing activities		
Purchase of equipment		(2,000)
Cash flows from financing activities		
Cash contributions from owners	$10,000	
Proceeds from bank loan	3,000	
Payment of cash dividend	(500)	
Net cash increase (decrease) from financing activities		12,500
Net increase (decrease) in cash balance		$ 6,000
Beginning cash balance		0
Ending cash balance		$ 6,000

E2–4

a. Balance sheet
b. Income statement
c. Balance sheet
d. Income statement
e. Balance sheet
f. Income statement
g. Balance sheet
h. Balance sheet
i. Balance sheet
j. Balance sheet
k. Income statement
l. Income statement
m. Balance sheet
n. Balance sheet
o. Balance sheet
p. Income statement
q. Balance sheet
r. Balance sheet

E2–5

	Ending Retained Earnings	=	Beginning Retained Earnings	+	Revenues	–	Expenses	–	Dividends
1988:	50[a]	=	0	+	550	–	X	–	10
							X = $490		
1989:	70[b]	=	50	+	X	–	525	–	30
					X = $575				
1990:	100	=	70	+	700	–	565	–	X
									X = $105

---
[a] 1988 ending Retained Earnings = 1989 beginning Retained Earnings.
[b] 1989 ending Retained Earnings = 1990 ending Retained Earnings.

E2–6

	Ending Cash Balance	=	Beginning Cash Balance	+	Net Cash from Operating Activities	+	Net Cash from Investing Activities	+	Net Cash from Financing Activities
1989:	10,000	=	0	+	2,000	+	X	+	14,000
							X = ($6,000)		
1990:	X	=	X	+	X	+	1,000	+	(4,000)
	X	=	10,000[a]	+	X	+	1,000	+	(4,000)
	3,000[b]	=	10,000	+	X	+	1,000	+	(4,000)
					X = ($4,000)				
1991:	9,000	=	3,000	+	3,000	+	(4,00)	+	X
									X = $7,000

---
[a] 1990 beginning cash balance = 1989 ending cash balance.
[b] 1990 ending cash balance = 1991 beginning cash balance.

E2–7

Tara & Sons
Statement of Cash Flows
For the Year Ended ________

Cash flows from operating activities		
Cash collections from services provided	$3,000	
Cash payments for expenses	(3,000)	
Net cash increase (decrease) from operating activities		$ 0
Cash flows from investing activities		
Purchase of machinery	(2,000)	
Net cash increase (decrease) from investing activities		(2,000)
Cash flows from financing activities		
Proceeds from owner contribution	5,000	
Payment of dividends	(2,000)	
Net cash increase (decrease) from financing activities		3,000
Increase (decrease) in cash balance		$1,000
Beginning cash balance		0
Ending cash balance		$1,000

E2–8

Transaction	Assets	=	Liabilities	+	Stockholders' Equity
(1)	+5,000				+5,000
(2)	+3,000				+5,000
	+2,000				
(3)	(3,000)		+3,000		(6,000)
(4)	+10,000		+8,000		
	(2,000)				
(5)	(2,000)				(2,000)

Tara & Sons
Income Statement
For the Year Ended ________

Revenues	$5,000
Expenses	6,000
Net loss	$1,000

Tara & Sons
Statement of Retained Earnings
For the Year Ended ________

Beginning retained earnings balance	$ 0
Less: Net loss	1,000
Dividends declared	2,000
Ending retained earnings deficit	$3,000

Tara & Sons
Balance Sheet
[date]

Assets		Liabilities & Stockholders' Equity	
Cash	$ 1,000	Accounts payable	$ 3,000
Accounts receivable	2,000	Long-term note payable	8,000
Property, plant & equipment	10,000	Contributed capital	5,000
		Retained earnings deficit	3,000
Total assets	$13,000	Total liabilities and stockholders' equity	$13,000

E2–9

Current liabilities are those obligations that will be settled through the use of current assets or the creation of new current liabilities. Current liabilities are generally considered to be liabilities that will be settled in the longer of one year or the company's operating cycle. Current assets are those assets that will be consumed or converted to cash in the longer of one year or the company's operating cycle. Consequently, comparing current assets to current liabilities provides an indication of a company's ability to meet its short-term debts. In this case, current assets were 2.89 and 2.14 times greater than current liabilities as of December 31, 1989 and December 31, 1990, respectively.

While comparing current assets to current liabilities provides a measure of a company's solvency, this measure is not perfect. A true test of a company's short-term solvency would be to compare the cash value of its current assets to the cash value of its current liabilities. For current liabilities, the book value is usually a good approximation of the cash value, since a company cannot, from a legal viewpoint, unilaterally change its debts. The situation is different for current assets though. The book value may or may not bear any relation to the cash value. Consequently, comparing current assets to current liabilities may not give an accurate measure of a company's solvency.

E2–10

	Method 1	**Method 2**	**Method 3**
Current ratio as of 12/31/90 ($23,500 ÷ $11,000)	2.14	2.14	2.14
Impact of method on current assets			
Cash	(4,000)	0	0
Accounts receivable	0	0	0
Inventory	4,000	4,000	4,000
Total impact on current assets	0	4,000	4,000
Impact of method on current liabilities			
Accounts payable	0	4,000	0
Total impact on current liabilities	0	4,000	0

Current ratio

Method 1
($23,500 + 0) ÷ ($11,000 + 0) 2.14

Method 2
($23,500 + $4,000) ÷ ($11,000 + $4,000) 1.83

Method 3
($23,500 + $4,000) ÷ ($11,000 + 0) 2.50

Method 1 would be acceptable to the company since the current ratio would exceed 2:1. However, using cash to purchase the inventory would virtually exhaust the company's cash balance which, in turn, might cause some solvency problems. Method 2 would not be acceptable to the company since the current ratio would drop below 2:1, thereby causing the company to violate its debt covenant. Method 3 would be acceptable to the company since the current ratio would exceed 2:1. This method should maximize the probability that the company would not violate its debt covenant. However, the company should consider the increased cost (i.e., interest) usually associated with a note payable. Overall, Method 3 appears to be the most feasible.

P2–1

Transaction	**Assets**	=	**Liabilities**	+	**Contributed Capital**	+	**Retained Earnings**
(1)	+1,000	=			+1,000		
(2)	+1,500	=	+1,500				
(3)	+300	=					
	(300)						
(4)	(200)	=					(200)
(5)	+500	=					+ 500
(6)		=	+100				(100)
(7)	(50)	=					(50)
	2,750	=	1,600	+	1,000	+	150

Note: Transactions (4), (5), (6), and (7) are initially recorded in temporary accounts and are closed into stockholders' equity through the Retained Earnings Account.

P2–2

	Accounts Affected	Assets	=	Liabilities	+	Stockholders' Equity
(1)	Cash	+1,000				
	Contributed Capital					+1,000
	Subtotal	1,000	=	0	+	1,000
(2)	Supplies Inventory	+ 150				
	Cash	(150)				
	Subtotal	1,000	=	0	+	0
(3)	Machinery	+ 1,500				
	Cash	(500)				
	Long-Term Note Payable			+ 1,000		
	Subtotal	2,000	=	1,000	+	0
(4)	Cash	(250)				
	Retained Earnings					(250)
	Subtotal	1,750	=	0	+	750
(5)	Accounts Receivable	+ 1,350				
	Retained Earnings					+ 1,350
	Subtotal	3,100	=	0	+	2,100
(6)	Cash	(1,100)				
	Marketable Securities	+ 1,100				
	Subtotal	3,100	=	0	+	0
(7)	Cash	+ 500				
	Accounts Receivable	(500)				
	Subtotal	3,100	=	0	+	0
(8)	Cash	+ 1,600				
	Marketable Securities	(1,100)				
	Retained Earnings					+ 500
	Subtotal	3,600	=	0	+	2,600
(9)	Long-Term Debt			(1,500)		
	Contributed Capital					+ 1,500
	Subtotal	0	=	(500)	+	4,100
(10)	Supplies Inventory	(75)				
	Retained Earnings					(75)
	Total	3,525	=	(500)	+	4,025

P2–3

Transaction	Account	Direction	Net Income	Net Cash Flow
(1)	Cash	+	NE	+
	Contributed Capital	+		
(2)	Inventory	+	NE	NE
	Accounts Payable	+		
(3)	Accounts Receivable	+	+	NE
	Fees Earned	+		
(4)	Depreciation Expense	+	–	NE
	Accumulated Depreciation	+		
(5)	Cash	+	NE	+
	Accounts Receivable	–		
(6)	Cash	–	NE	–
	Equipment	+		
(7)	Wages Payable	–	NE	–
	Cash	–		
(8)	Cash	+	+	+
	Fees Earned	+		
(9)	Cash	–	NE	–
	Long-Term Note Payable	–		
(10)	Cash	–	–	–
	Interest Expense	+		

Note: In Transactions (3) and (8), Fees Earned would be closed into Retained Earnings and increase Retained Earnings. In Transactions (4) and (10), the expenses would be closed into Retained Earnings and decrease Retained Earnings.

P2–4

1.	e	9.	a	17.	c
2.	e	10.	a	18.	a
3.	a	11.	c	19.	d
4.	a	12.	d	20.	b
5.	g	13.	c	21.	e
6.	c	14.	b	22.	e
7.	f	15.	e	23.	e
8.	c	16.	a		

X Company
Balance Sheet
[Date]

Assets			
Current assets			
Cash		XX	
Marketable securities		XX	
Accounts receivable	XX		
Less: Allowance for doubtful accounts	XX	XX	
Inventory		XX	
Prepaid rent		XX	
Total current assets			XX
Long-term investments			
Land		XX	
Investment fund for plant expansion		XX	
Total long-term investments			XX
Property, plant & equipment			
Property		XX	
Building	XX		
Less: Accumulated depreciation (building)	XX	XX	
Machinery and equipment	XX		
Less: Accumulated depreciation (mach & equip)	XX	XX	
Total property, plant, & equipment			XX
Intangible assets			
Patents		XX	
Trademarks		XX	
Total intangible assets			XX
Total Assets			XX
Liabilities and stockholders' equity			
Current liabilities			
Accounts payable		XX	
Wages payable		XX	
Dividend payable		XX	
Short-term note payable		XX	
Current portion due of long-term debt		XX	
Payments received in advance		XX	
Total current liabilities			XX
Long-term liabilities			
Bonds payable		XX	
Total long-term liabilities			XX
Stockholders' equity			
Contributed capital		XX	
Retained earnings		XX	
Total stockholders' equity			XX
Total liabilities and stockholders' equity			XX

P2–5

1.	e	6.	e	11.	e
2.	b	7.	e	12.	f
3.	e	8.	f	13.	f
4.	a	9.	c	14.	d
5.	e	10.	c	15.	c

X Company
Income Statement
For the Period Ended _______

Revenues			
Sales		XX	
Fees earned		XX	
Interest income		XX	
Dividend income		XX	
Gain on sale of marketable securities		XX	
Total revenues			XX
Expenses			
Cost of goods sold		XX	
Operating expenses			
Office salary expense	XX		
Insurance expense	XX		
Salesman commission expense	XX		
Depreciation expense	XX		
Office supplies expense	XX		
Advertising expense	XX		
Total operating expenses		XX	
Other expenses			
Interest expense	XX		
Loss on sale of equipment	XX		
Loss on sale of building	XX		
Total other expenses		XX	
Total expenses			XX
Net income			XX

P2–6

Johnson Company
Balance Sheet
December 31, 1989

Assets			
Current assets			
Cash		$ 5,500	
Marketable securities		35,000	
Accounts receivable	$125,000		
Less: Allowance for doubtful accounts	2,400	122,600	
Inventory		162,000[a]	
Total current assets			$325,100
Property, plant & equipment			
Buildings		35,000	
Less: Accumulated depreciation		8,000	
Total property, plant & equipment			27,000
Total assets			$352,100
Liabilities & stockholders' equity			
Current liabilities			
Accounts payable		$119,500	
Taxes payable		23,400	
Total current liabilities			$142,900
Long-term liabilities			
Long-term notes payable			69,100
Stockholders' equity			
Contributed capital		100,000[b]	
Retained earnings		40,100[c]	
Total stockholders' equity			140,100
Total liabilities & stockholders' equity			$352,100

[a] Inventory is reported at the lower of its cost or its market value.
[b] $100,000 = $12,500 shares x $8 per share.
[c] $40,100 = $60,000 cumulative earnings – $19,900 cumulative declared dividends.

P2–7

1988
Contributed Capital

Total assets = Total liabilities + Total stockholders' equity
($100 + $200 + $400 + $100 + $700) = ($200 + $500) + (Contributed capital + $400)
Contributed capital = $400

Net Income

Net income = Sales – Expenses
= $900 – $400
= $500

Dividends

Ending retained earnings = Beginning retained earnings + Sales – Expenses – Dividends
$400 = $0 + $900 – Dividends
Dividends = $100

1989

Inventory

Total assets = Total liabilities + Total stockholders' equity
($300 + $300 + Inventory + $300 + $600) = ($400 + $600) + ($400 + $800)
Inventory = $700

Expenses

Net income = Sales – Expenses
$400 = $1,000 – Expenses
Expenses = $600

Dividends

Ending retained earnings = Beginning retained earnings + Sales – Expenses – Dividends
$800 = $400 + $1,000 – $600 – Dividends
Dividends = $0

1990

Accounts Receivable

Total assets + Total liabilities + Total stockholders' equity
($200 + Accounts receivable + $500 + $400 + $800) = ($500 + $800) + ($600 + $300)
Accounts receivable = $300

Expenses

Net income = Sales – Expenses
($100) = $700 – Expenses
Expenses = $800

Dividends

Ending retained earnings = Beginning retained earnings + Sales – Expenses – Dividends
$300 = $800 + $700 – $800 – Dividends
Dividends = $400

1991

Accounts Payable

Total assets = Total liabilities + Total stockholders' equity
($500 + $700 + $400 + $400 + $700) = (Accounts payable + $700) + ($600 + $600)
Accounts payable = $800

Sales

Ending retained earnings = Beginning retained earnings = Sales – Expenses – Dividends
$600 = $300 + Sales – $600 – $100
Sales = $1,000

Net Income

Net income = Sales – Expenses
= $1,000 – $600
= $400

P2–8

	Assets					=	Liabilities			+	Stockholders' Equity	
	Cash	Accts Rec	Misc Rec	P, P&E	L-T Invest		Misc Pay	Notes Pay	L-T Mortgage		Contrib. Capital	Retained Earnings
(1)	+125,000					=				+	+125,000	
(2)	+185,000	+50,000				=				+		+235,000*
(3)	(175,000)					=	+25,000			+		(200,000)*
(4)	+35,000					=		+35,000		+		
(5)	(25,000)			+75,000		=			+50,000	+		
(6)						=	+15,000			+		−15,000
(7A)	(50,000)				+50,000	=				+		
(7B)	+4,000		+1,000			=				+		+5,000*
	99,000	50,000	1,000	75,000	50,000		40,000	35,000	50,000		125,000	25,000

* These transactions are operating transactions and would initially be recorded in temporary accounts and then closed into Retained Earnings.

Gordon and Gray, Unlimited
Balance Sheet
December 31, 1989

Assets		
Current assets		
Cash	$ 99,000	
Accounts receivable	50,000	
Miscellaneous receivables	1,000	
Total current assets		$150,000
Long-term investments		50,000
Property, plant, and equipment		75,000
Total assets		$275,000
Liabilities & Stockholders' Equity		
Current liabilities		
Miscellaneous payables	$ 40,000	
Short-term note payable	35,000	
Total current liabilities		$ 75,000
Long-term liabilities		50,000
Stockholders' equity		
Contributed capital	125,000	
Retained earnings	25,000	
Total stockholders' equity		150,000
Total liabilities and stockholders' equity		$275,000

Gordon and Gray, Unlimited
Income Statement
For the Year Ended December 31, 1989

Revenues		
Fees earned	$235,000	
Rent revenue	5,000	
Total revenues		$240,000
Operating expenses		200,000
Net income		$ 40,000

Gordon and Gray, Unlimited
Statement of Retained Earnings
For the Year Ended December 31, 1989

Beginning retained earnings balance (1/1/89)	$ 0
Plus: Net income	40,000
Less: Dividends	15,000
Ending retained earnings balance (12/31/89)	$ 25,000

Gordon and Gray, Unlimited
Statement of Cash Flows
For the Year Ended December 31, 1989

Cash flows from operating activities		
Cash sales	$185,000	
Cash collected from tenants	4,000	
Cash paid for expenses	(175,000)	
Net cash increase (decrease) due to operating activities		$ 14,000
Cash flows from investing activities		
Purchase of rental property	(50,000)	
Purchase of property	(25,000)	
Net cash increase (decrease) due to investing activities		(75,000)
Cash flows from financing activities		
Proceeds from owner contributions	125,000	
Proceeds from bank loan	35,000	
Net cash increase (decrease) due to financing activities		160,000
Increase (decrease) in cash balance		$ 99,000
Beginning cash balance		0
Ending cash balance		$ 99,000

P2–9

a. Current ratio

Current assets ÷ Current liabilities

($10,000 + $40,000) ÷ $20,000 = 2.50

Debt/equity ratio

Total liabilities ÷ Total stockholders' equity

($20,000 + $20,000) ÷ ($30,000 + $50,000) = .50

Book Value

(Total assets – Total liabilities) ÷ Shares outstanding

[$120,000 – ($20,000 + $20,000)] ÷ 12,000 shares = 6.67

b.

	Impact on Current Assets	Impact on Current Liabilities	Impact on Long-Term Liabilities	Impact on Stockholders' Equity
Issue stock	$0	$ 0	$ 0	$30,000
Long-term note	0	0	30,000	0
Open account	0	30,000	0	0

Current Ratio

Issue stock: ($10,000 + $40,000) ÷ $20,000 = 2.50

Long-term note: ($10,000 + $40,000) ÷ $20,000 = 2.50

Open account: ($10,000 + $40,000) ÷ ($20,000 + $30,000) = 1.00

Debt/Equity Ratio

Issue stock: ($20,000 + $20,000) ÷ ($30,000 + $50,000 + $30,000) = 0.36

Long-term note: ($20,000 + $20,000 + $30,000) ÷ ($30,000 + $50,000) = 0.875

Open Account: ($20,000 + $20,000 + $30,000) ÷ ($30,000 + $50,000) = 0.875

Book Value

Issue stock: [($120,000 + $30,000) – ($20,000 + $20,000)] ÷ (12,000 + 3,000 shares) = 7.33

Long-term note: [($120,000 + $30,00) – ($20,000 + $20,000 + $30,000)] ÷ 12,000 shares = 6.67

Open Account: [($120,000 + $30,000) – ($20,000 + $20,000 + $30,000)] ÷ 12,000 shares = 6.67

Financing Alternative	Current Ratio	Debt/Equity Ratio	Book Value per Share
1. Issue stock	2.50	.36	7.33
2. Long-term note	2.50	.875	6.67
3. Open account	1.00	.875	6.67

c. **Issue Stock:** Issuing stock is attractive because it impoves the company's debt/equity ratio. By decreasing this ratio, the company might become more attractive to creditors in the future, thereby allowing the company to borrow money at more favorable interest rates. Further, issuing stock, as opposed to issuing debt, will improve future cash flows. Stock does not require mandatory interest payments, and it never matures. On the negative side, issuing more stock has the potential to dilute the ownership rights of existing stockholders.

Long-Term Note: Issuing debt could place severe cash restrictions on the company. Every year the note is outstanding the company will incur $3,600 in interest charges. Also, the company will have to pay back the $30,000 when the note matures. If the company is unable to meet any of these obligations, it could be forced into bankruptcy. On the positive side, interest on the note is tax deductible, so issuing the note would decrease the company's cash outflows from income taxes. Further, with a long-term note, as opposed to a short-term note, the company has more time in which to generate cash to pay off the obligation.

Open Account: Purchasing the equipment on account would allow the company to avoid interest charges. However, the company would be placed in a severe financial bind by purchasing the equipment on account. The $30,000 must be repaid within 30 days, and the company currently has only $10,000. The company would have to raise an additional $20,000 either through operations or by selling some of its assets. Either solution may not be desirable. Diverting money from operations to pay off the obligation means the company will plow less of its earnings back into the business. If the company reduces the amount reinvested in the business, the company could suffer long-term negative consequences. Using money raised by selling assets may cause the company to hurt its base of operations, thereby hurting future operations.

Of the three options, issuing stock seems to be the most attractive.

d. The balance in Retained Earnings represents the excess of cumulative net income over cumulative net losses and declared dividends. Retained Earnings does not represent cash (or any other particular asset). Retained Earnings simply represents one source of funds for net assets. In other words, Retained Earnings is an accounting concept and does not indicate a company's financial wherewithal to purchase items or declare dividends. Items are purchased and dividends are paid with assets (usually cash). Since the company only has $10,000 in cash, it would have to use other assets to purchase the equipment and pay a dividend. In doing so, the company would hurt its future base of operations.

P2–10

Transaction	Net Income	Current Ratio	Working Capital	Debt/Equity Ratio
(1)	NE	+	+	–
(2)	NE	–	–	NE
(3)	NE	–	–	–
(4)	+	+	+	–
(5)	NE	–	–	+
(6)	NE	+	NE	–
(7)	NE	NE	NE	NE
(8)	–	–	–	+*
(9)	–	NE	NE	+*

* Transactions (8) and (9) increase expenses, thereby decreasing the net income amount closed into Retained Earnings. Since reducing Retained Earnings reduces stockholders' equity, Transactions (8) and (9) increase the debt/equity ratio.

P2–11

a. Assets are, for the most part, recorded at historical cost. Over a period of time the value of an item will change. For instance, the value of Eat and Run's property, plant, and equipment will most likely change as the items become older. Consequently, over time the cost of an item may have no relation to the item's market value. Since the cash a company would receive from selling an asset is based on the asset's market value, the book value of the asset is not an accurate indicator of a company's value.

b. The value of the firm would equal the sum of the fair market value of the assets less the sum of liabilities. The value of Eat and Run would, therefore, be as follows:

	Market Value
Cash	$ 25,000
Marketable securities	19,000
Accounts receivable	25,000
Inventory	33,000
Prepaid insurance	0
P, P & E	100,000
Other assets	0
Total market value of assets	$202,000
Less: Total liabilities	196,000
Value of Eat and Run	$ 6,000

c. If Eat and Run were to go bankrupt, the stockholders would receive anything left after all the assets were sold and the creditors were paid. In this case the fair value of the assets exceeds the total liabilities, so the stockholders would receive the residual, which would be $6,000. As a practical matter, Eat and Run might have to hire lawyers and accountants for the bankruptcy proceedings. If this were the case, the lawyers and accountants would have to be paid before the stockholders received anything. So in this particular case, there may be nothing left for the stockholders once the lawyers and accountants are paid.

P2–12

a.

Ryan & Brothers
Statement of Retained Earnings
For the Year Ended December 31, 1990

Beginning retained earnings balance (1/1/90)	$27,000
Plus: Net income	12,000
Less: Dividends declared	5,000
Ending retained earnings balance (12/31/90)	$34,000

b. Cash decreased by $7,000 (i.e., $25,000 – $32,000) during 1990

c.

Account	1989 Balance	1990 Balance	Change	Explanation
Cash	$ 32,000	$ 25,000	–$ 7,000	Operating, investing, and financing activities used more cash than they provided.
Accounts receivable	45,000	73,000	28,000	Sales on account exceeded cash collections from customers on open accounts receivable.
Inventory	42,000	31,000	–11,000	Ryan & Brothers sold more inventory than it purchased during 1990.
Prepaid insurance	3,000	4,000	1,000	Ryan & Brothers purchased additional insurance during 1990.
Land	61,000	42,000	–19,000	Ryan & Brothers sold land that had cost $19,000.
Building (net)	165,000	157,000	–8,000	The decrease in the book value of the building represents depreciation.
Equipment (net)	18,000	36,000	18,000	The book value decreased $4,000 due to depreciation, but the company also acquired an additional $22,000 in equipment.
Accounts payable	75,000	62,000	–13,000	Payments to suppliers on open accounts exceeded the purchase of inventory on account.
Salaries payable	8,000	6,000	2,000	The company paid the 12/31/89 balance during 1990. As of 12/31/90 the company had incurred but had not yet paid $6,000 in salaries. The net effect is a $2,000 decrease.
Interest payable	4,000	4,000	0	The company paid the 12/31/89 balance during 1990, but incurred an additional liability of $4,000 by 12/31/90.
Notes payable	72,000	82,000	10,000	A $10,000 note was issued to partially finance the acquisition of new equipment.
Contributed capital	180,000	180,000	0	No activity in the account.
Retained earnings	27,000	34,000	7,000	Ryan & Brothers generated net income during 1990 of $12,000 and declared dividends during 1990 of $5,000 for a net increase of $7,000.

C2-1

a. Nike, Inc. experienced higher profits as a result of decreased expenses and a lower tax rate. Because costs decreased more than revenues increased, profits tripled.

b. Accounting income is not equivalent to cash flow. It is possible that the increased revenues reported have not been collected in cash and/or there were more expenses paid in cash than in the previous year. Accordingly, you would not expect cash flows to triple.

c. Stockholders might expect a higher dividend, but the company may not pay one. It may not have more cash as a result of increased net income (see question [b]) or it may reinvest its cash instead of paying a dividend.

C2-2

a. The excerpt indicates that Cummins must comply with some restrictions imposed by its lenders. These restrictions do not permit the company to use its cash freely. It must maintain compliance with its loan agreements.

b. A bank or other creditor would impose such limits to protect itself from a loan default. Imposing requirements on the current ratio ensures that (or at least provides a structure whereby) funds will be available to meet loan repayments.

c. Financial accounting numbers are used directly to assess the company's compliance with the restrictions. For example, the balance sheet is used to compute the current ratio to determine if its is 1.25 or greater, the balance in Retained Earnings reveals compliance with dividend payments, and liabilities report any additional borrowing.

C2-3

a. A company could have negative cash flow by paying out more cash than was collected in revenues during a period from operating activities. Positive net income could occur simultaneously as a result of accruals of income (i.e., recording income when it is earned, even if it is before cash is received). The payment of dividends could be made simultaneously as well by using cash that has been retained in the past or, possibly, by taking out a loan.

b. A company could not continue this strategy over a long period of time. Its status as a going concern could be threatened by such a strategy. If the company continues to pay out more in dividends than it realizes in cash from operations, it will soon experience a cash deficit and will be unlikely to pay its obligations.

C2-4

a. Continuum's practice of capitalizing software development costs (i.e., not expensing them against the current year's income) results in a higher net income in the current period. Relative to other methods of reporting income, this provides a positive net income in an earlier time period. Because of this "front-ending," this practice could be viewed as "liberal."

b. (i) If the company had no (or low) revenues, expensing these costs would result in deficit (negative) earnings.

(ii) The company may view the costs as an investment that will yield benefits over time. Thus, they may amortize the costs in future periods when they collect revenue from selling software products.

(iii) If the company must comply with debt covenants or is concerned about credit ratings or bonus agreements, it has an incentive to report the highest possible income in the earliest time period.

c. Future problems could result from having to maintain this practice of capitalizing costs to keep the financial reports consistent. While it may be beneficial to capitalize software development costs in the early stages of a business entity's life, it may not continue to be beneficial in the future. Recognizing higher income in the earlier periods requires recognition of lower income in later periods. There is no change in the total amount of income over a long period, only in the timing of its recognition.

C2-5

Because of the many estimations and assumptions that are included in accounting numbers, it is inappropriate to interpret an unqualified opinion in this manner. A firm may choose to depreciate equipment over 10 years or 20 years. Each useful life may be defensible and result in different amounts of depreciation expense. Since the choice involves the occurrence of future events, which are uncertain, there is no way to determine which is right or wrong. The same is true for other numbers included on the financial statements. Accordingly, it is incorrect to presume that an unqualified opinion means "totally accurate."

CHAPTER 3 The Accounting Cycle

E3–1

Accounts	Debit	Credit
Cash	Increase	Decrease
Fees Earned	Decrease	Increase
Notes Payable	Decrease	Increase
Common Stock	Decrease	Increase
Interest Expense	Increase	Decrease
Office Equipment	Increase	Decrease
Unearned Rent Revenue	Decrease	Increase
Interest Payable	Decrease	Increase
Prepaid Rent	Increase	Decrease
Insurance Expense	Increase	Decrease
Rent Revenue	Decrease	Increase
Accounts Receivable	Increase	Decrease
Inventory	Increase	Decrease
Interest Receivable	Increase	Decrease
Dividends	Increase	Decrease

E3–2

Account	Debit	Credit	Financial Statement
Sales Revenue		X	Income Statement
Cash	X		Balance Sheet
Dividends Payable		X	Balance Sheet
Retained Earnings		X	Balance Sheet Statement of Retained Earnings
Depreciation Expense	X		Income Statement
Deferred Revenues		X	Balance Sheet
Inventory	X		Balance Sheet
Equipment	X		Balance Sheet
Common Stock		X	Balance Sheet
Marketable Securities	X		Balance Sheet
Fees Earned		X	Income Statement
Wage Expense	X		Income Statement
Cost of Goods Sold	X		Income Statement
Dividends	X		Statement of Retained Earnings
Accounts Receivable	X		Balance Sheet
Accounts Payable		X	Balance Sheet
Patent	X		Balance Sheet
Interest Expense	X		Income Statement
Rent Revenue		X	Income Statement

E3–3

	Accounting Significance	Explanation
(1)	No	Entries are made to record the value of events that have occurred. In this case, the new contract will affect the dollar value of future events, not past events.
(2)	Yes	This event represents the receipt of cash in exchange for issuing debt. Since this transaction alters the financial position of the firm, an entry is necessary. The entry would be Cash XX Bonds Payable XX
(3)	No	The retirement of an official does not influence the company's current financial position.
(4)	Yes	Receiving cash from a customer would change the company's financial position. The entry would be Cash XX Accounts Receivable XX
(5)	Yes	Payment of a liability will change a company's financial position. The entry would be Accrued Interest Payable XX Cash XX
(6)	No	Long-lived assets are reported at historical cost less accumulated depreciation. Increases in market value above the reported amounts are not reported because market values on long-lived assets are not objective (i.e., are not reliable).
(7)	Yes	The purchase of an insurance policy represents a change in the company's financial position. However, the value of the policy has no influence on the company. The appropriate entry would be Prepaid Insurance 1,500 Cash 1,500
(8)	No	Simply placing an order does not alter a company's financial position. The company's position does not change until it legally owns the goods.

E3–4

a.

Transaction	Account	Effect	Dollar Value
(1)	Equipment	Increase	$10,000
	Cash	Decrease	10,000
(2)	Marketable Securities	Increase	2,500
	Cash	Decrease	2,500
(3)	Cash	Increase	300
	Accounts Receivable	Increase	500
	Fees Earned	Increase	800
(4)	Cash	Increase	40,000
	Common Stock	Increase	40,000
(5)	Cash	Increase	200
	Accounts Receivable	Decrease	200
(6)	Wage Expense	Increase	700
	Cash	Decrease	700
(7)	Interest Expense	Increase	800
	Note Payable	Decrease	200
	Cash	Decrease	1,000
(8)	Dividend	Increase	700
	Dividend Payable	Increase	700

b.

	Account	Debit	Credit
(1)	Equipment	10,000	
	Cash		10,000
	To record purchase of equipment.		
(2)	Marketable Securities	2,500	
	Cash		2,500
	To record purchase of marketable securities.		
(3)	Cash	300	
	Accounts Receivable	500	
	Fees Earned		800
	To record sale of services.		
(4)	Cash	40,000	
	Common Stock		40,000
	To record issue of common stock.		
(5)	Cash	200	
	Accounts Receivable		200
	To record cash collection from customers.		

		Dr.	Cr.
(6)	Wage Expense	700	
	Cash		700
	To record wages incurred and paid.		
(7)	Interest Expense	800	
	Notes Payable	200	
	Cash		1,000
	To record payment of principal and interest.		
(8)	Dividends	700	
	Dividend Payable		700
	To record declaration of dividend.		

E3–5

a.

Pratt Printing Company
Unadjusted Trial Balance
For the Period Ended ________________

Accounts	**Dr.**	**Cr.**
Assets:		
Marketable Securities	$10,000	
Accounts Receivable	32,000	
Prepaid Expenses	9,000	
Equipment	30,000	
Liabilities:		
Accounts Payable		$15,000
Notes Payable		24,000
Stockholders' Equity:		
Common Stock		20,000
Retained Earnings		10,000
Dividends	4,000	
Revenues:		
Fees Earned		35,000
Other Revenues		8,000
Expenses:		
Advertising Expense	10,000	
Miscellaneous Expenses	15,000	
Interest Expense	2,000	
Totals	$112,000	$112,000

b.

Pratt Printing Company
Income Statement
For the Period Ended ________

Revenues		
Fees earned	$35,000	
Other revenue	8,000	
Total revenues		$43,000
Expenses		
Advertising expense	$10,000	
Miscellaneous expenses	15,000	
Interest expense	2,000	
Total expenses		27,000
Net income		$16,000

Pratt Printing Company
Statement of Retained Earnings
For the Period Ended ________

Beginning retained earnings balance	$10,000
Plus: Net income	16,000
Less: Dividends declared	4,000
Ending retained earnings balance	$22,000

Pratt Printing Company
Balance Sheet
[Date]

Assets		
Marketable securities		$10,000
Accounts receivable		32,000
Prepaid expenses		9,000
Equipment		30,000
Total assets		$81,000
Liabilities & stockholders' equity		
Liabilities		
Accounts payable	$15,000	
Notes payable	24,000	
Total Liabilities		$39,000
Stockholders' equity:		
Common stock	20,000	
Retained earnings	22,000	
Total stockholders' equity		42,000
Total liabilities & stockholders' equity		$81,000

E3–6

a.

Transaction	Assets	= Liabilities	+ Stockholders' Equity
(1)	Debit		Credit
(2)	Debit	Credit	
(3)	Debit		
	Credit		
(4)	Debit	Credit	
(5)	Debit		Credit
(6)	Credit		Debit
(7)	Credit	Debit	
(8)	Credit		Debit
(9)	Credit		
	Debit		
(10)	Debit		Credit
(11)	Credit		Debit

b.

Transaction	Common Stock	+ Retained Earnings	+ Revenues	– Expenses	– Dividends
(1)	Credit				
(5)			Credit		
(6)				Debit	
(8)					Debit
(10)			Credit		
(11)				Debit	

E3–7

a. Ending cash = Beginning cash + Cash receipts – Cash disbursements
= \$10,000 + \$122,500 – \$104,500
= \$28,000

b.

Miller Manufacturing
Statement of Cash Flows
For the Year Ended December 31, 1990

Cash flows from operating activities		
Cash collections from customers	$90,000	
Payment of salaries	(27,500)	
Payment of miscellaneous expenses	(14,000)	
Payment of rent	(9,000)	
Payment of interest	(3,000)	
Net cash increase (decrease) due to operating activities		$36,500
Cash flows from investing activities		
Proceeds from sale of land	7,500	
Purchase of long-term investments	(12,000)	
Purchase of equipment	(25,000)	
Net cash increase (decrease) due to investing activities		(29,500)
Cash flows from financing activities		
Proceeds from issue of common stock	15,000	
Proceeds from borrowing	10,000	
Payment of bank loan	(10,000)	
Payment of dividends	(4,000)	
Net cash increase (decrease) due to financing activities		11,000
Increase (decrease) in cash balance		$18,000
Beginning cash balance		10,000
Ending cash balance		$28,000

E3–8

1989

Ending retained earnings

Ending retained earnings = Beginning retained earnings + Revenues – Expenses – Dividends
= $0 + $900,000 – $450,000 – $75,000
= $375,000

Liabilities

Total liabilities = Total assets – Common stock – Retained earnings
= $700,000 – ($200,000 + $375,000)
= $125,000

1990

Total assets

Total assets = Total liabilities + Total owners' equity
= $150,000 + ($280,000 + $675,000)
= $1,105,000

Expenses

Ending retained earnings = Beginning retained earnings + Revenues – Expenses – Dividends
$675,000 = $375,000 + $850,000 – Expenses – $75,000
Expenses = $475,000

1991

Common stock

Common stock	=	Total assets – (Total liabilities + Retained earnings)
	=	$1,100,000 + ($120,000 + $700,000)
	=	$280,000

Dividends

Ending retained earnings	=	Beginning retained earnings + Revenues – Expenses – Dividends
$700,000	=	$675,000 + $900,000 – $475,000 – Dividends
Dividends	=	$400,000

E3–9

Account	Debit	Credit
Sales	450,000	
Rent Revenue	30,000	
Cost of Goods Sold		200,000
Depreciation Expense		25,000
Insurance Expense		80,000
Wage Expense		125,000
Income Summary		50,000
To close revenue and expense accounts into Income Summary.		
Income Summary	50,000	
Retained Earnings		50,000
To close Income Summary into Retained Earnings.		
Retained Earnings	100,000	
Dividends		100,000
To close Dividends into Retained Earnings.		

E3–10

a.

Account	Debit	Credit
Fees Earned	550	
Rent Revenue	900	
Income Summary		630
Interest Expense		70
Commission Expense		450
Advertising Expense		300
To close revenue and expense accounts into Income Summary.		
Income Summary	630	
Retained Earnings		630
To close Income Summary into Retained Earnings.		
Retained Earnings	800	
Dividends		800
To close Dividends into Retained Earnings.		

b.

Lake Forest Real Estate
Statement of Retained Earnings
For the Year Ended ________

Beginning retained earnings balance	$4,000
Plus: Net income	630
Less: Dividends declared	800
Ending retained earnings balance	$3,830

E3–11

a.	(1)	Cash	10,000	
		Common Stock		10,000
		To record issue of common stock.		
	(2)	Cash	2,400	
		Fees Earned		2,400
		To record services performed for cash.		
	(3)	Wage Expense	500	
		Cash		500
		To record wages incurred and paid.		
	(4)	Investment in Land	8,000	
		Cash		8,000
		To record investment in land.		
	(5)	Dividend	5,000	
		Cash		5,000
		To record payment of dividend.		
	(6)	Cash	3,000	
		Equipment		3,000
		To record sale of equipment.		
	(7)	Interest Expense	600	
		Note Payable	900	
		Cash		1,500
		To record principal and interest payment.		
	(8)	Miscellaneous Expenses	1,400	
		Cash		1,400
		To record miscellaneous expenses incurred and paid.		

b.

Cash

Beginning balance	5,000	8,000	Purchase of land
Issue of common stock	10,000	500	Wages
Services	2,400	5,000	Dividend payment
Sale of equipment	3,000	600	Interest payment
		900	Loan repayment
		1,400	Miscellaneous expenses
Ending Balance	4,000		

c.

Butler and Associates
Statement of Cash Flows
For the Month Ended January 31, 1990

Cash from operating activities		
Collections from customers	$2,400	
Payment of wages	(500)	
Payment of interest	(600)	
Payment of miscellaneous expenses	(1,400)	
Net cash increase (decrease) due to operating activities		($100)
Cash from investing activities		
Proceeds from sale of equipment	3,000	
Purchase of land	(8,000)	
Net cash increase (decrease) due to investing activities		(5,000)
Cash flows from financing activities		
Proceeds from issue of stock	10,000	
Repayment of note	(900)	
Dividend payment	(5,000)	
Net cash increase (decrease) due to financing activities		4,100
Increase (decrease) in cash balance		($1,000)
Beginning cash balance		5,000
Ending cash balance		$4,000

E3–12

Solution for parts (a), (b), and (c).

Transaction	Assets	= Liabilities+	Contributed Capital +	Retained Earnings +	Revenues –	Expenses–	Dividends	Equation Balance ?
Beg. Bal.	$750,000	$205,000	$300,000	$245,000	0	0	0	yes
(1)	150,000				150,000			
Subtotal	900,000	205,000	300,000	245,000	150,000	0	0	yes
(2)	88,000							
	(88,000)							
Subtotal	900,000	205,000	300,000	245,000	150,000	0	0	yes
(3)	(55,000)					55,000		
Subtotal	845,000	205,000	300,000	245,000	150,000	55,000	0	yes
(4)	(10,000)					10,000		
Subtotal	835,000	205,000	300,000	245,000	150,000	65,000	0	yes
(5)	(8,000)						8,000	
Subtotal	827,000	205,000	300,000	245,000	150,000	65,000	8,000	yes
(6)	175,000	75,000						
	(100,000)							
Subtotal	902,000	280,000	300,000	245,000	150,000	65,000	8,000	yes
(7)	(25,000)	5,000				30,000		
Subtotal	877,000	285,000	300,000	245,000	150,000	95,000	8,000	yes

d. Net income for 1991 is as follows:

Net income = Revenue – Expenses
= \$150,000 – \$95,000
= \$55,000

e. December 31, 1991 retained earnings = Beginning retained earnings + Net income – Dividends
= \$245,000 + \$150,000 – \$95,000 – \$8,000
= \$292,000

P3–1

Answers to (a), (b), and (c) combined in tabular form.

Account	Balance	Statement	Financial Classification	Debt
Cash	Debit	Balance sheet	Asset	Increase
Marketable Securities	Debit	Balance sheet	Asset	Increase
Unearned Rent Revenue	Credit	Balance sheet	Liability	Decrease
Common Stock	Credit	Balance sheet	Stockholders' equity	Decrease
Office Equipment	Debit	Balance sheet	Asset	Increase
Sales	Credit	Income statement	Revenue	Decrease
Prepaid Rent	Debit	Balance sheet	Asset	Increase
Bonds Payable	Credit	Balance sheet	Liability	Decrease
Retained Earnings	Credit	Balance sheet	Stockholders' equity	Decrease
Accounts Receivable	Debit	Balance sheet	Assets	Increase

P3–2

		Debit	Credit
a. (1)	Equipment	200,000	
	Cash		200,000
	To record purchase of equipment.		
(2)	Wage Expense	25,000	
	Cash		25,000
	To record wages incurred and paid.		
(3)	Cash	25,000	
	Accounts Receivable		25,000
	To record collection on open accounts receivable.		
(4)	Cash	15,000	
	Accounts Receivable	9,000	
	Fees Earned		24,000
	To record services rendered.		
(5)	Interest Expense	8,000	
	Note Payable	37,000	
	Cash		45,000
	To record interest and principal payment.		
(6)	Advertising Expense	5,000	
	Cash		5,000
	To record purchase of advertising.		
(7)	Building	250,000	
	Cash		100,000
	Long-Term Note Payable		150,00
	To record purchase of building.		

b. (1) None
(2) Wage Expense
(3) None
(4) Fees Earned
(5) Interest Expense
(6) Advertising Expense
(7) None

P3–3

		Debit	Credit
(a)	Cash	5,000	
	Accounts Receivable	20,000	
	Sales Revenue		25,000
	To record sale made for cash and on account.		
(b)	Inventory	10,000	
	Accounts Payable		10,000
	To record purchase of inventory on account.		
(c)	Accounts Payable	2,000	
	Cash		2,000
	To record payment to suppliers on open accounts.		
(d)	Equipment	50,000	
	Cash		20,000
	Notes Payable		30,000
	To record purchase of equipment.		
(e)	Rent Expense	1,000	
	Cash		1,000
	To record rent expense incurred and paid		
(f)	Cash	6,000	
	Accounts Receivable		6,000
	To record cash collection from customers on open accounts.		
(g)	Cash	18,000	
	Common Stock		18,000
	To record issue of common stock for cash.		

P3–4

a.

Transaction	Assets	=	Liabilities	+	Stockholders' Equity
(1)	5,000				5,000
(2)	2,000				
	(2,000)				
(3)	(1,000)		(1,000)		
(4)	5,000		5,000		
(5)	(3,000)				(3,000)
(6)	(500)				(500)

b.

	Accounts	Effect	Dollar Value
(1)	Cash	Increase	$5,000
	Fees Earned	Increase	5,000
(2)	Cash	Increase	2,000
	Accounts Receivable	Decrease	2,000
(3)	Liabilities	Decrease	1,000
	Cash	Decrease	1,000
(4)	Long-Term Assets	Increase	5,000
	Note Payable	Increase	5,000
(5)	Miscellaneous Expenses	Increase	3,000
	Cash	Decrease	3,000
(6)	Dividend	Increase	500
	Cash	Decrease	500

c.

		Debit	Credit
(1)	Cash	5,000	
	Fees Earned		5,000
	To record services performed.		
(2)	Cash	2,000	
	Accounts Receivable		2,000
	To record collection of cash on open accounts.		
(3)	Liabilities	1,000	
	Cash		1,000
	To record payment on outstanding liabilities.		
(4)	Long-Term Assets	5,000	
	Note Payable		5,000
	To record the purchase of long-lived assets.		
(5)	Miscellaneous Expenses	3,000	
	Cash		3,000
	To record expenses incurred and paid.		
(6)	Dividends	500	
	Cash		500
	To record the declaration and payment of dividends.		

d. (1) Fees Earned 5,000
Income Summary 2,000
Miscellaneous Expenses 3,000
To close revenue and expense accounts into Income Summary.

		Debit	Credit
d. (1)	Fees Earned	5,000	
	Income Summary		2,000
	Miscellaneous Expenses		3,000
	To close revenue and expense accounts into Income Summary.		
(2)	Income Summary	2,000	
	Retained Earnings		2,000
	To close Income Summary into Retained Earnings.		
(3)	Retained Earnings	500	
	Dividends		500
	To close Dividends into Retained Earnings.		

e.

Alexander Baseball Scouting
Income Statement
For the Month Ended January 31, 1991

Revenues	$5,000
Miscellaneous expenses	3,000
Net income	$2,000

Alexander Baseball Scouting
Statement of Retained Earnings
For the Month Ended January 31, 1991

Beginning retained earnings balance	$8,000
Plus: Net income	2,000
Less: Dividends declared	500
Ending retained earnings balance	$9,500

Alexander Baseball Scouting
Balance Sheet
January 31, 1991

Assets		Liabilities & Stockholders' Equity	
Cash	$ 7,500	Liabilities	$ 8,000
Receivables	5,000	Common stock	10,000
Long-term assets	15,000	Retained earnings	9,500
Total assets	$27,500	Total liab. & stockholders' equity	$27,500

Alexander Baseball Scouting
Statement of Cash Flows
For the Month Ended January 31, 1991

Cash flows from operating activities		
Cash collections from customers	$7,000	
Payment of expenses	(3,000)	
Net cash increase (decrease) due to operating activities		$4,000
Cash flows from investing activities		0
Cash flows from financing activities		
Repayment of liabilities	(1,000)	
Dividend payment	(500)	
Net cash increase (decrease) due to financing activities		(1,500)
Net increase in cash		2,500
Beginning cash balance		5,000
Ending cash balance		$7,500

Note: In preparing the statement of cash flows it was assumed that the liabilities arose from financing activities rather than from operating activities. Given the information provided, either assumption would be valid.

P3–5

Solution for parts (a), (b), and (d); the numbers in parentheses refer to the closing entries from part (c). Beginning balance is indicated by (BB); ending balance is indicated by (EB).

Retained Earnings

Debit	Credit
	148,000 (BB)
(c1) 17,000	
(c2) 8,000	
	123,000 (EB)

Income Summary

Debit	Credit
(c1) 17,000	
	17,000 (c2)
0	0

Dividends

Debit	Credit
8,000	
	8,000 (c3)
0	

Fees Earned

Debit	Credit
	75,000
(c1) 75,000	
	0

Rent Expense

Debit	Credit
12,000	
	12,000 (c1)
0	

Wage & Salary Expense

Debit	Credit
50,000	
	50,000 (c1)
0	

Other Expenses

Debit	Credit
30,000	
	30,000 (c1)
0	

		Debit	Credit
c. (c1)	Fees Earned	75,000	
	Income Summary	17,000	
	Wage and Salary Expense		50,000
	Rent Expense		12,000
	Other Expenses		30,000
	To close revenue and expense accounts into Income Summary.		
(c2)	Retained Earnings	17,000	
	Income Summary		17,000
	To close Income Summary into Retained Earnings.		
(c3)	Retained Earnings	8,000	
	Dividends		8,000
	To close Dividends into Retained Earnings.		

e. Ending retained earnings = Beginning retained earnings + Net income – Dividends
= $148,000 – ($17,000) – $8,000
= $123,000

P3–6

		Debit	Credit
a. (1)	Cash	100,000	
	Common Stock		100,000
	To record issue of common stock for cash.		
(2)	Rent Expense	36,000	
	Cash		36,000
	To record rent payments.		
(3)	Cash	40,000	
	Accounts Receivable	150,000	
	Fees Earned		190,000
	To record sale of services.		
(4)	Land	35,000	
	Cash		35,000
	To record purchase of land.		
(5)	Cash	75,000	
	Long-Term Note Payable		75,000
	To record borrowing.		
(6)	Salary Expense	90,000	
	Cash		90,000
	To record salaries incurred and paid.		
(7)	Other Expenses	35,000	
	Cash		35,000
	To record expenses incurred and paid.		

(8) Cash 60,000
  Accounts Receivable 60,000
  To record collection on open accounts.

(9) Dividends 20,000
  Cash 20,000
  To record declaration and payment of dividend.

b. The references (c1) – (c3) refer to the closing entries from part (c).

Cash

	Debit	Credit	
(BB)	0	36,000	(2)
(1)	100,000	35,000	(4)
(3)	40,000	90,000	(6)
(5)	75,000	35,000	(7)
(8)	60,000	20,000	(9)
(EB)	59,000		

Accounts Receivable

	Debit	Credit	
(BB)	0	60,000	(8)
(3)	150,000		
(EB)	90,000		

Land

	Debit	Credit	
(BB)	0		
(4)	35,000		
(EB)	35,000		

L-T Notes Payable

	Debit	Credit	
		0	(BB)
		75,000	(5)
		75,000	(EB)

Common Stock

	Debit	Credit	
		0	(BB)
		100,000	(1)
		100,000	(EB)

Retained Earnings

	Debit	Credit	
		0	(BB)
(c3)	20,000	29,000	(C2)
		9,000	(EB)

Dividends

	Debit	Credit	
(9)	20,000		
		20,000	(c3)
	0		

Fees Earned

	Debit	Credit	
		190,000	(3)
(c1)	190,000		
		0	

Salary Expense

	Debit	Credit	
(6)	90,000		
		90,000	(c1)
	0		

Rent Expense

	Debit	Credit	
(2)	36,000		
		36,000	(c1)
	0		

Other Expenses

	Debit	Credit	
(7)	35,000		
		35,000	(c1)
	0		

Income Summary

	Debit	Credit	
		29,000	(c1)
(c2)	29,000		
	0	0	

c. (c1) Fees Earned 190,000

		Debit	Credit
c. (c1)	Fees Earned	190,000	
	Income Summary		29,000
	Salary Expense		90,000
	Rent Expense		36,000
	Other Expenses		35,000
	To close revenues and expenses into Income Summary.		
(c2)	Income Summary	29,000	
	Retained Earnings		29,000
	To close Income Summary into Retained Earnings.		
(c3)	Retained Earnings	20,000	
	Dividends		20,000
	To close Dividends into Retained Earnings		

d.

Rix, Inc.
Income Statement
For the Year Ended December 31, 1990

Revenues		
Fees earned		$190,000
Operating expenses		
Salary expense	$90,000	
Rent expense	36,000	
Other expense	35,000	
Total operating expense		161,000
Net income		$ 29,000

Rix, Inc.
Statement of Retained Earnings
For the Year Ended December 31, 1990

Beginning retained earnings balance (1/1/90)	$ 0
Plus: Net income	29,000
Less: Dividends declared	20,000
Ending retained earnings balance (12/31/90)	$ 9,000

Rix, Inc.
Statement of Cash Flows
For the Year Ended December 31, 1990

Cash flows from operating activities		
Cash collections from customers	$100,000	
Cash paid for rent	(36,000)	
Cash paid for salaries	(90,000)	
Cash paid for other expenses	(35,000)	
Net cash increase (decrease) due to operating activities		($61,000)
Cash flows from investing activities		
Purchase of land	(35,000)	
Net cash increase (decrease) due to investing activities		(35,000)
Cash flows from financing activities		
Proceeds from stock issue	100,000	
Proceeds from debt issue	75,000	
Dividend payment	(20,000)	
Net cash increase (decrease) due to financing activities		155,000
Increase (decrease) in cash balance		$59,000
Beginning cash balance		0
Ending cash balance		$59,000

Rix, Inc.
Balance Sheet
As of December 31, 1990

Assets		Liabilities & Stockholders' Equity	
Cash	$ 59,000	Long-term notes payable	$ 75,000
Accounts receivable	90,000	Common stock	100,000
Land	35,000	Retained earnings	9,000
		Total liabilities &	
Total assets	$184,000	stockholders' equity	$184,000

P3–7

a.

Ed Hauser Consulting
Adjusted Trial Balance
For the Year Ended December 31, 1990

Accounts	**Dr.**	**Cr.**
Assets:		
Cash	10,000	
Accounts Receivable	12,000	
Land	5,000	
Equipment	20,000	
Liabilities:		
Accounts Payable		3,000
Wages Payable		4,000
Notes Payable		15,000
Stockholders' Equity:		
Common Stock		20,000
Retained Earnings		5,000
Revenues:		
Fees Earned		45,000
Expenses:		
Selling Expenses	25,000	
Administrative Expenses	18,000	
Dividends	2,000	
Totals	92,000	92,000

b.

Fees Earned	45,000	
Income Summary		2,000
Selling Expenses		25,000
Administrative Expenses		18,000
To close revenues and expenses into Income Summary.		
Income Summary	2,000	
Retained Earnings		2,000
To close Income Summary into Retained Earnings.		
Retained Earnings	2,000	
Dividends		2,000
To close Dividends into Retained Earnings.		

P3–8

		Account	Debit	Credit
a.	(1)	Wage Payable	4,000	
		Cash		4,000
		To pay wages incurred in previous period		
	(2)	Cash	10,000	
		Accounts Receivable	3,000	
		Fees Earned		13,000
		To record services performed.		
	(3)	Selling Expense	3,000	
		Cash		3,000
		To record wages incurred and paid		
	(4)	Cash	6,000	
		Accounts Receivable		6,000
		To record cash collection from customer.		
	(5)	Interest Expense	1,000	
		Note Payable	4,000	
		Cash		5,000
		To record principal and interest payment on note.		
	(6)	Cash	5,000	
		Land		5,000
		To record sale of land.		
	(7)	Accounts Payable	3,000	
		Cash		3,000
		To record payment to suppliers.		
	(8)	Equipment	3,000	
		Note Payable		3,000
		To record the purchase of machinery for a note.		
	(9)	Administrative Expenses	3,500	
		Cash		3,500
		To record expenses incurred and paid.		
	(10)	Dividends	1,000	
		Dividend Payable		1,000
		To record declaration of a dividend.		

b. The closing entries from part (d) are identified by (C1), (C2), and (C3).

Cash

(BB)	10,000	4,000	(1)
(2)	10,000	3,000	(3)
(4)	6,000	5,000	(5)
(6)	5,000	3,000	(7)
		3,500	(9)
(EB)	12,500		

Accounts Receivable

(BB)	12,000	6,000	(4)
(2)	3,000		
(EB)	9,000		

Land

(BB)	5,000		
		5,000	(4)
(EB)	0		

Equipment

(BB)	20,000		
(8)	3,000		
(EB)	23,000		

Accounts Payable

		3,000	(BB)
(7)	3,000		
		0	(EB)

Wages Payable

		4,000	(BB)
(1)	4,000		
		0	(EB)

Dividends Payable

		0	(BB)
		1,000	(10)
		1,000	(EB)

Notes Payable

		15,000	(BB)
(5)	4,000	3,000	(8)
		14,000	(EB)

Common Stock

		20,000	(BB)
		20,000	(EB)

Retained Earnings

		5,000	(BB)
(C3)	1,000	5,500	(C2)
		9,500	(EB)

Dividends

(9)	1,000		
		1,000	(C3)
	0		

Fees Earned

		13,000	(2)
(C1)	13,000		
		0	

Administrative Expenses

(2)	3,500		
		3,500	(C1)
	0		

Interest Expense

(5)	1,000		
		1,000	(C1)
	0		

Selling Expense

(6)	3,000		
		3,000	(C1)
	0		

Income Summary

(C2)	5,500	5,500	(C1)
	0	0	

c.

Ed Hauser Consulting
Trial Balance
For the Month Ended January 31, 1991

Account	Dr.	Cr.
Assets:		
Cash	12,500	
Accounts Receivable	9,000	
Equipment	23,000	
Liabilities:		
Dividends Payable		1,000
Notes Payable		14,000
Stockholders' Equity:		
Common Stock		20,000
Retained Earnings		5,000
Dividends	1,000	
Revenues:		
Fees Earned		13,000
Expenses:		
Interest Expense	1,000	
Selling Expense	3,000	
Administrative Expenses	3,500	
Total	53,000	53,000

d.

	Account	Dr.	Cr.
(C1)	Fees Earned	13,000	
	Income Summary		5,500
	Selling Expense		3,000
	Interest Expense		1,000
	Administrative Expenses		3,500
	To close revenues and expenses into Income Summary.		
(C2)	Income Summary	5,500	
	Retained Earnings		5,500
	To close Income Summary into Retained Earnings.		
(C3)	Retained Earnings	1,000	
	Dividends		1,000
	To close Dividends into Retained Earnings.		

e.

Ed Hauser Consulting
Final Trial Balance
For the Month Ended January 31, 1991

Account	**Dr.**	**Cr.**
Assets:		
Cash	12,500	
Accounts Receivable	9,000	
Equipment	23,000	
Liabilities:		
Dividends Payable		1,000
Notes Payable		14,000
Stockholders' Equity:		
Common Stock		20,000
Retained Earnings		9,500
Totals	44,500	44,500

f.

Ed Hauser Consulting
Income Statement
For the Month Ended January 31, 1991

Revenues		
Fees earned		$13,000
Expenses		
Selling expense	$3,000	
Administrative expenses	3,500	
Interest expense	1,000	
Total expenses		7,500
Net income		$ 5,500

Ed Hauser Consulting
Statement of Retained Earnings
For the Month Ended January 31,1991

Beginning retained earnings balance (Jan. 1, 1991)	$5,000
Plus: Net income	5,500
Less: Dividends	1,000
Ending retained earnings balance (Jan. 31, 1991)	$9,500

Ed Hauser Consulting
Statement of Cash Flows
For the Month Ended January 31,1991

Cash flows from operating activities		
Cash collections from customers	$16,000	
Cash paid for wages	(7,000)	
Cash paid for administrative expenses	(3,500)	
Cash paid for administrative supplies	(3,000)	
Cash paid for interest	(1,000)	
Net cash increase (decrease) due to operating activities		$ 1,500
Cash flows from investing activities		
Proceeds from sale of land	5,000	
Net cash increase (decrease) due to investing activities		5,000
Cash flows from financing activities		
Payment on debt	(4,000)	
Net cash increase (decrease) due to financing activities		(4,000)
Increase (decrease) in cash balance		$ 2,500
Beginning cash balance		10,000
Ending cash balance		$12,500

g.

Ed Hauser Consulting
Balance Sheet
January 31, 1991

Assets		Liabilities & Stockholders' Equity	
Cash	$12,500	Dividends payable	$ 1,000
Accounts receivable	9,000	Notes payable	14,000
Equipment	23,000	Contributed capital	20,000
		Retained earnings	9,500
Total Assets	$44,500	Total liabilities and stockholders' equity	$44,500

P3–9

Accounts	Adjusted Trial Balance Dr.	Adjusted Trial Balance Cr.	Closing Entries Dr.	Closing Entries Cr.	Final Trial Balance Dr.	Final Trial Balance Cr.
Assets:						
Cash	23,000				23,000	
Accounts Receivable	14,000				14,000	
Inventory	9,000				9,000	
Prepaid Expenses	2,000				2,000	
Long-Term Investments	15,000				15,000	
Machinery	35,000				35,000	
Building	54,000				54,000	
Liabilities:						
Accounts Payable		25,000				25,000
Interest Payable		4,000				4,000
Wages Payable		5,000				5,000
Short-Term Notes Payable		32,000				32,000
Long-Term Notes Payable		25,000				25,000
Stockholders' Equity:						
Common Stock		55,000				55,000
Retained Earnings		18,000	5,000[b] 7,000[c]			6,000
Revenues:						
Sales		85,000	85,000[a]			
Expenses:						
Cost of Goods Sold	35,000			35,000[a]		
Wage Expense	22,000			22,000[a]		
Advertising Expense	5,000			5,000[a]		
Insurance Expense	4,000			4,000[a]		
Miscellaneous Expenses	24,000			24,000[a]		
Dividends	7,000			7,000[a]		
Income Summary			5,000[a]	5,000[b]		
Total	249,000	249,000	102,000	102,000	152,000	152,000

[a] Entry to close revenues and expenses into Income Summary.
[b] Entry to close Income Summary into Retained Earnings.
[c] Entry to close Dividends into Retained Earnings.

P3–10

a. (1) Cash 500,000
Common Stock 500,000
To record issue of common stock.

(2) Rafts 72,000
Cash 10,000
Notes Payable 62,000
To record the purchase of six rafts.

(3) No journal entry is necessary.

(4) Cash 45,000
Accounts Receivable 105,000
Fees Earned 150,000
To record fees earned.

(5) No journal entry is necessary.

(6) Wage Expense 75,000
Cash 75,000
To record wage expense incurred and paid.

(7) Rent Expense 12,000
Cash 12,000
To record expense incurred and paid.

(8) Interest Expense 4,000
Cash 4,000
To record interest incurred and paid.

(9) Dividend 22,000
Cash 22,000
To record dividend payment.

b. The keys (C1), (C2), and (C3) refer to the closing entries posted from part (d).

Cash

Debit	Credit
(BB) 0	10,000 (2)
(1) 500,000	75,000 (6)
(4) 45,000	12,000 (7)
	4,000 (8)
	22,000 (9)
(EB) 422,000	

Accounts Receivable

Debit	Credit
(BB) 0	
(4) 105,000	
(EB) 105,000	

Rafts

Debit	Credit
(BB) 0	
(2) 72,000	
(EB) 72,000	

Notes Payable

Dr.	Cr.
	0 (BB)
	62,000 (2)
	62,000 (EB)

Common Stock

Dr.	Cr.
	0 (BB)
	500,000 (1)
	500,000 (EB)

Retained Earnings

Dr.	Cr.
	0 (BB)
(C3) 22,000	59,000 (C2)
	37,000 (EB)

Dividends

Dr.	Cr.
(9) 22,000	
	22,000 (C3)
0	

Fees Earned

Dr.	Cr.
	150,000 (4)
(C1) 150,000	
	0

Wage Expense

Dr.	Cr.
(6) 75,000	
	75,000 (C1)
0	

Rent Expense

Dr.	Cr.
(7) 12,000	
	12,000 (C1)
0	

Interest Expenses

Dr.	Cr.
(8) 4,000	
	4,000 (C1)
0	

Income Summary

Dr.	Cr.
	59,000 (C1)
(C2) 59,000	
0	0

c. The keys (C1), (C2), and (C3) refer to the closing entries from part (d).

Powell Rafting Company
Worksheet
For the Year Ended December 31, 1989

Accounts	**Adjusted Trial Balance** Dr.	Cr.	**Closing Entries** Dr.	Cr.	**Final Trial Balance** Dr.	Cr.
Assets:						
Cash	422,000				422,000	
Accounts Receivable	105,000				105,000	
Rafts	72,000				72,000	
Liabilities:						
Notes Payable		62,000				62,000
Stockholders' Equity:						
Common Stock		500,000				500,000
Retained Earnings		0	(C3) 22,000	(C2) 59,000		37,000
Dividends	22,000			(C3) 22,000		
Revenues:						
Fees Earned		150,000	(C1) 150,000			
Expenses:						
Wage Expense	75,000			(C1) 75,000		
Rent Expense	12,000			(C1) 12,000		
Interest Expense	4,000			(C1) 4,000		
Income Summary			(C1) 59,000	(C2) 59,000		
Total	712,000	712,000	231,000	231,000	599,000	599,000

d. (C1) Fees Earned 150,000
Income Summary 59,000
Interest Expense 4,000
Wage Expense 75,000
Rent Expense 12,000
To close revenues and expenses into Income Summary.

(C2) Income Summary 59,000
Retained Earnings 59,000
To close Income Summary into Retained Earnings.

(C3) Retained Earnings 22,000
Dividends 22,000
To close Dividends into Retained Earnings.

e.

Powell Rafting Company
Income Statement
For the Year Ended December 31, 1989

Revenues		
Fees earned		$150,000
Expenses		
Wage expense	$75,000	
Interest expense	4,000	
Rent expense	12,000	
Total expense		91,000
Net income		$ 59,000

Powell Rafting Company
Statement of Retained Earnings
For the Year Ended December 31, 1989

Beginning retained earnings balance (Jan. 1, 1989)	$ 0
Plus: Net income	59,000
Less: Declared dividends	22,000
Ending retained earnings balance (Dec. 31, 1989)	$37,000

Powell Rafting Company
Balance Sheet
December 31, 1989

Assets		Liabilities & Stockholders' Equity	
Cash	$422,000	Notes payable	$ 62,000
Accounts Receivable	105,000	Common stock	500,000
Rafts	72,000	Retained earnings	37,000
Total assets	$599,000	Total liabilities & stockholders' equity	$599,000

Powell Rafting Company
Statement of Cash Flows
For the Year Ended December 31, 1989

Cash flows from operating activities		
Cash collections from customers	$ 45,000	
Cash paid for wages	(75,000)	
Cash paid for rent	(12,000)	
Cash paid for interest	(4,000)	
Net cash increase (decrease) due to operating activities		($46,000)
Cash flows from investing activities		
Purchase of rafts	(10,000)	
Net cash increase (decrease) due to investing activities		(10,000)
Cash flows from financing activities		
Proceeds from stock issue	500,000	
Dividend payment	(22,000)	
Net cash increase (decrease) due to financing activities		478,000
Increase (decrease) in cash balance		$422,000
Beginning cash balance		0
Ending cash balance		$422,000

P3–11

a. Cash	10,000	
Accounts Receivable		10,000
To record collections from customers on open accounts.		
Cash	45,000	
Common Stock		45,000
To record issue of common stock.		
Wage Expense	5,000	
Cash		5,000
To record wages incurred and paid.		
Accounts Payable	7,000	
Cash		7,000
To record payment to suppliers on open accounts.		
Machinery	12,000	
Cash		12,000
To record purchase of machinery.		
Machinery	8,000	
Cash		8,000
To record purchase of machinery.		
Rent Expense	14,000	
Cash		14,000
To record rent incurred and paid.		

Accounts Receivable	100,000	
Sales		100,000
To record sales on account.		
Inventory	125,000	
Accounts Payable		125,000
To record purchase of inventory on account.		
Cost of Goods Sold	115,000	
Inventory		115,000
To record cost of inventory sold.		

b.

	Trial Balance		Closing Entries		Final Trial Balance	
Accounts	**Debit**	**Credit**	**Debit**	**Credit**	**Debit**	**Credit**
Assets:						
Cash	29,000				29,000	
Accounts Receivable	125,000				125,000	
Inventory	60,000				60,000	
Machinery	220,000				220,000	
Liabilities:						
Accounts Payable		208,000				208,000
Stockholders' Equity:						
Common Stock		150,000				150,000
Retained Earnings		110,000	34,000[b]			76,000
Revenues:						
Sales		100,000	100,000[a]			
Expenses:						
Rent Expense	14,000			14,000[a]		
Cost of Goods Sold	115,000			115,000[a]		
Wage Expense	5,000			5,000[a]		
Income Summary			34,000[a]	34,000[b]		
Totals	568,000	568,000	168,000	168,000	434,000	434,000

[a] Entry to close revenues and expenses into Income Summary.
[b] Entry to close Income Summary into Retained Earnings.

c.

Crozier Company
Income Statement
For the Year Ended December 31, 1989

Revenues		$100,000
Expenses		
Cost of goods sold	115,000	
Rent expense	14,000	
Wage expense	5,000	
Total expenses		134,000
Net loss		$34,000

Crozier Company
Statement of Retained Earnings
For the Year Ended December 31, 1989

Beginning retained earnings balance	$110,000
Less: Net loss	34,000
Ending retained earnings balance	$ 76,000

Crozier Company
Balance Sheet
December 31, 1989

Assets	
Cash	$ 29,000
Accounts receivable	125,000
Inventory	60,000
Machinery	220,000
Total assets	$434,000
Liabilities and stockholders' equity	
Accounts payable	$208,000
Common stock	150,000
Retained earnings	76,000
Total liabilities and stockholders' equity	$434,000

Crozier Company
Statement of Cash Flows
For the Year Ended December 31, 1889

Cash Flows from Operating Activities		
Cash collections from customers	$ 10,000	
Cash payments for rent	(14,000)	
Cash payments for wages	(5,000)	
Cash payments for inventory	(7,000)	
Net cash increase (decrease) due to operating activities		($16,000)
Cash flows from investing activities		
Purchase of machinery	(20,000)	
Net cash increase (decrease) due to investing activities		(20,000)
Cash flows from financing activities		
Proceeds from issue of common stock	45,000	
Net cash increase (decrease) due to financing activities		45,000
Increase (decrease) in cash balance		$ 9,000
Beginning cash balance		20,000
Ending cash balance		$29,000

P3–12

Cash Receipts Journal Page 1

Date	Account Credited	Post. Ref.	Credits: Other Accounts	Credits: Accounts Receivable	Credits: Sales	Cash Debits
(1)	Donna Smith	√		500		500
(2)	Loretta Jones	√		1,025		1,025
(4)	Jimmy Johnston	√		700		700
			0	2,225	0	2,225

Sales Journal Page 1

Date	Account Debited	Invoice Number	Post Ref.	Amount
(2)	Jimmy Johnston		√	300
				300

Accounts Receivable Subsidiary Ledger

Donna Smith

Date	Post Ref.	Debit	Credit	Balance
July 31				875
(1)	CR 1		500	375

Jimmy Johnston

Date	Post Ref.	Debit	Credit	Balance
July 31				1,100
(2)	SJ 1	300		1,400
(4)	CR 1		700	700

Loretta Jones

Date	Post Ref.	Debit	Credit	Balance
July 31				1,025
(3)	CR 1		1,025	0

General Ledger

Accounts Receivable

Date	Post Ref.	Debit	Credit	Balance: Debit	Balance: Credit
July 31				3,000	
August 31	CR 1		2,225	775	
August 31	SR 1	300		1,075	

P3–13

Cash Disbursements Journal							Page 1
					Debits		
Date	Check No.	Payee	Other Accounts Debited	Post Ref.	Other Account	Accounts Payable	Cash Credits
(1)	XX	M & S Supply		√		2,700	2,700
(2)	XX	Ellery Industries		√		1,000	1,000
(4)	XX	Thompson, Inc.	Inventory	√	200	300	500
					200	4,000	4,200

Purchases Journal					Page 1
Date	Account Credited	Post Ref.	Invoice Date	Terms	Amount
(3)	M & S Supply	√			700
					700

Accounts Payable Subsidiary Ledger

M & S Supply				
Date	Post Ref.	Debit	Credit	Balance
January 31	CD1			2,700
(1)	P1	2,700		0
(3)			700	700

Ellery Industries				
Date	Post Ref.	Debit	Credit	Balance
January 31				1,500
(2)	CD1	1,000		500

Thompson, Inc.				
Date	Post Ref.	Debit	Credit	Balance
January 31				800
(4)	CD1	300		500

General Ledger

Accounts Payable					
				Balance	
Date	Post Ref.	Debit	Credit	Debit	Credit
January 31					5,000
August 31	P1		700		5,700
August 31	CD1	4,000			1,700

C3-1

a. The amount at which the SBS system would be recorded on MCI's balance sheet is the amount MCI gave up to receive it. Since MCI "paid" $376 million in stock and took on a note for $104 million (the proceeds of which were paid to IBM), the amount on MCI's balance sheet for SBS would be $480 million, less miscellaneous assets received of $52 million, or $428 million.

b. The exchange increased assets by $480 million, liabilities by $104 million and stockholder's equity by $376 million. The accounting equation remained in balance, as it should for all transactions.

c. MCI's balance sheet would show new assets composed of $52 million in miscellaneous assets and $428 million ($480 million - $52 million) for SBS. Its liabilities now include a note payable for $104 million. Stockholders' equity reflects increased common stock of $376 million.

d.

Accounts	**Effect**	**Dollar Value**
Miscellaneous Assets (Asset)	+	$ 52 million
Investment in SBS (Asset)	+	428 million
Notes Payable (Liability)	+	104 million
Common Stock (Equity)	+	376 million

e.

Miscellaneous Assets	52,000,000	
Investment in SBS	428,000,000	
Notes Payable		104,000,000
Common Stock		376,000,000
To record acquisition of SBS from IBM.		

C3-2

a. Assets would increase by $1,934,799 and stockholders' equity (i.e., Retained Earnings) would increase by the same amount.

b.

Accounts	**Effect**	**Dollar Value**
Accounts Receivable	+	$1,934,799
Sales	+	1,934,799

c.

Accounts Receivable	1,934,799	
Sales		1,934,799
To record sales on account for the year.		

d.

Sales	1,934,799	
Income Summary		1,934,799
To close Sales to Income Summary.		

e. same as (d)

C3-3

a. Individual revenue and expense account balances are closed to the Income Summary account at the end of the accounting period. The balance in the Income Summary account then reflects net income for the period.

b. The amount appears as a credit.

c.

	Debit	Credit
Sales	1,850,231	
Expenses		1,757,498
Income Summary		92,733
To close income and expense accounts to Income Summary.		

d.

	Debit	Credit
Income Summary	92,733	
Retained Earnings		92,733
To close Income Summary to Retained Earnings.		

C3-4

a.

Adjusted Trial Balance	Debit	Credit
Assets	9,901,900	
Liabilities		5,131,200
Stockholders' Equity		4,570,600
Revenues		7,838,200
Expenses	7,638,100	
Total	17,540,000	17,540,000

b.

	Debit	Credit
Revenues	7,838,200	
Expenses		7,638,100
Income Summary		200,100
To close revenue and expense accounts to Income Summary.		
Income Summary	200,100	
Retained Earnings*		200,100
To close Income Summary to Retained Earnings.		

* Part of stockholders' equity

c.

Final Trial Balance	Debit	Credit
Assets	9,901,900	
Liabilities		5,131,200
Stockholders' Equity		4,770,700
Total	9,901,900	9,901,900

C3-5

a. Such a report would be included to provide assurance to shareholders that management has in place a system of internal controls to safeguard assets and that only authorized transactions are recorded in the accounting records.

b. **Competent and trustworthy employees** provide the best internal control system. **Clearly defined authority and responsibility** establish the levels of authority and provide a structure for the approval of transactions. **Segregation of duties** separates the record-keeping function from the physical control of assets. **Sufficient records and documentation** provide an "audit trail" so transactions can be followed through the internal control system. **Physical control of assets and records** provides protection from theft or destruction and tampering.

c. The company's **auditors** will rely on the system of internal control when they perform their audit. Because they will not re-examine every transaction which occurred during the period, they will necessarily presume that internal controls were in place and operating. **Stockholders** have an investment in the company and essentially own a portion of its assets. They will obviously be interested in the safeguarding of assets and in the accountability of management. **Creditors** often retain an interest in assets acquired with the proceeds of their loans. They will be interested in internal control procedures because they increase the probability that the loans they granted will be repaid. **Managers** would be interested in internal control because they do not have the resources to examine all transactions which occur everywhere in a large organization. Accordingly, they will rely on some level of internal control.

CHAPTER 4 Cash Flows, Accruals, and Adjusting Journal Entries

E4–1

a. Ending cash = Beginning cash + Cash receipts – Cash disbursements
= 10,000 + 112,500 – 94,500
= $28,000

b.

Miller Manufacturing
Statement of Cash Flows
For the Year Ended December 31, 1990

Cash flows from operating activities		
Cash collections from customers	$75,000	
Payment to suppliers for inventory	(34,000)	
Payment of salaries	(17,500)	
Payment of administrative expenses	(14,000)	
Payment of interest	(3,000)	
Net cash increase (decrease) due to operating activities		$6,500
Cash flows from investing activities		
Proceeds from long–term investments	12,500	
Purchase of equipment	(12,000)	
Net cash increase (decrease) due to investing activities		500
Cash flows from financing activities		
Proceeds from issue of common stock	15,000	
Proceeds from borrowing	10,000	
Repayment of bank boan	(10,000)	
Payment of dividends	(4,000)	
Net cash increase (decrease) due to financing activities		11,000
Increase (decrease) in cash balance		18,000
Beginning cash balance		10,000
Ending cash balance		$28,000

E4–2

a. (1) The entry is to record rent incurred but not yet paid.

(2) The entry is to record the expiration of a previously purchased insurance policy.

(3) The entry is to record the expiration of a portion of a fixed asset cost.

(4) The entry is to record interest revenue earned but not yet received.

(5) The entry is to record a liability for collections from customers for services not yet rendered. The cash collected had initially been recorded as Fees Earned.

b. (1) Accrual adjusting entry.

(2) Cost expiration adjusting entry.

(3) Cost expiration adjusting entry.

(4) Accrual adjusting entry.

(5) Cost expiration adjusting entry.

E4–3

Transaction	Classification
(1)	4
(2)	1
(3)	3
(4)	5
(5)	5
(6)	1
(7)	2
(8)	5
(9)	1
(10)	5
(11)	1
(12)	5

E4–4

a. 12/31/89 Wage Expense 15,000 *
Wages Payable 15,000
To record wages incurred, but not yet paid.

* $15,000 = $25,000 x (3 days in December ÷ 5 days total)

b. 1/2/90 Wages Expense 10,000
Wages Payable 15,000
Cash 25,000
To record payment of wages.

c.

	1989	1990	Total
Wage expense	$15,000	$10,000	$25,000
Cash outflow associated with wages.	0	25,000	25,000

d. The purpose of the adjusting journal entry on December 31, 1989 is to recognize an economic event that has not yet been captured by an exchange transaction. The economic event is that the Hurst Corporation incurred an expense. This event will not be captured in an exchange transaction until the subsequent period when the wages are actually paid to the employees. Consequently, an adjusting entry is required on December 31 to capture this economic event in the correct accounting period.

E4–5

a.

		Debit	Credit
12/31/90	Depreciation Expense	2,000 *	
	Accumulated Depreciation		2,000
	To record depreciation expense for 1990.		
12/31/91	Depreciation Expense	2,000 *	
	Accumulated Depreciation		2,000
	To record depreciation expense for 1991.		
12/31/92	Depreciation Expense	2,000 *	
	Accumulated Depreciation		2,000
	To record depreciation expense for 1992.		

---

* $2,000 = ($6,000 ÷ 3 years)

1990

Book Value: 1/1/90		$6,000
1990 Depreciation Expense	$2,000	
Accumulated Depreciation: 12/31/90		2,000
Book Value: 12/31/90		$4,000

1991

Book Value: 1/1/90		$6,000
1990 Depreciation Expense	$2,000	
1991 Depreciation Expense	2,000	
Accumulated Depreciation: 12/31/91		4,000
Book Value: 12/31/91		$2,000

1992

Book Value: 1/1/91		$6,000
1990 Depreciation Expense	$2,000	
1991 Depreciation Expense	2,000	
1992 Depreciation Expense	2,000	
Accumulated Depreciation: 12/31/92		6,000
Book Value: 12/31/92		0

b.

	1990	1991	1992	Total
Depreciation expense	$2,000	$2,000	$2,000	$6,000
Cash outflow associated with the purchase of the press.	6,000	0	0	6,000

c. The purpose of the adjusting journal entry at the end of each period is to recognize an economic event that has already been captured by an exchange transaction. The purpose of the adjusting journal entries is to allocate the cost of the printing press to the periods that benefited from the press. Since the press has a useful life of three years, it is assumed that the press will help generate revenues for three years. The cost of a fixed asset should be matched with the periods in which the fixed asset helps generate revenues. Consequently, an adjusting entry is required on December 31 of 1990, 1991, and 1992 to allocate the economic event to the correct accounting periods.

E4–6

a. Under cash–basis accounting, revenues are recognized when cash is received, and expenses are recognized when cash is disbursed. So in this case Oregon Forest Products would recognize the following expenses under cash–basis accounting.

Insurance Expense	$30,000
Supplies Expense	25,000
Rent Expense	7,000

Under accrual–basis accounting, revenues are recognized when earned and expenses are recognized when incurred. In some cases, cash–basis and accrual–basis will yield the same revenue and expense amounts, but this situation would simply be by coincidence. In most cases, the timing of cash disbursements does not coincide with when expenses are incurred. So in this case expenses do not equal the cash disbursed because Oregon Forest Products uses accrual–basis accounting rather than cash–basis accounting.

b. **Insurance**
Ending balance = Beginning balance + Insurance purchased – Insurance expense
= $0 + $30,000 – $24,000
= $6,000

Since the company acquired more insurance than it used during 1990, the company expects to receive future benefits from the remaining insurance. Consequently, the company has an asset, and the appropriate account title is Prepaid Insurance.

Supplies
Ending balance = Beginning balance + Supplies purchased – Supplies expense
= $0 + $25,000 – $11,000
= $14,000

Since the company acquired more supplies than it used during 1990, the company expects to receive future benefits from the remaining supplies. Consequently, the company has an asset, and the appropriate account title is Supplies Inventory.

Rent
Ending balance = Beginning balance + Cash disbursed for rent – Rent expense
= $0 + $7,000 – $12,000
= (5,000)

Since the company incurred more expenses than it disbursed in cash for rent, the company expects to have to fulfill the remaining obligation in the future. Consequently, the company has a liability, and the appropriate account title would be Rent Payable.

E4–7

		Debit	Credit
a.	Note Receivable	250,000	
	Cash		250,000
	To record loan to a customer.		

b.	Interest Receivable	7,500 *	
	Interest Revenue		7,500
	To accrue interest earned but not yet received.		

* $7,500 = $250,000 x 12% x 3/12

c.	Interest Receivable	30,000 *	
	Interest Revenue		30,000
	To accrue interest earned but not yet received.		

* $30,000 = $250,000 x 12% x 12/12

d.	Cash	310,000	
	Note Payable		250,000
	Interest Receivable		37,500
	Interest Revenue		22,500
	To record collection of interest and principal on note.		

Note: The entries for parts c and d assume that interest does not compound.

E4–8

a.

Kelly Retailing
Income Statement
For the Month Ended July 31, ____

Revenues		
Sales		$7,000
Expenses		
Cost of goods sold	$2,500	
Accrued expenses	3,000	
Total expenses		5,500
Net income		$1,500

Kelly Retailing
Statement of Cash Flows from Operating Activities
For the Month Ended July 31, ____

Cash from operating activities	
Cash collections from customers	$9,000
Payment for inventory	(3,000)
Net cash increase (decrease) due to operating activities	$6,000

b. Cash flows from operating activities is based upon the inflow and outflow of cash. Net income is based upon the accrual method of accounting. Under accrual accounting, revenue is recognized when it is earned, and expenses are recognized when incurred. Hence, cash flows do not trigger the recognition of revenues and expenses. Consequently, cash flows from operating activities and net income will only be equal by coincidence. The difference between the cash flows and net income can be explained as follows:

Net income		$1,500
Adjustments		
Collections on accounts receivable	$4,000	
Payments on accounts payable in excess of cost of goods sold	(500)	
Sales in excess of cash collected	(2,000)	
Expenses incurred but not yet paid	3,000	
Total adjustments		4,500
Net cash increase (decrease) due to operating activities		$6,000

E4–9

a.

	Debit	Credit
(1) Cash	17,500	
Common Stock		17,500
To record issue of common stock.		
(2) Cash	3,600	
Accounts Receivable		3,600
To record collection from customers.		
(3) Wage Expense	900	
Cash		900
To record wages incurred and paid.		
(4) Land	9,000	
Cash		9,000
To record purchase of land.		
(5) Dividend	4,000	
Cash		4,000
To record dividend payment.		
(6) Cash	5,000	
Equipment		5,000
To record sale of equipment.		
(7) Interest Expense	1,100	
Note Payable	900	
Cash		2,000
To record interest and principal payment.		
(8) Miscellaneous Expenses	2,500	
Cash		2,500
To record expenses incurred and paid.		

b.

Cash

Beginning balance (BB)	4,000	9,000	Purchase of land
Issue of common stock	17,500	900	Payment of wages
Customer collections	3,600	4,000	Dividend payment
Sale of equipment	5,000	1,100	Interest payment
		900	Loan repayment
		2,500	Payment of misc. expenses
Ending balance (EB)	11,700		

c.

Rahal and Watson
Statement of Cash Flows
For the Month Ended January 31, 1990

Cash flows from operating activities		
Cash collections from customers	$ 3,600	
Payments for wages	(900)	
Payments for interest	(1,100)	
Payment for miscellaneous expenses	(2,500)	
Net cash increase (decrease) due to operating activities		($900)
Cash flows from investing activities		
Proceeds from sale of equipment	5,000	
Purchase of land	(9,000)	
Net cash increase (decrease) due to Investing activities		(4,000)
Cash flows from financing activities		
Proceeds from issue of common stock	17,500	
Dividend payment	(4,000)	
Repayment of note payable	(900)	
Net cash increase (decrease) due to financing activities		12,600
Increase (decrease) in cash balance		7,700
Beginning Cash Balance		4,000
Ending Cash Balance		$11,700

E4–10

a.

Ephemeral Company
Income Statement
For the Years Ended 19XX and 19XX

	Year 1		Year 2	
Revenues				
Sales		$12,000		$16,000
Expenses				
Cost of goods sold	$3,000		$3000	
Rent expense	2,000		2,000	
Wage expense	5,000		5,000	
Total expenses		10,000		10,000
Net income		$ 2,000		$ 6,000

Ephemeral Company
Statement of Cash Flows
For the Years Ended 19XX and 19XX

		Year 1		Year 2
Cash flows from operating activities				
Cash collections from customers	$10,000		$18,000	
Payment of wages	(3,000)		(7,000)	
Payment for inventory	0		(6,000)	
Payment of rent	(4,000)		0	
Net cash increase (decrease) due to operating activities		$ 3,000		$ 5,000
Cash flows from investing activities		0		0
Cash flows from financing activities				
Proceeds from stockholders' contribution	10,000		0	
Payment to stockholders	0		(18,000)*	
Net cash increase (decrease) due to financing activities		10,000		(18,000)
Increase (decrease) in cash balance		13,000		(13,000)
Beginning Cash Balance		0		13,000
Ending Cash Balance		$13,000		$ 0

* $18,000 = Beginning cash balance + Net cash provided by operating activities + Cash flows from investing activities in Year 2 + Proceeds from stockholders' contributions in Year 2 .

b.

Performance Measure	**Year 1**	**Year 2**	**Total**
Net income	$2,000	$6,000	$8,000
Net cash from operating activities	3,000	5,000	8,000

E4–11

a.

J. M. F. Corporation
Income Statement
For the Year Ended December 31, 1990

Sales		$40,000
Expenses		
Cost of goods sold	$27,500	
Insurance expense	5,000	
Interest expense	2,500	
Total expenses		35,000
Net income		$ 5,000

J.M.F. Corporation
Statement of Cash Flows from Operating Activities
For the Year Ended December 31, 1990

Cash flows from operating activities			
Net income			$ 5,000
Adjustments			
Decrease in accounts receivable		$ 2,000	
Increase in inventory		(1,000)	
Decrease in accounts payable		(2,500)	
Decrease in prepaid insurance		500	
Decrease in interest payable		(200)	
Total adjustments			(1,200)
Net cash increase (decrease) due to operating activities			$ 3,800

OR

Cash provided by operating activities			
Cash sales		$40,000	
Cash collection on accounts receivable		2,000	
Cash increase due to operating activities			$42,000
Cash used for operating activities			
Cash paid for inventory			
Cost of goods sold	27,500		
Payments to suppliers on open accounts	2,500		
Increase in inventory	1,000		
Total cash paid for inventory		31,000	
Cash paid for insurance			
Insurance expense	5,000		
Decrease in prepaid insurance	(500)		
Total cash paid for insurance		4,500	
Cash paid for interest			
Interest expense	2,500		
Decrease in interest payable	200		
Total cash paid for interest		2,700	
Total cash increase due to operating activities			(38,200)
Net cash increase (decrease) due to operating activities			$ 3,800

E4–12

a.

Accounts	Unadjusted Trial Balance Dr.	Unadjusted Trial Balance Cr.	Adjusting Entries Dr.	Adjusting Entries Cr.	Adjusted Trial Balance Dr.	Adjusted Trial Balance Cr.	Closing Entries Dr.	Closing Entries Cr.	Final Trial Balance Dr.	Final Trial Balance Cr.
Cash	3,200				3,200				3,200	
Accounts Receivable	15,800				15,800				15,800	
Rent Receivable			(1) 500		500				500	
Inventory	18,000				18,000				18,000	
Prepaid Insurance	1,200			(2) 600	600				600	
Office Equipment	43,500				43,500				43,500	
Accumulated Depr.				(4) 1,000		1,000				1,000
Accounts Payable		8,500				8,500				8,500
Wages Payable				(3) 1,200		1,200				1,200
Bonds Payable		20,000				20,000				20,000
Common Stock		40,000				40,000				40,000
Retained Earnings								(C2) 10,900		10,900
Sales		30,600				30,600	(C1) 30,600			
Rent Revenue		1,100		(1) 500		1,600	(C1) 1,600			
Cost of Goods Sold	11,000				11,000			(C1) 11,000		
Wage Expense	7,500		(3) 1,200		8,700			(C1) 8,700		
Depreciation Expense			(4) 1,000		1,000			(C1) 1,000		
Insurance Expense			(2) 600		600			(C1) 600		
Income Summary							(C2) 10,900	(C1) 10,900		
Total	100,200	100,200	3,300	3,300	102,900	102,900	43,100	43,100	81,600	81,600

Balmer and Associates
Income Statement
For the Year Ended December 31, 1990

Revenues		
Sales	$30,600	
Rent Revenue	1,600	
Total Revenues		$32,000
Expenses		
Cost of goods sold	11,000	
Wage expense	8,700	
Depreciation expense	1,000	
Insurance expense	600	
Total Expenses		21,300
Net income		$10,900

Balmer and Associates
Statement of Retained Earnings
For the Year Ended December 31, 1990

Beginning retained earnings balance (1/1/90)	$ 0
Net income	10,900
Ending retained earnings balance (12/31/90)	$10,900

Balmer and Associates
Balance Sheet
December 31,1990

Assets	$ 3,200
Cash	15,800
Rent Receivable	500
Inventory	18,000
Prepaid insurance	600
Office equipment	43,500
Less: Accumulated depreciation	1,000
Total assets	$80,600
Liabilities and stockholders' equity	
Accounts payable	$ 8,500
Wages payable	1,200
Bonds payable	20,000
Common stock	40,000
Retained earnings	10,900
Total liabilities and stockholders' equity	$80,600

Balmer and Associates
Statement of Cash Flows
For the Year Ended December 31, 1990

Cash flows from operating activities		
Net income		$10,900
Adjustments		
Depreciation expense	$ 1,000	
Increase in accounts receivable	(15,800)	
Increase in rent receivable	(500)	
Increase in inventory	(18,000)	
Increase in prepaid insurance	(600)	
Increase in accounts payable	8,500	
Increase in wages payable	1,200	
Total adjustments		(24,200)
Net cash increase (decrease) due to operating activities		(13,300)
Cash flows from investing activities		
Purchase of office equipment	(43,500)	
Net cash increase (decrease) due to investing activities		(43,500)
Cash flows from financing activities		
Proceeds from bond issue	20,000	
Proceeds from stock issue	40,000	
Net cash increase (decrease) due to financing activities		60,000
Increase (decrease) in cash balance	$ 3,200	
Beginning cash balance (1/1/90)		0
Ending cash balance (12/31/90)		$ 3,200

P4–1

Entry	Classification	Assets	Liabilities	Stockholders' Equity	Revenues	Expenses
(1)	A	NE	+	–	NE	+
(2)	A	NE	+	–	NE	+
(3)	A	+	NE	+	+	NE
(4)	C	NE	–	+	+	NE
(5)	C	–	NE	–	NE	+
(6)	C	+	NE	+	NE	–
(7)	C	NE	+	–	–	NE

P4–2

		Debit	Credit
(a)	Supplies Expense	90,000	
	Supplies Inventory		90,000
	To record supplies used during the year.		
(b)	Rent Expense	1,500	
	Rent Payable		1,500
	To record rent expense incurred but not yet paid.		
(c)	Fees Earned	15,000	
	Unearned Service Revenues		15,000
	To adjust for fees collected but not yet earned.		
(d)	Depreciation Expense	50,000	
	Accumulated Depreciation		50,000
	To record depreciation expense for 1990.		
(e)	Interest Expense	500 *	
	Interest Payable		500
	To record interest incurred but not yet paid		

* $500 = $10,000 x 10% x 6/12

		Debit	Credit
(f)	Advertising Expense	25,000	
	Advertising Payable		25,000
	To record advertising incurred but not yet paid.		
(g)	Insurance Expense	125	
	Prepaid Insurance		125
	To record portion of insurance policy used during 1990.		

P4–3

		Debit	Credit
(1)	Rent Expense	800	
	Prepaid Rent		800
	To record expiration of prepaid rent.		
(2)	Prepaid Insurance	500	
	Insurance Expense		500
	To adjust for insurance paid for but not yet expired.		

(3) Depreciation Expense 2,200
Accumulated Depreciation 2,200
To record depreciation expense.

(4) Salary Expense 800
Salaries Payable 800
To record salaries incurred but not yet paid.

(5) Unearned Revenue 700
Fees Earned 700
To record fees earned.

P4–4

Annual interest expense = $24,000 x 10 % = $2,400

	Ending Payable		Beginning Payable		Interest Expense		Interest Paid
Case 1:	X X = $0	=	600	+	2,400	–	3,000
Case 2:	400	=	800	+	2,400	–	X X = $2,800
Case 3:	X X = $400	=	400	+	2,400	–	2,400
Case 4:	200	=	X X = $400	+	2,400	–	2,600
Case 5:	400	=	200	+	2,400	–	X X = $2,200
Case 6:	0	=	X X = $400	+	2,400	–	2,800

P4–5

a. 11/1/90 Cash 1,500
Rent Collected in Advance 1,500
To record rent collected in advance.

12/31/90 Rent Collected in Advance 1,000*
Rent Revenue 1,000
To record rent earned

* $1,000 = $1,500 x 2/3

b. 11/1/90 Cash 1,500
Rent Revenue 1,500
To record rent collected in advance.

12/31/90 Rent Revenue 500
Rent Collected in Advance 500
To adjust for rent collected but not earned.

c. 11/1/90 Prepaid Rent 1,500
Cash 1,500
To record rent payments for Nov., Dec., and Jan.

12/31/90 Rent Expense 1,000
Prepaid Rent 1,000
To record expiration of prepaid rent.

d. 11/1/90 Rent Expense 1,500
Cash 1,500
To record rent payments.

12/31/90 Prepaid Rent 500
Rent Expense 500
To adjust for rent paid but not yet expired.

P4–6

a. (1) Cash 240,000
Unearned Insurance Premiums 240,000
To record advance collection of premiums.

(2) Unearned Insurance Premiums 70,000
Premium Revenue 70,000
To record revenue earned.

(3) The purpose of the adjusting journal entry is to recognize an economic event that had previously been captured by an exchange transaction. Prustate collected the cash for the insurance premiums, but had not yet earned the revenue associated with the cash. Prustate recorded the exchange transaction as a liability. During the life of the insurance policy, Prustate will earn the revenue and reduce its liability. The adjusting journal entry simply records the fact that Prustate has earned some of the revenue and that the revenue must be allocated to the appropriate accounting period.

(4)

	1989	1990	1991	Total
Insurance Revenue	$ 70,000	$120,000	$50,000	$240,000
Cash Receipts	240,000	0	0	240,000

b. (1) Prepaid Insurance 240,000
Cash 240,000
To record purchase of insurance.

(2) Insurance Expense 70,000
Prepaid Insurance 70,000
To record expiration of insurance.

(3) The purpose of the adjusting journal entry is to recognize an economic event that had previously been captured by an exchange transaction. Jacob paid the cash for the insurance premiums, but had not yet incurred the expense associated with the cash. Jacob recorded the exchange transaction as an asset. During the life of the insurance policy, the policy will expire, thereby giving rise to an expense. The adjusting journal entry simply records the fact that a portion of the policy has expired and that the expense must be allocated to the appropriate accounting period.

(4)

	1989	1990	1991	Total
Insurance expense	$ 70,000	$120,000	$50,000	$240,000
Cash payments	240,000	0	0	240,000

P4–7

a. Cash 24,000
Unearned Premium Revenues 24,000
To record collection of premiums.

Unearned Premium Revenues 6,000
Premium Revenues 6,000
To record insurance premiums earned.

b. Cash 24,000
Premium Revenues 24,000
To record collection of premiums.

Premium Revenues 18,000
Unearned Premium Revenues 18,000
To record premiums not yet earned.

c. Prepaid Insurance 24,000
Cash 24,000
To record purchase of insurance.

Insurance Expense 6,000
Prepaid Insurance 6,000
To record expiration of insurance.

		Debit	Credit
d.	Insurance Expense	24,000	
	Cash		24,000
	To record purchase of insurance.		
	Prepaid Insurance	18,000	
	Insurance Expense		18,000
	To record insurance not yet expired.		

P4–8

		Debit	Credit
a.	Insurance Expense	50,000	
	Prepaid Insurance		50,000
	To record expiration of customer liability insurance.		
	Insurance Expense	60,000	
	Prepaid Insurance		60,000
	To record expiration of employee health insurance.		
	Insurance Expense	60,000	
	Prepaid Insurance		60,000
	To record expiration of storm damage insurance.		
	Insurance Expense	75,000	
	Prepaid Insurance		75,000
	To record expiration of storm damage insurance.		
	Insurance Expense	100,000	
	Prepaid Insurance		100,000
	To record expiration of fire insurance.		
	Insurance Expense	55,000	
	Prepaid Insurance		55,000
	To record expiration of fire insurance.		
	Insurance Expense	22,500	
	Prepaid Insurance		22,500
	To record expiration of fire insurance.		

b. Customer liability: No adjusting journal entry is necessary.

	Debit	Credit
Prepaid Insurance	60,000	
Insurance Expense		60,000
To record unexpired employee health insurance.		
Prepaid Insurance	20,000	
Insurance Expense		20,000
To record unexpired storm damage insurance.		
Prepaid Insurance	25,000	
Insurance Expense		25,000
To record unexpired storm damage insurance.		

Prepaid Insurance	200,000	
Insurance Expense		200,000
To record unexpired fire insurance.		
Prepaid Insurance	165,000	
Insurance Expense		165,000
To record unexpired fire insurance.		
Prepaid Insurance	67,500	
Insurance Expense		67,500
To record unexpired fire insurance.		

P4–9

a.

(1) Depreciation Expense	40,000	
Accumulated Depreciation		40,000
To record depreciation expense.		
(2) Cost of Goods Sold	80,000	
Inventory		80,000
To adjust inventory to goods on hand.		
(3) Rent Expense	7,000	
Prepaid Rent		7,000
To record expiration of prepaid rent.		
(4) Supplies Expense	17,000	
Supplies Inventory		17,000
To adjust supplies to goods on hand.		
(5) Wage Expense	15,000	
Wages Payable		15,000
To record wages incurred but not yet paid.		
(6) Rent Receivable	10,000	
Rent Revenue		10,000
To record rent revenue earned but not yet collected.		
(7) Interest Expense	2,500*	
Interest Payable		2,500
To record interest incurred but not yet paid.		

* $2,500 = $50,000 x 12% x 5/12

b. (C1)

		Debit	Credit
Sales		900,000	
Rent Revenue		10,000	
Income Summary		126,500	
	Cost of Goods Sold		730,000
	Supplies Expense		50,000
	Insurance Expense		49,000
	Wage Expense		158,000
	Depreciation Expense		40,000
	Interest Expense		2,500
	Rent Expense		7,000

To close revenues and expenses into Income Summary.

(C2)

		Debit	Credit
Retained Earnings		126,500	
	Income Summary		126,500

To close Income Summary into Retained Earnings.

(C3)

		Debit	Credit
Retained Earnings		20,000	
	Dividends		20,000

To close Dividends into Retained Earnings.

c.

J. Feeney, Inc.
Income Statement
For the Year Ended December 31,1990

Revenues			
Sales		$900,000	
Rent revenue		10,000	
Total revenue			$ 910,000
Expenses			
Cost of goods sold		730,000	
Operating expenses:			
Supplies expense	$ 50,000		
Wage expense	158,000		
Insurance expense	49,000		
Depreciation expense	40,000		
Rent expense	7,000		
Total operating expenses		304,000	
Interest expense		2,500	
Total expenses			1,036,500
Net income (loss)			($126,500)

J. Feeney, Inc.
Balance Sheet
December 31,1990

Assets		
Current assets		
Cash	$ 92,000	
Accounts receivable	178,000	
Inventory	120,000	
Prepaid rent	7,000	
Supplies inventory	58,000	
Rent receivable	10,000	
Total current assets		$465,000
Property, plant & equipment		
Plant and equipment	550,000	
Less: Accumulated depreciation	189,000	
Total property, plant & equipment		361,000
Total assets		$826,000
Liabilities and stockholders' equity		
Liabilities		
Accounts payable	$104,000	
Wages payable	15,000	
Interest payable	2,500	
Note payable	50,000	
Total liabilities		$171,500
Stockholders' equity		
Common stock	300,000	
Retained earnings	354,500	
Total stockholders' equity		654,500
Total liabilities and stockholders' equity		$826,000

P4-10

a. All T-accounts for P4-10 appear in this section. Transactions are keyed to numbers in parentheses. Adjusting journal entries are keyed to lowercase letters. Closing entries are keyed to (C1), (C2), and (C3).

Cash

	Debit	Credit	
(BB)	96,000		
(1a)	350,000	425,000	(3)
(5)	892,000	820,000	(6)
(7)	34,000	148,000	(8)
(9)	180,000	40,000	(11)
		65,000	(12)
(EB)	54,000		

Accounts Receivable

	Debit	Credit	
(BB)	178,000		
(1a)	1,250,000	892,000	(5)
(10)	72,000		
(EB)	464,000		

Inventory

	Debit	Credit	
(BB)	210,000		
(2)	788,000	800,000	(1b)
(EB)	198,000		

Interest Receivable

	Debit	Credit
(BB)	0	
(f)	1,620	
(EB)	1,620	

Prepaid Advertising

	Debit	Credit
(BB)	0	
(c)	25,000	
(EB)	25,000	

Prepaid Insurance

(BB)	68,000		
		40,800	(a)
(EB)	27,200		

Supplies Inventory

(BB)	50,000		
(4)	110,000	126,000	(b)
(EB)	34,000		

Notes Receivable

(BB)	0		
72,000	(10)		
(EB)	72,000		

Long–Term Investments

(BB)	150,000		
(12)	65,000	30,000	(7)
(EB)	185,000		

Equipment

(BB)	480,000		
(EB)	480,000		

Accum Depr (Equipment)

		98,000	(BB)
		48,000	(g)
		146,000	(EB)

Machinery

(BB)	950,000		
(EB)	950,000		

Accum Depr (Machinery)

		230,000	(BB)
		47,500	(g)
		277,500	(EB)

Patent

(BB)	75,000		
		12,500	(g)
(EB)	62,500		

Rent Payable

		0	(BB)
		6,000	(d)
		6,000	(EB)

Interest Payable

		0	(BB)
		3,025	(h)
		3,025	(EB)

Accounts Payable

		225,000	(BB)
(6)	820,000	788,000	(2)
		193,000	(EB)

Wages Payable

		68,000	(BB)
(3)	68,000	43,000	(e)
		43,000	(EB)

S–T Notes Payable

		0	(BB)
		110,000	(4)
		110,000	(EB)

Mortgage Payable

		300,000	(BB)
		300,000	(EB)

Bonds Payable

		500,000	(BB)
		500,000	(EB)

Common Stock

		500,000	(BB)
		180,000	(9)
		680,000	(EB)

Retained Earnings

		336,000	(BB)
(C2)	1,205		
(C3)	40,000		
		294,795	(EB)

Dividends

(BB)	0		
(11)	40,000		
		40,000	(C3)
(EB)	0		

Sales

		0	(BB)
		1,600,000	(1)
(C1)	1,600,000		
		0	(EB)

Cost of Goods Sold

(1b)	800,000		
		800,000	(C1)
(EB)	0		

Wage Expense

(3)	357,000		
(e)	43,000	400,000	(C1)
(EB)	0		

Advertising Expense

(8)	60,000	25,000	(c)
		35,000	(C1)
(EB)	0		

Rent Expense

(8)	36,000		
(d)	6,000	42,000	(C1)
(EB)	0		

Maintenance Expense

(8)	52,000		
		52,000	(C1)
(EB)	0		

Supplies Expense

(b)	126,000		
		126,000	(C1)
(EB)	0		

Insurance Expense

Debit	Credit
(a) 40,800	
	40,800 (C1)
(EB) 0	

Interest Expense

Debit	Credit
(h) 3,025	
	3,025 (C1)
(EB) 0	

Depreciation Exp (Equip)

Debit	Credit
(g) 48,000	
	48,000 (C1)
(EB) 0	

Depreciation Exp (Machinery)

Debit	Credit
(g) 47,500	
	47,500 (C1)
(EB) 0	

Amortization Exp (Patent)

Debit	Credit
(g) 12,500	
	12,500 (C1)
(EB) 0	

Interest Revenue

Debit	Credit
	1,620 (f)
(C1) 1,620	
	0 (EB)

Gain on Sale of Investment

Debit	Credit
	4,000 (7)
(C1) 4,000	
	0 (EB)

Income Summary

Debit	Credit
(C2) 33,975	33,975 (C1)
0	0

b. Entries are posted to the T-accounts in preceding section (a).

	Account	Debit	Credit
(1a)	Cash	350,000	
	Accounts Receivable	1,250,000	
	Sales		1,600,000
	To record sales.		
(1b)	Cost of goods sold	800,000	
	Inventory		800,000
	To record cost of inventory sold.		
(2)	Inventory	788,000	
	Accounts Payable		788,000
	To record purchase of inventory on account.		
(3)	Wage Expense	357,000	
	Wages Payable	68,000	
	Cash		425,000
	To record payment of wages.		
(4)	Supplies Inventory	110,000	
	Short–Term Note Payable		110,000
	To record purchase of supplies by note.		
(5)	Cash	892,000	
	Accounts Receivable		892,000
	To record collections on open accounts.		
(6)	Accounts Payable	820,000	
	Cash		820,000
	To record payments to suppliers for open accounts.		
(7)	Cash	34,000	
	Long–Term Investments		30,000
	Gain on Sale of Investment		4,000
	To record sale of investment.		

(8)	Advertising Expense	60,000	
	Rent Expense	36,000	
	Maintenance Expense	52,000	
	Cash		148,000
	To record expenses incurred and paid.		
(9)	Cash	180,000	
	Common Stock		180,000
	To record the receipt of a note receivable in payment of an open account.		
(10)	Notes Receivable	72,000	
	Accounts Receivable		72,000
	To record payment of open account by note.		
(11)	Dividends	40,000	
	Cash		40,000
	To record declaration and payment of a dividend.		
(12)	Long–Term Investment	65,000	
	Cash		65,000
	To record purchase of investments.		

c. Adjusting entries are keyed to lowercase letters in parentheses.

Accounts	Unadjusted Trial Balance		Adjusting Entries		Adjusted Trial Balance		Closing Entries		Final Trial Balance	
	Dr.	Cr.	Dr.	Cr.	Dr.	Cr.	Dr.	Cr.	Dr.	Cr.
Cash	54,000				54,000				54,000	
Accounts Receivable	464,000				464,000				464,000	
Interest Receivable			(f) 1,620		1,620				1,620	
Inventory	198,000				198,000				198,000	
Supplies Inventory	160,000			(b) 126,000	34,000				34,000	
Prepaid Insurance	68,000			(a) 40,800	27,200				27,200	
Prepaid Advertising			(c) 25,000		25,000				25,000	
Notes Receivable	72,000				72,000				72,000	
L–T Investments	185,000				185,000				185,000	
Equipment	480,000				480,000				480,000	
Accum Depr: Equip		98,000		(g) 48,000		146,000				146,000
Machinery	950,000				950,000				950,000	
Accum Depr: Mach		230,000		(g) 47,500		277,500				277,500
Patent	75,000			(g) 12,500	62,500				62,500	
Accounts payable		193,000				193,000				193,000
Wages Payable				(e) 43,000		43,000				43,000
Interest Payable				(h) 3,025		3,025				3,025
Rent Payable				(d) 6,000		6,000				6,000
S–T Notes Payable		110,000				110,000				110,000
Mortgage Payable		300,000				300,000				300,000
Bonds Payable		500,000				500,000				500,000
Common Stock		680,000				680,000				680,000
Retained Earnings		336,000				336,000	(C2) 1,205			
							(C3) 40,000			294,795
Dividends	40,000				40,000			(C3) 40,000		
Sales		1,600,000				1,600,000	(C1) 1,600,000			
Interest Revenue				(f) 1,620		1,620	(C1) 1,620			
Gain on Sale of Invest		4,000				4,000	(C1) 4,000			
Cost of Goods Sold	800,000				800,000			(C1) 800,000		
Wage Expense	357,000		(e) 43,000		400,000			(C1) 400,000		
Advertising Expense	60,000			(c) 25,000	35,000			(C1) 35,000		
Rent Expense	36,000		(d) 6,000		42,000			(C1) 42,000		
Maintenance Expense	52,000				52,000			(C1) 52,000		
Insurance Expense			(a) 40,800		40,800			(C1) 40,800		
Supplies Expense			(b) 126,000		126,000			(C1) 126,000		
Interest Expense			(h) 3,025		3,025			(C1) 3,025		
Amortization Expense			(g) 12,500		12,500			(C1) 12,500		
Depr Exp: Equipment			(g) 48,000		48,000			(C1) 48,000		
Depr Exp: Machinery			(g) 47,500		47,500			(C1) 47,500		
Income Summary							(C1) 1,025	(C2) 1,025		
Total	4,051,000	4,051,000	353,445	353,445	4,200,145	4,200,145	1,647,850	1,647,850	2,553,320	2,553,320

d. Entries are posted to the T-accounts in part (a).

(a) Insurance Expense	40,800*	
Prepaid Insurance		40,800
To record partial expiration of insurance.		

* $40,800 = $68,000 x 60%

(b) Supplies Expense	126,000 *		
Supplies Inventory		126,000	
To record supplies used.			

* $126,000 = ($50,000 beginning balance of supplies inventory + $110,000 supplies inventory acquired during 1990) – $34,000 of supplies on hand as of 12/31/90

(c) Prepaid Advertising	25,000		
Advertising Expense		25,000	
To record advertising to be used in subsequent periods.			
(d) Rent Expense	6,000 *		
Rent Payable		6,000	
To record rent incurred but not yet paid.			

* $6,000 = ($3,500 per month x 12 months) – $36,000 rent payment

(e) Wage Expense	43,000		
Wages Payable		43,000	
To record wages incurred but not yet paid			
(f) Interest Receivable	1,620 *		
Interest Revenue		1,620	
To record interest earned but not yet collected			

* $1,620 = $72,000 x 9% x 3/12

(g) Depreciation Expense: Equipment		48,000	
Depreciation Expense: Machinery		47,500	
Amortization Expense: Patent		12,500	
Accumulated Depreciation: Equipment			48,000
Accumulated Depreciation: Machinery			47,500
Patent			12,500
To record amortization of fixed and intangible assets.			
(h) Interest Expense	3,025 *		
Interest Payable		3,025	
To record interest incurred but not yet paid.			

* $3,025 = $110,000 x 9% x 110/360

e. Closing entries are posted to T-accounts in part (a).

	Account	Debit	Credit
(C1)	Sales	1,600,000	
	Interest Revenue	1,620	
	Gain on Sale of Investments	4,000	
	Income Summary	1,205	
	Cost of Goods Sold		800,000
	Wage Expense		400,000
	Advertising Expense		35,000
	Rent Expense		42,000
	Depreciation Expense: Machinery		47,500
	Depreciation Expense: Equipment		48,000
	Amortization Expense: Patent		12,500
	Maintenance Expense		52,000
	Supplies Expense		126,000
	Interest Expense		3,025
	Insurance Expense		40,800
	To close revenues and expenses into Income Summary.		
(C2)	Retained Earnings	1,205	
	Income Summary		1,205
	To close Income Summary into Retained Earnings.		
(C3)	Retained Earnings	40,000	
	Dividends		40,000
	To close Dividends into Retained Earnings.		

f.

J. D. F Company
Income Statement
For the Year Ended December 31, 1990

Revenues			
Sales			$1,600,000
Other revenues			
Interest revenue	$ 1,620		
Gain on sale of investments	4,000		
Total other revenues		5,620	
Total revenues			$1,605,620
Expenses			
Cost of goods sold		800,000	
Operating expenses			
Wages expense	400,000		
Advertising expense	35,000		
Rent expense	42,000		
Maintenance expense	52,000		
Supplies expense	126,000		
Insurance expense	40,800		
Depreciation expense: equipment	48,000		
Depreciation expense: machinery	47,500		
Amortization expense: patent	12,500		
Total operating expense		803,800	
Interest expense		3,025	
Total expense			1,606,825
Net income (loss)			($1,205)

J. D. F Company
Statement of Retained Earnings
For the Year Ended December 31, 1990

Beginning retained earnings balance (1/1/90)	$336,000
Less: Net loss	1,205
Dividends declared	40,000
Ending retained earnings balance (12/31/90)	$294,795

J. D. F. Company
Balance Sheet
December 31, 1990

Assets			
Current assets			
Cash		$ 54,000	
Accounts receivable		464,000	
Interest receivable		1,620	
Inventory		198,000	
Supplies inventory		34,000	
Prepaid insurance		27,200	
Prepaid advertising		25,000	
Notes receivable		72,000	
Total current assets			$ 875,820
Long–term investments			185,000
Fixed assets			
Equipment	$480,000		
Less: Accumulated depreciation	146,000	334,000	
Machinery	950,000		
Less: Accumulated depreciation	277,500	672,500	
Total fixed assets			1,006,500
Patent			62,500
Total assets			$2,129,820
Liabilities & stockholders' equity			
Current liabilities			
Accounts payable		$ 193,000	
Wages payable		43,000	
Rent payable		6,000	
Interest payable		3,025	
Note payable		110,000	
Total current liabilities			$ 355,025
Long–term liabilities			
Mortgage payable		300,000	
Bond payable		500,000	
Total long–term liabilities			800,000
Stockholders' equity			
Common stock		680,000	
Retained earnings		294,795	
Total stockholders' equity			974,795
Total liabilities & stockholders' equity			$2,129,820

J. D. F. Corporation
Statement of Cash Flows (Direct Method)
For the Year Ended December 31, 1990

Cash flows from operating activities		
Collections from customers on cash sales	$350,000	
Collection from customers on open accounts	892,000	
Payments for wages	(425,000)	
Payments to suppliers on open account	(820,000)	
Payment for advertising	(60,000)	
Payment for rent	(36,000)	
Payment for maintenance	(52,000)	
Net cash increase (decrease) due to operating activities		($151,000)
Cash flows from investing activities		
Purchase of investment	(65,000)	
Proceeds from sale of investment	34,000	
Net cash increase (decrease) due to investing activities		(31,000)
Cash flows from financing activities		
Proceeds from issue of common stock	180,000	
Payment of dividends	(40,000)	
Net cash increase (decrease) due to financing activities		140,000
Increase (decrease) in cash balance		(42,000)
Beginning cash balance (1/1/90)		96,000
Ending cash balance (12/31/90)		$ 54,000

g.

J.D.F. Corporation
Statement of Cash Flows (Indirect Method)
For the Year Ended December 31, 1990

Cash flows from operating activities		
Net loss		($1,205)
Adjustments		
Depreciation expense: equipment	$ 48,000	
Depreciation expense: machinery	47,500	
Amortization expense	12,500	
Gain on sale of investments	(4,000)	
Increase in accounts receivable	(286,000)	
Increase in notes receivable	(72,000)	
Decrease in inventory	12,000	
Decrease in accountspayable	(32,000)	
Decrease in wages payable	(25,000)	
Increase in prepaid advertising	(25,000)	
Increase in rent payable	6,000	
Decrease in supplies inventory	16,000	
Increase in note payable	110,000	
Decrease in prepaid insurance	40,800	
Increase in interest receivable	(1,620)	
Increase in interest payable	3,025	
Total adjustments		(149,795)
Net cash increase (decrease) due to operating activities		(151,000)
Cash flows from investing activities		
Purchase of investment	(65,000)	
Proceeds from sale of investment	34,000	
Net cash increase (decrease) due to investing activities		(31,000)
Cash flows from financing activities		
Proceeds from issue of common stock	180,000	
Payment of dividends	(40,000)	
Net cash increase (decrease) due to financing activities		140,000
Increase (decrease) in cash balance		(42,000)
Beginning cash balance (1/1/90)		96,000
Ending cash balance (12/31/90)		$54,000

P4–11

a.

Account	Balance	Balance Sheet Activity		Cash Flows
Sales	$54,000	Accounts Receivable	$6,000	
		Unearned Revenue	(2,000)	$58,000
Gain on sale	3,000		(3,000)	0
C O G S	(21,000)	Inventory	7,500	
		Accounts Payable	(2,800)	(16,300)
Wage exp	(12,000)	Wages Payable	(2,000)	(14,000)
Rent exp	(8,000)	Prepaid Rent	200	(7,800)
Misc exp	(5,400)	Miscellaneous Payables	1,500	(3,900)
Depr exp	(3,500)		3,500	0
Loss on sale	(1,500)		1,500	0
Total	$ 5,600		$10,400	$16,000

Note: Gains and losses arise from a bookkeeping entry. Hence no cash flows are associated with gains and losses; rather, cash flows are associated with the underlying event of selling an asset.

b.

Russo and Brothers
Statement of Cash Flows from Operating Activities (Indirect Method)
For the Year Ended December 31, 1990

Net income		$5,600
Adjustments		
Depreciation expense	$3,500	
Gain on sale of investment	(3,000)	
Loss on sale of machinery	1,500	
Decrease in accounts receivable	6,000	
Decrease in unearned revenue	(2,000)	
Decrease in inventory	7,500	
Decrease in accounts payable	(2,800)	
Decrease in wages payable	(2,000)	
Decrease in prepaid rent	200	
Increase in miscellaneous payables	1,500	
Total adjustments		10,400
Net cash increase (decrease) due to operating activities		$16,000

c. Cash inflow from sale of investment:

Cash inflow = Cost of investment sold – Loss on sale + Gain on sale
= Decrease in investment balance – Loss on sale + Gain on sale
= $2,000 – $0 + $3,000
= $5,000

d.

Cash	1,500	
Accumulated Depreciation	2,000 *	
Loss on Sale of Machinery	1,500	
Machinery		5,000
To record sale of machinery.		

* $2,000 = Depreciation expense – Increase in accumulated depreciation
= $3,500 – $1,500

C4-1

a. Depreciation is a subset of amortization. Amortization refers to systematically converting an asset to an expense over its life. This involves the use of cost-expiration adjusting journal entries at the end of each accounting period. These entries match expenses against the benefits produced by the asset. Depreciation is the process of amortizing the cost of a fixed asset.

b. $4,603,000,000 ÷ 40 = $115,075,000

Amortization Expense	115,075,000	
Goodwill and Trademarks		115,075,000
To record amortization of goodwill and trademarks.		

c. A shorter useful life would *increase* amortization expense in each period. A twenty-year useful life would result in an expense of ($4,603,000,000 ÷ 20) $230,150,000. So, income would have *decreased* by $115,075,000, ($230,150,000 – $115,075,000).

C4-2

a. Depreciation expense reduces accrual net income but not cash flow. In this case, where cash flows are below earnings, depreciation serves to "narrow the gap" between reported net income and cash flow (i.e., it reconciles part of the difference). However, the reported depreciation is not the only factor responsible for cash flow being below earnings. A number of other factors (e.g., increases in receivables, decreases in payables) may also have played a part.

b. Possible explanations include items that affect cash flow but not earnings, or vice versa. Some of these follow:

(i) Sales revenue billed and recorded as earned but not collected in cash.
(ii) The payment of previously accrued expenses.
(iii) The payment of a prior period's accounts payable.

c. Stockholders are interested in their company's cash flow because that is how they receive a return on their investment in the form of dividends. A substantial decrease in cash flow means there is less cash available for dividends, so share price might decline. Additionally, reduced cash flow may signal bad news about the company's prospects and may cause the stock to be valued by the market at a lower amount.

C4-3

a. The $60,000 would be classified as a cash-increasing financing activity.

b. First-year cash revenues would be classified as a cash-increasing operating activity.

c. The amount of $750,000 would appear as revenues on the income statement; $300,000 would appear on the cash flow statement as an operating activity; $450,000 would appear on the balance sheet as Accounts Receivable.

C4-4

a. The labilities which result from adjusting journal entries follow:

Wage and Salaries Payable
Interest Payable
Accrued Income Taxes Payable

b.

	Debit	Credit
Wages and Salary Expense	195,299	
Wages and Salaries Payable		195,299
To record accrued wages and salaries.		
Interest Expense	51,497	
Interest Payable		51,497
To record accrued interest.		
Income Tax Expense	52,010	
Accrued Income Taxes Payable		52,010
To record income tax expense.		

All three entries decrease stockholders' equity (increase expenses) and increase liabilities.

c.

Reported net income:		$446,623
Expenses *not* accrued:		
Wages	$195,299	
Interest	51,497	
Taxes	52,010	
		298,80
Net income without accruals:		$745,429

C4-5

a. Nordstrom's statement of cash flows was prepared using the indirect method, in that in "reconciles" accrual net income to cash provided by operating activities. The direct method would present the classification of dollar amounts affecting the cash account during the period.

b. Depreciation is added back because it is an expense (included in the computation of accrual net income) which does not require a cash outlay. It is not a source of cash, but rather a noncash expense.

c.

Account	Change
Accounts Receivable	Increased
Merchandise Inventory	Increased
Prepaid Expense	Increased
Accounts Payable	Increased
Accrued Salaries, Wages and Taxes	Increased
Accrued Expense	Increased
Income Tax Liabilities	Decreased

CHAPTER 5 The Economic and Measurement Fundamentals of Financial Accounting

E5–1

At the beginning of the period, $10,000 would allow the company to buy a "basket of goods." Due to the increase in the general price level, the same basket of goods would cost more than $10,000 at the end of the period. Therefore, the company would have less purchasing power at the end of the period than at the beginning of the period. The decrease in purchasing power would be computed as follows:

1. Compute the cost of the basket of goods at the end of the period:
   $10,000 x (1 + inflation rate)
   = $10,000 x 1.05
   = $10,500

2. Compute change in cost of the basket of goods from the end of the period to the start of the period:
   $10,500 – $10,000 = $500

This decrease in purchasing power would not be reflected in the company's financial statements. Accountants adhere to the **stable dollar assumption**, which means that changes in the general price level are ignored when determining the value of the company. This assumption allows users of financial statements to compare financial statements from different points in time.

E5–2

a. Each land acquisition would be recorded at the historical cost of $6,000 for a total of $12,000.

b. No, the company could not purchase the same basket of goods for $6,000 in 1990 as in 1975. To purchase the same basket of goods in 1990, the company would need $9,000 [i.e., $6,000 x (1 + 50%)]. Therefore, cash held by the company from 1975 to 1990 would be subject to an economic loss of $3,000.

c. There are two alternatives for reporting the value of the land if the stable dollar assumption is ignored. The first alternative is to report both pieces of land at 1975 dollars. The second alternative is to report both pieces of land at 1990 dollars. The two alternatives are shown below.

1975 land purchase		$ 6,000
1990 land purchase		
1990 cost	$6,000	
Price-level adjustment	÷ 1.5	
1990 land purchase at 1975 dollars		4,000
Total land at 1975 dollars		$10,000

1990 land purchase		$ 6,000
1975 land purchase		
1975 cost	$6,000	
Price-level adjustment	x 1.5	
1975 land purchase at 1975 dollars		9,000
Total land at 1990 dollars		$15,000

E5–3

	Historical Cost	Fair Market Value	Present Value	Replacement Cost
Cash		X		
Marketable Securities	X[a]	X[a]		
Inventories	X[a]	X[a]		
Prepaid Expenses	X			
Long-Term Investment	X[b]	X[b]	X[b]	
Notes Receivable			X	
Machinery	X			
Equipment	X			
Land	X			
Intangible Assets	X			
Short-Term Payables		X		
Long-Term Payables			X	

[a] Marketable securities and inventory are recorded at the lower of historical cost or fair market value.

[b] Long-term investments are carried on the books at historical cost fair market value or present value depending upon the type of investment.

E5–4

a. The most common point at which a company would recognize revenue is at the time of delivery. So in this case McKey and Company would recognize revenue on February 9. The journal entries that would be prepared each month would be as follows:

December:	No entries necessary.		
January:	No entries necessary.		
February:	Accounts Receivable	2,000	
	Sales		2,000
	To record sale of brackets.		
March:	Cash	2,000	
	Accounts Receivable		2,000
	To record collection on an open account.		

b. The four criteria for recognizing revenue are 1) the company has completed a significant portion of the production and sales effort, 2) the amount of revenue can be objectively measured, 3) the company has incurred the majority of costs and remaining costs can be reasonably estimated, and 4) cash collection is reasonably assured. Presumably McKey and Company is reasonably assured that Cascades Enterprises will eventually be able to pay the $2,000, or McKey would not have entered into the agreement with Cascade in the first place. On January 17 McKey has completed the entire production process, and the only remaining sales effort is to transfer physical possession of the brackets to Cascades Enterprises. Since McKey did complete this last important step on February 9, February 9 appears to be the appropriate date to recognize the revenue.

c. Under the appropriate conditions, revenue can be recognized at several points in time. Revenue can be recognized (1) during production, (2) at the completion of production, (3) at the point of delivery, or (4) when the cash is collected. Case 1 normally arises in long-term construction projects such as office buildings, bridges, and so forth. Case 2 arises where goods are manufactured to the exact specifications of a customer and the goods cannot be sold to another party. Case 3 is the most common point of revenue recognition. Case 4 arises when cash collection is not reasonably assured.

d. McKey's managers could be interested in the timing of revenue recognition due to incentives provided by contracts. For example, the managers may be paid a bonus based upon accounting income. A manager who is trying to maximize his/her bonus might prefer recognizing revenue in a particular period rather than in a different period. Another contract that might influence the actions of managers would be a debt covenant. If a debt covenant stipulates a maximum debt-to-equity ratio, and the company is nearing the ratio, the managers could improve the ratio by increasing stockholders' equity. One way to increase stockholders' equity is to increase net income. Consequently, speeding up the revenue recognition might prevent the company from violating a debt covenant.

E5–5

a. (1) Revenue recognition at the end of the project.

Gigantic Bridge Builders
Income Statement
For the Period Ended ________

	Period 1	Period 2
Revenues		
Revenues form long-term contracts	0	$500,000
Expenses		
Construction costs	0	350,000
Net income	0	$150,000

(2) Revenue recognized during production.

Gigantic Bridge Builders
Income Statement
For the Period Ended ________

	Period 1	Period 2
Revenues		
Revenue from long-term contracts	$357,143[a]	$142,857[b]
Expenses		
Construction costs	250,000	100,000
Net income	$107,143	$42,857

[a] $357,143 = ($250,000 ÷ $350,000) x $500,000
[b] $142,857 = $500,000 – $357,143 or ($100,000 ÷ $350,000) x $500,000

(3) Revenue recognized when payments are received.

Gigantic Bridge Builders
Income Statement
For the Period Ended __________

	Period 1	Period 2
Revenues		
Revenue from long-term contracts	$300,000	$200,000
Expenses		
Construction costs	250,000	100,000
Net income	$50,000	$100,000

Note: Costs are recognized as expenses in accordance with the matching principle.

b.

Assumption	Period 1 Net Income	Period 2 Net Income	Total Net Income
(1)	$ 0	$150,000	$150,000
(2)	107,143	42,857	150,000
(3)	50,000	100,000	150,000

E5–6

a.

	1990	1991	1992	1993	1994
Original cost	$15,000	$15,000	$15,000	$15,000	$15,000
Depreciation expense	3,000	3,000	3,000	3,000	3,000
Accumulated depreciation	3,000	6,000	9,000	12,000	15,000
Net book value	12,000	9,000	6,000	3,000	0

b. Since the truck has an estimated useful life of five years, it is assumed that JHP and Brothers will receive a benefit from using the truck in each of the five years. Consequently, JHP and Brothers will receive future benefits from the truck. According to the matching principle, costs should be matched against the benefits the costs help generate. Since the benefits from the truck will not be realized until future periods, the cost of the truck should be capitalized.

In order to receive the future benefits from using the truck, JHP and Brothers must continue to exist. In other words, JHP and Brothers is assumed to be a going concern. If accountants did not use the going concern assumption, it would be inappropriate to capitalize costs because the company may not exist when the expected benefits resulting from the cost are to be realized.

c. It is assumed that the truck will help generate a benefit (i.e. revenue) in each year of its useful life. Under the **matching principle**, the cost of an item should be allocated to the period(s) in which the cost helps generate a benefit for the company. In this particular case, the truck is expected to provide a benefit for five years. If the entire cost was expensed in 1990, then an improper matching of costs with the related benefits would arise in 1991–1994. However, by capitalizing the costs of the truck in 1990 and then allocating a portion of the cost to each of the next five years, JPH and Brothers is able to match the cost of the truck with each period in which the truck is expected to provide a benefit to the company.

E5–7

a. Costs that are expected to provide future benefits to a company are, by definition, an asset. Hence, all such costs should be capitalized. As these costs help generate benefits, such as revenue, the costs are recognized as expenses and matched with the corresponding benefits.

b. Capitalizing expenditures and subsequently amortizing these costs are not costless activities. A company incurs costs, such as bookkeepers' salaries, supplies, and so forth, when engaging in such activities. In certain instances, these bookkeeping costs may exceed the benefits derived from properly capitalizing and amortizing expenditures. This situation is most likely to arise when the amount of expenditure is very small in relation to some criteria such as total expenditures, net income, or total assets. Such an expenditure is so small that users of financial statements would not care whether the expenditure was capitalized or immediately expensed. The financial statement users' decision process would not be influenced by the accounting treatment give such expenditures. In these cases, a company would apply the concept of materiality to decide whether an expenditure should be capitalized or expensed.

E5–8

a. The expanded accounting equation is as follows:

Assets = Liabilities + Contributed capital + Beginning retained earnings
+ Net income – Declared dividends

(1) *Change in depreciation method.* Depreciation expense decreases net income and the book value of fixed assets by the same amount. Since the change in the depreciation method increased the book value of fixed assets by $5,000, the change in the depreciation method must have also increased net income $5,000 over the amount it otherwise would have been. Therefore, the effect on the accounting equation is to increase assets and increase net income $5,000.

(2) *Change in inventory method.* The cost of inventory is allocated either to the Cost of Goods Sold account or to the Inventory account. Hence, an increase in the balance of Inventory implies a decrease in the balance of Cost of Goods Sold. Since the change in inventory methods increased Inventory by $13,000, the change in inventory methods must have also decreased Cost of Goods Sold by $13,000. A decrease in an expense increases net income, so the change in inventory methods increased net income by $13,000. The effect on the accounting equation is to increase assets and increase net income $13,000.

b.

	1988	**1989**	**1990**	**1991**
Net income as reported	$20,000	$23,000	$22,000	$28,000
Effect of depreciation change	0	(5,000)	(5,000)	(5,000)
Effect of inventory change	0	0	0	(13,000)
Adjusted net income	$20,000	$18,000	$17,000	$10,000

The adjusted net income figures indicate that if the company had not changed accounting methods, it would have reported declining profits. In fact, the company would have only reported net income of $10,000 in 1991. The reported net income figures have been enhanced with accounting techniques rather than by sound economic health. Consequently, the company's performance would be viewed less positively.

c. Companies should adhere to the **principle of consistency**. This principle states that a company should use the same accounting principles from year to year. Such a practice promotes the comparability of the company's financial statements over time and also promotes user confidence in the viability of financial statements. If a company was free to switch accounting principles at will, financial statement users would place very little faith in the statements.

Under certain conditions, companies may switch accounting principles. The primary condition that must be met before a company may switch methods is the approval of the company's auditors. The company must convince its auditors that the environment it faces has changed sufficiently so that the new accounting principle, rather than the old principle, more appropriately reflects the company's financial position and performance.

P5–1

a.	1/1/90	Property	1,000	
		Cash		1,000
		To record purchase of property.		
	12/31/90	Cash	2,000	
		Property		1,000
		Gain on Sale of Property		1,000
		To record sale of property.		

b. The company would report a gain of $1,000.

c. No. During 1990 the purchasing power of money decreased by 12%. On December 31, 1990, it would require $1,120 [i.e., $1,000 x (1 + 12%)] to purchase the same basket of goods that $1,000 would purchase on January 1, 1990. The difference in purchasing power gives rise to an economic loss of $120. Therefore, $2,000 would not allow someone to purchase twice as many goods and services on December 31, 1990 as on January 1, 1990. To be able to buy twice as many goods and services, an individual would need $2,240.

d. The $1,000 gain can be broken down into two components—a gain due to the increase in the value of the property and a gain due to general inflation. Since $1,000 on January 1 is equivalent to $1,120 in purchasing power on December 31, $120 of the gain is due to general inflation. The remaining $880 of the gain is due to an increase if the value of the property, which represents an economic gain.

Accountants ignore the effects of inflation due to the **stable dollar assumption**. This assumption allows financial statement users to compare financial statements from different points in time. Further, the stable dollar assumption gives rise to more objective financial statements. In order to adjust for the effects of inflation, the inflation rate must be known. Should the adjustment be based on wholesale, retail, global, national, state, industry, or company-specific inflation rates? Company-specific rates are probably the most relevant rate, yet they are probably the most subjective. The other rates may not be relevant for some companies. If managers were allowed to select the appropriate rate for their company, they could manipulate the financial statements. On the other hand, if the FASB or SEC mandated the use of a particular inflation rate, the rate would not be relevant for many companies. Consequently, the choice of an inflation rate would be arbitrary and could lead to distortions in the financial statements.

The use of historical costs is arbitrary and also leads to distortions in the financial statements. However, the use of historical costs has at least two advantages over inflation-adjusted amounts. First, the use of historical costs eliminates a potential source of manipulation of financial statements by managers. Second, users may disagree on the appropriate inflation rate for a company, and historical-cost financial statements allow users to individually adjust the financial statements for their perceptions of inflation.

P5–2

a.

Date	Account	Debit	Credit
1/1	Notes Receivable	4,760	
	Cash		4,760
	To record loan to Treetop Enterprises.		
12/31	Cash	5,000	
	Notes Receivable		4,760
	Interest Revenue		240
	To record collection of principal and interest.		

b. Banking Corporation is better off at the end of the year than if the company had not invested the $4,760 on January 1. Overall, however, the company is worse off financially on December 31 than on January 1. To purchase the same basket of goods on December 31 as it could purchase for $4,760 on January 1, Banking Corporation would need $5,236 [i.e., $4,760 x (1 + 10%)]. In other words, the company would need an additional $476. By loaning the money to Treetop Enterprises during the year, Banking Corporation acquired $240. Hence, during the year the company became economically worse off by $236 (i.e., $476 – $240). Just to maintain its purchasing power, Banking Corporation would have to loan money at the inflation rate. To improve its purchasing power, Banking Corporation would have to loan money at a rate exceeding the inflation rate.

c. As indicated in Part (b), Banking Corporation actually lost $236 of purchasing power during the year. On the other hand, Treetop Enterprises gained purchasing power during the year. Treetop could have invested the $4,760 it borrowed in a basket of goods on January 1. On December 31, Treetop could sell the basket of goods for $5,236, repay Banking Corporation $5,000, and still have $236 left over. Consequently, Treetop Enterprises ended up with the better deal. Whenever the interest rate on a loan is less than the inflation rate, the borrower has an advantage. Whenever the interest rate on a loan exceeds the inflation rate, the creditor has an advantage.

Since accountants adhere to the **stable dollar assumption**, inflation is not reflected in financial statements. Consequently, the financial statements of Banking Corporation would indicate the company is better off by the amount of Interest Revenue, while the financial statements of Treetop Enterprises would indicate the company is worse off by the amount of Interest Expense.

P5–3

a.

	Cash Inflows From Sale	Cash Outflow for Replacement	Increase in Future Cash Flows	Total Cash Flows
ASSET A				
Option 1	$3,000	$ 0	($5,000)	($2,000)
Option 2	3,000	(2,000)	5,000	6,000
Option 3	0	0	0	0
ASSET B				
Option 1	1,000	0	(5,000)	(4,000)
Option 2	1,000	(4,000)	2,000	(1,000)
Option 3	0	0	0	0
ASSET C				
Option 1	6,000	0	(5,000)	1,000
Option 2	6,000	(7,000)	5,000	4,000
Option 3	0	0	0	0

Kathy made the correct decision with respect to Assets B and C, but not with respect to Asset A. As demonstrated above, Option 3 (i.e., retain the asset) yields the highest total cash flows for Asset B. For Asset C, Option 2 (i.e., selling and replacing the asset) yields the highest net cash flows. If Kathy were to sell and replace the asset, she would receive $6,000 but have to pay out $7,000. So initially, Kathy is facing a cash outflow of $1,000. Fortunately, the new asset would increase the present value of cash flows from future production by $5,000, thereby providing a net increase in cash flows of $4,000.

For Asset A, Option 2 (i.e., selling and replacing the asset) yields the highest net cash flows. Kathy increases her cash flows through this option in two ways. First, she can gain $5,000 from the present value of cash flows from future production by paying out the $2,000 replacement cost. Second, she can gain $1,000 because the fair market value of the old asset is $1,000 more than that of the new asset.

b. **The historical cost information should not be used in evaluating the officer's decisions. Historical costs represent sunk costs, and sunk costs should not be considered in future decisions. In evaluating the performance of a manager, we are interested in the cash flows generated by the manager. If the cash flow information is not available, then proxies for the cash flows must be used in the evaluation process. One such proxy is historical cost data, which may be helpful in computing net income. However, if the cash flow information is available, then this information should be used in evaluating the performance. Since the cash flow information is available in this case, the historical cost data can and should be ignored.**

c. Under generally accepted accounting principles, assets should be carried on the balance sheet at historical cost. Assuming that Kathy proceeds with her decision and keeps Assets A and B and replaces Asset C, the company should report the following amounts for each asset.

Asset A	$8,000
Asset B	3,000
Asset C	7,000

The company is applying the **principle of objectivity**, which states that financial accounting information must be verifiable and relaible and that the value of transactions be objective. In many cases, historical cost is the most objective of the potential valuation bases.

P5–4

a. Real sales did not actually double from 1989 to 1991. To compute the real percentage change in sales, inflation must be considered. Converting 1991 sales to 1989 dollars reveals that 1991 real sales were actually $36,364 [i.e. $40,000 ÷ (1 + 10%)]. Consequently, sales increased from 1989 to 1991 by $16,364, which is only an 81.8% increase in sales.

b. (1) 1991 sales in 1989 dollars = $40,000 ÷ (1 + 25%) = $32,000

(2) Real change in sales = 1991 sales in 1989 dollars – 1989 sales in 1989 dollars
= $32,000 – $20,000
= $12,000

(3) Real percentage change in sales = Real change in sales ÷ 1989 sales in 1989 dollars
= $12,000 ÷ $20,000
= 60%

c. The **stable dollar assumption** assumes that inflation does not exist. So under this assumption, sales actually doubled. However, once one realizes that the stable dollar assumption is simply an assumption that promotes the comparability of financial statements from different points in time and that it does not accurately reflect reality, one must consider price changes when comparing financial data from different points in time. It appears that Milton Smart thought the stable dollar assumption reflected reality.

P5–5

a. In this case, the purchase price should equal the stream of future cash flows discounted to reflect the time value of money. The purchase price would be calculated as follows:

Purchase price = Present value of future cash flows
= $3,000 x Present value of an ordinary annuity factor for $i = 10\%$ and $n = 10$
= $3,000 x 6.14457 (from Table 5 in Appendix A)
= $18,433.71

b. Book value represents the residual ownership interest in the company based upon the financial statement values. This residual interest is, by definition, total stockholders' equity. Therefore, the book value of Buyable Goods is $9,000 (i.e., $4,000 of common stock + $5,000 of retained earnings). Using the accounting equation, the book value can also be calculated as total assets less total liabilities.

c. The purchase value of a company can be different from the book value of the company for two reasons. First, the fair market value of individual assets and liabilities may be different than the book value of individual assets and liabilities. Book values are largely based upon historical costs, which ordinarily do not reflect fair market values. Second, a company is usually worth more than simply the sum of its parts. Due to synergy, assets and liabilities in a particular grouping are worth more than the sum of the individual assets and liabilities. For example, Pepsico has generated a great deal of name recognition and customer loyalty. Both of these items make Pepisco more valuable than its individual assets and liabilities. In other words, the purchase price of a company reflects the company as a whole, not simply as individual assets and liabilities. The excess of the total market value of the company over the book value of the individual assets and liabilities represents goodwill.

If an entity purchases another company, the purchaser is allowed to record goodwill in the amount equal to the purchase price over the net value of the individual assets and liabilities. The purchaser is allowed to recognize goodwill because the dollar amount is established through an exchange transaction and is, therefore, an objective amount. Recording goodwill on the purchase of another company is consistent with the **historical cost principle**. So in this case Mr. Black could record goodwill for the difference between the purchase price and the book value of Buyable Goods. This amount would be $9,433.71 (i.e., $18,433.71 – $9,000.00).

A company is not allowed to recognize goodwill on itself because the dollar value of goodwill would be subjective. Hence, any attempts by a company to recognize goodwill on itself would violate the **objectivity principle**.

P5–6

			Debit	Credit
a.	1/1/90	Rental Property	50,000	
		Cash		50,000
		To record purchase of an apartment house.		

The book value of the building equals the present value of cash inflows less the present value of cash outflows.

The economic value of the building is equal to the future cash flows discounted to reflect the time value of money. In this case, there are two types of future cash flows. The first type is annual cash flows, which is an annuity, while the second type is the cash flow from the sale of the building. The present values of these two cash flows are calculated below.

Present value of annual cash flows
= ($30,000 cash inflow – $20,000 cash outflow) x Present value of an ordinary annuity factor for $i = 8\%$ and $n = 10$
= $10,000 x 6.71008 (from Table 5 in Appendix A)
= $67,100.80

Present value of cash flow from sale of building
= $20,000 x Present value factor for $i = 8\%$ and $n = 10$
= $20,000 x .46319 (from Table 4 in Appendix A)
= $9,263.80

Total present value of future cash flows = $67,100.80 + $9,263.80
= $76,364.60

Since the present value of future cash flows exceeds the purchase price of $50,000, it appears that Barry made a wise investment.

b.

Barry Smith
Income Statement
For the Year Ended December 31, 1990

Rental revenue		$30,000
Expenses		
Management expenses	$20,000	
Depreciation expense	3,000	
Total expenses		23,000
Net income		$ 7,000

Barry Smith
Balance Sheet
As of December 31, 1990

Assets		Liabilities & Stockholders' Equity	
Cash	$10,000	Liabilities	$ 0
Building	50,000	Contributed capital	50,000
Less: Accumulated depreciation	3,000	Retained earnings	7,000
Total assets	$57,000	Total liabilities & stockholders' equity	$57,000

c. Present value of future cash flows on December 31, 1990:

Present value of annual rentals = $10,000 + ($10,000 x Present value of an ordinary annuity factor for $i = 8\%$ and $n = 9$)
= $10,000 + ($10,000 x 6.24689 from Table 5 in Appendix A)
= $10,000 + $62,468.90
= $72,468.90

Present value of building sale = ($20,000 x Present value factor for $i = 8\%$ and $n = 9$)
= $20,000 x .50025 (from Table 4 in Appendix A)]
= $10,005.00

Total present value = $72,468.90 + $10,005.00
= $82,473.90

Economic income = 12/31/90 present value – 1/1/90 present value
= $82,473.90 – $76,364.60 (from Part [a])
= $6,109.30

Accounting income differs from economic income because economic income incorporates the time value of money. Hence, economic income reflects that the purchasing power of $1.00 received on December 31, 1990 is not equivalent to the purchasing power of $1.00 received on December 31, 1995. Accounting income, through the stable dollar assumption, ignores the time value of money. Further, economic income considers future events (i.e., discounted future cash inflows and outflows) while accounting income only considers past events.

d. The book value of the building on December 31, 1990 equals the cost of the building less accumulated depreciation. Therefore, the book value is $47,000 (i.e., $50,000 – $3,000). The present value of the building equals the present value of future cash flows, which as of December 31, 1990 is $82,473.90 (from Part [c]).

P5–7

a. Book value on 12/31/90 = Total book value of assets – Total value of liabilities
= $62,000 – ($4,000 + $10,000)
= $48,000

b. The economic value of Hauser and Hall equals its future cash flows discounted to reflect the time value of money. Hauser and Hall have two streams of future cash flows. The first type is annual cash flows, which is an annuity, while the second type is the cash flow from the sale of the building. The present values of these two cash flows are calculated below.

Present value of annual cash flows
= $10,000 x Present value of an ordinary annuity factor for i = 10% and n = 10
= $10,000 x 6.14457 (from Table 5 in Appendix A)
= $61,445.70

Present value of cash flow from sale of building
= $40,000 x Present value factor for i = 10% and n = 10
= $40,000 x .38554 (from Table 4 in Appendix A)
= $15,421.60

Total present value of future cash flows = $61,445.70 + $15,421.60
= $76,867.30

c. Liquidation value = Total FMV of assets – Total value of liabilities
= $65,000 – ($4,000 + $10,000)
= $51,000

d. Book value is based upon the historical cost of individual assets. This value provides little indication of a company's value due to price changes. The problem is magnified as the company's assets age. Liquidation value is based upon the fair market values of individual assets and liabilities. This value provides an accurate measure for a company planning to cease operations. However, such a measure provides little indication for a company that is a going concern. Under the **going concern assumption**, accountants are concerned with providing accounting numbers for companies that will continue operating indefinitely.

Present value is based upon future cash flows; as such, it incorporates all nonquantifiable assets, such as employee loyalty and customer loyalty. This value more accurately reflects the economic value of a company since it captures items not included on a balance sheet under GAAP. Unfortunately, it is difficult, if not impossible, to accurately predict future cash flows. Hence, in most instances, present value amounts do not satisfy the **principle of objectivity**.

A difference between a company's book value and its economic value (i.e., present value of future cash flows) can arise for two reasons. First, this difference can be due to a difference between a company's book value and the fair market value of its individual assets and liabilities. The assets are usually carried on the books at their historical cost. However, over time the actual value of the assets would be expected to diverge from their historical cost.

Second, the difference between a company's book value and its economic value can be due to the the excess of the company's economic value over the fair market value of its net assets (i.e., total assets less total liabilities). The net assets are worth more grouped together than individually. Companies generate customer loyalty and name recognition that has value yet is not reflected in the value of any particular asset. This value is, however, reflected in its economic value. The excess of the company's economic value over the fair market value of its net assets represents goodwill. In this case, Hauser and Hall's goodwill would be $76,867.30 – $51,000.00, or $25,867.30.

P5–8

a. Ending retained earnings = Beginning retained earnings + Net income – Dividends
$20,000 = $8,000 + Net income – $0
Net income = $12,000

b. 1991 FMV = FMV of total assets – Total liabilities
= $84,000 – ($3,000 + $10,000)
= $71,000

1990 FMV = FMV of total assets – Total liabilities
= $65,000 – ($4,000 + $10,000)
= $51,000

1991 Net income = 1991 FMV – 1990 FMV
= $71,000 – $51,000
= $20,000

c. Present value of future cash flows on December 31, 1990:
Present value of annual cash flows
= $10,000 x Present value of an ordinary annuity factor for i = 10% and n = 10
= $10,000 x 6.14457 (from Table 5 in Appendix A)
= $61,445.70

Present value of cash flow from sale of building
= $40,000 x Present value factor for i = 10% and n = 10
= $40,000 x .38554 (from Table 4 in Appendix A)
= $15,421.60

Total present value of future cash flows = $61,445.70 + $15,421.60
= $76,867.30

Present value of future cash flows on December 31, 1991:
Present value of annual cash flows
= $10,000 + ($10,000 x Present value of an ordinary annuity factor for i = 10% and n = 9)
= $10,000 + ($10,000 x 5.75902 from Table 5 in Appendix A)
= $67,590.20

Present value of cash flow from sale of building
= $40,000 x Present value factor for i = 10% and n = 9
= $40,000 x .42410 (from Table 4 in Appendix A)
= $16,964.00

Total present value of future cash flows = $67,590.20 + $16,964.00
= $84,554.20

Economic income = PV on 12/31/91 – PV on 12/31/90
= $84,554.20 – $76,867.30
= $7,686.90

d. All three measures of income provide a performance measure for Hauser and Hall. Of the three measures, economic income is the only one that incorporates the time value of money. Consequently, holding everything else constant, economic income is probably more accurate than the other measures. Unfortunately, in the real world it is extremely rare that the future cash flows can be predicted with any reasonable degree of accuracy. So in the end, economic income is simply a guess based upon estimates of the timing and amount of future cash flows.

Lack of objectivity can also plague income computed using fair market values. If a strong market exists for each of the company's assets, such as with marketable securities, then the company could probably obtain reasonably accurate estimates of what it could receive for selling the assets. In this case, net income would be more relevant than income computed using historical costs, since more up-to-date values are being used. Unfortunately, it is not possible to find a market for all assets. For example, a manufacturing company may use highly specialized equipment in its production process. If no other company would use this equipment, does the equipment have a fair market value? Do we assign it a value of zero, assign it a scrap value, or assign it an arbitrary fair market value? The end result is that the value assigned to some assets will be arbitrary and not objective.

Computing net income under GAAP circumvents the problem of arbitrary values and lack of objectivity. The values assigned to assets are based upon their historical costs. Assets are usually acquired in arms-length transactions. Since each party would have opposing interests, the purchase price should accurately reflect the value of the asset on the purchase date. Furthermore, anybody examining the value of the asset could verify the historical cost. While using historical cost as a basis for valuing assets provides objective values, historical cost amounts can often be extremely outdated.

P5–9

a. **Assumption**	**Year 1**	**Year 2**	**Year 3**	**Year 4**
(1) Revenue recognized in proportion to monuments completed				
($2,400,000)(2/12)	$400,000			
($2,400,000)(6/12)		$1,200,000		
($2,400,000)(3/12)			$600,000	
($2,400,000)(1/12)				$200,000
(2) Revenue recognized in proportion to percentage of costs incurred				
($2,400,000)(380,000/1,140,000)	$800,000			
($2,400,000)(380,000/1,140,000)		$800,000		
($2,400,000)(285,000/1,140,000)			$600,000	
($2,400,000)(95,000/1,140,000)				$200,000
(3) Revenue recognized in proportion to cash collections				
($2,400,000)(600,000/2,400,000)	$600,000			
($2,400,000)(900,000/2,400,000)		$900,000		
($2,400,000)(300,000/2,400,000)			$300,000	
($2,400,000)(600,000/2,400,000)				$600,000

b. **Costs**

	Year 1	Year 2	Year 3	Year 4
(1) Costs under Method 1				
($1,140,000)(2/12)	$190,000			
($1,140,000)(6/12)		$570,000		
($1,140,000)(3/12)			$285,000	
($1,140,000)(1/12)				$ 95,000
(2) Costs under Method 2				
($1,140,000)(380,000/1,140,000)	$380,000			
($1,140,000)(380,000/1,140,000)		$380,000		
($1,140,000)(285,000/1,140,000)			$285,000	
($1,140,000)(95,000/1,140,000)				$ 95,000
(3) Costs under Method 3				
($1,140,000)(600,000/2,400,000)	$285,000			
($1,140,000)(900,000/2,400,000)		$427,500		
($1,140,000)(300,000/2,400,000)			$142,500	
($1,140,000)(600,000/2,400,000)				$285,000

Net Income

	Year 1	Year 2	Year 3	Year 4
(1) Net income under Method 1				
400,000 – 190,000	$210,000			
1,200,000 – 570,000		$630,000		
600,000 – 285,000			$315,000	
200,000 – 95,000				$105,000
(2) Net income under Method 2				
800,000 – 380,000	$420,000			
800,000 – 380,000		$420,000		
600,000 – 285,000			$315,000	
200,000 – 95,000				$105,000
(3) Net income under Method 3				
600,000 – 285,000	$315,000			
900,000 – 427,500		$472,500		
300,000 – 142,500			$157,500	
600,000 – 285,000				$315,000

c.

	Total Revenue	Total Cost	Total Net Income
Method 1	$2,400,000	$1,140,000	$1,260,000
Method 2	2,400,000	1,140,000	1,260,000
Method 3	2,400,000	1,140,000	1,260,000

P5–10

a. Year 1: Unbilled Sales 20,000*
Sales Revenue 20,000
To record sales at completion of production.

---

* $20,000 = 200 units produced x $100 per unit

Year 2: Unbilled Sales 20,000
Sales Revenue 20,000
To record sales at completion of production.

Year 3: Unbilled Sales 10,000
Sales Revenue 10,000
To record sales at completion of production.

b. Year 1: Accounts Receivable 15,000*
Sales Revenue 15,000
To record sales at delivery.

---

* $15,000 = 150 units delivered x $100 per unit

Year 2: Accounts Receivable 20,000
Sales Revenue 20,000
To record sales at delivery.

Year 3: Accounts Receivable 15,000
Sales Revenue 15,000
To record sales at delivery.

c.

	Year 1	Year 2	Year 3	Total
Assumption 1				
Revenues (from Part A)	$20,000	$20,000	$10,000	$50,000
Expenses	8,000*	8,000*	4,000*	20,000
Net income	$12,000	$12,000	$ 6,000	$30,000

---

* Expenses = Number of units produced x $40 per unit

	Year 1	Year 2	Year 3	Total
Assumption 2				
Revenues (from Part [b])	$15,000	$20,000	$15,000	$50,000
Expenses	6,000*	8,000*	6,000*	20,000
Net income	$ 9,000	$12,000	$ 9,000	$30,000

---

* Expenses = Number of units delivered x $40 per unit

P5–11

a.

Inventory Method	Depreciation Method	ABC Income	ABC Working Capital	XYZ Income	XYZ Working Capital
FIFO	Straight-line	$14,000	$13,000	$12,000	$15,000
FIFO	Accelerated	10,000	13,000	8,000	15,000
LIFO	Straight-line	9,000	8,000	7,000	10,000
LIFO	Accelerated	5,000	8,000	3,000	10,000

Note: Changes in the companies inventory balances affect net income through Cost of Goods Sold.

b. ABC has the highest net income and working capital under the combination of FIFO and straight-line depreciation, and XYZ also has the highest net income and working capital under the combination of FIFO and straight-line depreciation.

Managers could have many reasons for selecting one accounting method over another method. The manager is a party to many contracts that may rely on accounting numbers. For example, a manager may have an incentive compensation contract based upon accounting income. A company may have a debt covenant with a creditor that stipulates a minimum level of working capital (or some other relevant measure). Or a manager may have incentives to minimize the company's tax liability. To the extent that the accounting methods used for tax reporting must also be used for financial reporting, a manager may select those methods that provide a tax benefit. In selecting a particular accounting method, a manager will consider the factors that provide an incentive for selecting one method over another, and in the end the manager would be expected to select the accounting method that gives him/her the greatest benefit. In some cases, the accounting method selected by the manager may actually cause net income to decrease. The most likely reason for a manager to select an accounting method that would cause net income to decrease would be to minimize taxable income, thereby minimizing cash outflows for taxes.

c. As an investor, one must realize that different companies may face different environments. To the extent that two companies face different environments, we would expect them to select the accounting methods appropriate to their particular environments. Further, an investor must realize that managers have their own interests and will work to satisfy their interests. In some cases the interests of the managers will be congruent with the investors' interests, and in some cases they will not.

Generally accepted accounting principles allow companies to use different accounting methods because it is impossible to select a method that would be appropriate across different companies and environments. Consequently, companies are allowed to select those methods that they deem appropriate for their situation. To an investor, the underlying economic reality (i.e., expected future cash flows) of the company is of interest. Consequently, if companies use different accounting methods, the effects of the different methods must be considered so that the financial statements of the companies are comparable.

P5–12

a. **Costs Of Error 1:** If Jarvis requires disclosure of the lawsuit, and Jarvis' client does not lose the lawsuit, Jarvis could incur some costs. If the president of Jensen Repairs, Inc. is serious about not wanting the lawsuit disclosed and Jarvis goes ahead and discloses it, Jensen could fire Jarvis. In this case, Jarvis would lose the audit fees of its biggest client. If these audit fees make up a substantial portion of Jarvis' total revenues, it is even possible that the loss of Jensen Repairs, Inc. as a client could cause Jarvis to cease operations.

Costs of Error 2: If Jarvis does not require disclosure of the lawsuit, and Jarvis' client loses the lawsuit, Jarvis could incur some costs. If any of the stockholders or creditors relied on the financial statements and incurred a loss, these stockholders could sue Jarvis for their losses. Since the lawsuit could force Jensen Repairs, Inc. out of business, the potential losses to stockholders and creditors could be quite substantial. A Type 2 error could also damage Jarvis' reputation. Financial statement users might view Jarvis as a "low quality" auditor and might be unwilling to accept financial statements verified by Jarvis. Loss of reputation might cause some potential clients to no longer be interested in hiring Jarvis. Even if some new clients did hire Jarvis, they might demand a lower audit fee to compensate for a "lower quality" service. Furthermore, some of Jarvis' existing clients may no longer wish to engage him as their auditors. Consequently, it appears that the cost of a Type 2 error exceeds the cost of a Type 1 error.

Jarvis faces a tough decision, though. Although the cost of a Type 2 error appears higher, the probability that Jensen Repairs, Inc. will lose the lawsuit is not very likely. Which factor should Jarvis focus on: the cost of the errors or the probability of an adverse outcome? Luckily, Jarvis can refer to *Statement of Financial Accounting Standards No. 5,* "Accounting for Contingencies" for guidance on whether to disclose this lawsuit.

b. Expected cost of an error = Cost of an error x Probability of an error

Expected cost of a Type 1 error	=	$4,000 x 90%
	=	$3,600
Expected cost of a Type 2 error	=	$60,000 x 10%
	=	$6,000

Based upon the expected cost of each type of error, it appears that Jarvis should disclose the lawsuit.

c. Conservatism means that "when in doubt, understate rather than overstate." This statement means that when a company faces some uncertainty concerning how to value or record an event, the company should understate, rather than overstate, the financial health of the company. In this case, Jarvis has some doubt as to whether Jensen Repairs, Inc. will win or lose the pending lawsuit. Jarvis' framework focuses on the relative costs of errors. He wants to determine the cost of a Type 1 error compared to the cost of a Type 2 error. Since the cost of overstatement (i.e., a type 2 error) exceeds the cost of understatement (i.e., a Type 1 error), Jarvis should risk making a Type 1 error. Hence, due to Jarvis' doubt concerning the outcome of the lawsuit, he should understate the financial health of Jensen Repairs, Inc. by disclosing the lawsuit.

C5-1

a.

		Revenue
1988	3 other aircraft plus spare parts	$1,500,000,000
1989	3 747 – 400 ($135 million X 3)	405,000,000
1990	3 747 – 400 ($135 million X 3)	405,000,000
		$2,310,000,000

b.

1988	0
1989	0
1990	$2,310,000

c. Costs should be *capitalized.* They should not be recognized in the period in which they were expended. To do so would distort income and be inconsistent with the matching principle. Capitalized costs would be recognized when the associated revenues are recognized.

C5-2

a. Immediately expending goodwill will decrease net income in the period in which the purchase is made. In subsequent periods, income would increase as a result of *not* amortizing goodwill.

b. Requiring companies to expense goodwill would discourage purchases because of the large expense which must be recorded when goodwill exists in a transaction.

c. The FASB position that accounting policies follow rather then lead business decisions is appropriate.

d. The matching principle is being followed. The revenues generated by the combined companies should be charged with the expenses required to generate them. Systematically amortizing goodwill achieves this objective. Further, by capitalizing goodwill, it is implied that the company will continue in the future as a going concern.

C5-3

a. Air Canada might consider a legal action against the auditors who examined the books prior to the purchase. If Air Canada relied on the auditors' examination in making their decision to purchase the subsidiary, then they may have a defensible action.

b. Neither acted conservatively. Management of the subsidiary overvalued assets, and the auditors did not object.

c. Costs include not only the legal liability they face for misstating the financial statements but also more indirect costs such as loss of reputation, loss of clients, and inability to find new jobs.

C5-4

Revenue recognition refers to the recording of revenues when they are earned. Matching refers to charging income with expenses which were incurred to generate the revenues. The criteria for revenue recognition follow:

(i) The company must have completed a significant portion of the production and sales effort.

(ii) The amount of the revenues can be objectively measured.

(iii) The major portion of the costs have been incurred, and the remaining costs can be reasonably estimated.

(iv) The eventual collection of cash is reasonably assured.

Given these criteria, the proposal by the AICPA to defer a potion of current revenues is more consistent with these principles than established practice. Accordingly, deferred revenue should be established for each ticket sold and recognized as revenue when passengers use their "free" tickets. Related costs should be capitalized and matched against the revenue when it is recognized.

C5-5

a. 1987 net income without the changes would have been ($2,915 – $858) $2,057. The restated amounts would reflect the same accounting principles through time and therefore be more consistent than the reported amounts.

b. Reference to accounting changes would be included in the footnotes and the auditor's report, and their effect on income would be disclosed in a separate category on the income statement.

c. To achieve *uniform* application of depreciation methods between GE and IBM, an investor would have to remove the effects of the heightened depreciation charge from GE's statements or, equivalently, recompute IBM's depreciation using GE's method.

d. Uniformity refers to the application of the *same* accounting principles across companies (between IBM and GE). Consistency refers to the application of the same accounting principles *across time* for the *same* company.

CHAPTER 6 The Current Asset Classification, Cash, and Marketable Securities

E6–1

Item	Classification	Explanation
1	Cash	Money held in checking accounts is defined as cash, and there are no restrictions on the account.
2	Cash	Checks are considered cash unless the checks cannot be cashed until a later date (i.e., postdated). In this case, the check date has passed, so the checks are considered cash.
3	Investment	Certificates of deposit contain penalties for early withdrawal. Hence, this source of cash is not readily available.
4	Cash	Banks have the right to demand notice prior to a withdrawal from a savings account; Consequently, the cash in savings accounts is not, technically, readily available. However, since banks rarely exercise their right of prior notification, savings accounts are considered cash.
5	Cash	Petty cash is always considered cash.
6	Restricted Cash	The company does not have ready access to these funds. Consequently, their $50,000 should not be reported as cash. The portion of the $50,000 corresponding to short-term loans should be classified in current assets as restricted cash. The proper amount would be $15,000. The remaining $35,000 should be classified either as a long-term investment or as an other asset.
7	Cash	See (1).

E6–2

Item	Classification
1	a
2	c
3	b
4	c
5	c
6	b
7	a

E6–3

a.

Space City Enterprises
Bank Reconciliation
December 31, ____

		Per Books	Per Bank Statement
Cash balance (12/31)		$3,480	$3,280
Plus			
Deposits in transit			1,200
Collections (cash collected by bank)		730	
Less			
Outstanding checks			810
NSF checks	$480		
Bank service charges	60	540	
Correct cash balance		$3,670	$3,670

b. Cash	190	
Accounts Receivable	480	
Service Charge Expense	60	
Notes Receivable		730
To record events disclosed on bank statement.		

c. $3,670

E6–4

a.

Lowen, Incorporated
Bank Reconciliation
December 31, 1990

	Per Books	Per Bank Statement
Cash balance (12/31/90)	$6,100	$6,175
Plus		
Deposits in transit		900
Less		
Outstanding checks		1,000
Bank service charges	25	
Correct cash balance	$6,075	$6,075

b. Service Charge Expense	25	
Cash		25
To record bank service charge.		

c. $6,075

E6–5

a.

Morgan Company
Bank Reconciliation
As of December 31, 1991

		Per Books		Per Bank Statement
Cash balance (12/31/91)		$78,450		$85,270
Plus				
Deposits in transit			$42,015	
Bank error			4,500	46,515
Less				
Outstanding checks				56,335
Bank service charge	$ 500			
NFS check	2,500	3,000		
Correct cash balance		$75,450		$75,450

b.

Service Charge Expense	500	
Accounts Receivable	2,500	
Cash		3,000

To record events disclosed on bank statement.

c. $75,450

E6–6

a. **Deposits in Transit**

Deposits in Transit = August deposits per books – August deposits per bank statement
= August deposits per books – (August deposits per bank statement – August deposits per bank statement actually made in July)
= $33,700 – ($34,200 – $2,500)
= $33,700 – $31,700 = $2,000

Outstanding Checks

Outstanding Checks = Checks written in August per books – Checks written in August per books recorded by bank.
= Checks written in August per books – (Checks cleared in August per bank statement – Checks cleared in August per bank actually written in July)
= $32,000 – ($32,800 – $3,100)
= $32,000 – $29,700 = $2,300

b.

McDaniel and Sons
Bank Reconciliation
As of August 31, 1990

		Per Books	Per Bank Statement
Cash balance (8/3/1990)		$13,900	$12,450
Plus			
Deposits in transit			2,000
Note collected by bank		800	
Less			
Outstanding checks			2,300
NFS check	$2,500		
Bank service charge	50	2,250	
Correct cash balance		$12,150	$12,150

c. Accounts Receivable 2,500
Service Charge Expense 50
Notes Receivable 800
Cash 1,750
To record events disclosed on bank statement.

d. $12,150

E6–7

a.

Wordinger Manufacturing
Bank Reconciliation
As of June 30, 19XX

	Per Books		Per Bank Statement
Cash balance (6/30/XX)	$8,094		$22,495
Plus			
Deposits in transit			26,463[a]
Less			
Outstanding checks		$39,989[b]	
Bank error (check #105)		900	40,889
Service charge	25		
Correct cash balance	$8,069		$8,069

[a] $26,463 = $15,573 + $10,890
[b] $39,989 = $13,190 + $15,925 + $10,874

b. Service Charge Expense 25
Cash 25
To record bank service charge.

E6–8

a.

Entry	Debit	Credit
(1) Marketable Securities	50,000	
Cash		50,000
To record investment in IBM.		
(2) Marketable Securities	30,000	
Cash		30,000
To record investment in GM.		
(3) Cash	45,000	
Marketable Securities		37,500
Gain on Sale of Marketable Securities		7,500
To record sale of IBM stock.		
(4) Cash	1,000	
Dividend Revenue		1,000
To record receipt of dividend.		
(5) Marketable Securities	8,000	
Cash		8,000
To record investment in Xerox.		
(6) Cash	10,000	
Loss on Sale of Marketable Securities	2,500	
Marketable Securities		12,500
To record sale of IBM stock.		
(7) Cash	11,000	
Marketable Securities		8,000
Gain on Sale of Marketable Securities		3,000
To record sale of Xerox stock.		
(8) Cash	30,000	
Marketable Securities		30,000
To record sale of GM stock.		

b. Two types of transactions affected the income statement. First, the receipt of dividends from General Motors is considered to be revenue. Hence, the dividend increased net income by $1,000. Second, the sale of marketable securities for an amount different than the purchase price gives rise to a gain or a loss. Monroe Auto Supplies realized gains of $7,500 and $3,000 on the first sale of IBM stock and on the sale of Xerox stock, respectively, and realized a loss of $2,500 on the second sale of IBM stock. Therefore, the net effect of the gains and losses on net income was to increase net income by $8,000.

E6–9

a. The balance in Allowance for Unrealized Losses on Marketable Securities represents the excess of the portfolio's cost over the portfolio's market value. Since the account balance on December 31, 1990 of $50,000 is greater than the account balance on December 31, 1989 of $35,000, the difference between the portfolio's cost and market value is greater on December 31, 1990 than on December 31, 1989.

b. Unrealized Loss on Marketable Securities 15,000
Allowance for Unrealized Losses on Marketable Securities 15,000
To adjust marketable securities to LCM.

c. Applying the lower-of-cost-or-market (LCM) rule in 1990 gives rise to an unrealized loss of $15,000. This loss is reported on the income statement and reduces net income. Therefore, the LCM rule reduces net income by $15,000 in 1990.

E6–10

a. **1988**

Unrealized Loss on Marketable Securities	25,000	
Allowance for Unrealized Losses on Marketable Securities		25,000
To adjust marketable securities to LCM.		

1989

Unrealized Loss on Marketable Securities	10,000	
Allowance for Unrealized Losses on Marketable Securities		10,000
To adjust marketable securities to LCM.		

1990

Allowance for Unrealized Losses on Marketable Securities	35,000	
Recovery of Unrealized Losses on Marketable Securities		35,000
To adjust marketable securities to LCM.		

b. The balance in the Allowance for Unrealized Losses on Marketable Securities represents the excess of the aggregate cost over the aggregate market value. But since this account can never have a debit balance, the largest the account balance can be is zero. A balance of zero indicates that either (1) the aggregate cost exactly equals the aggregate market value or (2) the aggregate market value is greater than the aggregate cost. Therefore, we cannot determine whether the aggregate market value is greater than or equal to the aggregate cost as of December 31, 1990, but we can state that the aggregate market value is not less than the aggregate cost as of December 31, 1990.

E6–11

a.

	Wearever Fabrics	**Frames Corp.**	**Pacific Transport**	**Video Magic**
Short-term marketable securities	$800,000	$600,000	$640,000	$310,000

Note: The aggregate cost of the marketable securities is always reported in the Short-Term Marketable Securities account.

b.

	Wearever Fabrics	**Frames Corp.**	**Pacific Transport**	**Video Magic**
Unrealized losses on marketable securities	50,000	0	30,000	40,000

Note: The balance in the Allowance account should always equal the excess of the portfolio cost over the portfolio market value on the balance sheet date.

c. **Wearever Fabrics**

Allowance for Unrealized Losses on Marketable Securities	25,000	
Recovery of Unrealized Losses on Marketable Securities		25,000
To adjust marketable securities to LCM.		

Frames Corp.

Allowance for Unrealized Losses on Marketable Securities	10,000	
Recovery of Unrealized Losses on Marketable Securities		10,000
To adjust marketable securities to LCM.		

Pacific Transport

Unrealized Loss on Marketable Securities	30,000	
Allowance for Unrealized Losses on Marketable Securities		30,000
To adjust marketable securities for LCM.		

Video Magic

No entry is needed. The Allowance balance is currently $40,000 and the necessary Allowance balance is $40,000.

E6–12

a.

Marketable Securities	100,000	
Cash		100,000
To record investment in Waste Systems, Inc.		
Marketable Securities	50,000	
Cash		50,000
To record investment in Stowe Ski Supply.		
Marketable Securities	80,000	
Cash		80,000
To record investment in Edmunson Swimwear.		
Marketable Securities	75,000	
Cash		75,000
To record investment in Mandel Entertainment.		

b.

	Cost	12/31/90 Market Value	12/31/91 Market Value
Waste Systems, Inc	$100,000	$ 98,000	$ 90,000
Stowe Ski Supplies	50,000	55,000	40,000
Edmunson Swimwear	80,000	60,000	65,000
Mandel Entertainment	75,000	70,000	60,000
Totals	$305,000	$283,000	$255,000

Unrealized Loss on Marketable Securities	22,000*	
Allowance for Unrealized Losses on Marketable Securities		22,000
To adjust Marketable Securities to LCM.		

* $22,000 = Portfolio cost – Portfolio market value = $305,000 – $283,000

c. Unrealized Loss on Marketable Securities 28,000*
Allowance for Unrealized Losses on Marketable Securities 28,000
To adjust marketable Securities to LCM.

* $28,000 = Change in Allowance balance = ($305,000 – $255,000) – ($305,000 – $283,000)

E6–13

a. Emery Enterprises should not recognize any revenue on this investment. For investments in short-term marketable securities, revenue is only recognized if (1) dividends are earned or (2) the security is sold at a price above the acquisition cost (i.e., at a gain). Holding gains are not recognized under GAAP. Since Emery did not earn any dividends or sell any shares of Distinct, Inc., Emery should not recognize any revenue.

b.

Cash	720	
Marketable Securities		660
Gain on Sale of Marketable Securities		60
To record sale of marketable securities.		

Emery Enterprises would recognize the gain of $60 as income on its income statement.

c. Yes, if Emery Enterprises sold the Distinct Common Stock, Emery would recognize a gain of $60 (see Part [b]). Further, since the aggregate market value exceeds the aggregate cost (whether Emery sells Distinct or not), Emery would not need to recognize an unrealized loss on the marketable securities. Therefore, the net income would be increased by $60 if Emery sold its investment in Distinct.

d. Yes, in addition to recognizing the gain of $60 on the sale of the investment in Distinct, Emery's income would be affected by the lower-of-cost-or-market rule. If Emery did not sell the investment in Distinct, the portfolio cost would exceed the portfolio market value by $10 (i.e., $860 – $850). This amount would be reported on the income statement as Unrealized Losses on Marketable Securities. If Emery sold the investment in Distinct, the portfolio cost of $200 would then exceed the portfolio market value of $130 by $70. Hence, Unrealized Losses on Marketable Securities would be increased by $60. The net effect of selling Distinct would be to increase other revenues by $60 for the gain and to increase other expenses by $60 for the holding loss on the the remaining investment portfolio. Since these two items offset each other, net income would be unaffected. However, the components of the income statement would be affected.

E6–14

a.	(1)	1/28	Marketable Securities	120	
			Cash		120
			To record investment in Able Co.		
	(2)	2/18	Marketable Securities	500	
			Cash		500
			To record investment in Baker Co.		
	(3)	3/15	Cash	10	
			Dividend Revenue		10
			To record receipt of dividends.		
	(4)	4/29	Cash	65	
			Marketable Securities		60
			Gain on Sale of Marketable Securities		5
			To record sale of Able Co. stock.		
	(5)	5/18	Cash	40	
			Dividend Revenue		40
			To record receipt of dividends.		
	(6)	6/1	Cash	110	
			Loss on Sale of Marketable Securities	15	
			Marketable Securities		125
			To record sale Baker Co. stock.		

b.

	Cost	Market Value
Able (5 shares)	$ 60	$ 70
Baker (15 shares)	375	300
Total	$435	$370

Unrealized Loss on Marketable Securities	65*	
Allowance for Unrealized Losses on Marketable Securities		65
To adjust Marketable Securities to LCM.		

* $65 = $435 – $370

c.

Date	Income Statement Effect	Classification
1/28	$ 0	N/A
2/18	0	N/A
3/15	10	Other revenue
4/29	5	Other revenue (i.e., gain)
5/18	40	Other revenue
6/1	15	Other expense (i.e., loss)
6/30	65	Other expense (i.e., loss)
Total decrease	25	

		Debit	Credit
d.	Cash	70	
	Marketable Securities		60
	Gain on Sale of Marketable Securities		10
	To record sale of Able stock.		
	Unrealized Loss on Marketable Securities	75	
	Allowance for Unrealized Losses on Marketable Securities		75
	To adjust marketable securities to LCM.		

Entry	Income Statement Effect	Classification
1/28	$ 0	N/A
2/18	0	N/A
3/15	10	Other revenue
4/29	5	Other revenue (i.e., gain)
5/18	40	Other revenue
6/1	15	Other expense (i.e., loss)
6/30	10	Other revenue
6/30	75	Other expense (i.e., loss)
Total decrease	25	

e. The sale of Able shares did not affect net income, but did affect the components of the income statement. If the Able shares had not been sold on June 30, the net effect of Lido's investment activity on net income would have been ($25) (see Part [c]). If the Able shares had been sold on June 30, the net effect of Lido's investment activity on net income still would have been ($25) (see Part [d]). In applying the LCM rule, the portfolio cost is compared to the portfolio market value. Consequently, holding gains on one security are offset by holding losses on other securities. In this case, a $10 holding gain on the Able shares was offset against a $75 holding loss on the Baker shares. By selling the Able shares, Lido was able to recognize the $10 holding gain. But in selling these shares, Lido was no longer able to offset this holding gain against the $75 holding loss on the Baker shares. Consequently, in applying the LCM rule, Lido would have to recognize the entire $75 as an unrealized loss. So regardless of whether Lido sold the Able shares or held on to these shares the net effect on income would be ($65). In one case, Lido would report a Gain on Sale of Marketable Securities of $10 and an Unrealized Loss on Marketable Securities of ($75), while in the other case Lido would report an Unrealized Loss on Marketable Securities of ($65).

E6–15

a. Working capital = Current assets – Current liabilities
= $77,000 – $40,000
= $37,000

Current ratio = Current assets ÷ Current liabilities
= $77,000 ÷ $40,000
= 1.925

Quick ratio = (Cash + Marketable securities) ÷ Current liabilities
= ($12,000 + $35,000) ÷ $40,000
= 1.175

Yes, Susan is correct. If her estimates are correct, the company's current ratio will only be 1.925, which is less than the current ratio specified in the debt covenant.

b. Cash 47,040*

Marketable Securities 35,000

Gain on Sale of Marketable Securities 12,040

To record sale of marketable securities.

---

* $47,040 = $48,000 market value – ($48,000 x 2% brokerage fee)

Working capital = ($77,000 – $35,000 + $47,040) – $40,000
= $49,040

Current ratio = ($77,000 – $35,000 + $47,040) ÷ $40,000
= 2.226

Quick ratio = ($59,040 + $0) ÷ $40,000
= 1.476

c. Cash 47,040*

Marketable Securities 35,000

Gain on Sale of Marketable Securities 12,040

To record sale of marketable securities.

---

* $47,040 = $48,000 market value – ($48,000 x 2% brokerage fee)

Marketable Securities 48,960*

Cash 48,960

To record investment in marketable securities.

* $48,960 = $48,000 market value + ($48,000 x 2% brokerage fee)

Working capital = $89,040 – $40,000
= $49,040

Current ratio = $89,040 ÷ $40,000
= 2.226

Quick ratio = ($10,080 + $48,960) ÷ $40,000
= 1.476

d. Susan wants to insure that the company will not violate its debt covenant at the least possible cost. If the company sells the marketable securities, the company's current ratio exceeds the ratio specified in the debt covenant, but the company incurs a 2% brokerage fee. This approach is the lowest-cost alternative for Susan. Susan will then have to decide what to do with the proceeds from the sale of the securities. The company can either invest the money in the bank or in marketable securities. However, investing in marketable securities will cost the company an additional 2% brokerage fee to purchase the securities.

E6–16

a.

Tom Miller
Balance Sheet
December 31, 1989

Assets		Liabilities & Stockholders' Equity	
Cash	$2,552	Accounts payable	$1,500
Marketable securities	2,,448*	Contributed capital	5,000
Inventory	1,500	Retained earnings	0
		Total liabilities &	
Total assets	$6,500	stockholders' equity	$6,500

* $2,448 = (100 shares x $24) + (100 shares x $24 x 2% brokerage fee)

Larry Rogers
Balance Sheet
December 31, 1989

Assets		Liabilities & Stockholders' Equity	
Cash	$2,424[a]	Accounts payable	$1,500
Marketable securities	3,264[b]	Contributed capital	5,000
Inventory	1,500	Retained earnings	688[c]
		Total liabilities &	
Total assets	$7,188	stockholders' equity	$7,188

[a] $2,424 = $5,000 contributed by Larry – $2,448 for initial investment in Diskette + $3,136 in proceeds from sale of Diskette – $3,264 for reinvestment in Diskette

[b] $3,264 = (199 shares x $32) + (100 shares x $32 x 2% brokerage fee)

[c] $688 = [(100 shares x $32) – (100 shares x $32 x 2% brokerage fee)] – $2,448

b.

	Tom Miller	Larry Rogers
Net income	$ 0	$ 688
Working capital (i.e., current assets – current liabilities)	5,000	5,688
Current ratio (i.e., current assets ÷ current liabilities)	4.33	4.79

c. Larry Rogers appears to be in the better financial position. His balance sheet reports higher assets and stockholders' equity. Further, he generated more net income, has higher working capital, and a better current ratio.

d. Tom Miller is actually in a better financial position than Larry Rogers. Both of them own the exact same marketable securities, and both own $1,500 in inventory. But Tom has more cash because he chose to simply hold on to his investment and not incur the transaction costs of buying and selling. On the other hand, Larry sold and repurchased his securities, and each transaction cost him 2% of the transaction value.

P6–1

a. No. The $275,000 is comprised of the $225,000 in savings and checking accounts and the $50,000 compensating balance. The $225,000 can properly be classified as a current asset since no restrictions on the access or on the use of these funds exist. However, Print-O-Matic is restricted from using the $50,000 compensating balance. Since use of these funds is restricted, the $50,000 has to be disclosed separately from unrestricted cash. To determine whether the $50,000 should be classified as a current or as a noncurrent asset, one must determine the remaining length of the restriction. In this case the $50,000 is restricted until the loan matures on October 1, 1996. Consequently, these funds will not become available within the time frame of current assets, thereby not qualifying the $50,000 for classification as a current asset. The $50,000 should be classified as a noncurrent asset.

b. The concept of interest expense is viewed differently by economists and accountants. Economists would define interest expense as the total cost of borrowing. Such costs would include the actual interest charged on the borrowing plus an opportunity cost incurred from borrowing. In this case, the actual interest charged on the borrowing for 1991 was $6,250. Print-O-Matic also incurred an opportunity cost. By borrowing the money, the company lost the opportunity to invest the $50,000 compensating balance. Assuming that Print-O-Matic would have invested this money in its savings and checking accounts at an annual rate of 5%, the company incurred an opportunity cost of $625 (i.e., $50,000 x 5% x 1/4). The opportunity cost should be considered when making business decisions.

Accountants would define interest expense as the outflow of assets or the inflow of liabilities associated with borrowing. Since opportunity costs represent lost opportunities and do not represent outflows of assets or inflows of liabilities, opportunity costs are not properly classified as expenses. Consequently, accountants would classify only the $6,250 as interest expense for 1991.

P6–2

a.

Habitat Realty Company
Bank Reconciliation — Savings Account
June 30, 1990

	Per Books	Per Bank Statement
Cash balance (6/30/90)	$15,525	$14,375
Plus		
Interest earned	95	
Deposits in transit		3,645
Less		
Bank error		2,400*
Correct cash balance	$15,620	$15,620

* $2,400 = $1,200 transfers from savings to checking *not* recorded + $1,200 transfers from checking to savings *incorrectly* recorded.

Habitat Realty Company
Bank Reconciliation — Checking Account
June 30, 1990

		Per Books		**Per Bank Statement**
Cash balance (6/30/90)		$5,163		$ 998
Plus				
Deposits in transit			$1,809	
Bank error			2,400*	4,209
Interest earned		20		
Less				
Outstanding checks				1,088
Service charge—printing	$ 10			
Service charge	25			
Returned post-dated checks	1,029	1,064		
Correct cash balance		$4,119		$4,119

b. **Savings Account**

Cash	95	
Interest Revenue		95

To record interest earned on savings account.

Checking Account

Service Charge Expense	35	
Accounts Receivable	1,029	
Interest Revenue		20
Cash		1,044

To adjust Cash account to the correct balance.

c. The company should report the total of both the savings and checking accounts as cash. The amount would be $19,739.

P6–3

a.

Kirkwood Appliances
Bank Reconciliation
October 31, 1991

		Per Books		**Per Bank Statement**
Cash balance (10/31/91)		$10,315		$ 9,255
Plus				
Deposits in transit				4,350
Note collected by bank	$ 2,000			
Interest earned	125	2,125		
Less				
Outstanding checks			$1,795	
NSF checks	670			
Bank error			90	1,885
Service charge	50	720		
Correct cash balance		$11,720		$11,720

b.

Cash	1,405	
Accounts Receivable	670	
Service Charge Expense	50	
Notes Receivable		2,000
Interest Revenue		125
To correct Cash account to the correct balance.		

c. $11,720

P6–4

a.

Marketable Securities	26,000*	
Cash		26,000
To record purchase of marketable securities.		

---

* Houser Company	100 x $20	=	$ 2,000
Miller, Inc.	200 x $45	=	9,000
Letter Books	75 x $50	=	3,750
Nordic Equipment	150 x $75	=	11,250
Total			$26,000

b. **Houser Company**

Cash	1,500	
Marketable Securities		1,200
Gain on Sale of Marketable Securities		300
To record sale of marketable securities (Houser Company).		

Miller, Inc.

Cash	2,700	
Loss on Sale of Marketable Securities	1,350	
Marketable Securities		4,050
To record sale of marketable securities (Miller, Inc.).		

Letter Books

Cash	550	
Marketable Securities		500
Gain on Sale of Marketable Securities		50
To record sale of marketable securities (Letter Books).		

Nordic Equipment

Cash	13,775	
Marketable Securities		10,875
Gain on Sale of Marketable Securities		2,900
To record sale of marketable securities.		

c.

Cash	205	
Dividend Revenue		205
To record receipt of dividends.		

d.

Security	Numbers of Shares Held	Cost/Share	Market Value/Share	Total Cost	Total Market Value
Houser Company	40	$20	$25	$ 800	$1,000
Miller, Inc.	110	45	35	4,950	3,850
Letter Books	65	50	50	3,250	3,250
Nordic Equipment	5	75	90	375	450
Total				$9,375	$8,550

Unrealized Loss on Marketable Securities	825*	
Allowance for Unrealized Losses on Marketable Securities		825
To adjust Marketable Securities to LCM.		

* $825 = Change in Allowance balance = ($9,375 – $8,550) – $0

P6–5

a. Short-term marketable securities $205,000[a]
Less: Allowance for unrealized losses on marketable securities 15,000[b]
190,000

---

[a]

Security	Cost	12/31/90 Market Value
Rudnicki Corp.	$ 50,000	$ 45,000
Ultraplex Theaters	70,000	80,000
T. J. Investors	25,000	10,000
Cards & Gifts	60,000	55,000
Total	$205,000	$190,000

[b] $15,000 = Cost – Market value = $205,000 – $190,000

b. Marketable Securities 75,000
Cash 75,000
To record investment in Giant Food.

c. On the balance sheet, short-term marketable securities are reported at the lower-of-cost or market (LCM) value. The cost of the securities is reported in the Short-Term Marketable Securities account, and the securities are reduced to LCM through the Allowance for Unrealized Losses on Marketable Securities account. Hence, the amount that should be reported in Short-Term Marketable Securities is the cost of the short-term marketable securities. Since Easton Records intends to hold the investment in T. J. Investors longer than one year, it is not considered a short-term security. Therefore, the total cost that should be reported in the account Short-Term Marketable Securities is $255,000 (i.e., $50,000 + $70,000 + $60,000 + $75,000).

Allowance for Unrealized Losses on Marketable Securities 10,000*
Recovery of Unrealized Losses on Marketable Securities 10,000
To adjust Marketable Securities to LCM.

---

* $10,000 = Change in Allowance balance = $5,000 – $15,000. The $5,000 Allowance balance as of 12/31/91 is calculated as follows:

1. Market value of short-term marketable securities = $50,000 for Rudnicki + $75,000 for Ultraplex + $65,000 for Cards & Gifts + $60,000 for Giant Foods = $250,000
2. Cost of short-term marketable securities = $255,000 (from Part [c])
3. 12/31/91 Allowance balance = $255,000 – $250,000 = $5,000

P6–6

a. (1) 3/10/90 Marketable Securities 30,000
Cash 30,000
To record investment in Arctic Oil & Gas.

(2) 3/31/90 Marketable Securities 9,600
Cash 9,600
To record investment in Humphries Manufacturing.

(3) 5/26/90 Cash 1,250
Dividend Revenue 1,250
To record receipt of dividends.

(4) 7/10/90 Marketable Securities 18,000
Cash 18,000
To record investment in Kingsman Games Company.

(5) 9/11/90 Cash 28,000
Marketable Securities 24,000
Gain on Sale of Marketable Securities 4,000
To record sale of Arctic Oil & Gas stock.

(6) 9/27/90 Cash 5,000
Loss on Sale of Marketable Securities 1,000
Marketable Securities 6,000
To record sale of Humphries Manufacturing stock.

(7) 10/19/90 Marketable Securities 25,000
Cash 25,000
To record investment in Quimby, Inc.

(8) 11/6/90 Cash 250*
Dividend Revenue 250
To record dividend earned and received.

* $250 = (1,000 shares purchased – 800 shares sold) x $1.25 per share

(9) 12/8/90 Cash 10,500*
Marketable Securities 9,600
Gain on Sale of Marketable Securities 900
To record sale of Arctic Oil & Gas and Humphries Manufacturing stock.

Computation for adjusting journal entry on 12/31/90:

Security	Numbers of Shares Held	Cost/Share	Market Value/Share	Total Cost	Total Market Value
Arctic Oil & Gas	0	$30	$32	$ 0	$ 0
Humphries Manufacturing	0	12	14	0	0
Kingsman Games Company	1,000	18	15	18,000	15,000
Quimby, Inc.	1,000	25	26	25,000	26,000
Total				$43,000	$41,000

12/31/90	Unrealized Loss on Marketable Securities	2,000*	
	Allowance for Unrealized Losses on Marketable Securities		2,000
	To adjust Marketable Securities to LCM.		

* $2,000 = $43,000 – $41,000

b. Marketable securities $43,000
Less: Allowance for unrealized losses on Marketable Securities 2,000
$41,000

c.

Transaction		Income Statement Impact	Explanation
(1)	3/10	$ 0	
(2)	3/31	0	
(3)	5/26	1,250	Dividend revenue
(4)	7/10	0	
(5)	9/11	4,000	Gain on sale of marketable securities
(6)	9/27	1,000	Loss on sale of marketable securities
(7)	10/19	0	
(8)	11/6	250	Dividend revenue
(9)	12/8	900	Gain on sale of marketable securities
	12/31	2,000	Holding loss on investment portfolio
	Net increase	$3,400	

P6–7

a. **1989**

Marketable Securities	320,000[a]	
Cash		320,000
To record investment in marketable securities.		
Unrealized Loss on Marketable Securities	15,000[a]	
Allowance for Unrealized Losses on Marketable Securities		15,000
To adjust Marketable Securities to LCM.		

1990

Marketable Securities	55,000[a]	
Cash		55,000
To record investment in marketable securities.		
Cash	80,000	
Loss on Sale of Marketable Securities	20,000	
Marketable Securities		100,000[a]
To record sale of marketable securities.		
Unrealized Loss on Marketable Securities	7,000[a]	
Allowance for Unrealized Losses on Marketable Securities		7,000
To adjust Marketable Securities to LCM.		

1991

	Debit	Credit
Marketable Securities	85,000[a]	
Cash		85,000
To record investment in marketable securities.		
Cash	15,000	
Marketable Securities		10,000[a]
Gain on Sale of Marketable Securities		5,000
To record sale of marketable securities.		
Allowance for Unrealized Losses on Marketable Securities	12,000	
Recovery of Unrealized Losses on Marketable Securities		12,000
To adjust Marketable Securities to LCM.		

[a] The dollar amounts for the entries are derived from the following T-accounts.

Marketable Securities

Date		Debit	Credit	Date
1/1/89		0		
1989	W =	320,000		
12/31/89		320,000		
1990	X =	55,000	100,000[b]	1990
12/31/90		275,000		
1991	Y =	85,000	10,000[c]	1991
12/31/91		350,000		

Allowance for Unrealized Losses on Marketable Securities

Date	Debit		Credit	Date
			0	1/1/90
		W =	15,000	1989
			15,000	12/31/89
		X =	7,000	1990
			22,000	12/31/90
1991	$12,000			
			10,000	12/31/91

[b] $100,000 = $80,000 cash + $20,000 loss on sale
[c] $10,000 = $15,000 cash – $5,000 gain on sale

b.

	1989	1990	1991
Gain on sale of marketable securities	$ 0	$ 0	$ 5,000
Loss on sale of marketable securities	0	20,000	0
Unrealized losses from LCM rule	15,000	7,000	0
Recoveries of unrealized losses from LCM rule	0	0	12,000
Increase (decrease)	($15,000)	($27,000)	$17,000

P6–8

a. Marketable Securities 23,400*
Cash 23,400
To record investment in marketable securities.

* Security	Number of Shares	Price Per Share	Total Cost
Crozier Can Company	250	$10	$ 2,500
Hamilton Housewares	100	25	2,500
Watson Manufacturing	200	15	3,000
St. Clair Computers	300	48	14,400
Cummings Moving Company	50	20	1,000
Total			$23,400

		Debit	Credit
12/31/91	Cash	9,000	
	Marketable Securities		3,000
	Gain on Sale of Marketable Securities		6,000
	To record sale of Watson Manufacturing stock.		
12/31/91	Marketable Securities	9,000	
	Cash		9,000
	To record investment in marketable securities.		

b. Marketable Securities 23,400
Cash 23,400
To record investment in marketable securities.

c.

Security	Levy Company Cost	Levy Company Market Value	Guyer Books Cost	Guyer Books Market Value
Crozier Can Company	$ 2,500	$ 3,000	$ 2,500	$ 3,000
Hamilton Housewares	2,500	2,000	2,500	2,000
Watson Manufacturing	9,000	9,000	3,000	9,000
St. Clair Computers	14,400	3,000	14,400	3,000
Cummings Moving Company	1,000	1,050	1,000	1,050
Total	$29,400	$18,050	$23,400	$18,050

Levy Company

Unrealized Loss on Marketable Securities 11,350*
Allowance for Unrealized Losses on Marketable Securities 11,350
To adjust Marketable Securities to LCM.

* $11,350 = change in allowance balance = ($29,400 – $18,050) – $0

Guyer Books

Unrealized Loss on Marketable Securities 5,350*
Allowance for Unrealized Losses Marketable Securities 5,350
To adjust Marketable Securities to LCM.

* $5,350 = change in allowance balance = ($23,400 – $18,050) – $0

	Levy Company	Guyer Books
Gain on sale	$ 6,000	$ 0
Unrealized losses from LCM rule	11,350	5,350
Net decrease	$ 5,350	$5,350

d. Levy Company reports a gain of $6,000, but this gain is completely offset by an increase in the reported unrealized loss. Therefore, the net effect on the income statement of holding these securities is the same for both companies. If we focus just on the marketable securities held by each company, Levy appears to hold a more valuable portfolio because its cost is greater than the portfolio held by Guyer Books. However, Guyer Books can use its unrealized gain on Watson manufacturing to offset unrealized losses on other investments.

In reality, the two companies are in the same economic condition. Both companies own exactly the same investments. However, if we consider the cash payments associated with acquiring the securities, Guyer Books would be in a better economic condition than Levy Company. By selling and repurchasing an investment, Levy Company paid an additional $6,000 for its investment portfolio, thereby reducing its available cash by $6,000. Further, Levy Company incurred transaction costs (i.e., brokerage fees, etc.) that it could have avoided if it had simply held on to the investment in Watson Manufacturing.

e. Accountants adhere to the lower-of-cost-or-market rule because of conservatism. Errors of understatement are less costly than errors of overstatement to managers and auditors.

P6–9

a.

Security	Numbers of Shares Held	Cost/Share	Market Value/Share	Total Cost	Total Market Value
Desk Publishing	1,000	$10	$13	$10,000	$13,000
T. Brown, Inc.	750	12	11	9,000	8,250
Cityscapes	1,500	20	17	30,000	25,500
Wilson Cribs	100	80	60	8,000	6,000
Total				$57,000	$52,750

(1) Portfolio cost = $57,000
Portfolio market value = 52,750

(2) Allowance balance = Excess of portfolio cost over portfolio market value
= $57,000 – $52,750
= $4,250

(3) Change in Allowance balance = 12/31/90 Balance – 3/10/90 Balance
= $4,250 – $0
= $4,250 increase

(4) Unrealized Loss on Marketable Securities 4,250
Allowance for Unrealized Losses on Marketable Securities 4,250
To adjust Marketable Securities to LCM.

			Debit	Credit
b.	1/10/91	Marketable Securities	18,750	
		Cash		18,750
		To record investment in Chicago Bakery.		
	3/6/91	Cash	12,600	
		Marketable Securities		9,000
		Gain on Sale of Marketable Securities		3,600
		To record sale of investment in Desk Publishing.		
	5/23/91	Cash	28,500	
		Loss on Sale of Marketable Securities	1,500	
		Marketable Securities		30,000
		To record sale of investment in Cityscapes.		
	6/15/91	Marketable Securities	50,000	
		Cash		50,000
		To record investment in Eagle Air Freight.		
	9/20/91	Cash	8,000	
		Marketable Securities		8,000
		To record sale of investment in Wilson Cribs.		
	12/1/91	Marketable Securities	10,000	
		Cash		10,000
		To record investment in Rix Scooters.		

c.

Security	Numbers of Shares Held	Cost/Share	Market Value/Share	Total Cost	Total Market Value
Desk Publishing	100	$10	$ 16	$ 1,000	$ 1,600
T. Brown, Inc..	750	12	10	9,000	7,500
Cityscapes	0	20	20	0	0
Wilson Cribs	0	80	89	0	0
Chicago Bakery	1,250	15	20	18,750	25,000
Eagle Air Freight	1,000	50	45	50,000	45,000
Rix Scooters	500	20	22	10,000	11,000
Total				$88,750	$90,100

(1) Portfolio cost = \$88,750
Portfolio market value = \$90,100

(2) Allowance balance = Excess of portfolio cost over portfolio market value
= \$88,750 – \$90,100
= \$0 Since the market value exceeds the cost, cost will be used for financial reporting purposes.

(3) Change in Allowance balance = 12/31/91 Balance – 12/31/90 Balance
= \$0 – \$4,250
= \$4,250 decrease

	Debit	Credit
(4) Allowance for Unrealized Losses on Marketable Securities	4,250	
Recovery of Unrealized Losses on Marketable Securities		4,250
To adjust Marketable Securities to LCM.		

C6-1

a. Working capital = Current assets ≈ Current liabilities
= \$528,950 – \$157,626 = \$371,324

Current ratio = Current assets] Current labilities
= \$528,950 ÷ \$157,626 = 3.3557

Quick ratio = (Cash + Accounts receivable) ÷ Current liabilities
= (\$11,182 + \$238,930) ÷ \$157,626 = 1.5867

Note: The quick ratio can be calculated several different ways. The most common formula is (Cash + Marketable Securities) ÷ Current liabilities. An alternative formula is the one used.

b. A covenant that specifies maintenance of working capital is directed at ensuring repayment of a loan. Recall that working capital is composed of current assets less current liabilities, or net current assets. Current assets are those assets that will be converted to cash within a year or the operating cycle, whichever is longer. Accordingly, specifying a certain level of working capital is a method of ensuring that some level of cash will be available to meet loan obligations. Failure to adhere to the covenant may make the loan immediately due and may jeopardize relationships with creditors if future financing is required.

C6-2

a. Working capital (WC) = Current assets – Current liabilities

	WC	Excess
1986:	\$296.8	\$ 96.8
1987:	507.9	307.9
1988:	417.5	217.5

b. On July 1, 1988, Quaker Oats had \$217,500,000 "excess" working capital. This is *not* all in cash. Their available cash is \$91,200,000. In order to purchase \$600,000,000 of land and buildings *and* comply with a minimum \$200,000,000 working capital requirement, Quaker Oats could use the following financing scheme for purchasing the assets:

(1) Pay \$91,200,000 in cash
(2) Issue a note payable for the balance of \$508,800,000. (Some would have to be long-term to avoid violating the covenant.)

Note that they would want to pay out less than their entire cash balance, which would increase the amount of the note payable.

C6-3

a. A potential investor is interested in the solvency of a company. Accordingly, an investor would want to know about any existing restrictions on a reported cash balance.

b. Because the cash will be "converted" to a noncurrent asset on January 3, the restricted cash at December 31 would be disclosed as noncurrent.

c. The amount of cash used in the calculation of working capital, the current ratio, and the quick ratio would be reduced by the amount of the restriction, \$15 million.

d. The increase in cash and the decrease in short-term investment offset each other, and working capital is unaffected. The repayment of the loan results in a decrease in current assets and a decrease in current liabilities. *Total* working capital will not be affected. Ratios, such as the current and quick ratios, however, will be affected.

C6-4

a. The lower-of-cost-or-market rule requires that marketable equity securities be reflected on the balance sheet at either their historical cost or their current market value, whichever is lower. Clabir viewed the price included in the oral agreement from U.S. Industries as a market value instead of the NYSE price.

b. The SEC considered Clabir's method of accounting improper principally because they used a restricted definition of "market" (i.e., U.S. Industries' offer) which favored nonconservative accounting practices.

c. Reasons why Clabir's management might have chosen such a method include the original purchase of stock at a substantially higher price, which, when compared to the offered price, resulted in a lower loss than if the NYSE valuation had been used. Clabir may have motives for reducing the loss, which include debt covenants or bonus arrangements. It is possible, however, that management may indeed consummate the deal with U.S. Industries, which would justify their actions. The SEC action highlights the valuation questions and also provides a signal about the management of Clabir that may or may not be justified.

   It may be true that Clabir's management was "window dressing." Using the higher valuation decreased the recorded loss and made their income higher. On the other hand, their action may be entirely valid because they intend to follow through on the offer from U.S. Industries. More facts are necessary to determine what the appropriate valuation should have been.

C6-5

a. As the auditors for Saxon Industries, Fox & Co. assumes some legal liability with regard to the issuance of their opinion on Saxon's financial statements. If International Paper and Borden relied on the auditor's opinion in extending credit to Saxon, then Fox must assume the liability for the consequences of their opinion. If Fox & Co. acted correctly and fulfilled their obligation for an audit, then it is not their fault if the creditors did not accurately assess the information. The same is true for the stockholders of Saxon. It would be necessary to gather more facts related to this case in order to determine who is at fault.

b. The auditor should always maintain objectivity and never intentionally report the position of a company as either better or worse than it actually is. Further, the actual numbers are the representations of the company's management, which include an auditor's opinion regarding the fairness of the presentation. International Paper and Borden may have filed similar suits, anyway, but it is unlikely because in situations of understatements, the plaintiffs have no out-of-pocket losses.

c. Lower-of-cost-or-market reflects the fact that the costs of overstatement, especially in the form of legal liability, exceeds the costs of understatement.

CHAPTER 7 Short-Term Receivables

E7–1

	Date	Account	Debit	Credit
a.	5/1/91	Accounts Receivable	50,000	
		Sales		50,000
		To record sale of lobster.		
	5/5/91	Accounts Receivable	20,000	
		Sales		20,000
		To record sale of cod.		
	5/6/91	Cash	48,500	
		Cash Discount	1,500	
		Accounts Receivable		50,000
		To record cash collection from customer.		
	5/31/91	Cash	20,000	
		Accounts Receivable		20,000
		To record cash collection from customer.		
b.	5/1/91	Accounts Receivable	48,500	
		Sales		48,500
		To record sale of lobster.		
	5/5/91	Accounts Receivable	19,400	
		Sales		19,400
		To record sale of cod.		
	5/6/91	Cash	48,500	
		Accounts Receivable		48,500
		To record cash collection from customer.		
	5/31/91	Cash	20,000	
		Accounts Receivable		19,400
		Cash Discount Not Taken		600
		To record cash collection from customer.		

E7–2

	Date	Account	Debit	Credit
a.	12/12	Accounts Receivable	30,000	
		Sales		30,000
		To record sale on account.		
	12/31	Adjusting entry: No adjusting entry is necessary.		
	1/5	Cash	30,000	
		Accounts Receivable		30,000
		To record cash collection from customer.		

b. 12/12 Accounts Receivable 29,400 *
Sales 29,400
To record sale on account.

---

* $29,400 = $30,000 – ($30,000 x 2% discount)

12/31 Adjusting entry
Accounts Receivable 600
Cash Discounts Not Taken 600
To record expiration of discount period.

1/5 Cash 30,000
Accounts Receivable 30,000
To record cash collection from customer.

c.

	Gross Method	Net Method
Sales	$30,000	$29,400
Less: Cash discounts	0	N/A
Net sales	$30,000	$29,400
Other revenue: Cash discounts not taken	0	600
Net income	$30,000	$30,000

d. The net method of accounting for cash discounts captures the economic substance of the transaction, and records the initial sale and receivable at the cash value of the transaction, which is in accordance with good measurement theory. Consequently, net sales under the net method represents only the cash value of the sale. On the other hand, under the gross method of accounting for cash discounts, net sales may or may not represent the cash value of the sale. If all customers pay within the discount period, then net sales will be identical under both methods, and net sales under the gross method equals the cash value of the sale.. But if some customers fail to pay within the discount period, the "finance charge" for delaying payment is mixed with sales, and net sales will not equal the cash value of the sale. Since net sales can, and often will, differ between the two methods, the gross profit of the same company would be different depending upon which method was employed to account for cash discounts.

Further, the net method provides more accessible information regarding whether customers are taking advantage of cash discounts and the amount of discounts not taken. Under the net method, any discount not taken is recorded in the account Cash Discounts Not Taken. While the same information can be obtained under the gross method, the calculation is much more cumbersome. The balance in Cash Discounts would have to be compared to the product of the discount rate times sales. However, this measure may not be accurate since the Cash Discount balance may include discounts on sales made at the end of the last accounting period.

e. For the same series of transactions, both the net and gross methods of accounting for cash discounts yield the same net income figure. However, the components of net income will be different under the two methods. Under the gross method, any discounts not taken are buried in net sales, thereby allowing a company to report a higher gross profit. However, this amount will be immaterial for most companies. If Mayliner's annual sales equal $1 million, then the total value of potential discounts is $20,000. Consequently, most companies simply select the least costly method to account for cash discounts.

Using the gross method to account for cash discounts is less costly than using the net method. The net method requires an adjusting entry at the end of the accounting period for all cash discounts that have expired. This entry necessitates detailed tracking of accounts receivables, which can be quite costly. However, with the availability of computers, the task of tracking and identifying receivables outside the discount period will become easier and less costly. So in the future, the net and gross methods may be equally easy to use. But due to inertia and the cost of implementing a computer system to track receivables, companies may still not switch to the net method. The benefits of using the net method will simply not exceed the costs of switching.

E7–3

		Debit	Credit
a.	Bad Debt Expense	60,000 *	
	Allowance for Doubtful Accounts		60,000
	To record bad debt expense.		

* $60,000 = $3,000,000 x 2%

		Debit	Credit
b.	Bad Debt Expense	55,000 *	
	Allowance for Doubtful Accounts		55,000
	To record bad debt expense.		

* $55,000 = $2,750,000 x 2%

c. **1990**

	Debit	Credit
Bad Debt Expense	87,000 *	
Allowance for Doubtful Accounts		87,000
To record bad debt expense.		

* $87,000 = $57,000 estimated uncollectible + $30,000 actually written off

1991

	Debit	Credit
Bad Debt Expense	78,000 *	
Allowance for Doubtful Accounts		78,000
To record bad debt expense.		

* $78,000 = $80,000 estimated uncollectible + $55,000 actually written off – $57,000 beginning balance in the Allowance account.

E7–4

		Debit	Credit
a.	Allowance for Doubtful Accounts	205,000	
	Accounts Receivable		205,000
	To write off uncollectible accounts.		
	Accounts Receivable	50,000	
	Allowance for Doubtful Accounts		50,000
	To record recovery of accounts previously written off.		
	Bad Debt Expense	125,000	
	Allowance for Doubtful Accounts		125,000
	To record bad debt expense.		

b. Ending Allowance balance = Beginning Allowance balance + Bad debt expense – Write–offs + Recoveries

$350,000 = Beginning Allowance balance + $125,000 – $205,000 + $50,000

Beginning Allowance balance = $380,000

E7–5

		Debit	Credit
a.	Bad Debt Expense	38,240 *	
	Allowance for Doubtful Accounts		38,240
	To record bad debt expense.		

* $38,240 = Sales x 4% = $956,000 x 4%

b. Ending allowance balance = Beginning Allowance balance + Bad debt expense – Write–offs + Recoveries

= $45,000 + $38,240 – $20,000 + 0

= $63,240

		Debit	Credit
c.	Bad Debt Expense	35,000 *	
	Allowance for Doubtful Accounts		35,000
	To record bad debt expense.		

* $35,000 = $60,000 estimated to be uncollectible + $20,000 written off – $45,000 beginning balance in the Allowance account.

E7–6

a. Ending Allowance balance = Beginning Allowance balance + Bad debt expense + Recoveries – Write–offs

$830 = $750 + ($75,300 x 3%) + 55 – Write–offs

Write–offs = $2,234

		Debit	Credit
b.	Accounts Receivable	75,300	
	Sales		75,300
	To record sales on account.		
	Accounts Receivable	55	
	Allowance for Doubtful Accounts		55
	To record recoveries of accounts previously written off.		

		Debit	Credit
	Allowance for Doubtful Accounts	2,234	
	Accounts Receivable		2,234
	To record write off of accounts deemed uncollectible.		
	Bad Debt Expense	2,259*	
	Allowance for Doubtful Accounts		2,259
	To record bad debt expense.		

* $2,259 = credit sales x 3% = $75,300 x 3%

		Debit	Credit
	Cash	71,721*	
	Accounts Receivable		71,721
	To record cash collections from customers.		

* $71,721 = beginning balance in Accounts Receivable + $75,300 of credit sales + $55 of recoveries – $2,234 of write–offs – $9,400 ending balance in Accounts Receivable

c. Ending Allowance balance = Beginning Allowance balance – Write–offs + Recoveries + Bad debt expense

$830 = $2,750 – $2,000 + 55 – Bad debt expense

Bad debt expense = $2,025

E7–7

a. **No Discount Account Used**

Date	Account	Debit	Credit
12/1	Notes Receivable	7,000	
	Cash		7,000
	To record loan to Slayden Brothers.		
12/31	Adjusting entry		
	Interest Receivable	70*	
	Interest Revenue		70
	To record interest earned but not yet collected.		

* $70 = ($7,000 x 12%) x 1/12

Date	Account	Debit	Credit
3/1	Cash	7,210	
	Notes receivable		7,000
	Interest receivable		70
	Interest revenue		140
	To record collection on loan from Slayden Brothers.		

Discount Account Used

Date	Account	Debit	Credit
12/1	Note receivable	7,210*	
	Cash		7,000
	Discount on Note Receivable		210

* $7,210 = $7,000 + [($7,000 x 12%) x 3/12]

Date	Account	Debit	Credit
12/31	Adjusting entry		
	Discount on Note Receivable	70	
	Interest Revenue		70
	To record amortization of discount.		

3/1	Cash	7,210	
	Discount on Note Receivable	140	
	Notes Receivable		7,210
	Interest Revenue		140
	To record collection on loan from Slayden Brothers.		

b. Methods 1 and 2 have the same monetary affect on the financial statements. As of December 31, Method 1 reports a balance of $7,000 and $70 for Notes Receivable and Interest Receivable, respectively, for a total of $7,070 in current assets. As of the same date, Method 2 reports a balance of $7,210 for Notes Receivable, but also reports a balance in Discount on Notes Receivable of $140, which partially offsets the $7,210. Consequently, a total of $7,070 is reported in current assets under this method as well. Interest is earned at the same rate and at the same time under both methods, so the choice of method does not affect the income statement. The only difference between the two methods is the method of disclosure on the balance sheet.

E7–8

a. The balance in the Allowance account represents the estimated dollar amount currently in Accounts Receivable that will prove to be uncollectible. The Allowance account is a permanent account that partially offsets the balance in Accounts Receivable. Since the Allowance account is a permanent account, its balance carries over from year to year. Consequently, this account would be expected to have a preadjustment balance, because of the balance carried over from the previous year. Further, the balance from the previous year would be affected by write–offs of customers' accounts as uncollectible and by recoveries of customers' accounts previously written off as uncollectible.

b. The balance in the Allowance account represents the estimated dollar amount currently in Accounts Receivable that will prove to be uncollectible. Since the controller estimated from her analysis that $195,000 of customers' accounts would prove to be uncollectible, the Allowance balance should be a credit of $195,000.

c.	Bad Debt Expense	95,000 *	
	Allowance for Doubtful Accounts		95,000
	To record bad debt expense.		

* $95,000 = $195,000 in estimated uncollectibles – $100,000 preadjustment balance in the Allowance account.

E7–9

a.	Bad Debt Expense	40,000	
	Allowance for Doubtful Accounts		40,000
	To record bad debt expense.		
b.	Bad Debt Expense	55,000	
	Allowance for Doubtful Accounts		55,000
	To record bad debt expense.		

E7–10

Account Age	Balance	Noncollection Probability	Uncollectible Amount
Current	$200,000	2%	$ 4,000
1–45 days	110,000	5%	5,500
46–90 days	68,000	8%	5,440
> 90 days	25,000	15%	3,750
Total			$18,690

a.	Bad Debt Expense	3,690 *	
	Allowance for Doubtful Accounts		3,690
	To record bad debt expense.		

* $3,690 = $18,690 – $15,000

Bad Debt Expense	19,690 *	
Allowance for Doubtful Accounts		19,690
To record bad debt expense.		

* $19,690 = $18,690 – $10,000 beginning balance – $3,000 of recoveries + $14,000 of write–offs

P7–1

a.	7/5	Accounts Receivable	147,000 *	
		Sales		147,000
		To record sales on account.		

* $147,000 = $150,000 – ($150,000 x 2%)

7/21	Accounts Receivable	78,400	
	Sales		78,400
	To record sales on account.		

* $78,400 = $80,000 – ($80,000 x 2%)

	7/31	Cash	78,400	
		Accounts Receivable		78,400
		To record cash collection from customer.		
	7/31	Adjusting journal entry		
		Accounts Receivable	3,000	
		Cash Discount Not Taken		3,000
		To record expiration of sales discount period.		
	8/30	Cash	150,000	
		Accounts Receivable		150,000
		To record cash collection from customer.		
b.	7/5	Accounts Receivable	150,000	
		Sales		150,000
		To record sales on account.		

Date	Account	Debit	Credit
7/21	Accounts Receivable	80,000	
	Sales		80,000
	To record sales on account.		
7/31	Cash	78,400	
	Cash Discount	1,600	
	Accounts Receivable		80,000
	To record cash collection from customer.		
7/31	Adjusting journal entry: No adjusting journal entry is necessary.		
8/30	Cash	150,000	
	Accounts Receivable		150,000
	To record cash collection from customer.		

P7–2

	Date	Account	Debit	Credit
a.	5/2	Accounts Receivable	9,700 *	
		Sales		9,700
		To record sale on account.		

* $9,700 = $10,000 – ($10,000 x 3%)

	Date	Account	Debit	Credit
	5/10	Accounts Receivable	19,400 *	
		Sales		19,400
		To record sale on account.		

* $19,400 = $20,000 – ($20,000 x 3%)

	Date	Account	Debit	Credit
	5/13	Cash	9,700	
		Accounts Receivable		9,700
		To record cash collection from customer.		
	5/31	Adjusting entry		
		Accounts Receivable	600	
		Cash Discount Not Taken		600
		To adjust for expiration of sales discount period.		
	6/18	Cash	20,000	
		Accounts Receivable		20,000
		To record collection on an open account.		
b.	5/2	Accounts Receivable	10,000	
		Sales		10,000
		To record sale on account.		
	5/10	Accounts Receivable	20,000	
		Sales		20,000
		To record sale on account.		

	Date	Account	Debit	Credit
	5/13	Cash	9,700	
		Cash Discount	300	
		Accounts Receivable		10,000
		To record cash collection from customer.		
	5/31	Adjusting entry: No adjusting entry is necessary.		
	6/18	Cash	20,000	
		Accounts Receivable		20,000
		To record cash collection from customer.		
c.	5/10	Accounts Receivable		19,400
		Sales		19,400
		To record sale on account.		
	5/20	Cash	14,550	
		Accounts Receivable		14,550
		To record partial cash collection from customer.		
	5/31	Adjusting entry		
		Account Receivable	150 *	
		Cash Discount Not Taken		150
		To adjust expiration of sales discount period.		

* Step 1: Compute remaining outstanding balance
= $19,400 – $14,550
= $$4,850

Step 2: Compute gross amount associated with remaining outstanding balance
$4,850 = gross amount – (gross amount x 3%)
$4,850 = 97% x gross amount
gross amount = $5,000

Step 3: Compute amount of discount forfeited = Gross amount x 3%
= $5,000 x 3%
= $5,150

	Date	Account	Debit	Credit
	6/27	Cash	5,000	
		Accounts Receivable		5,000
		To record cash collection from customer.		
d.	5/10	Accounts Receivable	20,000	
		Sales		20,000
		To record sale on account.		
	5/20	Cash	14,550	
		Cash Discount	450 *	
		Accounts Receivable		15,000
		To record cash collection from customer.		

* $450 = [$14,550 ÷ (1 – discount rate of 3%)] x 3%

5/31 Adjusting entry: No adjusting journal entry is necessary.

6/27	Cash	5,000	
	Accounts Receivable		5,000
	To record cash collection from customer.		

P7–3

a. (1)	3/3	Accounts Receivable	1,200	
		Sales		1,200
		To record sale on account.		
(2)	3/8	Accounts Receivable	800	
		Sales		800
		To record sale on account.		
(3)	3/11	Cash	1,176	
		Cash Discount	24*	
		Accounts Receivable		1,200
		To record cash collection from customer.		

* $24 = $1,200 x 2% discount

(4)	3/28	Cash	800	
		Accounts Receivable		800
		To record cash collection from customer.		
(5)	3/29	Accounts Receivable	1,600	
		Sales		1,600
		To record sale on account.		
b. (1)	3/3	Accounts Receivable	1,176	
		Sales		1,176
		To record sale on account.		
(2)	3/8	Accounts Receivable	784	
		Sales		784
		To record sale on account.		
(3)	3/11	Cash	1,176	
		Accounts Receivable		1,176
		To record cash collection from customer.		
(4)	3/28	Cash	800	
		Accounts Receivable		784
		Cash Discount Not Taken		16
		To record cash collection from customer.		
(5)	3/29	Accounts Receivable	1,568	
		Sales		1,568
		To record sale on account.		

c. Ordinarily the gross and net methods give rise to the same net income figure. However, the components of net income under the two methods may differ. Under the net method, Cash Discounts reduce the amount recorded for Sales, thereby resulting in the sales amount always reflecting the net amount of the sales. If customers do not take their discounts, the forfeited discount amount is reported separately as an Other Revenue and Expense Item on the income statement. Therefore, Sales is always stated at the net amount of the sale. Under the gross method, sales are always recorded at the gross amount of the sale. Only those cash discounts actually taken by customers reduce gross sales. Therefore, unlike the net method, cash discounts not taken are buried in the sales amount under the gross method.

The only time that the gross and net methods do not result in the same net income figure, as in this case, is when a customer purchases something prior to the end of the accounting period, the discount period does not expire until after the end of the accounting period, and the customer has not settled the account by the end of the accounting period. In such cases, the gross method reports the gross amount of the sale, and the net method reports the net amount of the sale. The difference will not be reconciled until either the customer settles the account within the discount period, or the discount period expires. Hence, net income is $32 higher under the gross method than under the net method due to the sale to CCC Company.

d. The annual interest rate of forfeiting a cash discount is calculated as follows:

Annual rate = Cash discount rate x (365 days ÷ Number of days receipts collected after the end of the discount period
= 2% x (365 ÷ 10 days)
= 73%

Since BBB can borrow money at an annual interest rate of 14%, BBB should have borrowed money at the 14% rate and paid its obligation to QNI Corporation. BBB would have saved itself some interest costs by borrowing the money rather than forfeiting the cash discount.

P7–4

a. **1988**

Allowance for Doubtful Accounts	7,000	
Accounts Receivable		7,000
To record write–off of accounts deemed uncollectible.		
Bad Debt Expense	5,400 *	
Allowance for Doubtful Accounts		5,400
To record bad debt expense.		

* $5,400 = $180,000 x 3%

1989

Allowance for Doubtful Accounts	9,000	
Accounts Receivable		9,000
To record write–off of accounts deemed uncollectible.		
Bad Debt Expense	6,000 *	
Allowance for Doubtful Accounts		6,000
To record bad debt expense.		

* $6,000 = $200,000 x 3%

1990

Allowance for Doubtful Accounts	10,000	
Accounts Receivable		10,000
To record write–off of accounts deemed uncollectible.		
Bad Debt Expense	6,150 *	
Allowance for Doubtful Accounts		6,150
To record bad debt expense.		

* $6,150 = $205,000 x 3%

b.

January 1, 1988 balance	$10,000	
Write–offs during 1988	(7,000)	
1988 bad debt expense	5,400	
December 31, 1988 balance		$8,400
Write–offs during 1989		(9,000)
1989 bad debt expense		6,000
December 31, 1989 balance		$15,400
Write–offs during 1990		(10,000)
1990 bad debt expense		6,150
December 31, 1990 balance		$ 1,550

c. Stable Toddlers should consider increasing the percentage of credit sales that is considered uncollectible. From 1988 through 1990, write–offs exceeded bad debt expense, with the difference increasing over time. Write–offs as a percentage of credit sales increased from 3.89% (i.e., $7,000 ÷ $180,000) in 1988 to 4.88% (i.e., $10,000 ÷ $205,000) in 1990. This trend indicates that the December 31, 1990 balance in Allowance for Doubtful Accounts is probably understated, thereby causing an overstatement of the company's assets. A more appropriate bad debt percentage would appear to be 4.5% to 5.0% of credit sales.

d. Under the direct write–off method, bad debt expense is recognized when a customer's account is deemed to be uncollectible and written off. Since Stable Toddlers, Inc. wrote off customer's accounts in the amounts of $7,000, $9,000, and $10,000 in 1988, 1989, and 1990, respectively, the company would recognize these same amounts as bad debt expense in each of those years. Comparing these amounts to the amounts recorded for bad debt expense under the allowance method used in Part (a) indicates that the allowance method, in this case, gave rise to lower bad debt expense in each year. Over the three-year period, Bad Debt Expense under the allowance method would have been $8,450 less than Bed Debt Expense under the direct write-off method. However, as noted in Part (c), the reason that write–offs exceeded bad debt expense was that the company was using too low of an uncollectible percentage.

P7–5

a.

Bad Debt Expense	40,500 *	
Allowance for Doubtful Accounts		40,500
To record bad debt expense.		

* $40,500 = net sales x 3% = [$1,500,000 – ($100,000 + $50,000)] x 3%

b. Ending Allowance balance = Beginning Allowance balance + Bad debt expense + Recoveries – Write–offs
= $65,000 + $40,500 (from Part [a]) + $0 – $70,000
= $35,500

c. Bad Debt Expense 55,500 *
Allowance for Doubtful Accounts 55,500
To record bad debt expense.

* $55,500 = net sales x 3% = [$2,000,000 – ($125,000 + $25,000)] x 3%

d. Ending Allowance balance = Beginning Allowance balance + Bad debt expense + Recoveries – Write–offs
= $35,500 (from Part [b]) + $55,500 (from Part [c]) + $0 – $85,000
= $86,000

P7–6

a.

Johnson Company
Income Statement
For the Year Ended December 31, 1990

Sales	$200,000
Cost of goods sold	102,000
	$ 98,000
Expenses	115,000*
Net income (Loss)	$ 17,000

Johnson Company
Balance Sheet
December 31, 1990

Cash	$ 5,000
Accounts receivable	35,000
Other assets	40,000
Total assets	$80,000
Current Liabilities	$13,000
Long-term note payable	80,000
Stockholders' equity	(13,000)
Total liabilities and stockholders' equity	$80,000

* $115,000 = $65,000 (reported expenses) + $50,000 (bad debt expense associated with the Litzenberger account)

After considering the adjustment for potential bad debts, Johnson generated a net loss for 1990. Therefore, it appears than Johnson Company did not have a very successful first year of operations.

b. Auditors have their own interests. They must consider factors affecting their own well–being. One item that could adversely affect auditors' well–being is being the defendant in a lawsuit. If the auditors did not require an adjustment for the Litzenberger account, and Litzenberger was subsequently unable to pay its debt, users of the Johnson's financial statements could sue the auditors for any losses incurred. Conservatism, which states "when in doubt, understate rather than overstate," applies to this situation. Since the auditors are uncertain as to whether Johnson Company will ever collect the money from Litzenberger, the auditors would prefer to understate Johnson Company's financial health rather than overstate it.

c. While it is true that Litzenberger is still operating, Johnson's CFO is ignoring the revenue recognition principle and the matching principle. Under the revenue recognition principle, revenue should not be recognized if post–sales costs can not be adequately estimated (subject to materiality). In this case, the actual bad debt cost associated with Litzenberger will not occur until a subsequent period. However, if this cost cannot be adequately estimated, Johnson Company should not even recognize the revenue from the sale to Litzenberger. Assume that Johnson Company can adequately estimate the bad debt cost. In this case Johnson Company is allowed to recognize the revenue. But under the matching principle, all costs associated with generating revenue should be matched against those revenues. Hence, any costs associated with making a sale, whether incurred in the current period or in subsequent periods, should be recorded in the period of the sale. Since the bad debt cost is associated with generating revenue, Johnson Company should record the bad debt cost in the current period as an expense.

P7–7

a. Based upon the auditor's findings, Finley, Ltd. should make the following entries.

Fees Earned	$10,000	
Accounts Receivable		$10,000
To remove a sale on account incorrectly recorded.		
Bad Debt Expense	$2,400 *	
Allowance for Uncollectibles		$2,400
To adjust for estimated bad debts.		

* $2,400 = [($68,000 – $10,000) x 10%] – $3,400

Using these entries, the effect of the auditor's findings on 1990 Fees Earned, Accounts Receivable, Allowance for Doubtful Accounts, current ratio, working capital, and net income can be determined as follows.

Fees Earned: Fees Earned would decrease from $240,000 to $230,000.

Accounts Receivable: Accounts Receivable would decrease from $68,000 to $58,000.

Allowance for Uncollectibles: This account should have a balance equal to 10% of the <u>new</u> Accounts Receivable balance. The correct balance would be $5,800, or an increase of $2,400.

Current Ratio: The current ratio before the auditor's findings was 1.62 (i.e., $105,000 ÷ $65,000). Current assets after these findings would be $92,600 (i.e., $105,000 – $10,000 decrease in Accounts Receivable – $2,400 increase in Allowance for Doubtful Accounts). Current liabilities would be unaffected by the auditor's findings. So the new current ratio would be 1.42 (i.e., $92,600 ÷ $65,000).

Working Capital: Working capital would decrease from $40,000 (i.e., $105,000 – $65,000) to $27,600 (i.e., $92,600 – $65,000).

Net Income: Net income would decrease by the reduction in Fees Earned of $10,000 and by the increase in Bad Debt Expense of $2,400. The new net income would be $2,600.

b. Prior to the auditor's findings, Finley, Ltd. was in compliance with its debt covenants. However, after correcting the books for the auditor's findings, Finley, Ltd. has violated both requirements of its debt covenants. The company's current ratio has fallen to 1.42, which is below 1.5 as specified in the loan agreement. Further, the company declared dividends equal to 192.3% of the adjusted net income. It appears that one possible explanation for Finley's decision to record the sale and not record an adequate amount for bad debts was to avoid violating its debt covenants.

P7–8

a.	(1)	7/6/88	Bad Debt Expense	10,000	
			Accounts Receivable		10,000
			To write off an account deemed uncollectible.		
	(2)	2/3/89	Bad Debt Expense	50,000	
			Accounts Receivable		50,000
			To write off an account deemed uncollectible.		
	(3)	9/11/89	Bad Debt Expense	25,000	
			Accounts Receivable		25,000
			To write off an account deemed uncollectible.		
	(4)	3/24/90	Accounts Receivable	5,000	
			Bad Debt Expense		5,000
			To record the recovery of an account previously written off.		
		3/24/90	Cash	5,000	
			Accounts Receivable		5,000
			To record cash collection from a customer.		
	(5)	8/8/91	Bad Debt Expense	75,000	
			Accounts Receivable		75,000
			To write off an account deemed uncollectible.		
	(6)	12/2/91	Bad Debt Expense	5,000	
			Accounts Receivable		5,000
			To write off an account deemed uncollectible.		
	(7)	9/19/92	Bad Debt Expense	90,000	
			Accounts Receivable		90,000
			To write off an account deemed uncollectible.		
b.	(1)	7/6/88	Allowance for Doubtful Accounts	10,000	
			Accounts Receivable		10,000
			To write off an account deemed uncollectible.		
		12/31/88	Bad Debt Expense	80,000*	
			Allowance for Uncollectibles		80,000
			To record bad debt expense.		

* $80,000 = $1,000,000 in sales x 8%

	(2)	2/3/89	Allowance for Doubtful Accounts	50,000	
			Accounts Receivable		50,000
			To write off an account deemed uncollectible.		

	Date	Account	Debit	Credit
(3)	9/11/89	Allowance for Doubtful Accounts	25,000	
		Accounts Receivable		25,000
		To write off an account deemed uncollectible.		
	12/31/89	Bad Debt Expense	78,000	
		Allowance for Doubtful Accounts		78,000
		To record bad debt expense.		
(4)	3/24/90	Accounts Receivable	5,000	
		Allowance for Doubtful Accounts		5,000
		To record the recovery of an account previously written off.		
	3/24/90	Cash	5,000	
		Accounts receivable		5,000
		To record cash collection from a customer.		
	12/31/90	Bad Debt Expense	82,000	
		Allowance for Doubtful Accounts		82,000
		To record bad debt expense.		
(5)	8/8/91	Allowance for Doubtful Accounts	75,000	
		Accounts Receivable		75,000
		To write off an account deemed uncollectible.		
(6)	12/2/91	Allowance for Doubtful Accounts	5,000	
		Accounts Receivable		5,000
		To write off an account deemed uncollectible.		
	12/31/91	Bad Debt Expense	82,560	
		Allowance for Doubtful Accounts		82,560
		To record bad debt expense.		
(7)	9/19/92	Allowance for Doubtful Accounts	90,000	
		Accounts Receivable		90,000
		To write off an account deemed uncollectible.		
	12/31/92	Bad Debt Expense	79,200	
		Allowance for Doubtful Accounts		79,200
		To record bad debt expense.		

1/28/88 Allowance balance	$ 0
1988 Recoveries	0
1988 Write–offs	(10,000)
1988 Bad debt expense	80,000

12/31/88 Allowance balance	$70,000
1989 Recoveries	0
1989 Write–offs	(75,000)
1989 Bad debt expense	78,000

12/31/89 Allowance balance	$73,000
1990 Recoveries	5,000
Write–offs	(0)
1990 bad debt expense	82,000

12/31/90 Allowance balance	$160,000
1991 Recoveries	0
1991 Write–offs	(80,000)
1991 bad debt expense	82,560
12/31/91 Allowance balance	$162,560
1992 Recoveries	0
1992 Write–offs	(90,000)
1992 Bad debt expense	79,200
12/31/92 Allowance balance	$151,760

c.

	1988	1989	1990	1991	1992
Direct write–off method					
Bad debt expense	$ 10,000	$ 75,000	$ (5,000)	$ 80,000	$ 90,000
Accounts receivable value	950,000	900,000	1,200,000	1,175,000	1,095,000
Allowance method					
Bad debt expense	80,000	78,000	82,000	82,560	79,200
Accounts receivable value*	880,000	827,000	1,040,000	1,012,440	943,240

* Under the allowance method, the net value of Accounts Receivable equals the balance in Accounts Receivable less the balance in Allowance for Doubtful Accounts.

	Direct Write–off	Allowance
Total bad debt expense	$250,000	$401,760

The allowance method provides a measure of net income consistent with both the revenue recognition and the matching principles. Over the five–year period, Grace Linen Service wrote off a total of $212,000 in Accounts Receivable from sales made in prior years. Under the direct method, the $212,000 did not reduce revenue in the year of the sale. Hence, net income in each individual year was misstated. Under the allowance method, bad debt expense is computed based upon the year's sales. Consequently, the allowance method, while an estimate, provides better matching of expenses with the associated revenues.

P7–9

			Debit	Credit
a. (1)	1/4	Short–Term Note Receivable	525,000	
		Sales		525,000
		To record sale in exchange for a note.		
(2)	2/15	Account Receivable	665,000	
		Sales		665,000
		To record sales on account.		
(3)	3/5	Cash	235,000	
		Accounts Receivable		235,000
		To record cash collection from a customer.		
(4)	3/29	Allowance for Doubtful Accounts	98,000	
		Accounts Receivable		98,000
		To write off an account deemed uncollectible.		

No.	Date	Account	Debit	Credit
(5)	4/15	Accounts Receivable	500,000	
		Sales		500,000
		To record sales on account.		
(6)	4/23	Cash	485,000	
		Cash Discount	15,000	
		Accounts Receivable		500,000
		To record cash collection from a customer.		
(7)	5/30	Accounts Receivable	15,000	
		Allowance for Doubtful Accounts		15,000
		To record recovery of an account previously written off.		
		Cash	15,000	
		Accounts Receivable		15,000
		To record cash collection from a customer.		
(8)	6/4	Cash	542,500	
		Short–Term Notes Receivable		525,000
		Interest Revenue		17,500
		To record collection of principal and interest on an outstanding note receivable.		

* $17,500 = $525,000 x 8% x 5/12

No.	Date	Account	Debit	Credit
(9)	6/27	Accounts Receivable	750,000	
		Sales		750,000
		To record sales on account.		
(10)	7/1	Cash	788,000	
		Cash Discount	12,000[a]	
		Accounts Receivable		800,000[b]
		To record collection on an open account.		

[a] Step 1: Cash collected on 6/27 sale = 788,000 – $400,000
= $388,000

Step 2: Compute gross amount of 6/27 sale collected.

Cash collected = gross amount of sale – (gross amount of sale x discount)

$388,000 = gross amount – (gross Amount x 3%)

$388,000 = 97% x gross amount

gross amount = $400,000

Step 3: Compute cash discount:

Cash discount = gross amount x discount percentage

= $400,000 x 3%

= $12,000

[b] $800,000 = $400,000 from 2/15 sale + $400,000 gross amount of sale from 6/27 sale (see preceding computations).

(11) 8/31	Allowance for Doubtful Accounts	146,000	
	Accounts Receivable		146,000
	To write off accounts deemed uncollectible.		
(12) 9/18	Cash	200,000	
	Accounts Receivable		200,000
	To record cash collection from customer.		
(13) 10/30	Accounts Receivable	200,000	
	Sales		200,000
	To record sales on account.		
(14) 11/12	Accounts Receivable	28,000 *	
	Allowance for Doubtful Accounts		28,000
	To record the recovery of an account previously written off.		

* $28,000 = $43,000 (initial balance written off) – $15,000 (amount previously collected).

	Cash	20,000	
	Accounts Receivable		20,000
	To record cash collection from customer.		
(15) 12/20	Accounts Receivable	150,000	
	Sales		150,000
	To record sales on account.		

b.

Bad Debt Expense	67,950 *	
Allowance for Doubtful Accounts		67,950
To record bad debt expense.		

* $67,950 = Total credit sales x 3%
= ($665,000 + $500,000 + $750,000 + $200,000 + $150,000) x 3%.

c. Ending Allowance balance = Beginning Allowance balance + Bad debt expense + Recoveries – Write–offs
= $500,000 + $67,950 + 43,000 – $244,000
= $366,950

Ending Accounts Receivable balance = Beginning Accts Rec balance + Credit sales + Recoveries – Cash collections – Write–offs
= $3,750,000 + $2,265,000 + $43,000 – $1,770,000 – $244,000
= $4,044,000

P7–10

a.

(1) 1/29	Notes Receivable	45,000	
	Sales		45,000
	To record sale in exchange for a note.		

		Date	Account	Debit	Credit
	(2)	3/1	Notes Receivable	10,000	
			Cash		10,000
			To record a loan to an employee.		
	(3)	4/29	Cash	46,125	
			Notes Receivable		45,000
			Interest Revenue		1,125 *
			To record cash collection on a note.		

* $1,125 = $45,000 x 10% x 3/12.

		Date	Account	Debit	Credit
	(4)	5/31	Notes Receivable	15,000	
			Accounts Receivable		15,000
			To record conversion of account receivable to a note.		
	(5)	7/14	Cash	5,000	
			Notes Receivable	20,000	
			Sales		25,000
			To record a sale.		
	(6)	10/31	Cash	15,562.50	
			Notes Receivable		15,000.00
			Interest Revenue		562.50 *
			To record cash collection on a note.		

* $562.50 = $15,000 x 9% x 5/12.

		Date	Account	Debit	Credit
	(7)	12/1	Notes Receivable	30,000	
			Sales		30,000
			To record sale in exchange for a note.		
	(8)	12/31	Cash	11,000	
			Notes Receivable		10,000
			Interest Revenue		1,000 *
			To record cash collection on employee loan.		

* $21,000 = $10,000 x 12% x 10/12.

		Date	Account	Debit	Credit
		12/31	Adjusting Entry		
			Interest Receivable	1,300 *	
			Interest Revenue		1,300
			To accrued interest earned, but not yet received.		

* $1,300 = ($20,000 on 7/14 note x 12% x 5.5/12) + ($30,000 on 12/1 note x 8% x 1/12).

		Date	Account	Debit	Credit
b.	(1)	1/29	Notes Receivable	46,125	
			Sales		45,000
			Discount on Notes Receivable		1,125
			To record sale in exchange for a note.		
	(2)	3/1	Notes Receivable	11,000	
			Cash		10,000
			Discount on Notes Receivable		1,000
			To record loan to an employee.		

			Debit	Credit
(3)	4/29	Cash	46,125	
		Discount on Notes Receivable	1,125	
		Notes Receivable		46,125
		Interest Revenue		1,125
		To record cash collection on a note.		
(4)	5/31	Notes Receivable	15,562.50	
		Accounts Receivable		15,000.00
		Discount on Notes Receivable		562.50
		To record conversion of account receivable to a note.		
(5)	7/14	Cash	5,000	
		Notes Receivable	21,200	
		Sales		25,000
		Discount on Notes Receivable		1,200 *
		To record sale.		

* $1,200 = $20,000 x 12 % x 6/12.

			Debit	Credit
(6)	10/31	Cash	15,562.50	
		Discount on Notes Receivable	562.50	
		Notes Receivable		15,562.50
		Interest Revenue		562.50
		To record cash collection on a note.		
(7)	12/1	Notes Receivable	30,300	
		Sales		30,000
		Discount on Notes Receivable		300 *
		To record sale in exchange for a note.		

* $300 = $30,000 x 8% x 45/360.

			Debit	Credit
(8)	12/31	Cash	11,000	
		Discount on Notes Receivable	1,000	
		Notes Receivable		11,000
		Interest Revenue		1,000
		To record cash collection on a note.		
	12/31	Adjusting Entry		
		Discount on Notes Receivable	1,300	
		Interest Revenue		1,300
		To record interest revenue.		

* $1,300 = ($20,000 on 7/14 note x 12% x 5.5/12) + ($30,000 on 12/1 note x 8% x 1/12).

P7–11

Account Age	Balance	Noncollection Probability	Uncollectible Amount
Current	$3,050,000	1%	$230,500
1–30 days	1,500,000	3%	45,000
31–100 days	650,000	10%	65,000
101–200 days	250,000	15%	37,500
> 200 days	100,000	45%	45,000
Total			$223,000

a.	Bad Debt Expense	23,000 *	
	Allowance for Doubtful Accounts		23,000
	To record bad debt expense.		

* $23,000 = $223,000 – $200,000

b.	Bad Debt Expense	173,000 *	
	Allowance for Doubtful Accounts		173,000
	To record bad debt expense.		

* $173,000 = $223,000 – $200,000 beginning balance – $300,000 of recoveries + $450,000 of write–offs

P7–12

a.	Bad Debt Expense	515,000 *	
	Allowance for Doubtful Accounts		515,000
	To record bad debt expense.		

* $515,000 = $12,875,000 x 4%

b.

Account Age	Balance	Noncollection Probability	Uncollectible Amount
Current	$3,870,000	1.25%	$ 48,375
1–30 days	2,578,000	2.75%	70,895
31–90 days	1,364,000	8.50%	115,940
91–150 days	743,000	14.00%	104,020
> 150 days	549,000	50.00%	274,500
Total			$613,730

Bad Debt Expense	749.730 *	
Allowance for Doubtful Accounts		749,730
To record bad debt expense.		

* $749,730 = $613,730 – $514,000 beginning balance in the Allowance account + $650,000 of accounts written off

Account Age	Balance	Noncollection Probability	Uncollectible Amount
Current	$3,870,000	2.25%	$ 87,075
1–30 days	2,578,000	3.75%	96,675
31–90 days	1,364,000	9.50%	129,580
91–150 days	743,000	15.00%	111,450
> 150 days	549,000	51.00%	279,990
Total			$704,770

Bad Debt Expense	840,770 *	
Allowance for Doubtful Accounts		840,770
To record bad debt expense.		

* $840,770 = $704,770 – $514,000 beginning balance in the Allowance account + $650,000 of accounts written off

d. Companies that use the percent–of–sales method to estimate bad debts should consider periodically using the aging method to examine the accuracy of the estimates for several reasons. First, the aging method identifies slow–moving accounts that may require additional collection efforts. Further, the dollar amount of any particular aging classification indicates the maximum amount that the company should expend in trying to collect the accounts. Second, an aging can help a company define its credit policies. For example, if an aging identifies a particular customer as a consistently slow payer, the company may decide to no longer extend credit to this customer. If an aging indicates a large percentage of old accounts, this information could be used to decide whether to offer cash discounts and the terms of such discounts. Finally, an aging can indicate the accuracy of the percent–of–sales method. A detailed analysis of Accounts Receivable will usually provide a more accurate estimate for the required balance in Allowance for Doubtful Accounts than the percent–of–sales method. The estimated Allowance balance using the aging method can be compared to the balance obtained using the percent–of–sales method. Significant differences would indicate a need to revise the percent of sales considered uncollectible.

e. As a general rule, a company would not want to expend more resources in collecting accounts than it expects to collect. By performing an aging of accounts receivable, a company estimates the total amount, by age classification, expected to be uncollectible. These estimated uncollectible amounts represent the maximum amount a company would want to spend for collecting old accounts. For example, using the aging from Part (b), Bremen Brewery would want to spend no more than the following (by age classification)

Age Classification	Maximum Collection Costs
Current	$ 48,375
1–30 Days Past Due	70,895
31–90 Days Past Due	115,940
91–150 Days Past Due	104,020
>150 Days Past Due	274,500

In some cases, a company may ignore this information in deciding how much to expend for collection purposes and spend more to collect old accounts. In these cases the justification for the "excess" expenditures is to send a signal to all customers that late payments or nonpayment of accounts will not be tolerated. By sending this signal, the company hopes to increase its future receivables turnover and to decrease its future bad debt write–offs.

P7–13

a. Bad Debt Expense 15,000 *
   Allowance for Doubtful Accounts 15,000
  To record bad debt expense.

* $15,000 = (Total credit sales of $11,940,000 x 2%) – (Total credit sales for Jan. through Nov. of $11,190,000 x 2%)

OR

$15,000 = December credit sales of $750,000 x 2%

b. Ending Allowance balance = Beginning Allowance balance + Annual bad debt expense + Recoveries – Write–offs
= $70,000 + ($11,940,000 x 2%) + $0 – $239,000
= $69,800

c. Ending accounts receivable balance = Beginning accounts receivable balance + Credit sales + Recoveries – Cash collections –Write–offs
$3,250,000 (from the aging) = Beginning Accts Rec balance + $11,940,000 +$0 – $12,126,000 – $239,000
Beginning accts receivable balance = $$3,675,000

d.

Account Age	Balance	Noncollection Probability	Uncollectible Amount
Current	$ 700,000	2.0%	$ 14,000
1–30 days	1,200,000	5.5%	66,000
31–75 days	550,000	10.0%	55,000
> 75 days	800,000	25.0%	200,000
Total			$335,000

Bad Debt Expense 280,200 *
   Allowance for Doubtful Accounts 280,200
  To record bad debt expense.

* $280,200 = $335,000 – $70,000 beginning balance in the allowance account – $223,800 of monthly adjusting entries for bad debt expense + $239,000 of accounts written off.

e. Some companies use the percent–of–sales method to estimate bad debts but also periodically use the aging method. Companies would use the two methods for several reasons. The percent–of–sales method is very easy and comparatively inexpensive to use. Further, the percent–of–sales method emphasizes revenues and expenses, since estimated bad debts are a function of revenues. For these reasons a company is more apt to use the percent–of–sales method than the aging method.

Additionally, the aging method can be very costly and time–consuming. For all but the smallest companies, preparing an aging of Accounts Receivable requires a computerized accounting system. However, in return for this increased cost and time, the aging method provides several types of useful information. First, the aging method identifies slow–moving accounts, which may require additional collection efforts. Further, the dollar amount of any particular aging classification indicates the maximum amount that the company should expend in trying to collect the accounts. A company would generally not want to spend more to collect an account than it expects to ultimately collect.

Second, an aging can help a company define its credit policies. For example, if an aging identifies a particular customer as a consistently slow payer, the company may decide to no longer extend credit to this customer. If an aging indicates a large percentage of old accounts, this information could be used to decide whether to offer cash discounts and the terms of such discounts.

Finally, an aging can indicate the accuracy of the percent–of–sales method. A detailed analysis of Accounts Receivable will usually provide an accurate estimate for the required balance in Allowance for Doubtful Accounts. This estimated balance can be compared to the balance obtained using the percent–of–sales method. Significant differences would indicate a need to revise the percent of sales considered uncollectible. To obtain this information, companies will periodically prepare an aging of Accounts Receivable.

C7–1

a. Each participating company must have prepared an aging schedule. An aging schedule categorizes individual accounts in terms of the length of time each has been outstanding (e.g., 30–60 days; 61–90 days; etc.).

b.

Age	%Amt.	$Amount	%Uncollectible	$Uncollectible
Current	78.5%	$51,444,190	1%	$ 514,442
30-60	16.5%	10813,110	4%	432,524
60+	%%	3,276,700	20%	655,340
		$65,534,000		$1,602,306

The bad debt estimate is $1,602,306

c.

Balance, allowance for doubtful accounts (Dr.)	$ 840,000
Desired balance	1,602,306
	$2,442,306

Journal entry

Bad Debt Expense	2,442,306	
Allowance for Doubtful Accounts		2,442,306
To record estimated bad debts.		

C7–2

a. Sales volume may increase if buyers are enticed with the 2% discount for immediate cash payment. Only those buyers who have cash could take advantage of the discount terms. The benefit of greater unit sales is traded off against a lower profit margin per unit. If the discount rate were too high, some profit margin might be eroded. The marginal cost to the retailer of offering the discount would be greater than the benefit of receiving the cash sooner.

b. If paid in 10 days: $500 – (2% x $500) = $490
If paid in 20 days, payment would be $500. The rate of interest would be (10/500) x (365/10) = 73%.
If paid in 30 days, payment would also be $500. The interest rate would be (10/500) x (365/20) = 36.5%.

C7–3

a. Uncollectible percentage = Bad debt expense ÷ Credit sales

1985: $224 ÷ ($24,274 x 62%) = 1.49%
1986: $350 ÷ ($24,811 x 61%) = 2.31%
1987: $291 ÷ ($25,875 x 59%) = 1.91%

b.

	1985	1986	1987
Beg. Bal. (Cr.)	$200	$238	$345
Bad Debt Expense	224	350	291
Write-offs	186	243	256
Ending Bal. (Cr.)	$238	$345	$380

Journal Entries

	1985		1986		1987	
Bad Debt Expense	224		350		291	
Allowance for Doubtful Accts.		224		350		291
To record bad debt expense.						
Allowance for Doubtful Accounts	186		243		256	
Accts. Rec.		186		243		256
To write off A/R.						

Estimates have been consistently over their experience because the amount of provision for bad debts (i.e., bad debt expense) exceeds the actual write-off. Sears' auditors might not encourage them to lower their estimate because it is conservative. However, accuracy in estimating the provision is important and desirable.

C7–4

a.

Reserve for Loan Losses	222,000,000	
Loan Loss Expense		222,000,000
To reduce previously recorded loan loss.		

This practice is highly unusual because recovering loan loss expenses already recognized is rare. It would normally only happen if a company dramatically improved its collection efforts.

b. Subsidy payments from the U.S. government to farmers would have reduced the likelihood of Farm Credit's loans being uncollectible. Accordingly, they could argue that they had previously recognized too much loan loss expense, because they will now realize more of their loans than they previously anticipated.

c. Price Waterhouse may have felt that even though the subsidy payment had been promised, it may not be received.

C7–5

a. When a debt is "called," it is immediately due and must be paid. First Republic was experiencing decreased collections and therefore may not have the cash available to repay a called loan.

b. Loan write-offs could decrease the amount of current and noncurrent assets, which could decrease certain ratios including, for example, the current ratio. If such ratios fall below the amounts specified in a debt covenant, the debt could be called.

c. If it appears likely the loan will be called and the bank does not have funds to repay it, the auditors may qualify their opinion on the basis that the entitv will not be able to continue as a going concern.

CHAPTER 8 Merchandise Inventory

E8–1

	Date	Account	Debit	Credit
a.	10/10	Inventory	35,000	
		Accounts Payable		35,000
		To record inventory purchase on account.		
	10/11	Inventory	20,000	
		Accounts Payable		20,000
		To record inventory purchase on account.		
	10/20	Accounts Payable	35,000	
		Cash		33,950*
		Purchase Discount		1,050
		To record payment to supplier.		

* $33,950 = $35,000 – ($35,000 x 3% discount)

	Date	Account	Debit	Credit
	10/30	Accounts Payable	20,000	
		Cash		20,000
		To record payment to supplier.		
b.	10/10	Inventory	33,950*	
		Accounts Payable		33,950
		To record inventory purchase on account.		

* $33,950 = $35,000 – ($35,000 x 3% discount)

	Date	Account	Debit	Credit
	10/11	Inventory	19,400*	
		Accounts Payable		19,400
		To record inventory purchase on account.		

* $19,400 = $20,000 – ($20,000 x 3% discount)

	Date	Account	Debit	Credit
	10/20	Accounts Payable	33,950	
		Cash		33,950
		To record payment to supplier.		
	10/30	Accounts Payable	19,400	
		Purchase Discount Lost	600	
		Cash		20,000
		To record payment to supplier.		

E8–2

	Date	Account	Debit	Credit
a.	3/3	Inventory	196,000*	
		Accounts Payable		196,000
		To record inventory purchase on account.		

* $196,000 = $200,000 – ($200,000 x 2% discount)

3/10	Inventory	176,400*	
	Accounts Payable		176,400
	To record inventory purchase on account.		

* $176,400 = $1800,000 – ($180,000 x 2% discount)

3/20	Accounts Payable	176,400	
	Cash		176,400
	To record payment to supplier.		
3/31	Adjusting Entry		
	Purchase Discount Lost	4,000	
	Accounts Payable		4,000
	To record expiration of purchase discount period.		
4/25	Accounts Payable	200,000	
	Cash		200,000
	To record payment to supplier.		
b. 3/3	Inventory	200,000	
	Accounts Payable		200,000
	To record inventory purchase on account.		
3/10	Inventory	180,000	
	Accounts Payable		180,000
	To record inventory purchase on account.		
3/20	Accounts Payable	180,000	
	Cash		176,400
	Purchase Discount		3,600
	To record payment to supplier.		
3/31	Adjusting Entry: No adjusting journal entry is necessary.		
4/25	Accounts Payable	200,000	
	Cash		200,000
	To record payment to supplier.		

E8–3

a. **12/31/90**

Purchase discounts

Cost of goods available = Beginning inventory + Purchases – Purchase discounts
$135,000 = $100,000 + $50,000 – Purchase discounts
Purchase discounts = $15,000

Ending inventory

Cost of goods sold = Cost of goods available – Ending inventory
$10,000 = $135,000 – Ending inventory
Ending inventory = $125,000

12/31/91

Cost of goods available for sale

Cost of goods available	=	Beginning inventory + Purchases – Purchase discounts
	=	\$125,000 + \$60,000 – \$5,000
	=	\$180,000

OR

Cost of goods sold	=	Cost of goods available – Ending inventory
\$45,000	=	Cost of goods available for sale – \$135,000
Cost of goods available	=	\$180,000

12/31/92

Beginning inventory

1992 Beginning inventory	=	1991 Ending inventory
	=	\$135,000

Purchase discounts

Cost of goods available	=	Beginning inventory + Purchases – Purchase discounts
\$190,000	=	\$135,000 + \$75,000 – Purchase discounts
Purchase discounts	=	\$20,000

Ending inventory

Cost of goods sold	=	Cost of goods available – Ending inventory
\$80,000	=	\$190,000 – Ending inventory
Ending inventory	=	\$110,000

OR

1992 Ending inventory	=	1993 Beginning inventory
	=	\$110,000

12/31/93

Purchases

Cost of goods available	=	Beginning inventory + Purchases – Purchase discounts
\$155,0000	=	\$110,000 + Purchases – \$10,000
Purchases	=	\$55,000

Cost of goods sold

Cost of goods sold	=	Cost of goods available – Ending inventory
	=	\$155,000 – \$75,000
	=	\$80,000

	Closing Entry 12/31/90		**Closing Entry 12/31/91**	
Inventory (ending)	125,000		135,000	
Cost of Goods Sold	10,000		45,000	
Purchase Discounts	15,000		5,000	
Purchases		50,000		60,000
Inventory (beginning)		100,000		125,000
To record COGS and ending inventory.				

	Closing Entry 12/31/92		Closing Entry 12/31/93	
Inventory (ending)	110,000		75,000	
Cost of Goods Sold	80,000		80,000	
Purchase Discounts	20,000		10,000	
Purchases		75,000		55,000
Inventory (beginning)		135,000		110,000
To record COGS and ending inventory.				

E8–4

a Error in ending inventory = Error in beginning inventory + Error in purchases – Error in COGS

–$10,000 = $0 + $0 – Error in COGS
Error in COGS = $10,000

Ending inventory is understated by $10,000 as of December 31, 1989, while COGS is overstated by $10,000 for the year ended December 31, 1989.

b. Error in ending inventory = Error in beginning inventory + Error in purchases – Error in COGS

$5,000 = –$10,000 + $0 – Error in COGS
Error in COGS = –$15,000

Ending inventory is overstated by $5,000 as of December 31, 1990, while COGS is understated by $15,000 for the year ended December 31, 1990.

	1989	1990	Total
c. Error in COGS	$10,000	–$15,000	$5,000

The $10,000 overstatement of ending inventory in 1989 reverses itself during 1990. Consequently, for the two-year period, only the $5,000 overstatement of inventory on December 31, 1990 affects COGS. By the end of 1991, this $5,000 error will also have reversed itself.

E8–5

a. (1) The goods were shipped F.O.B. shipping point, so legal title passes to the buyer on the shipping date of December 30, 1990. Since Austin is the buyer, Austin has legal title to the inventory as of December 31, 1990.

(2) The goods were shipped F.O.B. destination, so legal title passes to the buyer on January 2, 1991. Since Austin is the seller, not the buyer, Austin still has legal title to the inventory as of December 31, 1990.

(3) The goods were shipped F.O.B. shipping point, so legal title passes to the buyer on December 31, 1990. Since Austin is the seller, not the buyer, Austin does not have legal title to the inventory as of December 31, 1990.

(4) The goods were shipped F.O.B. destination, so legal title passes to the buyer on January 3, 1991. Since Austin is the buyer, Austin does not have legal title to the inventory as of December 31, 1990.

(5) The goods were shipped F.O.B. destination, so legal title passes to the buyer on December 31, 1990. Since Austin is the buyer, Austin has legal title to the inventory as of December 31, 1990.

b. (1) Inventory would not have been on hand.
(2) Inventory would not have been on hand.
(3) Inventory would not have been on hand.
(4) Inventory would not have been on hand.
(5) Inventory would have been on hand.

c. (1) Increase inventory by $50,000.
(2) Increase inventory by $25,000.
(3) No adjustment to inventory is necessary.
(4) No adjustment to inventory is necessary.
(5) No adjustment to inventory is necessary.

E8–6

a.

Ending inventory	=	Beginning inventory + Net purchases – Cost of goods sold
$50,000	=	$32,000 + ($84,000 + $3,500) – COGS
COGS	=	$69,500

Inventory (ending)	50,000	
Cost of Goods Sold	69,500	
Purchases		84,000
Transportation–In		3,500
Inventory (beginning)		32,000
To record COGS and ending inventory.		

b.

Ending inventory	=	Beginning inventory + Net purchases – Cost of goods sold
$52,000	=	$32,000 + ($84,000 + $3,500) – COGS
COGS	=	$67,500

Under the perpetual method, COGS is recorded for every sale. Therefore, at the end of the year no adjusting entry is necessary to record COGS. But since ending inventory per the books does not equal ending inventory per the physical count, the following adjusting entry is necessary at the end of the year.

Inventory Shrinkage	2,000	
Inventory		2,000
To record inventory shrinkage.		

c. Under the perpetual method, the inventory account is decreased, and the COGS account is increased for every sale. Consequently, the balance in COGS represents the sum of the cost of inventory for all sales. No other items are recorded in the COGS account, thus any discrepancy between the balance in the Inventory account and ending inventory per a physical count indicates inventory shrinkage. The access to this information is an advantage of the perpetual method.

Under the periodic method, COGS is not computed until the end of the accounting period. Further, COGS is computed as the difference between cost of goods available for sale and ending inventory per a physical count. So COGS is a "plug" amount and is not based upon actual sales transactions. Consequently, under the periodic method, COGS will include any inventory shortages.

E8–7

a. If Marian wants to maximize profits and ending inventory, she should give the customer the lowest-priced coat (i.e., Coat 4). If she gives the customer Coat 4, Marian would report the following gross profit and ending inventory.

Gross profit		Ending inventory	
Revenues	$10,000	Coat 1	$ 7,200
COGS of Coat 4	7,000	Coat 2	7,600
Gross profit	$ 3,000	Coat 3	8,000
		Total	$22,800

Marian may have several reasons to maximize profits and ending inventory. If Marian's Furs has borrowed money and entered into debt covenants, the debt covenants may contain clauses stipulating a certain current ratio, debt/equity ratio, and so forth. By maximizing profits and inventory, Marian can also minimize the probability that she will violate one of these ratios, thereby decreasing the chance that she will violate her debt covenants. Further, if Marian has a bonus linked to accounting earnings, she could maximize her bonus by maximizing profits.

b. If Marian wants to minimize profits and ending inventory, she should give the customer the highest-priced coat (i.e., Coat 3). If she gives the customer Coat 3, Marian would report the following gross profit and ending inventory.

Gross profit		Ending inventory	
Revenues	$10,000	Coat 1	$ 7,200
COGS of Coat 3	8,000	Coat 2	7,600
Gross profit	$ 2,000	Coat 3	7,000
		Total	$21,800

The most likely reason Marian would want to minimize profits and ending inventory is to minimize taxes. Minimizing profits would minimize current tax payments, thereby minimizing the present value of future tax payments. Further, some states charge taxes on a company's assets, thereby providing an incentive to minimize assets.

E8–8

Units available for sale = Units in beginning inventory + Units purchased
= 12 + (8 + 25 + 10 + 20 + 30)
= 105 Units

Cost of goods available for sale = Cost of beginning inventory + Cost of goods purchased
= (12 x $5.50) + [(8 x $5.75) + (25 x $5.80) + (10 x $6.00)
+ (20 x $6.05) + (30 x $6.20)
= $624.00

a. **LIFO cost flow assumption**

Cost of goods sold

Sale 1	(8 x $5.75) + (7 x $5.50)	=	$ 84.50
Sale 2	(10 x $6.00) + (13 x $5.80)	=	135.40
Sale 3	(20 x $6.05) + (6 x $5.80)	=	155.80
Sale 4	(6 x $5.80) + (4 x $5.50)	=	56.80
Total cost of goods sold			$432.50

Shortage expense = [(105 units available to sell – 74 units sold) – 28 units on hand] x $6.20
= $18.60

Ending inventory = Cost of goods available for sale – Cost of goods sold – Shortage expense
= $624.00 – $432.50 – $18.60
= $172.90

b. **FIFO cost flow assumption**

Cost of goods sold

Sale 1	(12 x $5.50) + (3 x $5.75)	=	$ 83.25
Sale 2	(5 x $5.75) + (18 x $5.80)	=	133.15
Sale 3	(7 x $5.80) + (10 x $6.00) + (9 x $6.05)	=	155.05
Sale 4	(10 x $6.05)	=	60.50
Total cost of goods sold			$431.95

Shortage expense = (1 x $6.05) + (2 x $6.20)
= $18.45

Ending Inventory = $624.00 – $431.95 – $18.45
= $173.60

c. **Averaging cost flow assumption:**

	Transaction			Balance		
Date	**Units**	**Unit Cost**	**Total Cost**	**Total Cost**	**Total Units**	**Unit Cost**
Beg Inv				$ 66.00	12	$ 5.50
1/2	8	$ 5.75	$ 46.00	112.00	20	5.60
3/10	(15)	5.60	(84.00)	28.00	5	5.60
5/30	25	5.80	145.00	173.00	30	5.767
8/14	10	6.00	60.00	233.00	40	5.825
10/29	(23)	5.825	(133.98)	99.02	17	5.825
11/18	20	6.05	121.00	220.02	37	5.9465
12/8	(26)	5.9465	(154.61)	65.41	11	5.9465
12/11	(10)	5.9465	(59.47)	5.94	1	5.94
12/27	30	6.20	186	191.94	31	6.19
Shrinkage	(3)	6.19	18.57	173.37	28	6.19

Cost of goods sold = $ 84.00 + $133.98 + $154.61 + $59.47
= $432.06

Shrinkage expense = 3 units x $6.19 = $18.57

Ending inventory = $173.37

E8–9

a. **1. FIFO cost flow assumption**

Cost of goods sold = (75 units x $450) + (60 units x $500) + (15 units x $600)
= $33,750 + $30,000 + $9,000
= $72,750

Gross profit = Sales – Cost of goods sold
= (150 units x $1,000) – $72,750
= $77,250

Ending inventory = (50 units x $600)
= $30,000

2. Averaging cost flow assumption:

Cost per unit = [(75 units x $450) + (60 units x $500) + (65 units x $600)]
÷ (75 units + 60 units + 65 units)
= $513.75 per unit

Cost of goods sold = (150 units x $513.75)
= $77,062.50

Gross profit = Sales – Cost of goods sold
= (150 units x $1,000) – $77,062.50
= $72,937.50

Ending inventory = 50 units x $513.75
= $25,687.50

3. LIFO cost flow assumption

Cost of goods sold = (65 units x $600) + (60 units x 500) + (25 units x $450)
= $39,000 + $30,000 + $11,250
= $80,250

Gross profit = Sales – Cost of goods sold
= (150 units x $1,000) – $80,250
= $69,750

Ending inventory = (50 units x $450)
= $22,500

b. If the monitors are identical, customers would be indifferent between any two monitors. Hence, Vinnie could simply give a customer the monitor that allows him to either maximize or minimize cost of goods sold, thereby maximizing or minimizing gross profit.

If Vinnie wants to maximize net income, he would give the customers the lowest-priced monitors first, followed by the second lowest-priced monitors, and so forth. Since the cost of the monitors is increasing, this strategy is identical to the FIFO cost flow assumption. Therefore, the highest gross profit Vinnie could report is $77,250 (from Part [a]). Vinnie may want to maximize net income for several reasons. First, if Vinnie receives any incentive compensation, such as a bonus, that is tied to net income, then he can maximize his compensation by maximizing net income. Second, if Vinnie has any existing debt covenants, they may specify a maximum debt/equity ratio. By increasing net income, Vinnie would increase equity, thereby decreasing his debt/equity ratio. In this manner, Vinnie decreases the probability that he will violate the debt covenant. Finally, if Vinnie is in the process of trying to obtain debt, potential creditors may use net income as a factor in determining whether or not to loan money to Vinnie or what interest rate to charge.

If Vinnie wants to minimize net income, he would give the customers the highest-priced monitors first, followed by the second highest-priced monitors, and so forth. Since the cost of the monitors is increasing, this strategy is identical to the LIFO cost flow assumption. Therefore, the lowest gross profit Vinnie could report is $69,750 (from Part [a]). The most likely reason Vinnie would want to minimize net income is for tax purposes. If he uses the same set of books for tax and financial reporting purposes, then by minimizing book income, Vinnie minimizes taxable income. Minimizing taxable income, in turn, minimizes the present value of future cash outflows for taxes.

E8–10

a. **(1) LIFO cost flow assumption**

Year	Calculation	Amount
1986	6,000 units x $10	$ 60,000
1987	(12,000 units x $15) + (3,000 units x $10)	210,000
1988	3,000 units x $16	48,000
1989	9,000 units x $20	180,000
1990	(2,000 units x $22) + (1,000 units x $20) + (2,000 units x $16) + (1,000 units x $10)	106,000
Total		$604,000

(2) FIFO cost flow assumption

Year	Calculation	Amount
1986:	6,000 units x $10	$ 60,000
1987	(4,000 units x $10) + (11,000 units x $15)	205,000
1988	(1,000 units x $15) + (2,000 units x $16)	47,000
1989	(3,000 units x $16) + (6,000 units x $20)	168,000
1990	(4,000 units x $20) + (2,000 units x $22)	124,000
Total		$604,000

(3) Averaging cost flow assumption

Year	Calculation			Amount
1986	Cost per unit	=	$100,000 ÷ 10,000 units = $10 per unit	
	COGS	=	6,000 units x $10	$ 60,000
1987	Cost per unit	=	[(4,000 x $10) =(12,000 x $15)] ÷ 16,000 units	
		=	$13.75 per unit	
	COGS	=	15,000 units x $13.75	206,250
1988	Cost per unit	=	[(1,000 x $13.75) + (5,000 x $16)] ÷ 6,000 units	
		=	$15.625 per unit	
	COGS	=	3,000 units x $15.625	46,875
1989	Cost per unit	=	[(3,000 x $15.625) + (10,000 x $20)] ÷ 13,000 units	
		=	$18.99.04 per unit	
	COGS	=	9,000 units x $18.99.04	170,914
1990	Cost per unit	=	[(4,000 x $18.9904) + (2,000 x $22)] ÷ 6,000 units	
		=	19.9936 per unit	
	COGS	=	6,000 units x $19.9936	119,961
Total				$604,000

b. Over the life of a company, Cost of Goods Sold would be the same regardless of the cost flow assumption employed. Over the life of a business, all the units of inventory will be sold. Consequently, all costs associated with inventory will be expensed. The choice of a cost flow assumption only affects the allocation of inventory costs to particular accounting periods, but does not affect total inventory costs.

c. Assume that accounting earnings equals tax earnings. Over the life of a business, a company's total earnings is the same regardless of the cost flow assumption employed. Therefore, a company's total tax liability over the company's life is the same, regardless of the cost flow assumption employed. The choice of a cost flow assumption does, however, affect the allocation of inventory costs to particular years. These different cost allocations give rise to different earnings in particular years. The different earnings amounts under different cost flow assumptions then give rise to different tax liabilities (i.e., cash outflows) in particular years. Due to the time value of money, the timing of cash flows affects the present value of the total tax payments.

In times of inflation, the LIFO cost flow assumption gives rise to lower earnings in the early years of a company's life, while the FIFO cost flow assumption gives rise to lower earnings in the later years of a company's life. Consequently, LIFO results in lower tax payments in a company's early years and FIFO results in higher tax payments in a company's early years. The timing of the tax payments means that the present value of tax payments under LIFO is less than the present value of tax payments under FIFO. In times of deflation, the opposite situation arises. The present value of tax payments under FIFO is less than the present value of tax payments under LIFO.

E8–11

a. **Perpetual/FIFO**

Date	Cost of Inventory Purchased	Cost of Inventory Sold	Inventory Balance
Beg Inv	15,000 x $ 5		$ 75,000
2/15	10,000 x $10		175,000
3/15		15,000 x $ 5	100,000
4/25	15,000 x $15		325,000
5/10		10,000 x $10	225,000
9/18	10,000 x $20		425,000
10/9		(15,000 x $15) + (10,000 x $20)	0
11/1	30,000 x $25		750,000
2/2		25,000 x $25	125,000
12/7	15,000 x $30		575,000

COGS = $1,225,000
Ending inventory = $ 575,000

b. **Periodic/FIFO**

Units available = Units in beginning inventory + units purchased
= 15,000 + 80,000
= 95,000 units

Units sold = 75,000

Units in ending inventory = Units available – Units sold
= 95,000 – 75,000
= 20,000 units

Cost of goods available = Cost of goods in beginning inventory + Cost of goods purchased
= (15,000 x $5) + [(10,000 x $10) + (15,000 x $15)
+ (10,000 x $20) + (30,000 x $25) + (15,000 x $30)]
= $1,800,000

Ending inventory = (15,000 x $30) + (5,000 x $25)
= $575,000

COGS = Cost of goods available – cost of ending inventory
= $1,550,000 – $575,000
= $1,225,000

c. **Perpetual/LIFO**

Date	Cost of Inventory Purchased	Cost of Inventory Sold	Inventory Balance
Beg Inv.	15,000 x $ 5		$ 75,000
2/15	10,000 x $10		175,000
3/15		(10,000 x $10) + (5,000 x $5)	50,000
4/25	15,000 x $15		275,000
5/10		10,000 x $15	125,000
9/18	10,000 x $20		325,000
10/9		(10,000 x $20) +(5,000 x $15) + (10,000 x $5)	0
11/1	30,000 x $25		750,000
12/2		25,000 x $25	125,000
12/7	15,000 x $30		575,000

COGS = $1,225,000
Ending inventory = $ 575,000

Note: Perpetual/LIFO yielded the same COGS and ending inventory value as periodic/FIFO and perpetual/FIFO. Ordinarily this would not happen. But in this case, the company did not maintain a large surplus of inventory. Consequently, the company never created any LIFO layers. When a company "turns" its inventory rapidly and consumes its LIFO layers, perpetual/LIFO may effectively be identical to FIFO.

d. **Periodic/LIFO**

Units available = 95,000 units (from Periodic/FIFO)

Units sold = 75,000 units (from Periodic/FIFO)

Units in ending inventory = 20,000 units (from Periodic/FIFO)

Cost of goods available = $1,800,000 (from Periodic/FIFO)

Ending inventory = (15,000 x $5) + (5,000 x $10)
= $125,000

COGS = Cost of goods available – cost of ending inventory
= $1,800,000 – $125,000
= $1,675,000

E8–12

a. Inventory turnover = COGS ÷ Average inventory
1988 ($42,000 x 40%) ÷ [($5,000 + $9,000) ÷ 2] = 2.40 times
1989 ($53,000 x 40%) ÷ [($9,000 + $10,000) ÷ 2] = 2.23 times
1990 ($55,000 x 40%) ÷ [($10,000 + $12,000) ÷ 2] = 2.00 times

b. Days supply = 365 ÷ Inventory turnover
1988 365 ÷ 2.40 = 152 days
1989 365 ÷ 2.23 = 163 days
1990 365 ÷ 2.00 = 182.5 days

c. The inventory is turning over more slowly each year. This trend may indicate obsolete or slow moving inventory. Since carrying inventory can be costly, management should look more closely into this trend.

E8–13

a. (1) Number of units available = Number of units in beginning inventory + number of units purchased
= 10,000 units + 79,000 units
= 89,000 units

(2) Number of units sold = 46,000 units

(3) Number of units in ending inventory = Number of units available – Number of units sold
= 89,000 units – 46,000 units
= 43,000

b.

	(1) Periodic FIFO	(2) Periodic Averaging	(3) Periodic LIFO
Sales	$2,000,000	$2,000,000	$2,000,000
Cost of goods sold	805,000[a]	1,162,921[b]	1,520,000[c]
Gross profit	1,195,000	837,079	480,000
Operating expenses	250,000	250,000	250,000
Net income	$ 945,000	$ 587,079	$ 230,000

[a] $1,805,000 = (10,000 x $10) + (12,000 x $15) + (15,000 x $20) + (9,000 x $25)
[b] $1,162,880 = {[(10,000 x $10) + (12,000 x $15) + (15,000 x $20) + (18,000 x $25) + (14,000 x $30) + (20,000 x $40)] ÷ 89,000 units} x 46,000 units
[c] $1,520,000 = (20,000 x $40) + (14,000 x $30 + (12,000 x $25)

	(4) Perpetual FIFO	(5) Perpetual Averaging	(6) Perpetual LIFO
Sales	$2,000,000	$2,000,000	$2,000,000
Cost of goods sold	805,000[a]	906,543[b]	1,100,000[c]
Gross profit	1,195,000	1,093,457	900,000
Operating expenses	250,000	250,000	250,000
Net income	$2,945,000	$2,843,457	$2,650,000

[a] Sale 1 = (10,000 x $10) = $100,000
Sale 2 = (12,000 x $15) + (8,000 x $20) = 340,000
Sale 3 = (7,000 x $20) + (9,000 x $25) = 365,000
Total $805,000

[b] The following table was used to calculate COGS under the perpetual averaging method.

	Transaction			Balance		
Date	Units	Unit	Total	Total	Total	Unit
Beg Inv				$ 100,000	10,000	$10.0000
2/10	12,000	$15.0000	$180,000	280,000	22,000	12.7273
5/20	(10,000)	12.7273	(127,273)	152,727	12,000	12.7273
6/30	15,000	20.0000	300,000	452,727	27,000	16.7677
9/10	18,000	25.0000	450,000	902,727	45,000	20.0606
10/9	(20,000)	20.0606	(401,212)	501,515	25,000	20.0606
11/1	14,000	30.0000	420,000	921,515	39,000	23.6286
12/8	(16,000)	23.6286	(378,058)	543,457	23,000	23.6286
12/9	20,000	40.0000	800,000	1,343,457	43,000	31.2436

COGS = $127,273 + $401,212 + $378,058 = $906,543

[c] Sale 1 = (10,000 x $15) = $ 150,000
Sale 2 = (18,000 x $25) + (2,000 x $20) = 490,000
Sale 3 = (14,000 x $30) + (2,000 x $20) = 460,000
Total $1,100,000

E8–14

a. and b.

Company	Market Value	Carrying Value
Wheaton	$35,600	$32,300
Loners	63,100	63,100
Flowe	16,000	16,000
Roberts	7,100	6,500
Strayling	22,900	22,900

c. **Wheaton**
Since cost is lower than market value and the inventory is already on the books at cost, no journal entry is necessary.

Loners

Loss on Inventory Writedown	1,100*	
Inventory		1,100
To adjust inventory to LCM.		

* $1,100 = Cost – Market value = $64,200 – $63,100

Flowe

Loss on Inventory Writedown	1,400*	
Inventory		1,400
To adjust inventory to LCM.		

* $1,400 = $17,400 – $16,000

Roberts
Since cost is lower than market value, and the inventory is already on the books at cost, no journal entry is necessary.

Strayling

Loss on Inventory Writedown	3,400*	
Inventory		3,400
To adjust inventory to LCM.		

* $3,400 = $26,300 – $22,900

P8–1

a. **Gross Method**

12/15	Inventory	4,000	
	Accounts Payable		4,000
	To record inventory purchase on account.		
12/26	Inventory	6,000	
	Accounts Payable		6,000
	To record inventory purchase on account.		
12/31	No adjusting journal entry is necessary.		

Net method

12/15	Inventory	3,920*	
	Accounts Payable		3,920
	To record inventory purchase on account.		

* $3,920 = $4,000 – ($4,000 x 2% discount)

12/26	Inventory	5,880*	
	Accounts Payable		5,880
	To record inventory purchase on account.		

* $5,880 = $6,000 – ($6,000 x 2% discount)

		Debit	Credit
12/31	Adjusting entry		
	Purchase Discount Lost	80	
	Accounts Payable		80
	To record expiration of discount period on 12/15 purchase.		

b. Since none of the inventory had been sold, the only difference betttween the two methods is the $80 from the lost purchase discount. Under the gross method this $80 is still included as inventory so assets and net income are both overstated by $80. If the inventory from the December 15 purchase had been sold, this $80 would flow through to Cost of Goods Sold and net income under the net and gross methods would be the same, although the components of net income would be different.

c. Gross profit equals revenues minus Cost of Goods Sold. Since none of the inventory was sold, there is no revenue or COGS associated with these two transactions. Consequently, gross profit is correctly stated. If the inventory had been sold, gross profit would be misstated for any discount not taken. Discounts not taken are technically not a cost of inventory and should not be reported as part of COGS.

d. **Gross Method**

		Debit	Credit
1/2	Accounts Payable	4,000	
	Cash		4,000
	To record payment to supplier.		
1/2	Accounts Payable	6,000	
	Cash		5,880
	Purchase Discount		120
	To record payment to supplier.		

Net Method

		Debit	Credit
1/2	Accounts Payable	4,000	
	Cash		4,000
	To record payment to supplier.		
1/2	Accounts Payable	5,880	
	Cash		5,880
	To record payment to supplier.		

P8–2

a.

		Debit	Credit
3/5	Inventory	14,700*	
	Accounts Payable		14,700
	To record inventory purchased on account.		

* $14,700 = $15,000 – ($15,000 x 2% discount)

		Debit	Credit
3/10	Inventory	29,400	
	Accounts Payable		29,400
	To record inventory purchases on account.		
3/13	Accounts Payable	14,700	
	Cash		14,700
	To record payment to supplier.		

	Date	Account	Debit	Credit
	3/31	Adjusting entry		
		Purchase Discount Lost	600	
		Accounts Payable		600
		To record expiration of discount period on March 10 inventory purchase.		
	7/18	Accounts Payable	30,000	
		Cash		30,000
		To record payment to supplier.		
b.	3/5	Inventory	15,000	
		Accounts Payable		15,000
		To record inventory purchased on account.		
	3/10	Inventory	30,000	
		Accounts payable		30,000
		To record inventory purchased on account.		
	3/13	Accounts Payable	15,000	
		Cash		14,700
		Purchase Discount		300
		To record payment to supplier.		
	3/31	No adjusting journal entry is necessary.		
	7/18	Accounts Payable	30,000	
		Cash		30,000
		To record payment to supplier.		
c.	3/10	Same as Part (a)		
	3/19	Accounts Payable	19,600*	
		Cash		19,600
		To record payment to supplier.		

* $19,600 = ($30,000 x 2/3) – [($30,000 x 2/3) x 2% discount]

	Date	Account	Debit	Credit
	3/31	Adjusting entry		
		Purchase Discount Lost	200*	
		Accounts Payable		200
		To record expiration of discount period on March 10 inventory purchase.		

* $200 = ($29,400 – $19,600) x 2% discount

	Date	Account	Debit	Credit
	8/7	Accounts Payable	10,000	
		Cash		10,000
		To record payment to supplier.		
d.	3/10	Same as Part (b)		
	3/19	Accounts Payable	20,000	
		Cash		19,600
		Purchase Discount		400
		To record payment to supplier.		

3/31	No adjusting journal entry is necessary.		
8/7	Accounts Payable	10,000	
	Cash		10,000
	To record payment to supplier.		

P8–3

	1989	1990	1991
Sales	$85,000	$90,000	$100,000
Cost of goods sold*	42,000	37,000	54,000
Gross profit	43,000	53,000	46,000
Expenses	20,000	32,000	37,000
Net income	$23,000	$21,000	$ 9,000

* Error in ending inventory = Error in beginning inventory + Error in purchases – Error in COGS

1989
$2,000 = $0 + $ – Error in COGS
Error in COGS = ($2,000). Therefore, COGS as reported is understated $2,000.
Correct COGS = ($40,000) + ($2,000) = ($42,000)

1990
($3,000) = $2,000 + $0 – Error in COGS
Error in COGS = $5,000 Therefore, COGS as reported is overstated $5,000
Correct COGS = ($42,000) + $5,000 = ($37,000)

1991
$1,000 = ($3,000) + $0 – Error in COGS
Error in COGS = ($4,000) Therefore, COGS as reported is understated $4,000.
Correct COGS = ($50,000) + ($4,000) = ($54,000)

P8–4

a.

Rodman and Sons
Income Statement
For the Year Ended December 31, 1990

Sales	$200,000
Cost of goods sold	118,000*
Gross profit	82,000
Selling and administrative expenses	40,000
Net income	$ 42,000

* $118,000 = $130,000 – $12,000 of consigned inventory

Rodman and Sons
Balance Sheet
As of December 31, 1990

Assets		Liabilities and Stockholders' Equity	
Cash	$ 35,000	Current Liabilities	$ 30,000[b]
Inventory	62,000[a]	Long–term liabilities	50,000
Noncurrent assets	120,000	Stockholders' equity	137,000[c]
		Total liabilities and	
Total assets	$217,000	stockholders' equity	$217,000

[a] $62,000 = $40,000 + $10,000 goods in transit + $12,000 of consigned inventory.
[b] $30,000 = $20,000 + $10,000 goods in transit. Since Rodman and Sons has legal title to this merchandise on 12/31, the company must record the related liability.
[c] $137,000 = $125,000 + $12,000 of consigned inventory.

b. No. Under the FIFO cost flow assumption, ending inventory always represents the costs of the most recently purchased goods regardless of whether it is calculated using the periodic or perpetual method, while COGS always represents the costs of the oldest inventory purchased regardless of whether it is calculated using the periodic or perpetual method. Hence, the choice of the periodic or perpetual method makes no difference in the amounts reported for ending inventory and COGS.

P8–5

a. and b.

		Inventory		Accounts Payable
Reported amounts		$2,345,000		$778,000
Adjustments				
(1)	No effect		No effect	
(2)	(55,000)		No effect	
(3)	12,000 [a]		18,000	
(4)	60,000 [b]		No Effect	
(5)	No effect		30,000	
(6)	50,000		No effect	
Total adjustments		67,000		48,000
Adjusted Amounts		$2,412,000		$826,000

[a] $12,000 = 2/3 x $18,000. The remaining $6,000 would be allocated to COGS.
[b] $60,000 = 80% x $75,000

P8–6

a.		
Inventory (ending)	500,000	
Cost of Goods Sold	1,155,000	
Purchases		980,000
Inventory (beginning)		675,000
To record COGS and ending inventory.		

b. (1) Since the shipping terms are F.O.B. shipping point, legal title to the merchandise passes to Chung Graphics on 12/30/90 (i.e., the shipping date). The goods were not received until 1/4/91 and thus were not included in the 12/31/90 physical count of inventory. Inventory should be increased by $35,000 for these goods in transit.

(2) Legal title to these goods passed to Chung Graphics on 12/29/90 (i.e., the shipping date). The goods were included in the 12/31/90 physical inventory since they were received prior to the close of business on 12/31/90. Since the goods were included in the physical count, and they legally belong to Chung, no adjustment is necessary.

(3) Chung Graphics did not have physical possession of the merchandise on 12/31/90, so the merchandise was not included in the physical count. Legal title to the merchandise passed to Chung on 1/2/91 (i.e., date received) under the shipping terms. Since Chung did not include the merchandise in its physical count and did not legally own the goods as of 12/31/90, the books are correctly stated, and no adjustment is necessary.

(4) Title to these goods passed from Chung to the buyer on 12/29/90 (i.e., the shipping date). Chung Graphics did not have physical possession of these goods on 12/31/90, so they were not included in the physical count. Since Chung did not include the goods in its physical count and did not legally own them as of 12/31/90, the books are correctly stated, and no adjustment is necessary.

(5) Title to these goods passed from Chung to the buyer on 12/31/90 (i.e., the date they were received by the buyer). Chung Graphics did not have physical possession of these goods on 12/31/90, so they were not included in the physical count. Since Chung did not include the goods in its physical count and did not legally own them as of 12/31/90, the books are correctly stated and no adjustment is necessary.

(6) Title to these goods passed from Chung to the buyer on 1/3/91 (i.e., the date they were received by the buyer). Chung Graphics did not have physical possession of these goods on 12/31/90, so they were not included in the physical count. Since Chung did not include the goods in its physical count but still legally owned them as of 12/31/90, the books are incorrectly stated. Inventory is currently understated by $15,000, and COGS is currently overstated by $15,000.

c. After considering the effect of these inventory transactions, the appropriate entry to record these transactions would be as follows.

Inventory	50,000	
Cost of Goods Sold		15,000
Accounts Payable		35,000
To record impact of goods in transit.		

The inventory balance as of December 31, 1990 should be $550,000 which represents the $500,000 amount per the physical count plus $50,000 for goods in transit legally owned by Chung.

P8–7

a.

Lumbermans and Associates
Income Statements
For the Year Ended December 31,____

	FIFO	Averaging	LIFO
Sales	$55,000	$55,000	$55,000
COGS	29,400[a]	32,110[b]	34,700[c]
Gross profit	25,600	22,890	20,300
Other expenses	15,000	15,000	15,000
Income before taxes	10,600	7,890	5,300
Income taxes	3,180	2,367	1,590
Net income	$57,420	$55,523	$53,710

[a] Units sold = Units in beginning inventory + Units purchased – Units in ending inventory
= 15,000 + 22,000 – 11,000 = 26,000
$29,400 = (15,000 x $1) + (5,000 x $1.20) + (6,000 x $1.40)
[b] Cost per unit = Cost of goods available for sale ÷ Units available for sale.
= [$15,000 + (5,000 x $1.20) + (8,000 x $1.40) + (9,000 x $1.50)]
÷ (15,000 units + 22,000 units purchased) = $1.235 per unit
$32,110 = Cost per unit x units sold = $1,235 per unit x 26,000 units
[c] $34,700 = (9,000 x $1.50) + (8,000 x $1.40) + (5,000 x $1.20) + (4,000 x $1.00)

b. By using LIFO rather than FIFO, Lumbermans and Associates would save $1,590 (i.e., $3,180 – $1,590) in taxes.

c. Ending inventory at market value = 11,000 units x $1.35 per unit = $14,850

Lower–of–cost or market value

	FIFO	Averaging	LIFO
Cost	$16,300[a]	$13,585[b]	$11,000[c]
Market value	14,850	14,850	14,850
Excess of cost over market value (cannot be negative)	$ 1,450	0	0

[a] $16,300 = (9,000 units x $1.50) + (2,000 units x $1.40)
[b] $13,585 = 11,000 units x $1.235
[c] $11,000 = 11,000 units x $1.00

Journal entries

FIFO method

	Debit	Credit
Loss on Inventory Writedown	1,450	
Inventory		1,450
To adjust inventory to LCM.		

Averaging method: No entry is necessary

LIFO method: No entry is necessary

d.

Lumbermans and Associates
Income Statements
For the Year Ended December 31,_____

	FIFO	Averaging	LIFO
Sales	$55,000	$55,000	$55,000
COGS	39,900[a]	37,596[b]	35,900[c]
Gross profit	15,100	17,404	19,100
Other expenses	15,000	15,000	15,000
Income before taxes	100	2,404	410
Income taxes	30	721	1,230
Net income	$55,070	$51,683	$52,870

[a] $39,900 = (15,000 x $1.60) + (5,000 x $1.50) + (6,000 x $1.40)
[b] Cost per unit = [(15,000 x $1.60) + (5,000 x $1.50) + (8,000 x $1.40) + (9,000 x $1,20)]
÷ 37,000 units = $1.446 per unit
$37,596 = 26,000 units x $1.446 per unit
[c] $35,900 = (19,000 x $1.20) + (8,000 x $1.40) + (5,000 x $1.50) + (4,000 x $1.60)

The LIFO cost flow assumption gives rise to the highest net income in this case. Under FIFO, the oldest costs flow into COGS before the most recent costs. Under LIFO, the most recent costs flow into COGS before the older costs. Under the averaging method, all the costs are averaged to determine COGS. In this case, the cost of the inventory is decreasing, so the LIFO cost flow assumption uses lower, newer costs in computing COGS than the other two methods. Since these lower costs flow into COGS under LIFO, the older, higher costs flow into ending inventory.

P8–8

IBT
Income Statements
For the Year ended December 31, 1990

	Part (a)	Part (b)
Sales	$40,000	$ 40,000
COGS	17,400[a]	24,000[b]
Gross profit	22,600	16,000
Other epxenses	20,000	20,000
Income (Loss) before taxes	2,600	(4,000)
Income taxes	780	1,200[c]
Net income (Loss)	$ 1,820	$ (2,800)

[a] $17,400 = (400 units x $30) + (200 x units $15) + (200 units x $12)
[b] $24,000 = (800 units $30
[c] Since the company generated a net loss before taxes, the company will have a tax benefit. Therefore, the income tax benefit reduces the company's net loss.

c. The primary advantage of purchasing the additional 400 units on December 20 is the effect on income taxes. Under Part (a), IBT would have to pay $780 in income taxes. However, under Part (b), IBT would receive a tax benefit of $1,200. So the net difference between the income statements of Parts (a) and (b) is $1,980 in taxes saved. Since income taxes represent a cash flow, the strategy of acquiring the additional 400 units would save IBT $1,980 in cash from income taxes.

Unfortunately, this tax savings is not without a cost. To obtain this tax savings, IBT had to purchase 400 additional units at a total cost of $12,000. If IBT was planning on acquiring at least 400 units some time in the near future, then the cost of the tax savings is not $12,000; rather the cost is the return lost on an alternative use of the $12,000. If IBT was not planning on acquiring additional inventory, then the cost of obtaining the tax savings would be the entire $12,000 plus the opportunity cost of not investing the $12,000.

P8–9

a.

	Current Assets	+	Current Liabilities	=	Current Ratio
FIFO	$40,000[a]		$18,000		2.22
LIFO	30,000[b]		18,000		1.67
Decrease					.55

[a] $40,000 = $15,000 in cash + $25,000 in inventory.
[b] $30,000 = $15,000 in cash + $15,000 in inventory.

b.

	FIFO		LIFO	
Sales		$80,000		$80,000
Cost of goods sold				
Beginning inventory	$20,000		$20,000	
Purchases	40,000		40,000	
Ending inventory	25,000		15,000	
Cost of goods sold		35,000		45,000
Gross profit		45,000		35,000
S & A expense		20,000		20,000
Income before taxes		25,000		15,000
Income tax		7,500		4,500
Net income		$17,500		$10,500

Change in gross profit = $45,000 – $35,000 = $10,000
Change in net income = $17,500 – $10,500 = $7,000

c. Tax dollars saved = $7,500 – $4,500 = $3,000.

d. Using LIFO can have several disadvantages. First, LIFO requires a company to maintain records for older inventory acquisitions. This practice usually results in higher bookkeeping costs. Second, to avoid "eating into" a LIFO layer, managers may purchase inventory at a time or at a cost that is not advantageous to the company. Third, LIFO can adversely affect a company's and/or manager's contracts. A company's debt covenant may stipulate a minimum current ratio, or level of working capital. These both would all be lower under LIFO than under FIFO (assuming inflation). Also, using LIFO reduces net income during inflationary periods. If a manager has an incentive contract linked to net income, the manager's compensation will decrease. Finally, the lower net income achieved under LIFO may mislead current and potential investors into believing that the company is performing poorly (although current research indicates that this last point is not likely).

P8–10

a. LIFO layers

1980	14,000 units	x	$5 per unit	=	$ 70,000
1991	500 units	x	$85 per unit	=	42,500
Total					$112,500

b.

Ruhe Auto Supplies
Income Statement
For the Year Ended December 31, 1993

Revenue		$3,000,000
Cost of goods sold		
Beginning inventory	$ 112,500	
Purchases	902,500	
Cost of goods available for sale	1,015,000	
Ending inventory	20,000*	
Cost of goods sold		995,000
Gross profit		2,005,000
Operating expenses		800,000
Income before income taxes		1,205,000
Income taxes		361,500
Net Income		$ 843,500

* $20,000 = 4,000 units from 1980 $5.

The company's income tax liability is $361,500 and its net income is $843,500.

c.

Revenue		$3,000,000
Cost of goods sold		
Beginning inventory	$ 112,500	
Purchases	1,900,000[a]	
Cost of goods available for sale	2,012,500	
Ending inventory	112,500[b]	
Cost of goods sold		1,900,000
Gross profit		1,100,000
Operating expenses		800,000
Net income before taxes		300,000
Income taxes		90,000
Net Income		$ 210,000

[a] $1,900,000 = (9,500 units + 10,500 units) x $95
[b] $112,500 = (14,000 units x $5) + (500 units x $85)

Purchasing an additional 10,500 units of inventory on December 31, 1993 would cost Ruhe Auto Supplies $997,500. By incurring these costs, the company would only save $271,500 in taxes. So on the face of it, it appears that it would not be a wise decision to acquire these additional units of inventory. However, if Ruhe Auto Supplies was planning to acquire additional inventory early in 1994 anyway, then it might not be a bad decision to acquire the inventory at the end of 1993 to lower the company's taxes.

P8–11

a. LIFO cost flow assumption

Entry	Account	Debit	Credit
(1) 1/3	Purchases	160,000	
	Accounts Payable		160,000
	To record inventory purchased on account.		
(2) 1/3	Cash	100,000	
	Sales		100,000
	To record cash sales.		
(3) 1/9	Accounts Receivable	200,000	
	Sales		200,000
	To record sales on account.		
(4) 1/10	Accounts Payable	160,000	
	Cash		156,800
	Purchase Discount		3,200*
	To record payment to supplier.		

* $3,200 = $160,000 x 2% discount.

Entry	Account	Debit	Credit
(5) 1/15	Purchases	248,500	
	Cash		73,500
	Accounts Payable		175,000
	To record inventory purchases.		
(6) 1/19	Purchases	182,000	
	Accounts Payable		182,000
	To record inventory purchases.		
(7) 1/23	Accounts Payable	87,500	
	Cash		85,750
	Purchase Discount		1,750*
	To record payment to supplier.		

* $1,750 = $87,500 x 2% discount.

Entry	Account	Debit	Credit
(8) 1/27	Purchases	56,000	
	Cash		56,000
	To record inventory purchased on account.		
(9) 1/28	Accounts Payable	87,500	
	Cash		87,500
	To record payment to supplier.		
(10) 1/28	Accounts Payable	182,000	
	Cash		178,360
	Purchase Discount		3,640*
	To record payment to supplier on an open account.		

* $3,640 = $182,000 x 2% discount.

(11) 1/29	Cash	360,000	
	Sales		360,000
	To record cash sales.		
(12) 1/30	Accounts Receivable	300,000	
	Sales		300,000
	To record sales on account.		
(13) 1/31	Purchases	30,000	
	Cash		30,000
	To record inventory purchased for cash.		
(14) 1/31	Freight–in	28,000	
	Accounts Payable*		28,000
	To record freight bill.		

* Accounts Payable was credited because freight is related to inventory.

1/31	Adjusting entry		
	Inventory (ending)	336,825*	
	Cost of Goods Sold	454,085	
	Purchase Discount	8,590	
	Purchases		676,500
	Freight–in		28,000
	Inventory (beginning)		95,000
	To record COGS and ending inventory.		

* Ending inventory was calculated using the following table.

Date	Number of Units	Unit Cost	Freight Cost[a] Per Unit	Purchase Discount Per Unit	Total Unit Cost	Total Cost
Beg Inv	5,000	$19.00	$0.00	$ 0.00	$ 19.00	$ 95,000
1/3	8,000	20.00	1.00	0.40	20.60	164,800
1/15	10,000	24.85[b]	1.00	0.175[c]	25.675	256,750
1/19	7,000	26.00	1.00	0.52	26.48	185,360
1/27	2,000	28.00	1.00	0.00	29.00	58,000
1/31	1,000	30.00	1.00	0.00	31.00	31,000
Total	33,000					$790,910

[a] The total freight bill of $28,000 must be allocated to all purchases covered by the freight bill. Since only the 28,000 units purchased during 1990 were covered by the freight bill, each unit purchased is allocated $1.00.

[b] $24.85 unit cost = [(3,000 units x $24.50) + (7,000 x $25.00)] ÷ 10,000 units.

[c] $0.175 Discount per unit = Total discount ÷ 10,000 units = $1,750 ÷ 10,000 units.

Ending inventory = (5,000 units x $19.00) + (8,000 units x $20.60)
+ (3,000 units x $25.675) = $336,825

b. **FIFO cost flow assumption**

All entries throughout January would be identical under the FIFO and LIFO cost flow assumptions using the periodic method. The only difference would be in the adjusting entry to record COGS and ending inventory.

1/31	Adjusting entry		
	Inventory (ending)	428,410*	
	Cost of Goods Sold	362,500	
	Purchase Discount	8,590	
	Purchases		676,500
	Freight–in		28,000
	Inventory (beginning)		95,000
	To record COGS and ending inventory.		

---

* The computations for ending inventory are based upon the table used in Part (a)
$428,410 = (1,000 units x $31.00) + (2,000 units x $29.00) + (7,000 units x $26.48)
+ (6,000 units x $25.675)

P8–12

a.

Date	Cost of Inventory Purchased	Cost of Inventory Sold	Inventory Balance
Beg Inv	12,000 x $10		$120,000
2/10	10,000 x 15		270,000
5/10		10,000 units x $15	120,000
6/30	15,000 x 20		420,000
9/10	17,000 x 25		845,000
10/9		(17,000 units x $25) + (3,000 units x $20)	360,000
11/1	14,000 x 30		780,000
12/8		(14,000 units x $30) + (2,000 units x $20)	320,000
12/9	5,000 x 40		520,000

Cost of goods sold = $1,095,000
Inventory shrinkage = 1,000 units x $40 = $40,000
Ending inventory = $520,000 – Inventory shrinkage = $520,000 – $40,000 = $480,000

b.

Date	Cost of Inventory Purchased	Cost of Inventory Sold	Inventory Balance
Beg Inv	12,000 x $10		$120,000
2/10	10,000 x 15		270,000
5/10		10,000 x $10	170,000
6/30	15,000 x 20		470,000
9/10	17,000 x 25		895,000
10/9		(2,000 x $10) + (10,000 x $15) + (8,000 x $20)	565,000
11/1	14,000 x 30		985,000
12/8		(7,000 units x $20) + (9,000 units x $25)	620,000
12/9	5,000 x 40		820,000

Cost of goods sold = $795,000
Inventory shrinkage = 1,000 units x $25 = $25,000
Ending inventory = $520,000 – Inventory shrinkage = $820,000 – $25,000 = $795,000

c.

Inventory (ending)	795,000*	
Cost of Goods Sold	820,000	
Purchases		1,495,000
Inventory (beginning)		120,000
To record COGS and ending inventory.		

* $795,000 = (5,000 units x $40) + (14,000 units x $30) + (7,000 units x $25)

Under the periodic method, a company does not maintain a running balance of inventory. All the company knows is its beginning inventory and net purchases; it does not know its cost of goods sold. Cost of goods sold is estimated at year end by taking a physical count of inventory and deducting the cost of ending inventory per the physical count from the cost of goods available. Hence, any inventory shortage is buried in Cost of Goods Sold. So F. S. Larson would not disclose anything for inventory shortage under the periodic method.

P8–13

a. (1) **Periodic method/FIFO assumption**

6/10	Purchases	20,000	
	Accounts Payable		20,000
	To record purchase on account.		
12/31	Inventory (ending)	7,000*	
	Cost of Goods Sold	18,000	
	Purchases		20,000
	Inventory (beginning)		5,000
	To record COGS and ending inventory		

* $7,000 = 700 units x $10

(2) Periodic method/LIFO assumption

6/10	Purchases	20,000	
	Accounts Payable		20,000
	To record purchases on account.		
12/31	Inventory (ending)	3,500*	
	Cost of Goods Sold	21,500	
	Purchases		20,000
	Inventory (beginning)		5,000
	To record COGS and ending inventory.		

* $3,500 = 700 units x $5

(3) Perpetual method/FIFO assumption

3/8	Cost of Goods Sold	4,500*	
	Inventory		4,500
	To record cost of inventory sold.		

* $4,500 = 900 units x $5.

6/10	Inventory	20,000	
	Accounts Payable		20,000
	To record purchases on account.		
7/19	Cost of Goods Sold	11,500*	
	Inventory		11,500
	To record cost of inventory sold		

* $11,500 = (100 units x $5) + (1,100 units x $10)

12/1	Cost of Goods Sold	2,000*	
	Inventory		2,000
	To record cost of inventory sold.		

* $2,000 = 200 units x $10

(4) Perpetual method/LIFO assumption

3/8	Cost of Goods Sold	4,500*	
	Inventory		4,500
	To record cost of inventory sold.		

* $4,500 = 900 units x $5

6/10	Inventory	20,000	
	Accounts Payable		20,000
	To record purchases on account.		
7/19	Cost of Goods Sold	12,000*	
	Inventory		12,000
	To record cost of inventory sold.		

* $12,000 = 1,200 units x $10

12/1	Cost of Goods Sold	2,000*	
	Inventory		2,000
	To record cost of inventory sold.		

* $2,000 = 200 x $10

	Periodic		Perpetual	
	FIFO	LIFO	FIFO	LIFO
Cost of goods sold	$18,000	$21,500	$18,000	$18,500
Ending inventory	7,000	3,500	7,000	6,500

The FIFO cost flow assumption under both the periodic and perpetual methods yields the lowest COGS and highest ending inventory. In times of inflation, FIFO yields lower COGS than LIFO. The LIFO assumption under the periodic method yields the highest COGS and lowest ending inventory. This assumption/method combination allocates the most recent inventory costs to COGS.

c. Under the periodic method, a running balance of Inventory and Cost of Goods Sold is not maintained throughout the accounting period. The ending inventory balance is determined by a physical count of the inventory on hand at the end of the accounting period. Using this information, along with beginning inventory and net purchases, Cost of Goods Sold can be computed. In other words the total cost of goods available for sale is used to compute COGS. Consequently, individual purchases of inventory are not allocated to specific sales of inventory.

Under the perpetual method, a running balance of Inventory and COGS is maintained throughout the accounting period. At the end of the accounting period, the balance in the Inventory account should equal the inventory on hand. Under this method, sufficient information is available to allocate specific inventory purchases to specific sales of inventory. In other words, the periodic method basically assumes that all sales take place on the last day of the accounting period, while the perpetual method basically assumes that each sale takes place on the actual sale date. Since LIFO assigns the most recent inventory cost incurred prior to the sale to COGS, different inventory costs are assigned to COGS under the periodic and perpetual methods

P8–14

a. **Periodic method**

(1)	Purchases–Movie Videos	9,000	
	Accounts Payable		9,000
	To record inventory purchased on account.		
(2)	Cash	4,000	
	Sales–Movie		4,000
	To record cash sales.		
(3)	Purchases–Music Videos	2,400	
	Accounts Payable		2,400
	To record inventory purchased on account.		
(4)	Purchases–Movie Videos	5,400	
	Accounts Payable		5,400
	To record inventory purchased on account.		
(5)	Purchases–Movie Videos	2,000	
	Accounts Payable		2,000
	To record inventory purchased on account.		

		Debit	Credit
(6)	Cash	10,000	
	Sales–Movie		10,000
	To record cash sales.		
(7)	Cash	9,000	
	Sales–Movie		9,000
	To record cash sales.		
(8)	Purchases–Movie Videos	8,800	
	Accounts Payable		8,800
	To record inventory purchased on account.		
(9)	Cash	3,500	
	Sales–Music		3,500
	To record cash sales.		
(10)	Cash	18,000	
	Sales–Movie		18,000
	To record cash sales.		
(11)	Purchases–Movie Videos	5,000	
	Accounts Payable		5,000
	To record inventory purchased on account.		
	Freight–in: Movie Videos	800[a]	
	Freight–in: Music Videos	100[b]	
	Accounts Payable		900
	To record freight charges on inventory.		

[a] $800 = (600 + 300 + 100 + 400 + 200 movie videos purchased) x 50¢
[b] $100 = (200 music videos purchased x 50¢

Adjusting entries

	Debit	Credit
Movie Video Inventory (end)	12,825*	
Cost of Goods Sold–Movie	20,775	
Purchases–Movie Videos		30,200
Freight–in: Movie Videos		800
Movie Video inventory (beg)		2,600
To record COGS and ending inventory.		

* $12,825 = (200 x $13) + (600 x $15) + (50 x $18) + (650 x 50¢)

Note: 200 of the units in ending inventory were already in beginning inventory. Therefore, the freight charge of 50¢ per unit was not charged to these 200 units.

		Debit	Credit
	Music Video Inventory (end)	1,750*	
	Cost of Goods Sold–Music	1,250	
	Purchases–Music Videos		2,400
	Freight–in: Music Videos		100
	Music Video Inventory (beg)		500
	To record COGS and ending inventory.		

* $1,775 = (50 x $10) + (100 x $12) + (100 x 50¢)

Note: 50 of the units in ending inventory were already in beginning inventory. Therefore, the freight charge of 50¢ per unit was not charged to these 50 units.

Perpetual method

		Debit	Credit
(1)	Movie Video Inventory	9,000	
	Accounts Payable		9,000
	To record inventory purchased on account.		
(2a)	Cash	4,000	
	Sales–Movie		4,000
	To record cash sales.		
(2b)	Cost of Goods Sold–Movie	1,500*	
	Movie Video Inventory		1,500
	To record cost of inventory sold.		

* $1,500 = 100 videos x $15.

		Debit	Credit
(3)	Music Video Inventory	2,400	
	Accounts Payable		2,400
	To record inventory purchased on account.		
(4)	Music Video Inventory	5,400	
	Accounts Payable		5,400
	To record inventory purchased on account.		
(5)	Movie Video Inventory	2,000	
	Accounts Payable		2,000
	To record inventory purchased on account.		
(6a)	Cash	10,000	
	Sales–Movie		10,000
	To record cash sales.		
(6b)	Cost of Goods Sold–Movie	4,700*	
	Movie Video Inventory		4,700
	To record cost of inventory sold.		

* $4,700 = (100 videos x $20) + (150 videos x $18)

		Debit	Credit
(7a)	Cash	9,000	
	Sales–Movies		9,000
	To record cash Sales.		

		Debit	Credit
(7b)	Cost of Goods Sold–Movie	3,450*	
	Movie Video Inventory		3,450
	To record cost of inventory sold.		

* $3,450 = (150 videos x $18) + (50 videos x $15)

		Debit	Credit
(8)	Movie Video Inventory	8,800	
	Accounts Payable		8,800
	To record inventory purchased on account.		
(9a)	Cash	3,500	
	Sales–Music		3,500
	To record cash sales.		
(9b)	Cost of Goods Sold–Music	1,200*	
	Music Video Inventory		1,200
	To record cost of inventory sold.		

* $1,200 = 100 videos x $12.

		Debit	Credit
(10a)	Cash	18,000	
	Sales–Movie		18,000
	To record cash sales.		
(10b)	Cost of Goods Sold–Movie	8,800*	
	Movie Video Inventory		8,800
	To record cost of inventory sold.		

* $8,800 = 400 videos x $22

		Debit	Credit
(11)	Movie Video Inventory	5,000	
	Accounts Payable		5,000
	To record inventory purchased on account.		
	Movie Video Inventory	800	
	Music Video Inventory	100	
	Accounts Payable		900
	To record freight on inventory.		
	Cost of Goods Sold–Movie	475[a]	
	Cost of Goods Sold–Music	50[b]	
	Movie Video Inventory		475
	Movie Video Inventory		50
	To record cost of freight on videos sold.		

[a] $475 = (100 + 250 + 200 + 400 movie videos sold) x 50¢
[b] $450 = 100 music videos sold x 50¢

Note: The freight cost could have been recorded for each individual transaction rather than making one entry for the entire year.

b. **Periodic Method**

Entries A – K would be identical to Part (a) under the periodic method.

Freight–in: Movie Videos	800	
Freight–in: Music Videos	100	
Accounts Payable		900
To record freight charges on inventory		

Adjusting entry—movie videos		
Movie Video Inventory (end)	18,925*	
Cost of Goods Sold–Movie	14,675	
Purchases–Movie Videos		30,200
Freight–in: Movie Videos		800
Movie Videos Inventory (beg)		2,600
To record COGS and ending inventory.		

* $18,925 = (200 x $25) + (400 x $22) + (100 x $20) + (150 x $18) + (850 x 50¢)

Note: There were 950 movie videos sold during 1990. However, the freight charge of 50¢ per unit was only allocated to 750 of these units. The remaining 200 units were from beginning inventory and the $13 unit cost already included a charge for freight.

Adjusting entry—music videos		
Music Video Inventory (end)	1,875*	
Cost of Goods Sold-Music	1,125	
Purchases-Music Videos		2,400
Freight-in: Music Videos		100
Music Videos Inventory (beg)		500
To record COGS and ending inventory.		

* $1,875 = (150 x $12) + (150 x 50¢)

Note: There were 100 movie videos sold during 1990. However, the freight charge of 50¢ per unit was only allocated to 50 of these units. The remaining 50 units were from beginning inventory, and the $13 unit cost already included a charge for freight.

Perpetual Method

(1) Entry for perpetual method is the same as in Part (a).

(2a) Entry for perpetual method is the same as in Part (a).

(2b)	Cost of Goods Sold-Movie	1,300*	
	Movie Video Inventory		1,300
	To record cost of inventory sold.		

* $1,300 = 100 videos x $13.

(3) Entry is the same as in Part (a).

(4) Entry is the same as in Part (a).

(5) Entry is the same as in Part (a).

(6a) Entry is the same as in Part (a).

		Debit	Credit
(6b)	Cost of Goods Sold-Movie	3,550*	
	Movie Video Inventory		3,550
	To record cost of inventory sold.		

* $3,550 = (100 videos x $13) + (150 videos x $15)

(7a) Entry is the same as in Part (a).

		Debit	Credit
(7b)	Cost of Goods Sold-Movie	3,000*	
	Movie Video Inventory		3,000
	To record cost of inventory sold.		

* $3,000 = 200 videos x $15

(8) Entry is the same as in Part (a).

(9a) Entry is the same as in Part (a).

		Debit	Credit
(9b)	Cost of Goods Sold-Music	1,100*	
	Music Video Inventory		1,100
	To record cost of inventory sold.		

* $1,100 = (50 videos x $10) + (50 videos x $12)

(10a) Entry is the same as in Part (a).

		Debit	Credit
(10b)	Cost of Goods Sold-Movie	6,450*	
	Movie Video Inventory		6,450
	To record cost of inventory sold.		

* $6,450 = (250 videos x $15) + (150 videos x $18)

(11) Entry is the same as in Part (a).

Adjusting entry to allocate freight charges

	Debit	Credit
Movie Video Inventory	425 [a]	
Music Video Inventory	75 [b]	
Cost of Goods Sold-Movie	375 [c]	
Cost of Goods Sold-Music	25 [d]	
Accounts Payable		900
To record freight charges on inventory.		

[a] $425 =850 units in ending inventory x 50¢

[b] $75 =150 units in ending inventory x 50¢

[c] $375 = (450 units sold – 200 units sold from beginning inventory) x 50¢

[d] $25 = (100 units sold – 50 units sold from beginning inventory) x 50¢

c. By maximizing Cost of Goods Sold, Starfire Video would minimize its net income and, hence, minimize its tax payments. LIFO allocates the most recent inventory costs to Cost of Goods Sold, while FIFO allocates the older inventory costs to Cost of Goods Sold. In times of rising prices, the more recent inventory costs will be greater than the older inventory costs, so the LIFO cost flow assumption will minimize taxes compared to FIFO. Further, the periodic method under LIFO allocates the inventory costs acquired closest to year end, while the perpetual method under LIFO allocates the inventory costs acquired closest to the sale of inventory. Therefore, to minimize tax payments during times of rising prices, a company should use the LIFO cost flow assumption in combination with the periodic method.

P8–15

a.

Item	**Market Value**	**Historical Cost**	**LCM**
Item A	$ 50	$ 60	$ 50
Item B	60	55	55
Item C	74	77	74
Item D	45	44	44
Item E	40	50	40
Item F	39	40	39
Item G	12	8	8
Item H	8	5	5
Total	$328	$339	$315

Babbit Plumbing should report $315 for inventory under the LCM method.

b.

Loss on Valuation of Inventory	24*	
Inventory		24
To adjust inventory to LCM.		

* $24 = $339 – $315

C8–1

a. Loss on Write-down of Inventory 12,000,000
Inventory 12,000,000
To write down inventory to market value.

	Debit	Credit
Loss on Write-down of Inventory	12,000,000	
Inventory		12,000,000
To write down inventory to market value.		

This is not a realized loss because the inventory has not been sold. It is, however, a recognized loss.

b. In period 1, the loss is $12,000,000 (the write down). In period 2, there is income of $8,000,000. The net loss over the two periods is $4,000,000.

	Debit	Credit
Accounts Receivable (or Cash)	48,000,000	
Sales Revenue		48,000,000
To record sale of inventory.		

	Debit	Credit
Cost of Goods Sold	40,000,000	
Inventory		40,000,000
To record cost of goods sold.		

c. Because the lower-of-cost-or-market rule gives differential treatment to price decreases and price increases, and because it forces the recognition of loss before it is realized, it may provide inconsistent measures of net income. However, such conservative accounting treatments are employed in response to the liability faced by those who provide and audit financial statements. The costs associated with understating inventories and profits are typically less than the potential costs of overstating.

C8–2

a. A potential investor would be interested in the inventory method used because it has a direct impact on Cost of Goods Sold, and the resultant net income amount. Since the company can switch to a different method, the difference between them is relevant information to an investor. Further, because different companies use different methods, such a practice enhances the comparability among companies. Providing such information also allow investors to examine the impact of different cost flow assumptions on ratios, working capital, and debt covenant compliance.

b. If FIFO had been used, a higher inventory amount would have been reflected and, accordingly, a lower cost of goods sold amount. Under FIFO, income would have increased by $96.3 million.

c. Armstrong would have paid $28,890,000, (30% x $96.3 million) in additional taxes if it used FIFO.

d. During a period of rising inventory costs, using the LIFO method puts the more recent and higher cost into Cost of Goods Sold. The ending inventory is valued at the (lower) earlier prices.

C8–3

a. Liquidating LIFO inventory involves charging “old” lower costs to current income. Thus, sales reflect a higher profit margin.

b. The tax liability would have increased as a result of its higher income.

c. GM could have avoided the LIFO liquidation by switching methods or by increasing the amount of inventory through heightened production or increased purchases.

C8–4

The tradeoffs involved in choosing from the inventory cost flow assumptions are divided into two categories: (1) income and asset measurement and (2) economic consequences. In terms of income and asset measurement, neither LIFO nor FIFO is clearly preferred. LIFO is a better application of the matching principle than FIFO. FIFO, however, produces a more current measure of inventory on the balance sheet.

Economic consequences are broad. The method of inventory costing directly impacts taxes and can result in substantially different tax liabilities. There are potential liquidity problems that may be created when using FIFO, because of resultant "paper profits' that are not supported with cash flows. LIFO requires more bookkeeping procedures and is generally more costly to implement. Using LIFO can result in grossly overstated net income amounts when inventory levels are cut back. During a period of rising prices, FIFO produces higher net income and accordingly may increase income-based compensation for managers. Finally, managers may choose FIFO because they believe the capital market will place a higher value on their resultant higher net income.

C8–5

a. Inventories could have been inflated while Cost of Goods Sold could be decreased with the same journal entry. Such an entry could be described as an adjustment and not be the subject of controversy. The result would be to show a higher inventory cost, and lower Cost of Goods Sold, which produces a higher net income.

b. Inventory errors correct themselves over a two-year period. Consequently, if inventory and profits are overstated in one year, profits will be understated in the next period. Unless Saxon does something, it will report lower profits in the next period. To avoid reporting lower profits, Saxon would have to once again inflate the value of ending inventory.

c. The auditors assume liability regarding the fairness of amounts reflected in the financial statements. Since inventory is such a material component of assets, they should have been scrutinized by the auditors and the "inflation" entry should have been found. The stockholders have a right to sue the auditor. Further, the auditors have "deep pockets' and may be more capable of providing a larger settlement to the plaintiffs.

CHAPTER 9 Long–Lived Assets

E9–1

Objective	Straight–Line	Sum-of-the-Years'-Digits	Double-Declining Balance	Activity Method
(a)	x[a]	x[a]	x[a]	x[a]
(b)	x	x	x	x
(c)			x	x[b]
(d)			x	
(e)			x	
(f)	x			
(g)	x			x[c]
(h)	x	x	x	x

[a] Under certain conditions, all four methods could meet this objective. However, for the straight–line method, the sum-of-the-years'-digits method, and the double-declining-balance method, this objective will only be met by chance. The activity method will always meet this objective because depreciation is based upon the actual use of the asset.

[b] It is possible that the activity method would generate the largest net income in the last year of an asset's useful life. However, this result would be due to the company's use patterns of the asset and would not be due to the depreciation method per se.

[c] See note (b). The same rationale would hold in this case too.

E9–2

a. Lowery, Inc. should capitalize all costs associated with getting the equipment in a serviceable condition and location. These costs would be the actual purchase price of $850,000, the transportation cost of $50,000, and the insurance cost of $10,000. Therefore, the total cost of the equipment is $910,000.

b. The depreciation base equals the cost of the fixed asset that the company does not expect to recover over the asset's useful life. Since the asset had a total cost of $910,000 and can be expected to be sold for $75,000 at the end of its useful life, Lowery, Inc. can expect not to recover $835,000. Therefore, the depreciation base is $835,000. The depreciation base always equals the capitalized cost of the fixed asset less its estimated salvage value.

c. The amount that will be depreciated over the life of a fixed asset is the asset's depreciation base. The depreciation base equals the amount of future benefits that the company will consume. The outflow of future benefits (i.e., assets) are expenses, in this case depreciation expense. Therefore, the total amount that Lowery, Inc. will depreciate over the equipment's useful life is $835,000.

E9–3

	Lot 1	Lot 2	Lot 3	Lot 4
Revenue	$40,000	$30,000	$15,000	$15,000
Expenses	32,000*	24,000*	12,000*	12,000*
Net Income	$ 8,000	$ 6,000	$ 3,000	$ 3,000

* Expenses were calculated as follows:

1. Calculate total market value.
   Total Market value = $40,000 + $30,000 + $15,000 + $15,000 = $100,000
2. Allocate costs to each lot based upon relative market values.
   Lot 1 = $80,000 x (40,000/100,000) = $32,000
   Lot 2 = $80,000 x (30,000/100,000) = $24,000
   Lot 3 = $80,000 x (15,000/100,000) = $12,000
   Lot 4 = $80,000 x (15,000/100,000) = $12,000

E9–4

a. Maintenance
b. Maintenance
c. Maintenance
d. Betterment
e. Maintenance
f. Maintenance
g. Betterment
h. Maintenance
i. Betterment

Note: The classification of these expenditures is quite subjective. Some accountants might very well classify some of these expenditures differently. For example, the cost of the muffler in (h) could be argued to be a betterment expenditure if the reduced noise allows workers to work more efficiently, thereby increasing the productive capacity of the machine.

E9–5

		Debit	Credit
a.	Computer System	385,000	
	Cash		385,000
	To record acquisition of computer system.		

Note: Capitalizing the $10,000 of training costs could be debated. But, without incurring these costs, the computer system would not be serviceable. Hence, the training costs meet the requirement to be capitalized as part of the fixed asset.

b.

	Straight-Line	Sum-of-the-Years'	Double-Declining
1989	$ 60,000	$100,000	$154,000
1990	60,000	80,000	92,400
1991	60,000	60,000	53,600
1992	60,000	40,000	0
1993	60,000	20,000	0
Total	$300,000	$300,000	$300,000

		Debit	Credit
c.	Depreciation Expense	154,000	
	Accumulated Depreciation		154,000
	To record depreciation expense.		

E9–6

a. **Straight-line depreciation**

Depreciation per year = (Cost – Salvage value) ÷ Useful life
= (145,000 – 20,000) ÷ 4 years.
= $31,250 per year for 1989, 1990, 1991, and 1992.

Sum-of-the-years'-digits depreciation

Depreciation per year = (Cost – Salvage value) x Depreciation factor

1989 = ($145,000 – $20,000) x 4/10 = $50,000
1990 = ($145,000 – $20,000) x 3/10 = $37,500
1991 = ($145,000 – $20,000) x 2/10 = $25,000
1992 = ($145,000 – $20,000) x 1/10 = $12,500

Double-declining-balance depreciation

Date	Depreciation Factor	Depreciation Expense[a]	Cost	Accumulated Depreciation	Book Value
1/1/89			$145,000	$ 0	$145,000
12/31/89	50%	$72,500	145,000	72,500	72,500
12/31/90	50%	36,250	145,000	108,750	36,250
12/31/91	50%	16,250[b]	145,000	125,000	20,000
12/31/92	50%	0	145,000	125,000	20,000

[a] Depreciation expense = Book value at beginning of the period x Depreciation factor

[b] Book value x Depreciation factor = $36,250 x 50% = $18,125
If Benick Industries depreciated $18,125 in 1991, the asset's book value would drop below its salvage value. Therefore, depreciation expense for 1991 must be $16,250.

b. A manager should consider the costs and benefits associated with each depreciation method. The most likely benefit is the impact of depreciation methods on income taxes. An accelerated method decreases the present value of tax payments. However, there is no requirement that a company use the same depreciation method for financial and tax reporting. A manager should also consider the bookkeeping costs associated with each method. However, with computers the bookkeeping costs should be relatively consistent across methods. Finally, since the choice of depreciation methods affects net income, managers might want to consider the impact of the depreciation methods on contracts such as debt covenants and incentive compensation contracts.

E9–7

a. **Expense immediately**

Income Statements	**1993**	**1992**	**1991**
Revenues	$50,000	$50,000	$50,000
Amortization	0	0	30,000
Other expenses	20,000	20,000	20,000
Net Income	$30,000	$30,000	$ 0

Balance Sheets	**12/31/93**	**12/31/92**	**12/31/91**
Assets			
Current assets	$100,000	$70,000	$40,000
Long–lived assets (including land)	50,000	50,000	50,000
Total assets	$150,000	$120,000	$90,000
Liabilities & stockholders' equity			
Liabilities	$ 35,000	$ 35,000	$35,000
Stockholders' equity	115,000	85,000	55,000
Total liabilities & stockholders' equity	$150,000	$120,000	$90,000

Amortize over two years

Income Statements	**1993**	**1992**	**1991**
Revenues	$50,000	$ 50,000	$50,000
Amortization	0	(15,000)	15,000
Other expenses	20,000	20,000	20,000
Net income	$30,000	$ 15,000	$15,000

Balance Sheets	**12/31/93**	**12/31/92**	**12/31/91**
Assets			
Current assets	$100,000	$ 70,000	$ 40,000
Long–lived assets (including land)	50,000	50,000	65,000
Total assets	$150,000	$120,000	$105,000
Liabilities & stockholders' equity			
Liabilities	$ 35,000	$ 35,000	$ 35,000
Stockholders' equity	115,000	85,000	70,000
Total liabilities & stockholders' equity	$150,000	$120,000	$105,000

Amortize over three years

Income Statements	**1993**	**1992**	**1991**
Revenues	$50,000	$50,000	$50,000
Amortization	10,000	10,000	10,000
Other expenses	20,000	20,000	20,000
Net income	$20,000	$20,000	$20,000

Balance Sheets	12/31/93	12/31/92	12/31/91
Assets			
Current assets	$100,000	$ 70,000	$ 40,000
Long–lived assets (including land)	50,000	60,000	70,000
Total assets	$150,000	$130,000	$110,000
Liabilities & stockholders' equity			
Liabilities	$ 35,000	$ 35,000	$ 35,000
Stockholders' equity	115,000	95,000	75,000
Total liabilities & stockholders' equity	$150,000	$130,000	$110,000

b.

	1993	1992	1991	Total
Method 1	$30,000	$30,000	$ 0	$60,000
Method 2	30,000	15,000	15,000	60,000
Method 3	20,000	20,000	20,000	60,000

c. The balance sheet under all three methods report identical amounts for each balance sheet account. Since the asset was fully amortized by December 31, 1993, the method used to amortize the asset does not affect the amounts reported on the balance sheet.

E9–8

a. An asset's book value equals the asset's initial capitalized value less the associated accumulated depreciation. With straight-line depreciation, accumulated depreciation equals depreciation expense per year times the number of years the asset has been used. Therefore, the asset's book value would be calculated as follows:

Depreciation expense per year = (Cost – Salvage value) ÷ Useful life
= ($15,000 – $3,000) ÷ 5 years
= $2,400 per year.

Book value = Capitalized cost – Accumulated depreciation
= $15,000 – ($2,400 x 3 years)
= $7,800

b. Depreciation expense = [(Cost – Accumulated depreciation) – Salvage value]
÷ Remaining useful life
= (Book value – Salvage value) ÷ Remaining useful life
= ($7,800 – $3,000) ÷ 5 remaining years
= $960

Depreciation expense	960	
Accumulated Depreciation		960
To record depreciation expense		

E9–9

a. **Activity Method**
Depreciation expense per mile = ($25,000 – $5,000) ÷ 200,000 miles = 0.1/mile

Depreciation Expense	4,800	
Accumulated Depreciation		4,800
To record depreciation expense.		
Depreciation Expense	3,500	
Accumulated Depreciation		3,500
To record depreciation expense.		
Depreciation Expense	4,000	
Accumulated Depreciation		4,000
To record depreciation expense.		
Depreciation Expense	2,500	
Accumulated Depreciation		2,500
To record depreciation expense.		
Depreciation Expense	3,500	
Accumulated Depreciation		3,500
To record depreciation expense.		
Depreciation Expense	1,000	
Accumulated Depreciation		1,000
To record depreciation expense.		
Cash	3,000	
Accumulated Depreciation	19,300	
Loss on Sale of Truck	2,700	
Truck		25,000
To record sale of truck.		

b. **Straight–line Method**
Depreciation expense per year = ($25,000 – $5,000) ÷ 5 years = $4,000/year.

Depreciation Expense	4,000	
Accumulated Depreciation		4,000
To record depreciation expense.		

Note. This entry would be made each year for five years. No entry would be made in Year 6 since the truck's useful life ended in Year 5.

Cash	3,000	
Accumulated Depreciation	20,000	
Loss on Sale of Truck	2,000	
Truck		25,000
To record sale of truck.		

E9–10

a.

Item	Land	Land Improvements	Building
Tract of land	$80,000		
Demolition of warehouse	15,000		
Scrap from warehouse	(5,000)		
Construct building			$140,000
Driveway and parking lot		$22,000	
Landscaping	4,000		
Total	$94,000	$22,000	$140,000

b. Land. Land is assumed to have an indefinite life, so it is never depreciated.

Land Improvements

Depreciation Expense: Land Improvements	1,100*	
Accumulated Depreciation: Land Improvements		1,100
To record depreciation on land improvements.		

* $1,100 = ($22,000 – $0) ÷ 20 years

Building

Depreciation Expense: Building	7,000*	
Accumulated Depreciation: Building		7,000
To record depreciation on building.		

* $7,000 = ($140,000 – $0) ÷ 20 years

E9–11

a. and b.

Stork Freight Company
Income Statement
For the Year Ended______

	12-Year Useful Life		6 -Year Useful Life	
Revenues		$47,000,000		$47,000,000
Expenses				
Operating expenses	$25,000,000		$25,000,000	
Depreciation expense	1,250,000		2,500,000	
Total expenses		26,250,000		27,500,000
Net income		$20,750,000		$19,500,000

The percentage decrease in net income would be approximately 6% [i.e. ($19,500,000 – $20,750,000) ÷ $20,750,000].

c.

		12-Year Useful Life		6-Year Useful Life
Net income		$20,750,000		$19,500,000
Dividend payout percentage	x	70%	x	70%
Dividends		$14,525,000		$13,650,000

The difference in dividends due simply to using different estimated useful lives for the planes would be $875,000 (i.e. $14,525,000 – $13,650,000).

E9–12

	Debit	Credit
a. Cash	275,000	
Accumulated Depreciation: Office Equipment	300,000	
Office Equipment		500,000
Gain on Sale of Fixed Assets		75,000
To record sale of office equipment.		

	Debit	Credit
b. Cash	105,000	
Accumulated Depreciation: Office Equipment	300,000	
Loss on Sale of Fixed Assets	95,000	
Office Equipment		500,000
To record sale of office equipment.		

E9–13

	Debit	Credit
a. Accumulated Depreciation: Equipment	19,600*	
Loss on Disposal of Equipment		5,400
Equipment		25,000
To record disposal of equipment.		

* Under the double-declining-balance depreciation method, depreciation expense equals the fixed asset's book value at the beginning of the period times the depreciation factor. Accumulated depreciation was calculated using the following table.

Date	Depreciation Factor	Depreciation Expense	Cost	Accumulated Depreciation	Book Value
1/1/88			$25,000	$ 0	$25,000
12/31/88	40%	$10,000	25,000	10,000	15,000
12/31/89	40%	6,000	25,000	16,000	9,000
12/31/90	40%	3,600	25,000	19,600	5,400
12/31/91	40%	400	25,000	20,000	5,000
12/31/92	40%	0	25,000	20,000	5,000

	Debit	Credit
b. Accumulated Depreciation: Equipment	20,000*	
Loss on Disposal of Equipment	5,000	
Equipment		25,000
To record retirement of equipment.		

* See table in Part (a).

		Debit	Credit
c.	Cash	8,000	
	Accumulated Depreciation: Equipment	19,600*	
	Equipment		25,000
	Gain on Sale of Equipment		2,600
	To record sale of equipment.		

* See table in Part (a).

		Debit	Credit
d.	Equipment (new)	30,000	
	Accumulated Depreciation: Equipment	20,000*	
	Loss on Trade–in of Fixed Asset	3,000	
	Cash		28,000
	Equipment (old)		25,000
	To record trade–in of equipment.		

* See table in Part (a).

E9–14

a.

Year	Depr. Exp. Per Books	Correct Depr. Exp.	Annual Difference	Cumulative Difference
1990	$200,000	$40,000	$160,000	$160,000
1991	0	40,000	(40,000)	120,000
1992	0	40,000	(40,000)	80,000
1993	0	40,000	(40,000)	40,000

b. After adjusting entries are prepared and posted on December 31, 1992, Accumulated Depreciation will be understated by $120,000.

c. After adjusting entires, but before closing entries, have been prepared and posted on December 31, 1992, Retained Earnings will be understated by $120,000.

d. After adjusting entires and closing entries have been prepared and posted on December 31, 1992, Retained Earnings will be understated by $80,000.

E9–15

		Debit	Credit
a.	Oil Inventory (Depletion)	600,000*	
	Oil Deposits		600,000
	To record depletion.		

* $600,000 = ($2,000,000 ÷ 100,000 barrels) x 30,000 barrels extracted

	Debit	Credit
Cost of Goods Sold	200,000*	
Oil Inventory		200,000
To record cost of inventory sold.		

* $200,000 = ($2,000,000 ÷ 100,000 barrels) x 10,000 barrels sold

b. Oil Inventory (Depletion) 1,000,000*
Oil Deposits 1,000,000
To record depletion.

* $1,000,000 = ($2,000,000 ÷ 100,000 barrels) x 50,000 barrels extracted.

Cost of Goods Sold 1,300,000*
Oil Inventory 1,300,000
To record cost of inventory sold.

* $1,300,000 = ($2,000,000 ÷ 100,000 barrels) x 65,000 barrels sold.

c. Oil deposits $400,000
Oil inventory 100,000

E9–16

a. Mandel Corporation should capitalize these costs. Assets are defined as items that are expected to provide future economic benefits to the entity. Organizational costs are costs incurred by an entity prior to starting operations. Examples of such costs are legal fees to incorporate, accountants' fees to set up an accounting system, and so forth. Without incurring these costs, most companies could not be in business. Consequently, organizational costs allow a company to be in business, thereby helping it to generate future benefits. Since these costs help in generating future benefits, they should most definitely be capitalized.

b. Theoretically, organizational costs should be amortized over their useful life. In the extreme, organizational costs provide a benefit over the entire life of a company. Since under the going concern assumption accountants assume that entities will exist indefinitely, it would seem that organizational costs should be amortized over an indefinite period. Since this position is not practical, the accounting profession has decided that organizational costs should be amortized over a pertiod not to exceed forty years.

Assuming that Mandel Corporation amortizes its organizational costs over the maximum period of forty years, the appropriate adjusting journal entry for a single year would be as follows:

Amortization Expense 1,125
Organization Costs 1,125
To amortize organization costs.

c. As mentioned in Part (b), organization costs provide benefits over the life of the comapany. Under the going concern assumption, the company is assumed to exist indefinitely. If the company is assumed to exist indefinitely and if organization costs provide benefits over the life of the company, then these costs should provide an indefinite benefit. Consequently, organization costs should provide a benefit for an indefinite period of time, which implies that they should be reported as an asset (i.e. future benefit) indefinitely. But if organization costs are amortized, the asset will at some point in time have a zero balance. This situation contradicts the matching principle and the concept of an asset. The only way to adhere to the matching principle and the concept of an asset is to capitalize organization costs and not allocate the cost to future periods.

d. A patent gives a company the exclusive right to use or market a particular product or process, thereby providing it with an expected future benefit. Consequently, the costs incurred to acquire a patent should be capitalized as an asset and amortized over the patent's useful life.

e. Research and development costs may or may not provide a company with future benefits. The company will not know whether or not a particular R & D expenditure will provide a future benefit until some time in the future. Due to the uncertainty of projecting the usefuless of a given R & D expenditure, the FASB, in *Statement of Financial Accounting Standards No. 2*, "Accounting for Research and Development Costs", requires companies to expense R & D costs in the year in which they are incurred.

f. Engaging in research and development activities can lead companies to develop new products or processes that will provide them with future benefits. In such cases, the R & D costs should, theoretically, be capitalized. The R & D costs would then be allocated to those periods in which the costs helped generate a benefit. From a practical standpoint, however, this matching of costs with the associated benefits is not readily possible. For example, consider a company that spends $10,000,000 trying to develop a more efficient manufacturing process. The company's attempts end in failure, but the company acquires some new technology from its R & D activities that permit it to develop a revolutionary new product ten years later. In this case, it is clear that the $10,000,000 eventually provided a future benefit. But this information is only available with hindsight. At the time the $10,000,000 was expended, all the company knew was that the R & D project was a failure. So while capitalizing R & D costs and then amortizing the costs over their useful lives is theoretically superior to immediately expensing the R & D costs, immediately expensing R & D costs is extremely practical and lessens a manager's ability to manipulate the financial statements.

E9–17

a. (1) North Robotics should report the costs incurred in acquiring the patent as an asset. Therefore, the $50,000 legal and filing fees should be capitalized as an asset in 1990. Since it is company policy not to amortize intangible assets in the year of acquisition, the company would report the entire $50,000 as an asset on December 31, 1990.

(2) Since North Robotics successfully defended its patent, the patent is still expected to provide a future benefit to the company. Hence, the company should continue to carry the patent on its books as an asset. The amount it should report for the patent as of December 31, 1991 should be the cost of acquiring and defending the patent less the portion of these costs that have been amortized. Therefore, North Robotics should report $200,000 on its balance sheet (i.e., $50,000 in legal and filing fees + $200,000 in legal fees to defend the patent – $50,000 in amortization).

(3)		
Amortization Expense	50,000	
Patent		50,000
To record amortization of patent.		

b. (1) Since the lawsuit did not take place until 1991, North Robotics should still report the patent at $50,000 on its books. However, since North Robotics was probably aware of the lawsuit, it might want to disclose the lawsuit and the potential effect on the company's financial statements as a contingent liability.

(2) Since North Robotics was unsuccessful in defending its patent, the company no longer has the exclusive right to use or market its robotics arm. Therefore, the patent no longer provides the company with any future benefits. Since the patent no longer provides any future benefits, it should be written off in 1991.

(3)		
Loss on Patent	50,000	
Legal Expenses	200,000	
Patent		50,000
Cash		200,000
To record legal fees to defend patent and to write off patent.		

P9–1

a. Stonebrecker should capitalize all costs incurred that were necessary to get the equipment in a serviceable condition and location. The capitalizable costs are (1) the $1,000,000 purchase price, (2) the $25,000 of transportation costs incurred by Stonebrecker, (3) the $5,000 of transportation insurance, (4) the $40,000 in installation fees, (5) the $20,000 to reinforce the floor, and (6) the $10,000 in employee downtime. Some accountants may disagree with capitalizing the last two items; however, theoretically, these costs are necessary to get the equipment in usable condition. Therefore, the total dollar amount that should be capitalized for the equipment is $1,100,000.

b.		
Equipment	1,100,000	
Cash		1,100,000
To record acquisition of equipment.		

c. The depreciation base represents the capitalized cost of a fixed asset that the company does not expect to recover over the asset's useful life. Since the capitalized cost of the equipment is $1,100,000 and the company expects to sell the equipment for $100,000 after ten years, the company does not expect to recover $1,000,000 of the capitalized cost. Thererfore, the depreciation base of the equipment is $1,000,000.

d. Every depreciation method will result in the same total dollar amount being depreciated over the fixed asset's useful life. Under every method, the depreciation base will be depreciated. While each method gives rise to the same total depreciation, the timing of depreciation charges varies across depreciation methods. The straight–line method allocates the depreciation evenly across time, while the sum–of–the–years'–digits method and the double–declining–balance method allocate the depreciation base more rapidly to the early years of the asset's useful life and more slowly to the later years of the asset's useful life.

P9–2

a.

Asset	1/1/89 FMV	Relative FMV	x	Purchase Price	=	Cost Allocation
Building	$ 300,000	300/1,200		$1,000,000		$ 250,000
Office equip	150,000	150/1,200		1,000,000		125,000
Crane 1	75,000	75/1,200		1,000,000		62,500
Crane 2	75,000	75/1,200		1,000,000		62,500
Land	600,000	600/1,200		1,000,000		500,000
Total	$1,200,000	1,200/1,200		$1,000,000		$1,000,000

Building	250,000	
Office equipment	125,000	
Cranes	125,000	
Land	500,000	
Cash		1,000,000
To record lump–sum purchase of assets.		

b.

Depreciation Expense: Building	8,750[a]	
Depreciation Expense: Office Equipment	30,000[b]	
Depreciation Expense: Cranes	19,000[c]	
Accumulated Depreciation: Building		8,750
Accumulated Depreciation: Office Equipment		30,000
Accumulated Depreciation: Cranes		19,000
To record depreciation expense.		

[a] \$8,750 = (\$250,000 – \$75,000) ÷ 20 years
[b] \$30,000 = (\$125,000 – \$35,000) ÷ 3 years
[c] \$19,000 = [\$125,000 – (\$15,000 + \$15,000)] ÷ 5 years

c.

Building	250,000	
Less: Accumulated depreciation	35,000[a]	215,000
Office equipment	125,000	
Less: Accumulated depreciation	90,000[b]	35,000
Cranes	125,000	
Less: Accumulated depreciation	76,000[c]	49,000
Land	500,000	

[a] \$35,000 = [(\$250,000 – \$75,000) ÷ 20 years] x 4 years
[b] \$90,000 = [(\$125,000 – \$35,000) ÷ 23 years] x 3 years (i.e., carry at salvage value)
[c] \$76,000 = [(\$125,000 – \$30,000) ÷ 25 years] x 4 years

P9–3

a. Cost = Purchase price + Transportation + Installation
= \$900,000 + \$100,000 + \$130,000 = \$1,130,000

b. **Sum-of-the-years'-digits method**

Depreciation Expense: Equipment	432,000*	
Accumulated Depreciation: Equipment		432,000
To record depreciation expense.		

* \$432,000 = (\$1,130,000 – \$50,000) x 4/10

Double–declining–balance method

Depreciation Expense: Equipment	565,000*	
Accumulated Depreciation: Equipment		565,000
To record depreciation expense.		

* \$565,000 = \$1,130,000 x 50%

Straight–line method

Depreciation Expense: Equipment	270,000*	
Accumulated Depreciation: Equipment		270,000
To record depreciation expense.		

* \$270,000 = (\$1,130,000 – \$270,000) ÷ 4 years

c. **Sum–of–the–years'–digits method**

Cash	250,000	
Accumulated Depreciation: Equipment	756,000*	
Loss on Sale of Equipment	124,000	
Equipment		1,130,000
To record sale of equipment.		

* $756,000 = [($1,130,000 – $50,000) x 4/10] + [($1,130,000 – $50,000) x 3/10]

Double-declining-balance method

Cash	250,000	
Accumulated Depreciation: Equipment	847,500*	
Loss on Sale of Equipment	32,500	
Equipment		1,130,000
To record sale of equipment.		

* $847,500 = ($1,130,000 x 50%) + {[$1,130,000 – ($1,130,000 x 50%)] x 50%}
= (1,130,000 x 50%) + [(1,130,000 – 565,000) x 50%]

Straight-line method

Cash	250,000	
Accumulated Depreciation: Equipment	540,000*	
Loss on Sale of Equipment	340,000	
Equipment		1,130,000
To record sale of equipment.		

* $540,000 = [($1,130,000 – $50,000) ÷ 4 years] x 2 years

P9–4

a. When fixed assets are acquired in exchange for a long–term note, the fixed asset should be recorded at the present value of the future cash payments. The present value of these payments represents the cash value of the transaction today. In this particular case, the future cash flows are four payments of $100,000 each with the first payment due immediately and with the remaining payments being made at the end of each year for the next three years. The present value of these payments is calculated as follows:

Present value = $100,000 + ($100,000 x Present value of an ordinary annuity factor for i = 10% and n = 3)
= $100,000 + ($100,000 x 2.48685 from Table 5 in Appendix A)
= $100,000 + $248,685
= $348,685

Therefore, the equipment should be capitalized at $348,685.

b.

Depreciation Expense: Equipment	59,737*	
Accumulated Depreciation: Equipment		59,737
To record depreciation expense.		

* $59,737 = ($348,685 – $50,000) ÷ 5 years

c. Cash 90,000
Accumulated depreciation: Equipment 238,948*
Loss on Sale of Equipment 19,737
Equipment 348,685
To record sale of equipment.

* $238,948 = [($348,685 – $50,000) ÷ 5 years] x 4 years

P9–5

a. Dryer 45,000
Cash 45,000
To record purchase of a dryer.

b. In deciding how to account for service and repair costs, one must consider the effect of the cost on (1) the useful life of the asset, (2) the quantity of units produced by the asset, or (3) the quality of units produced by the asset. If the costs increase one of the above items, the y provide a future benefit to the company. Consequently, the costs should be capitalized and amortized over the asset's life. If the costs do not increase one of the above items, they do not provide a future benefit, and they should be expensed immediately. In this particular case, the $10,000 overhaul increased both the dryer's efficiency and useful life. Consequently, the $10,000 should be capitalized as follows:

Dryer 10,000
Cash 10,000
To record dryer overhaul.

The annual service cost of $500 and the major repair cost of $2,500 are incurred simply to maintain the dryer in operating condition, not to improve it. Consequently, these costs should be expensed as incurred as follows:

Repair Expense 3,000
Cash 3,000
To record repairs.

c. **1989 through 1992**
Depreciation expense = (Cost – Salvage value) ÷ Useful life
= ($45,000 – $5,000) ÷ 5 years = $8,000

1993 through 1996
Depreciation expense = {[(Cost – Accumulated depreciation) + Betterments] – Salvage value} ÷ Remaining useful life.
= {[($45,000 – $32,000) + $10,000] – $5,000} ÷ 4 years
= $4,500

P9–6

a. Building 1,500,000
Cash 1,500,000
To record purchase of building.

b. Building 200,000
Cash 200,000
To record new roof.

c. Depreciation Expense 50,500*
Accumulated Depreciation 50,500
To record depreciation expense.

* $50,500 = {[($1,500,000 – $540,000 Accumulated depreciation) + $200,000] – $150,000 Salvage value} ÷ Remaining life of 20 years.

d. Cash 1,200,000
Accumulated Depreciation 843,000*
Building 1,700,000
Gain on Sale of Building 343,000
To record sale of building.

* $843,000 = ($54,000 x 10 years for 1989 through 1998) + ($50,500 x 6 years for 1999 through 2004)

Note. The above entry assumes that the adjusting entry to record depreciation expense for 2004 had already been recorded. If this entry had not yet been made, the appropriate entry to record the sale is as follows:

Cash 1,200,000
Accumulated Depreciation 792,500
Depreciation Expense 50,500
Building 1,700,000
Gain on Sale of Building 343,000
To record sale of building.

P9–7

a.

	Capitalized Cost	–	Depreciation	=	Book Value
Straight–line	$150,000		$ 60,000[a]		$90,000
Sum-of-the-years'-digits	150,000		87,273[b]		62,727
Double-declining-balance	150,000		100,848[c]		49,152

[a] $60,000 = ($150,000 – $30,000) ÷ 10 years] x 5 years
[b] $87,273 = ($120,000 x 10/55) + ($120,000 x 9/55) + ($120,000 x 8/55) + ($120,000 x 7/55) + ($120,000 x 6/55)
[c] Accumulated depreciation was taken from the following table.

Date	Multiplication Factor	Depreciation Expense	Capitalized Cost	Accumulated Depreciation	Book Value
1/1/85			$150,000	$ 0	$150,000
12/31/85	20%	$30,000	150,000	$ 30,000	120,000
12/31/86	20%	24,000	150,000	54,000	96,000
12/31/87	20%	19,200	150,000	73,200	76,800
12/31/88	20%	15,360	150,000	88,560	61,440
12/31/89	20%	12,288	150,000	100,848	49,152

b. Depreciation Expense	7,500*	
Accumulated Depreciation		7,500
To record depreciation expense.		

* $7,500 = (Book value – Salvage value) ÷ Remaining useful life
= ($90,000 – $30,000) ÷ 8 years

P9–8

a. Every depreciation method depreciates the same amount over the useful life of the fixed asset. Depreciation methods only vary the timing of depreciation charges. Therefore, both the straight-line method and the double-declining-balance method will give rise to the same depreciation over the four-year useful life of this equipment. The following table shows that the total depreciation under the two methods is the same.

Method	Year 1	Year 2	Year 3	Year 4	Total
Straight line[a]	$ 3,750	$3,750	$3,750	$3,750	$15,000
Double declining balance[b]	10,000	5,000	0	0	15,000

[a] $3,750 = ($20,000 – $5,000) ÷ 4 years

[b]

Date	Depreciation Factor	Depreciation Expense	Historical Cost	Accumulated Depreciation	Book Value
1/1/89			$20,000	$ 0	$20,000
12/31/89	50%	$10,000	20,000	10,000	10,000
12/31/90	50%	5,000	20,000	15,000	5,000
12/31/91	50%	0	20,000	15,000	5,000
12/31/92	50%	0	20,000	15,000	5,000

b. Since, as demonstrated in Part (a), both depreciation methods give rise to the same depreciation over the fixed asset's life, net income over the asset's life must also be the same. Therefore, total taxes will be the same regardless of which depreciation method a company selects. The following shows that the total net income and total taxes are the same under the two methods.

Method	Year 1	Year 2	Year 3	Year 4	Total
Straight-line					
Revenues	$100,000	$100,000	$100,000	$100,000	$400,000
Depreciation expense	3,750	3,750	3,750	3,750	15,000
Other expenses	60,000	60,000	60,000	60,000	240,000
Net income before taxes	36,250	36,250	36,250	36,250	145,000
Income taxes	10,875	10,875	10,875	10,875	43,500
Net income	$ 25,375	$ 25,375	$ 25,375	$ 25,375	$101,500
Double-declining-balance					
Revenues	$100,000	$100,000	$100,000	$100,000	$400,000
Depreciation expense	10,000	5,000	0	0	15,000
Other expenses	60,000	60,000	60,000	60,000	240,000
Net income before taxes	30,000	35,000	40,000	40,000	145,000
Income taxes	9,000	10,500	12,000	12,000	43,500
Net income	$ 21,000	$ 24,500	$ 28,000	$ 28,000	$101,500

c. The double–declining–balance method is preferred for tax purposes because this method defers tax payments. Under this depreciation method, more depreciation is taken in the early years of an asset's life than in later years. Increasing depreciation in an asset's early life reduces net income which, in turn, reduces income taxes (see Part [b]). The reduction in income taxes is offset by higher taxes in the later years of an asset's life. However, due to the time value of money, deferring taxes is beneficial.

d. **Straight-line-method**

Present value = \$10,875 from Part (b) x Present value of an ordinary annuity factor for i = 10% and n = 4
= \$10,875 x 3.16986 (from Table 5 in Appendix A)
= \$34,472.23

Double-declining-balance method

Present value = (\$9,000 x Present value factor for i = 10% and n = 1) +(\$10,500 x Present value factor for i = 10% and n = 2) + (\$12,000 x Present value factor for i = 10% and n = 3) + (\$12,000 x Present value factor for i = 10% and n = 4)
= (\$9,000 x .90909) + (\$10,500 x .82645) + (\$12,000 x .75132) + (\$12,000 x .68301)
= \$8,181.81 + \$8,677.73 + \$9,015.84 + \$8,196.12
= \$34,071.50

Ellery and Son would save \$400.73 (i.e. \$34,472.23 – \$34,071.50) in taxes on just this one asset by using the double–declining–balance method rather than the sraight–line method.

P9–9

a., b., and c.

	(a) Straight-Line Depreciation (10-year life)	(b) Double-Declining Balance Depreciation	(c) Straight-Line Depreciation (5-year life)
Tax Payments			
Revenues	\$ 250,000	\$ 250,000	\$ 250,000
Depreciation expense	(10,000)[a]	(20,000)[b]	(20,000)[c]
Other expenses	(140,000)	(140,000)	(140,000)
Net income before taxes	100,000	90,000	90,000
Income taxes[d]	(32,000)	(28,800)	(28,800)
Net income	\$ 68,000	\$ 61,200	\$ 61,200
Bonus payment			
Net income	\$68,000	\$61,200	\$61,200
Bonus percentage	x 8%	x 8%	x 8%
Bonus amount	\$ 5,440	\$ 4,896	\$ 4,896
Dividend payment			
Net income	\$68,000	\$61,200	\$61,200
Dividend payout percentage	x 75%	x 75%	x 75%
Dividend Amount	\$51,000	\$45,900	\$45,900

[a] \$10,000 = (\$10,000 – 0) ÷ 10 years
[b] \$20,000 = (\$100,000 x 20%
[c] \$20,000 = (\$100,000 – 0) ÷ 5 years
[d] Income taxes = 32% x Net income before taxes.

P9–10

a. The amount that should be capitalized for an asset acquired in exchange for a long–term note payable is the present value of the future cash flows specifed in the note. Therefore, the machinery should be recorded on the books at $105,340.

b. and c.

	(b) 10–Year Life	(c) 5–Year Life
Revenues	$ 100,000	$ 100,000
Depreciation expense	(10,534)	(21,068)
Other expenses	(40,000)	(40,000)
Net income	$ 49,466	$ 38,932
Bonus		
Net income	$49,466	$38,932
Bonus percentage	x 10%	x 10%
Bonus amount	$ 4,947	$ 3,893
Maximum Dividends		
Net income	$49,466	$38,932
Dividend payout percentage	x 50%	x 50%
Maximum dividends	$24,733	$19,466

d. In general, Morley would prefer a long estimated useful life. A longer estimated useful life increases his wealth. Increasing the estimated life increases the present value of the company's net income, thereby increasing the present value of Morley's bonus. In this particular case, increasing the estimated useful life from five years to ten years increases Morley's bonus by $1,054. Further, if Morley owned any stock in the company, he would receive more dividends (assuming the company paid the maximum allowable dividends) as the estimated life increased.

e. Without restrictions on paying dividends, Weatherly could, in the extreme, sell off all of its assets and pay out the proceeds as dividends. The creditors would then be left with an empty shell and would lose their investments. The restrictions force Weatherly to maintain a certain level of assets, thereby insuring a source of funds to meet the debt obligation as it matures.

P9–11

a.

	Debit	Credit
Truck	18,000	
Cash		18,000
To record purchase of a truck.		

b.

	Depreciation Per Books	Correct Depreciation	Difference
1988	$18,000	$ 0	$18,000
1989	0	4,000*	4,000

* $4,000 = ($18,000 – $6,000) ÷ 3 years

Therefore, in 1988 expenses were overstated by $18,000, so net income was understated by $18,000. In 1989 expenses were understated by $4,000, so net income was overstated by $4,000.

c.

	Depreciation Per Books	Correct Depreciation	Difference
1988	$18,000	$ 0	$18,000
1989	0	12,000*	12,000

* $12,000 = $18,000 x 66.67%

Therefore, in 1988 expenses were overstated by $18,000, so net income was understated by $18,000. In 1989 expenses were understated by $12,000, so net income was overstated by $12,000.

P9–12

		Debit	Credit
a.	Plant Equipment	750,000	
	Cash		750,000
	To record purchase of plant equipment.		

b. JoyDon Enterprises uses the sum-of-the-years'-digits method of depreciation. This method is the only depreciation method that would result in a balance in Accumulated Depreciation of $490,000 as of December 31, 1987. The following table shows how the balance of $490,000 was obtained.

Year	Depreciation Factor	Depreciation Base	Depreciation Expense	Accumulated Depreciation
1986	4/10	$700,000	$280,000	$280,000
1987	3/10	$700,000	210,000	490,000

		Debit	Credit
c.	Depreciation Expense: Plant	280,000	
	Accumulated Depreciaition: Plant Equipment		280,000
	To record depreciation expense.		
d.	Depreciation Expense: Plant Equipment	210,000	
	Accumulated Depreciation: Plant Equipment		210,000
	To record depreciation expense.		
e.	Cash	85,000	
	Accumulated Depreciation. Plant Equipment	140,000*	
	Plant Equipment		200,000
	Gain on Sale of Plant Equipment		25,000
	To record Sale of Plant Equipment.		

* $140,000 = [($200,000 – $0) x 4/10] + [($200,000 – $0) x 3/10]

		Debit	Credit
f.	Plant Equipment	450,000*	
	Cash		450,000
	To record purchase of plant equipment.		

* $450,000 was calculated using the following equation:
Ending plant equipment = Beginning plant equipment + Plant equipment acquired – Plant equipment disposed.

g. Depreciation Expense: Plant Equipment 240,000*
    Accumulated Depreciation: Plant Equipment 240,000
  To record depreciation expense.

---

* $240,000 can be calculated in various ways; two possible methods follow.

1. Depreciation expense can be inferred from the Accumulated Depreciation accounts as follows: Ending accumulated depreciation = Beginning accumulated depreciation + Current depreciation expense – Accumulated depreciation associated with fixed assets disposed of during the period.

2. $240,000 = (Remaining depreciation base of assets acquired on 1/1/86 x 2/10)
   + (Depreciation base of assets acquired on 1/1/88 x 5/15)
   = [($750,000 – $200,000 from Part (e) – $50,000 Salvage value) x 2/10]
   + [($450,000 from Part (f) – $30,000 Salvage value) x 5/15]

P9–13

a.

Cash	325,000	
Accumulated Depreciation	240,000*	
Machinery		500,000
Gain on Sale of Machinery		65,000
To record sale of machinery.		

---

* $240,000 = [($500,000 – $100,000) ÷ 5 years] x 3 years

b.

Depreciation Expense	40,000*	
Accumulated Depreciation		40,000
To record depreciation expense for 1/1 to 6/30.		

---

* $40,000 = [($500,000 – $100,000) ÷ 5 years] x 1/2 year

Cash	320,000	
Accumulated Depreciation	280,000	
Machinery		500,000
Gain on Sale of Machinery		100,000
To record sale of machinery.		

c. **FMV of asset received**

Land	210,000	
Accumulated Depreciation	240,000	
Loss on Trade–in	225,000	
Machinery		500,000
Cash		175,000
To record trade of machinery for land.		

FMV of assets given up

Land	250,000*	
Accumulated Depreciation	240,000	
Loss on Trade–in	185,000	
Machinery		500,000
Cash		175,000
To record trade of machinery for land.		

* $250,000 = Cash given up + Appraised value of machinery given up

P9–14

a.

Drilling Equipment	625,000	
Mobile Home	24,000	
Cash	649,000	
To record acquisition of assets for drilling fields.		

b. **1989**

Minerals Inventory	187,500*	
Drilling Equipment (or Accumulated Depletion)		187,500
To record depletion of drilling equipment.		
Cost of Goods Sold	187,500*	
Minerals Inventory		187,500
To record cost of oil sold.		

* $187,500 = ($625,000 ÷ 2,000,000 barrels) x 600,000 barrels

1990

Minerals Inventory	234,375*	
Drilling Equipment (or Accumulated Depletion)		234,375
To record depletion of drilling equipment.		
Cost of Goods Sold	234,375*	
Minerals Inventory		234,375
To record cost of oil sold.		

* $234,375 = ($625,000 ÷ 2,000,000 barrels) x 750,000 barrels

1991

Minerals Inventory	203,125*	
Drilling Equipment (or Accumulated Depletion)		203,125
To record depletion of drilling equipment.		
Cost of Goods Sold	203,125*	
Minerals Inventory		203,125
To record cost of oil sold.		

* $203,125 = ($625,000 ÷ 2,000,000 barrels) x 650,000 barrels

Note: Since all the oil was immediately sold, the depletion could have been allocated directly to Cost of Goods Sold, rather than first being allocated to Minerals inventory.

c. **1989**

Depreciation Expense	3,000*	
Accumulated Depreciation		3,000
To record depreciation expense.		

1990

Depreciation Expense	3,000*	
Accumulated Depreciation		3,000
To record depreciation expense.		

1991

Depreciation Expense	3,000*	
Accumulated Depreciation		3,000
To record depreciation expense.		

---

* $3,000 = ($24,000 – $3,000) ÷ 7 years.

Different methods are used to allocate the costs of the drilling equipment and the mobile home based upon the link between the asset and the oil field. The drilling equipment is site–specific. Hence, its useful life is identical to the productive life of the oil field. Under the matching principle, the activity method provides the best matching of the costs with the associated benefits. On the other hand, the mobile home is not site–specific; it has a useful life beyond this oil field. The activity method would not be appropriate for the mobile home because the productive capabilities of future oil fields on which the mobile home may be used are not yet known. Consequently, Garmen Oil Company must select either the straight–line method or an accelerated method to depreciate the mobile home.

d. **Depletion**

1989

Minerals Inventory	187,500*	
Drilling Equipment (or Accumulated Depletion)		187,500
To record depletion of drilling equipment.		
Cost of Goods Sold	187,500*	
Minerals Inventory		187,500
To record cost of oil sold.		

---

*$187,500 = ($625,000 ÷ 2,000,000 barrels) x 600,000 barrels

1990

Minerals Inventory	234,375	
Loss on Oil Field	203,125*	
Drilling Equipment (or Accumulated Depletion)		437,500
To record depletion of drilling equipment.		
Cost of Goods Sold	234,375	
Minerals Inventory		234,375
To record cost of oil sold.		

---

* Since the well is dry, the drilling equipment will provide no future benefit; hence, the remaining cost of $203,125 [i.e., ($625,000 – ($187,500 + $234,375)] should be expensed.

1991

No journal entries are necessary.

Depreciation

Since the mobile home is not site–specific, the entries for depreciation would be the same as in Part (c).

P9–15

a. Assets are, for the most part, recorded at historical cost. The historical cost of a particular asset is constant over time. However, the fair market value of that same asset fluctuates over time. Consequently, the fair market value of assets can be less than, equal to, or greater than the historical cost of the assets at any point in time.

b. Diversified would pay more for Specialists due to synergy. Specialists' assets considered as a package are worth more than their individual value. Synergy arises because certain "assets" are not included on a company's balance sheet. Items that cannot be given a value (i.e., cannot be quantified) are omitted from a balance sheet. Examples are customer loyalty and name recognition.

c.

Assets	1,200,000	
Goodwill	550,000	
Liabilities		250,000
Cash		1,500,000
To record purchase of Specialists, Inc.		

d. If Diversified desires to maximize net income, the company would want to minimize its expenses. Consequently, Diversified would amortize the goodwill over the maximum allowable period, which is forty years. The appropriate journal entry on December 31, 1990 follows.

Amortization Expense	13,750*	
Goodwill		13,750
To amortize goodwill.		

* $13,750 = $550,000 ÷ 40 years

e. Presumably a company will not pay more for an item than the item is worth. If a portion of an item's value is due to nonquantifiable items, such as customer loyalty or name recognition, there is no reason to suspect that these nonquantifable items will decrease in value over time. Further, there is no reason to suspect that these items will not continue to provide benefits for an indefinite period of time. If the benefits are expected to continue for an indefinite period of time, then they should remain on the books as an asset. Consequently, it would appear that no expense is associated with goodwill.

C9–1

a. It will be necessary to assign a cost to the hotel and land that was sold. The cost could be established on the basis of the fair market value of the two hotels and the land, determined by an independent appraiser.

b.

Cash	110,000,000	
Hotel		75,000,000
Land		17,000,000
Gain on Sale		18,000,000
To record sale of hotel and land.		

c. For the purchasing company, it would be necessary to allocate the total $110 million cost to the hotel and land. This could be done on an appraised fair market value. The land without the hotel would be appraised first; the difference would be the value of the hotel.

d. Cost of hotel: $110,000,000 – $43,000,000 = $67,000,000

Depreciation (assuming no salvage value): $67,000,000 ÷ 25 = $2,680,000

C9–2

a. Depreciation rate = (100 ÷ 15) x 2 = 13.33%.

Year	Depreciation	Accum Depreciation	Balance
0			$850.00
1	$113.31	$113.31	736.69
2	98.20	211.51	638.49
3	85.11	296.62	553.38
4	73.77	370.39	479.61
5	63.93	434.32	415.68

b.

Cash	500,000,000	
Accum. Depr. ($434,320,000 ÷ 2)	217,160,000	
Reservation System ($850,000,000 ÷ 2)		425,000,000
Gain on Sale		292,160,000
To record sale of half of reservation system.		

c. Total accumulated depreciation = ($850,000,000 ÷ 15) x 5 = $283,333,333

Cash	500,000,000	
Accumulated Depreciation	141,666,667	
Reservation System		425,000,000
Gain on Sale		216,666,667
To record sale of half of reservation system.		

d. Using double-declining-balance gives rise to the highest gain because it recognizes more depreciation and thus reduces the carrying of the asset more than straight-line.

e. DDB: $292,160,000 – $217,160,000 = $75,000,000
SL: $216,666,667 – $141,666,667 = $75,000,000

C9–3

a. Annual depreciation charge: $75,000,000 ÷ 10 = $7,500,000
Loss on sale in 1988: $29,000,000 – [$75,00,000 – (3 x $7,500,000)] = – $23,500,000

	1986	1987	1988
Leaserevenue	$100.00	$100.00	$100.00
Depreciation	7.50	7.50	7.50
Expenses	60.00	60.00	60.00
Loss on sale			23.50
Net income	$ 32.50	$ 32.50	$ 9.00

b. Depreciation expense = (Cost – Salvage value) x SYD factor

1986:	$75,000,000 x 10/55 =	$13,636,000
1987:	$75,000,000 x 9/55 =	12,273,000
1988:	$75,000,000 x 8/55 =	10,909,000
Accumulated depreciation		$36,818,000

Loss on sale = $29,000,000 – ($75,000,000 – $36,818,000)
= $9,182,000

	1986	1987	1988
Lease revenue	$100.000	$100.000	$100.000
Depreciation	13.636	12.273	10.909
Expenses	60.000	60.000	60.000
Loss on sale			9.182
Net income	$ 26.364	$ 27.727	$ 19.909

c.

	1986	1987	1988
Straight-line (Net income x 30%)	$9.75	$9.75	$2.70
Sum-of-year's-digits (Net income x 30%)	7.91	8.32	5.97

d. Straight-line: Present value = ($9.75 x .90909) + ($9.75 x .82645) + ($2.70 x .75131)
= $18.95

Sum-of-years' digits: Present value = ($7.91 x .90909) + ($8.32 x .82645) + ($5.97 x .75131)
= $18.55

Using sum-of-years'-digits provides a present value tax savings of $400,000 over using straight-line.

C9–4

a. Nonprofit organizations are evaluated on the basis of how they distribute their funds. Requiring them to record depreciation causes several problems. It will result in a deficit of expenses over receipts if the organization maintains its spending pattern. Spending, or distribution of funds, would necessarily have to decrease if depreciation must be recorded. Further, recording depreciation may decrease the ability of the organization to raise funds through bond issuances or private donations because of the appearance of a deficit.

b. Most institutions rely on bond financing. Investors may not purchase the bonds, or require a higher return by purchasing them at a discount, should the rating on the bonds fall. Accordingly, the institutions are interested in the reactions of the bond rating agencies.

c. If the accounting rule is a generally accepted accounting procedure and a client did not comply, the auditor would be required to qualify the audit opinion to be in conformance with generally accepted auditing standards.

d. A spending limit could easily be incorporated into a bond covenant. Lenders may require that their creditors not spend amounts in excess of their receipts. If institutions fail to record depreciation and their audit opinion is qualified, their "true" spending (which includes depreciation) would be below their receipts, and they would be in violation of their bond covenants.

C9–5

a. The main issue to be considered is whether the capital expenditure is a betterment or for maintenance. If it is a betterment, the expenditure must increase the asset's useful life, improve the quality of the asset's output, increase the quantity of the asset's output, or reduce the costs associated with operating the asset.

b. The amount may be immaterial.

c. The book value of the "old" plant plus the expenditure for refurbishment will be depreciated over the estimated remaining useful life of the "new" plant.

CHAPTER 10 Current Liabilities, Contingencies, Retirement Costs, and Deferred Income Taxes

E10–1

a.

	Current Assets	Current Liabilities
	$15,000	$12,000
1.	2,000	2,000
2.	(1,200)	(1,200)
3.	0	1,800
4.	0	(2,200)*
Total	$15,800	$12,400

* In accordance with *SFAS Statement No. 6,* "Classification of Short-Term Obligations Expected to Be Refinanced," short-term obligations should be excluded from current liabilities if (1) the company intends to refinance the obligation on a long–term basis and (2) the company can demonstrate the ability to refinance the obligation on a long–term basis.

Current ratio = Current assets ÷ Current liabilities
= $15,800 ÷ $12,400
= 1.27

E10–2

a. Present value = $25,000 x [(1 + 12%) – 10/365]
= $25,000 x .99690
= $24,922.50

b. Accounts payable is not carried at its present value on the balance sheet due to materiality and cost/benefit considerations. Since payables usually turn over relatively quickly, the difference between the face value and the present value is small. This difference would be too small to influence the decision process of financial statement users, so the difference is immaterial. Further, the cost of computing the present value and amortizing the resulting discount would exceed the benefits because the discount (i.e., the excess of the face value over the present value) amount is so small.

E10–3

Since the loan must be repaid in ten years, the loan would be classified as a long-term liability. Consequently, the loan would not affect total current liabilities.

a. Current ratio = Current assets ÷ Current liabilities
= ($130,000 + $50,000) ÷ $80,000
= 2.25

Current assets cannot fall below 1.5 times current liabilities. Therefore, dividing current assets by 1.5 indicates the maximum level that Darrington and Darling can allow current liabilities to grow to without violating the debt covenant. So current liabilities can grow to $120,000 (i.e., $180,000 ÷ 1.5).

b. Current ratio = ($130,000 + $20,000) ÷ $80,000
= 1.875

Using the same logic as in Part (a), the current liabilities can grow to $100,000 (i.e., $150,000 ÷ 1.5).

c. Current ratio = ($130,000 + $0) ÷ $80,000
= 1.625

Using the same logic as in Part (a), the current liabilities can grow to $86,666.67 (i.e., $130,000 ÷ 1.5).

E10–4

	Current Assets	Current Liabilities	Net Income
Reported balances	$24,000	$15,000	$7,500
Adjustments			
Rent	2,200		2,200
Wages		4,000[a]	4,000[b]
Interest		50[b]	50[b]
Adjusted balances	$26,200	$19,050	$5,650

[a] $4,000 = $6,000 x 10/15
[b] $50 = $600 x 12% x 15/360

Current ratio = Current assets ÷ Current liabilities
= $26,200 ÷ $19,050
= 1.375

Net income = $5,650

E10–5

a. 12/1 Cash 19,250
Discount on Notes Payable 750
Notes Payable 20,000
To record loan from First Bank and Trust.

b. 12/31 Interest Expense 250*
Discount on Notes Payable 250
To record amortization of discount.

* $250 = $750 x 30/90 days

Alton Department Store should disclose the note payable on its balance sheet as follows.

Notes payable	$20,000
Less: Discount on notes payable	500
	$19,500

c. Interest rate = ($750/$19,250) x (360/90)
= 15.58% (rounded)

Check: $750 = $19,250 x 15.58% x 90/360

d. The actual, or effective, interest rate is determined by comparing the cash payments for interest to the actual cash received. The cash payments for interest equal the stated interest rate times the face value of the note. Therefore, for the stated and effective interest rates to be equal, the actual cash received and the face value of the note must be equal. In this case, the interest of $750 was deducted up front, thereby making the actual cash received less than the face value.

E10–6

a. Lacey Treetoppers has to make a total of fifteen payments of $10,000 each. As of December 31, 1990, the company has made the payments for 1986, 1987, 1988, 1989, and 1990. Consequently, Lacey Treetoppers has a total of ten payments remaining. The remaining liability of $100,000 must be allocated between the amounts that will mature within the time frame of current liabilities and the amounts that will not mature within that time. As of December 31, 1990, only $10,000 will become due within the next year. This $10,000 should be classified on the balance sheet under current liabilities as Current Maturities of Long-Term Debt. The remaining $90,000 should be classified on the balance sheet under long-term debt.

b. Current liabilities are defined as those liabilities that will be settled through the use of current assets or through the creation of other current liabilities. If a liability is to be settled through noncurrent assets or through long-term refinancing, then the liability should be classified as long-term debt. In this case, Lacey Treetoppers has basically two options in trying to avoid classifying the upcoming $10,000 installment payment as a current liability. The first option is to negotiate with the creditor to refinance the payment on a long-term basis. The second option is to intend to pay off the $10,000 using noncurrent assets. For example, the company could create a sinking fund to service the entire obligation. Since the sinking fund would be classified as a long-term investment, the corresponding liability would be classified as long-term debt.

Lacey Treetoppers may also be able to avoid violating its debt covenants by increasing its current assets to offset the increase in current liabilities. Assume that Lacey Treetoppers intends to pay off the upcoming installment payment by selling off investments in marketable securities classified as long–term. Since these securities would be sold off within one year, the marketable securities should be reclassified as a current asset. Consequently, current assets would be increased to offset the increase in current liabilities.

E10–7

			Debit	Credit
a.	(1)	Cash	200	
		Damage Deposit		200
		To record collection of damage deposit.		
	(2)	Damage Deposit	48	
		Cash		48
		To record damage repairs.		
	(3)	Damage Deposit	152	
		Cash		152
		To record refund of damage deposit.		

b. A damage deposit is collected to cover the cost of any repairs necessary due to damage caused by the tenant. Any amount collected in excess of repair costs must be returned to the tenant. So the deposit represents an amount that may have to be paid to another entity. Hence, by definition, the deposit represents a liability, not revenue.

E10–8

a. Cash	22,000	
Deferred Revenue		22,000
To record sale of gift certificates.		
b. Deferred Revenue	13,000	
Sales		13,000
To record redemptions of gift certificates.		
Cost of Goods Sold	8,000	
Inventory		8,000
To record cost of inventory sold.		

c. Ending balance = Beginning balance + Gift certificates sold – Gift certificates redeemed

1990
Ending balance = $0 + $22,000 – $13,000
= $9,000

1991
Ending balance = $9,000 + $15,000 – $20,000
= $4,000

E10–9

a. Linson Motor Services withheld certain items from Ed's pay. These items were amounts owed by Ed to other entities. Rather than Ed paying these amounts directly, Linson Motor Services acts as a collection agency. The company collects these amounts from Ed and later remits the amounts to the appropriate entities.

b. Wage Expense	3,063	
Social Security Taxes Payable		230
Withholding Taxes Payable		523
Payable to United Way		25
Savings Withholdings Payable		50
Cash		2,235
To record payroll.		
c. Social Security Taxes Payable	230	
Withholding Taxes Payable	523	
Payable to United Way	25	
Savings Withholdings Payable	50	
Cash		828
To record payment of payroll liabilities.		

E10–10

	Date	Account	Debit	Credit
a.	4/15	Income Tax Expense	17,000	
		Cash		17,000
		To record quarterly tax payment.		
	6/15	Income Tax Expense	17,000	
		Cash		17,000
		To record quarterly payment.		
	9/15	Income Tax Expense	17,000	
		Cash		17,000
		To record quarterly payment.		
	12/15	Income Tax Expense	17,000	
		Cash		17,000
		To record quarterly payment.		
b.	12/31	Income Tax Expense	5,100*	
		Income Tax Liability		5,100
		To record income taxes incurred but not yet paid.		

* $5,100 = ($215,000 x 34%) – ($17,000 x 4)

E10–11

a. Since Thor Power brought the lawsuit, Thor Power is facing a gain contingency. Gain contingencies are ordinarily not disclosed in the financial statements or in the footnotes to the financial statements due to conservatism. However, if it is probable that Thor Power will realize the gain contingency, then it is acceptable to disclose the contingency in the footnotes to the financial statements.

b. The way Regional Supply should account for this lawsuit depends upon (1) whether an adverse outcome to the lawsuit is remote, reasonably possible, or probable and (2) whether the amount of the loss, given an adverse outcome, is reasonably estimable. To record an economic event, the amount of the event must be known. If the amount of the potential loss on the lawsuit is not known, it is impossible for Regional Supply to accrue a contingent liability. At best, the company could disclose in a footnote that the company is currently involved in a lawsuit. Assume that the amount of the loss is reasonably estimable. If an adverse outcome is remote, then the company can ignore the lawsuit in preparing its financial statements. If an adverse outcome is reasonably possible, then the company should disclose the lawsuit in a footnote. Finally, if an adverse outcome is probable, then the company should accrue the contingent liability. In this case, it appears that the amount of the loss is reasonably estimable. Regional Supply must decide whether "a greater than 50% chance" of losing the lawsuit means that it is reasonably possible or probable that the company will lose the lawsuit.

c. Thor Power and Regional Supply would account for this lawsuit differently due to conservatism. Under conservatism the basic rule is "if in doubt on how to record an economic event, put your worst foot forward." In other words, record the event in a way that is least favorable to the company. Since doubt exists on who will win the lawsuit, this event qualifies for conservatism. For Thor Power disclosing or recording the potential gain would put it in a better position than not disclosing or recording it. Consequently, Thor Power should probably ignore this event for financial statement purposes. For Regional Supply, the opposite is true. Disclosing or accruing the lawsuit presents the event in the least favorable way.

E10–12

a. The owners of a company usually want the managers to maximize net income. However, the owners of a company are unable to observe the day-to-day activities of the company's managers. The owners and managers of a company also have their own goals. Consequently, the owners are unsure that the managers are taking actions in the best interests of the owners. If the owners and managers had similar goals, then the managers would be expected to take actions that the owners would approve. One way to achieve this goal congruence is to make maximizing net income desirable to managers. If the managers were to receive bonuses linked to net income, then they would be expected to try to increase net income. So a company would institute a bonus plan to try to align the goals of managers and owners.

If Stice Brothers earned net income of $130,000, then the amount allocated to the bonus pool would be computed as follows.

($130,000 – $100,000) x 10% = $3,000

The appropriate journal entry would be

	Debit	Credit
Bonus Expense	3,000	
Bonus Liability		3,000
To record bonus liability.		

b. The managers of the company are not eligible for a bonus unless net income exceeds $100,000. So if net income is only $90,000, nothing would be allocated to the bonus pool.

Assume that Stice Brothers eventually loses this lawsuit and that the company will have to pay the entire $40,000. If Stice Brothers accrues the loss now, net income will be reduced by $40,000, and no additional losses will have to be recorded when the lawsuit is actually settled. Since nothing will be allocated to the bonus pool this year anyway, accruing the loss this year does not affect this year's bonus. Since no additional losses will have to be recorded in future years, accruing the loss this year will not affect future bonuses.

If, however, Stice Brothers simply discloses the loss now, the company will have to record the $40,000 loss when the lawsuit is settled. Since nothing will be allocated to the bonus pool this year anyway, simply disclosing the loss this year does not affect this year's bonus. However, future years' bonuses could be decreased. Assume that in the year the lawsuit is settled, net income exceeds $100,000. Any item that reduces net income also reduces the allocation to the bonus pool. Consequently, simply disclosing the lawsuit could have economic consequences to the managers. By accruing the loss this year, the managers are increasing the probability that they will receive a bonus in a future year.

E10–13

		Debit	Credit
a. (1)	Cash	50,000	
	Sales		50,000
	To record cash sales.		
(2)	Warranty Expense	4,000*	
	Contingent Warranty Liability		4,000
	To record warranty expense.		

* $4,000 = 200 engines x $20 per engine.

(3) 1990

	Debit	Credit
Contingent Warranty Liability	1,200	
Cash, Parts or Wages Payable		1,200
To record repairs under warranty.		

1991

	Debit	Credit
Contingent Warranty Liability	2,800	
Cash, Parts or Wages Payable		2,800
To record repairs under warranty.		

b.

	Contingent Loss		Expense as Incurred	
	1990	1991	1990	1991
Sales	$50,000	$0	$50,000	$ 0
Warranty expense	4,000	0	1,200	2,800
Net income	$46,000	$0	$48,800	$2,800

Net income over the two–year period is the same under both methods. This will always be the case as long as estimated warranty costs equal actual warranty costs. The difference between the two methods is in the allocation of the warranty costs to particular accounting periods. Treating the warranty costs as contingent liabilities results in better matching of expenses with revenues.

E10–14

a. **Year 1**

	Debit	Credit
Pension Expense	10,000	
Cash		10,000
To record contribution to pension.		

Year 2

	Debit	Credit
Pension Expense	10,000	
Cash		10,000
To record contribution to pension.		

Year 3

	Debit	Credit
Pension Expense	10,000	
Cash		10,000
To record contribution to pension.		

b. The pension liability equals the difference between the amount necessary to fund the benefits and the amount already paid into the pension plan. In this case, the liability would be $15,000 (i.e., $45,000 – $30,000).

E10–15

a.

	Debit	Credit
Income Tax Expense	32,000[a]	
Income Tax Liability		26,000[b]
Deferred Income Taxes		6,000
To record income tax expense and liability		

---

[a] $32,000 = $80,000 x 40%
[b] $26,000 = $65,000 x 40%

b. Income Tax Expense 24,000[a]
Income Tax Liability 19,500[b]
Deferred Income Taxes 4,500
To record income tax expense and liability.

	Debit	Credit
Income Tax Expense	24,000[a]	
Income Tax Liability		19,500[b]
Deferred Income Taxes		4,500
To record income tax expense and liability.		

[a] $24,000 = $80,000 x 30%
[b] $19,500 = $65,000 x 30%

c. Generally accepted accounting principles differ from the Internal Revenue Code. The two sets of accounting principles/procedures usually yield different income amounts. However, over the life of a company, total net income should, for all practical purposes, be the same. So the total expense recognized over the life of the entity should equal the total tax liability incurred over the life of the entity. If in a particular year the tax expense exceeds the tax liability, then in a subsequent year the tax liability must exceed the tax expense to balance out. So the balance in Deferred Income Taxes represents the amount that the entity will have to pay in the future to balance the timing differences between its tax expense and its tax liability.

The balance in Deferred Income Taxes is directly linked to the tax rate. The lower the rate, the smaller the difference between the tax expense and tax liability. Consequently, there is a smaller amount that must be balanced out over the life of the entity.

P10–1

a., b., and c.

	(a) Classification		Amount	
			(b)	(c)
Item	Current Liability	Long-Term Liability	Current Liability	Long-Term Liability
(1)	X		$250,000	
(2)		X		$ 50,000
(3)	X	X	75,000	425,000
(4)	X		10,000	
(5)	X		25,000	
(6)	X		15,000	
(7)		X		125,000
(8)	X		80,000	
Total			$455,000	$600,000

P10–2

The balance sheet of Sealby, immediately after the bank loan and purchase of equipment would be

Assets		Liabilities and Stockholders' Equity	
Current assets	$ 260,000[a]	Current liabilities	125,000[c]
Noncurrent assets	1,860,000[b]	Long–term liabilities	775,000[d]
		Capital stock	1,000,000
		Retained earnings	220,000
Total assets	$2,120,000	Total liabilities and stockholders' equity	$2,120,000

[a] $260,000 = $120,000 + $140,000 in cash.
[b] $1,860,000 = $1,500,000 + $360,000 in purchased equipment.
[c] $125,000 = $100,000 + $25,000 in current maturities of the new note.
[d] $775,000 = $300,000 + $475,000 in long–term maturities of the new note.

The current ratio after recording the bank loan and the purchase of the equipment would be

Current ratio	=	Current assets ÷ Current liabilities
	=	$260,000 ÷ $125,000
	=	2.08

Declaring and paying a dividend would decrease current assets. Current assets cannot fall below $250,000 (i.e., $125,000 x 2) if Sealby is to avoid violating its debt covenant. Since current assets are currently $260,000, Sealby could declare and pay a dividend of $10,000. This dividend would decrease current assets to $250,000 and retained earnings to $210,000.

P10–3

a. (1)	Bad Debt Expense	1,000*	
	Allowance for Doubtful Accounts		1,000
	To record bad debt expense.		

* $1,000 = ($50,000 x 6%) – $2,000 Balance in the Allowance account

(2)	Warranty Expense	7,000	
	Warranty Liabilities		7,000
	To record warranty expense.		
(3)	Deferred Revenue	10,000	
	Revenue		10,000
	To record revenue earned.		
(4)	Other Current Liabilities	5,000	
	Long–Term Liabilities		5,000
	To reclassify liabilities.		
(5)	Income Tax Expense	3,000	
	Income Tax Payable		3,000
	To record income tax expense.		

(6)	Loss on Lawsuit	10,000*	
	Short–Term Contingent Liability		10,000
	To record potential loss of lawsuit.		

---

* Assumes that 60% is considered probable. If 60% was only considered reasonably possible, the $10,000 would not be accrued, but would, instead, be disclosed in a footnote.

b. Current ratio = Current assets ÷ Current liabilities
= ($40,000 + $50,000 – $3,000 + $52,000) ÷ ($30,000 + $15,000 + $12,000
+ $5,000 + $3,000)
= $139,000 ÷ $65,000
= 2.138

c. Current ratio = $139,000 (from Part [b]) ÷ ($65,000 + $10,000)
= $139,000 ÷ $75,000
= 1.853

d. The company's auditors must first consider the directives of the FASB. *SFAS Statement No. 5*, "Accounting for Contingencies," addresses contingent liabilities. This pronouncement states that if a contingent liability is both reasonably estimable and probable, then the liability must be accrued. But if the contingent liability is reasonably estimable and only reasonably possible, or if it is not reasonably estimable, then the liability only has to be disclosed in a footnote. Finally, if a contingency is remotely likely, then the contingent liability does not have to be disclosed. Since *SFAS Statement No. 5* does not provide a definition of probable, reasonably possible, or remote, judgment must be used in converting a probability estimate to one of these categories. One factor that may greatly influence the auditor's judgment is his/her legal liability regarding each classification.

Assume that the company loses the lawsuit. If the liability was considered remotely likely and, hence, not disclosed, the auditor would be legally liable to financial statement users. If the liability was considered reasonably possible and, hence, disclosed in the footnotes, the auditor could, potentially, still face legal action from the financial statement users. The users could argue that the auditor should have required the lawsuit to be accrued. Finally, if the liability was considered probable and, hence, accrued, the financial statement users were provided with the correct information and the auditor would not face any legal liability.

Assume that the company wins the lawsuit. If the liability was considered remotely likely, the financial statement users were provided with the correct information. The managers of the company would also be happy because the company was not made to appear worse off than it actually was. If the liability was considered reasonably possible and only disclosed in the footnotes, it is doubtful that many financial statement users incurred out-of-pocket losses due to the disclosure. Some potential investors or creditors might have foregone transacting with the company, but these people only incurred opportunity losses. People cannot sue for opportunity losses. The managers might be somewhat upset that the potential loss was disclosed in the footnotes. This disclosure might make it more difficult to attract capital. However, since the contingent liability was only disclosed in the footnotes and was not accrued, the liability would not affect any of the manager's contracts such as debt covenants or bonus contracts. Finally, if the contingent liability was accrued, the auditor would probably not face any legal liability because the auditor took the most conservative action. However, the managers would probably be upset. Since the contingent liability was accrued, liabilities would be increased, and the company would have to report a loss on the income statement. Accruing the liability could decrease the manager's bonus and could also place the company in default on its debt covenants.

The auditor faces two conflicting interests. The auditor must consider his/her legal liability to financial statement users. On the other hand, the manager pays the audit fees. If the auditor demands that the contingent liability be accrued, the manager may fire the auditor. The auditor must trade off these two conflicting interests in trying to decide whether or not to accrue a contingent liability. In most cases, the cost of legal liability will probably be greater than lost audit fees and damage to the auditor's reputation. In this particular case, a 60% probability of losing the lawsuit would probably be considered either reasonably possible or probable. So at the minimum, the auditor should require disclosure of the contingent liability in the footnotes.

P10–4

a.	12/15	Cash	2,100	
		Unearned Rent Revenue		1,200
		Damage Deposit		900
		To record collection of first month's rent and damage deposit.		
b.	12/30	Damage Deposit	220	
		Cash		220
		To record damage repairs.		
c.	12/31	Unearned Rent Revenue	1,200	
		Rent Revenue		1,200
		To record rent revenue earned.		
d.	1/10	Damage Deposit	80	
		Cash		80
		To record refund of balance of damage deposit.		

P10–5

a.	Cash	48.15	
	Sales Tax Payable		3.15*
	Sales		45.00
	To record cash sales.		

* $48.15 = Sales price + (Sales price x 7%)
Sales price = $48.15 ÷ 1.07 = $45.00
Sales Tax = $48.15 – $45.00 = $3.15

b.	Sales Tax Payable	3.15	
	Cash		3.15
	To record remittance of sales tax to government.		

P10–6

a. (1) FICA = Gross wages x 7.5%
= $1,000,000 x 7.5% = $75,000

(2) Federal income taxes = Gross wages x 9.0%
= $1,000,000 x 9.0% = $90,000

b. Take–home pay = Gross pay – Withholdings
= $1,000,000 – ($21,000 + $75,000 + $90,000) = $814,000

c.

	Debit	Credit
Wage Expense	1,000,000	
Insurance Withholding Payable		21,000
FICA Payable		75,000
Income Tax Withholding Payable		90,000
Wages Payable		814,000
To record wages incurred but not yet paid.		

d.

	Debit	Credit
Wages Payable	814,000	
Cash		814,000
To record payment of wages.		

P10–7

a.

Date	Account	Debit	Credit
April	Income Tax Expense	18,570	
	Income Tax Liability	15,000	
	Cash		33,750
	To record tax payment.		
June	Income Tax Expense	18,750	
	Cash		18,750
	To record quarterly tax payment.		
Sept.	Income Tax Expense	18,750	
	Cash		18,750
	To record quarterly tax payment.		
Dec.	Income Tax Expense	18,750	
	Cash		18,750
	To record quarterly tax payment.		

b.

Date	Account	Debit	Credit
12/31	Income Tax Expense	15,000*	
	Income Tax Liability		15,000
	To record income tax incurred but not yet paid.		

---

* $15,000 = ($300,000 x $30%) – ($18,750 x 4)

P10–8

a. From an accounting standpoint, the Floor Wax Shop must consider generally accepted accounting principles. The company would find authoritative guidance in *SFAS Statement No. 5*, "Accounting For Contingencies."

From an economic standpoint, the Floor Wax Shop must consider the costs and benefits of the different ways to report this lawsuit. If the lawsuit is not disclosed or accrued and the company subsequently loses the lawsuit, the company could be sued by the financial statement users. If the lawsuit is disclosed, then it is less likely that financial statement users would be able to sue the company. Also, any contracts already in place, such as debt covenants or bonuses, would not be affected by a footnote disclosure of the lawsuit. However, disclosing the lawsuit may make it difficult to attract new capital. Some suppliers may also be wary of extending credit, thereby requiring the Floor Wax Shop to pay cash for purchases or sign interest–bearing notes. In either case, the Floor Wax Shop could encounter cash flow problems. If the lawsuit is accrued, it is extremely unlikely that any financial statement users would be able to sue the company. However, in addition to the problems mentioned by disclosing the footnote, accruing the lawsuit would also affect existing contracts. Accruing the lawsuit might also be considered an admission of guilt to the court; so accruing the loss might become a self–fulfilling prophecy.

b. The Floor Wax Shop should accrue the lawsuit for two reasons. First, the contingent liability meets the requirements established in *SFAS Statement No. 5*, "Accounting For Contingencies," for accruing contingent liabilities. It is **probable** that the Floor Wax Shop will lose the lawsuit, and the amount of the loss is **reasonably estimable**. Second, accruing the loss minimizes the auditors' legal exposure.

c. The Floor Wax Shop would have made the following entry to accrue the lawsuit on December 31, 1990.

Contingent Loss on Lawsuit	896,000	
Contingent Liability		896,000
To accrue contingent liability.		

When the lawsuit is settled on August 12, 1991 for $675,000, the Floor Wax Shop should make the following entry.

Contingent Liability	896,000	
Cash		675,000
Recovery of a Contingent Loss		221,000
To record settlement of contingent liability.		

The entry to record the contingent liability on December 31 was an estimate; $896,000 was the best estimate at that point in time given all the available information. On August 12, new information became available that allowed a revision of the estimated loss. Changes in estimates are handled prospectively (i.e., in the current and future periods). Consequently, a prior period adjustment is not necessary.

P10–9

a.

Cash or Accounts Receivable	280,000	
Sales		280,000
To record sales.		

b. 5/30	Contingent Warranty Liability	3,000	
	Cash		1,350
	Parts		1,650
	To record warranty costs incurred.		
9/2	Contingent Warranty Liability	5,000	
	Cash		2,250
	Parts		2,750
	To record warranty costs incurred.		
11/15	Contingent Warranty Liability	6,000	
	Cash		2,700
	Parts		3,300
	To record warranty costs incurred.		

c. Warranty Expense	26,250*	
Contingent Warranty Liability		26,250
To record warranty expense.		

* $26,250 = 35 cars x $750 per car

d. Ending balance = Beginning balance + Warranty expense − Warranty costs incurred
= $3,000 + $26,250 (from Part [d]) − ($3,000 + $5,000 + $6,000)
= $15,250

e. Under the matching principle, all costs that are incurred in generating revenue should be matched to those revenues. The matching principle does not distinguish between costs incurred before or after the sale. Consequently, both presale and postsale costs should be matched with the associated revenue. The problem with matching postsale costs to the associated revenue is that the costs have not yet been incurred. The concept of contingencies guides the recognition of postsale costs. Only those costs that are **reasonably estimable** and **probable** are recognized at the time the revenue is recognized. In the case of warranties, a company can usually use company-specific data or industry-specific data to estimate the average cost that will subsequently be incurred to repair merchandise under warranty. However, if a company expects to incur material warranty costs but cannot reasonably estimate the amount, it is debatable whether the company should recognize the revenue in the current period. Under the revenue recognition principle, one of the criteria for recognizing revenue is that postsales costs can be reasonably estimated. If this criterion cannot be met and the amount is material, a company should probably delay recognizing the revenue.

P10–10

a.

	1990		1991	
Cash	40,000		56,000	
Sales		40,000		56,000
To record cash sales.				
Promotion Expense	400[a]		560[b]	
Contingent Promotion Liability		400		560
To record warranty expense.				

[a] $400 = 20,000 boxes x 10% x $1.00 per refund ÷ 5 boxtops per refund
[b] $560 = 28,000 boxes x 10% x $1.00 per refund ÷ 5 boxtops per refund

	1990		1991	
Contingent Promotion Liability	300[a]		400[b]	
Cash		300		400
To record payment of refunds.				

[a] $300 = 1,500 boxes ÷ 5 boxtops per refund x $1.00 per refund
[b] $400 = 2,000 boxes ÷ 5 boxtops per refund x $1.00 per refund

b. Ending balance = Beginning balance + Warranty liability – Refund payments

1990
Ending balance = $0+ $400 – $300 = $100

1991
Ending balance = $100 + $560 – $400 = $260

P10–11

a. **1986**

Income Tax Expense	14,250[a]	
Deferred Income Taxes		750
Income Tax Liability		13,500[b]
To record income tax expense and liability.		

[a] $14,250 = ($50,000 – $2,500) x 30%.
[b] $13,500 = ($50,000 – $5,000) x 30%.

1987

Income Tax Expense	14,250*	
Income Tax Liability		14,250
To record income tax expense and liability.		

* $14,250 = ($50,000 – $2,500) x 30%.

1988

Income Tax Expense	14,250	
Deferred Income Taxes	375	
Income Tax Liability		14,625*
To record income tax expense and liability.		

* $14,625 = ($50,000 – $1,250) x 30%.

1989

Income Tax Expense	14,250	
Deferred Income Taxes	375	
Income Tax Liability		14,625
To record income tax expense and liability.		

Year	Balance in Deferred Income Taxes
1986	$750
1987	750
1988	375
1989	0

b. **1986**
Same as in Part (a)

1987
Same as in Part (a).

1988

Deferred Income Taxes	250*	
Gain on Deferred Income Taxes		250
To record change in statutory tax rate.		

---

* $250 = Excess depreciation x (Change in tax rate)
= $2,500 x (30% – 20%) = $250

Income Tax Expense	9,500	
Deferred Income Taxes	250	
Income Tax Liability		9,750*
To record income tax expense and liability.		

---

* $9,750 = ($50,000 – $1,250) x 20%.

1989

Income Tax Expense	9,500	
Deferred Income Taxes	250	
Income Tax Liability		9,750
To record income tax expense and liability.		

Year	Balance in Deferred Income Taxes
1986	$750
1987	750
1988	250
1989	0

The balance in Deferred Income Taxes represents amounts that a company will, theoretically, have to pay the government in the future as timing differences, such as depreciation, between book and taxable income reverse themselves. If the government lowers the tax rate, then the tax liability in future periods when the timing differences reverse themselves will be lower than the associated tax expense recorded on the books when the older tax rate was still in effect. Therefore, the amount of tax expense recorded in prior periods was "incorrect", and the company should adjust its books for the decrease in the expense. If the misstatement is considered to be an error, then a prior period adjustment is necessary. But if the misstatement is considered to be a change in estimate (which is the more likely view), then the correction would be handled prospectively and reported as a gain in the current period. In this particular case, the gain from the change in the tax rate was $250.

c. **1986**
Same as Part (a).

1987

Income Tax Expense	13,500[a]	
Income Tax Liability		12,750[b]
Deferred Income Taxes		750
To record income tax expense and liability.		

[a] \$13,500 = [\$50,000 – (\$2,500 + \$2,500)] x 30%
[b] \$12,750 = [\$50,000 – (\$2,500 + \$5,000)] x 30%

1988

Income Tax Expense	13,500	
Deferred Income Taxes	375	
Income Tax Liability		13,875*
To record income tax expense and liability.		

* \$13,875 = [\$50,000 – (\$1,250 + \$2,500)] x 30%.

1989

Income Tax Expense	12,750[a]	
Income Tax Liability		12,750[b]
To record income tax expense and liability.		

[a] \$12,750 = [\$50,000 – (\$2,500 – \$2,500 – \$2,500)] x 30%
[b] \$12,750 = [\$50,000 – (\$1,250 + \$1,250 + \$5,000)] x 30%

Year	Balance in Deferred Income Taxes
1986	\$ 750
1987	1,500
1988	1,125
1989	1,125

If a company uses different depreciation methods for calculating book and taxable income, it is possible that the Deferred Income Tax account will remain on the company's books indefinitely. If a company continues to acquire fixed assets, the deferred income taxes resulting from new assest will exceed the deferred income taxes reversed from prior accounting periods in the period in which new assets are acquired. Consequently, the balance in Deferred Income Taxes will grow over time.

P10–12

a.

	1986		1987	
Pension Expense	20,000		20,000	
Cash		16,000[a]		16,000[a]
Pension Liability		4,000		4,000
To record funding of pension liability.				

	1988		1989	
Pension Expense	20,000		20,000	
Cash		18,000[b]		18,000[b]
Pension Liability		2,000		2,000
To record funding of pension liability.				

	1990	
Pension Expense	20,000	
Cash		20,000[c]
To record funding of pension.		

[a] $16,000 = $20,000 x 80%
[b] $18,000 = $20,000 x 90%
[c] $20,000 = 20,000 x 100%.

b.

Year	Liability Amount
1986	$ 4,000
1987	4,000
1988	2,000
1989	2,000
1990	0
12/31/90 Balance	$12,000

C10–1

a.

	1987	1986
Working Capital	255.4	243.6
Current Ratio	1.54	1.69

For both years, the company is in compliance with its debt covenant, but the current ratio as of the end of 1987 is only slightly above the constraint.

b. If the company violated the debt covenant, the lender could require that the debt be repaid immediately, or it might place some additional restrictions on the company and ask that it develop a plan to comply with the restrictions.

c. If purchased for cash, the working capital and current ratio would be unaffected, because inventory is included in current assets. If purchased on account, current assets and current liabilities would increase by $40 million. The total working capital would remain unchanged, but the current ratio would fall to 1.498, which is in violation of the covenant.

C10–2

a. The payments in advance are deferred revenues because they are collections from customers in advance of revenue recognition as described in the notes.

b.

Cash	XXX	
Customers' Advance Payments		XXX
To record receipt of cash from customers.		
Customers' Advance Payments	XXX	
Revenue		XXX
To record revenue for products shipped.		

This approach records revenue when the company considers it earned. In this case, this occurs when products are shipped.

c. The company is able to control the recognition of revenue by controlling when the products are shipped; thus it is able to directly impact earning per share. The initial receipt of advances does not affect EPS, increases both current assets and current liabilities (which may increase or decrease the current ratio), and increases the debt/equity ratio. The recognition of revenue increases EPS, increases the current ratio and decreases the debt/equity ratio. The debt/equity ratio includes all debt: current and long-term.

C10–3

a.

Warranty Expense	3,907,600,000	
Contingent Warranty Liability		3,907,600,000
To record warranty expense and liability.		

The amount is determined by estimating the amount of expense that is associated with the warranty that was extended to goods sold during the year.

b.

Contingent Warranty Liability	7,500,000	
Cash (or other payables or supplies)		7,500,000
To record warranty costs incurred during the year.		

c. If a loss is viewed as probable, and the amount of the loss can be estimated, the potential loss and associated liability should be accrued on the financial statements, and the nature of the loss should be described in the footnotes. Warranties represent a potential expense that, based on experience, is likely to occur. Accordingly, it is afforded treatment similar to loss contingencies.

d. Because the amount of contingencies can be determined by management, they would be able to directly impact the financial ratios. Because estimates are an inherent apart of loss contingencies, management is still within GAAP in recording them.

C10–4

a. 1984: Since amount was not estimable, but the loss was possible, it should be disclosed in the footnotes. No journal entry is required.

1986:	Loss on Lawsuit	9,500,000	
	Payable for Lawsuit		9,500,000
	To record liability for lawsuit.		

The nature of the loss should be disclosed in the footnotes.

1987:	Interest Expense	1,045,000	
	Payable for Lawsuit		1,045,000
	To record interest on judgment.		
1988:	Interest Expense	1,045,000	
	Payable for Lawsuit		1,045,000
	To record interest on judgment.		
	Payable for Lawsuit	11,590,000	
	Cash		11,590,000
	To record payment of lawsuit.		

b. The contingent liability would be recorded as a current liability, if it is to be paid within the time period defining current assets. Otherwise, it should be included as a long-term liability.

C10–5

a. Deferred income taxes result from the different accounting methods used to calculate taxable income and accounting (book) income, to which the same tax rate is applied. They are considered long-term liabilities because they generally take longer than one year to "reverse."

b. Deferred income taxes accumulate to such large amounts because they are principally related to firms' investments in fixed assets, which are a material component of a firm's financial statements. As firms keep growing and investments in fixed assets each year exceed retirements, the deferred income tax amount increases.

c. Debt/Total assets = \$8218.1 ÷ \$9022.7 = .91

Management could argue that it had not violated the covenant by excluding deferred income taxes, which are not *really* debt, and claiming that current liabilities are supported by current assets.

C10–6

a. Medical and Life Insurance Expense 2,260,000,000
   Accrued Insurance Liability 2,260,000,000
   To record accrued medical and life insurance expense.

Medical and Life Insurance Expense	2,260,000,000	
Accrued Insurance Liability		2,260,000,000
To record accrued medical and life insurance expense.		

b. If the company was required to accrue this liability immediately after emerging from Chapter 11, it might have forced them into violations of their new debt covenants. By recording it before negotiating new credit agreements, the company will already have the liability reflected on its books, and it will not force them into automatic violation of their debt covenants.

c. By taking the charges during bankruptcy, the company is protected from these creditors while it takes time to work out a reorganization plan. Accordingly, taking the charges during the bankruptcy proceeding allows more time for the payment of the indebtedness. Further, taking write-offs now avoids having to take them in the future, which will increase future income. Recently, the FASB has proposed requiring companies to recognize and accrue post-retirement health care costs. LTV might be avoiding taking the big charge in 1992 when the standard is planned to be a requirement.

C10–7

a. Using incentive compensation schemes provides top management with a motivation to maximize the goals of the board of directors as representatives of the stockholders. If the board of directors would like net income to be as high as possible, making a manger's pay a percentage of net income provides him or her with the incentive to maximize net income.

b. If managers are compensated with stock, they will obviously want to protect and maximize the value of the stock. In doing so, they protect themselves and also help other sotckholders.

c. Stockholders generally vote upon the provisions of incentive compensation plans. The plans are usually based on some measure of net income, which creates the incentive for managers to manage net income either through accounting methods or investment and financing palns.

C10–8

a. The company must intend to use current assts to repay the current liabilities, or intend to creat new current lliabilities.

b. The debt should be classified as long-term because it will not use current assets or creat new current liabilities to refinance it. The company will use long-term notes.

c. Such a refinancing strategy may be used to improve the current ratio and avoid violating debt covenants. The debt/total assets ratio will remain unchanged.

CHAPTER 11 Long–Term Liabilities: Notes, Bonds, and Leases

E11–1

a. Roseton Enterprises' debt/equity ratio is currently 1.25 [i.e., ($200,000 + $300,000) ÷ $400,000]. The company's loan agreement specifies that debt can be twice stockholders' equity. Consequently, the company's debt cannot exceed $800,000. Since Roseton Enterprises already has $500,000 in debt, the company can borrow an additional $300,000.

b. By definition, Roseton Enterprises will settle its December 31, 1990 current liabilities sometime during 1991. The company will probably also incur new current liabilities as of December 31, 1991. Since no information is provided as to the expected amount of current liabilities as of December 31, 1991, a reasonable assumption is that these liabilities will remain at $200,000. Consequently, Roseton Enterprises would have total debt of $500,000 and total stockholders' equity of $550,000 (i.e., $400,000 + $950,000 in revenues – $800,000 in expenses). The company could now borrow a total of twice $550,000, or $1,100,000. Roseton Enterprises could, therefore, borrow an additional $600,000.

c. At the end of 1991, Roseton Enterprises would have $200,000 in current liabilities and $300,000 in long–term debt for total debt of $500,000, and it would have $450,000 in stockholders' equity (i.e., $400,000 + $950,000 in revenues – $800,000 in expenses – $100,000 in declared dividends). The company could now borrow a total of twice $450,000 or $900,000. Consequently, Roseton Enterprises could borrow an additional $400,000.

If Roseton Enterprises declares, but does not pay, the $100,000 dividend, the company's debt/equity ratio will be affected. Dividends that are declared but not yet paid are typically classified as current liabilities. Consequently, Roseton Enterprises would have $300,000 in current liabilities and $300,000 in long–term liabilities for total liabilities of $600,000, and it would have $450,000 in stockholders' equity. The company could now borrow a total of twice $450,000 or $900,000. Consequently, Roseton Enterprises could borrow an additional $300,000. Declaring, but not paying, the dividend as opposed to declaring and paying the dividend reduced the amount of money that the company could borrow on a dollar–for–dollar basis.

E11–2

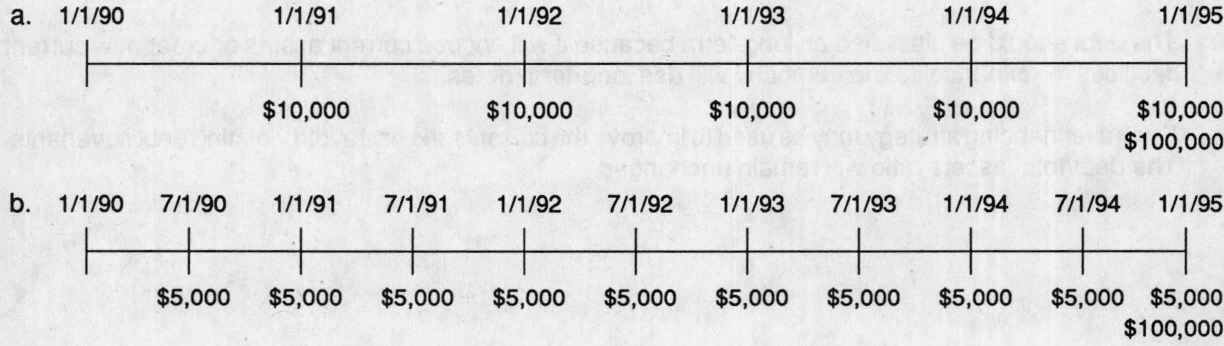

c. Total present value = Present value of face value + Present value of periodic interest payments

(1) Annual interest payments

Total present value = (\$100,000 x Present value factor for i = 10% and n = 5)
+ (\$10,000 x Present value of an ordinary annuity factor for i = 10% and n = 5)
= (\$100,000 x .62092 from Table 4, App.A) + (\$10,000 x 3.79079 from Table 5, App.A)
= \$62,092 + \$37,908
= \$100,000

(2) Semiannual interest payments

Total present value = (\$100,000 x Present value factor of 1 for i = 5% and n = 10)
+ (\$5,000 x Present value of an ordinary annuity factor for i = 5% and n = 10)
= (\$100,000 x .61391 from Table 4, App.A) + (\$5,000 x 7.72173 from Table 5, App. A)
= \$ 61,391 + \$38,609
= \$100,000

E11–3

Note	Issue Value
1	Par value
2	Premium
3	Discount
4	Premium

E11–4

Total present value = Present value of face value + Present value of interest payments

Note 1
Total present value = (\$1,000 x Present value factor for i = 10% and n = 2)
+ [(\$1,000 x 0%) x Present value of an ordinary annuity factor for i = 10% and n = 2]
= (\$1,000 x .82645 from Table 4 in App. A) + 0
= \$826.45

Note 2
Total present value = \$5,000 x Present value factor for i = 8% and n = 5)
+ [(\$5,000 x 0%) x Present value of an ordinary annuity factor for i = 8% and n = 5]
= (\$5,000 x .68058 from Table 4 in App. A) + 0
= \$3,402.90

Note 3

Total present value = \$8,000 x Present value factor for i = 12% and n = 5)
+ [(\$8,000 x 5%) x Present value of an ordinary annuity factor for i = 12% and n = 5]
= (\$8,000 x .56743 from Table 4 in App. A) + (\$400 x 3.60478 from Table 5 in App. A)
= \$4,539.44 + \$1,441.91
= \$5,981.35

Note 4

Total present value = \$3,000 x Present value factor for i = 8% and n = 8)
+ [(\$3,000 x 8%) x Present value of an ordinary annuity factor for i = 8% and n = 8]
= (\$3,000 x .54027 from Table 4 in App. A) + (\$240 x 5.74664 from Table 5 in App. A)
= \$1,620.81 + \$1,379.19
= \$3,000.00

Note 5

Total present value = \$10,000 x Present value factor for i = 6% and n = 10)
+ [(\$10,000 x 10%) x Present value of an ordinary annuity factor for i = 6% and n = 10]
= (\$10,000 x .55839 from Table 4 in App. A) + (\$1,000 x 7.36009 from Table 5 in App. A)
= \$5,583.90 + \$7.360.09
= \$12,943.99

E11–5

a.

Cash	5,674	
Discount on Notes Payable	4,326	
Bonds Payable		10,000
To record the issue of a note.		

b. Interest Expense = Book value of debt x Effective interest rate
= (\$10,000 – \$4,326) x 12%
= \$680.88

c. Balance sheet value = Face value – Discount on notes payable
= \$10,000 – (\$4,326 – \$680.88)
= \$6,354.88

d. Interest expense is computed as the product of the debt's book value times the effective interest rate. For a note issued at a discount, the book value will increase over time until the book value equals the face value immediately before the note matures. Since the book value is greater at the beginning of Year 2 than it was at the beginning of Year 1, and the effective interest rate is constant, the interest expense recognized by AAA in the second year will be greater than the interest expense recognized in the first year.

As proof, interest expense for Year 2 = \$6,354.88 (from Part [c]) x 12%
= \$762.58

This amount exceeds the interest expense for Year 1 computed in Part (b).

e. Since the note has not yet matured, the same logic used in Part (d) can be applied to this question. Consequently, the interest expense recognized by AAA in the third year will be greater than the interest expense recognized in the second year.

As proof, interest expense for Year 3 = Book value at beginning of Year 3 x 12%
= [$10,000 – ($4,326 – $680.88 – $762.58)] x 12%
= $854.10

This amount exceeds the interest expense for Year 2 computed in Part (d).

E11–6

a. Stated interest rate = 8%

Cash	5,000	
Notes Payable		5,000
To record issue of notes payable.		
Interest Expense	400	
Cash		400
To record interest payment.		
Interest Expense	400	
Cash		400
To record interest payment.		
Notes Payable	5,000	
Cash		5,000
To record repayment of notes payable.		

b. Stated interest rate = 0%

Face value	$5,000.00
Present value (i = 8%, n = 2)	
Present value of face value ($5,000 x .85734 from Table 4 in App.A)	4,286.70
Discount on notes payable	$ 713.30

Cash	4,286.70	
Discount on Notes Payable	713.30	
Notes Payable		5,000.00
To record issue of notes payable.		
Interest Expense	342.94	
Discount on Notes Payable		342.94
To record interest expense incurred.		
Interest Expense	370.36	
Discount on Notes Payable		370.36
To record interest expense incurred.		
Notes Payable	5,000.00	
Cash		5,000.00
To record repayment on notes payable.		

c. Stated interest rate = 6%

Face value		$5,000.00
Present value (i = 8%, n = 2)		
Present value of face value ($5,000 x .85734 from Table 4 in App. A)	$4,286.70	
Present value of interest payments [($5,000 x 6%) x 1.78326 from Table 5 in App. A]	534.99	
Total present value		4,821.69
Discount on notes payable		$ 178.31

Cash	4,821.69	
Discount on Notes Payable	178.31	
Notes Payable		5,000.00
To record issue of notes payable.		
Interest Expense	385.74[a]	
Discount on Notes Payable		85.74[b]
Cash		300.00[c]
To record interest payment.		

[a] $385.74 = Book value x Effective interest rate = ($5,000 – $178.31) x 8%.
[b] $ 85.74 = Interest expense – Interest payment
[c] $300.00 = Face value x Stated interest rate = $5,000 x 6%

Interest Expense	392.57*	
Discount on Notes Payable		92.57
Cash		300.00
To record interest payable.		

* $392.57 = [$5,000 – ($178.31 – $85.74)] x 8%

Notes Payable	5,000.00	
Cash		5,000.00
To record repayment of notes payable.		

E11–7

a. Total present value = Present value of face value + Present value of periodic interest payments

(1) **Discount rate** = 8%
Present value = ($5,000 x Present value factor for i = 8% and n = 2)
+ ($400 x Present value of an ordinary annuity factor for i = 8% and n = 2)
= ($5,000 x .85734 from Table 4 in App. A) + ($400 x 1.78326 from Table 5 in App.A)
= $4,286.7 + $713.30
= $5,000

(2) **Discount rate** = **10%**
Present value = ($5,000 x Present value factor for i = 10% and n = 2)
+ ($400 x Present value of an ordinary annuity factor for i = 10% and n = 2)
= ($5,000 x .82645 from Table 4 in App. A) + ($400 x 1.73554 from Table 5 in App. A)
= $4,132.25 + $694.22
= $4,826.47

(3) **Discount rate** = **12%**
Present value = ($5,000 x Present value factor for i = 12% and n = 2)
+ ($400 x Present value of an ordinary annuity factor for i = 12% and n = 2)
= ($5,000 x .79719 from Table 4 in App. A) + ($400 x 1.69005 from Table 5 in App. A)
= $3,985.95 + $676.02
= $4,661.97

b. The effective interest rate is the interest rate that equates the undiscounted future cash flows with the present value of the future cash flows. In this case, the undiscounted future cash flows are (1) the $5,000 face value due in two years and (2) the interest payments of $400 due at the end of each year for two years, while the present value of the note is the proceeds of $4,826. From Part (a), a discount rate of 10% equates the future cash flows and the proceeds. Therefore, the effective interest rate is 10%.

c. If Wilmes Floral Supplies originally borrowed $5,000, the $5,000 would be the present value of the future cash flows. From Part (a), a discount rate of 8% equates the future cash flows with $5,000. The effective interest rate would, therefore, be 8%. Anytime the proceeds equal the face value, the effective interest rate equals the stated interest rate.

E11–8

a. The building should be capitalized at the cash value of the transaction. In this particular case, the cash value of the transaction would be assumed to equal the building's appraised value. Therefore, the building should be recorded at $550,125.

b. Total present value = Present value of face value

(1) **Discount rate** = **6%**
Present value = ($693,000 x Present value factor for i = 6% and n = 3)
= ($693,000 x .83962 from Table 4 in App. A)
= $581,857

(2) **Discount rate** = **8%**
Present value = ($693,000 x Present value factor for i = 8% and n = 3)
= ($693,000 x .79383 from Table 4 in App.A)
= $550,125

(3) **Discount rate** = **10%**
Present value = ($693,000 x Present value factor for i = 10% and n = 3)
= ($693,000 x .75132 from Table 4 in App. A)
= $520,665

c. The effective interest rate is the interest rate that equates the undiscounted future cash flows with the present value of the future cash flows. In this case, the undiscounted future cash flow is the $693,000 face value due in three years, while the present value of the note is the value of the building, or $550,125. From Part (b), a discount rate of 8% equates the future cash flows and the proceeds. Therefore, the effective interest rate is 8%.

E11–9

a.

Interest expense	=	Effective interest rate x Book value of debt at beginning of the period
$8,280	=	Effective interest rate x ($100,000 – $7,280)
Effective interest rate	=	9% (rounded)

b.

	Debit	Credit
Interest Expense	8,280	
Discount on Notes Payable		1,280
Cash		7,000
To record interest payment.		

E11–10

a. **Bond A**

Face value	$200,000	
Present value (i = 4%, n = 40)		
PV of face value ($200,000 x .20829 from Table 4 in App. A)	$41,658	
PV of interest payments [($200,000 x 4%) x 19.79277 from Table 5 in App. A]	158,342	
Total present value (i.e., proceeds)		200,000
Discount/premium		$200,000

Bond B

Face value	$500,000	
Present value (i = 4%, n = 40)		
PV of face value ($500,000 x .20829 from Table 4 in App. A)	$104,145	
PV of interest payments [($500,000 x 5%) x 19.79277 from Table 5 in App. A]	494,819	
Total present value (i.e., proceeds)		598,964
Premium	$598,964	

Bond C

Face value		$800,000
Present value (i = 5%, n = 30)		
PV of face value ($800,000 x .23138 from Table 4 in App. A)	$185,104	
PV of interest payments [($800,000 x 4%) x 15.37245 from Table 5 in App. A)	491,918	
Total present value (i.e., proceeds)		677,022
Discount		$122,978

b. The balance sheet value of the liability will remain constant over the life of Bond A since there is no associated discount or premium. The balance sheet value of the liability will decrease over the life of Bond B since there is a premium associated with this bond issue. Over the life of the bond issue, the premium will be amortized. Since the premium balance is added to the face value of the bond to determine the book value of the liability, any reduction in the premium balance will reduce the book value. The balance sheet value of the liability will increase over the life of Bond C since there is a discount associated with this bond issue. Over the life of the bond issue, the discount will be amortized. Since the discount balance is deducted from the face value of the bond to determine the book value of the liability, any reduction in the discount balance will increase the book value.

c. Interest expense is computed as book value at the beginning of the accounting period times the effective interest rate per period. The effective interest rate is constant over the life of the bond issue for each of these bond issues. Hence, the only factor that could affect whether the interest expense recognized each period increases, decreases, or remains constant over the life of the bond is the book value.

As discussed in Part (b), the book value of Bond A will remain constant over the life of the bond issue. Consequently, the interest expense recognized in each accounting period will remain constant over the life of Bond A. As discussed in Part (b), the book value of Bond B will decrease over the life of the bond issue. Consequently, the interest expense recognized in each accounting period will decrease over the life of Bond B. As discussed in Part (b), the book value of Bond C will increase over the life of the bond issue. Consequently, the interest expense recognized in each accounting period will increase over the life of Bond C.

E11–11

a. These bonds will be issued at par value. Discounts or premiums arise because investors must earn the effective interest rate on their investments. Since investors cannot adjust the stated interest rate, the investors adjust the amount that they will pay for a bond. When the stated interest rate equals the effective interest rate, the bond already pays the investors the effective interest rate. Consequently, the investors do not need to adjust the amount that they will pay for the bond, and the investors will pay the par (or face) value for the bonds.

As proof:

Face value		$10,000
Present value (i = 6%, n = 20)		
PV of face value		
($10,000 x .31180 from Table 4 in App. A)	$3,118	
PV of interest payments		
[($10,000 x 6%) x 11.46992 from Table 5 in App. A]	6,882	
Total present value		10,000
Discount/premium		$ 0

b.

Cash	10,000	
Bonds Payable		10,000
To record issue of bonds for cash.		

c.

6/30/90	Interest Expense	600[a]	
	Cash		600[b]
	To record interest payment.		

[a] $600 = Book value x Effective interest rate per period = $10,000 x 6%
[b] $600 = Face value x Stated interest rate per period = $10,000 x 6%

12/31/90	Interest Expense	600	
	Cash		600
	To record interest payment.		

d. Balance sheet value = Face value – Associated discount + Associated premium
= $10,000 – 0 + 0
= $10,000

e. Present value (i = 6%, n = 18)

PV of face value		
($10,000 x .35034 from Table 4 in App. A.)	$ 3,503.40	
PV of interest payments		
[($10,000 x 6%) x 10.82760 from Table 5 in App. A.]	6,496.60	
Total present value	$10,000.00	

E11–12

a. Face value		$1,500,000
Present value (i = 5%, n = 10)		
PV of face value		
($1,500,000 x .61391 from Table 4 in App. A.)	$920,865	
PV of interest payments		
[($1,500,000 x 4%) x 7.72173 from Table 5 in App. A]	463,304	
Total present value		1,384,169
Discount		$ 115,831

7/1/90	Cash	1,384,169	
	Discount on Bonds Payable	115,831	
	Bonds Payable		1,500,000
	To record issue of bonds.		

b. 12/31/90	Interest Expense	69,208.45[a]	
	Discount on Bonds Payable		9,208.45[c]
	Interest Payable		60,000.00[b]
	To accrue interest payable.		

[a] $69,208.45 = Book value x Effective rate per period = $1,384,169 x 5%
[b] $60,000.00 = Face value x Stated rate per period = $1,500,000 x 4%
[c] $ 9,208.45 = $69,208.45 – $60,000.00

c. Balance sheet value as of 12/31/90 = Face value – Discount as of 12/31/90
= $1,500,000.00 – ($115,831.00 – $9,208.45)
= $1,393,377.50

d. Present value (i = 5%, n = 29)

PV of face value	
($1,500,000 x ..64461 from Table 4 in App. A.)	$ 966,915
PV of interest payments	
[($1,500,000 x 4%) x 7.10782 from Table 5 in App A]	426,469
Total present value	$1,272,889

E11–13

a. Market value of bonds = (\$10,000 x Present value factor for i = 4% and n = 8)
+ [(\$10,000 x 5%) x Present value of an ordinary annuity factor for i = 4% and n = 8]
= (\$10,000 x .73069 from Table 4 in App.A) + (\$500 x 6.73274 from Table 5 in App. A)
= \$7,306.90 + \$3,366.37
= \$10,673.27

Since the bonds were issued at face value, the effective interest rate on the date of issue equaled the stated interest rate, and there was no discount or premium associated with the bonds. When bonds are issued at face value, the bonds are carried on the books at face value until the bonds mature. Consequently, the book value of these bonds is \$10,000. Since the market value of the bonds now exceeds \$10,000, Treadway has experienced an economic loss. If Treadway wanted to retire the bonds, it would cost the company \$10,673.27 rather than \$10,000.00 The amount of the loss is the excess of the bond's market value over the bond's book value, or \$673.27.

b. Market value of bonds = (\$10,000 x Present value factor for i = 6% and n = 8)
+ [(\$10,000 x 5%) x Present value of an ordinary annuity factor for i = 6% and n = 8]
= (\$10,000 x .62741 from Table 4 in App. A) + (\$500 x 6.20979 from Table 5 in App. A)
= \$6,274.10 + \$3,104.90
= \$9,379.00

Now the market value of the bonds is less than their book value. If Treadway Motors wanted to retire the bonds through the bond market it would have to pay less then their book value. Therefore, the effective liability of the company has decreased, which implies that the company has experienced an economic gain. The gain would be the excess of the bonds' book value over the bonds' market value or \$621.00.

c. Companies experience economic gains and losses when their wealth changes. In the case of bonds, their market value indicates the company's effective obligation on the bonds at that particular point in time. If the market value exceeds book value, then the company experiences a decrease in wealth; if the market value is less than book value, then the company experiences an increase in wealth.

E11–14

a.

Cash	505,000	
Interest Payable		5,000*
Bonds Payable		500,000
To record issue of bonds.		

* \$5,000 = Face value x Stated rate per period x Proportion of period until issued
= \$500,000 x 6% x 1/6

b. Interest Expense 25,000[a]
Interest Payable 5,000
Cash 30,000[b]
To record interest payment.

[a] $25,000 = (Book value x Effective rate per period) – Interest payable
= ($500,000 x 6%) – $5,000
[b] $30,000 = Face value x Stated rate per period = $500,000 x 6%

E11–15

a. Cash paid to redeem the bonds = Face value x 101%
= $500,000 x 101%
= $505,000

	Debit	Credit
Bonds Payable	500,000	
Loss on Redemption	17,000	
Discount on Bonds Payable		12,000*
Cash		505,000
To record redemption of bonds.		

* $12,000 = Face value – Book value = $500,000 – $488,000

b.

	Debit	Credit
Bonds Payable	500,000	
Premium on Bonds Payable	2,000*	
Loss on Redemption	3,000	
Cash		505,000
To record redemption of bonds.		

* $2,000 = Book value – Face value = $502,000 – $500,000

E11–16

a.

	Debit	Credit
Interest Expense	4,822.70[a]	
Cash		4,000.00[b]
Discount on Bonds		822.70
To record interest payment.		

[a] $4,822.70 = Book value x Effective interest rate per period = $96,454 x 5%
[b] $4,000.00 = Face value x Stated interest rate per period = $100,000 x 4%

b.

	Debit	Credit
Bonds Payable	100,000.00	
Loss on Retirement of Bonds Payable	973.30	
Discount on Bonds Payable		2,723.30*
Cash		98,250.00
To record retirement of bonds payable.		

* $2,723.30 = Discount balance as of 12/31/90 – Discount amortized from 1/1/91 to 7/1/91
= $3,546.00 – $822.70 (from Part [a])

E11–17

a. Annual rental expense = Rental expense per car x Number of cars
= \$3,500 x 100 cars
= \$350,000

b. Present value of lease payments = \$3,500 per car x 100 cars x Present value of an ordinary annuity factor for $i = 8\%$, $n = 5$
= \$ 350,000 x 3.99271 from Table 5 in App.A
= \$1,397,448.50

Automobiles	1,397,448.50	
Lease Liability		1,397,448.50
To record capital lease.		

c. Interest Expense = Lease obligation x 8%
= \$1,397,448.50 x 8%
= \$111,795.88

Depreciation expense = Cost of automobiles ÷ 5 years
= \$1,397,448.50 ÷ 5
= \$279,489.70

Total rental expense = Interest expense + Depreciation expense
= \$111,795.88 + \$279,489.70
= \$391,285.58

d. Classifying the lease as an operating lease would give rise to both higher net income and a lower debt/equity ratio. The total rental expense under the operating lease method during 1991 would be \$350,000 (from Part [a]) while the total rental expenses under the capital lease method during 1992 would be \$391,285.58 (from Part [c]). Since the operating lease method gives rise to lower expenses than the capital lease method, the operating lease method would also give rise to higher net income. Future obligations under operating leases are not disclosed on the face of the balance sheet. Consequently, an operating lease would not affect a company's debt/equity ratio. On the other hand, the present values of future lease obligations are recorded under capital leases. Consequently, a capital lease results in increased liabilities, thereby increasing the debt/equity ratio.

e. Off-balance-sheet financing refers to financing agreements that require future payments, yet are structured so that these future obligations do not have to be disclosed on the face of the balance sheet as liabilities. If a lease is structured so that it does not meet any of the criteria for a capital lease, then it will be classified as an operating lease. Operating leases do not require any disclosure on the face of the balance sheet for the future obligations under the lease agreement. Consequently, by structuring a lease agreement as an operating lease, the lessee can engage in off-balance-sheet financing.

E11–18

a. Since the face value of the bank loan equals the proceeds of the loan (i.e., $74,694), the effective interest rate is equal to the stated interest rate. Therefore, the appropriate effective interest rate for Frederickson Motors for a twenty–year borrowing arrangement is 12%. This rate should also be used for the lease.

The annual lease payments would be an ordinary annuity for $i = 12\%$ and $n = 20$. Setting up the following formula and solving for the payment amount gives us the annual lease payment that would equate the two financing options.

$74,694 = Lease Payment x Present value of an ordinary annuity factor for $i = 12\%$ and $n = 20$
$74,694 = Lease Payment x 7.46944 (from Table 5 in App. A)
Lease Payment = $10,000 (rounded)

b. With the lease payment, Frederickson Motors would pay $10,000 at the end of each year for twenty years. With the bank loan, Frederickson Motors would make interest payments of $8,963.28 (i.e., $74,694 x 12%) at the end of each year for twenty years and a payment of $74,694 at the end of Year 20. The essential difference between the two financing arrangements is that a portion of every lease payment is applied against the outstanding principal balance, while the interest payments under the bank loan do not reduce the principal balance.

c. **Option 1**

Building	74,694	
Notes Payable		74,694
To record acquisition of a building.		

Option 2

Assets Acquired Under Capital Leases	74,694	
Obligations Under Capital Leases		74,694
To record capital lease of building.		

Option 3
Under an operating lease, the building would not be capitalized. Instead, on every lease–payment date, Frederickson Motors would debit Lease Expense or Rent Expense for $10,000 and credit Cash for the same amount.

d.

Payment	Interest Expense[a]	Principal Reduction[b]	Principal
			$74,694.00
$10,000.00	$8,963.28	$1,036.72	73,657.28
10,000.00	8,838.87	1,161.13	72,496.15

[a] Interest expense = Principal x Effective interest rate of 12%
[b] Principal reduction = $10,000.00 – Interest expense

e. Present value = $10,000 x Present value of an ordinary annuity factor for $i = 12\%$ and $n = 18$
= $10,000 x 7.24967 (from Table 5 in App. A)
= $72,496.70

The present value of the future lease payments equals the amount reported on the balance sheet calculated in Part (d).

E11–19

Total present value = Present value of face value + Present value of interest payments
= (Face value x Present value factor) + (Periodic interest payment
x Present value of an ordinary annuity factor)

Note 1

Since the proceeds (i.e., present value) equal the face value, we know that the effective rate equals the stated rate. Consequently, the effective rate for Note 1 is 8%.

As proof:

Present value (i =8%, n = 5)	
PV of face value	
($10,000 x .68058 from Table 4 in App.A)	$ 6,805.80
PV of interest payments	
[($10,000 x 8%) x 3.9927 from Table 5 in App.A]	3,194.20
Total present value (i.e., proceeds)	$10,000.00

Note 2

$37,594 = ($100,000 x Present value factor) + [($100,000 x 0%) x Present value of an ordinary annuity factor]

PV factor = $37,594 ÷ $100,000
= .37594

Examining Table 4 in App.A (i.e, present value of $1 table) for n = 7, we find that the effective rate is 15%.

Note 3

$922 = ($1,000 x Present value factor) + [($1,000 x 7%) x Present value of an ordinary annuity factor]

Since the proceeds (i.e., present value) are less than the face value, we know that the note was issued at a discount. Consequently, the effective rate must be more than the stated rate.

Try i = 8% for n = 5

($1,000 x .68058 from Table 4 in App. A) + [($1,000 x 7%) x 3.99271 from Table 5 in App.A]
= $680.58 + $279.49
= $960.07

Try i = 9% for n = 5

($1,000 x .64993 from Table 4) + [($1,000 x 7%) x 3.88965 from Table 5]
= $649.93 + $272.27
= $922 (rounded)

Therefore, the annual effective interest rate must be 9%.

Bond 1

$11,635 = $10,000 x Present value factor) + [($10,000 x 3%) x Present value of an ordinary annuity factor]

Since the proceeds are greater than the face value, we know that the bond was issued at a premium. Consequently, the effective rate is less than the stated rate.

Try i = 2% for n = 20

($10,000 x .67297 from Table 4 in App.A) + [($10,000 x 3%) x 16.35143 from Table 5 in App. A]
= $6,729.7 + $4,905.43
= $11,635 (rounded)

The effective rate per period is 2%. Since there are two interest periods per year, the annual effective interest rate is 4%.

Bond 2

$45,710 = ($50,000 x Present value factor) + [($50,000 x 4.5%) x Present value of an ordinary annuity factor]

Since the proceeds (i.e., present value) are less than the face value, we know that the note was issued at a discount. Consequently, the effective rate must be more than the stated rate.

Try i = 6% for n = 40

($50,000 x .09722 from Table 4) + [($50,000 x 4.5%) x 15.04630 from Table 5]
= $4,861 + $33,854
= $38,715

Try i = 5% for n = 40

($50,000 x .14205 from Table 4) + [($50,000 x 4.5%) x 17.15909 from Table 5]
= $7,102.50 + $38,607.95
= $45,710 (rounded)

The effective rate per period is 5%. Since there are two interest periods per year, the annual effective interest rate is 10%.

E11–20

a. Assume 1 bond with a face value of $1,000.

Present value = ($1,000 x Present value factor for n = 16)
+ [($1,000 x 4%) x Present value of an ordinary annuity factor for n =16]

($1,000 x 89.16%) = ($1,000 x Present value factor for n = 16) + [($1,000 x 4%)
x Present value of an ordinary annuity factor for n =16]

Try i = 6% per period for 16 periods (i.e., an annual return of 12%)

($1,000 x .39365 from Table 4) + [($1,000 x 4%) x 10.10590 from Table 5]
= $393.65 + $404.24
= $797.89

To earn an annual return of 12% on your investment, you would not be willing to pay more than $797.89. Since the bonds are selling for $891.60 (i.e., $1,000 x 89.16%), you would not be be able to earn your desired return, and you should not purchase these bonds.

b. Since the present value is less than the face value, the bonds are being issued at a discount. Consequently, the effective interest rate is greater than the stated rate but less than an annual rate of 12%

Try i = 5% for n = 16

($1,000 x .45811 from Table 4) + [($1,000 x 4%) x 10.83777 from Table 5]
= $458.11 + $433.51
= $891.62

The effective rate per period is 5%. Since there are two interest periods per year, the annual effective interest rate is 10%. At this rate, you would be indifferent to purchasing these bonds.

P11–1

a. The present value of the future cash flows of this note equals $20,000. Since the effective rate of 12% equals the stated rate of 12%, the note will be issued at par value. Consequently, the face value of this note would be $20,000.

b. The present value of the future cash flows of this note equals $20,000. Since the effective rate of 12% exceeds the stated rate of 0%, the note will be issued at a discount. The task is to determine what amount of cash paid at the end of two years discounted at 12% would equal $20,000. In other words,

$20,000 = (Face value x Present value factor for i = 12%, n = 2)
= Face value x .79719 (from Table 4 in App. A)
Face value = $25,088 (rounded)

Consequently, the face value of this note would be $25,088.

c. **Note A**

Cash	20,000	
Notes Payable		20,000
To record issue of note payable for cash.		

Note B

Cash	20,000	
Discount on Notes Payable	5,088	
Notes Payable		25,088
To record issue of note payable for cash.		

d. **Note A**

Account	Debit	Credit
Interest Expense	2,400*	
Cash		2,400*
To record interest payment.		

* $2,400 = $20,000 x 12%

Account	Debit	Credit
Notes Payable	20,000	
Cash		20,000
To record principal repayment on note payable.		

Note B

Account	Debit	Credit
Interest Expense	2,688*	
Discount on Notes Payable		2,688
To amortize discount on notes payable.		

* $2,688 = Book value x Effective rate = [$25,088 – ($5,088 – $2,400)] x 12%

Account	Debit	Credit
Notes Payable	25,088.00	
Cash		25,088.00
To record principal repayment on note payable.		

P11–2

a. The bonds will be issued at a discount. The bond market has determined that purchasers of Hartl Enterprises' bonds should earn a return on their investment of 12%. However, Hartl Enterprises is only offering interest equal to 10%. Since the stated interest rate cannot be changed, the only way that the investors can earn their 12% return is to invest a smaller amount in Hartl Enterprises, but still receive the same future cash flows. Consequently, the bonds will be issued at a price that allows the investors to earn a return of exactly 12% on their investment.

b.

Face value		$5,000
Present value (i = 6%, n = 20)		
PV of face value		
($5,000 x .31180 from Table 4 in App. A)	$1,559	
PV of interest payments		
[($5,000 x 5%) x 11.46992 from Table 5 in App. A]	2,867	
Total present value		4,426
Discount		$ 574

Account	Debit	Credit
Cash	4,426	
Discount on Bonds Payable	574	
Bonds Payable		5,000
To record issue of bonds.		

c. Interest Expense 132.78[a]
Discount on Bonds Payable 7.78[b]
Interest Payable 125.00[c]
To accrue interest payable.

---

[a] $132.78 = Book value x Effective rate per period x Portion of period outstanding
= $4,426 x 6% x 1/2

[b] $7.78 = Interest expense – Interest payable

[c] $125.00 = Face value x Stated rate per period x Portion of period outstanding
= $5,000 x 5% x 1/2

d. Interest Expense 132.78
Interest Payable 125.00
Discount on Bonds Payable 7.78
Cash 250.00
To record interest payment.

P11–3

a. L–T debt/equity ratio = Total long–term liabilities ÷ Total stockholders' equity
= $40,000 ÷ $100,000
= 0.4

b. Proceeds = Present value of future cash flows discounted at 11% for 5 periods
= $40,000 x .59345 (from Table 4 in App.A)
= $23,738

If Connerty Corporation borrows this $40,000, its L–T debt/equity ratio would be .637 [i.e., ($40,000 + $23,738) ÷ $100,000].

c. Proceeds = Present value of future cash flows discounted at 4% for 40 periods
= Present value of the face value + Present value of interest payments
= ($40,000 x .20829 from Table 4 in App. A) + [($40,000 x 5%) x 19.79277 (from Table 5 in App. A
= $8,331.60 + $39,585.54
= $47,917.14

If Connerty Corporation issues these bonds, its L–T debt/equity ratio would be .879 [i.e., ($40,000.00 + $47,917.14) ÷ $100,000].

P11–4

a. **Note A**

Face value		$10,000
Present value (*i* = 12%, *n* = 5)		
PV of face value		
($10,000 x .56743 from Table 4 in App A)	$5,674	
PV of interest payments		
[($10,000 x 0%) x 3.60478 from Table 5 in App. A]	0	
Total present value (i.e., proceeds)		5,674
Discount		$ 4,326

Note B		
Face value		$35,000
Present value (i = 9%, n = 7)		
PV of face value		
($35,000 x .54703 from Table 4)	$19,145	
PV of interest payments		
[($35,000 x 6%) x 5.03295 from Table 5]	10,569	
Total present value (i.e., proceeds)		29,714
Discount		$ 5,286

Note C		
Face value		$50,000
Present value (i = 5%, n = 20)		
PV of face value		
($50,000 x .37689 from Table 4)	$18,844.50	
PV of interest payments		
[($50,000 x 5%) x 12.46221 from Table 5]	31,155.50	
Total present value (i.e., proceeds)		50,000
Discount/premium		$ 0

b. **Note A**

Cash	5,674	
Discount on Notes Payable	4,326	
Notes Payable		10,000
To record issue of note payable for cash.		

Note B

Cash	29,714	
Discount on Notes Payable	5,286	
Notes Payable		35,000
To record issue of note payable for cash.		

Note C

Cash	50,000	
Notes Payable		50,000
To record issue of note payable for cash.		

c.

Interest Expense	2,500.00	
Cash		2,500.00
To record interest payment.		

d. **Note B**

Interest Expense	2,674.26[a]	
Discount on Notes Payable		574.26[b]
Cash		2,100.00[c]
To record interest payment.		

---

[a] $2,674.26 = Book value x Effective rate per period =($35,000 – $5,286) x 9%
[b] $74.26 = Interest expense – Interest payment
[c] $2,100.00 = Face value x Stated rate per period = $35,000 x 6%

Note C

Interest Expense	2,500.00	
Cash		2,500.00
To record interest payment.		

e.

Interest Expense	680.88*	
Discount on Notes Payable		680.00
To amortize discount on notes payable.		

* $680.88 = Book value x Effective rate per period =($10,000 – $4,326) x 12%

P11–5

a. The building should be capitalized at the sum of the present value of both notes payable. The present value of the notes would be computed as follows.

Note 1

Present value = Present value of face value discounted at 8% for 6 periods
= $465,000 x .63017 (from Table 4 in App. A)
= $293,029.05

Note 2

Present value = (Present value of the face value discounted 8% for 3 periods)
+ (Present value of the interest payments discounted 8% for 3 periods)
= ($500,000 x .79383 from Table 4) + [($500,000 x 9%) x 2.57710 from Table 5]
= $396,915.00 + $115,969.50
= $512,884.50

Total present value = $293,029.05 + $512,884.50
= $805,913.55

b.

Building	805,913.55	
Discount on Notes Payable (for Note 1)	171,970.95[a]	
Premium on Notes Payable (for Note 2)		12,884.50[b]
Notes Payable		965,000.00
To record purchase of building in exchange for notes.		

[a] $155,170.50 = Face value – Present value = $465,000.00 – $293,029.05
[b] $12,884.50 = Present value – Face value = $512,884.50 – $500,000.00

c. **Note 1**

Interest Expense	23,442.32*	
Discount on Notes Payable		23,442.32
To amortize discount on notes.		

* $23,442.32 = Book value x Effective interest rate = ($465,000.00 – $171,970.05) x 8%

Note 2

Interest Expense	41,030.76[a]	
Premium on Notes Payable	3,969.24[b]	
Cash		45,000.00[c]
To record interest payment.		

---

[a] $41,030.76 = Book value x Effective interest rate = ($500,000.00 + $12,884.50) x 8%
[b] $3,969.24 = Interest payment – Interest expense = $45,000.00 – $41,030.76
[c] $45,000.00 = Face value x Stated interest rate = $500,000 x 9%

P11–6

a. **The effective interest rate can be calculated in two ways. The first way is by solving for *i* in each of the following equations.**

Note A: $37,566 = $50,000 x $(1 + i)^{-3}$
Note B: $50,000 = [$50,000 x $(1 + i)^{-3}$] + {($50,000 x 10%) x {[1 – $(1 + i)^{-3}$] ÷ *i* }}
Note C: $45,027 = [$50,000 x $(1 + i)^{-3}$] + {($50,000 x 10%) x {[1 – $(1 + i)^{-3}$] ÷ *i* }}

The second way is by trial and error. Simply plug an interest rate into the equations above until the right–hand side of the equation equals the left–hand side. The annual effective interest rate for each note is 10%.

b.

	Interest Expense (Note A) [a]	**Interest Expense (Note B)** [b]	**Interest Expense (Note C)** [c]
Year 1	$ 3,756.60	$ 5,000.00	$ 4,502.70
Year 2	4,132.26	5,000.00	4,652.97
Year 3	4,545.14	5,000.00	4,817.33
Total	$12,434.00	$15,000.00	$13,973.00

Interest expense = Book value x Effective rate = (Face value – Discount) x Effective rate

---

[a] $3,756.60 = ($50,000 – $12,434) x 10%
$4,132.26 = [$50,000 – ($12,434 – $3,756.60)] x 10%
$4,545.14 = [$12,434 – ($3,576.60 + $4,132.26)]}

[b] $5,000.00 = ($50,000 – 0) x 10%

[c] $4,502.70 = ($50,000 – $4,973) x 10%
$4,652.97 = {$50,000 – [$4973 – ($4,502.70 – $3,000.00)] x 10%
$4,817.33 = {$4,973 – [($4,502.70 – $3,000.00) + ($4,652.97 – $3,000.00)]

c. **Note A**

	Return	**Expense**	**Income**
Year 1	$4,507.92[a]	$3,756.60	$ 751.32
Year 2	5,048.87[b]	4,132.26	916.61
Year 3	5,654.73[c]	4,545.14	1,109.59

Note: The following answers assume that any money generated from investing the proceeds is reinvested at 12%.

---

[a] $4,507.92 = $37,566 x 12%
[b] $5,048.87 = ($37,566 + $4,507.92) x 12%
[c] $5,654.73 = ($37,566 + $4,507.92 + $5,048.87) x 12%

Note B

	Return	Expense	Income
Year 1	$6,000.00[a]	$5,000.00	$1,000.00
Year 2	6,720.00[b]	5,000.00	1,720.00
Year 3	7,526.40[c]	5,000.00	2,526.40

[a] $6,000.00 = $50,000 x 12%
[b] $6,720.00 = ($50,000 + $6,000) x 12%
[c] $7,526.40 = ($50,000 + $6,000 + $6,720) x 12%

Note C

	Return	Expense	Income
Year 1	$5,403.24[a]	$4,502.70	$ 900.54
Year 2	6,051.63[b]	4,652.97	1,398.66
Year 3	6,777.82[c]	4,817.33	1,960.49

[a] $5,403.24 = $45,027 x 12%
[b] $6,051.63 = ($45.027 + $5,403.24) x 12%
[c] $6,777.82 = ($45.027 + $5,403.24 + $6,051.63) x 12%

d. Total debt = Current liabilities as of 12/31/90 + (L–T liabilities as of 12/31/90 + Face value of notes payable – Discount balance)

Total stockholders' equity = Stockholders' equity as of 12/31/90 + Net income

Debt/equity ratio = Total debt ÷ Total stockholders' equity

	Debt/equity (Note A)	Debt/equity (Note B)	Debt/equity (Note C)
12/31/91	4.270	4.516	4.418
12/31/92	4.277	4.279	4.278
12/31/93	4.271	3.972	4.086

e. Cherrington Sons must consider at least four factors in deciding which note to issue. First, the company must consider the income that can be earned from the proceeds. Since Note B provides the largest proceeds, this note provides the highest net income. Second, the company must consider the cash outflow effects of each note. If the company did not have sufficient cash on hand to meet an interest or principal payment, it could be forced into bankruptcy. Since each note requires a payment at maturity of $50,000, the only difference between the notes is the periodic interest payments. In this case, Note A requires the lowest interest payments. Third, the company must consider the immediate effects on its debt/equity ratio. If the company has any existing debt with debt agreements, one of the notes may cause the company to violate the debt agreement. In this case, Note A results in the lowest current debt/equity ratio. Finally, the company must consider the trend in the debt/equity ratio over time. If the company needs or desires to issue additional debt in the future, it might be constrained by its future debt/equity ratio. Creditors might be wary of a company with too high of a debt/equity ratio. In this case, the decrease in the debt/equity ratio is greatest for Note B.

P11–7

a. The amount of interest payments = Face value of debt x Stated interest rate
= $800,000 x 10%
= $80,000

b. When the note payable was issued, the stated interest rate did not equal the effective interest rate; the effective interest rate exceeded the stated interest rate. Consequently, the proceeds from the note were less than par value, so that the entity loaning to Rix Driving Range and Health Club would actually earn the effective interest rate on its money. The excess of the face value over the proceeds gave rise to the Discount on Notes Payable and, from Rix's viewpoint, this account effectively represents prepaid interest. Over the life of the note, this discount will be amortized to Interest Expense. Consequently, the difference between the balance in Interest Expense and the cash paid out for interest payments represents the amortization of the Discount on Notes Payable.

c. Interest expense = Book value at beginning of the period x Effective interest rate
$95,000 = ($800,000 – $70,000) x Effective interest rate
Rate = 13%

d.

Interest Expense	95,000	
Discount on Notes Payable		15,000
Cash		80,000
To record interest payment.		

P11–8

a.

Face value		$10,000
Present value (*i* = 10%, *n* = **30**)		
PV of cash payment at maturity ($10,000 x .05731 from Table 4 in App. A)	$ 573.10	
PV of cash interest payments [($10,000 x 9%) x 9.42691 from Table 5 in App. A]	8,484.21	
Total present value		9,057.31
Discount on bonds		$ 942.69

b.

Face value		$10,000
Present value (*i* = 10%, *n* = **29**)		
PV of cash payment at maturity ($10,000 x .06304 from Table 4)	$ 630.40	
PV of cash interest payments [($10,000 x 9%) x 9.36961 from Table 5]	8,432.64	
Total present value		9,063.04
Discount on bonds		$ 936.96

The present value of the cash flows on these bonds as of December 31, 1990, using the effective interest rate on the date the bonds were originally issued, represents the book value of the bonds as of December 31, 1990.

c. The difference of $5.73 in present values from June 30, 1990 and December 31, 1990 represents the change in book value of these bonds for this six–month period. The change in book value would be captured by the amortization of the Discount on Bonds Payable account.

d.

Interest Expense	905.73[a]	
Discount on Bonds Payable		5.73[b]
Cash		900.00[c]
To record interest payment.		

[a] $905.73 = Book Value x Effective rate per period = $9,057.31 x 10%
[b] $5.73 = Interest Expense – Interest payment
[c] $900.00 = Face value x Stated rate per period = $10,000 x 9%

The amount of discount on bonds payable is identical in Part (c) and Part (d). Under the effective–interest method, bonds are carried on the balance sheet at their present value (based upon the effective rate at the initial date of issue) at that particular point in time. Hence, it makes no difference if one computes the present value of the cash outflows associated with bonds or applies the effective–interest method; both methods will yield identical financial statements.

P11–9

a. To compute the amount of money that Ross Running Shoes must invest on June 30, 1990, the future cash flows must be discounted at the investment rate of 8%. Since the investment rate is an annual rate, and interest is paid semi–annually, the rate must be adjusted to a six–month rate of 4%. Therefore, i = 4% and n = 6.

Present value = Present value of face value + Present value of interest payments
= ($5,000 x .79031 from Table 4 in App. A) + [($5,000 x 5%) x 5.24214 from Table 5 in App. A]
= 3,951.55 + $1,310.50
= $5,262.00 (rounded)

b.

Interest Expense	210.48[a]	
Premium on Notes Payable	39.52[b]	
Cash		250.00[c]
To record interest payment.		

[a] $210.48 = Book Value x Effective rate per period = ($5,000 + $262) x 4%
[b] $39.52 = Interest expense – Interest payment
[c] $250.00 = Face value x Stated rate per period = $5,000 x 5%

c.

Interest Expense	206.33[a]	
Premium on Notes Payable	43.67[b]	
Cash		250.00[c]
To record interest payment.		

[a] $206.33 = Interest payment – Premium amortization
[b] $43.67 = Total premium ÷ Number of 6–month periods = $262.00 ÷ 6 periods
[c] $250.00 = Face value x Stated rate per period = $5,000 x 5%

d. Under the effective–interest method, the company will recognize interest expense during 1990 of $210.48 (from Part [b]). Under the straight–line method, the company will recognize interest expense during 1990 of $206.33 (from Part [c]). Consequently, the straight–line method results in lower expenses and, hence, higher net income than the effective–interest method in the early periods of a note issued at a premium.

e. Over the life of a note or bond, both the effective–interest method and the straight–line method will amortize the entire discount or premium balance. Consequently, over the life of a note or bond, both methods will amortize exactly the same amount of discount or premium. As noted in Part (d), for notes issued at a premium, the straight–line method will recognize lower interest expense than the effective–interest method in the early years of the note's life. This "excess" interest expense recognized under the effective–interest method will eventually have to be offset if both methods are to recognize the same amount of interest expense over the life of the note. To offset this "excess" interest expense, the straight–line method must recognize higher interest expense in the later years of a note issued at a premium than the effective–interest method would recognize. Consequently, the effective–interest method will recognize lower interest expense and, hence, higher net income in the later years of a note issued at a premium.

P11–10

a. **Note A**

1/1/90

Present value (i = 10%, n = 3)	
PV of face value ($1,000 x .75132)	$751.32
PV of interest payment [($1,000 x 8%) x 2.48685]	198.95
Total present value	$950.27

12/31/90

Present value (i = 10%, n = 2)	
PV of face value ($1,000 x .82645)	$826.45
PV of interest payment [($1,000 x 8%) x 1.73554]	138.85
Total present value	$965.30

12/31/91

Present value (i = 10%, n = 1)	
PV of face value ($1,000 x .90909)	$909.09
PV of interest payment [($1,000 x 8%) x .90909]	72.73
Total present value	$981.82

Note B

1/1/90

Present value (i = 10%, n = 3)	
PV of face value ($1,000 x .75132)	$ 751.32
PV of interest payment [($1,000 x 10%) x 2.48685]	248.68
Total present value	$1,000.00

12/31/90

Present value (i = 10%, n = 2)	
PV of face value ($1,000 x .82645)	$ 826.45
PV of interest payment [($1,000 x 10%) x 1.73554]	173.55
Total present value	$1,000.00

12/31/91

Present value (i = 10%, n = 1)	
PV of face value ($1,000 x .90909)	$ 909.09
PV of interest payment [($1,000 x 10%) x .90909]	90.91
Total present value	$1,000.00

Note C

1/1/90

Present value (i = 8%, n = 3)	
PV of face value ($1,000 x ..79383)	$ 793.83
PV of interest payment [($1,000 x 10%) x 2.57710]	257.71
Total present value	$1,051.54

12/31/90

Present value (i = 10%, n = 2)	
PV of face value ($1,000 x .85734)	$ 857.34
PV of interest payment [($1,000 x 10%) x 1.78326]	178.33
Total present value	$1,035.67

12/31/91

Present value (i = 10%, n = 1)	
PV of face value ($1,000 x .92593)	$ 925.93
PV of interest payment [($1,000 x 10%) x .92593]	92.59
Total present value	$1,018.52

b.

Date	Interest Expense	Payment Amount	Disc/Prem Amort	Face Value	Disc/Prem Balance	Book Value
Note A						
1/1/90				$1,000.00	$49.73	$950.27
12/31/90	$95.03	$80.00	$15.03	1,000.00	34.70	965.30
12/31/91	96.53	80.00	16.53	1,000.00	18.17	981.83
12/31/92	98.17	80.00	18.17	1,000.00	0.00	1,000.00
Note B						
1/1/90				1,000.00	0.00	1,000.00
12/31/90	100.00	100.00	0.00	1,000.00	0.00	1,000.00
12/31/91	100.00	100.00	0.00	1,000.00	0.00	1,000.00
12/31/92	100.00	100.00	0.00	1,000.00	0.00	1,000.00
Note C						
1/1/90				1,000.00	51.54	1,051.54
12/31/90	84.12	100.00	15.88	1,000.00	35.66	1,035.66
12/31/91	82.85	100.00	17.15	1,000.00	18.52	1,018.52
12/31/92	81.48	100.00	18.52	1,000.00	0.00	1,000.00

c.

Date	Interest Expense	Payment Amount	Disc/Prem Amort	Face Value	Disc/Prem Balance	Book Value
Note A						
1/1/90				$1,000.00	$49.73	$950.27
12/31/90	$96.58	$80.00	$16.58	1,000.00	33.15	966.85
12/31/91	96.58	80.00	16.58	1,000.00	16.57	983.43
12/31/92	96.57	80.00	16.57	1,000.00	0.00	1,000.00
Note B						
1/1/90				1,000.00	0.00	1,000.00
12/31/90	100.00	100.00	0.00	1,000.00	0.00	1,000.00
12/31/91	100.00	100.00	0.00	1,000.00	0.00	1,000.00
12/31/92	100.00	100.00	0.00	1,000.00	0.00	1,000.00
Note C						
1/1/90				1,000.00	51.54	1,051.54
12/31/90	82.82	100.00	17.18	1,000.00	34.36	1,034.36
12/31/91	82.82	100.00	17.18	1,000.00	17.18	1,017.18
12/31/92	82.82	100.00	17.18	1,000.00	0.00	1,000.00

d. Compare Part (b) to Part (a) and Part (c) to Part (a). The effective–interest method maintains the net book value of the liability equal to the present value of the future cash flows of the liability throughout its life. On the other hand, the straight–line method does not maintain this equality. Further, under the effective–interest method, interest expense is always the same percentage of the outstanding debt throughout the life of the liability. This constant relationship arises because interest expense is computed as the book value times the effective interest rate, and since the effective interest rate is constant, interest expense remains a constant percentage of the liability. The straight–line method does not give rise to this constant relationship between interest expense and the outstanding liability, as evidenced by the amounts reported under interest expense in Part (c).

P11–11

a. Cash	808,000	
Bonds Payable		800,000
Interest Payable		8,000*
To record issue of bonds.		

* $8,000 = $800,000 x 6% x 1/6

b. Interest Expense	40,000*	
Interest Payable		40,000
To accrue interest expense.		

* $40,000 = $800,000 x 6% x 5/6

c. Interest Payable	48,000	
Cash		48,000
To record interest payment.		

P11–12

a. Cash Paid = Face Value x 102%
= $500,000 x 102%
= $510,000

Bonds Payable	500,000	
Premium on Bonds Payable	12,600	
Cash		510,000
Gain on Redemption		2,600
To record redemption of bonds.		

b. Cash Paid = Face Value x 110%
= $500,000 x 110%
= $550,000

Bonds Payable	500,000	
Premium on Bonds Payable	12,600	
Loss on Redemption	37,400	
Cash		550,000
To record redemption of bonds.		

c. Interest Expense	15,378[a]	
Premium on Bonds Payable	4,622[b]	
Cash		20,000[c]
To record interest payment.		

[a] $15,378 = Book Value x Effective rate per period = $512,600 x 3%
[b] $4,622 = Interest expense – Interest payment
[c] $20,000 = Face value x Stated rate per period = $500,000 x 4%

d. Cash Paid = Face Value x 107%
= $500,000 x 107%
= $535,000

Bonds Payable	500,000	
Premium on Bonds Payable	7,978*	
Loss on Redemption	27,022	
Cash		535,000
To record redemption of bonds.		

---

*$7,978 = Premium balance on 1/1/90 – Premium amortized from 1/1/90 to 6/30/90
= $12,600 – $4,622 (from Part [c])

P11–13

a. Face value		$ 10,000
Present value (i = 8%, n = 10)		
PV of face value		
($10,000 x .46319 from Table 4 in App. A)	$4,631.90	
PV of interest payments		
[($10,000 x 7%) x 6.71008 from Table 5 in App. A]	4,697.06	
Total present value		9,328.96
Discount		$ 671.04

Cash	9,328.96	
Discount on Bonds Payable	671.04	
Bonds Payable		10,000
To record issue of bonds.		

b. Interest Expense	746.32[a]	
Discount on Bonds Payable		46.32[b]
Cash		700.00[c]
To record interest payment.		

---

[a] $746.32 = Book value x Effective rate per period = $9,328.96 x 8%
[b] $46.32 = Interest expense – Interest payment.
[c] $700.00 = Face value x Stated rate per period = $10,000 x 7%

c. As of June 30, 1992, the bonds have a remaining life of five six–month periods until they mature.

Option 1: Repurchase the bonds through the bond market.

Present value (i = 6%, n = 5)	
PV of face value (i = 6%, n = 5)	
($10,000 x .74726 from Table 4)	$ 7,472.60
PV of interest payments	
[($10,000 x 7%) x 4.21236 from Table 5]	2,948.65
Total present value (i.e., repurchase price)	$10,421.25

Option 2: Repurchase the bonds using the call provision.

Repurchase price = Face value x 103.5%
= $10,000 x 103.5%
= $10,350.00

In this case, Ficus Tree Farm would have to use less cash to redeem the bonds using the call provision than to repurchase them through the bond market. Consequently, the company should use the call provision to redeem the bonds.

d. Assume that a company wishes to redeem all outstanding bonds prior to maturity. It is unlikely that it could accomplish this goal by repurchasing the bonds through the bond market. Some bondholders would simply be unwilling to sell the bonds. It is costly for bondholders to sell their bonds and reinvest. They incur transaction costs (i.e., brokerage fees, etc.) when selling investments. It is also time-consuming (an opportunity cost) to research new investment opportunities. Bondholders would also consider the tax implications of selling their bonds. If the bondholder would have to recognize any gains on the sale of the bond, these gains would be considered taxable income. To avoid these taxes, the bondholder may prefer to simply hold the bond. By exercising a call provision, a company can compel all bondholders to surrender their bonds. Consequently, if a company wishes to retire all outstanding bonds, the company will have to resort, at least partially, to exercising any relevant call provisions.

e.

	Debit	Credit
Bonds Payable	10,000.00	
Loss on Redemption	749.30	
Discount on Bonds Payable		399.30*
Cash		10,350.00
To record redemption of bonds.		

*

Date	Interest Expense	Payment Amount	Discount Amort	Face Value	Discount Balance	Book Value
1/1/90				10000.00	671.03	9328.97
6/30/90	746.32	700.00	46.32	10000.00	624.71	9375.29
1/1/91	750.02	700.00	50.02	10000.00	574.69	9425.31
6/30/91	754.02	700.00	54.02	10000.00	520.66	9479.34
1/1/92	758.35	700.00	58.35	10000.00	462.32	9537.68
6/30/92	763.01	700.00	63.01	10000.00	**399.30**	9600.70

P11–14

a. Face value $100,000
Present value (i = 6%, n = 8)
PV of face value
($100,000 x .62741 from Table 4 in App. A) $62,741
PV of interest payments
[($100,000 x 4%) x 6.20979 from Table 5 in App. A) 24,839
Total present value 87,580
Discount on bonds payable $ 12,420

Date	Interest Expense[a]	Cash Payment[b]	Unamortized Discount[c]	Book Value[d]
6/30/90			12420.00	87580.00
12/31/90	5254.80	4000.00	11165.20	88834.80
6/30/91	5330.09	4000.00	9835.11	90164.89
12/31/91	5409.89	4000.00	8425.22	91574.78
6/30/92	5494.49	4000.00	6930.73	93069.27
12/31/92	5584.16	4000.00	5346.58	94653.42
6/30/93	5679.21	4000.00	3667.37	96332.63
12/31/93	5779.96	4000.00	1887.41	98112.59
6/30/94	5887.41	4000.00	0.00	100000.00

[a] Interest expense = Book value at the beginning of the period x 6%
[b] Cash payment = Face value x stated rate per period = $100,000 x 4%
[c] Unamortized discount = Unamortized discount at the beginning of the period + Cash payment – Interest expense.
[d] Book value = Face value – Unamortized discount

b. **Cash outflows**
Total interest payments = $4,000 x 8 payments
= $32,000

Total principal payment = $100,000 on maturity of the bonds

Total cash outflows = $32,000 + $100,000
= $132,000

Cash inflows
Cash inflows = Proceeds received upon issuance of the bonds
= $87,580

Therefore, cash outflows exceeded cash inflows by $44,420.

c. **Cash outflows**

Post-tax interest payments = $4,000 x (1 – tax rate)
= $4,000 x (1 – 34%)
= $2,640

Total post-tax interest payments = $2,640 x 8 payments
= $21,120

Total principal payment = $100,000 on maturity of the bonds

Total cash outflows = $21,120 + $100,000
= $121,120

Cash inflows

Cash inflows = Proceeds received upon issuance of the bonds
= $87,580

Therefore, cash outflows exceeded cash inflows by $33,540.

d. **Cash outflows**

Post-tax interest payments = $2,640 (from Part [c])

Present value of post-tax payments = $2,640 x Present value of an ordinary annuity factor for $i = 6\%$, $n = 8$
= $2,640 x 6.20979 (from Table 5 in Appendix A)
= $16,394 (rounded)

Total principal payment = $100,000 on maturity of the bonds

Present value of principal payment = $62,741 (from Part [a])

Total cash outflows = $16,394 + $62,741
= $79,135

Cash inflows

Cash inflows = Proceeds received upon issuance of the bonds
= $87,580 (from Part A)

Therefore, cash inflows now exceed cash outflows by $8,445.

P11–15

a. Present value of lease payments = FMV of equipment
= $59,890.65

OR

= Present value of lease payments
= $15,000 x Present value of an ordinary annuity factor for $i = 8\%$, $n = 5$
= $15,000 x 3.99271 (from Table 5 in App. A)
= $59,890.65

Date	Balance Sheet Value of Equipment[a]	Leasehold Obligation[b]	Interest Expense[c]	Depreciation Expense[d]	Rent Expense	Total Expense
001/1/90	$59,890.65	$59,890.65				
12/31/90	47,912.52	49,681.90	$4,791.25	$11,978.13	$0.00	$16,769.38
12/31/91	35,934.39	38,656.45	3,974.55	11,978.13	0.00	15,952.68
12/31/92	23,956.26	26,748.97	3,092.52	11,978.13	0.00	15,070.65
12/31/93	11,978.13	13,888.89	2,139.92	11,978.13	0.00	14,118.05
12/31/94	0.00	0.00	1,111.11	11,978.13	0.00	13,089.24

[a] Balance sheet value of equipment = Value of equipment on 1/1/90 – Accumulated depreciation

[b] Leasehold obligation = Leasehold obligation at beginning of the period – ($15,000 rental payment – Interest expense for the period)

[c] Interest expense = Leasehold obligation at beginning of the period x 8%

[d] Depreciation expense = $59,890.65 ÷ 5 years

b.

Date	Balance Sheet Value of Equipment	Leasehold Obligation	Interest Expense	Depreciation Expense	Rent Expense	Total Expense
1/1/90	$0.00	$0.00				
12/31/90	0.00	0.00	$0.00	$0.00	$15,000.00	$15,000.00
12/31/91	0.00	0.00	0.00	0.00	15,000.00	15,000.00
12/31/92	0.00	0.00	0.00	0.00	15,000.00	15,000.00
12/31/93	0.00	0.00	0.00	0.00	15,000.00	15,000.00
12/31/94	0.00	0.00	0.00	0.00	15,000.00	15,000.00

P11–16

a. Debt/equity ratio = Total liabilities ÷ Stockholders' equity
= (Current liabilities + L-T liabilities) ÷ Stockholders' equity
= $30,000 ÷ $40,000
= 0.75

b. Present value of lease payments = $5,000 x Present value of an ordinary annuity factor for $i = 12\%$, $n = 5$
= $5,000 x 3.60478 (from Table 5 in App. A)
= $18,023.90

Debt/equity ratio = ($30,000 + $18,023.90) ÷ $40,000
= 1.20

c.

	Rent Expense	Interest Expense	Depreciation Expense	Total Expenses
Operating lease	$5,000.00	$ 0.00	$ 0.00	$5,000.00
Capital lease	0.00	2,162.87	3,604.78	5,767.65

d. There are two primary reasons why Thompkins Laundry might want to arrange the terms of the lease agreement so that the lease would be classified as an operating lease rather than as a capital lease. First, lease obligations under an operating lease are not disclosed on the face of the balance sheet. Consequently, operating leases are essentially off-balance-sheet financing and will not affect any existing debt covenants. Second, in this case the capital lease classification results in higher expenses and, hence, lower net income in 1991 than the operating lease classification. Decreased net income would adversely affect any contracts, such as the manager's incentive contract, written on the basis of reported net income.

To avoid classifying this lease as a capital lease, Thompkins Laundry would have to arrange the terms so that the lease did not meet any of the criteria for capital leases. Consequently, the company would have to arrange the terms so that:

(1) the present value of the lease payments is less than the fair market value of the lease property;
(2) the term of the lease is less than 75% of the leased property's life;
(3) the lessee does not have the right either during or at the expiration of the lease agreement to purchase the property from the lessor at a nominal amount; or
(4) ownership of the property is not transferred to the lessee from the lessor by the end of the lease term.

P11–17

a.

Equipment	8,802	
Discount on Notes Payable	1,198	
Notes Payable		10,000
To record purchase of equipment in exchange for a note.		

b. Present value = Present value of maturity payment + Present value of periodic payments

$8,802 = ($10,000 x Present value factor) + ($500 x Present value of an ordinary annuity factor)

Since the present value of $8,802 is less than the face value, we know that the note was issued at a discount. Consequently, the effective rate is greater than the stated rate. We also know that the stated rate is 5% (i.e., $500 ÷ $10,000 face value).

Try $i = 6\%$ for $n = 5$.

($10,000 x .74726 from Table 4 in App. A) + ($500 x 4.21236 from Table 5 in App. A)
= $7,473 + $2,106
= $9,579

Try $i = 8\%$ for $n = 5$

($10,000 x .68058 from Table 4) + ($500 x 3.99271 from Table 5)
= 6,805.80 + 1,996.36
= $8,802 (rounded)

Therefore, the effective interest rate on the note is 8%.

c. Interest Expense	704[a]	
Discount on Notes Payable		204[b]
Cash		500
To record interest payment.		

[a] \$704 = Book value x Effective rate per period = (\$10,000 – \$1,198) x 8%
[b] \$204 = Interest expense – Interest payment

d. 12/31/90 Net book value = Face value – 12/31/90 Discount on notes payable
= \$10,000 – (\$1,198 – \$204)
= \$9,006

P11–18

a. If the bonds are currently selling for par value, then the stated interest rate is identical to the effective interest rate. Since the stated interest rate on Lowers and Sons' bonds is 9%, the effective interest rate on these bonds is also 9%. The effective rate is determined by two factors: the risk-free return and a risk premium. These two factors are added together to determine the appropriate effective rate. The following equation can be used to solve for the maximum risk premium.

Effective rate = Risk-free rate + Risk premium
9% = 7% + Risk premium
Maximum risk premium = 2%

b. Assume an individual bond with a face value of \$1,000. The appropriate annual effective interest rate would now be 12% (i.e., 7% risk-free rate + 5% risk premium), so the appropriate effective rate per period would now be 6%. The number of periods would be ten.

Total present value = (\$1,000 x .55839 from Table 4 in App. A)
+ [(\$1,000 x 4.5%) x 7.36009 from Table 5 in App. A]
= \$558.39 + \$331.20
= \$889.59

Given the new risk premium of 5%, the bonds should be selling for \$889.59.

c. The decrease in the prime rate would tend to increase bond prices. Changes in the prime rate or discount rate normally indicate a change in the risk-free rate. Since the risk-free rate is a component of the effective interest rate, and the effective interest rate is used to discount the future cash flows associated with bonds, any indication that the risk-free rate has changed would cause a change in bond prices. Specifically, a decrease in the prime rate signals a decrease in the risk-free rate, thereby decreasing the effective interest rate. Decreasing the effective interest rate relative to the stated rate makes bonds appear to be a more attractive investment alternative, so the demand for the bonds will increase. One method to compensate for the increased demand for bonds is to increase prices until supply and demand are once again equal. At this price, the investors will earn a return on their investment equal to the effective interest rate.

If the prime rate decreased 1%, the new annual riskless rate of return would be 6%. Since the annual risk premium is still 2%, the annual effective rate on these bonds would now be 8%. A single bond would now be selling for

Total present value	=	($1,000 x .67556 from Table 4)
	+	[($1,000 x 4.5%) x 8.11090 from Table 5]
	=	$675.56 + $364.99
	=	$1,040.55

Prior to the decrease in the prime rate, the same bond was selling for par value (or $1,000). Consequently, the decrease in the prime rate by 1% caused the price of a single bond to increase by $40.55.

C11–1

a. A debenture is an *unsecured* bond. Thus, should the company not repay the bonds, investors do not have security in any assets that could be sold to repay them. For this reason, unsecured bonds are riskier than secured bonds. Investors are compensated for this risk via a higher return (effective interest rate) on debentures. Accordingly, these bonds would be priced lower than secured bonds, which means they provide a higher return.

b. A company might repurchase its outstanding debt in order to reduce the amount of long-term debt reported on its balance sheet. This may improve some financial ratios and assist the company in meeting any exiting covenant requirements from other lenders. If the general level of interest rates falls, a company may reissue its debt to take advantage of decreased interest rates.

c. Assets would decrease as cash was paid to the bondholders. Liabilities would decrease as the debt was retired. Stockholders' equity would decrease because the company is paying out $957.50 for bonds with a current carrying value of $875.00 Thus, there is a loss on the repurchase of $82.50 per $1000 bond.

d. The amount paid for each bond on August 2 would be

Promised repayment	$957.50
Accrued interest	
($1000 x 8.5% x 79/365)	18.40
Total	$975.90

C11–2

a. The bonds were issued at a discount (i.e., less than their face amount).

b.

Cash (.99325 x $200,000,000)	198,650,000	
Discount on Bonds Payable	1,350,000	
Bonds Payable		200,000,000
To record issuance of bonds.		

c. The effective interest rate is the rate that equates the proceeds from the bond issue with its future cash outflows. In the present case, the annual rate that equates the proceeds of $198,650,000 with the payment of $200,000,000 at the end of sixty six-month periods and with the payments of $10,000,000 at the end of each six-month period for sixty periods is approximately 10.08%, or 10% rounded.

d.

Interest Expense	10,011,960*	
Discount on Bonds Payable		11,960
Cash		10,000,000
To record interest payment.		

* $10,011,960 = $198,650,000 x (10.08% ÷ 2)

e. The present value of $200,000,000 in fifty-eight six-month periods and of fifty-eight semiannual payments of $10,000,000 discounted using an annual rate of 12.07% is $166,843,040. The balance sheet value on this same date is $198,674,520. These two values are different because a different discount rate was used to calculate the present values. In the case of the market price, the effective rate as of July 1, 1989 was used while in the case of the bookvalue, the effective rate on the date the bonds were issued was used.

f. The July 1, 1989 interest payment would have increased the bonds carrying value to $198,674,520. Accordingly, there would be a gain on the redemption of $31,831,480 (i.e., $198,674,520 – $166,843,040). The appropriate entry is

Bonds Payable	200,000,000	
Discount on Bonds Payable		1,325,480
Gain on Redemption		31,831,480
Cash		166,843,040
To record redemption of bonds.		

g. The gain results solely from a change in the level of interest rates in the market. The gain would not have been recognized if BP America had not redeemed the bonds when interest rates rose.

C11–3

a. If an investor is not in need of periodic cash payments, a noninterest-bearing obligation that provides a competitive rate of return is an attractive investment.

b. The rate that discounts $200 million due in eight years to $66,480,000 is 14.75% (or 15%, rounded).

c. If a company does not expect to have cash flows to support periodic interest payments, it is to its advantage to issue bonds with a stated rate of zero.

d. 5% stated rate

Present value of $200,000,000 received in 8 years	
$200,000,000 x .32690	$ 65,380,000
Present value of periodic interest payments	
($200,000,000 x 5%) x 4.48732	44,873,200
Issue price	$110,253,200

18% stated rate

Present value of $200,000,000 received in 8 years	
$200,000,000 x .32690	$ 65,380,000
Present value of periodic interest payments	
($200,000,000 x 18%) x 4.48732	161,540,000
Issue price	$226,920,000

C11–4

a. The effective interest rate on both arrangements is the discount rate that equates a $6 million payment for fifteen years to $45,636,480: 10%

b.

Cash	45,636,480	
Note Payable		45,636,480
To record receipt from note.		
Airplane	45,636,480	
Cash		45,638,480
To record purchase of airplances.		

c.

Airplane	45,636,480	
Lease Liability		45,636,480
To record lease arrangement.		

d. Both approaches have similar effects on the financial statements. Both increase assets by the purchase price of the airplane and increase liabilities for the amount of the loan or the present value of the lease liability. Depreciation of the airplane would be included on the financial statements under both approaches.

e. No journal entry is required if the transaction is treated as an operating lease.

f. Alternative 2 would be a form of off-balance-sheet financing if the lease is classified as an operating lease. United might want to pursue this approach to keep from increasing its indebtedness and affecting related ratio measures. This might be done to remain compliant with other debt covenant or in general to appear less risky to outside investors and creditors.

C11–5

a. The rating assigned to a bond is an assessment of its riskiness. If a bond has a low rating, it is deemed to be risky, and investors who purchase it will require a higher return as a risk premium. This would most likely be achieved by issuing the bond at a larger discount. If the rating is upgraded, the price of the bond will increase (which reduces its effective interest rate), because the risk premium is determined to be smaller.

b. If bonds can be issued at an effective rate that is lower than the rate on an outstanding loan, it makes sense to issued bonds and repay the loan. This effectively extends the period over which the original debt is to be repaid. The balance sheet would be unaffected by the transaction, as the face amount of the bonds equals the amount of the loan. Differential effects would occur in the periodic recording of a lower interest expense.

c. If MGM/UA used the proceeds to purchase additional plant assets, both assets and liabilities would increase. Standard & Poor's might consider the asset purchase more risky then simply replacing the financing of exiting assets. Accordingly, they may not have upgraded the rating.

CHAPTER 12 Stockholders' Equity

E12–1

a. Debt capital = Total liabilities
= $52,000 + $35,000
= $87,000

Contributed capital = Preferred stock + Common stock + Additional paid-in capital: common stock – Treasury stock
= $50,000 + $80,000 + ($50,000 + $100,000) – $80,000
= $200,000

Earned capital = Retained earnings
= $113,000

The portions of Schmitt's assets provided by debt, contributed capital, and earned capital are, therefore, 21.75%, 50%, and 28.25%, respectively.

b. Debt/equity = Total liabilities ÷ Total stockholders' equity
= Total liabilities ÷ (Contributed capital + Earned capital)
= $87,000 ÷ ($200,000 + $113,000)
= .278

Debt/equity = Total liabilities ÷ Total stockholders' equity
= (Total liabilities + Contributed capital from preferred stock) ÷ (Contributed capital from common stock + Earned capital – Treasury stock)
= ($87,000 + $50,000 + $50,000) ÷ ($80,000 + $100,000 + $113,000 – $80,000)
= .878

c. Most states restrict the dollar amount of dividends to either the balance in Retained Earnings or the balance in Retained Earnings less any treasury stock. So in this case, Schmitt and Associates, Inc. would either be restricted to $113,000 or $33,000 depending upon the state.

E12–2

a. Accounts	b. Effect on Account	c. Effect on Total Stockholders' Equity
(1) Common stock	Increase	Increase
Additional paid-in capital: common stock	Increase	
(2) None	N/A	No effect
(3) Treasury stock	Increase	Decrease
(4) Common stock	Increase	No effect
Additional paid-in capital: common stock	Increase	
Retained earnings	Decrease	
(5) Treasury stock	Decrease	Increase
Additional paid-in capital: treasury stock	Increase	
(6) None	N/A	No effect
(7) Retained earnings	Increase	Increase
(8) Retained earnings *	Decrease	Decrease

* The declaration of a property dividend does not directly affect Retained Earnings. A loss account is increased for the writedown of the asset to its market value. The Dividend account is increased for the fair value of the declared dividend. Both of these accounts will be closed into the Retained Earnings account during the closing process. The net effect on the Retained Earnings account will be to reduce its balance.

E12–3

	Debit	Credit
(1) No entry is necessary.		
(2) Cash	200,000	
Common Stock		50,000
Additional Paid-in Capital: Common Stock		150,000
To record issue of common stock.		
(3) Cash	5,000,000	
Preferred Stock		2,500,000
Additional Paid-in Capital: Preferred Stock		2,500,000
To record issue of preferred stock.		
(4) Cash	7,500,000	
Preferred Stock		7,500,000
To record issue of preferred stock.		

E12–4

	Account	Debit	Credit
a.	Treasury Stock	12,500	
	Cash		12,500
	To record acquisition of treasury stock.		

b. Debt/equity = Total liabilities ÷ Total stockholders' equity

Before

Debt/equity = $450,000 ÷ $430,000
= 1.05

After

Debt/equity = $450,000 ÷ ($430,000 – $12,500)
= 1.08

c. Earnings per share = Net income ÷ Outstanding shares

Before

EPS = $120,000 ÷ 5,000 shares
= $24 per share

After

EPS = $120,000 ÷ (5,000 shares issued – 500 treasury shares)
= $26.67 per share

E12–5

	Account	Debit	Credit
a. (1)	Cash	500,000	
	Common Stock		250,000
	Additional Paid-in Capital: Common Stock		250,000
	To record the issue of common stock.		
(2)	Cash	60,000	
	Preferred Stock		60,000
	To record the issue of preferred stock.		
(3)	Treasury Stock	45,000	
	Cash		45,000
	To record the repurchase of common stock.		
(4)	Cash	18,000	
	Treasury Stock		15,000
	Additional Paid-in Capital: Treasury Stock		3,000
	To record the reissue of treasury stock.		
(5)	Cash	5,000	
	Additional Paid-in Capital: Treasury Stock	3,000	
	Retained Earnings	7,000	
	Treasury Stock		15,000
	To record the reissue of treasury stock.		

b. Preferred stock ($9 no par value, 5,000 shares outstanding)

Preferred stock ($9 no par value, 5,000 shares outstanding)	$ 60,000
Common stock ($10 par, 25,000 shares issued and 24,000 outstanding)	250,000
Additional paid-in capital: common stock	250,000
Retained earnings	493,000 *
Treasury stock	(15,000)
Total stockholders' equity	$1,038,000

* $493,000 = $500,000 net income – $7,000 (from entry [5])

E12–6

a. (1) Treasury Stock 15,000
Cash 15,000
To record purchase of treasury stock.

	Debit	Credit
(1) Treasury Stock	15,000	
Cash		15,000
To record purchase of treasury stock.		
(2) Cash	1,000	
Retained Earnings	6,500	
Treasury Stock		7,500
To record reissue of treasury stock as compensation.		

Note: Depending upon the terms of the employees' compensation package, it may be appropriate to debit Wage Expense for $6,500 rather than debiting for $6,500 Retained Earnings.

	Debit	Credit
(3) Cash	8,250	
Treasury Stock		7,500
Additional paid-in Capital: Treasury Stock		750
To record reissue of treasury stock.		

Common stock	$40,000
Additional paid-in capital	
Common stock	5,000
Treasury stock	750
Retained earnings	23,500
Total stockholders' equity	$69,250

b. A total of $750 of additional paid-in capital is attributed to treasury stock. This amount would be recorded in the account Additional Paid-in Capital: Treasury Stock. Under the cost method, this amount represents the amount of proceeds received in excess of the acquisition cost of the treasury stock reissued.

E12–7

a. Treasury Stock 2,850,000
Cash 2,850,000
To record acquisition of treasury stock.

b.	
Common stock	$1,000,000
Additional paid-in capital: common stock	1,500,000
Retained earnings	4,300,000
Treasury stock	(2,850,000)
Total stockholders' equity	$3,950,000

c. When common stock is initially issued, it is recorded at the value of the assets received. In this case AAA Corporation received $25 per share for 100,000 shares, for a total of $2,500,000. This $2,500,000 was allocated between the accounts Common Stock and Additional Paid-in Capital: Common Stock. Under the cost method of accounting for treasury stock, acquiring treasury stock does not cause the amount recorded for the initial issue of common stock to be adjusted. The treasury stock is simply recorded at the value of the assets given up. So if the value of the assets given up to acquire the treasury stock exceeds the value of the assets received when the common stock was initially issued, then the Treasury Stock balance will exceed contributed capital. In this case the treasury stock was acquired at $95 per share, so Treasury Stock should exceed contributed capital by $70 per share for the 30,000 shares held in treasury.

E12–8

a. Book value per share = Total common stockholders' equity ÷ Number of shares outstanding
= $130,000 ÷ 10,000 shares
= $13.00 per share

b. Book value per share = [$130,000 + (5,000 shares x $15)] ÷ 15,000 shares
= $13.67 per share

c. Book value per share = [$130,000 + (5,000 shares x $10)] ÷ 15,000 shares
= $12.00 per share

d. Book value per share = [$130,000 – (5,000 x $15)] ÷ 5,000 shares
= $11.00 per share

e. Book value per share = [$130,000 – (5,000 x $10)] ÷ 5,000 shares
= $16.00 per share

f. Issuing stock either increases or decreases the book value of common stock. Whether issuing stock increases or decreases the book value depends upon the issue price of the new stock. If new stock is issued at a price above the preissue book value, then issuing the stock increases the book value. Alternatively, if new stock is issued at a price below the preissue book value, then issuing the stock decreases the book value.

g. Purchasing treasury stock either increases or decreases the book value of common stock. Whether purchasing treasury stock increases or decreases the book value depends upon the acquisition price of the treasury stock. If treasury stock is acquired at a price above the preissue book value, then purchasing treasury stock decreases the book value. Alternatively, if treasury stock is acquired at a price below the preissue book value, then purchasing the treasury stock increases the book value.

E12–9

		Debit	Credit
a.	Cash	300	
	Preferred Stock		300
	To record issue of preferred stock.		
b.	Cash	120	
	Common Stock		100
	Additional Paid-in Capital: Common Stock		20
	To record issue of common stock.		
c.	Cash	30	
	Treasury Stock		20
	Additional Paid-in Capital: Treasury Stock		10
	To record reissue of treasury stock.		

E12–10

a. **Date of declaration**

Marketable Securities	1,500,000*	
Gain on Appreciation of Marketable Securities		1,500,000
To record appreciation on marketable securities.		

* $1,500,000 = 100,000 shares x ($60 – $45)

Property Dividend	6,000,000	
Dividend Payable		6,000,000
To record property dividend declaration.		

Date of record
No journal entries are necessary.

Date of payment

Dividend Payable	6,000,000	
Marketable Securities		6,000,000
To record payment of property dividend.		

b. **Date of declaration**

Loss on Marketable Securities	2,000,000*	
Marketable Securities		2,000,000
To record decrease in value of marketable securities.		

* $1,500,000 = 100,000 shares x ($80 – $60)

Property Dividend	6,000,000	
Dividend Payable		6,000,000
To record property dividend declaration.		

Date of record
No journal entries are necessary.

Date of payment

Dividend Payable	6,000,000	
Marketable Securities		6,000,000
To record payment of property dividend.		

c. **Entry to record sale of securities**

Cash	6,000,000	
Loss on Sale of Marketable Securities	2,000,000	
Marketable Securities		8,000,000
To record decrease in value of marketable securities.		

Date of declaration

Cash Dividend	6,000,000	
Dividend Payable		6,000,000
To record cash dividend declaration.		

Date of record

No journal entries are necessary.

Date of payment

Dividend Payable	6,000,000	
Cash		6,000,000
To record payment of cash dividend.		

E12–11

a. Only those shares that are both issued and outstanding are eligible to receive dividends. Since Enerson has 275,000 shares of common stock issued, but 25,000 of those shares are held in treasury, the total number of common shares outstanding and, hence, eligible for a dividend is 250,000 shares.

b. **Date of declaration**

Cash Dividend	5,000,000*	
Dividend Payable		5,000,000
To record cash dividend declaration.		

* $5,000,000 = 250,000 shares (from Part [a]) x $20 per share.

Date of record

No journal entry is necessary.

Date of payment

Dividend Payable	5,000,000	
Cash		5,000,000
To record payment of cash dividend.		

c. **Date of declaration**

Marketable Securities	500,000*	
Gain on Appreciation of Marketable Securities		500,000
To record appreciation on marketable securities.		

* $50,000 = 50,000 shares x ($55 – $45)

Property Dividend	2,750,000	
Dividend Payable		2,750,000
To record property dividend declaration.		

Date of record
No journal entries are necessary.

Date of payment

Dividend Payable	2,750,000	
Marketable Securities		2,750,000
To record payment of property dividend.		

E12–12

a. Each year the preferred stockholders are entitled to $5 for each share of preferred stock outstanding. Since 5,000 shares are outstanding, total dividends to preferred stockholders should be $25,000 per year.

Year	Dividends Declared	Dividends to Preferred	Dividends to Common
1986	$ 0	$ 0	$ 0
1987	40,000	25,000 (for 1986)	0
		15,000 (for 1987)	
1988	100,000	10,000 (for 1987)	65,000
		25,000 (for 1988)	
1989	20,000	20,000 (for 1989)	0
1990	20,000	5,000 (for 1989)	0
		15,000 (for 1990)	

b. The balance in dividends in arrears equals the dividends not declared and not paid to which the preferred stockholders are entitled.

12/31/86 balance = $25,000

12/31/87 balance = $10,000

12/31/88 balance = $ 0

12/31/89 balance = $ 5,000

12/31/90 balance = $10,000

c. Dividends in arrears should not be considered a liability. A liability represents the probable future sacrifice of assets. In the case of dividends, too much uncertainty exists whether there will actually be a future sacrifice of assets. A company may choose to reinvest its profits back into the company, or the company may not be financially sound enough to pay a dividend. This uncertainty is only resolved when the Board of Directors actually declares the dividend.

Preferred stockholders are only entitled to receive their dividend when the company declares a dividend. If the Board of Directors never declares a dividend, then the preferred stockholders are not entitled to receive one; thus, no liability exists until the dividend is actually declared.

E12–13

		Debit	Credit
a.	Stock Dividend	7,000*	
	Common Stock		1,000
	Additional paid-in Capital: Common Stock		6,000
	To record 5% stock dividend.		

* $7,000 = (Number of outstanding shares x 5%) x $35 per share
= (5,000 shares issued – 1,000 shares in treasury) x 5% x $35 per share.

		Debit	Credit
b.	Stock Dividend	10,000*	
	Common Stock		10,000
	To record a 50% stock dividend.		

* $20,000 = Number of shares outstanding x 50% x $5 par value per share
= 4,000 shares x 50% x $5

		Debit	Credit
c.	Stock Dividend	20,000*	
	Common Stock		20,000
	To record 100% stock dividend.		

* $40,000 = Number of shares outstanding x 100% x $5 par value per share
= 4,000 shares x 100% x $5

d. No journal entry is necessary. However, the company should prepare a memorandum entry stating that the par value has decreased from $5 to $2.50 per share and that 8,000 shares of common stock are now issued and outstanding.

e. Ratio = (Common stock + Additional paid-in capital – Treasury stock)
÷ Retained earnings

Prior to entries
($25,000 + $50,000 – $12,000) ÷ $30,000 = 2.10

After entry (a)
[($25,000 + $1,000) + ($50,000 + $6,000) – $12,000] ÷ ($30,000 – $7,000) = 3.04

After entry (b)
[($25,000 + $10,000) + $50,000 – $12,000] ÷ ($30,000 – $10,000) = 3.65

After entry (c)
[($25,000 + $20,000) + $50,000 – $12,000] ÷ ($30,000 – $20,000) = 8.30

After entry (d)
($25,000 + $50,000 – $12,000) ÷ $30,000 = 2.10

E12–14

a. Stock Dividend 85,000
Common Stock 10,000
Additional Paid-in Capital: Common Stock 75,000
To record 20% stock dividend.

	Debit	Credit
Stock Dividend	85,000	
Common Stock		10,000
Additional Paid-in Capital: Common Stock		75,000
To record 20% stock dividend.		

When a company declares an ordinary stock dividend, the fair market value of the new shares issued is transferred from Retained Earnings, via the Dividend account, to the contributed capital accounts. Since in most states dividends are restricted to the balance in Retained Earnings (or Retained Earnings less Treasury Stock), any decrease in its account balance decreases the amount of potential dividends. So from the stockholders' viewpoint a stock dividend is not attractive because it decreases potential future dividends.

The primary reason that a company would declare an ordinary stock dividend is as a publicity gesture. Some companies take great pride in being able to "promote" the company's dividend-paying history. If a company finds itself short of cash and still wants to be able to claim that it paid a dividend, then the company can maintain its dividend-paying streak by declaring a stock dividend.

b. **Option (2)**

	Debit	Credit
Stock Dividend	25,000	
Common Stock		25,000
To record 50% stock dividend.		

Option (3)

	Debit	Credit
Stock Dividend	50,000	
Common Stock		50,000
To record stock split in form of a stock dividend.		

c. Issuing a large stock dividend or declaring a stock split does not inherently increase or decrease a company's value. After a large stock dividend or a stock split, a company's value is allocated over a larger number of shares, so each share is worth less. If each share is worth less, then each share should sell for a lower price. If a company's stock is trading at too high a price, the average investor will not be able to invest in the company. If the price of the company's stock was lowered, trading in the company's stock would be stimulated. Consequently, a company can lower the price of its stock and stimulate trading in its stock by declaring and issuing a large stock dividend or a stock split.

E12–15

a. Appropriating retained earnings serves to restrict a portion of retained earnings from the payment of future dividends. Appropriations of retained earnings usually arise for two reasons. First, a creditor requires the borrower to appropriate retained earnings. Such appropriations prevent the borrower from paying "excessive" dividends to the stockholders, thereby reducing the amount of the cash available to repay creditors. Second, a company may decide to restrict future dividends and use the cash that would have otherwise been used to pay dividends to finance plant expansions and so forth. In this particular case, the company appropriated retained earnings for both of these reasons.

Auditors would require that appropriations of retained earnings be disclosed in the financial statement because they affect the magnitude of a company's future dividends. The magnitude of future dividends is information that current and potential investors desire. Failure to adequately disclose such information could cause investors to lose money on their investments and, consequently, to sue the auditor.

b. Retained Earnings 650,000
    Restricted Retained Earnings 650,000
  To restrict a portion of retained earnings.

c. Common stock XX
Additional paid-in capital: common stock XX
Retained earnings
  Restricted 650,000
  Unrestricted 150,000
Total stockholders' equity XX

d. The company can only declare a dividend equal to the unrestricted portion of retained earnings, which is $150,000.

E12–16

	Debit	Credit
a. Cash	50,000	
Building	40,000	
Land	60,000	
Capital, Bob		50,000
Capital, Tom		100,000
To record partnership formation.		

	Debit	Credit
b. Income Summary	15,000	
Capital, Bob		5,000*
Capital, Tom		10,000*
To close Income Summary to the capital accounts.		

* Net income is distributed to the capital accounts based upon the relative proportion of the capital accounts. One-third of the total capital was provided by Bob, so one-third of net income is allocated to Bob. Two-thirds of the total capital was provided by Tom, so two-thirds of net income is allocated to Tom.

	Debit	Credit
c. Capital, Bob	35,000	
Capital, Tom	30,000	
Cash		65,000
To record partner withdrawals.		

	Debit	Credit
d. Income Summary	30,000	
Capital, Bob		6,000*
Capital, Tom		24,000*
To close Income Summary into the capital accounts.		

* As of 12/31/90, Bob had $20,000 in his capital account (i.e., the initial $50,000 investment + $5,000 net income from 1989 – $35,000 withdrawal during 1990), while Tom had $80,000 in his capital account (i.e., $100,000 + $10,000 – $30,000). So Bob has contributed 20% of the total capital, and Tom has contributed 80% of the contributed capital. The net income is allocated to the partners based upon this 20/80 split.

e. Assets	$130,000	Liabilities	$ 0
		Capital, Bob	26,000
		Capital, Tom	104,000
Total assets	$130,000	Total equities	$130,000

E12–17

a. A corporation is a distinct legal entity; consequently, corporations can be sued. A stockholder in a corporation is usually only legally liable for his/her investment in the company. So a stockholder enjoys limited liability; the corporation serves as a legal shield for the stockholders.

Although corporations offer stockholders limited legal liability, corporations do suffer from some drawbacks, particularly small corporations. First, stockholders are subject to double taxation. As a legal entity, a corporation must pay taxes on its net income. This net income flows into retained earnings and will eventually be distributed as dividends. The stockholder who receives the dividend must pay taxes on it. Second, small corporations might have trouble securing loans without sacrificing stockholders' limited liability. Creditors may be afraid that a small corporation will be unable to generate sufficient cash flows to repay the loan. The only way that the creditor will agree to provide the financing is if the owners personally guarantee the loan. Once the owner(s) personally guarantee the loan, they face unlimited liability.

b. (1) Incorporates the business

Corporate taxes				
Federal taxes	=	$850,000 x 34%	=	$289,000	
State taxes	=	$850,000 x 20%	=	$170,000	
Total corporate taxes	=				$459,000
Personal taxes					
Federal taxes	=	$95,000 x 28%	=	$ 26,600	
State taxes	=	$95,000 x 15%	=	$ 14,250	
Total personal taxes	=				$ 40,850
Total taxes					$499,850

(2) Remains as a partnership

Corporate taxes					$ 0
Personal taxes					
Federal taxes	=	$850,000 x 28%	=	$238,000	
State taxes	=	$850,000 x 15%	=	$127,500	
Total personal taxes	=				$365,500
Total taxes					$365,500

(3) Incorporates the business

Corporate taxes					
Federal taxes	=	($850,000 – $95,000) x 34%	=	$256,700	
State taxes	=	($850,000 – $95,000) x 20%	=	$151,000	
Total corporate taxes	=				$407,700
Personal taxes					
Federal Taxes	=	$95,000 x 28%	=	$26,600	
State Taxes	=	$95,000 x 15%	=	$14,250	
Total personal taxes	=				$ 40,850
Total taxes					$448,550

P12–1

a. Cash 100,000
   Preferred Stock 100,000
   To record issue of preferred stock.

Debt/equity = Total liabilities ÷ Total stockholders' equity
= $250,000 ÷ ($330,000 + $100,000)
= .58

b. Debt/equity = ($250,000 + $100,000) ÷ $330,000
= 1.06

c. If management classifies the stock as stockholders' equity, then the company will not be in violation of its debt agreement. However, if management classifies the stock as debt, then the company will be in violation of its debt agreement. Since violating debt agreements can be quite costly to both the company and managers, managers have incentives to classify the stock as stockholders' equity.

The terms of the preferred stock make it appear to be more similar to debt than to equity. For example, the stock has a specified rate, does not participate in the benefits of ownership (i.e., does not vote and does not participate in profits), and has a fixed life. Based upon these factors, it appears that the stock is in substance actually debt and should be classified as such.

Auditors will consider the costs and benefits to themselves, the financial statement users, and the company in deciding how to classify the preferred stock. Auditors are normally better off by having events recorded in the most conservative manner. In this case, the most conservative manner of recording the stock would be to classify it as debt. Classifying the stock in this way decreases the probability that financial statement users will suffer out-of-pocket losses and be able to sue the auditors. Consequently, the auditors would probably prefer that the stock be classified as debt.

P12–2

a. The balance in the Common Stock account represents the number of shares of common stock issued times the par value per share. Since the balance of $300,000 represents 50,000 shares, the par value per share is $6.

b. Book value = (Total stockholders' equity – Contributed capital from preferred stockholders)
÷ Number of common shares outstanding
= ($540,000 – $50,000) ÷ 45,000 shares
= $10.89

c. Since 50,000 shares have been issued, and only 45,000 shares are outstanding, 5,000 shares are held in treasury. The balance of $40,000 in treasury stock represents the cost of 5,000 shares. Consequently, the average price of the treasury stock was $8.

d. If the company reissues the treasury stock at $10 per share, the company would make the following entry.

Cash 50,000
   Treasury Stock 40,000
   Additional Paid-in Capital: Treasury Stock 10,000
   To record the reissue of treasury stock.

Therefore, stockholders' equity would be increased by $50,000.

Debt/equity ratio
The company's debt/equity ratio is calculated as Total debt ÷ Total stockholders' equity. This ratio would decrease, since the numerator would be unchanged, while the denominator would increase.

Book value
The book value is calculated as Total stockholders' equity ÷ Number of common shares outstanding. In this case, the numerator would increase by $50,000, and the denominator would increase by the 5,000 shares reissued. The book value would now be

($540,000 – $50,000 + $50,000) ÷ (45,000 + 5,000) = $10.80

Since the book value prior to the reissue was $18.89 (see Part [b]), the company's book value would decrease.

EPS
Earnings per share is calculated as Net income ÷ Number of common shares outstanding. If the company did not reissue the stock, its EPS would be

$45,000 ÷ 45,000 shares = $1 per share.

The reissue of treasury stock has no effect on net income, but does increase the number of common shares outstanding. So the company's EPS would decrease. Its EPS would now be

$45,000 ÷ (45,000 + 5,000) = $0.90 per share.

e. If the company purchases an additional 5,000 shares, it would make the following entry.

Treasury Stock	50,000	
Cash		50,000
To record the acquisition of treasury stock.		

Therefore, total stockholders' equity would decrease by $50,000.

Debt/equity ratio
The numerator of this ratio is unchanged by acquiring treasury stock, while the denominator would decrease. So the company's debt/equity ratio would increase.

Book value
Total common stockholders' equity would decrease by $50,000, while the number of common shares outstanding would decrease by 5,000 shares. The book value would now be

($540,000 – $50,000 – $50,000) ÷ (45,000 – 5,000) = $11.00

Since the book value would be $10.89 if it did acquire the stock, the company's book value would increase.

EPS
Net income is not affected by acquiring treasury stock, but the number of common shares outstanding would decrease by 5,000 shares. The company's EPS would now be

$45,000 ÷ (45,000 – 5,000) = $1.125 per share.

Since the company's EPS would be $1 per share (see Part [d]) if it did not reissue the stock, reissuing the stock would cause its EPS to increase.

P12–3

(1) Cash	700,000	
Common Stock		700,000
To record the issue of common stock.		
(2) Cash	700,000	
Common Stock		10,000
Additional Paid-in Capital: Common Stock		690,000
To record the issue of common stock.		
(3) Cash	700,000	
Common Stock		100,000
Additional Paid-in Capital: Common Stock		600,000
To record the issue of common stock.		
(4) Cash	750,000	
Preferred Stock		750,000
To record the issue of preferred stock.		

(5) Par value has accounting significance in that it is used to determine the amount that is allocated to the related paid-in capital accounts to the Common Stock or the Preferred Stock account when stock is issued. Economically, par value has little significance. Par values were initially established to protect creditors. Par value represents the amount that stockholders are liable to creditors. However, par values are usually very small amounts, such as $1.00 or even $0.01. So par value no longer has much economic significance.

P12–4

a. Dividends are only paid on the shares that are both issued and outstanding. In this case, 75,000 shares have been issued, but 10,000 of these shares are held as treasury stock. So only 65,000 shares are eligible to participate in a dividend.

b. (1) Cash dividend

Date of declaration

Cash Dividend	975,000	
Dividend Payable		975,000
To record dividend declaration.		

Date of record

No journal entry is necessary

Date of payment

Dividend Payable	975,000	
Cash		975,000
To record dividend payment.		

(2) Property dividend

Date of declaration

Marketable Securities	195,000*	
Gain on Appreciation of Securities		195,000
To adjust property to fair market value.		

* $195,000 is computed as follows:
1. Number of shares to be distributed = 65,000 shares of outstanding common stock ÷ 5 = 13,000 shares.
2. Total appreciation = Appreciation per share x Number of shares
   = ($75 – $60) x 13,000 shares

Property Dividend	975,000*	
Dividend Payable		975,000
To record dividend declaration.		

* $975,000 = Number of shares to be distributed x Fair market value per share
= 13,000 shares x $75 per share

Date of record
No journal entry is necessary

Date of payment

Dividend Payable	975,000	
Marketable Securities		975,000
To record dividend payment.		

c. Stock Dividend

Stock Dividend	650,000[a]	
Common Stock		130,000[b]
Additional Paid-in Capital: Common Stock		520,000
To record declaration and distribution of stock dividend.		

[a] $650,000 is calculated as follows:
1. Number of shares to be distributed = Number of shares outstanding x 20%
   = 65,000 x 20% = 13,000 shares
2. Value of dividend = Fair market per share x Number of shares to be distributed
   = $50 per share x 13,000 shares

[b] $130,000 = Number of shares to be distributed x Par value per share
= 13,0000 shares x $10 per share.

d. Cash

Cash	975,000	
Marketable Securities		780,000
Gain on Sale of Marketable Securities		195,000
To record the sale of marketable securities.		

Date of Declaration

Cash Dividend	975,000	
Dividend Payable		975,000
To record dividend declaration.		

Date of Record
No journal entry is necessary.

Date of Payment

Dividend Payable	975,000	
Cash		975,000
To record dividend payment.		

There is no economic difference between declaring the dividend as a dividend in kind or selling the property and then declaring a cash dividend. In both cases, the company is declaring a dividend based upon the fair market value of the property. Both procedures would result in the same financial statements. The amount of dividends would be identical, total assets (and its components) would be identical, and net income would be identical under the two different procedures. The only difference is that with a dividend in kind, the adjustment of the property to its fair market value gives rise to a gain on appreciation of marketable securities while in the second procedure, the adjustment gives rise to a gain on the sale of marketable securities. Hence, the only difference is in the account title used to record the appreciation.

P12–5

a. Each share of preferred stock is entitled to 10% of the par value or $5.00. Since there are 15,000 shares, preferred stockholders are entitled to a total of $75,000 for any particular year.

Year	Total Dividends Declared	Dividends to Preferred	Dividends to Common	Dividend per Share (Preferred)	Dividend per Share (Common)
1984	$ 65,000	$65,000	$ 0	$4.33	$0.00
1985	100,000	75,000	25,000	5.00	0.50
1986	70,000	70,000	0	4.67	0.00
1987	50,000	50,000	0	3.33	0.00
1988	125,000	75,000	50,000	5.00	1.00
1989	110,000	75,000	35,000	5.00	0.70
1990	99,000	75,000	24,000	5.00	0.48

b.

Year	Total Dividends Declared	Dividends to Preferred	Dividends to Common	Dividend per Share (Preferred)	Dividend per Share (Common)
1984	$ 65,000	$65,000 (for 1984)	$ 0	$4.33	$0.00
1985	100,000	10,000 (for 1984)	15,000	5.67	0.30
		75,000 (for 1985)			
1986	70,000	70,000 (for 1986)	0	4.67	0.00
1987	50,000	5,000 (for 1986)	0	3.33	0.00
		45,000 (for 1987)			
1988	125,000	30,000 (for 1987)	20,000	7.00	0.40
		75,000 (for 1988)			
1989	110,000	75,000 (for 1989)	35,000	5.00	0.70
1990	99,000	75,000 (for 1990)	24,000	5.00	0.48

c.

Year	Total Dividends Declared	Dividends to Preferred		Dividends to Common	Dividend per Share (Preferred)	Dividend per Share (Common)
1984	$ 65,000	$65,000	(for 1984)	$ 0	$4.33	$ 0.00
1985	100,000	10,000	(for 1984)	7,500	6.17	0.15
		75,000	(for 1985)			
		7,500*	(participating)			
1986	70,000	70,000	(for 1986)	0	4.67	0.00
1987	50,000	5,000	(for 1986)	0	3.33	0.00
		45,000	(for 1987)			
1988	125,000	30,000	(for 1987)	12,500	7.50	0.25
		75,000	(for 1988)			
		7,500*	(participating)			
1989	110,000	75,000	(for 1989)	27,500	5.50	0.55
		7,500*	(participating)			
1990	99,000	75,000	(for 1990)	16,500	5.50	0.33
		7,500*	(participating)			

* $7,500 = 15,000 shares x $50 Par value x 1% Participation rate.

P12–6

a. The maximum cash dividend that Cotter Company could declare given its current financial position would be $25,000. This amount represents the cash that the company currently has on hand. If the company wishes to declare a larger cash dividend, it would have to sell some of its assets or borrow cash, thereby altering its financial position.

b. In most states a company can not legally declare a dividend that exceeds the balance in Retained Earnings. Since Cotter Company has a balance in Retained Earnings (after closing entries) of $288,000, this amount is the maximum amount that the company could legally declare as a dividend. With an ordinary stock dividend, the fair market value of the common stock is allocated from Retained Earnings to contributed capital. Since the company's common stock is currently selling for $40 per share, the company could distribute an additional 7,200 shares (i.e., $288,000 ÷ $40 per share). These shares equal 14.4% of the 50,000 shares already outstanding. Since stock dividends are not considered to be a large stock dividend until the distribution of shares exceeds 20% to 25% of outstanding shares, the distribution of the 7,200 shares would be considered an ordinary stock dividend.

c. **Cash Dividend**

	Debit	Credit
Cash Dividend	25,000	
Cash		25,000
To record declaration and payment of cash dividend.		

Stock Dividend

	Debit	Credit
Stock Dividend	288,000	
Common Stock		72,000
Additional Paid-in Capital: Common Stock		216,000
To record stock dividend.		

d. If the company sold its marketable securities, the company would receive the market value of $50 per share. Since the company owns 2,500 shares, Cotter Company would receive $125,000. Combining this $125,000 with the $25,000 of cash already on hand would allow Cotter Company to declare and pay a cash dividend of $150,000.

P12–7

a. If Stevenson Enterprises declares the ordinary stock dividend, the company would make the following journal entry:

Dividend	150,000*	
Common Stock		36,000
Additional Paid-in Capital: Common Stock		114,000
To record 10% stock dividend.		

* $150,000 = (60,000 shares outstanding x 10%) x $25 per share

Common stock ($6 par value, 650,000 shares authorized, 76,000 shares issued, 66,000 shares outstanding, and 10,000 shares held as treasury stock)	$ 456,000
Additional paid-in capital: Common stock	639,000
Retained earnings (after closing entries)	545,000
Treasury stock	(100,000)
Total stockholders' equity	$1,540,000

b. If Stevenson Enterprises declares a 2-for-1 stock split in the form of a 100% stock dividend, the company would make the following entry:

Stock Dividend	360,000*	
Common Stock		360,000
To record a stock split in the form of a stock dividend.		

* $360,000 = (60,000 shares outstanding x 100%) x $6 per share

Common stock ($6 par value, 650,000 shares authorized, 130,000 shares issued, 120,000 shares outstanding, and 10,000 shares held as treasury stock)	$ 780,000
Additional paid-in capital: common stock	525,000
Retained earnings (after closing entries)	335,000
Treasury stock	(100,000)
Total stockholders' equity	$1,540,000

c. If Stevenson Enterprises declares the ordinary stock dividend, the appropriate journal entry would be the same as the entry in Part (a). If Stevenson Enterprises declares the stock split in the form of a dividend after the ordinary stock dividend, the company would have to make the following entry:

Stock Dividend	396,000*	
Common Stock		396,000
To record a stock split in the form of a stock dividend.		

* $396,000 = [(60,000 shares initially outstanding + 6,000 shares issued and outstanding from ordinary stock dividend) x 100%] x $6 per share

Common stock ($6 par value, 650,000 shares authorized, 142,000 shares issued, 132,000 shares outstanding, and 10,000 shares held as treasury stock)	$ 852,000
Additional paid-in capital: common stock	639,000
Retained earnings (after closing entries)	149,000
Treasury stock	(100,000)
Total stockholders' equity	$1,540,000

d. If Stevenson Enterprises declares the stock split in the form of a stock dividend, then the appropriate journal entry would be the same as the entry in Part (b). If Stevenson Enterprises then declares the ordinary stock dividend, the company would have to make the following entry:

Stock Dividend	300,000*	
Common Stock		72,000
Additional Paid-in Capital: Common Stock		228,000
To record 10% stock dividend.		

* $300,000 = [(60,000 shares initially outstanding + 60,000 shares issued in stock split) x 10%] x $25 per share

Common stock ($6 par value, 650,000 shares authorized, 142,000 shares issued, 132,000 shares outstanding, and 10,000 shares held as treasury stock)	$ 852,000
Additional paid-in capital: common stock	753,000
Retained earnings (after closing entries)	35,000
Treasury stock	(100,000)
Total stockholders' equity	$1,540,000

P12–8

a. (1) Treasury Stock	215,000	
Cash		215,000
To record the acquisition of treasury stock.		
(2) Cash	38,000	
Preferred Stock (10%)		20,000
Additional Paid-in Capital: Preferred Stock (10%)		18,000
To record issue of preferred stock.		
(3) Cash	1,125,000	
Retained Earnings	17,500	
Treasury Stock		1,142,500*
To record the reissue of treasury stock.		

* $1,142,500 = [(4,500 shares x $230 per share) + (500 shares x $215 per share)]

(4) 10% Preferred Cash Dividend	202,000[a]	
12% Preferred Cash Dividend	180,000[b]	
Common Cash Dividend	368,000	
Dividends Payable		750,000
To record dividend declaration.		

[a] $200,000 = [(Par value for 1988 x 10%) + (Par value for 1989 x 10%)]
= [(1,000,000 x 10%) + (1,020,000 x 10%)]

[b] $180,000 = (Par value for 1989 x 12%) = $1,500,000 x 12%

(5) Dividends Payable	750,000	
Cash		750,000
To record payment of dividend.		

(6) No journal entry is needed. A memorandum entry should be made stating that the company's common stock now has a par value of $10 per share and that 350,000 shares are now issued and 42,000 shares (after entries [a] and [c]) are held in treasury.

b. Preferred stock (10%, $100 par value, cumulative)	$ 1,020,000
Preferred stock (12%, $100 par value, non-cumulative)	1,500,000
Common stock ($10 par value, 500,000 shares authorized, 350,000 shares issued, and 40,000 shares held in treasury)	3,500,000
Additional paid-in capital	
Preferred stock (10%)	1,068,000
Preferred stock (12%)	1,275,000
Common stock	2,345,000
Retained earnings	4,387,500 *
Treasury stock	(4,822,500)
Total stockholders' equity	$10,273,000

* $4,387,500 = $4,256,000 – $17,500 (entry [c]) – $750,000 (dividends declared) + $899,000 (net income)

P12–9

a. Number of shares issued = Increase in par value ÷ Par value per share
= ($200,000 – $110,000) ÷ $100 per share
= 900 shares

Average issue price = Increase in contributed capital ÷ Number of shares
= (Increase in par value + Increase in additional paid-in capital) ÷ 900 shares
= [($200,000 – $110,000) + ($150,000 – $35,000)] ÷ 900 shares
= $227.78 per share

b. Number of shares issued = ($900,000 – $750,000) ÷ $10 per share
= 15,000 shares

Average issue price = [(900,000 – $750,000) + ($465,000 – $298,000)] ÷ 15,000 shares
= $21.13 per share

c.

Treasury Stock	110,000	
Cash		110,000
To record acquisition of treasury stock.		

Average repurchase price = Total repurchase price ÷ Number of shares held in treasury
= $110,000 ÷ 5,000 shares
= $22.00 per share

d. Prior to the repurchase of the treasury stock, the book value of outstanding shares was

Total common stockholders equity ÷ Number of shares outstanding
= ($1,830,000 + $110,000) ÷ 90,000 shares
= $21.56 per share

After the repurchase of the treasury stock, the book value of outstanding shares was $21.56 per share (i.e., $1,830,000 ÷ 85,000 shares outstanding). So repurchasing the treasury stock decreased the book value per share by $0.03.

P12–10

a. Number of shares issued = Change in total par value ÷ Par value per share
= ($110,000 – $70,000) ÷ $10 per share
= 4,000 shares

b. Average issue price = Cash received ÷ Number of shares issued
= (Change in total par value + Change in additional paid-in capital: common stock) ÷ 4,000 shares (from Part [a])
= [($110,000 – $70,000) – ($625,000 – $500,000)] ÷ 4,000 shares
= $41.25 per share

c. Ending retained earnings = Beginning retained earnings + Net income – Dividends declared – Treasury stock adjustments
$975,000 = 250,000 + 2,000,000 – Dividends declared – 0*
Dividends declared = $1,275,000

---

* Since the balance in Additional Paid-in Capital: Treasury Stock increased during 1988, we know that, on average, Voce Corporation reissued the treasury stock for an amount greater than what the company paid for the stock. Since Retained Earnings is only adjusted for treasury stock transactions when the stock is reissued for an amount less than for what it was acquired, there is no treasury stock adjustment to Retained Earnings during 1988.

d. Total dividends declared = $1,275,000 (from Part [c])

Dividends to preferred stockholders = Dividends in arrears + Current dividends
= Dividends for 1987 + Dividends for 1988
= ($400,000 x 10%) + ($400,000 x 10%)
= $80,000

Dividends to common stockholders = Total dividends – Dividends to preferred
= 1,275,000 – $80,000
= $1,195,000

e.

Treasury Stock	105,000	
Cash		105,000
To record the acquisition of treasury stock.		

f.

Cash	90,000	
Treasury Stock		21,000
Additional Paid-in Capital: Treasury Stock		69,000
To record reissue of treasury stock.		

g. Reissue price per share = Cash received ÷ Number of shares reissued
= $90,000 ÷ 300 shares*
= $300.00 per share

---

* The number of shares reissued is computed as follows:
1. Cost of shares = $105,000 ÷ 1,500 shares = $70 per share.
2. Number of shares reissued = Change in treasury stock balance ÷ $70 per share
= ($105,000 – $84,000) ÷ $70 per share
= 300 shares

P12–11

	Debit	Credit
a. (1) Cash	1,500,000	
Common Stock		600,000
Additional Paid-in Capital: Common Stock		900,000
To record issue of common stock.		
(2) Stock Dividend	300,000*	
Common Stock		300,000
To record 50% stock dividend.		

---

* $300,000 = 50,000 shares outstanding x 50% x $12 par value per share.

	Debit	Credit
(3) Cash	2,700,000	
Common Stock		720,000
Additional Paid-in Capital: Common Stock		1,980,000
To record issue of common stock.		
(4) Treasury Stock	765,000	
Cash		765,000
To record acquisition of treasury stock.		
(5) Cash	275,000	
Treasury Stock		255,000
Additional Paid-in Capital: Treasury Stock		20,000
To record reissue of treasury stock.		

(6) No journal entry is necessary. The company should make a memorandum entry stating that the par value per share has been adjusted to $4 and that the total number of shares issued has been adjusted to 405,000 shares, of which 375,000 shares are outstanding, and 30,000 shares are held in treasury at an adjusted cost of $17 per share.

	Debit	Credit
(7) Cash	160,000	
Treasury Stock		136,000*
Additional Paid-in Capital: Treasury Stock		24,000
To record reissue of treasury stock.		

---

* $136,000 = 8,000 shares x acquisition price per share = 8,000 shares x $17 per share

	Debit	Credit
(8) Cash Dividend	100,000	
Dividend Payable		100,000
To record dividend declaration.		
(9) Dividend Payable	100,000	
Cash		100,000
To record payment of dividend.		

(10) Cash	60,000	
Treasury Stock		34,000*
Additional Paid-in Capital: Treasury Stock		26,000
To record reissue of treasury stock.		

* $34,000 = 2,000 shares x $17 per share

b.

Common stock ($4 par value, 1,000,000 shares authorized, 405,000 shares issued, and 20,000 shares held in treasury)	$1,620,000
Additional paid-in capital	
Common stock	2,880,000
Treasury stock	70,000
Retained earnings	220,000 [a]
Treasury stock	(340,000)[b]
Total stockholders' equity	$4,450,000

[a] $220,000 = Cumulative net income – Cumulative declared dividends
= ($400,000 + $100,000 + $100,000 + $20,000) – ($300,000 from entry [2] + $100,000 from entry [8])

[b] ($340,000) = $765,000 (from entry [4]) – $255,000 (from entry [5]) – $136,000 (from entry [7]) – $34,000 (from entry [10])

P12–12

a. Only shares that are both issued and outstanding are eligible to vote to elect a board of directors. If the current board could reduce the number of shares held by investors other than themselves, then they would control a greater proportion of the shares outstanding. Consequently, the board would decrease the probability that Vadar, Inc. could takeover Edmonds. One way that the board could consolidate its ownership position is to reacquire the company's common stock from other investors.

If the current board could consolidate its ownership so that it controlled 50% plus one share of the outstanding shares, they could completely block Vadar, Inc.'s takeover attempt. In this particular case, the current board members own 140,000 shares (i.e., 35% x 400,000 shares outstanding). To allow the board to completely control the company without the board members personally acquiring any additional shares, the total number of shares outstanding could not exceed 279,999 [i.e., (140,000 shares x 2) – 1 share]. Since 260,000 shares are currently held by non-board investors, and the non-board members can only control a total of 139,999 shares (i.e., 279,999 shares – 140,000 shares held by board members), the company would have to repurchase 120,001 shares of the company's stock.

b. The company will need to pay $50 per share for 120,001 shares (from Part [a]). Consequently, the company will need at least $6,000,050 in cash. Edmonds currently has insufficient cash to repurchase all 120,001 shares. If the board wants to block Vadar's takeover attempt by repurchasing some of its common stock, the company will have to borrow additional cash.

c.

Assets		Liabilities and Stockholders' Equity	
Cash	$ 1,149,950*	Liabilities	$ 5,250,000
Other current assets	4,200,000	Common stock	8,000,000
Noncurrent assets	8,220,000	Retained earnings	6,320,000
		Treasury stock	(6,000,050)
Total Assets	$13,569,950	Total liabilities and stockholders' equity	$13,569,950

* $1,149,950 = $3,150,000 Cash on hand + $4,000,000 Cash borrowed – $6,000,050 Cash paid out for stock

P12–13

a.

	Debit	Credit
Loss on Writedown of Fixed Assets	50,000	
Fixed Assets		50,000
To record writedown of obsolete fixed assets.		

b. **Alternative 1**

	Debit	Credit
Cash	650,000	
Current Assets		200,000
Fixed Assets		450,000
To record liquidation of assets.		
Cash Dividends	250,000	
Cash		250,000
To record dividend declaration.		
Liabilities	400,000	
Cash		400,000
To record payment of liabilities.		

Alternative 2

	Debit	Credit
Cash	650,000	
Current Assets		200,000
Fixed Assets		450,000
To record liquidation of assets.		
Cash Dividends	400,000	
Cash		400,000
To record dividend declaration.		
Liabilities	250,000	
Cash		250,000
To record payment of liabilities.		

Alternative 3

Cash	650,000	
Current Assets		200,000
Fixed Assets		450,000
To record liquidation of assets.		
Treasury Stock	250,000	
Cash		250,000
To record acquisition of treasury stock.		
Liabilities	400,000	
Cash		400,000
To record payment of liabilities.		

Alternative 4

Cash	650,000	
Current Assets		200,000
Fixed Assets		450,000
To record liquidation of assets.		
Treasury Stock	650,000	
Cash		650,000
To record acquisition of treasury stock.		

c. In the event of a liquidation, creditors have the first claim on the company's assets. Consequently, obligations to creditors should be settled in full before the stockholders receive any residual assets. In alternatives (2) and (4), the board of directors has proposed circumventing the law and has planned to distribute assets to the stockholders first and then distribute the residual assets, if any, to the creditors. The creditors could sue the company and probably force the stockholders to return the "excess" dividends, which would then be used to satisfy the creditors' claims.

P12–14

a. **Option 1**

Cash	200,000	
Delivery Truck	50,000	
Capital, Shannon Cummings		120,000
Capital, Patrick Cummings		130,000
To record formation of partnership.		

Option 2

Cash	200,000	
Delivery Truck	50,000	
Common Stock		200,000
Additional Paid-in Capital: Common Stock		50,000
To record formation of the corporation.		

Option 3

Cash	200,000	
Delivery Truck	50,000	
Common Stock (Stated Value)		150,000
Additional Paid-in Capital: Common Stock		100,000
To record formation of the corporation.		

Option 4

	Debit	Credit
Cash	200,000	
Delivery Truck	50,000	
Common Stock		250,000
To record formation of the corporation.		

b.

	Debit	Credit
Income Summary	45,000	
Capital, Shannon Cummings		21,600[a]
Capital, Patrick Cummings		23,400[b]
To record income allocation to owners.		

---

[a] $21,600 = [$120,000 ÷ ($120,000 + $130,000)] x $45,000 net income
[b] $23,400 = [$130,000 ÷ ($120,000 + $130,000)] x $45,000 net income

c. **Shannon**

Net cash inflow = Gross cash withdrawal x (1 – tax rate)
= $21,600 (from Part [b]) x (1 – 33%)
= $14,472

Patrick

Net cash inflow = $23,400 (from Part [b]) x (1 – 33%)
= $15,678

d. **Dividend declaration**

After tax net income = $45,000 x (1 – tax rate)
= $45,000 x (1 – 34%)
= $29,700

	Debit	Credit
Cash Dividends	29,700	
Dividends Payable		29,700
To declare a cash dividend.		

e. **Individual cash flows**

Shannon

Net cash inflow = Gross cash inflow x (1 – tax rate)
= {[$120,000 ÷ ($120,000 + $130,000)] x $29,700} x (1 – 33%)
= $14,256 x 67%
= $9,551.52

Patrick

Net cash inflow = {[$130,000 ÷ ($120,000 + $130,000)] x $29,700} x (1 – 33%)
= $15,444 x 67%
= $10,347.48

f. Double taxation refers to the number of times that the profits of a corporation are ultimately taxed. Since a corporation is a legal entity, it must pay taxes on its profits. Any dividends that the corporation distributes to its shareholders are also subject to taxation. In the case of the dividends, though, the taxes are borne by the shareholders. Consequently, a corporation's profits are taxed twice: once when the corporation earns the income and once when the shareholders receive their dividends.

The liability of partners and stockholders is different. Partners are personally liable for the debts of each partner. Stockholders are usually only liable for the amount invested in the corporation. Hence, in options (2), (3), and (4), the stockholders are only liable for the fair market value of the assets contributed to the corporation.

C12–1

a. Cash 54,000,000
   Common Stock 3,600,000
   Additional Paid-in-Capital 50,400,000
 To record issuance of stock.

b.

	Before	After
Common stock ($1 par value)	$ 12,000,000	$ 15,600,000
Additional paid-in capital: common stock	108,000,000	158,400,000
Total contributed capital	$120,000,000	$174,000,000

c. The number of authorized shares that can be issued is specified in the articles of incorporation. The issuance of new shares is permitted without stockholder approval, as long as the number of shares outstanding does not exceed the authorized amount. If this issuance did, then the stockholders and board of directors would have to approve a new level of authorized shares, because it increases the dispersion (dilutes) of the ownership of the company.

d. Reasons for issuing equity instead of debt include the lack of a required interest payment, the residual claim of shareholders (i.e., the company is not *required* to return any face value on the investment) and it has the appearance of making the company look less risky, because an equity issue decreases the debt/equity ratio.

C12–2

a. April 10 Dividends 4,100,000
   Dividends Payable 4,100,000
 To record declaration of dividend.

May 2 No entry required.

June 1 Dividends Payable 4,100,000
   Cash 4,100,000
 To record payment of dividends.

b.

	April 10	May 2	June 1
Current ratio	Decrease	No effect	Indeterminant*
Working capital	Decrease	No effect	No effect
Debt/equity	Increase	No effect	Decrease

* If current ratio > 1, then transaction will increase it. If < 1, current ratio will decrease.

c. Dividends serve to reduce Retained Earnings, which are a measure of the assets generated through profitable operations. Not all companies with large profits may have cash available to pay a dividend.

d. Factors considered by boards of directors include the nature, financial condition, and desired image of the company, as well as legal constraints. The amount to pay may be restricted by available cash or by debt covenants and state law.

C12–3

a. The distribution of shares in Acme Steel was a property dividend. It was paid in a form other than cash (i.e., securities owned by Interlake).

b.

Declaration:	Property Dividend	131,477	
	Dividend payable		131,477
	To record declaration of dividend.		
Record:	No entry required.		
Payment:	Dividend Payable	131,477	
	Marketable Securities		131,477
	To record payment of property dividend.		

c. The balance sheet value was $131,477, because no gain or loss was recorded.

d. The fair market value of the stock distributed was $131,477.

C12–4

a. The number of shares outstanding prior to the dividend was 24,660,000 ÷ 1.37 = 18,000,000. The number of shares issued was 6,660,000.

b.

Stock Dividend (6,660,000 x $15)	99,900,000	
Common Stock (6,660,000 x $5)		33,300,000
Additional Paid-in Capital		66,600,000
To record stock dividend.		

c. Value before stack dividend: 18,000,000 x $15 = $270,000,000
Value per share after dividend: $270,000,000 ÷ 24,660,000 = $10.95 per share.

d. After the stock dividend, Mr. Jones owned 1.37 x 900,000 = 1,233,000 shares. The percent of the company owned before was (900,000 ÷ 18,000,000) 5%. The percent owned after was (1,233,000 ÷ 24,660,000) 5%. The percentage owned does not change as a result of a stock dividend. Similarly, the value of the investment does not change either, assuming the market price adjusted proportionately to the increase in the number of shares outstanding.

e. A stock dividend does not represent an economic exchange between a corporation and its shareholders. It merely splits the shareholder interests into smaller pieces. The total value of the company and its assets and liabilities remain unchanged.

f. A company may issue a stock dividend for several reasons, which include giving the appearance of paying a dividend when there is limited cash on hand, decreasing the market price of the shares outstanding, and expanding the number of shares outstanding without selling new stock.

C12–5

a. 100 X 3/2 = 150.

b. The stock price would increase by one-half to reflect the fact that the same total value of the company is split into twice as many pieces as before. The increase in the following day may be due to other factors, not related to the split. It may have increased the demand for the stock by reducing the per share value. More investors can afford the stock after the split.

c. Companies split their stock mainly to decrease the market price of the stock, perhaps in a effort to heighten trading, which may increase the price of the stock. No entry is made for a stock split because it does not represent an economic transaction. No assets or liabilities are exchanged, only the par value of the already outstanding stock is affected.

C12–6

a. A treasure stock purchase decreases the number of shares outstanding in the market. This decrease, when the value of the company is relatively unchanged, could lead to a higher share price. Earnings per share would also increase, as there would be fewer number of shares in the denominator when computing it.

b. The threat of acquisition is reduced because there are fewer shares available for acquisition in the market. Shares are concentrated in the hands of fewer shareholders.

c. Debt may be increased because the company may have to issue debt to get cash with which to purchase the treasury stock. Doing so increases the total level of debt and the debt/equity ratio. The debt/equity ratio would have an increased numerator and a decreased denominator, intensifying the effect.

d. The effect of acquiring treasury stock on the company's debt and debt/equity ratio increases the company's riskiness. Consequently, credit-rating services would view the company as more risky and lower the company's credit rating accordingly.

C12–7

a. A hybrid security is one that has characteristics of both debt and equity. Certain kinds of preferred stock are considered hybrid because they include features such as a promised dividend payment, which may or may not be cumulative. This is similar to interest on debt, but the security is technically classified as equity.

b. A credit rating may be protected by issuing hybrid securities because the company is able to obtain more capital funds without increasing its debt burden, which may make it appear more risky.

c. A company near its debt covenant in terms of a debt/equity or debt/asset ratio would leave the ratios the same or improved by the issuance of a hybrid security instead of bonds.

d. Hybrid securities generally do not carry a voting privilege. Accordingly, the company is able to obtain capital without diluting control of the company.

CHAPTER 13 Long-Term Investments

E13–1

a. **Stated rate = 10%**

Face value		$5,000.00
Present value (i = 10%, n = 2)		
Present value of maturity receipt ($5,000 x .82645 from Table 4 in App. A)	$4,132.24	
Present value of interest receipts [($5,000 x 10%) x 1.73554 from Table 5 in App. A]	867.76	
Total present value		5,000.00
Discount/premium		$ 0.00

Therefore, the amount of cash that was loaned is $5,000.00.

Stated rate = 0%

Face value		$5,000.00
Present value (i = 10%, n = 2)		
Present value of maturity receipt ($5,000 x .82645 from Table 4)	$4,132.24	
Present value of interest receipts [($5,000 x 0%) x 1.73554 from Table 5]	0.00	
Total present value		4,132.24
Discount		$ 867.76

Therefore, the amount of cash that was loaned is $4,132.24.

Stated rate = 6%

Face value		$5,000.00
Present value (i = 10%, n = 2)		
Present value of maturity receipt ($5,000 x .82645 from Table 4)	$4,132.24	
Present value of interest receipts [($5,000 x 6%) x 1.73554 from Table 5]	520.66	
Total present value		4,652.90
Discount		$ 347.10

Therefore, the amount of cash that was loaned is $4,652.90.

b. **Stated rate = 10%**

Notes Receivable	5,000.00	
Cash		5,000.00
To record loan made to Barner Brothers.		

Stated rate = 0%

Notes Receivable	5,000.00	
Cash		4,132.24
Discount on Notes Receivable		867.76
To record loan made to Barner Brothers.		

Stated rate = 6%

Notes Receivable	5,000.00	
Cash		4,652.90
Discount on Notes Receivable		347.10
To record loan made to Barner Brothers.		

E13–2

a. **Note A**

Face value		$2,000.00
Present value (*i* = 10%, *n* = 3)		
Present value of maturity receipt ($2,000 x .75132 from Table 4 in App. A)	$1,502.64	
Present value of interest receipts [($2,000 x 0%) x 2.48685 from Table 5 in App. A]	0.00	
Total present value		1,502.74
Discount		$ 497.36

Note B

Face value		$4,000.00
Present value (*i* = 8%, *n* = 4)		
Present value of maturity receipt ($4,000 x .73503 from Table 4)	$2,940.12	
Present value of interest receipts [($4,000 x 0%) x 3.31213 from Table 5]	0.00	
Total present value		2,940.12
Discount		$1,059.88

Note C

Face value		$7,000.00
Present value (*i* = 4%, *n* = 4)		
Present value of maturity receipt ($7,000 x .85480 from Table 4)	$5,983.60	
Present value of interest receipts [($7,000 x 4%) x 3.62990 from Table 5]	1,016.40	
Total present value		7,000.00
Discount/premium		$ 0.00

Note D

Face value		$9,000.00
Present value (*i* = 8%, *n* = 6)		
Present value of maturity receipt ($9,000 x .63017 from Table 4)	$5,671.53	
Present value of interest receipts [($9,000 x 6%) x 4.62288 from Table 5]	2,496.35	
Total present value		8,167.88
Discount		$ 832.12

Note E

Face value		$5,000.00
Present value (*i* = 8%, *n* = 10)		
Present value of maturity receipt ($5,000 x .46319 from Table 4)	$2,315.95	
Present value of interest receipts [($5,000 x 8%) x 6.71008 from Table 5]	2,684.05	
Total present value		5,000.00
Discount/premium		$ 0.00

b. **Note A**

Notes Receivable	2,000.00	
Cash		1,502.74
Discount on Notes Receivable		497.36
To record acceptance of note receivable.		

Note B

Notes Receivable	4,000.00	
Cash		2,940.12
Discount on Notes Receivable		1,059.88
To record acceptance of note receivable.		

Note C

Notes Receivable	7,000.00	
Cash		7,000.00
To record acceptance of note receivable.		

Note D

Notes Receivable	9,000.00	
Cash		8,167.88
Discount on Notes Receivable		832.12
To record acceptance of note receivable.		

Note E

Notes Receivable	5,000.00	
Cash		5,000.00
To record acceptance of note receivable.		

E13–3

a. **Bond A**

Face value		$20,000.00
Present value (i = 5%, n = 6)		
PV of face value		
($20,000 x .74622 from Table 4 in App. A)	$14,924.35	
PV of interest receipts		
[($20,000 x 5%) x 5.07569 from Table 5 in App. A]	5,075.65	
Total present value		20,000.00
Discount/premium		$ 0.00

Therefore, the price of Bond A will be $20,000.00.

Bond B

Face value		$15,000.00
Present value (i = 5%, n = 20)		
PV of face value		
($15,000 x .37689 from Table 4)	$5,653.35	
PV of interest receipts		
[($15,000 x 4%) x 12.46221 from Table 5]	7,477.33	
Total present value		13,130.68
Discount		$ 1,869.32

Therefore, the price of Bond B will be $13,130.68.

Bond C

Face value		$7,000.00
Present Value ($i = 5\%$, $n = 10$)		
PV of face value		
($7,000 x .61391 from Table 4)	$4,297.37	
PV of interest receipts		
[($7,000 x 6%) x 7.72173 from Table 5]	3,243.13	
Total present value		7,540.50
Premium		$ 540.50

Therefore, the price of Bond C will be $7,450.50.

b. Weatherton Enterprises invested in Bond A at its face value; consequently, there is no discount or premium associated with this investment. Since there is no discount or premium to amortize over the life of the investment, the book value of Bond A will remain constant over time.

Weatherton Enterprises acquired Bond B below its face value; consequently, there is a discount associated with this investment. The discount is deducted from the bond's face value to calculate the bond's book value. Since the discount will be amortized over the life of the bond, the discount balance will decrease over the life of the bond. So over time a decreasing amount will be deducted from the face value. Consequently, the book value of Bond B will increase over time.

Weatherton Enterprises acquired Bond C above its face value; consequently, there is a premium associated with this investment. The premium is added to the bond's face value to calculate the bond's book value. Since the premium will be amortized over the life of the bond, the premium balance will decrease over the life of the bond. So over time a decreasing amount will be added to the face value. Consequently, the book value of Bond C will decrease over time.

c. Interest revenue is calculated by multiplying the effective interest rate per period by the book value of the bond at the beginning of the period. For all three bond investments, the effective interest rate per period is constant over time at 5% per period. Consequently, the only factor that will affect whether interest revenue changes over time is the book value of the bond.

For Bond A, the book value is constant over time. Multiplying a constant percentage times a constant amount implies that the interest revenue recognized on Bond A will remain constant over time. For Bond B, the book value will increase over time. Multiplying a constant percentage times an increasing amount implies that the interest revenue recognized on Bond B will increase over time. For Bond C, the book value will decrease over time. Multiplying a constant percentage times a decreasing amount implies that the interest revenue recognized on Bond C will decrease over time.

E13–4

a.

Notes Receivable	10,000.00	
Cash		5,674.00
Discount on Notes Receivable		4,326.00
To record loan made to Watson, Inc.		

b. Interest revenue = Book value x Effective interest rate
= ($10,000 – $4,326) x 12%
= $680.88

c. Book value = Face value – Discount on notes receivable
= $10,000 – ($4,326 – $680.00)
= $6,354.88

d. The interest revenue recognized in the second year will be greater than the interest revenue recognized in the first year. Interest revenue equals the book value of the note times the effective interest rate. Since the book value increases over time as the discount is amortized, and since the effective rate is constant over time, interest revenue must increase over time.

In the second year, the interest revenue would be calculated as follows:

Interest revenue = [$10,000 – ($4,326 – $680.88)] x 12% = $762.58.

Therefore, interest revenue will be $81.70 greater in the second year than in the first year of the note's life.

e. Using the same reasoning as in Part D, the interest revenue will be greater in the third year than it was in the second year. In the third year, the interest revenue would be calculated as follows:
Interest revenue = {$10,000 – [$4,326 – ($680.88 + $762.58)]} x 12% = $854.10.

Therefore, interest revenue will be $91.52 greater in the third year than in the second year of the note's life.

E13–5

a. **Effective rate = 8%**

Face value		$5,000.00
Present value (i = 8%, n = 2)		
Present value of maturity receipt		
($5,000 x .85734 from Table 4 in App. A)	$4,286.70	
Present value of interest receipts		
[($5,000 x 8%) x 1.78326 from Table 5 in App. A]	713.30	
Total present value		5,000.00
Discount/premium		$ 0.00

Effective rate = 10%

Face value		$5,000.00
Present value (i = 10%, n = 2)		
Present value of maturity receipt		
($5,000 x .82645 from Table 4)	$4,132.25	
Present value of interest receipts		
[($5,000 x 8%) x 1.73554 from Table 5]	694.22	
Total present value		4,826.47
Discount		$ 173.53

Effective rate = 12%

Face value		$5,000.00
Present value (i = 12%, n = 2)		
Present value of maturity receipt		
($5,000 x .79719 from Table 4)	$3,985.95	
Present value of interest receipts		
[($5,000 x 8%) x 1.69005 from Table 5]	676.02	
Total present value		4,661.97
Discount		$ 338.03

b. The effective interest rate equals 10%. In Part (a) discounting the future cash flows using an effective rate of 10% resulted in a present value of these cash flows of $4,826 (rounded). Since this is the amount that Bodinger Financial Services loaned to Weyton Industries, it implies that the effective rate of the note is 10%.

c. **January 1, 1990**

Face value		$5,000.00
Present value (i = 10%, n = 2)		
Present value of maturity receipt ($5,000 x .82645 from Table 4)	$4,132.25	
Present value of interest receipts [($5,000 x 8%) x 1.73554 Table 5]	694.22	
Total present value		4,826.47
Discount		$ 173.53

January 1, 1991

Face value		$5,000.00
Present value (i = 10%, n = 1)		
Present value of maturity receipt ($5,000 x .90909 from Table 4)	$4,545.45	
Present value of interest receipts [($5,000 x 8%) x .90909 from Table 5]	363.64	
Total present value		4,909.09
Discount		$ 90.91

d.

Date	Account	Debit	Credit
1/1/90	Notes Receivable	5,000.00	
	Cash		4,826.47
	Discount on Notes Receivable		173.53
	To record loan to Weyton Industries.		
12/31/90	Cash	400.00	
	Discount on Notes Receivable	82.65[a]	
	Interest Revenue		482.65[b]
	To record receipt of interest.		

[a] $482.65 = Book value x Effective interest rate
= $4,826.47 x 10%

[b] $ 82.65 = Interest revenue – Interest received in cash
= $482.65 – $400.00

Date	Account	Debit	Credit
12/31/91	Cash	400.00	
	Discount on Notes Receivable	90.88[a]	
	Interest Revenue		490.88[b]
	To record receipt of interest.		

[a] $ 90.88 = Remaining Discount on Notes Receivable balance to be discounted
= Discount on Notes Receivable balance as of 1/1/90 – Discount amortized during 1990 = $173.53 – $82.65

[b] $490.88 = Interest received in cash + Discount amortized
= $400.00 + $90.88

Account	Debit	Credit
Cash	5,000.00	
Notes Receivable		5,000.00
To record collection on note receivable.		

e. Book value as of 1/1/91 = Book value as of 1/1/90 – Discount balance as of 1/1/91
= $5,000.00 – ($173.53 – $82.65)
= $4,909.12

This amount approximately equals the present value of the future cash flows as of January 1, 1991 calculated in Part (c). The amounts are different by $0.03, which is due to rounding. These amounts are equal because the effective-interest method results in long-term notes being carried on the balance sheet at the present value of their future cash flows discounted using the effective rate on the date the notes were accepted.

E13–6

a. The stated interest rate equals the effective interest rate. Consequently, Christie Sohn purchased the bonds at face value.

b.

		Debit	Credit
	Bond Investment	5,000	
	Cash		5,000
	To record purchase of bonds.		

c.

		Debit	Credit
6/30	Cash	300[a]	
	Interest Revenue		300[b]
	To record receipt of interest.		

[a] $300 = Face value x Stated interest rate per period = $5,000 x 6%
[b] $300 = Book value x Effective interest rate per period = $5,000 x 6%

		Debit	Credit
12/31	Cash	300	
	Interest Revenue		300
	To record receipt of interest.		

d. Book value = Face value – Discount on Notes Receivable + Premium on Notes Receivable
= $5,000 – 0 + 0
= $5,000

e. If the annual effective interest rate is 8%, the effective rate is less than the stated rate. Consequently, Christie Sohn purchased the bonds above their face value (i.e., at a premium). The amount paid for the bonds is $5,811.07, which is calculated as follows:

Face value		$5,000.00
Present value (i = 4%, n = 10)		
PV of face value		
($5,000 x .67556 from Table 4 in App. A)	$3,377.80	
PV of interest receipts		
[($5,000 x 6%) x 8.11090 from Table 5 in App. A]	2,433.27	
Total present value		5,811.07
Premium		$ 811.07

		Debit	Credit
1/1/90	Bond Investment	5,000.00	
	Premium on Bond Investment	811.07	
	Cash		5,811.07
	To record purchase of bonds.		

6/30/90	Cash	300.00[a]	
	Interest Revenue		232.44[b]
	Premium on Bond Investment		67.56[c]
	To record receipt of interest.		

[a] $300.00 = Face value x Stated interest rate per period = $5,000 x 6%
[b] $232.44 = Book value x Effective interest rate per period
= ($5,000 + $811.07) x 4%
[c] $67.56 = Cash received – Interest revenue = $300.00 – $232.44

12/31/90	Cash	300.00	
	Interest Revenue		229.74[a]
	Premium on Bond Investment		70.26[b]
	To record receipt of interest.		

[a] $229.74 = Book value x Effective interest rate per period
= [$5,000 + ($811.07 – $67.56)] x 4%
[b] $70.26 = Cash received – Interest revenue = $300.00 – $229.74

Book value as of 12/31/90 = {$5,000 + [$811.07 – ($67.56 + $70.26)]}
= $5,673.25

f. If the annual effective interest rate is 16%, the effective rate is greater than the stated rate. Consequently, Christie Sohn purchased the bonds below their face value (i.e., at a discount). The amount paid for the bonds is $4,328.97, which is calculated as follows:

Face value		$5,000.00
Present value ($i = 8\%$, $n = 10$)		
PV of face value4		
($5,000 x .46319 from Table 4)	$2,315.95	
PV of interest receipts		
[($5,000 x 6%) x 6.71008 from Table 5]	2,013.02	
Total present value		4,328.97
Discount		$ 671.03

1/1/90	Bond Investment	5,000.00	
	Cash		4,328.97
	Discount on Bond Investment		671.03
	To record purchase of bonds.		

6/30/90	Cash	300.00[a]	
	Discount on Bond Investment	46.32[b]	
	Interest Revenue		346.32[c]
	To record receipt of interest.		

[a] $300.00 = Face value x Stated interest rate per period = $5,000 x 6%
[b] $46.32 = Interest revenue – Cash received = $346.32 – $300.00
[c] $346.32 = Book value x Effective interest rate per period
= ($5,000 – $671.03) x 8%

12/31/90 Cash	300.00	
Discount on Bond Investment	50.02[a]	
Interest Revenue		350.02[b]
To record receipt of interest.		

[a] \$50.02 = Interest revenue – Cash received = \$350.02 – \$300.00
[b] \$229.74 = Book value x Effective interest rate per period
= [\$5,000 – (\$671.03 – \$46.32)] x 8%

Book value as of 12/31/90 = {\$5,000 – [\$671.03 – (\$46.32 + \$50.02)]}
= \$4,425.31

E13–7

a. Interest revenue = Book value at the beginning of the period x Effective interest rate
\$828 = [(\$10,000 – \$800) x Effective interest rate]

Effective interest rate = 9.0%

b. The appropriate journal entry on an interest receipt date is

Cash	XX	
Discount on Notes Receivable	XX	
Interest Revenue		XX

We know that the credit to Interest Revenue was \$828 for 1990. The debit to Discount on Notes Receivable can be inferred from the change in the account balance from the end of 1989 to the end of 1990. The debit was for \$200. If the credit to Interest Revenue was \$828, and the debit to the discount account was \$200, then the debit to Cash for interest received in cash was \$628.

The interest received in cash is calculated as the face value of the note times the stated interest rate. So

\$628 = (\$10,000 x Stated interest rate)

Stated interest rate = 6.28%

c.

Cash	628	
Discount on Notes Receivable	200	
Interest Revenue		828
To record receipt of interest.		

d. Under the effective-interest method, the book value of the note receivable equals the present value of the note using the effective interest rate on the date the note was accepted. Therefore, the present value of the note equals the face value of the note less the associated discount. The present value is \$10,000 – \$600, or \$9,400.

E13–8

Percentage of Ownership in Investee Company	Are the securities marketable? Yes	No
1. Less than 20%	LCM	Cost
2. 20% to 50%	Equity	Equity
3. Greater than 50%	Consolidated	Consolidated

E13–9

a. (1) This investment should be classified as a long-term investment and accounted for using the equity method. Hartney Consulting owns 40% of the investee's common stock, which indicates that they can exert some control over the company, and Hartney Consulting intends to hold the investment for five years.

(2) This investment should be classified as a long-term investment and accounted for using the consolidated method. Hartney owns greater than 50% of the investee, and it appears that Hartney Consulting has no intention of disposing of the investment within the time frame of current assets.

(3) This investment should be classified as a long-term investment and accounted for using the cost method. To be classified as a short-term investment, a ready market for the securities must exist, so that the investor can dispose of the investment at any time. In this case, Hartney Consulting could not dispose of the investment when it desires.

(4) This investment should be classified as a long-term investment and accounted for using the equity method. Hartney Consulting owns 45% of the investee's common stock, which indicates that they desire to exert some control over the company, and Hartney Consulting intends to hold the investment for five years.

(5) This investment should be classified as a long-term investment and accounted for using the cost method. To be classified as a short-term investment, a ready market for the securities must exist, so that the investor can dispose of the investment at any time. In this case, Hartney Consulting could not dispose of the investment when it wishes.

(6) This investment should be classified as a long-term investment and accounted for using the equity method. Although Hartney Consulting owned less than 20% of the investee for a portion of the year, it owned greater than 20% of the investee as of December 31, 1990. Furthermore, the company intends to hold the investment for four years.

b. To be classified as a short-term marketable equity investment, the equity investment must meet two criteria. First, the investor must intend to dispose of the investment within the time frame of current assets. Second, a ready market for the securities must exist. A ready market for the investment enables the investor to dispose of the investment at any time. In the case of nonmarketable equity securities, the investor may not be able to dispose of the investment when it wishes. Since too much uncertainty exists as to whether the investor could actually dispose of nonmarketable investments within the time frame of current assets, the investment should be classified as a long-term investment. To account for equity investments using the lower-of-cost-or-market (LCM) method, the market value of the equity securities must be known. With nonmarketable equity securities, no market value exists. Consequently, nonmarketable equity securities are accounted for using the cost method rather than the LCM method.

E13–10

(1)	Long-Term Investment in Equity Securities	250,000	
	Cash		250,000
	To record investment in Thayers International.		
(2)	Long-Term Investment in Equity Securities	1,000,000	
	Cash		1,000,000
	To record investment in Bayne International.		
(3)	Dividend Receivable	20,000	
	Dividend Revenue		20,000
	To record dividend earned, but not yet received.		
(4)	Cash	150,000	
	Loss on Sale of Investment	50,000	
	Long-Term Investment in Equity Securities		200,000
	To record sale of Bayhe Enterprises stock.		
(5)	Cash	320,000	
	Long-Term Investment in Equity Securities		200,000
	Gain on Sale of Investment		120,000
	To record sale of Thayers International stock.		

E13–11

a. (1)	Long-Term Investment in Equity Securities	250,000	
	Cash		250,000
	To record investment in Thayers International.		
(2)	Long-Term Investment in Equity Securities	1,000,000	
	Cash		1,000,000
	To record investment in Bayne International.		
(3)	Dividend Receivable	20,000	
	Dividend Revenue		20,000
	To record dividend earned, but not yet received.		

		Debit	Credit
(4)	Cash	150,000	
	Loss on Sale of Investment	50,000	
	Long-Term Investment in Equity Securities		200,000
	To record sale of Bayhe Enterprises stock.		
(5)	Cash	320,000	
	Long-Term Investment in Equity Securities		200,000
	Gain on Sale of Investment		120,000
	To record sale of Thayers International stock.		

b.

Securities	Shares Held	Cost	Market Value
Thayers	2,000	$ 50,000	$ 54,000
Bayhe	20,000	800,000	640,000
Total		$850,000	$694,000

	Debit	Credit
Unrealized Loss on Long-Term Equity Investment	156,000*	
Allowance for Unrealized Loss on Long-Term Equity Investment		156,000
To adjust long-term equity investments to LCM.		

* $156,000 = Change in allowance balance = ($850,000 – $694,000) – $0

E13–12

a. The balance in the allowance account represents the excess of the aggregate (i.e., portfolio) cost of long-term equity investments over the aggregate market value of long-term equity investments. On December 31, 1990, the allowance account had a balance of $55,000, which indicates that the aggregate cost exceeded the aggregate market value by $55,000. On December 31, 1991, the allowance account had a balance of $40,000, which indicates that the aggregate cost exceeded the aggregate market value by $40,000. Therefore, the difference between the portfolio cost and portfolio market value was greater on December 31, 1990 than on December 31, 1991.

b.

	Debit	Credit
Allowance for Unrealized Loss on Long-Term Equity Investment	15,000	
Unrealized Loss on Long-Term Equity Investment		15,000
To adjust long-term equity investments to LCM.		

c. Unlike short-term marketable equity securities, applying the lower-of-cost-or-market rule to long-term marketable equity securities does not affect net income. Changes in the difference between the aggregate cost and aggregate market value of long-term marketable equity securities flow through the stockholders' equity section of the balance sheet, not through the income statement. Therefore, the Unrealized Loss on Long-Term Equity Investment account is a permanent account that is carried on the balance sheet. Since the long-term portfolio is carried at the lower-of-cost-or-market value, the Unrealized Loss account can never have a credit balance.

E13–13

a. Finny, Inc. must consider the differences between debt and equity investments. Debt investments are usually characterized by a formal contract that specifies the maturity date of the investment, its maturity value, and its periodic cash flows. On the other hand, equity investments are not usually characterized by a formal contract. Consequently, an equity investment has no definite life, no definite maturity value, and no definite periodic cash flows. Debt investments are also usually characterized by senior claims on the investee's assets in the case of bankruptcy; equity investments only represent a residual claim on the investee's assets. These factors imply that an equity investment is more risky than a debt investment and that an equity investment should provide a larger return than a debt investment, holding everything else constant. Consequently, Finny, Inc. must determine which investment provides the appropriate risk/return tradeoff.

b.

Long-Term Investment in Equity Securities	1,000,000	
Cash		1,000,000
To record investment in Abby Lane Music Company.		

Since Finny, Inc. owns more than 20% of the investee's common stock, Finny should use the equity method to account for this investment. The intent underlying the equity method is to carry the investment at cost adjusted for changes in the investor's proportion of the investee's net assets. Dividends declared by the investee reduce the investee's net assets, which causes the investor's proportion of the investee's net assets to decrease. Consequently, under the equity method, the Investment account is reduced for the investor's portion of any dividends declared by the investee. Dividends declared by the investee are effectively an exchange of assets from the investor's viewpoint.

c.

Bond Investment	1,000,000	
Cash		975,000
Discount on Bond Investment		25,000
To record bond investment in Watson Enterprises.		

d.

Long-Term Investment in Equity Securities	500,000	
Bond Investment	500,000	
Cash		987,500*
Discount on Bond Investment		12,500
To record equity investment in Abby Lane and bond investment in Watson Enterprises.		

* $987,500 = (25,000 shares x $20 per share) + (50% x $975,000 of bonds)

Finny, Inc. now owns 12.5% of Abby Lane Music Company. Since this percentage is less than 20% of the investee's outstanding stock, Finny should use either the lower-of-cost-or-market (LCM) method or the cost method to account for this investment. The decision as to which method to use depends upon whether the stock of Abby Lane is marketable. If its stock is marketable, then Finny should use the LCM method to account for the investment. If its stock is not marketable, then Finny should use the cost method.

E13–14

a. Since Transit Canada owns less than 20% of the investees' outstanding common stock and since the investments are in marketable securities, these two investments should be accounted for using the lower-of-cost-or-market value method. The entry to record the acquisition of the two investments would be

Long-Term Investment in Equity Securities	16,000	
Cash		16,000
To record long-term investment in Lansing, Inc.		
Long-Term Investment in Equity Securities	1,200	
Cash		1,200
To record long-term investment in Melmen Company.		

b. 1. Portfolio cost as of 12/31/89 = (500 shares x $32) + (100 shares x $12) = $17,200
Portfolio market value as of 12/31/89 = (500 shares x $30) + (100 shares x $13) = $16,300
2. Excess of cost over market value = $17,200 – $16,300 = $900
3. Change in excess of cost over market value = $900 – $0 = $900 increase
4. The appropriate adjusting journal entry on December 31, 1989 would be

Unrealized Loss on Long-Term Equity Investments	900	
Allowance for Unrealized Loss on Long-Term Investments		900
To adjust long-term equity securities to LCM.		

c. 1. Portfolio cost as of 12/31/90 = $17,200
Portfolio market value as of 12/31/90 = (500 shares x $33) + (100 shares x $6) = $17,100
2. Excess of cost over market value = $17,200 – $17,100 = $100
3. Change in excess of cost over market value = $900 – $100 = $800 decrease
4. The appropriate adjusting journal entry would be

Allowance for Unrealized Loss on Long-Term Equity Investments	800	
Unrealized Loss on Long-Term Equity Investments		800
To adjust long-term equity securities to LCM.		

d. Book value equals the value of the long-term equity investments accounted for using the lower-of-cost-or-market method. The portfolio market value is less than the portfolio cost, so the securities are valued at the portfolio market value. In this case, the portfolio market value is $17,100 (from Part [c]) as of December 31, 1990.

e. If the stocks of Lansing, Inc. and Melmen Company are not actively traded, then the investment in these two companies should be accounted for using the cost method. The entry to record the acquisition of the securities would be the same under the cost method as the entry under the lower-of-cost-or-market method. Under the cost method, the investments are carried on the books at the cost of the investment. Consequently, no adjusting journal entry is necessary as of December 31, 1989 or as of December 31, 1990 to recognize temporary changes in the aggregate market value of the investments. Since the investments are carried on the books at cost, the book value of these two investments as of December 31, 1990 would be equal to their cost, or $17,200.

E13–15

a.

Date	Account	Debit	Credit
1/1/89	Long-Term Investment in Equity Securities	180,000	
	Cash		180,000
	To record long-term investment in Reilly manufacturing.		
1989	Cash	15,000	
	Long-Term Investment in Equity Securities		15,000
	To record receipt of dividends under the equity method.		
12/31/89	Long-Term Investment in Equity Securities	12,000*	
	Income from Long-Term Equity Investment		12,000
	To record revenue earned from investment under the equity method.		

* $12,000 = $40,000 of investee net income x 30%

Date	Account	Debit	Credit
1990	Cash	15,000	
	Long-Term Investment in Equity Securities		15,000
	To record receipt of dividends under the equity method.		
12/31/89	Loss on Long-Term Equity Investment	2,400	
	Long-Term Investment in Equity Securities		2,400
	To record loss from investment under the equity method.		

b.

Cost of investment	$180,000	
Portion of investee's 1989 net income	12,000	
Portion of dividends declared by investee during 1989	15,000	
Book value of investment as of December 31, 1989		$177,000
Portion of investee's 1990 net loss		2,400
Portion of dividends declared by investee during 1990		15,000
Book value of investment as of December 31, 1990		$159,600

E13–16

a. Since Mainmont Industries owns 40% of Tumbleweed Construction, 40% of Tumbleweed Construction's net income "flows through" to Mainmont Industries' income statement. Consequently, Tumbleweed Construction's total net income for 1990 would be $30,000 (i.e., $12,000 ÷ 40%).

b.

Long-term investment in equity securities: 12/31/89	$25,000
40% of Tumbleweed Construction's 1990 net income	12,000
40% of Tumbleweed Construction's 1990 declared dividends	x
Long-Term investment in equity securities: 12/31/90	$29,000

Mainmont Industries' portion of the dividends declared by Tumbleweed Construction during 1990 was $8,000. Since this amount represents 40% of the total dividends declared by Tumbleweed, the total dividends declared by Tumbleweed were $20,000 (i.e., $8,000 ÷ 40%).

	Debit	Credit
c. Cash	8,000	
Long-Term Investment in Equity Securities		8,000
To record receipt of dividends under the equity method.		
Long-Term Investment in Equity Securities	12,000	
Income from Long-Term Equity Securities		12,000
To record revenue earned from investments under the equity method.		

E13–17

	Debit	Credit
a. Accounts Receivable	30,000	
Inventory	80,000	
Plant and Equipment	280,000	
Goodwill	115,000	
Payables		120,000
Cash		385,000
To record purchase of Lipley Company.		

b. Goodwill amortized in year 1 = $115,000 ÷ 40 years
= $2,875

c. The net book values of assets and liabilities represent the amounts at which the assets and liabilities are carried on the balance sheet. Some assets are carried at historical cost, net realizable value, or lower-of-cost or market value. If the fair market value exceeds these other valuation bases, then the net fair market value of Lipley's assets and liabilities could exceed their book value.

Multiplex is purchasing all of Lipley Company. Consequently, Multiplex is not only purchasing the net assets of Lipley, but it is also purchasing the nonquantifiable items that make Lipley a viable company. These nonquantifiable items include customer loyalty, name recognition, and employee skills and loyalty. These items make Lipley more valuable than the sum of its quantifiable assets and liabilities. Therefore, Multiplex is willing to pay more for Lipley Company than the sum of its individual assets and liabilities, due to synergy.

P13–1

Note 1: The effective interest rate equals the stated interest rate, so this note would sell at par value.

Note 2: The effective interest rate is greater than the stated interest rate, so this note will not be "attractive" to potential investors. Therefore, to attract investors, the note will sell at a discount. The note should sell for a price at which the investor will earn exactly the effective interest rate of 8% on his or her investment.

Note 3: The situation is the same as with Note 2, so this note will also sell at a discount. Note 3 should sell for a price at which the investor will earn exactly the effective interest rate of 15% on his or her investment.

Note 4: The effective interest rate is less than the stated interest rate, so this note will be "attractive" to investors. Since demand to invest in this note will exceed the supply, the bond will sell at a premium. Note 4 should sell for a price at which the investor will earn exactly the effective interest rate of 8.1% on his or her investment.

P13–2

January 1, 1989		
Face value		$10,000
Present value (i = 6%, n = 2)		
PV of face value		
($10,000 x .89000 from Table 4 in App. A)	$8,900	
PV of interest receipts		
[($10,000 x 0%) x 1.83339 from Table 5 in App. A)	0	
Total present value		8,900
Discount		$ 1,100
December 31, 1989		
Face value		$10,000
Present value (i = 6%, n = 1)		
PV of face value		
($10,000 x .94340 from Table 4)	$9,434	
PV of interest receipts		
[($10,000 x 0%) x .94340 from Table 5)	0	
Total present value		9,434
Discount		$ 566

b. Notes Receivable	10,000	
Cash		8,900
Discount on Notes Receivable		1,100
To record receipt of note receivable.		
c. Discount on Notes Receivable	534*	
Interest Revenue		534
To record interest earned.		

* $534 = Book value x Effective interest rate per period
= ($10,000 – $1,100) x 6%

Book value as of 12/31/89 = [$10,000 – ($1,100 – $534)]
= $9,434

d. Discount on Notes Receivable	550*	
Interest Revenue		550
To record interest earned.		

* $550 = Total discount ÷ Number of periods = $1,100 ÷ 2 periods

Book value as of 12/31/89 = [$10,000 – ($1,100 – $550)] = $9,450

e. Compare the book value computed in Part (c) to the present value of the future cash flows as of December 31, 1989 computed in Part (a) and also compare the book value computed in Part (d) to the present value of the future cash flows as of December 31, 1989 computed in Part (a). The book value computed using the effective-interest method (i.e., Part [c]) equals the present value of the future cash flows, while the book value computed using the straight-line method (i.e., Part [d]) does not. The effective-interest method is, therefore, preferred to the straight-line method because the effective-interest method results in notes and bonds being carried on the balance sheet at the present value of the future cash flows discounted using the effective interest rate on the date the note or bond was acquired.

P13–3

a. (1)

Face value		$5,000.00
Present value (i = 12%, n = 6)		
PV of face value		
($5,000 x .50663 from Table 4 in App. A)	$2,533.15	
PV of interest receipts		
[($5,000 x 12%) x 4.11141 from Table 5 in App. A]	2,466.85	
Total present value		5,000.00
Discount/premium		$ 0.00

Notes Receivable	5,000	
Cash		5,000
To record loan to West Ore Corporation.		

(2)

Cash	600[a]	
Interest Revenue		600[b]
To record receipt of interest.		

[a] $600 = Face value x Stated interest rate = $5,000 x 12%
[b] $600 = Book value x Effective interest rate = $5,000 x 12%

(3)

Cash	5,000	
Notes Receivable		5,000
To record receipt of principal payment from West Ore Corporation.		

b. (1)

Face value		$5,000.00
Present value (i = 12%, n = 6)		
PV of face value		
($5,000 x .50663 from Table 4)	$2,533.15	
PV of interest receipts		
[($5,000 x 6%) x 4.11141 from Table 5]	1,233.42	
Total present value		3,766.57
Discount/premium		$1,233.43

Notes Receivable	5,000	
Cash		3,766.57
Discount on Notes Receivable		1,233.43
To record loan to West Ore Corporation.		

(2)

Cash	300.00[a]	
Discount on Notes Receivable	151.99[b]	
Interest Revenue		451.99[c]
To record receipt of interest.		

[a] $300 = Face value x Stated interest rate = $5,000 x 6%
[b] $151.99 = Interest revenue – Cash received = $451.99 – $300.00
[c] $451.99 = Book value x Effective interest rate
= ($5,000 – $1,233.43) x 12%

3. Cash	5,000	
Notes Receivable		5,000
To record receipt of principal payment from West Ore Corporation.		

c. (1) Face value		$5,000.00
Present Value (i = 12%, n = 6)		
PV of face value ($5,000 x .50663 from Table 4)	$2,533.15	
PV of interest receipts [($5,000 x 0%) x 4.11141 from Table 5]	0.00	
Total present value		2,533.15
Discount		$2,466.85

Notes Receivable	5,000	
Cash		2,533.15
Discount on Notes Receivable		2,466.85
To record loan to West Ore Corporation.		

(2) Discount on Notes Receivable	303.98	
Interest Revenue		303.98*
To record receipt of interest.		

* $303.98 = Book value x Effective interest rate
= ($5,000 – $2,466.85) x 12%

(3) Cash	5,000	
Notes Receivable		5,000
To record receipt of principal payment from West Ore Corporation.		

P13–4

a. **Discount rate = 8%**

Face value		$12,000.00
Present value (i = 8%, n = 3)		
PV of face value ($12,000 x .79383 from Table 4 in App. A)	$9,525.96	
PV of interest receipts [($12,000 x 6%) x 2.5771 from Table 5 in App. A)	1,855.51	
Total present value		11,381.47
Discount		$ 618.53

Discount rate = 10%

Face value		$12,000.00
Present value (i = 10%, n = 3)		
PV of face value ($12,000 x .75132 from Table 4)	$9,015.84	
PV of interest receipts [($12,000 x 6%) x 2.48685 from Table 5)	1,790.53	
Total present value		10,806.37
Discount		$ 1,193.63

Discount rate = 12%

Face value		$12,000.00
Present value (i = 12%, n = 3)		
PV of face value		
($12,000 x .71178 from Table 4)	$8,541.36	
PV of interest receipts		
[($12,000 x 6%) x 2.40183 from Table 5)	1,729.32	
Total present value		10,270.68
Discount		$1,729.32

The effective interest rate is 10%. Using a discount rate of 10%, the present value of the future cash flows specified in the note equals $10,806 (rounded). This amount is the same as the amount of the accounts receivable that was converted to a note.

b.

		Debit	Credit
	Notes Receivable	12,000	
	Accounts Receivable		10,806
	Discount on Notes Receivable		1,194
	To record conversion of an open account to a note.		

c.

Date	Account	Debit	Credit
12/31/90	Interest Receivable	120.00[a]	
	Discount on Notes Receivable	60.10[b]	
	Interest Revenue		180.10[c]
	To record interest earned.		

[a] $120.00 = Face value x stated interest rate x 2/12
= $12,000 x 6% x 2/12

[b] $60.10 = Interest revenue – Interest receivable

[c] $180.10 = Book value x Effective interest rate x 2/12
= ($12,000 – $1,194) x 10% x 2/12

Date	Account	Debit	Credit
10/31/91	Cash	720.00	
	Discount on Notes Receivable	300.50	
	Interest Receivable		120.00
	Interest Revenue		900.50
	To record receipt of interest.		
12/31/91	Interest Receivable	120.00	
	Discount on Notes Receivable	66.11	
	Interest Revenue		186.11
	To record interest earned.		
10/31/92	Cash	720.00	
	Discount on Notes Receivable	330.55	
	Interest Receivable		120.00
	Interest Revenue		930.55
	To record receipt of interest.		
12/31/92	Interest Receivable	120.00	
	Discount on Notes Receivable	72.79	
	Interest Revenue		192.79
	To record interest earned.		

10/31/93	Cash	720.00	
	Discount on Notes Receivable	363.95	
	Interest Receivable		120.00
	Interest Revenue		963.95
	To record receipt of interest.		

d. 11/1/93	Cash	12,000	
	Notes Receivable		12,000
	To record receipt of principal payment.		

P13–5

a. Face value — $100,000

a. Face value		$100,000
Present value (i = 12%, n =2)		
PV of face value		
($100,000 x .79719 from Table 4 in App. A)	$79,719	
PV of interest receipts		
[($100,000 x 4%) x 1.69005 from Table 5 in App. A]	6,760	
Total present value		86,479
Discount		$13,521

b. Cash	10,000	
Notes Receivable	100,000	
Discount on Notes Receivable		13,521
Sales		96,479
To record sale of merchandise.		

c.

Date	Cash Received[a]	Interest Revenue[b]	Discount Amortized[c]	Face Value	Discount Balance	Book Value
4/1/90				$100,000.00	$13,521.00	$ 86,479.00
3/31/91	$4,000.00	$10,377.48	$6,377.48	100,000.00	7,143.52	92,856.48
3/31/92	4,000.00	11,143.52	7,143.52	100,000.00	0.00	100,000.00
4/1/92	100,000.00			0.00	0.00	0.00

[a] Cash received = Face value x 4%
[b] Interest Revenue = Book value at beginning of the period x 12%
[c] Discount amortized = Interest revenue – Cash received.

12/31/90	Interest Receivable	3,000.00*	
	Discount on Notes Receivable	4,783.11*	
	Interest Revenue		7,783.11*
	To record interest earned.		

* Amounts equal 75% of the amounts listed on the schedule for 3/31/91

3/31/91	Cash	4,000.00	
	Discount on Notes Receivable	1,594.37*	
	Interest Receivable		3,000.00
	Interest Revenue		2,594.37*
	To record receipt of interest.		

* Amounts equal the amounts listed on the schedule for 3/31/91 less the associated amounts from the 12/31/90 entry.

12/31/91	Interest Receivable	3,000.00*	
	Discount on Notes Receivable	5,357.64*	
	Interest Revenue		8,357.64*
	To record interest earned.		

* Amounts equal 75% of the amounts listed on the schedule for 3/31/92.

3/31/92	Cash	4,000.00	
	Discount on Notes Receivable	1,785.88*	
	Interest Receivable		3,000.00
	Interest Revenue		2,785.88*
	To record receipt of interest.		

* Amounts equal the amounts listed on the schedule for 3/31/92 less the associated amounts from the 12/31/91 entry.

4/1/92	Cash	100,000	
	Notes Receivable		100,000
	To record collection of principal.		

d. Johnson House Supplies would be indifferent between accepting a cash payment of $96,479 and accepting a cash payment of $10,000 plus the note receivable. Since the present value of the note is $86,479 (from Part [a]), the total present value of accepting $10,000 plus the note receivable would be $96,479. Consequently, the present value of both of these options is $96,479.

P13–6

a. **Discount rate = 6%**

Face value		$693,000.00
Present value (i = 6%, n = 3)		
PV of face value		
($693,000 x .83962 from Table 4 in App. A)	$581,856.66	
PV of interest receipts		
[($693,000 x 0%) x 2.67301 from Table 5 in App. A]	0.00	
Total present value		581,856.66
Discount		$111,143.34

Discount rate = 8%

Face value		$693,000.00
Present value (i = 8%, n = 3)		
PV of face value		
($693,000 x .79383 from Table 4)	$550,124.19	
PV of interest receipts		
[($693,000 x 0%) x 2.57710 from Table 5]	0.00	
Total present value		550,124.19
Discount		$142,875.81

Discount rate = 10%

Face value		$693,000.00
Present value (i = 10%, n = 3)		
PV of face value		
($693,000 x .75132 from Table 4)	$520,664.76	
PV of interest receipts		
[($693,000 x 0%) x 2.48685 from Table 5]	0.00	
Total present value		520,664.76
Discount		$172,335.24

The building has a fair market value of $550,125 which represents the cash value of the transaction. Using a discount rate of 8%, the future cash flows specified in the note equal approximately $550,125. Consequently, the appropriate effective interest rate is 8%.

b.

Notes Receivable	693,000	
Accumulated Depreciation	100,000	
Building		500,000
Discount on Notes Receivable		142,875
Gain on Disposal of Building		150,125
To record sale of building.		

c.

12/31/91	Discount on Notes Receivable	44,010*	
	Interest Revenue		44,010
	To record interest earned.		

* $44,010 = Book value x Effective interest rate = ($693,000 – $142,875) x 8%.

12/31/92	Discount on Notes Receivable	47,530.80*	
	Interest Revenue		47,530.80
	To record interest earned.		

* $47,530.80 = [$693,000 – ($142,875 –$44,010)] x 8%.

12/31/93	Discount on Notes Receivable	51,333.20*	
	Interest Revenue		51,333.20
	To record interest earned.		

* $51,333.20 = $142,875 – ($44,010 + $47,530.80).

1/1/94	Cash	693,000	
	Notes Receivable		693,000
	To record collection of principal.		

If a note is non-interest bearing (as it is in this case), then the balance in the account Discount on Notes Receivable represents the amount of interest revenue that will be recognized over the remaining life of the note.

P13–7

a.	Face value		$100,000.00
	Present value (i = 6%, n = 6)		
	PV of face value		
	($100,000 x .70496 from Table 4 in App. A)	$70,496.00	
	PV of interest receipts		
	[($100,000 x 4%) x 4.91732 from Table 5 in App. A]	19,669.28	
	Total present value		90,165.28
	Discount		$ 9,834.72

b.	Bond Investment	100,000.00	
	Cash		90,165.28
	Discount on Bond Investment		9,834.72
	To record investment in bonds.		

c.

Date	Cash Received[a]	Interest Earned[b]	Increase in Bond Investment[c]	Bond Investment
12/31/90				$ 90,165.28
6/30/91	$ 4,000.00	$5,409.92	$1,409.92	91,575.20
12/31/91	4,000.00	5,494.51	1,494.51	93,069.71
6/30/92	4,000.00	5,584.18	1,584.18	94,653.89
12/31/92	4,000.00	5,679.23	1,679.23	96,333.12
6/30/93	4,000.00	5,779.99	1,779.99	98,113.11
12/31/93	4,000.00	5,886.89	1,886.89	100,000.00
12/31/93	100,000.00			0.00

[a] Cash received = Face value x Stated interest rate per period
= $100,000 x 4%.

[b] Interest earned = Bond investment at beginning of period x 6%.

[c] Increase in bond investment = Interest earned – Cash received.

d.	6/30/91	Cash	4,000.00	
		Discount on Bond Investment	1,409.92	
		Interest Revenue		5,409.92
		To record receipt of interest.		
	12/31/91	Cash	4,000.00	
		Discount on Bond Investment	1,494.51	
		Interest Revenue		5,494.51
		To record receipt of interest.		

Date	Account	Debit	Credit
6/30/92	Cash	4,000.00	
	Discount on Bond Investment	1,584.18	
	Interest Revenue		5,584.18
	To record receipt of interest.		
12/31/92	Cash	4,000.00	
	Discount on Bond Investment	1,679.23	
	Interest Revenue		5,679.23
	To record receipt of interest.		
6/30/93	Cash	4,000.00	
	Discount on Bond Investment	1,779.99	
	Interest Revenue		5,779.99
	To record receipt of interest.		
12/31/93	Cash	4,000.00	
	Discount on Bond Investment	1,886.89	
	Interest Revenue		5,886.89
	To record receipt of interest.		
e. 12/31/93	Cash	100,000	
	Bond Investment		100,000
	To record collection of principal.		

P13–8

a. **July 1, 1989**

Face value		$10,000.00
Present value (i = 5%, n = 3)		
PV of face value		
($10,000 x .86384 from Table 4 in App. A)	$8,638.40	
PV of interest receipts		
[($10,000 x 3%) x 2.72325 from Table 5 in App. A]	816.98	
Total present value		9,455.38
Discount		$ 544.62

December 31, 1989

Face value		$10,000.00
Present value (i = 5%, n = 2)		
PV of face value4		
($10,000 x .90703 from Table 4)	$9,070.30	
PV of interest receipts		
[($10,000 x 3%) x 1.85941 from Table 5]	557.82	
Total present value		9,628.12
Discount		$ 371.88

June 30, 1990

Face value		$10,000.00
Present value (i = 5%, n = 1)		
PV of face value		
($10,000 x .95238 from Table 4)	$9,523.80	
PV of interest receipts		
[($10,000 x 3%) x .95238 from Table 5]	285.71	
Total present value		9,809.51
Discount		$ 109.49

December 31, 1990

Face value		$10,000.00
Present value (i = 5%, n = 0)		
PV of face value		
($10,000 x 1.00)	$10,000.00	
PV of interest receipts		
[($10,000 x 0%) x 1.00]	0.00	
Total present value		10,000.00
Discount		$ 0.00

b.

Bond Investment	10,000.00	
Cash		9,455.38
Discount on Bond Investment		544.62
To record investment in bonds.		

c.

Date	Interest Revenue[a]	Cash Interest Received[b]	Book Value of Bond Investment
6/30/89			$ 9,455.38
12/31/89	$472.77	$300.00	9,628.15
6/31/90	481.41	300.00	9,809.56
12/31/90	490.44	300.00	10,000.00

[a] Interest revenue = Book value of bond investment x 5%.
[b] Cash received = Face value x 3%.

d. Compare the book value of the bond investment in Part (c) to the corresponding present value of future cash flows calculated in Part (a). The book value of the bond investment equals the present value of the future cash flows (adjusted for rounding differences). Consequently, bond investments are carried on the balance sheet at the present value of the future cash flows under the effective-interest method. The appropriate discount factor used to calculate the present value of the future cash flows is the effective interest rate on the date that the bonds were purchased.

P13–9

a. (1) The bonds were purchased below their face value (i.e., at a discount). Bonds sell at a discount when the effective interest rate is greater than the stated interest rate. When the effective interest rate exceeds the stated interest rate, the bond offers a return less than the required return given the riskiness of the investment. Consequently, demand for the bond is less than the supply. To equate the supply of the bonds with the demand for them, the price is reduced until the investors will earn the the effective interest rate on their investments.

(2) **Annual discount rate = 8%**

Face value		$200,000.00
Present value (i = 4%, n = 20)		
PV of face value		
($200,000 x .45639 from Table 4 in App. A)	$ 91,278.00	
PV of interest receipts		
[($200,000 x 5%) x 13.59033 from Table 5 in App. A]	135,903.30	
Total present value		227,181.30
Premium		$ 27,181.30

Annual discount rate = 10%

Face value		$200,000.00
Present value (i = 5%, n = 20)		
PV of face value		
($200,000 x .37689 from Table 4)	$ 75,378.00	
PV of interest receipts		
[($200,000 x 5%) x 12.46221 from Table 5]	124,662.00	
Total present value		200,000.00
Discount/premium		$ 0.00

Annual discount rate = 12%

Face value		$200,000.00
Present value (i = 6%, n = 20)		
PV of face value		
($200,000 x .31180 from Table 4)	$ 62,360.00	
PV of interest receipts		
[($200,000 x 5%) x 11.46992 from Table 5]	114,699.20	
Total present value		177,059.20
Discount		$ 22,940.80

The effective interest rate is the interest rate that equates the discounted future cash flows and the purchase price of the bonds. In this case, the purchase price equals $177,060. Using a discount rate of 12% results in the discounted future cash flows being equal to the purchase price. Consequently, the appropriate annual effective interest rate is 12%.

(3) Bond Investment	200,000.00	
Cash		177,060.00
Discount on Bond Investment		22,940.00
To record investment in bonds.		

(4) Cash	10,000.00[a]	
Discount on Bond Investment	623.60[b]	
Interest Revenue		10,623.60[c]
To record receipt of interest.		

---

[a] $10,000.00 = Face value x Interest rate per period
= $200,000 x 5%.

[b] $623.60 = Interest revenue – Cash received

[c] $10,623.60 = Book value x Effective interest rate per period
= ($200,000 – $22,940) x 6%

b. (1) Price of the bonds would be $227,181.30, from Part (a[1]).

(2)

Bond Investment	200,000.00	
Premium on Bond Investment	27,181.30	
Cash		227,181.30
To record investment in bonds.		

(3)

Cash	10,000.00[a]	
Premium on Bond Investment		912.75[b]
Interest Revenue		9,087.25[c]
To record receipt of interest.		

[a] $10,000.00 = Face value x Interest rate per period
= $200,000 x 5%.
[b] $912.75 = Cash received – Interest revenue
[c] $9,087.25 = Book value x Effective interest rate per period
= ($200,000 + $27,181.30) x 4%

P13–10

a. On the date of purchase, the annual effective interest rate was 10%, while the annual stated interest rate was 14%. Since the stated interest rate was greater than the effective interest rate, these bonds offered an interest rate greater than the riskiness of the investment warranted. Consequently, this investment was attractive to investors, thereby driving up the demand for these bonds. Since the supply of the bonds was fixed, the price of the bonds increased and stabilized at the point where investors would earn exactly the effective interest rate on their investments. Therefore, the bonds sold for an amount greater than their face value (i.e., at premium).

b.

Face value		$100,000.00
Present value (i = 5%, n = 20)		
PV of face value ($100,000 x .37689 from Table 4 in App. A)	$37,689.00	
PV of interest receipts [($100,000 x 7%) x 12.46221 from Table 5 in App. A]	87,235.47	
Total present value		124,924.47
Premium		$ 24,924.47

The entry to record the bond investment would be

Bond Investment	100,000.00	
Premium on Bond Investment	24,924.47	
Cash		124,924.47
To record investment in bonds.		

c.

12/31/89	Cash	7,000.00[a]	
	Premium on Bond Investment		753.78[b]
	Interest Revenue		6,246.22[c]
	To record receipt of interest.		

[a] $7,000.00 = Face value x Stated interest rate per period = $100,000 x 7%
[b] $753.78 = Cash received – Interest revenue
[c] $6,246.22 = Book value x Effective interest rate per period
= ($100,000.00 + $24,924.47) x 5%

6/30/90	Cash	7,000.00[a]	
	Premium on Bond Investment		791.47[b]
	Interest Revenue		6,208.53[c]
	To record receipt of interest.		

[a] $7,000.00 = Face value x Stated interest rate per period = $100,000 x 7%
[b] $791.47 = Cash received – Interest revenue
[c] $6,208.53 = Book value x Effective interest rate per period
= [$100,000.00 + ($24,924.47 – $753.78) x 5%

d. If Hussin Imports sells the bonds, they will sell for an amount equal to the future cash flows for the remaining 18 six-month periods discounted at an annual rate of 6%. This rate would be adjusted to a six-month interest rate of 3%. The selling price would, therefore, be

Face value		$100,000.00
Present value (***i* = 3%, *n* = 18**)		
PV of face value ($100,000 x .58739 from Table 4)	$58,739.00	
PV of interest receipts [($100,000 x 7%) x 13.75351 from Table 5]	96,274.57	
Total present value		155,013.57
Premium		$ 55,013.57

If the company decides to sell the bonds, it would receive $155,013.57 in cash. This amount represents a gain of $31,634.35 over the carrying value of the bonds on July 1, 1990. Although the company would realize a gain on the sale of the bonds, the actual decision to buy or hold the bonds hinges upon (1) the cash needs of the company and (2) alternative investment opportunities. The company is currently earning a return of 10% on its investment (i.e., the effective interest rate on the date of purchase). If the company sold the bonds and tried to reinvest the proceeds in a similar-risk company, Hussin Imports could only earn a return of 6% on its investment. The company should also consider the tax ramifications of recognizing a gain. A gain would increase the company's taxable income, thereby increasing the company's tax liability. So unless the company has an urgent need for cash, it should probably not sell the investment. Even if the company has an urgent need for cash, it should investigate borrowing opportunities. If the company can borrow money at an interest rate less than 10%, it may be better off borrowing money and holding its bond investment. Furthermore, the interest incurred on the borrowed money would be tax deductible and reduce the company's tax liability.

e. Cash	155,013.57	
Bond Investment		100,000.00
Premium on Bond Investment		23,379.22
Gain on Sale of Bond Investment		31,634.35
To record sale of bond investment.		

f. If Hussin Imports sells the bonds, the bonds will sell for an amount equal to the cash flows of the remaining 18 six-month periods, discounted at an annual rate of 12%. This rate would be adjusted to a six-month interest rate of 6%. The selling price would be calculated as follows:

Face value		$100,000.00
Present value (***i* = 6%, *n* = 18**)		
PV of face value		
($100,000 x .35034 from Table 4)	$35,034.00	
PV of interest receipts		
[($100,000 x 7%) x 10.82760 from Table 5]	75,793.20	
Total present value		110,827.20
Premium		$ 10,827.20

The entry to record the sale of the bonds would be

Cash	110,827.20	
Loss on Sale of Bond Investment	12,552.02	
Bond Investment		100,000.00
Premium on Bond Investment		23,379.22
To record sale of bond investment.		

P13–11

a. **1988**

Unrealized Loss on Long-Term Equity Investments	40,000	
Allowance for Unrealized Losses on Long-Term Equity Investments		40,000
To adjust long-term investments to LCM.		

1989

Unrealized Loss on Long-Term Equity Investments	10,000	
Allowance for Unrealized Losses on Long-Term Equity Investments		10,000
To adjust long-term investments to LCM.		

1990

Allowance for Unrealized Losses on Long-Term Equity Investments	50,000	
Unrealized Loss on Long-Term Equity Investments		50,000
To adjust long-term investments to LCM.		

b. Under the lower-of-cost-or-market rule, long-term marketable equity securities are carried on the books at the lower of cost or market value. If the aggregate cost exceeds the aggregate market value, the Allowance account is used to adjust the portfolio of long-term marketable equity securities from its cost to its market value. The balance in the Allowance account represents the excess of the aggregate cost over the aggregate market value of long-term marketable equity securities. Since the balance in the Allowance account on December 31, 1990 is zero, it can be inferred that the aggregate market value is not less than the aggregate cost.

If the aggregate market value were less than the aggregate cost, the Allowance account would have a credit balance. If the aggregate market value were equal to or greater than the aggregate cost, the allowance account would have a balance of zero. Consequently, it can be inferred that the aggregate cost is not greater than the aggregate market value, but it is not possible to infer whether the aggregate cost is equal to or less than the aggregate market value.

P13–12

a. Acme Households uses the lower-of-cost-or-market method. We can infer that the company uses this method since it uses an Allowance for Unrealized Loss on Long-Term Equity Investments account.

b. The balance in Long-Term Investment in Equity Securities increased by $5,000 during 1990. If Acme did not sell any long-term securities during 1990, then the entire $5,000 increase represents the cost of long-term securities purchased by Acme during 1990.

The balance in Long-Term Investment in Equity Securities represents the cost of long-term equity investments, while the balance in Allowance for Unrealized Loss on Long-Term Equity Investments represents the excess of the aggregate cost over the aggregate market value of long-term equity investments. Since the latter account balance decreased from $1,200 to $700 during 1990, the excess of the aggregate cost over the aggregate market value decreased $500 during 1990. Therefore, the aggregate cost of long-term equity investments decreased in relation to the aggregate market value of long-term equity investments during 1990.

c.

Allowance for Unrealized Loss on Long-Term Equity Investments	500	
Unrealized Loss on Long-Term Equity Investments		500
To adjust long-term equity securities to LCM.		

Both of these accounts are balance sheet accounts; consequently, adjusting long-term equity securities to LCM does not affect the income statement. Unrealized Loss on Long-Term Equity Investments is disclosed as part of stockholders' equity on the balance sheet. Consequently, changes in this account affect a company's debt/equity ratio. The account is a contra-stockholders' equity account, implying that decrease in its balance increases total stockholders' equity. In this case, the account balance decreased, so the company's debt/equity ratio also decreased.

d. The entry to record the sale of the investments would be

Cash	28,000	
Long-Term Investment in Equity Securities		25,000
Gain on Sale of Securities		3,000
To record sale of long-term equity securities.		

As of December 31, 1991, the account Allowance for Unrealized Loss on Long-Term Equity Investments should have a zero balance. Since the balance of $700 carried over from December 31, 1990, an adjusting journal entry is necessary. The adjusting journal entry to adjust the portfolio to LCM would be

Allowance for Unrealized Loss on Long-Term Equity Investments	700	
Unrealized Loss on Long-Term Equity Securities		700
To adjust long-term equity securities to LCM.		

P13–13

Since Sparrow Electronics owns less than 20% of each of the investees, and since each of the investees' stock is considered to be marketable, these investments should be accounted for using the lower-of-cost-or-market method.

2/2	Cash	7,500	
	Dividend Receivable		7,500
	To record receipt of dividend.		
3/19	Cash	80,000	
	Long-Term Investments in Equity Securities		50,000
	Gain on Sale of Long-Term Equity Securities		30,000
	To record sale of long-term securities.		
5/29	Long-Term Investment in Equity Securities	28,000	
	Cash		28,000
	To record investment in Heinekin, Inc.		
6/30	Dividend Receivable	16,000*	
	Dividend Revenue		16,000
	To record dividends earned on investments.		

* $16,000 = $2.00 per share x (10,000 shares owned as of 1/1/90 – 2,000 shares sold on 3/19)

7/10	Cash	16,000	
	Dividend Receivable		16,000
	To record receipt of dividend.		
11/27	Long-Term Investment in Equity Securities	135,000	
	Cash		135,000

To record investment in Beck Enterprises.

12/31 1. Portfolio Cost
(8,000 shares of Beck x $25 per share) + (3,000 shares of Beck x $45 per share) + (5,000 shares of Moosehead x $20 per share) + (3,000 shares of Heinekin x $25 per share) + (1,000 shares of Heinekin x $28 per share) = $538,000

Portfolio Market Value
(11,000 shares of Beck x $42.50 per share) + (5,000 shares of Moosehead x $28.00 per share) + (4,000 shares of Heinekin x $24.00 per share) = $703,500

2. Excess of portfolio cost over portfolio market value
= $538,000 – $703,500
= $0 (Marketable securities are recorded at the lower-of-cost-or-market value; therefore, the securities cannot be recorded above cost.)

3. Change in excess of cost over market value
= $0 – $8,000 = $8,000 decrease

4. The appropriate adjusting journal entry would be

Allowance for Unrealized Loss on Long-Term Equity Investments	8,000	
Unrealized Loss on Long-Term Equity Investments		8,000
To adjust long-term equity securities to LCM.		

P13–14

a. The account Allowance for Unrealized Loss on Long-term Equity Investments only applies to long-term marketable equity securities. Consequently, only the long-term marketable equity securities owned as of December 31, 1989 should be used to calculate the December 31, 1989 account balance. Therefore, the investments that should be considered are Langley, Inc., Valley Corporation, Boston Celtics, and Enterprise Flights.

Portfolio Cost = $110,000 + $150,000 + $50,000 + $300,000 = $610,000
Portfolio Market Value = $105,000 + $135,000 + $75,000 + $285,000 = $600,000

Allowance balance = Excess of portfolio cost over portfolio market value
= $610,000 – $600,000
= $10,000

b.

Cash	272,000	
Loss on Sale of Long-Term Equity Investment	28,000	
Long-Term Investment in Equity Securities		300,000
To record sale of long-term equity securities.		

c.

Long-Term Investment in Equity Securities	200,000	
Cash		200,000
To record investment in Newton Labs.		
Cash	25,000	
Dividends Receivable	3,000	
Dividend Revenue		28,000
To record dividends earned on investments.		

d. As of December 31, 1990, the following investments should be accounted for using the lower-of-cost-or-market method: Langley, Inc., Valley Corporation, Boston Celtics, and Newton Labs.

Portfolio Cost = $110,000 + $150,000 + $50,000 + $200,000 = $510,000
Portfolio Market Value = $120,000 + $125,000 + $60,000 + $50,000 = $355,000

Excess of portfolio cost over portfolio market value
= $510,000 – $355,000
= $155,000

Change in excess of cost over market value
= $155,000 – $10,000 = $145,000 increase

Unrealized Loss on Long-Term Equity Investments	145,000	
Allowance for Unrealized Losses on Long-Term Equity Investments		145,000
To adjust long-term marketable equity securities to LCM.		

e.

Investments in long-term equity securities	$765,000 *
Allowance for unrealized losses on long-term equity securities	(155,000)
	$610,000

* $765,000 = Portfolio cost of long-term marketable equity securities + Portfolio cost of long-term nonmarketable equity securities
= $510,000 + ($175,000 + $80,000)

P13–15

a. Under the lower-of-cost-or-market method, the investment is carried on the books at the lower of its cost or market value as of the balance sheet date. Adjustments of the investment portfolio do not "flow through" to the income statement; they are disclosed in the stockholders' equity section of the balance sheet. Dividends declared by the investee are recognized as income to the investor in the period the dividends are declared.

(1)

Masonite Tires
Balance Sheet
January 1, 1990

Noninvestment assets	$120,000	Liabilities	$ 70,000
L-T investment in securities	40,000	Stockholders' equity	90,000
Total	$160,000	Total	$160,000

(2) During 1990, Masonite Tires would make the following original and adjusting journal entries under the lower-of-cost-or-market method:

Cash	85,000	
Revenues		85 000
To record noninvestment revenues.		
Expenses	50,000	
Cash		50,000
To record expenses.		

Cash (25% x $10,000)	2,500	
Dividend Revenue		2,500
To record dividends earned and received from investments.		

Unrealized Loss on Long-Term Equity Investments	4,000	
Allowance for Unrealized Losses on Long-Term Equity Investments		4,000
To adjust long-term equity investments to LCM.		

Masonite Tires
Income Statement
For the Year Ended December 31, 1990

Revenues	
Revenue	$85,000
Dividend revenue	2,500
Expenses	50,000
Net income	$37,500

Masonite Tires
Balance Sheet
December 31, 1990

Assets	$157,500	Liabilities	$ 70,000
L-T investment in securities	$ 40,000	Stockholders' equity	123,500*
Allowance for unrealized losses	(4,000)		
Total	$193,500	Total	$193,500

* $123,500 = $90,000 Beginning balance + $37,500 Net income – $4,000 Increase in unrealized losses on long-term equity securities.

(3) During 1991, Masonite Tires would make the following original and adjusting journal entries:

Cash	75,000	
Revenues		75,000
To record noninvestment revenues.		

Expenses	70,000	
Cash		70,000
To record expenses.		

Cash (25% x $15,000)	3,750	
Dividend Revenue		3,750
To record dividends earned and received from investments.		

Allowance for Unrealized Losses on Long-Term Equity Investments	4,000	
Unrealized Loss on Long-Term Equity Investments		4,000
To adjust long-term equity investments to LCM.		

Masonite Tires
Income Statement
For the Year Ended December 31, 1991

Revenues	
Revenue	$75,000
Dividend revenue	3,750
Expenses	70,000
Net income	$ 8,750

Masonite Tires
Balance Sheet
As of December 31, 1991

Noninvestment assets	$166,250	Liabilities	$ 70,000
L-T investment in securities	40,000	Stockholders' Equity	136,250*
Total	$206,250	Total	$206,250

* $136,250 = $123,500 Beginning balance + $8,750 Net income + $4,000 Decrease in unrealized loss on long-term equity securities.

b. Under the equity method, an investment is initially recorded at its cost and subsequently adjusted for changes in the investe's net assets. Therefore, any net income or loss generated by the investee and any dividends declared by the investee causes the investment account to be adjusted.

(1)

Masonite Tires
Balance Sheet
As of January 1, 1990

Noninvestment assets	$120,000	Liabilities	$ 70,000
L-T investment in securities	40,000	Stockholders' equity	90,000
Total	$160,000	Total	$160,000

(2) During 1990, Masonite Tires would make the following original and adjusting journal entries:

Cash	85,000	
Revenues		85,000
To record noninvestment revenues.		
Expenses	50,000	
Cash		50,000
To record expenses.		
Cash (25% x $10,000)	2,500	
Long-Term Investment in Equity Securities		2,500
To record investor's portion of dividends declared by investee.		
Long-Term Investment in Equity Securities	3,750	
Revenue from Long-Term Investments (25% x $15,000)		3,750
To record investor's portion of investee's net income.		

Masonite Tires
Income Statement
For the Year Ended December 31, 1990

Revenues	
Revenue	$85,000
Revenue from L-T investments	3,750
Expenses	50,000
Net income	$38,750

Masonite Tires
Balance Sheet
As of December 31, 1990

Assets	$157,500	Liabilities	$ 70,000
L-T investment in securities	41,250	Stockholders' equity	128,750
Total	$198,750	Total	$198,750

(3) During 1991, Masonite Tires would make the following original and adjusting journal entries:

Cash	75,000	
Revenues		75,000
To record noninvestment revenues.		
Expenses	70,000	
Cash		70,000
To record expenses.		
Cash (25% x $15,000)	3,750	
Long-Term Investment in Equity Securities		3,750
To record investor's portion of dividends declared by investee.		
Long-Term Investment in Equity Securities	5,000	
Revenue from Long-Term Investments (25% x $20,000)		5,000
To record investor's portion of investee's net income.		

Masonite Tires
Income Statement
For the Year Ended December 31, 1991

Revenues	
Revenue	$75,000
Revenue from L-T investments	5,000
Expenses	70,000
Net income	$10,000

Masonite Tires
Balance Sheet
As of December 31, 1991

Noninvestment assets	$166,250	Liabilities	$ 70,000
Investment in L-T securities	42,500	Stockholders' equity	138,750
Total	$208,750	Total	$208,750

c. Using the equity method versus the lower-of-cost-or-market method may be desirable due to debt covenants and incentive compensation. Under the equity method, a portion of the investee's net income flows through to the investor's income statement and through the closing process into stockholders' equity. This increase in stockholders' equity will, holding everything else constant, decrease the investor's debt/equity ratio. In this problem, Masonite's debt/equity ratio as of December 31, 1990 and 1991 is lower under the equity method than under the lower-of-cost-or-market method. Further, increased net income would be desirable to management if they receive incentive compensation based on net income.

In some cases owning 20% of a company does not constitute substantial influence over the investee. To be able to substantially influence a company means that Masonite must be able to influence general corporate policy, dividend policy, and so forth. If another investor owns a larger percentage of the company than Masonite, that investor could exert more influence than Masonite. In the extreme, some other investor may own 80% of the investee while Masonite owns the remaining 20%. In such a case, Masonite could not exert a substantial influence on the investee and should not account for the investment using the equity method.

P13–16

	Date	Account	Debit	Credit
a.	1/10	Long-Term Investment in Equity Securities	500,000	
		Cash		500,000
		To record investment in Wharton, Inc.		
	1/28	Long-Term Investment in Equity Securities	100,000	
		Marketable Securities		100,000
		To reclassify investment from short-term to long-term.		
	2/5	Long-Term Investment in Equity Securities	7,500,000	
		Cash		7,500,000
		To record investment in St. Clair International.		
	4/13	Cash	6,000	
		Dividend Revenue		6,000
		To record dividends earned and received on investments.		
	6/26	Cash	55,000	
		Long-Term Investment in Equity Securities		50,000
		Gain on Sale of Long-Term Equity Securities		5,000
		To record sale of long-term investment.		
	7/18	Long-Term Investment in Equity Securities	3,000,000	
		Cash		3,000,000
		To record investment in Crozier Limited.		

Date	Account	Debit	Credit
8/1	Cash	18,000	
	Dividend Receivable		18,000
	To record receipt of dividends earned previously.		
10/9	Cash	300,000	
	Loss on Sale of Long-Term Equity Securities	50,000	
	Long-Term Investment in Equity Securities		350,000
	To record sale of long-term investment.		
10/10	Dividend Receivable	315,000	
	Long-Term Investment in Equity Securities		315,000
	To record dividends earned on investments under equity method.		
10/30	Cash	315,000	
	Dividend Receivable		315,000
	To record receipt of dividends earned previously.		
12/20	Long-Term Investment in Equity Securities	48,000	
	Cash		48,000
	To record investment in Wharton, Inc.		

b. All of the securities are considered to be marketable, so they should be accounted for using either the lower-of-cost-or-market (LCM) method or the equity method. Rankin owns less than 20% of Wharton, Inc. and Hamilton Hardware Manufacturers. Consequently, the LCM method should be used to account for these two investments. Rankin owns more than 20% of the remaining investees, so the equity method should be used to account for the remaining investments.

Wharton, Inc. and Hamilton Hardware

Portfolio Cost
(9,000 shares of Wharton x $50 per share) + (1,000 shares of Wharton x $48 per share) + (4,000 shares of Hamilton x $25 per share) = $598,000

Portfolio Market Value
(10,000 shares of Wharton x $53 per share) + (4,000shares of Hamilton x $17.50 per share) = $600,000

Excess of portfolio cost over portfolio market value
= $598,000 – $600,000
= $0 (Under the LCM rule, the investment portfolio cannot be recorded above its cost. Therefore, the excess of the cost over the market value cannot be negative.)

Change in the allowance account = $0 – $17,000 = $17,000 decrease

The appropriate adjusting journal entry would be

Account	Debit	Credit
Allowance for Unrealized Losses on Long-Term Equity Securities	17,000	
Unrealized Loss on Long-Term Equity Securities		17,000
To adjust long-term equity securities to LCM.		

St. Clair International

Account	Debit	Credit
Loss on Long-Term Investments	187,500	
Long-Term Investment in Equity Securities		187,500
To record Rankin's portion of investee's net loss.		

Crozier Limited

Account	Debit	Credit
Long-Term Investment in Equity Securities	300,000	
Income from Long-Term Equity Investments		300,000
To record Rankin's portion of investee's net income.		

Long-Term Investments

Long-Term Investment in Equity Investments	$10,895,500*
Allowance for Unrealized Loss on Long-Term Equity Securities	0
	$10,895,500

---

* $10,895,500 = Beginning balance + Investments during 1990 – Sales of investments during 1990 + Reclassification of investments from short-term to long-term-Adjustments for dividends under the equity method + Adjustments for investees' net income under the equity method
= $350,000 + ($500,000 + $7,500,000 + $3,000,000 + $48,000) – ($50,000 + $350,000)
+ $100,000 – $315,000 + ($300,000 – $187,500)

The balance in Allowance for Unrealized Losses on Long-Term Equity Securities is zero because the portfolio cost of long-term marketable securities is less than the portfolio market value of long-term marketable securities. Under the LCM method, the portfolio of long-term marketable equity securities cannot be carried on the books above its cost.

P13–17

a.

	Account	Debit	Credit
(1)	Long-Term Investment in Equity Securities	150,000	
	Cash		150,000
	To record investment in Seely Freight Company.		
(2)	Long-Term Investment in Equity Securities	500,000	
	Cash		500,000
	To record investment in American Surgical Corporation.		
(3)	Long-Term Investment in Equity Securities	360,000	
	Cash		360,000
	To record investment in Lambert Athletic Equipment.		
(4)	Dividend Receivable	30,000	
	Dividend Revenue		30,000
	To record dividends earned.		
(5)	Cash	354,000	
	Long-Term Investment in Equity Securities		300,000
	Gain on Sale of Long-Term Investments		54,000
	To record sale of long-term investment.		
(6)	Cash	30,000	
	Dividend Receivable		30,000
	To record collection of a previously declared dividend.		

		Debit	Credit
(7)	Cash	20,000	
	Dividend Revenue		20,000
	To record dividend earned and collected.		
(adj a)	Allowance for Unrealized Loss on Long-Term Equity Investment	5,000*	
	Unrealized Loss on Long-Term Equity Investment		5,000
	To adjust long-term marketable securities to LCM.		

*Portfolio cost of marketable securities = $0
Portfolio market value of marketable securities = 0
Excess of portfolio cost over portfolio market value = $0

Change in allowance balance = $0 – $5,000 = $5,000 decrease

The long-term investment section of the balance sheet as of December 31, 1990 would be as follows:

Long-term investments $1,010,000*

* $1,010,000 = cost of Seely + cost of American Surgical + cost of Lambert Athletic

Since the investments are not marketable, and since Peeples Plastic owns less than 20% of each company, the investments are accounted for using the cost method. Under the cost method, the only transactions that would affect the income statement would be the dividends earned from the investments and the sale of any investments at a gain or at a loss. For the portfolio of long-term marketable equity securities accounted for using the LCM method (i.e., Bench Restaurant Supply), the adjustment of the investment portfolio to LCM does not "flow through" to the income statement, it "flows through" to the stockholders' equity section on the balance sheet. Consequently, the effect of these transactions on the income statement would be

Dividend revenue	$ 50,000
Gain on sale of long-term investment	54,000
	$104,000

b.

		Debit	Credit
(1)	Long-Term Investment in Equity Securities	150,000	
	Cash		150,000
	To record investment in Seely Freight Company.		
(2)	Long-Term Investment in Equity Securities	500,000	
	Cash		500,000
	To record investment in American Surgical Corporation.		
(3)	Long-Term Investment in Equity Securities	360,000	
	Cash		360,000
	To record investment in Lambert Athletic Equipment.		
(4)	Dividend Receivable	30,000	
	Dividend Revenue		30,000
	To record dividends earned.		
(5)	Cash	354,000	
	Long-Term Investment in Equity Securities		300,000
	Gain on Sale of Long-Term Investments		54,000
	To record sale of long-term investment.		

		Debit	Credit
(6)	Cash	30,000	
	Dividend Receivable		30,000
	To record collection of a previously declared dividend.		
(7)	Cash	20,000	
	Dividend Revenue		20,000
	To record dividend earned and collected.		
(adj a)	Unrealized Loss on Long-Term Equity Investment	67,500*	
	Allowance for Unrealized Loss on Long-Term Equity Investment		67,500
	To adjust long-term marketable securities to LCM.		

*Portfolio cost of marketable securities	=	$1,010,000
Portfolio market value of marketable securities	=	937,500
Excess of portfolio cost over portfolio market value	=	$ 72,500

Change in allowance balance = $72,500 – $5,000 = $67,500 increase

The long-term investment section of the balance sheet would be as follows

Long-Term Investments	$1,010,000
Allowance for Unrealized Loss on Long-Term Equity Securities	72,500
	$ 937,500

Since the investments are marketable, and Peeples Plastic owns less than 20% of each company, the investments are accounted for using the lower-of-cost-or-market (LCM) method. Under the LCM method, the only transactions that would affect the income statement would be the dividends earned from the investments and the sale of any investments at a gain or at a loss. For the portfolio of long-term marketable equity securities accounted for using the LCM method, the adjustment of the investment portfolio to LCM does not "flow through" to the income statement; it "flows through" to the stockholders' equity section on the balance sheet. Consequently, the effect of these transactions on the income statement would be

Dividend revenue	$ 50,000
Gain on sale of long-term investment	54,000
	$104,000

c.

		Debit	Credit
(1)	Long-Term Investment in Equity Securities	150,000	
	Cash		150,000
	To record investment in Seely Freight Company.		
(2)	Long-Term Investment in Equity Securities	500,000	
	Cash		500,000
	To record investment in American Surgical Corporation.		
(3)	Long-Term Investment in Equity Securities	360,000	
	Cash		360,000
	To record investment in Lambert Athletic Equipment.		
(4)	Dividend Receivable	30,000	
	Long-Term Investment in Equity Securities		30,000
	To record dividends earned.		

		Debit	Credit
(5)	Cash	354,000	
	Long-Term Investment in Equity Securities		300,000
	Gain on Sale of Long-Term Investments		54,000
	To record sale of long-term investment.		
(6)	Cash	30,000	
	Dividend Receivable		30,000
	To record collection of a previously declared dividend.		
(7)	Cash	20,000	
	Long-Term Investment in Equity Securities		20,000
	To record dividend earned and collected.		
(adj a)	Allowance for Unrealized Loss on Long-Term Equity Investment	5,000*	
	Unrealized Loss on Long-Term Equity Investment		5,000
	To adjust long-term marketable securities to LCM.		

*Portfolio cost of marketable securities = $0
Portfolio market value of marketable securities = 0
Excess of portfolio cost over portfolio market value = $0

Change in allowance balance = $0 – $5,000 = $5,000 decrease

		Debit	Credit
(adj b)	Long-Term Investment in Equity Securities	125,000*	
	Income from Long-Term Equity Securities		125,000
	To record revenue earned on investment in Seely Freight.		

* $125,000 = 25% x $500,000

		Debit	Credit
(adj c)	Long-Term Investment in Equity Securities	22,500*	
	Income from Long-Term Equity Securities		22,500
	To record revenue earned on investment in American Surgical.		

* $22,500 = 25% x $90,000

		Debit	Credit
(adj d)	Loss on Long-Term Equity Investment	75,000*	
	Long-Term Investment in Equity Securities		75,000
	To record loss incurred on investment in Lambert Athletic.		

* $75,000 = 25% x $300,000

The long-term investment section of the balance sheet would be as follows:

Long-term investments $1,032,500*

* $1,032,500 = Cost of Seely + Cost of American Surgical + Cost of Lambert Athletic
+ Adjustments for investees' net income – Adjustments for dividends declared by investees
= $150,000 + $500,000 + $360,000 + ($125,000 + $22,500 – $75,000)
– ($20,000 + $30,000)

Since Peeples Plastic owns more than 20% of each company, the investments are accounted for using the equity method. Under the equity method, the only transactions that would affect the income statement would be the net income or net loss of the investee that "flows through" to the investor's income statement, and sales of investments at a gain or at a loss. For the portfolio of long-term marketable equity securities accounted for using the LCM method, the adjustment of the investment portfolio to LCM does not "flow through" to the income statement; it "flows through" to the stockholders' equity section on the balance sheet. Consequently, the effect of these transactions on the income statement would be

Income on long-term investments	$147,500
Loss on long-term investments	75,000
Gain on sale of long-term investment	54,000
	$126,500

P13–18

a.

Group	Accounting Treatment
A	LCM
B	Cost
C	Equity
D	Equity
E	Effective-Interest

b.

		Debit	Credit
(1)	Cash	10,000	
	Dividend Receivable		10,000
	To record collection of dividends previously declared.		
(2)	Long-Term Investment in Equity Securities	200,000	
	Cash		200,000
	To record investment in Rising Moon Company.		
(3)	Dividend Receivable	2,000	
	Dividend Revenue		2,000
	To record dividends earned on investments.		
(4)	Cash	45,000	
	Long-Term Investment in Equity Securities		38,000
	Gain on Sale of Long-Term Investments		7,000
	To record sale of long-term investment.		

(5)

Face value		$250,000
Present value (i = 6%, n = 2)		
PV of maturity payment		
($250,000 x .89000 from Table 4 in App. A)	$222,500	
PV of interest payments		
[($250,000 x 0%) x 1.83339 from Table 5 in App. A]	0	
Total present value		222,500
Discount		$ 27,500

Notes Receivable	250,000	
Sales		222,500
Discount on Notes Receivable		27,500
To record sale of merchandise.		

(6)	Cash	2,000	
	Dividend Receivable		2,000
	To record collection of dividend previously earned.		
(7)	Cash	35,000	
	Long-Term Investment in Equity Securities		35,000
	To record collection of dividends under the equity method.		
(8)	Cash	40,000[a]	
	Premium on Bond Investment		7,080[b]
	Interest Revenue		32,920[c]
	To record receipt of interest on bond investment.		

[a] $40,000 = Face value x Stated interest rate per period = $800,000 x 5%
[b] $7,080 = Cash received – Interest revenue
[c] $32,920 = Book value x Effective interest rate per period = ($800,000+ $23,000) x 4%

(9)	Long-Term Investment in Equity Securities	50,000	
	Cash		50,000
	To record investment in Ruhe Art Supplies.		
(10)	Cash	21,000	
	Dividend Revenue		3,500
	Long-Term Investment in Equity Securities		17,500
	To record collection of dividends from investments.		

c. **Group A:** Entry to adjust Group A to LCM.

Portfolio cost = Portfolio cost as of 1/1/90 + Cost of securities purchased during 1990 – Cost of securities sold during 1990
= $720,000 + $50,000 of Ruhe Art Supplies – $38,000 of Cotter Can
= $732,000

Portfolio market value = $190,000 + $100,000 + $140,000 + $165,000
= $595,000

Excess of portfolio cost over portfolio market value = $732,000 – $595,000
= $137,000

Change in allowance balance = $137,000 – (1/1/90 portfolio cost – 1/1/90 portfolio market value)
= $137,000 – ($720,000 – $715,000)
= $132,000 increase

Unrealized Loss on Long-Term Equity Investments	132,000	
Allowance for Unrealized Losses on Long-Term Equity Investments		132,000
To adjust long-term marketable equity securities to LCM.		

Group B: No adjusting journal entries are necessary for the investments.

Group C: Entry to record investor's portion of investee's net income or loss.

Long-Term Investment in Equity Securities	238,750*	
Income from Long-Term Equity Investments		238,750
To record revenue from investment in Laidig Research Lab.		

* $238,750 = $955,000 x 25%

Loss on Long-Term Equity Investments [30% x ($250,000)]	75,000	
Long-Term Investment in Equity Securities		75,000
To record loss from investment in Lake Smelting.		

Loss on Long-Term Equity Investments [25% x ($60,000)]	15,000	
Long-Term Investment in Equity Securities		15,000
To record loss from investment in Manning Electronics.		

Group D: Entry to record investor's portion of investee's net income or loss.

Long-Term Investment in Equity Securities (30% x $140,000)	42,000	
Income from Long-Term Equity Investments		42,000
To record revenue from investment in Guyer Drilling.		

Long-Term Investment in Equity Securities (35% x $90,000)	31,500	
Income from Long-Term Equity Investments		31,500
To record revenue from investment in Tallman Fabrics.		

Group E: Entries to record accrued interest revenue.

Interest Receivable	40,000.00	
Premium on Bond Investment		7,363,20[a]
Interest Revenue		32,636.80[b]
To accrue interest on bond investment.		

[a] $7,363.20 = Interest receivable – Interest revenue = $40,000 – $32,636.80

[b] $32,636.80 = Book value x Effective interest rate per period
= [$800,000 + ($23,000 – $7,080)] x 4%

Discount on Notes Receivable	7,787.50*	
Interest Revenue		7,787.50
To accrue interest on note receivable.		

* $7,787.50 = Book value x Effective interest rate
= ($250,000 – $27,500) x 6% x 7/12

d.

	Dividend Revenue	Interest Revenue	Gains (Losses) on Sales of L-T Investments	Revenue (Losses) from Long-Term Investments
Group A				
Ricks Construction	$ 0	$ 0	$ 0	0
International Machines	0	0	0	0
Ruhe Art Supplies	1,000	0	0	0
Cotter Can Company	0	0	7,000	0
Group B				
Greenwell, Inc.	0	0	0	0
Hurst Publishing	2,000	0	0	0
Anderson Paint	2,500	0	0	0
Vitale Foods	0	0	0	0
Rising Moon Cola	0	0	0	0
Group C				
Laidig Research	0	0	0	238,750
Lake Smelting	0	0	0	(75,000)
Manning Electronics	0	0	0	(15,000)
Group D				
Guyer Drilling	0	0	0	42,000
Tallman Fabrics	0	0	0	31,500
Group E				
Flash Air Freight	0	65,557	0	0
Hahn Broadcasting	0	7,788	0	0

e. Long-term investments

Long-term equity investments (ownership < 20%)	$1,477,000	
Allowance for unrealized loss on long-term equity investments	137,000	$1,340,000
Long-term equity investments (ownership ≥ 20%)		2,629,750
Notes receivable	250,000	
Discount on notes receivable	19,713	230,287
Bond investments	800,000	
Premium on bond investments	8,557	808,557
Total long-term investments		$5,008,594

Supporting Schedules

	1/1/90 Carrying Value	1990 Additions	1990 Deductions	12/31/90 Carrying Value
Group A				
Ricks Construction	$ 200,000	$ 0	$ 0	$ 200,000
International Machines	250,000	0	0	250,000
Ruhe Art Supplies	80,000	50,000	0	130,000
Cotter Can Company	190,000	0	(38,000)	152,000
Total	$ 720,000	$ 50,000	($38,000)	$ 732,000
Group B				
Greenwell, Inc.	$ 150,000	$ 0	$ 0	$ 150,000
Hurst Publishing	225,000	0	0	225,000
Anderson Paint	110,000	0	0	110,000
Vitale Foods	60,000	0	0	60,000
Rising Moon Cola	0	200,000	0	200,000
Total	$ 545,000	$200,000	$ 0	$ 745,000
Total of Groups A and B	$1,265,000	$250,000	($38,000)	$1,477,000
Group C				
Laidig Research	$ 695,000	$238,750	($10,000)	$ 923,750
Lake Smelting	395,000	0	(75,000)	320,000
Manning Electronics	500,000	0	(15,000)	485,000
Total	$1,590,000	$238,750	($100,000)	$1,728,750
Group D				
Guyer Drilling	$ 540,000	$ 42,000	($7,500)	$ 574,500
Tallman Fabrics	330,000	31,500	($35,000)	326,500
Total	$ 870,000	$ 73,500	($42,500)	$ 901,000
Total of Groups C and D	$2,460,000	$312,250	($142,500)	$2,629,750
Group E				
Flash Air Freight	$ 823,000	$ 0	($14,443)	$ 808,557
Hahn Broadcasting	0	230,287*	0	230,287
Total	$ 823,000	$230,287	$(14,443)	$1,038,844

* $235,850 = $250,000 Face value of note – ($27,500 Discount associated with note on date accepted – $7,787 Discount amortized on 12/31/90)

P13–19

a. Assets	86,000	
Goodwill	40,000	
Liabilities		64,000
Cash		62,000
To record purchase of Martin Monthly.		

Belden, Ltd.
Consolidated Balance Sheet
January 1, 1990

Tangible assets	$204,000	Liabilities	$154,000
Goodwill	40,000	Stockholders' equity	90,000
Total	$244,000	Total	$244,000

b. 1990 Goodwill amortization = $40,000 ÷ 40 years = $1,000

c. Long-Term Investment in Equity Securities 62,000
    Cash 62,000
  To record investment in Martin Monthly.

Belden, Ltd.
Consolidated Balance Sheet
January 1, 1990

Noninvestment assets	$118,000	Liabilities	$ 90,000
Investment in L-T securities	62,000	Stockholders' equity	90,000
Total	$180,000	Total	$180,000

Under the equity method, Belden, Limited would also have to make the following entries during 1990.

Cash 10,000
    Long-Term Investment in Equity Securities 10,000
  To record dividends from investments.

Long-Term Investment in Equity Securities 15,000
    Revenue from Long-Term Equity Investment 15,000
  To record revenue earned on investment.

d. Debt/equity ratio = Liabilities ÷ Stockholders' equity

Purchase method: $154,000 ÷ $90,000 = 1.71
Equity method: $90,000 ÷ $90,000 = 1.00

Belden's debt/equity ratio is considerably lower if the investment is accounted for using the equity method than if it is accounted for using the purchase method. If Belden has any existing debt covenants that specify a maximum debt/equity ratio, the method used to account for this investment might affect whether or not Belden violates its debt covenant. The probability that Belden will violate any existing debt covenant is greater if the investment is accounted for using the purchase method than if it is accounted for using the equity method.

C13–1

a. An important assumption made to ensure that bonds and other debt investments are being carried at the present value of the contractual future cash inflows is that the effective interest rate is constant throughout the life of the investment. Further, it is assumed that Sears will hold the bonds until maturity.

b. Because the bonds were purchased at an amount higher than their face value, they will earn a lower rate of interest than the stated amount. Accordingly, the effective rate is less than the stated rate.

c.

Beginning balance, 12/31/86	$11,377
Amortization of premium [($11,377 x 10%) – ($10,000 x 12%)]	– 62
Ending balance, 12/31/87	–14,204
Increase in bond investment 1987	$ 2,889

d. The effective rate of return would be less than that experienced by Sears because the market price of the bonds is greater than the original cost. The effective rate of interest may vary for a variety of reasons that include changes in other types of interest rates, inflation and risk.

Cash	15,000	
Bond Investments		14,204
Gain on Investment		796
To record sale of bond investment.		

C13–2

a. The percent of ownership must be less than 50%. Otherwise, the companies would be consolidated with Northern's statement.

b. Companies in which Norton holds less than 20% are recorded at cost instead of lower-of-cost-or-market; thus there is a departure from generally accepted accounting principles. The amounts may be recorded at cost because of materiality.

c. Under certain conditions, greater than 50% investments in subsidiaries do not have to be consolidated into a parent's financial statement. When the nature of the subsidiary is significantly different from that of the parent, the subsidiaries may not have to be consolidated. If the subsidiary carries a large amount of debt (e.g., a financing subsidiary), such treatment may represent off-balance-sheet financing. However, the FASB has taken steps recently to limit this practice by requiring the consolidation of all wholly-owned subsidiaries.

C13–3

a. The level of ownership must be less than 20%. If it were over 20%, the equity method would be applied. If it were over 50% the investment would be consolidated into the parent's financial statements.

b. The market value exceeds cost at the end of 1985. Accordingly, there is no need to recognize unrealized losses.

Allowance for Unrealized Loss on Long-Term Equity Inv.	200,000	
Unrealized Loss on Long-Term Equity Investment		200,000
To record the recovery of equity investment classified as long-term.		

c. There is no loss to record in 1986. The market value exceeds cost.

d.	Cash	7,000,000	
	Marketable securities	4,860,000	
	Gain on sale of securities		2,140,000
	To record sale of marketable securities.		

C13–4

When applying the equity method, the Investment account is increased for the parent's share of the subsidiary's net income and decreased for any dividends received. This method presumes the parent's ability to significantly influence the operating decisions and management policies of the subsidiary. Accordingly, the income and dividends of the subsidiary are reflected as if the parent and the subsidiary were one. Equity method accounting is often referred to as "one-line consolidations." The only cash receipts by the parent are the dividends, yet the parent records income for its share of the subsidiary's reported net income; thus the argument can be made that the income included by the parent is not backed by cash receipts. It is important that investors and creditors be aware of how the subsidiary's reported net income was determined, so they can assess the quality of the subsidiary's earnings. The equity method may also be a way of keeping debt off the balance sheet.

C13–5

In the case of financing subsidiaries, it would be to the parent's benefit to apply the equity method instead of consolidating the subsidiary's financial statements into its own. If the subsidiary has issued debt in order to raise capital which it then loans to the parent's customers to finance sales, it would be beneficial for the parent not have to include the debt of the finance subsidiary in its financial statement. Even though the debt exists and may be 100% owned by the parent, keeping it off the parent's statements maintains financial ratios at acceptable levels, does not cause debt covenants to be violated, and increases future levels of reported net income. The FASB has recently taken steps to limit this practice by requiring the consolidation of wholly-owned subsidiaries.

CHAPTER 14 The Complete Income Statement

E14–1

a. (1) IS [a]
(2) N
(3) N
(4) IS [a]
(5) IS [a]
(6) IS [a]
(7) IS [a]
(8) SR [b]
(9) SR
(10) IS [a]
(11) IS [a]
(12) IS [a]

---

[a] Since each of these items is used to calculate net income, each item will be closed into Retained Earnings as part of the closing process. Consequently, each of these items will also be disclosed on the statement of retained earnings through net income.

[b] When a company declares a property dividend, the property is adjusted to its fair market value, and the company records a gain or loss on the adjustment. This gain or loss is then disclosed on the income statement. So declaring a property dividend would also be included on the income statement to the extent that any gain or loss on the adjustment of the property is recognized.

b. (1) 4
(2) N/A
(3) N/A
(4) 1
(5) 1
(6) 2
(7) 3 (although depending upon the circumstances it might instead be considered 2)
(8) N/A (if any gain or loss was recognized on the adjustment of the property to its fair market value, the gain or loss would be considered 2)
(9) N/A
(10) 1 (although this could also be considered 2)
(11) 1
(12) 1

E14–2

a. (1) 1
(2) 4
(3) 3
(4) 5
(5) 4
(6) 5
(7) 1
(8) 1
(9) 2
(10) 5
(11) 5
(12) 5
(13) 1
(14) 4
(15) 3

b. As the transactions move from 1 to 5, they move away from exchanges with owners toward exchanges with third parties involving the company's central, ongoing activities. Equity investors and debt investors are considered providers of capital that allows the company to operate. However, the company does not exist to draw capital from the equity and debt owners; it exists to provide goods and/or services to other entities. Providing goods and/or services is considered the company's operations.

E14–3

a. (1) **50% of net income**
Maximum dividend = 50% x $182,800
= $91,400

(2) **50% of income before change in accounting method**
Maximum dividend = 50% x $130,800
= $65,400

(3) **50% of income before extraordinary items**
Maximum dividend = 50% x $108,800
= $54,400

(4) **50% of income from operations**
Maximum dividend = 50% x $150,000
= $75,000

b. The bank requires restrictions on dividend payments to increase the probability that Worthy Manufacturing will have sufficient cash to meet its interest and principal payments. More stringent restrictions on dividends decrease the amount that Worthy Manufacturing can potentially pay out as dividends, thereby increasing the probability that the company will have sufficient cash to meet its obligations to the bank. In this particular case, basing the dividend restriction on income from operations provides the most stringent dividend restriction.

Further, managers have greater ability to manipulate items disclosed after income from operations than those items disclosed before income from operations. For example, the decision to sell assets and realize gains is completely at a manager's discretion, as is a change in accounting principle resulting in an increase in net income. Therefore, basing the dividend restriction on income from operations limits management's ability to manipulate the restriction.

E14–4

a. (1) Capital
(2) Operating
(3) Operating
(4) Capital
(5) Capital

Mayheim Company
Income Statement
For the Year Ended December 31, 1990

Fees earned	$45,000
Expenses	24,000
Net income	$21,000

b.

Mayheim Company
Income Statement
For the Year Ended December 31, 1991

Net book value: December 31, 1991	$102,000	
Net book value: January 1, 1990	55,000	
Increase in net assets		$47,000
Less: Stock issued		32,000
Plus: Dividends declared		6,000
Net Income		$21,000

c. The transaction view provides more information to financial statement users than the capital-maintenance view. Under the capital-maintenance view, only the change in net book value, adjusted for stock issuances and dividend declarations, is disclosed. Under the transaction view, similar transactions are summarized and grouped together. Such groupings can be disclosed in such a manner as to more fully explain the company's performance during the accounting period.

d. Under the transaction view, every transaction must be classified as either an operating transaction or as a capital transaction. It is not always easy to classify transactions into one of these categories. On the other hand, under the capital-maintenance view, a transaction only has to be evaluated as to whether it affects the company's net book value or not, and if so, whether it affects contributions from or distributions to owners.

E14–5

a. 12/31/89 Net book value = 1/1/89 Net book value + Value of stock issued – Value of dividends declared + Net income
= $50,000 + $30,000 – $10,000 + $22,160
= $92,160

b.

Bentley Brothers
Income Statement
For the Year Ended December 31, 1989

Net book value: December 31, 1989	$92,160	
Less: Net book value: January 1, 1989	50,000	
Change in net assets		$42,160
Less: Stock issued		30,000
Plus: Dividends declared		10,000
Net income		$22,160

E14–6

a.

Cash	785,000	
Liabilities	1,200,000	
Assets		1,850,000
Gain on Disposal of Business Segment		135,000
To record sale of business segment.		
Gain on Disposal of Business Segment	45,900*	
Income Tax Liability		45,900
To record income tax liability on disposal of business segment.		

* $45,900 = $135,000 Gain on disposal x 34%.

Income Tax Liability	5,100*	
Loss on Operations of Discontinued Segment		5,100
To record income tax benefit on net loss of discontinued segment.		

* $5,100 = $15,000 Net loss x 34%.

b.

Discontinued operations		
Loss on operations of discontinued segment (net of tax benefit of $5,100)	9,900	
Gain on disposal of business segment (net of $45,900 in taxes)	89,100	
Discontinued operations		79,200

E14–7

a. Loss on Destruction of Inventory 2,750,000
Inventory 2,750,000
To record destruction of inventory due to earthquake.

b. Loss on Destruction of Inventory (extraordinary) 2,750,000
Inventory 2,750,000
To record destruction of inventory due to earthquake.

Income Tax Liability 935,000*
Loss on Destruction of Inventory (extraordinary) 935,000
To record reduction in tax liability due to loss of inventory.

---

* $935,000 = $2,750,000 x 34%

c. If the earthquake is considered both an unusual and infrequent event, then the loss should be classified as an extraordinary loss. If the loss is considered to be unusual or infrequent in nature, but not both, then it should be classified as other revenues and expenses. If the loss is considered to be both usual and frequent in nature, then it should be disclosed as part of operations. In most cases, losses due to earthquakes are considered extraordinary.

d. If Paxson Company's plant was located in San Francisco, then the magnitude of the earthquake would have to be considered. To be considered an extraordinary loss, the events that gave rise to the loss must be both unusual in nature and occur infrequently. In San Francisco, minor earthquakes are not infrequent; they are expected to occur occasionally. Consequently, if this loss was due to a minor earthquake, it would not be considered to be extraordinary. Since earthquakes are not usual (i.e., part of the company's normal operations), the loss should not be considered as part of operations. Instead the loss should be classified as an other expense. Alternatively, if the damage was due to a major earthquake, it might qualify as an extraordinary loss. Major earthquakes, such as the 1906 and 1989 earthquakes that devastated the Bay area, are both unusual and infrequent.

E14–8

a.

Income from continuing operations (after taxes)	$4.20
Disposal of business segment *	1.00
Extraordinary Item	(1.40)
Changes in accounting method	1.20
Net earnings per share	$5.00

b.

Income from continuing operations (after taxes)	$2.10
Disposal of business segment *	.50
Extraordinary item	(.70)
Changes in accounting method	.60
Net earnings per share	$2.50

c.

Income from continuing operations (after taxes)	$1.05
Disposal of business segment *	.25
Extraordinary item	(.35)
Changes in accounting method	.30
Net earnings per share	$1.25

---

* The EPS disclosure for the disposal of the business segment includes both the income from the disposed segment and the gain on the sale of the disposed segment.

E14–9

a. If a lawsuit is considered to be an unusual but not infrequent event, then it would be classified under other expenses and losses. Consequently, the loss from the lawsuit would be used to compute net income from continuing operations.

Bonus = 10% x [($850,000 – $580,000) x (1 – tax rate)]
= 10% x [$270,000 x (1 – 34%)]
= $17,820

b. If the loss from the lawsuit is considered to be extraordinary, then the loss would not be used to compute net income from continuing operations.

Bonus = 10% x [$850,000 x (1 –tax rate)]
= 10% x [$850,000 x (1 – 34%)]
= $56,100

c. Gain not considered to be extraordinary

Bonus = 10% x [($850,000 + $580,000) x (1 – tax rate)]
= 10% x [$1,430,000 x (1 – 34%)]
= $94,380

Gain considered to be extraordinary

Bonus = 10% x [$850,000 x (1 – tax rate)]
= 10% x [$850,000 x (1 – 34%)]
= $56,100

d. Income figures are often included in ratios which are, in turn, incorporated into debt covenants or used as the basis for awarding incentive compensation to managers. If the income figures included in debt covenants or in incentive contracts stipulate between income from continuing operations and net income, then the decision as to whether to classify an event as extraordinary or not can have economic consequences. As demonstrated in Parts (a) through (c), how a loss is classified can have a profound effect on the magnitude of a manager's bonus.

E14–10

a.

Selmo Consolidated
Income Statement
For the Year Ended December 31, 19XX

Revenue		
Operating revenue	$87,000	
Other revenue	5,200	$92,200
Expenses		
Operating expenses		32,500
Income from continuing operations (before taxes)		59,700
Income tax expense		20,298
Income from continuing operations		39,402
Discontinued Operations		
Income earned by discontinued segment (net of taxes of $1,020)	1,980	
Loss on disposal of discontinued segment (net of tax benefit of $7,140)	(13,860)	
Discontinued operations		(11,880)
Income before extraordinary items		$27,522
Extraordinary loss (net of tax benefit of $1,700)		(3,300)
Income before change in accounting method		$24,222
Effect of change in accounting method (net of taxes of $4,250)		8,250
Net income		$32,472

b.

Selmo Consolidated
Statement of Retained Earnings
For the Year Ended December 31, 19XX

Beginning retained earnings balance: January 1, 19XX	$72,000
Plus: Net income	32,472
Less: Dividends declared	18,000
Ending retained earnings balance: December 31, 19XX	$86,472

E14-11

a.

Watson Company
Income Statement
For the Year Ended December 31, 1989

Sales revenue	$1,375,000	
Cost of goods sold	495,000	
Gross profit		$880,000
Expenses		
Administrative expenses	100,000	
Depreciation expense	250,000	
Selling expenses	189,000	
Total expenses		539,000
Income from operations		341,000
Other revenues and expenses		
Rent revenue	360,000	
Loss on sale of fixed assets	105,000	
Total other revenues and expense		255,000
Income from continuing operations (before taxes)		596,000
Income taxes		(202,640)
Income from continuing operations		393,360
Extraordinary loss (net of tax benefit of $68,680)		(133,320)
Net income		$260,040

b.

Watson Company
Statement of Retained Earnings
For the Year Ended December 31, 1989

Beginning retained earnings balance: January 1, 1989	$867,000
Plus: Net income	260,040
Less: Dividends	450,000
Ending retained earnings balance: December 31, 1989	$677,040

c. If Watson Company had no tax liability as of January 1, 1989 and made no tax payments during 1990, then the company's tax liability as of December 31, 1990 would equal the sum of the intraperiod tax allocations. Watson company incurred $202,640 in taxes associated with income from continuing operations. The extraordinary loss provided a tax benefit, thereby reducing income taxes by $68,680. Therefore, the company's total tax liability as of December 31, 1989 is $133,960.

P14–1

a. (1) Operating
(2) Operating
(3) Operating
(4) Capital
(5) Operating
(6) Operating
(7) Operating
(8) Capital
(9) Capital

b. (1) Normal and recurring
(2) Normal and recurring
(3) Other revenues and expenses
(4) Issues and payments of debt
(5) Normal and recurring
(6) Other revenues and expenses
(7) Changes in accounting principles
(8) Exchanges with owners
(9) The sale of the securities would be classified as purchases, sales, and exchanges or assets other than inventory, while the loss would be classified as other revenues and expenses.

c. Items (2), (3), (5), (6), (7), and (9) would all be disclosed on the income statement as follows.

(2) $500,000 would be disclosed as operating revenues, while the $375,000 would be disclosed as cost of goods sold, which is an operating expense.
(3) Minor earthquakes are not infrequent in San Francisco, although they are unusual. Consequently, the $100,000 would be disclosed as part of other revenues and expenses.
(5) $143,000 would be disclosed as operating expenses.
(6) It appears that the company is frequently sued, but lawsuits are unusual. Consequently, the $10,000 would be disclosed as part of other revenues and expenses.
(7) The effect of the change in accounting methods would be disclosed, net of any tax effect, after extraordinary items and before net income.
(9) The amount of the loss would be disclosed as part of other revenues and expenses.

P14–2

a. Bonus = 20% x (Income from operations before interest expense – Interest expense)
= 20% x [$1,300,000 – ($1,000,000 x 10% Interest rate)]
= $240,000

b. Bonus = 20% x (Income from operations before interest expense – Interest expense)
= 20% x ($1,300,000 – 0)
= $260,000

c. The decision whether to finance the plant expansion through an equity issue or through a debt issue is worth $20,000 to the managers. If the company issues equity instead of debt, the managers will receive an additional $20,000 in bonuses. While issuing equity is in the best interests of the managers, this option may not be in the best interests of the existing stockholders. It is possible that issuing additional stock will dilute the ownership interests of the existing stockholders. Further, the interest payments on debt are tax deductible. Hence, issuing debt would reduce cash outflows for taxes, thereby increasing the amount of cash the company has available to reinvest in the company or to pay dividends.

d. Bonus = 20% x Income from operations
= 20% x $1,300,000
= $260,000

In this case the bonus is identical under either financing option. Consequently, the manner in which the expansion is financed does not affect the managers' bonuses, so the managers will, hopefully, base their decision on factors that will be more relevant to the stockholders.

P14–3

a. (1) Capital
(2) Operating
(3) Capital
(4) Operating
(5) Capital
(6) Capital
(7) Capital

b.

Raleigh Corporation
Income Statement
For the Year Ended December 31, 1990

Fees earned		$450,000
Expenses		
Wage expense	$125,000	
Supplies expense	25,000	
Depreciation expense	50,000	
Miscellaneous expense	75,000	
Total expenses		275,000
Net income		$175,000

c.

Raleigh Corporation
Income Statement
For the Year Ended December 31, 1990

Net assets: December 31, 1990	$290,000	
Less: Net assets February 10, 1990	0	
Increase in net assets		$290,000
Less: Stock issued		125,000
Add: Dividends declared		10,000
Net income		$175,000

P14–4

a.

	Income Statement	Classification
Sales	Yes	Usual and frequent
Sales returns	Yes	Usual and frequent
Cost of goods sold	Yes	Usual and frequent
Dividends	No	N/A
Rent expense	Yes	Usual and frequent
Wage payable	No	N/A
Loss on sale of food service division	Yes	Disposal of segment *
Loss incurred by food service division	Yes	Disposal of segment *
Depreciation expense	Yes	Usual and frequent
Cumulative effect of change in depreciation methods	Yes	Changes in accounting
Gain on land appropriated by government	Yes	Unusual and infrequent
Insurance expense	Yes	Usual and frequent
Inventory	No	N/A
Administrative expenses	Yes	Usual and frequent
Prepaid insurance	No	N/A
Gain on sale of marketable securities	Yes	Unusual or infrequent

* The Loss on Sale of Food Services Division and the Loss Incurred by Food Services Division would be classified as a disposal of a business segment only if the food services division meets the requirements of a business segment as defined under GAAP. If the food services division does not meet these requirements, then the Loss on Sale of Food Services Division would be classified as part of other revenues and expenses. The Loss Incurred by Food Services Division would be broken down into its components (i.e., revenues and expenses) and reported as part of operating revenues and expenses.

b.

Crozier Industries
Income Statement
For the Year Ended December 31, 1990

Revenue		
Sales revenue	$987,000	
Less: Sales returns	9,000	
Gain on sale of marketable securities	142,000	
Total revenue		$1,120,000
Expenses		
Cost of goods sold	456,000	
Rent expense	90,000	
Depreciation expense	100,000	
Insurance expense	12,000	
Administrative expenses	109,000	
Total expenses		767,000
Income from continuing operations (Before taxes)		353,000
Income taxes		120,020
Income from continuing operations		232,980
Discontinued operations		
Loss on operations of discontinued segment (net of tax benefit of $3,400)	(6,600)	
Loss on disposal of discontinued segment (net of tax benefit of $680)	(1,320)	
Discontinued operations		(7,920)
Income before extraordinary items		$225,060
Extraordinary gain on appropriated land (net of taxes of $32,980)		64,020
Income before effect of accounting changes		$289,080
Cumulative effect of change in accounting principle (net of tax benefit of $45,900)		89,100
Net income		$199,980

P14–5

a. (1) Hurricanes are unusual, but they occur relatively frequently in Florida. Consequently, this loss should not be classified as an extraordinary item. Instead, it should be disclosed gross of taxes as part of other revenues and expenses.

(2) A loss on the disposal of a business segment is not considered an extraordinary item. This item should be disclosed net of taxes as a separate item on the income statement after income from continuing operations, but before extraordinary items.

(3) This loss appears to be both unusual and infrequent; consequently, it should be classified as an extraordinary item on the income statement. Extraordinary items should be disclosed net of any tax effect.

(4) Writing off an open account receivable as uncollectible should not be disclosed on the income statement. Under GAAP, a company should use the allowance method to account for bad debts. Under the allowance method, write-offs of uncollectible accounts affect only balance sheet accounts.

(5) Floods are unusual, and they occur relatively infrequently in Arizona; consequently, this loss should be classified as an extraordinary item on the income statement. Extraordinary items should be disclosed net of any tax effect.

b. Extraordinary items

Loss to employee destruction (net of tax benefit of $79,900)	$155,100
Loss due to flood (net of tax benefit of $30,600)	59,400

P14–6

a. (1) The extraordinary loss and the extraordinary gain would both be disclosed on the income statement, net of taxes, after discontinued operations, but before the effect of the change in accounting method.

(2) The sale of inventory would be disclosed on the income statement (gross of taxes) as part of operating revenues. The associated cost of inventory sold would be disclosed on the income statement (gross of taxes) as part of operating expenses.

(3) The loss on disposal of business segment would be disclosed on the income statement, net of taxes, as part of discontinued operations, which is disclosed after income from continuing operations, but before extraordinary items.

(4) The income effect due to change in accounting method would be disclosed as the last item before net income on the income statement, net of the tax effect.

(5) The advertising expense would be disclosed on the income statement (gross of taxes) as part of operating expenses.

(6) The income earned by the disposed business segment would be disclosed on the income statement, net of taxes, as part of discontinued operations, which is disclosed after income from continuing operations, but before extraordinary items.

b. Extraordinary items

Extraordinary loss (net of tax benefit of $85,000)	$165,000
Extraordinary gain (net of taxes of $18,700)	36,300
Discontinued operations	
Loss on disposal of business segment (net of tax benefit of $34,000)	66,000
Income earned by disposed business segment (net of taxes of 51,000)	99,000
Effect of change in accounting method (net of taxes of $27,200)	52,800

c.

Income from continuing operations (after taxes)	$4.00
Disposal of business segment	.33 [a]
Extraordinary items	(1.29)[b]
Effect of changes in accounting methods	.53
Net earnings per share	$3.57

[a] .33 = (Loss on disposal + Income from disposed segment) ÷ 100,000 shares
= [($66,000) + $99,000] ÷ 100,000 shares

[b] (1.29) = (Extraordinary loss + Extraordinary gain) ÷ 100,000 shares
= [($165,000) + $36,300] ÷ 100,000 shares

P14–7

a.

Income from continuing operations (before taxes)	$850,000
Income taxes	289,000
Income from continuing operations	561,000
Extraordinary loss (net of tax benefit of $45,900)	89,100
Net income	$471,900

b. Income tax expense = Income taxes on net income generated during 1989
= Income taxes on income from continuing operations + Income tax effect of extraordinary loss
= $289,000 from part (a) + ($45,900) from Part (a)
= $243,100

c.

B, J&R Company
Statement of Retained Earnings
For the Year Ended December 31, 1989

Beginning retained earnings balance: January 1, 1989	$1,259,000
Plus: Net income	471,900
Less: Dividends declared	175,000
Ending retained earnings balance: December 31, 1989	$1,555,900

d. The balance in the Income Tax Liability account would equal the entire amount owed to the government for income taxes as of December 31, 1989. B, J&R have two sources of income taxes during 1989. The first source is the income tax on income from continuing operations in the amount of $289,000 (from Part [a]). The second source is the income tax benefit on the extraordinary loss in the amount of $45,900 (from Part [a]). Therefore, B, J&R owe $243,100 in income taxes as of December 31, 1989, which equals the amount calculated in Part (b).

The income tax liability as of December 31, 1989 equals the 1989 income tax expense for two reasons. First, the company's income under GAAP equals its taxable income under the IRS Code. Since these two amounts are equal, the company has no deferred taxes (i.e., interperiod tax allocations). Second, the company made no tax payments during 1989, so the entire obligation must be disclosed as a liability.

P14–8

a.

	Straight-line	Double-declining
1985	$ 70,000[a]	$150,000[b]
1986	70,000	120,000
1987	70,000	96,000
1988	70,000	76,800
Total	$280,000	$442,800

[a] $70,000 = ($750,000 – $50,000 Salvage value) ÷ 10 years
[b] Depreciation expense = Book value x [2 x (1/10 years)]

b.

Loss on Change of Accounting Method	162,800*	
Accumulated Depreciation		162,800
To record effect of change in accounting method.		

* $162,800 = $442,800 – $280,000

Income Tax Liability	55,352*	
Loss on Change of Accounting Method		55,352
To record tax benefit of change in accounting method.		

* $55,352 = $162,800 x 34%

c. The cumulative effect of this change in accounting method would be disclosed as the last item on the income statement before net income. It would be disclosed net of the related tax effect.

P14–9

a. K mart presents comparative consolidated statements of income, consolidated statements of cash flows, and consolidated statements of stockholders' equity for the fiscal years ended January 28, 1987, January 27, 1988, and January 25, 1989. Further, the corporation presents comparative consolidated balance sheets as of January 27, 1988 and January 25, 1989.

b. K mart did not report any extraordinary items on its consolidated income statement for the fiscal years ended January 27, 1988, and January 25, 1989; however, it did report an extraordinary loss of $16,000,000 for the fiscal year ended January 28, 1987. According to footnote J, this loss is due to the early extinguishment of long-term debt.

c. The consolidated income statements do not report a cumulative effect of a change in accounting principle/method. Further, the audit report and footnotes does not mention any change in accounting principles. It appears, therefore, that K mart did not change any accounting principles/methods during the 1986, 1987, or 1988 fiscal years.

d. K mart reported four types of revenues: (1) sales, (2) licensee fees and rental income, (3) equity in income of affiliated retail companies, and (4) interest income. The corporation report net revenue for the fiscal year ended January 25, 1989 of $27,688,000,000.

e. According to the consolidated statements of shareholders' equity, K mart declared dividends during the 1988 fiscal year of $264,000,000. Based upon a comparison between dividends declared and net income in the fiscal years 1986, 1987, and 1988, it appears that K mart pays out dividends equal to approximately 33% of net income.

f. K mart presented cost of goods sold as a single line item on the consolidated statements of income.

g. K mart reported five general types of expenses: (1) cost of merchandise sold, (2) selling, (3) general administrative expenses, (4) advertising expense, (5) interest expense, and (6) income taxes. Interest expense was divided into interest on debt and interest on capital lease obligations.

h. Both income from continuing operations and net income have increased over the last three fiscal years. Both have increased approximately 40% over the last three fiscal years.

i. K mart did not report any discontinued operations on its consolidated income statement for the fiscal years ended January 27, 1988, and January 25, 1989; however, it did report a gain of $28,000,000 on discontinued operations for the fiscal year ended January 28, 1987. According to footnote B, K mart disposed of Furr's Cafeterias, Inc. and Bishop Buffets, Inc. in December 1986. This footnote also states that during 1988, K mart continued disposing of its discontinued insurance operations.

j. K mart uses a single-step, income statement so it is difficult to determine which items are unusual or infrequent, but not both. Items included on its income statement that are commonly considered to be unusual or infrequent, but not both are equity in income of affiliated retail companies, interest income, and interest expense. Licensee fees and rental income might also be considered unusual.

k. According to the consolidated balance sheets and statements of shareholders' equity, K mart had no restricted retained earnings as of January 25, 1989. However, according to footnote (j), K mart has restricted retained earnings due to revolving credit agreements. Of the $4,345 million reported for Retained Earnings on the balance sheet, $2,351 million is unrestricted and $1,994 is restricted.

l.

	Fiscal Year		
	1988	1988	1987
Continuing operations	$4.00	$3.40	$2.84
Discontinued operations	0	0	.14
Extraordinary item	0	0	.08
Changes in accounting principle/method	0	0	0

P14–10

Microbiology Labs
Income Statement
For the Year Ended December 31, 1989

Sales revenue	$10,000,000	
Cost of goods sold	2,500,000	
Gross profit		$ 7,500,000
Operating expenses		750,000
Income from operations		6,750,000
Loss on sale of office equipment		60,000
Income from continuing operations (Before taxes)		6,690,000
Income taxes		2,274,600
Income from continuing operations		4,415,400
Disposal of business segment		
Gain on disposal of assets (net of taxes of $136,000)	264,000	
Income from operations of disposed segment (net of taxes of $102,000)	198,000*	
Disposal of business segment		462,000
Income before extraordinary items		4,877,400
Extraordinary items:		
Loss on retirement of bonds (net of tax benefit of $34,000)	66,000	
Loss due to insect infestation (net of tax benefit of $272,000)	528,000	
Extraordinary items		594,000
Income before changes in accounting methods		4,283,400
Cumulative effect of change in accounting method (net of taxes of $85,000)		165,000
Net income		$4,448,400

Earnings per Share

Income from continuing operations	$4.42
Disposal of business segment	.46
Extraordinary items	.59
Cumulative effect of change in accounting method	.16
Net earnings per share	$4.45

* $198,000 = [Sales of discontinued segment – Cost of goods sold of discontinued segment – Operating expenses of discontinued segment] x (1 – 34% Tax rate)

P14–11

a. **Adjusting journal entries**

	Debit	Credit
(1) Inventory (ending)	510,000	
Cost of Goods Sold	707,000	
Purchases		750,000
Inventory (beginning)		467,000
To record ending inventory and COGS.		
(2) Bad Debt Expense	55,000*	
Allowance for Doubtful Accounts		55,000
To record bad debt expense.		

* $55,000 = $105,000 – $50,000 Balance in allowance for doubtful accounts

	Debit	Credit
(3) Depreciation Expense	89,000	
Accumulated Depreciation		89,000
To record depreciation of fixed assets.		
(4) Insurance Expense	20,000	
Prepaid Insurance		20,000
To record expiration of insurance policy.		
(5) Interest Expense	50,000	
Interest Payable		50,000
To accrue interest on bonds.		
(6) Income Tax Expense	17,340*	
Income Tax Liability		17,340
To accrue income taxes.		

* $17,340 = Income from continuing operations x 34%
= [(Sales + Other revenues) – (Operating expenses + Other expenses)] x 34%
= [($1,276,000 + $76,000) – ($707,000 + $100,000 + $255,000 + $75,000 + $55,000 + $89,000 + $20,000)] x 34%

Closing Entries

		Debit	Credit
C1	Sales	1,276,000	
	Gain on Sale of Land	76,000	
	Income Summary	2,640	
	Cost of Goods Sold		707,000
	Administrative Expenses		100,000
	Selling Expenses		255,000
	Interest Expense		75,000
	Bad Debt Expense		55,000
	Depreciation Expense		89,000
	Insurance Expense		20,000
	Income Tax Expense		17,340
	Extraordinary Loss		21,120[a]
	Cumulative Effect of Change in Accounting Method		15,180[b]
	To close revenues and expenses into Income Summary.		

[a] \$21,120 = Extraordinary loss x (1 – tax rate) = \$32,000 x (1 – 34%)
[b] \$15,180 = Cumulative effect of change x (1 – tax rate) = \$23,000 x (1 – 34%)

		Debit	Credit
C2	Retained Earnings	2,640	
	Income Summary		2,640
	To close Income Summary into Retained Earnings.		
C3	Retained Earnings	135,000	
	Dividends		135,000
	To close Dividends into Retained Earnings.		

b.

Laidig Industries
Income Statement
For the Year Ended December 31, 1989

Revenues		
Sales	$1,276,000	
Gain on sale of fixed assets	76,000	
Total revenues		$1,352,000
Expenses		
Cost of goods sold	707,000	
Administrative expenses	100,000	
Selling expenses	255,000	
Depreciation expense	89,000	
Bad Debt expense	55,000	
Insurance expense	20,000	
Interest expense	75,000	
Total expenses		1,301,000
Income from continuing operations		51,000
Income taxes		17,340
Income from continuing operations		33,660
Extraordinary loss (net of tax benefit of $10,880)		21,120
Income before change in accounting method		12,540
Less: Cumulative effect of change in accounting method (net of tax benefit of $7,820)		15,180
Net loss		$2,640

Earnings per Share:

Income from continuing operations	$0.07
Extraordinary loss	0.04
Less: Cumulative effect of change in accounting method	0.03
Net earnings per share	$0.00

c.

Laidig Industries
Statement of Retained Earnings
For the Year Ended December 31, 1989

Beginning retained earnings balance: January 1, 1989	$673,000
Less: Net loss	(2,640)
Dividends declared	(135,000)
Ending retained earnings: December 31, 1989	$535,360

C14–1

a. Earnings announcements are made in publications because they are information to investors and creditors and are used by them to make investment decisions.

b. Record earnings are good news. Accordingly, the stock price would be expected to rise. Further, the earnings exceeded analysts' expectations, which is even better news.

c. An investor would be interested in the components of net income to determine if the record earnings are the result of an extraordinary item, an accounting change, or some other nonpermanent feature. An investor would like to know whether the new earnings level is going to persist in the future.

C14–2

a.

Net book value, 1987 ($4,480.5 – $2,906.2)	$1,574.3
Net book value, 1986 ($3,939.4 – $2,580.1)	–1,359.3
Change in net assets	215.0
Less: proceeds from stock issue	18.8
Net income for 1987	$ 196.2

b. If the company had decreased its common stock by $12 million, the net income number would be larger. It would have been ($215.0 + $12) $227 million, an increase of $30.8 million ($18.8 + $12).

c. The transaction view produces a breakdown of items that comprise performance (i.e., revenues and expenses). When transactions are treated separately, they can be grouped into different categories and disclosed in a manner that more fully explains why a company did or did not achieve high performance during a period. A problem associated with the transaction view is classifying a transaction as an operating or capital transaction.

C14–3

a. Income from nonelectric sources would not be included in the operating section of the income statement. If the income is infrequent and unusual, it would be reported as an extraordinary gain, as a separate line item. Most likely, it is infrequent *or* unusual and reported in "other gains and losses."

b. These expenditures would be considered capital transactions because they are investments made in the current period that are expected to provide benefits in future periods.

c. Capital transactions are associated mainly with the investing and financing activities of a business. This includes the purchase and sale of long-term assets, and the issuance and repurchases of common stock and debt. Generally, these transactions do not initially affect the income statement. Operating transactions represent the actions that give rise to net income, and always involve accounts on the income statement.

C14–4

a.

Inventories	496,000,000	
Cumulative Gain from Accounting Change		496,000,000
To record the cumulative effect of a change in inventory methods.		

Cumulative Gain from Accounting Change	215,000,000	
Income Tax Liability		215,000,000
To record tax liability on accounting change.		

b. The amount of gain reported was ($496,000,000 – $215,000,000) $281,000,000.

c. The gain would be reported net of tax as a separate line item on the income statement. There would also be information related to the change in the footnotes and the audit report.

d. From management's viewpoint, the pros associated with a change in accounting method include the ability to manage the numbers on the financial statements. Conversely, management must be concerned that readers will not be confused by the changes or view them as a way of artificially increasing net income, thereby reducing the credibility of the financial statements.

C14–5

a. To be classified as extraordinary, the event must have been both unusual in nature and infrequent in occurrence.

b. If the eruptions continue periodically, they may not be viewed as infrequent in occurrence and any losses arising from eruptions would then cease to qualify as extraordinary.

c. The entire loss would have been [$36 million ÷ (1 – 48%)] $69.23 million.

Loss from Volcano Eruption	69,230,000	
Timberland		69,230,000
To record extraordinary loss from eruption of volcano.		
Income Tax Liability	33,230,000	
Loss from Volcano Eruption		33,230,000
To record tax effect associated with loss.		

C14–6

a. Standard & Poor's may have viewed the charge as different from previous years and felt including it would distort comparisons from year to year. Value Line may have felt that the exclusion of the charge would be a distortion of the income for the year.

b. The income statement is comprised of several categories. Revenues and expenses that are both usual and frequent are classified as operations. Revenues and expenses that are either usual or frequent, but not both, are classified as other revenues and expenses and considered part of continuing operations. Following continuing operations are special items. Such items are extraordinary items (which are both unusual and infrequent), discontinued operations, and the cumulative effect of accounting changes. All items listed after continuing operations are disclosed net of the associated tax effect.

c. The problem of grouping items on an income statement becomes most relevant when comparative statements are used to asses compliance with other contracts, such as debt covenants. If the classification changes from year to year, comparability is lost, and a company may change from being compliant with debt provisions to violating them. A careful analysis of all items included on an income statement should be part of a complete examination.

CHAPTER 15 The Statement of Cash Flows

E15–1

(1) Investing activity
(2) Financing activity
(3) Operating activity
(4) Financing activity
(5) Investing activity
(6) Investing activity (for the cash paid for the building)
Financing activity (for the mortgage payable)
(7) Financing activity (for the principal payment)
Operating activity (for the interest payment)
(8) Operating activity
(9) Financing activity
(10) Operating activity

E15–2

(1) Not included—does not affect cash

Allowance for Doubtful Accounts	XX	
Accounts Receivable		XX

(2) Investing activity

(3) Financing activity

(4) Not included—does not affect cash

Notes Receivable	XX	
Accumulated Depreciation—Building	XX	
Building		XX

(5) Not included—does not affect cash

Dividend	XX	
Dividend Payable		XX

(6) Not included—does not affect cash

Bonds Payable	XX	
Common Stock		XX

(7) Investing activity

(8) Not included—does not affect cash

Dividend	XX	
Common Stock		XX
Additional Paid-in Capital: Common Stock		XX

(9) Not included—does not affect cash

Depreciation Expense	XX	
Accumulated Depreciation		XX

(10) Operating activity

(11) Not included—does not affect cash

Inventory	XX	
Accounts Payable		XX

(12) Operating activity

(13) Not included—does not affect cash

Land	XX	
Accumulated Depreciation: Building	XX	
Building		XX

(14) Financing activity

(15) Operating activity

E15–3

Change in cash = Cash from operations + Cash from investments + Cash from financing

AAA

– $12 = $380 + Investments – $180
Investments = –$212

This company appears to be following a policy of maintaining a relatively constant cash balance. The company also appears to be relying primarily on operating activities to provide cash to finance the acquisition of nonoperating assets and to finance the repayment of debt or acquisition of treasury stock.

BBB

Change in cash = $219 – $450 + $240
= $9

This company appears to be following a policy of maintaining a relatively constant cash balance. This company also appears to be using cash from operating activities and from borrowings to purchase nonoperating assets.

CCC

–$137 = Operations – $414 + $7
Operations = $270

This company appears to be following a policy of using large amounts of cash generated in prior periods to acquire nonoperating assets. This company also appears to disdain borrowing money.

DDD

$420 = $150 – $130 + Financing
Financing = $400

This company appears to be following a policy of acquiring large amounts of cash in the current period. The company acquired this cash primarily through borrowings.

EEE

$92 = Operating – $120 – $100
Operating = $312

This company appears to be following a policy of acquiring moderate amounts of cash in the current period through operating activities. The company used some of this cash to acquire nonoperating assets and to repay existing debts or to acquire treasury stock.

E15–4

(1) Depreciation Expense	100,000	
Accumulated Depreciation		100,000
To record depreciation.		

Under the direct method, depreciation expense is not included on the statement of cash flows. However, under the indirect method, depreciation expense is included under operating activities as an adjustment to net income to arrive at net cash flows from operating activities.

(2) Cash	250,000	
Common Stock		100,000
Additional Paid-in Capital: Common Stock		150,000
To record issue of common stock.		

The $250,000 would be included in the financing activities section as an inflow of cash.

(3) Marketable Securities	425,000	
Cash		425,000
To record purchase of marketable securities.		

Marketable securities are nonoperating assets for most businesses. Consequently, the purchase of these securities for cash would be disclosed in the investing activities section as an outflow of cash.

(4) Prepaid Insurance	27,000	
Cash		27,000
To record purchase of insurance.		

The $27,000 would be included in the operating activities section as an outflow of cash.

(5) Building	200,000	
Cash		10,000
Mortgage Payable		190,000
To record purchase of a building.		

The $10,000 (the amount paid in cash as a down payment) would be included under investing activities as an outflow of cash. The mortgage would be disclosed in the footnotes to the financial statements or in a supplemental schedule to the statement of cash flows.

E15–5

a.

1. (b) and (i)
2. (x)
3. (d), (j), and (l)
4. (n) and (h)
5. (f)
6. (o)
7. (q)
8. (e), (k), (r), and (u) ([v] might also be used if the company does not use a discount or premium on bonds payable account)
9. (s)
10. (w)

b. **Sales Revenue**

1. An increase in Unearned Sales Revenue would be added to accrual-basis sales.
2. An increase in Accounts Receivable would be deducted from accrual-basis sales.
3. An increase in Allowance for Doubtful Accounts by itself has no effect on accrual-basis sales. However, one must analyze the account to determine whether the company had any write-offs or recoveries of previously written off accounts during the year. Write-offs would be deducted from accrual-basis sales, while recoveries would be added to accrual-basis sales to arrive at cash collections from sales

Cost of Goods Sold

1. An increase in Accounts Payable would be deducted from accrual-basis COGS.
2. An increase in Merchandise Inventory would be added to accrual-basis COGS.

Interest Expense

1. An increase in Interest Payable would be deducted from accrual-basis interest expense.
2. An increase in Discount on Bonds Payable does not affect interest expense per se; it indicates that the company issued additional bonds at less than face value. However, the net increase in the discount is comprised of two components. First, the discount balance increases for the discount associated with the new bonds issued. Second, the discount balance decreases for the amount of the discount balance amortized during the accounting period. Since the amount of the amortized discount flows into interest expense, the amount of the discount amortized would be deducted from accrual-basis interest expense. Consequently, the discount account would have to be analyzed in depth to determine the magnitude of these two components. The same applies to Premium on Bonds Payable.
3. An increase in Prepaid Interest would be added to accrual-basis interest expense.

E15–6

a. (1) Direct method

	Hamilton Hardware	Crozier Crafts	Watson Glass
Sales	$900,000	$900,000	$900,000
Cost of goods sold	400,000	400,000	400,000
Other expenses	200,000	200,000	200,000
Cash flows from operating activities	$300,000	$300,000	$300,000

(2) Indirect method

	Hamilton Hardware	Crozier Crafts	Watson Glass
Net income	$200,000	$160,000	$100,000
Plus: Depreciation	100,000	140,000	200,000
Cash flows from operating activities	$300,000	$300,000	$300,000

b. Cash flows from operating activities differ from net income due to depreciation expense. Cash flows from operating activities measure all the cash inflows and outflows associated with a company's operating assets and liabilities. Net income measures the inflows and outflows of all assets and liabilities, not just cash from operating activities. In this particular case, the only difference between cash flows from operating activities and net income is depreciation. Depreciation is the systematic allocation of the cost of fixed assets. Since depreciation is simply the allocation of the asset's cost, depreciation does not affect cash flows

c. Disagree. Many people think that depreciation expense represents a fund established to finance future acquisitions of fixed assets. If this belief is correct, it would follow that companies using accelerated depreciation methods would have more cash available than companies that use straight-line depreciation. However, as demonstrated in Part (a), depreciation expense has absolutely no effect on the cash flows from operating activities. All three companies have the same cash flows, even though each company uses a different method to compute depreciation. One must remember that depreciation is simply the allocation of the cost of fixed assets. Cash flows associated with fixed assets arise when fixed assets are acquired or sold, not when the cost of the fixed asset is allocated to expenses.

E15–7

		Debit	Credit
a.	(1) Cash	10,000	
	Contributed Capital		10,000
	To record capital contributed by owners.		
	(2) Cash	60,000	
	Payable to Bank		60,000
	To record loan from bank.		
	(3) Property, Plant, & Equipment	20,000	
	Cash		20,000
	To record purchase of long-lived assets.		
	(4) Inventory	40,000	
	Cash		30,000
	Accounts Payable		10,000
	To record purchase of inventory.		
	(5) Cash	15,000	
	Accounts Receivable	65,000	
	Sales		80,000
	To record sales.		
	Cost of Goods Sold	25,000	
	Inventory		25,000
	To record cost of inventory sold.		

(6) Operating Expenses	20,000	
Payable to Bank	5,000	
Dividend	2,000	
Cash		27,000
To record cash disbursements.		

(7) Operating Expenses	10,000	
Operating Expenses Payable		10,000
To record expenses incurred but not yet paid.		

b.

Balance Sheet
December 31, 1991

Assets		Liabilities & Stockholders' Equity	
Cash	$ 8,000	Accounts payable	$ 10,000
Accounts receivable	65,000	Operating expenses payable	10,000
Inventory	15,000	Payable to bank	55,000
Property, plant, & equipment	20,000	Contributed capital	10,000
		Retained earnings	23,000
Total assets	$108,000	Total Liabilities & Stockholders' Equity	$108,000

Income Statement
For the Year Ended December 31, 1991

Sales	$80,000
Cost of goods sold	25,000
Operating expenses	30,000
Net income	$25,000

Statement of Retained Earnings
For the Year Ended December 31, 1991

Beginning retained earnings balance: January 1, 1991	$ 0
Net income	25,000
Less: Dividends	2,000
Ending retained earnings: December 31, 1991	$23,000

c.

Cash

(BB)		0			
(1)	(contributed capital)	10,000	20,000	(3)	(fixed asset purchase)
(2)	(proceeds from loan)	60,000	30,000	(4)	(inventory purchase)
(5)	(inventory sale)	15,000	20,000	(6)	(operating expense payment)
			5,000	(6)	(principal repayment)
			2,000	(6)	(dividend payment)
(EB)		8,000			

Statement of Cash Flows
For the Year Ended December 31, 1991

Cash from operating activities		
Cash collections from sales	$ 15,000	
Cash paid for inventory	(30,000)	
Cash paid for expenses	(20,000)	
Net cash increase (decrease) due to operating activities		($35,000)
Cash from investing activities		
Purchase of fixed assets		(20,000)
Cash from financing activities		
Proceeds from issuing equity	10,000	
Proceeds from issuing debt	60,000	
Principal repayment on debt	(5,000)	
Payment of dividend	(2,000)	
Net cash increase (decrease) due to financing activities		63,000
Net increase (decrease) in cash		$8,000
Beginning cash balance: January 1, 1991		0
Ending cash balance: December 31, 1991		$8,000

d.

Statement of Cash Flows
For the Year Ended December 31, 1991

Cash from operating activities			
Net Income		$25,000	
Less: Increase in accounts receivable	($65,000)		
Increase in inventory	(15,000)		
Plus: Increase in accounts payable	10,000		
Increase in operating expense payable	10,000		
Total adjustments		(60,000)	
Net cash increase (decrease) due to operating activities			($35,000)
Cash from investing activities			
Purchase of long-lived assets			(20,000)
Cash from financing activities			
Proceeds from issuing equity		10,000	
Proceeds from issuing debt		60,000	
Principal repayment on debt		(5,000)	
Payment of dividend		(2,000)	
Net cash increase (decrease) due to financing activities			63,000
Net increase (decrease) in cash			$8,000
Beginning cash balance: January 1, 1991			0
Ending cash balance: December 31, 1991			$8,000

E15–8

		Debit	Credit
a. (1)	Cash	4,000	
	Common Stock		4,000
	To record issue of common stock.		
(2)	Inventory	6,500	
	Accounts Payable		6,500
	To record inventory purchase on account.		
(3)	Equipment	3,400	
	Cash		3,400
	To record purchase of equipment.		
(4)	Cash	10,000	
	Accounts Receivable		10,000
	To record receipts from customers.		
(5)	Accounts Payable	5,000	
	Cash		5,000
	To record payment to suppliers.		
(6)	Dividend	3,000	
	Cash		3,000
	To record declaration and payment of dividend.		
(7)	Rent Expense	6,000	
	Prepaid Rent	6,000	
	Cash		12,000
	To record disbursement for rent.		
(8)	Cash	61,000	
	Accounts Receivable	39,000	
	Sales		100,000
	To record sales.		
(9)	Miscellaneous Expenses	45,000	
	Cash		45,000
	To record payment of expenses.		
(10)	Cash	25,000	
	Land		20,000
	Gain on Sale of Land		5,000
	To record sale of land.		

b.

Cash

(BB)	25,000		
(1)	4,000	3,400	(3)
(4)	10,000	5,000	(5)
(8)	61,000	3,000	(6)
(10)	25,000	12,000	(7)
		45,000	(9)
(EB)	$56,600		

c.

Driftwood Ship Builders
Statement of Cash Flows
For the Year Ended December 31, 1991

Cash flows from operating activities		
Cash collections from customers	$ 71,000	
Cash payments for rent	(12,000)	
Cash payments for miscellaneous expenses	(45,000)	
Cash payments for inventory	(5,000)	
Net cash increase (decrease) due to operating activities		$ 9,000
Cash flows from investing activities		
Proceeds from sale of land	25,000	
Purchase of equipment	(3,400)	
Net cash increase (decrease) due to investing activities		21,600
Cash flows from financing activities		
Proceeds from issue of common stock	4,000	
Dividend payment	(3,000)	
Net cash increase (decrease) due to financing activities		1,000
Net increase (decrease) in cash		$31,600
Beginning cash balance: January 1, 1991		25,000
Ending cash balance: December 31, 1991		$56,600

E15–9

Insurance

Ending prepaid insurance = Beginning prepaid insurance + Insurance purchases – Insurance expense

$7,000 = $4,000 + Insurance purchases – $3,000

Insurance purchases = $6,000

Wages

Ending wages payable = Beginning wages payable + Wage expense – Wages paid

$6,000 = 0 + $9,000 – Wages paid

Wages paid = $3,000

E15–10

a. Cost of ending machinery = Cost of beginning machinery + Cost of machinery purchased – Cost of machinery sold

$30,000 = $20,000 + Machinery purchased – $5,000

Machinery purchased = $15,000

b. When the machinery was sold during 1991, Johnson and Daley, Inc. would prepare the appropriate entry using the following format.

Cash	XX	
Accumulated Depreciation	XX	
Machinery		XX
Gain on Sale of Machinery		XX

We can find the cash collected for the sale of the machinery by first calculating the other three amounts.

Machinery
It is given that the cost of the machinery sold was $5,000.

Gain on sale of machinery
It is given that the gain on the sale was $2,000.

Accumulated depreciation
Ending accumulated depreciation = Beginning accumulated depreciation + Depreciation expense – Accumulated depreciation on machinery sold

$15,000 = $12,000 + $7,000 – Accumulated depreciation on machinery sold

Accumulated depreciation on machinery sold = $4,000

From the entry given above,
Cash = Cost of machinery sold + Gain on sale of machinery – Accumulated depreciation on machinery sold
= $5,000 + $2,000 – $4,000
= $3,000

c.

Cash	3,000	
Accumulated Depreciation	4,000	
Machinery		5,000
Gain on Sale of Machinery		2,000
To record sale of machinery.		

E15–11

1. Direct method

The first step in calculating the cash flows from operating activities is to calculate the cash inflows and outflows associated with each income statement account. These calculations are given below.

Cash collections from sales

Cash collections = Sales – Ending accounts receivable + Beginning accounts receivable + Ending deferred revenue – Beginning deferred revenue
= \$45,000 – \$4,000 + \$6,000 + \$0 – \$3,000
= \$44,000

Cash disbursements for inventory

a. Inventory Purchased
Ending inventory = Beginning inventory + Net purchases – Cost of goods sold
\$9,000 = \$12,000 + Net Purchases – \$30,000

Net purchases = \$27,000

b. Disbursements for inventory
Ending accounts payable = Beginning accounts payable + Inventory purchases – Payments
\$3,000 = \$4,000 + \$27,000 – Payments

Payments = \$28,000

Cash disbursements for wages

Ending wages payable = Beginning wages payable + Wage expense – Wages paid
\$1,800 = \$700 + \$3,000 – Wages paid

Wages paid = \$1,900

Cash disbursements for advertising

Ending prepaid advertising = Beginning prepaid advertising + Advertising purchased – Advertising expense
\$3,000 = \$1,000 + Advertising purchased – \$1,000

Advertising purchased = \$3,000

Cash flows from operating activities	
Sales	\$ 44,000
COGS	(28,000)
Wages	(1,900)
Advertising	(3,000)
Net cash increase (decrease) due to operating activities	\$ 11,100

2. Indirect method

Cash flows from operating activities		
Net income		$ 9,000
Adjustments		
Depreciation	$ 2,000	
Decrease in accounts receivable	2,000	
Decrease in deferred revenues	(3,000)	
Decrease in inventory	3,000	
Decrease in accounts payable	(1,000)	
Increase in wages payable	1,100	
Increase in prepaid advertising	(2,000)	
Total adjustments		2,100
Net cash increase (decrease) due to operating activities		$11,100

E15–12

L. L Corn and Company
Statement of Cash Flows
For the Year Ended December 31, 1991

Cash from operating activities		
Cash collections from sales	$ 35,000	
Cash paid for operating assets	(2,000)	
Cash paid on operating liabilities	(7,000)	
Cash paid for expenses	(34,000)	
Net cash increase (decrease) due to operating activities		($8,000)
Cash from investing activities		
Proceeds from sale of assets[a]		10,000
Cash from financing activities		
Payment of dividends	(2,000)	
Proceeds from issue of debt[b]	2,000	
Repurchase of common stock[c]	(5,000)	
Net cash increase (decrease) due to financing activities		(5,000)
Net increase (decrease) in cash		($3,000)
Beginning cash balance: January 1, 1991		8,000
Ending cash balance: December 31, 1991		$ 5,000

[a] Proceeds from sale of assets = Decrease in nonoperating assets. Since no gain on sale of assets or loss on sale of assets is reported, one must assume that the book value of the assets sold equaled the proceeds from the sale.
[b] Proceeds from issue of debt = Increase in nonoperating liabilities
[c] Repurchase of common stock = Decrease in contributed capital

E15–13

Jones Supply House
Statement of Cash Flows
For the Year Ended December 31, 1991

Cash from operating activities		
Cash collections from sales	$ 59,000	
Cash collections from operating assets	7,000	
Cash from operating liabilities	5,000	
Cash paid for expenses	(61,000)	
Net cash increase (decrease) due to operating activities		$10,000
Cash from investing activities		
Purchase of assets[a]		(4,000)
Cash from financing activities		
Proceeds from equity issue[b]	5,000	
Payment on debt[c]	(4,000)	
Payment of dividends	(3,000)	
Net cash increase (decrease) due to financing activities		(2,000)
Net increase (decrease) in cash		$ 4,000
Beginning cash balance: January 1, 1991		5,000
Ending cash balance: December 31, 1991		$ 9,000

[a] Purchase of assets = Increase in nonoperating assets
[b] Proceeds from the issue of equity = Increase in contributed capital
[c] Payment on debt = Decrease in nonoperating liabilities

E15–14

Accrual-basis sales

Sales = Cash collections from sales + Ending accounts receivable – Beginning accounts receivable – Ending deferred revenue + Beginning deferred revenue
= $65,000 + $3,000 – $9,000 – $4,000 + $2,000
= $57,000

Accrual-basis COGS

COGS = Cash disbursements for inventory – Ending inventory + Beginning inventory + Ending accounts payable – Beginning accounts payable
= $40,000 – $15,000 + $10,000 + $7,000 – $4,000
= $38,000

Accrual-basis wage expense

Wage expense = Cash disbursements for wages + Ending wages payable – Beginning wages payable
= $6,000 + $2,100 – $1,300
= $6,800

Accrual-basis advertising expense

Advertising expense = Cash disbursements for advertising – Ending prepaid advertising + Beginning prepaid advertising
= $1,000 – $5,000 + $8,000
= $4,000

Depreciation expense

Depreciation Exp. = Ending accumulated depreciation – Beginning accumulated depreciation
= $8,000 – $3,000
= $5,000

Net income	
Sales	$57,000
Less: Cost of goods sold	38,000
Wage expense	6,800
Advertising expense	4,000
Depreciation expense	5,000
Net income	$ 3,200

P15–1

Transaction	Section	Inflow	Outflow	Amount
(1)	Operating		√	$ 50,000
(2)	N/A			
(3)	Operating		√	50,000
(4)	Investing	√		95,000
(5)	Operating		√	15,000
	Financing		√	75,000
(6)	N/A			
(7)	Financing	√		150,000
(8)	N/A			
(9)	Financing	√		470,000
(10)	Investing		√	100,000
(11)	N/A			

P15–2

Transaction	Section	Inflow	Outflow	Amount
(1)	Operating	√		$ 50,000
(2)	Investing		√	20,000
(3)	Operating		√	65,000
(4)	N/A			
(5)	Operating	√		10,000
	Investing	√		90,000
(6)	Operating	√		30,000
(7)	Financing		√	50,000
(8)	Financing		√	70,000
(9)	Operating		√	25,000
(10)	Financing		√	300,000
(11)	N/A			
(12)	N/A			
(13)	N/A			

P15–3

a. (1) Cash of $1,000 provided
(2) Cash of $10,000 used
(3) Cash of $9,000 used
(4) Cash of $5,000 provided
(5) Cash of $2,500 provided
(6) Cash of $3,000 provided
(7) Cash not affected
(8) Cash not affected
(9) Cash of $500 used
(10) Cash not affected
(11) Cash not affected
(12) Cash not affected
(13) Cash not affected

b. (1) Investing
(2) Investing
(3) Operating
(4) Financing
(5) The collection on the note receivable could be considered either an operating activity (if the note was originally accepted in a sales transaction or as payment of an open accounts receivable) or an investing activity (if the note was accepted for any other reason). The cash collected for the interest on the note would be classified as an operating activity.
(6) Operating
(7) N/A
(8) N/A
(9) Operating
(10) N/A
(11) N/A
(12) N/A
(13) N/A

P15–4

Trans.	Effect on Cash	Section of Statement	Explanation
(1)	$ 50,000	Operating	Operations is defined in terms of the company's ongoing central activities.
(2)	($ 55,000)	Operating	Cash payments for operating expenses
(3)	$100,000	Investing	Sale of a long-term asset

Note: If the company uses the indirect method to prepare the statement of cash flows, the loss on sale of fixed assets of $15,000 would also be included in the operating activities section as an adjustment to net income to arrive at net cash flows from operating activities.

Trans.	Effect on Cash	Section of Statement	Explanation
(4)	No effect	N/A	Dividends in kind do not affect cash
(5)	($500,000)	Financing	Stock repurchase
(6)	($100,000)	Operating	Cash payment for operating assets

(7)	No effect	N/A	The transaction did not affect cash
(8)	($500,000)	Investing	Cash payment for an investment in equity securities
(9)	$202,000	Financing company.	Issuing debt provides financing to the
(10)	No effect	N/A	Accruals do not affect cash from operations

P15–5

a. **1988**

Ending cash balance = Beginning cash balance + Change in cash
= $0 + $88
= $88

Cash from operating activities = Change in cash – Cash from investing activities – Cash from financing activities
= $88 – (–$500) – $900
= –$312

1989

Beginning cash balance = Ending cash balance – Change in cash
= $86 – (–$2)
= $88

Cash from investing activities = Change in cash – Cash from operating activities – Cash from financing activities
= –$2 – (–$202) – $300
= –$100

1990

Change in cash = Ending cash balance – Beginning cash balance
= $176 – $86
= $90

Cash from operating activities = Change in cash – Cash from investing activities – Cash from financing activities
= $90 – $100 – (–$150)
= $140

b. Ruttman Enterprises began operations during 1988. As part of its start-up phase, the company appears to have issued large amounts of stock or debt to finance the acquisition of nonoperating assets, to cover the cash used by operating activities during the start-up phase, and to provide a cash surplus for future years. During 1989, the company once again issued large amounts of stock or debt to finance the acquisition of nonoperating assets and to cover the cash used by operating activities. However, the company only acquired enough additional financing to meet these needs; it did not acquire an excessive amount of financing. By 1990 the company was generating cash from its operating activities and was able to dispose of some of its nonoperating assets. These cash inflows were then used to retire some of the company's debt or to reacquire some of its outstanding stock.

P15–6

Case 1

Buildings

	Debit	Credit	
(BB)	800,000		
(Purchase)	200,000	X	(Sale)
(EB)	750,000		

Accumulated Depreciation

	Debit	Credit	
		90,000	(BB)
(Sale)	Y	30,000	(Depr Exp)
		30,000	(EB)

X = Cost of buildings sold = $250,000

Y = Accumulated depreciation on buildings sold = $90,000

Cash

	Debit	Credit	
(Sale)	160,000	200,000	(Purchase)

Depreciation Expense

Debit	Credit
30,000	

Proceeds from sale = Cost of building sold – Related accumulated depreciation
= 250,000 – 90,000 = $160,000
(This solution assumes that there was no gain or loss on the sale of the building)

In the statement of cash flows for 1994, Webb Industries would report the following items under cash flows from investing activity.

Proceeds from the sales of buildings	$ 160,000
Purchase of a building	(200,000)

Case 2

Equipment

	Debit	Credit	
(BB)	400,000		
(Purchase)	X	50,000	(Sale)
(EB)	500,000		

Accumulated Depreciation

	Debit	Credit	
		85,000	(BB)
(Sale)	Y	10,000	(Depr Exp)
		75,000	(EB)

X = Cost of Equipment Purchased
= $150,000

Y = Accumulated depreciation on equipment sold = $20,000

Cash

	Debit	Credit	
(Sale)	35,000	150,000	(Purchase)

Proceeds from sale = Book value of equipment sold + Gain on sale
= ($50,000 – $20,000) + $5,000 = $35,000

Depreciation Expense

Debit	Credit
10,000	

Gain on Sale of Equipment

Debit	Credit	
	5,000	(Sale)

In the statement of cash flows for 1994, Webb Industries would report the following items under cash flows from investing activity.

Proceeds from the sale of equipment	$ 35,000
Purchase of equipment	(150,000)

Case 3

Land

	Debit	Credit	
(BB)	250,000		
(Purchase)	Y	X	(Sale)
(End Bal)	250,000		

Cash

	Debit	Credit	
(Sale)	300,000	Y	(Purchase)

Gain on Sale of Land

Debit	Credit
	75,000

X = Cost of land sold = Proceeds on the sale – Gain on the sale
= $300,000 – $75,000 = $225,000
Y = Cost of land purchased = Ending balance – Beginning balance + Cost of land sold
= $225,000

In the statement of cash flows for 1994, Webb Industries would report the following items under cash flows from investing activity.

Proceeds from the sale of land	$ 300,000
Purchase of land	(225,000)

Case 4

Buildings

	Debit	Credit	
(BB)	800,000		
(Exchange)	600,000	X	(Sale)
(EB)	750,000		

Accumulated Depreciation

	Debit	Credit	
		90,000	(BB)
(Sale)	Y	30,000	(Depr Exp)
		30,000	(EB)

X = Cost of buildings sold = $650,000

Y = Accumulated depreciation on buildings sold = $90,000

Land

	Debit	Credit	
(BB)	250,000		
(Purchase)	W	150,000	(Exchange)
(EB)	250,000		

W = Cost of Land Purchased = 150,000

Depreciation Expense

Debit	Credit
30,000	

Gain on Disposal of Land

Debit	Credit	
	450,000	(Exchange)

Cash

(Sale of Building)	560,000	150,000	(Purchase of Land)

Proceeds from sale = Cost of building sold – Related accumulated depreciation
= $650,000 – $90,000 = $560,000
(This solution assumes that there was no gain or loss on the sale of the building)

In the statement of cash flows for 1994, Webb Industries would report the following items under cash flows from investing activity.

Proceeds from the sale of building	$560,000
Purchase of land	150,000

P15–7

1. Total number of shares issued = Change in balance of common stock account ÷ Par value per share of common stock
= ($128,000 – $100,000) ÷ $1 per share
= 28,000 shares

2. Number of shares issued for cash = Total number of shares issued – (Shares issued as stock dividend + Shares issued in exchange for land)
= 28,000 shares – {[(100,000 shares issued on 1/1/90 – 4,000 shares held as treasury stock on 1/1/90]) x 20%] + 6,000 shares exchanged for land}
= 28,000 shares – (19,200 shares + 6,000 shares)
= 2,800 shares

3. Cash received = Change in common stock account + Change in additional paid–in capital: common stock account due to issue of common stock for cash.
= ($128,000 – $100,000) + [($55,000 – $12,000) + $38,400[a] – $12,000[b]]
= $20,600

---

[a] $38,400 represents the additional paid-in capital from the 20% stock dividend. The company distributed 19,200 shares (see Part [2]), and the fair market value at the time was $3 per share. One dollar was allocated to the Common Stock account, while the remaining $2 was allocated to the Additional Paid-in Capital account.
[b] $12,000 represents the additional paid-in capital from exchanging stock for land.

P15–8

a. Ending accounts receivable = Beginning accounts receivable + Net sales – Cash collections

1990

$100,000 = $0 + (Gross sales – $20,000) – $350,000
Gross sales = $470,000

1991

$150,000 = $100,000 + (Gross sales – $25,000) – $500,000
Gross sales = $575,000

b. Ending inventory = Beginning inventory + Net purchases – Cost of goods sold
$110,000 = $125,000 + Net purchases – $375,000
Net purchases = $360,000

Ending accounts payable = Beginning accounts payable + Net purchases – Cash payments
$115,000 = $105,000 + $360,000 – Cash payments
Cash payments = $350,000

c. Ending prepaid insurance = Beginning prepaid insurance + Insurance purchased – Insurance expense

1990

= $0 + $65,000 – $35,000
= $30,000

1991

= $30,000 + $80,000 – $50,000
= $60,000

P15–9

Accrual-basis sales

Accrual sales = Collections from customers – Change in accounts receivable
= $24,000 – ($3,000)
= $27,000

Accrual-basis COGS

Accrual COGS = Payments to suppliers – Change in inventory – Change in accounts payable
= ($13,000) – ($3,000) – $2,000
= ($12,000)

Accrual-basis operating expenses

Accrual expenses = Payments for expenses – Change in accrued payables
= ($9,000) – ($2,000)
= ($7,000)

Battery Builders, Inc.
Income Statement

Sales	$ 27,000
Cost of goods sold	(12,000)
Depreciation expense	(4,000)
Other operating expenses	(7,000)
Gain on sale of equipment	2,000
Net income	$ 6,000

P15–10

a.

Pendleton Enterprises
Statement of Cash Flows from Operating Activities
For the Years Ended December 31, 1989, 1990, and 1991

	1991	1990	1989
Cash collections from customers and sales	$ 9,000	$13,000	$ 4,000
Cash payments for expenses and to suppliers	(12,000)	(8,000)	(4,000)
Net cash increase (decrease) due to operating activities	($3,000)	$ 5,000	$ 0

b.

Pendleton Enterprises
Statement of Cash Flows from Operating Activities
For the Years Ended December 31, 1989, 1990, and 1991

	1991	1990	1989
Cash collections from customers and sales	$ 9,000	$ 9,000	$ 8,000
Cash payments for expenses and to suppliers	(12,000)	(8,000)	(4,000)
Net cash increase (decrease) due to operating activities	($3,000)	$ 1,000	$ 4,000

c.

Pendleton Enterprises
Statement of Cash Flows from Operating Activities
For the Years Ended December 31, 1989, 1990, and 1991

	1991	1990	1989
Cash collections from customers and sales	$ 9,000	$ 13,000	$ 4,000
Cash payments for expenses and to suppliers	(12,000)	(11,000)	(1,000)
Net cash increase (decrease) due to operating activities	($3,000)	$ 2,000	$ 3,000

d. Managers can manipulate cash flows from operating activities by manipulating the timing of cash collections and cash payments associated with operating activities. By comparing parts (a) and (b) and parts (a) and (c), it is obvious that these types of manipulations offset themselves in the next period. So if a manager wants to continue manipulating cash flows from operating activities, the manager will have to manipulate the timing of cash inflows and outflows every year.

P15–11

Watson and Holmes Detective Agency
Statement of Cash Flows—Direct Method
For the Year ended December 31, 1991

Cash flows from operating activities		
Cash collections from customers	$ 34,500 *	
Cash paid for inventory	(22,000)	
Cash paid for interest	(3,800)	
Cash paid for other expenses	(8,000)	
Net cash increase (decrease) due to operating activities		$ 700
Cash flows from investing activities		
Purchase of long-lived assets	(2,000)	
Net cash increase (decrease) due to investing activities		(2,000)
Cash flows from financing activities		
Cash paid for dividends	(700)	
Proceeds from issuance of common stock	4,000	
Net cash increase (decrease) due to financing activities		3,300
Net increase in cash		$ 2,000
Beginning cash balance: January 1, 1991		8,000
Ending cash balance: December 31, 1991		$10,000

* $34,500 = $40,000 revenues – $3,000 increase in accounts receivable + $500 increase in allowance for doubtful accounts – $2,000 bad debt expense – $1,000 decrease in deferred revenues

Watson and Holmes Detective Agency
Statement of Cash Flows—Indirect Method
For the Year ended December 31, 1991

Cash flows from operating activities			
Net income		$ 2,000	
Adjustments			
Depreciation	$ 2,000		
Increase in allowance for doubtful accounts	500		
Increase in accounts payable	1,000		
Decrease in discount on note payable	200		
Increase in accounts receivable	(3,000)		
Increase in inventory	(1,000)		
Decrease in deferred revenues	(1,000)		
Total adjustments		(1,300)	
Net cash increase (decrease) due to operating activities			$ 700
Cash flows from investing activities			
Purchase of fixed assets		(2,000)	
Net cash increase (decrease) due to investing activities			(2,000)
Cash flows from financing activities			
Cash paid for dividends		(700)	
Proceeds from issuance of common stock		4,000	
Net cash increase (decrease) due to financing activities			3,300
Increase in cash			$2,000
Beginning cash balance: January 1, 1991			8,000
Ending cash balance: December 31, 1991			$10,000

P15–12

		Debit	Credit
a. (1)	Cash	50,000	
	Common Stock		50,000
	To record issue of common stock.		
(2)	Inventory	20,000	
	Accounts Payable		20,000
	To record purchase of inventory on account.		
(3)	Prepaid Rent	6,000	
	Cash		6,000
	To record rent payment.		
(4)	Furniture	30,000	
	Cash		20,000
	Long-Term Notes Payable		10,000
	To record purchase of furniture.		
(5a)	Accounts Receivable	31,500	
	Sales		31,500
	To record sales on account.		

		Debit	Credit
(5b)	Cost of Goods Sold	9,000	
	Inventory		9,000
	To record cost of inventory sold.		
(6)	Accounts Payable	10,000	
	Cash		10,000
	To record payment to suppliers on open accounts.		
(7)	Cash	10,000	
	Accounts Receivable		10,000
	To record collections from customers on open accounts.		
(8)	Miscellaneous Expenses	9,000	
	Cash		9,000
	To record expenses incurred and paid.		
(9)	Depreciation Expense	5,000	
	Accumulated Depreciation		5,000
	To adjust for depreciation.		
(10)	Interest Expense	1,000	
	Accrued Interest Payable		1,000
	To record interest incurred but not yet paid.		
(11)	Dividends	3,000	
	Dividends Payable		3,000
	To record declaration of dividends.		
(12)	Rent Expense	3,000	
	Prepaid Rent		3,000
	To adjust for expired rent.		

b.

Lumbard and Brothers
Income Statement
For the Year ended December 31, 1989

Sales	$31,500
Less: Cost of goods sold	9,000
Depreciation expense	5,000
Rent expense	3,000
Interest expense	1,000
Miscellaneous expenses	9,000
Net income	$ 4,500

Lumbard and Brothers
Statement of Retained Earnings
For the Year ended December 31, 1989

Beginning retained earnings balance: January 1, 1989	$ 0
Net income	4,500
Dividends	3,000
Ending retained earnings balance: December 31, 1989	$1,500

Lumbard and Brothers
Balance Sheet
December 31, 1989

Assets		Liabilities & Stockholders' Equity	
Cash	$15,000	Accounts payable	$10,000
Accounts receivable	21,500	Accrued interest payable	1,000
Inventory	11,000	Dividend payable	3,000
Prepaid rent	3,000	Long-term notes payable	10,000
Furniture	30,000	Common stock	50,000
Less: Accum. depreciation	5,000	Retained earnings	1,500
Total assets	$75,500	Total Liabilities & stockholders' equity.	$75,500

Lumbard and Brothers
Statement of Cash Flows—Indirect Method
For the Year ended December 31, 1989

Cash flows from operating activities			
Net income		$4,500	
Adjustments			
Depreciation	$ 5,000		
Increase in accounts receivable	(21,500)		
Increase in inventory	(11,000)		
Increase in prepaid rent	(3,000)		
Increase in accounts payable	10,000		
Increase in interest payable	1,000		
Total adjustments		(19,500)	
Net cash increase (decrease) due to operating activities			($15,000)
Cash flows from investing activities			
Purchase of furniture		(20,000)	
Net cash increase (decrease) due to investing activities			(20,000)
Cash flows from financing activities			
Proceeds from issuance of common stock		50,000	
Net cash increase (decrease) due to financing activities			50,000
Net increase (decrease) in cash			$15,000
Beginning cash balance: January 1, 1989			0
Ending cash balance: December 31, 1989			$15,000

c. Working capital = Current assets – Current liabilities
= ($15,000 + $21,500 + $11,000 + $3,000) – ($10,000 + $1,000 + $3,000)
= $50,500 – $14,000
= $36,500

Current ratio = Current assets ÷ Current liabilities
= $50,500 ÷ $14,000
= 3.61

d. Working capital = ($50,500 – $10,000 cash) – ($14,000 – $10,000 accounts payable)
= $40,500 – $4,000
= $36,500

Current ratio = $40,500 ÷ $4,000
= 10.125

Net cash flows used by operating activities = –$15,000 from Part (b) – $10,000
= –$25,000

P15–13

a. **Cash collections from marketing revenue**

Ending accounts receivable = Beginning accounts receivable + Marketing revenue – Cash collections

$150,000 = $100,000 + $1,000,000 – Cash collections

Cash collections = $950,000

Cash paid for salaries

Since no related balance sheet account exists as of December 31, 1991 or as of December 31, 1992, it is safe to assume that the entire Salary Expense balance was paid in cash. Therefore, the cash paid for salaries equals $250,000.

Cash paid for supplies

Ending office supply inventory = Beginning office supply inventory + Office supply purchases – Office supplies expense

$75,000 = $100,000 + Office supply purchases – $175,000

Office supply purchases = $150,000

Cash paid for depreciation

Depreciation is the allocation of the cost of a fixed asset. Depreciation does not provide cash or use cash; hence, cash-basis depreciation expense is <u>always</u> zero.

Cash paid for insurance

Ending prepaid insurance = Beginning prepaid insurance + Insurance purchases – Insurance expense

$50,000 = $10,000 + Insurance purchases – $60,000

Insurance purchases = $100,000

Cash paid for rent

Ending rent payable	=	Beginning rent payable + Rent expense – Rent paid
$20,000	=	$0 + $120,000 – Rent paid
Rent paid	=	$100,000

This method would be more similar to directly computing net cash flows from operating activities since the actual cash flows for each component of operating activities are being computed. Under the indirect method, net cash flows for operating activities are computed by adjusting net income.

b.

Net income		$295,000
Adjustments		
Decrease in office supplies inventory	$ 25,000	
Depreciation expense	100,000	
Increase in rent payable	20,000	
Increase in accounts receivable	(50,000)	
Increase in prepaid insurance	(40,000)	
Total adjustments		55,000
Net cash increase (decrease) due to operating activities		$350,000

This method is similar to the indirect method since net income is adjusted for the change in each operating account on the balance sheet to arrive at cash flows from operating activities. The magnitudes of these adjustments are the same as in Part (a). However, in Part (a) each of these adjustments was related to a component of operating activity, whereas in Part (b) each adjustment is related to net income.

c.

Income Statement		Adjustments Required/Indirect Method		Operating Cash Flows Direct Method
Revenue	$1,000,000	Less: Increase in accts rec	$ 50,000	$ 950,000
Salary exp	(250,000)	None	0	(250,000)
Office supplies exp	(175,000)	Less: Decrease in office supplies inventory	25,000	(150,000)
Depreciation exp	(100,000)	Plus: Depreciation expense	100,000	0
Insurance exp	(60,000)	Less: Increase in prepaid insurance	40,000	(100,000)
Rent exp	(120,000)	Plus: Increase in rent payable	20,000	(100,000)
Net income	$ 295,000	Cash provided by operating activities		$ 350,000

P15–14

Johnson Vending Company
Balance Sheet
December 31, 1992

Assets		
Cash	$350,000	
Short-term marketable securities	250,000	
Less: Allowance for unrealized losses on marketable securities	10,000	
Accounts receivable	75,000	
Inventory	115,000	
Prepaid insurance	5,000	
Total current assets		$ 785,000
Fixed assets	650,000	
Less: Accumulated depreciation	100,000	
Total long-term assets		550,000
Total Assets		$1,335,000
Liabilities and Stockholders' Equity		
Accounts payable	$ 50,000	
Wages payable	15,000	
Bonds payable	200,000	
Less: Discount on bonds payable	5,000	
Total liabilities		$ 260,000
Common stock ($10 par value)	100,000[a]	
Additional paid-in capital: Common stock	75,000	
Retained earnings	900,000[b]	
Total owners' equity		1,075,000
Total liabilities and stockholders' equity		$1,335,000

[a] $100,000 = $10 par value x 10,000 shares. The excess cash received over par value is credited to Additional Paid-in Capital: Common Stock.
[b] $900,000 = $1,000,000 in net income – $100,000 in dividends

P15–15

a. (1) Johnson Vending Company generated net income during 1992 of $1,000,000, while the company's net cash flows provided by operating activities were $980,000.

(2) The market value of short-term marketable equity securities was equal to $240,000. Under GAAP, short-term marketable equity securities are recorded at the lower of their aggregate cost or aggregate market value. When the portfolio's market value has decreased during the accounting period, the company would have to make the following entry:

Unrealized Loss on Marketable Securities	XX	
Allowance for Unrealized Loss on Marketable Securities		XX

Since such a loss is disclosed on the statement of cash flows, we know that the market value of the company's portfolio decreased by $10,000 during 1992. Johnson Vending Company began operations in 1992, so this loss represents the entire balance necessary in the related Allowance account. Since the cost of the company's portfolio was $250,000, its market value must be $240,000.

(3) $75,000. The company issued 10,000 shares with a par value of $10 each. Hence, the total par value of the stock issued was $100,000. The excess of cash received over the total par value was $75,000. The excess cash received over par value was credited to Additional Paid-in Capital: Common Stock.

(4) Issuing stock to investors is a financing activity. An item that might attract an investor to select a particular stock is dividends. Since paying dividends is associated with attracting and maintaining financing, dividend payments should be classified as a financing activity.

(5) Depreciation represents the allocation of fixed asset costs to expense and is used to compute accrual-basis income under GAAP. However, depreciation neither uses nor provides cash flows, so Depreciation Expense does not affect net cash flows from operating activities. Since Depreciation Expense of $100,000 had already been deducted from revenues to arrive at net income, adding $100,000 back to net income causes the net effect of Depreciation Expense on net cash flows from operating activities to be zero.

(6) Net income under GAAP is an accrual concept and, as such, net income does not measure cash flows from operating activities. By analyzing balance sheet accounts that are related to the components of the income statement, net income can be converted to cash flows from operating activities.

(a) Depreciation: See question (5).

(b) Accounts Receivable: See question (7).

(c) Accounts Payable: Accounts Payable is related to the purchase of inventory on account. An increase in Accounts Payable implies that some of the inventory purchased on account still requires payment. Consequently, Cost of Goods Sold overstates the cash actually disbursed for inventory.

(d) Inventory: An increase in Inventory implies that the company acquired more inventory than it sold. This additional amount was either purchased on account or for cash. If it was purchased on account an examination of Accounts Payable is necessary to determine the actual cash disbursed for inventory. If it was purchased for cash, this amount would have to be added to COGS (i.e., deducted from net income).

(e) Prepaid Insurance: An increase in Prepaid Insurance implies that the company acquired additional insurance during the year. Assuming that the additional insurance was acquired for cash, the amount paid for the additional insurance should be used in computing cash flows from operating activities. Since Insurance Expense has already been used to compute net income, the amount necessary to adjust net income to cash flows is the difference between the balance in Insurance Expense and the additional insurance acquired.

(f) Wages Payable: Wages Payable is increased by incurring wages. Hence, Wage Expense arises from two sources—wages incurred and paid in cash or wages incurred but not yet paid. In computing cash flows from operating activities, the correct amount to use are the wages paid in cash. Since, Wage Expense was used to compute net income that portion of Wage Expense that represents wages incurred but not yet paid (i.e., an increase in Wages Payable) must be added back to net income to arrive at cash flows from operating activities.

(g) Unrealized Loss on Marketable Securities: Losses are deducted from revenues to compute net income. However, losses (and gains) do not provide or use cash; they are simply "paper" profits, so they should not be used to compute net cash flows from operating activities. Since the loss has already been deducted in computing net income, the loss must be added back to net income to arrive at net cash flows from operating activities.

(7) Cash collections on sales were less than accrual-basis sales. Cash collections on sales equal accrual-basis sales plus beginning Accounts Receivable less ending Accounts Receivable. In this case, beginning Accounts Receivable was zero (since the company began in operations in 1992), while ending Accounts Receivable was $105,000. Consequently, cash collections were $105,000 less than accrual-basis sales. An increase in Accounts Receivable implies that the company made sales on account during the year and that some of the corresponding receivables had not been collected as of year end.

b. Johnson Vending Company uses the indirect method for its statement of cash flows. The indirect and direct methods only affect the cash from operating activities section of the statement of cash flows. With the direct method, the actual cash inflows and outflows associated with each component of operating activities are reported on the face of the statement of cash flows. With the indirect method, net income is reported on the face of the statement of cash flows, and is then adjusted for (1) operating activities used to compute net income that did not affect cash flows and (2) operating activities that did affect cash flows but were not used to compute net income. Since the company's statement of cash flows begins with net income and is adjusted for these items, it appears that the company uses the indirect method.

P15–16

Lewis Manufacturing Industries
Statement of Cash Flows—Direct Method
For the Year Ended December 31, 1994

Cash from operating activities		
Cash collections from sales and accounts receivable	$ 100,000 [a]	
Cash paid to suppliers for inventory	(100,000)	
Cash paid for wages	(12,000)	
Cash paid for supplies	(4,000)	
Cash paid for interest	(10,000)	
Net cash increase (decrease) due to operating activities		($26,000)
Cash flows from investing activities		
Proceeds on sale of fixed assets	130,000 [b]	
Proceeds from sale of marketable securities	50,000 [c]	
Net cash increase (decrease) due to investing activities		180,000
Net cash flows from financing activities		0
Net increase (decrease) in cash due to financing activities		$154,000
Beginning cash balance: January 1, 1994		593,000
Ending cash balance: December 31, 1994		$747,000

[a] Cash collections include changes in both Accounts and Notes Receivable.

[b] Proceeds on sale of fixed assets are computed as follows:

Cost of machinery & equipment sold	$ 150,000
Less: Related accumulated depreciation	10,000
Book value of machinery & equipment sold	$ 140,000
Less: Loss on sale of fixed assets (per income statement)	10,000
Proceeds on sale of fixed assets	$ 130,000

[c] Proceeds from sale of marketable securities are computed as follows:

Decrease in marketable securities	$ 55,000
Less: Loss on sale of marketable securities (per income statement)	5,000
Proceeds from sale	$ 50,000

Lewis Manufacturing Industries
Statement of Cash Flows—Indirect Method
For the Year Ended December 31, 1994

Cash from operating activities			
Net income			$ 37,000
Adjustments			
Decrease in inventory	$ 25,000		
Depreciation	25,000		
Decrease in discount on bonds payable	5,000		
Decrease in supplies inventory	2,000		
Loss on sale of fixed assets	10,000		
Loss on sale of marketable securities	5,000		
Increase in accounts receivable	(50,000)		
Increase in notes receivable	(50,000)		
Decrease in accounts payable	(35,000)		
Total adjustments		(63,000)	
Net cash increase (decrease) due to operating activities			($26,000)
Cash flows from investing activities			
Proceeds on sales of fixed assets		130,000	
Proceeds from sale of marketable securities		50,000	
Net cash increase (decrease) due to investing activities			180,000
Net cash increase (decrease) due to financing activities			0
Net increase in cash			$154,000
Beginning cash balance: January 1, 1994			593,000
Ending cash balance: December 31, 1994			$747,000

P15–17

Conlon Restaurant Supply Company
Statement of Cash Flows—Direct Method
For the Year Ended December 31, 1994

Cash flows from operating activities		
Cash collections from customers	$ 165,000	
Cash paid to suppliers	(194,000)	
Cash paid for interest	(13,000)	
Net cash increase (decrease) due to operating activities		($42,000)
Cash flows from investing activities		
Proceeds from sale of plant equipment	90,000 [a]	
Purchase of plant equipment	(25,000)[a]	
Net cash increase (decrease) due to investing activities		65,000
Cash flows from financing activities		
Proceeds from common stock issue	50,000 [b]	
Payment of dividends	(20,000)[c]	
Net cash increase (decrease) due to financing activities		30,000
Net increase in cash		$ 53,000
Beginning cash balance: January 1, 1994		120,000
Ending cash balance: December 31, 1994		$173,000

[a] Explanation of activity involving plant equipment

Ending plant equip = Beginning plant equip + Purchases – Equipment sold
$275,000 = $350,000 + Purchases – $100,000
Purchases = $25,000

Proceeds from sale of equipment = Book value of assets sold + Gain on the sale
Proceeds = [(Asset cost – Accumulated depreciation on asset sold) + Gain on sale]
Proceeds = [($100,000 – $20,000) + $10,000] = $90,000

[b] Proceeds from issue of common stock = Increase in common stock + Increase in additional paid-in capital: common stock
= $25,000 + $25,000 = $50,000

[c] Dividends = Beginning retained earnings + Net income – Ending retained earnings
= $194,000 + $37,000 – $211,000 = $20,000

Conlon Restaurant Supply Company
Statement of Cash Flows—Indirect Method
For the Year Ended December 31, 1994

Cash flows from operating activities			
Net income		$ 37,000	
Adjustments			
Depreciation	$12,000		
Decrease in accounts receivable	5,000		
Decrease in prepaid insurance	10,000		
Increase in accounts payable	6,000		
Increase in inventory	(100,000)		
Decrease in premium on bonds payable	(2,000)		
Gain on sale of plant equipment	(10,000)		
Total adjustments		(79,000)	
Net cash increase (decrease) due to operating activities			($42,000)
Cash flows from investing activities			
Proceeds from sale of plant equipment		90,000	
Purchase of plant equipment		(25,000)	
Net cash increase (decrease) due to investing activities			65,000
Cash flows from financing activities			
Proceeds from common stock Issue		50,000	
Payment of dividends		(20,000)	
Net cash increase (decrease) due to financing activities			30,000
Net increase (decrease) in cash			$ 53,000
Beginning cash balance: January 1, 1994			120,000
Ending cash balance: December 31, 1994			$ 173,000

P15–18

a. **1993**

Cash collections from customers		
Sales for cash: (65% x $5,590,000)	$3,633,500	
Cash collections from accounts receivable[a]	4,936,500	
Total cash collections from customers		$8,570,000[b]
Cash Payments for Expenses		
Salary: Salary expense – Salary payable = $1,794,000 – $145,000	$1,649,000	
Advertising	710,000	
Administrative expenses	832,000	
Janitorial expense	120,000	
Supplies expense: Supplies expense – Supply inventory payable = $299,000 – $67,000	232,000	
Total cash paid for expenses		(3,543,000)
Net cash increase (decrease) due to operating activities		$ 5,027,000

[a] Cash collections = Sales on account – Δ Accounts receivable
= [35% x $5,590,000] – (–$2,980,000) = $4,936,500

[b] An alternative approach to calculating the $8,570,000 is to add the decrease in Accounts Receivable during 1993 of $2,980,000 to the 1993 sales of $5,590,000.

1994

Cash collections from customers		
Sales for cash: (25%)($5,967,000)	$1,491,750	
Cash collections from accounts receivable[a]	2,803,500	
Total cash collections from customers		$4,295,250[b]
Cash payments for expenses		
Salary: Salary expense – Ending salary payable + Beginning salary payable = $1,794,000 – $25,000 + $145,000	$2,145,000	
Advertising: Advertising expense – Advertising payable = $755,000 – $50,000	705,000	
Administrative expenses	898,000	
Janitorial expense	132,000	
Supplies expense: Supplies expense + Beginning supply inventory payable = $299,000 + $67,000	348,000	
Total cash paid for expenses		($4,228,000)
Net cash increase (decrease) due to operating activities		$67,250

[a] Cash collections = Sales on account – Δ Accounts receivable
= (75% x 5,967,000) – $1,671,750 = $2,803,500

[b] This amount can also be calculated as 1994 sales of $5,967,000 less the increase in Accounts Receivable during 1994.

b. The first thing that must be explained to the stockholders is the nature of dividends. Dividends are paid out of assets, not out of net income. If a company has insufficient assets or has alternative uses for its assets, it will be unable to declare a cash dividend or a dividend in kind. While net income is a measure of the net assets that have flowed into the company during the year from operating activities, these net assets may be in a form, such as inventory or accounts receivable, that cannot easily be distributed to stockholders. Hence, net income only provides a low-quality indication of potential dividends; a better indication of a firm's potential ability to declare dividends is the net cash flows from operating activities.

In this particular case, 1993 was a good year for the Rudnicki Engineering Firm. The company generated $597,000 in net income and $5,027,000 (see Part [a]) in cash flows from operating activities. The large cash flows are due primarily to the collection of receivables that were outstanding at the beginning of the year and were not associated at all with 1993 net income. 1994 was also a good year with respect to net income; the company generated an income of $638,000. However, as demonstrated in Part (a), the company only realized a net cash flow from operating activities of $67,250. The low cash flows (compared to 1993 cash flows) are due to (1) a larger proportion of sales being on account compared to 1993 and (2) customers not promptly paying their accounts. As a board member you felt that the 1994 cash flows were insufficient to both fund future operations and pay a dividend.

P15–19

a. **Original entries**

		Debit	Credit
(1a)	Cash	2,050,000	
	Sales		2,050,000
	To record cash sales.		
(1b)	Cost of Goods Sold	875,000	
	Inventory		875,000
	To record cost of inventory sold.		

	Account	Debit	Credit
(2a)	Cash	1,500,000	
	Common Stock ($15 par value)		750,000
	Additional Paid-in Capital: Common Stock		750,000
	To record issue of common stock.		
(2b)	Cash	102,000	
	Preferred Stock (10%, $100 par value)		100,000
	Additional Paid-in Capital: Preferred Stock		2,000
	To record issue of preferred stock.		
(3)	Fixed Assets	750,000	
	Cash		750,000
	To record purchase of fixed assets.		
(4a)	Accounts Receivable	880,000	
	Sales		880,000
	To record sales on account.		
(4b)	Cost of Goods Sold	490,000	
	Inventory		490,000
	To record cost of inventory sold.		
(4c)	Cash	500,000	
	Accounts Receivable		500,000
	To record cash collections on open accounts.		
(5a)	Inventory	2,000,000	
	Accounts Payable		2,000,000
	To record inventory purchased on account.		
(5b)	Accounts Payable	1,075,000	
	Cash		1,075,000
	To record payment to suppliers for open accounts.		
(6)	Miscellaneous Expenses	500,000	
	Cash		500,000
	To record payment for miscellaneous expenses.		
(7)	Prepaid Insurance	80,000	
	Cash		80,000
	To record purchase of insurance.		
(8)	Marketable Securities	250,000	
	Cash		250,000
	To record investment in marketable securities.		
(9)	Cash	29,200[a]	
	Bonds Payable		20,000[b]
	Premium on Bonds Payable		9,200
	To record issue of bonds.		

---

[a] $29,200 = 20 bonds x $1,000 face value per bond x 146%
[b] $20,000 = 20 bonds x $1,000 face value per bond

		Debit	Credit
(10)	Dividends	100,000	
	Dividend Payable		100,000
	To record dividend declaration.		
(11)	Land	40,000	
	Common Stock ($15 par value)		15,000
	Additional Paid-in Capital: Common Stock		25,000
	To record acquisition of land for common stock.		
(12)	Interest Expense	1,460[a]	
	Premium on Bonds Payable	140	
	Cash		1,600[b]
	To record interest payment.		

[a] $1,460 = [(10% ÷ 2) x $29,200]
[b] $1,600 = [(16% ÷ 2) x $20,000]

Adjusting Entries

		Debit	Credit
(a)	Depreciation Expense	140,000*	
	Accumulated Depreciation		140,000
	To record depreciation for 1993.		

* $140,000 = [($750,000 – $50,000) ÷ 5 years]

		Debit	Credit
(b)	Insurance Expense	20,000	
	Prepaid Insurance		20,000
	To adjust for insurance expired.		
(c)	Unrealized Loss on Short-Term Marketable Securities	25,000	
	Allowance for Unrealized Loss on Short-Term Marketable Securities		25,000
	To adjust marketable securities to LCM.		
(d)	Miscellaneous Expenses	75,000	
	Accrued Miscellaneous Expense Payable		75,000
	To record expenses incurred but not yet paid.		
(e)	Bad Debt Expense	70,400*	
	Allowance for Doubtful Accounts		70,400
	To record bad debt expense.		

* $70,400 = 8% x $880,000

		Debit	Credit
(f)	Loss on Inventory Writedown	5,000	
	Inventory		5,000
	To adjust inventory for LCM.		

b. **Closing Entries**

		Debit	Credit
(C1)	Sales	2,930,000	
	Income Summary		2,930,000
	To close Sales to Income Summary.		
(C2)	Income Summary	2,201,860	
	Miscellaneous Expenses		575,000
	Cost of Goods Sold		1,365,000
	Interest Expense		1,460
	Bad Debt Expense		70,400
	Depreciation Expense		140,000
	Insurance Expense		20,000
	Loss on Writedown of Inventory		5,000
	Unrealized Loss on Short-Term Marketable Securities		25,000
	To close expenses to Income Summary.		

Note: Entries (C1) and (C2) could be combined into one journal entry.

		Debit	Credit
(C3)	Income Summary	728,140	
	Retained Earnings		728,140
	To close Income Summary to Retained Earnings.		
(C4)	Retained Earnings	100,000	
	Dividends		100,000
	To close Dividends to Retained Earnings.		

Cash

(BB)	0		
(1a)	2,050,000	750,000	(3c)
(1b)	1,500,000	1,075,000	(5b)
(2b)	102,000	500,000	(6)
(4c)	500,000	80,000	(7)
(9)	29,200	250,000	(8)
		1,600	(12)
(EB)	1,524,600		

Marketable Securities

(BB)	0		
(8)	250,000		
(EB)	250,000		

Accounts Receivable

(BB)	0		
(4a)	880,000	500,000	(4c)
(EB)	380,000		

Allow for Loss/Mkt Sec

		0	(BB)
		25,000	(c)
		25,000	(EB)

Allow for Doubtful Accounts

		0	(BB)
		70,400	(e)
		70,400	(EB)

Inventory

(BB)	0		
(5a)	2,000,000	875,000	(1b)
		490,000	(4b)
		5,000	(f)
(EB)	630,000		

Prepaid Insurance

(BB)	0		
(7)	80,000	20,000	(b)
(EB)	60,000		

Fixed Assets

(BB)	0		
(3)	750,000		
(EB)	750,000		

Accounts Payable

Debit	Credit
	0 (BB)
(5b) 1.075,000	2,000,000 (5a)
	925,000 (EB)

Land

Debit	Credit
(BB) 0	
(11) 40,000	
(EB) 40,000	

Accumulated Depreciation

Debit	Credit
	0 (BB)
	140,000 (a)
	140,000 (EB)

Dividend Payable

Debit	Credit
	0 (BB)
	100,000 (10)
	100,000 (EB)

Misc. Expenses Payable

Debit	Credit
	0 (BB)
	75,000 (d)
	75,000 (EB)

Bonds Payable

Debit	Credit
	0 (BB)
	20,000 (9)
	20,000 (EB)

Premium on Bonds Payable

Debit	Credit
	0 (BB)
(10) 140	9,200 (9)
	9,060 (EB)

Preferred Stock

Debit	Credit
	0 (BB)
	100,000 (2b)
	100,000 (EB)

Common Stock

Debit	Credit
	0 (BB)
	750,000 (2a)
	15,000 (11)
	765,000 (EB)

Retained Earnings

Debit	Credit
	0 (BB)
(C4) 100,000	728,140 (C3)
	628,140 (EB)

APIC: Preferred Stock

Debit	Credit
	0 (BB)
	2,000 (2b)
	2,000 (EB)

APIC: Common Stock

Debit	Credit
	0 (BB)
	750,000 (2a)
	25,000 (11)
	775,000 (EB)

Dividends

Debit	Credit
(BB) 0	
(10) 100,000	
	100,000 (C4)
(EB) 0	

Sales

Debit	Credit
	0 (BB)
	2,050,000 (1a)
	880,000 (4a)
(C1) 2,930,000	
	0 (EB)

Cost of Goods Sold

Debit	Credit
(BB) 0	
(1b) 875,000	
(4b) 490,000	
	1,365,000 (C2)
(EB) 0	

Miscellaneous Expenses

Debit	Credit
(BB) 0	
(6) 500,000	
(d) 75,000	
	575,000 (C2)
(EB) 0	

Interest Expense

Debit	Credit
(BB) 0	
(10) 1,460	
	1,460 (C2)
(EB) 0	

Insurance Expense

Debit	Credit
(BB) 0	
(b) 20,000	
	20,000 (C2)
(EB) 0	

Depreciation Expense

Debit	Credit
(BB) 0	
(a) 140,000	
	140,000 (C2)
(EB) 0	

Bad Debt Expense

Debit	Credit
(BB) 0	
(e) 70,400	
	70,400 (C2)
(EB) 0	

Loss on Inventory Writedown

Debit	Credit
(BB) 0	
(f) 5,000	
	5,000 (C2)
(EB) 0	

Unrealized Loss on S-T Mkt Sec

Debit	Credit
(BB) 0	
(c) 25,000	
	25,000 (C2)
(EB) 0	

Income Summary

Debit	Credit
(BB) 0	
(C2) 2,201,860	2,930,000 (C1)
(C3) 728,140	
(EB) 0	

c.

Adams Photographic Equipment
Income Statement
For the Year Ended December 31, 1993

Sales revenue	$2,930,000	
Cost of goods sold	1,365,000	
Gross profit		$1,565,000
Operating expenses		
Depreciation expense	140,000	
Bad debt expense	70,400	
Insurance expense	20,000	
Miscellaneous expenses	575,000	
Total operating expenses		805,400
Income from operations		759,600
Nonoperating expenses and losses		
Interest expense	1,460	
Loss on writedown of inventory	5,000	
Unrealized loss on short-term marketable securities	25,000	
Total nonoperating expenses and losses		31,460
Net income		$ 728,140

Adams Photographic Equipment
Balance Sheet
As of December 31, 1993

Assets		
Current assets		
Cash	$1,524,600	
Marketable securities (net of allowance for unrealized losses of $25,000)	225,000	
Accounts receivable (net of allowance for doubtful accounts of $70,400)	309,600	
Inventory	630,000	
Prepaid insurance	60,000	
Total current assets		$2,749,200
Land		40,000
Fixed assets	750,000	
Less: accumulated depreciation	140,000	610,000
Total assets		$3,399,200
Liabilities and Stockholders' Equity		
Current Liabilities		
Accounts payable	$925,000	
Miscellaneous expenses payable	75,000	
Dividends payable	100,000	
Total current liabilities		$1,100,000
Bonds payable	20,000	
Premium on bonds payable	9,060	29,060
Stockholders' equity		
Preferred stock	100,000	
Common stock	765,000	
Additional paid-in capital:		
Preferred stock	2,000	
Common stock	775,000	
Retained earnings	628,140	
Total stockholders' equity		2,270,140
Total liabilities and stockholders' equity		$3,399,200

d.

Adams Photographic Equipment
Statement of Cash Flows—Direct Method
For the Year Ended December 31, 1993

Cash flows from operating activities		
Cash collections from sales	2,550,000	
Cash paid for inventory	(1,075,000)	
Cash paid for interest	(1,600)	
Cash paid for insurance	(80,000)	
Cash paid for miscellaneous expenses	(500,000)	
Net cash increase (decrease) due to operating activities		$893,400
Cash flows from investing activities		
Purchase of marketable securities	(250,000)	
Purchase of fixed assets	(750,000)	
Net cash increase (decrease) due to investing activities		(1,000,000)
Cash flows from financing activities		
Proceeds from issue of bonds	29,200	
Proceeds from issue of preferred stock	102,000	
Proceeds for issue of common stock	1,500,000	
Net cash increase (decrease) due to financing activities		1,631,200
Net increase (decrease) in cash		$1,524,600
Beginning cash balance: January 1, 1993		0
Ending cash balance: December 31, 1993		$1,524,600

Adams Photographic Equipment
Statement of Cash Flows—Indirect Method
For the Year Ended December 31, 1993

Cash flows from operating activities			
Net income		$ 728,140	
Adjustments			
Increase in accounts receivable	($380,000)		
Increase in inventory	(630,000)		
Increase in prepaid insurance	(60,000)		
Decrease in premium on bonds	(140)		
Increase in accounts payable	925,000		
Depreciation expense	140,000		
Increase in miscellaneous expenses payable	75,000		
Bad debt expense	70,400		
Unrealized loss on short-term marketable securities	25,000		
Total adjustments		165,260	
Net cash increase (decrease) due to operating activities			$893,400
Cash flows from investing activities			
Purchase of marketable securities		(250,000)	
Purchase of fixed assets		(750,000)	
Net cash increase (decrease) due to investing activities			(1,000,000)
Cash flows from financing activities			
Proceeds from issue of bonds		29,200	
Proceeds from issue of preferred stock		102,000	
Proceeds for issue of common stock		1,500,000	
Net cash increase (decrease) due to financing activities			1,631,200
Net increase (decrease) in cash			$1,524,600
Beginning cash balance: January 1, 1993			0
Ending cash balance: December 31, 1993			$1,524,600

P15–20

a. **Original Entries**

(1)	Cash	198,000	
	Gain on Sale of Marketable Securities		18,000
	Marketable Securities		180,000
	To record sale of marketable securities.		
(2a)	Accounts Receivable	4,243,000	
	Sales		4,243,000
	To record sales on account.		
(2b)	Cost of Goods Sold	2,476,000	
	Inventory		2,476,000
	To record cost of inventory sold.		
(3)	Short-term Notes Payable	100,000	
	Interest Expense	5,000	
	Cash		105,000
	To record interest and principal payment on debt.		
(4)	Cash	150,000	
	Treasury Stock		125,000
	Additional Paid-in Capital: Treasury Stock		25,000
	To record reissue of treasury stock.		
(5a)	Interest Expense	27,000[a]	
	Discount on Bonds Payable		2,000
	Cash		25,000[b]
	To record interest payment on bonds (6/30).		

[a] $27,000 = Book value x Effective rate per period = ($500,000 – $50,000) x 6%
[b] $25,000 = Face value x Stated rate per period = $500,000 x 5%

(5b)	Interest Expense	27,120*	
	Discount on Bonds Payable		2,120
	Cash		25,000
	To record interest payment on bonds (12/31).		

* $27,120 = Book value x Effective rate per period = [$500,000 – ($50,000 – $2,000 from entry (1e) x 6%

(6)	Inventory	3,180,000	
	Cash		80,000
	Accounts Payable		3,100,000
	To record purchase of inventory.		
(7)	Land	500,000	
	Cash		500,000
	To record purchase of land.		
(8)	Cash	75,000	
	Long-Term Investment in Equity Securities		75,000
	To record receipt of dividend from Lewis, Inc.		

		Debit	Credit
(9)	Miscellaneous Expenses	947,000	
	Rent Payable	10,000	
	Cash		957,000
	To record payment of rent and miscellaneous expenses.		
(10)	Cash	4,550,000	
	Accounts Receivable		4,550,000
	To record collection from customers on open accounts.		
(11)	Accounts Payable	2,320,000	
	Cash		2,320,000
	To record payment to suppliers on open accounts.		
(12)	Dividend	200,000	
	Dividend Payable	250,000	
	Cash		450,000
	To record dividend declaration and payment.		
(13)	Cash	100,000	
	Unearned Sales Revenue		100,000
	To record collections in advance from customers.		
(14)	Marketable Securities	355,000	
	Cash		355,000
	To record acquisition of marketable securities.		
(15)	Cash	7,250	
	Accumulated Depreciation: Plant & Equipment	50,000	
	Plant & Equipment		50,000
	Gain on Sale of Fixed Assets		7,250
	To record sale of fixed assets.		
(16)	Allowance for Doubtful Accounts	18,000	
	Accounts Receivable		18,000
	To record writeoff of accounts deemed uncollectible.		

Adjusting Entries

		Debit	Credit
(a)	Allowance for Unrealized Loss on Marketable Securities	5,000	
	Recovery of Unrealized Loss on Marketable Securities		5,000
	To adjust marketable securities to LCM.		

* $5,000 in decrease in allowance balance = $0 – $5,000

(b)	Bad Debt Expense	20,500*	
	Allowance for Doubtful Accounts		20,500
	To record estimated bad debt expense.		

* The amount of the adjusting entry is calculated as follows:

1. Ending accounts receivable = $600,000 beginning balance + $4,243,000 (from entry [2a]) – $4,550,000 (from entry [10]) – $18,000 (from entry [16]) = $275,000
2. Unadjusted allowance balance = $25,000 beginning balance – $18,000 (from entry [16]) = $7,000
3. Adjusted allowance balance = Ending accounts receivable x 15% = $275,000 X 10% = $27,500
4. Bad debt expense = Adjusted allowance balance – Unadjusted allowance balance = $27,500 – $7,000 = $20,500

(c)	Loss on Long-Term Equity Investment	15,000	
	Long-Term Investment in Equity Securities		15,000
	To adjust for net income earned by investee.		
(d)	Depreciation Expense: Building	19,000*	
	Accumulated Depreciation: Building		19,000
	To record depreciation on building.		

* $19,000 = [($125,000 – $24,000 accumulated depreciation) – $6,000 salvage value] ÷ 5 years

(e)	Depreciation Expense: Plant & Equipment	100,000*	
	Accumulated Depreciation: Plant & Equipment		100,000
	To record depreciation on plant and equipment.		

* $100,000 = {[($868,000 – $50,000 of equipment sold) – ($82,000 – $50,000 of depreciation on equipment sold)] – $86,000 salvage value]} ÷ 7 years

(f)	Insurance Expense	12,000	
	Prepaid Insurance		12,000
	To record portion of insurance that expired.		
(g)	Amortization Expense	5,000	
	Patent		5,000
	To record amortization of patent.		
(h)	Rent Expense	20,000	
	Rent Payable		20,000
	To accrue rent expense.		

b. (C1)

		Debit	Credit
	Sales	4,243,000	
	Recovery of Unrealized Loss on Marketable Securities	5,000	
	Gain on Sale of Marketable Securities	18,000	
	Gain on Sale of Plant & Equipment	7,250	
	Income Summary		599,630
	Cost of Goods Sold		2,476,000
	Interest Expense		59,120
	Insurance Expense		12,000
	Depreciation Expense: Building		19,000
	Depreciation Expense: Plant & Equipment		100,000
	Miscellaneous Expenses		967,000
	Amortization Expense		5,000
	Bad Debt Expense		20,500
	Loss on Long-Term Equity Investment		15,000
	To close revenues and expenses into Income Summary.		
(C2)	Retained Earnings	599,630	
	Income Summary		599,630
	To close Income Summary into Retained Earnings.		
(C3)	Retained Earnings	200,000	
	Dividends		250,000
	To close Dividends into retained Earnings.		

c.

Wallace Corporation
Income Statement
For the Year Ended December 31, 1994

Sales		$4,243,000	
COGS		2,476,000	
Gross profit			$1,767,000
Operating expenses			
Miscellaneous expenses		967,000	
Insurance expense		12,000	
Depreciation expense: Building		19,000	
Depreciation expense: Plant & Equipment		100,000	
Amortization (patent) expense		5,000	
Bad debt expense		20,500	
Total operating expenses			1,123,500
Income from operations			643,500
Nonoperating revenues and gains			
Gain on sale of marketable securities	18,000		
Gain on sale of plant & equipment	7,250		
Recovery of unrealized loss on marketable securities	5,000		
Total nonoperating revenues and gains		30,250	
Nonoperating expenses and losses:			
Interest expense	59,120		
Loss on long-term equity investment.	15,000		
Total nonoperating expenses and losses		74,120	
Total nonoperating income (loss)			43,870
Net income			$599,630

d.

Cash

(BB)	57,000		
(1)	198,000	105,000	(3)
(4)	150,000	25,000	(5a)
(8)	75,000	25,000	(5b)
(10)	4,550,000	80,000	(6)
(13)	100,000	500,000	(7)
(15)	7,250	957,000	(9)
		2,320,000	(11)
		450,000	(12)
		355,000	(14)
(EB)	320,250		

e.

Wallace Corporation
Statement of Cash Flows—Direct Method
For the Year Ended December 31, 1994

Cash flows from operating activities		
Cash collections from customers	$4,650,000	
Cash paid for inventory	(2,400,000)	
Cash paid for miscellaneous expenses	(957,000)	
Cash paid for interest expense	(55,000)	
Net cash increase (decrease) due to operating activities		$1,238,000
Cash flows from investing activities		
Proceeds from sale of marketable securities	198,000	
Proceeds from investee dividends	75,000	
Proceeds from sale of fixed assets	7,250	
Purchase of marketable securities	(355,000)	
Purchase of land	(500,000)	
Net cash increase (decrease) due to investing activities		(574,750)
Cash flows from financing activities		
Proceeds from sale of treasury stock	150,000	
Payment of note	(100,000)	
Dividend payment	(450,000)	
Net cash increase (decrease) due to financing activities		(400,000)
Net increase in cash		$ 263,250
Beginning cash balance		57,000
Ending cash balance		$ 320,250

Wallace Corporation
Statement of Cash Flows—Indirect Method
For the Year Ended December 31, 1994

Cash flows from operating activities			
Net income		$ 599,630	
Adjustments			
Depreciation expense: Building	$ 19,000		
Depreciation expense: P & E	100,000		
Amortization expense	5,000		
Loss on equity investment	15,000		
Gain on sale of marketable securities	(18,000)		
Gain on sale of fixed assets	(7,250)		
Recovery on marketable securities	(5,000)		
Decrease in accounts receivable	325,000		
Increase in allowance for doubtful accounts	2,500		
Increase in inventory	(704,000)		
Decrease in prepaid insurance	12,000		
Increase in accounts payable	780,000		
Increase in rent payable	10,000		
Increase in unearned sales revenue	100,000		
Decrease in discount on notes payable	4,120		
Total adjustments		638,370	
Net cash increase (decrease) due to operating activities			$1,238,000
Cash flows from investing activities			
Proceeds from sale of marketable aecurities	198,000		
Proceeds from investee dividends	75,000		
Proceeds from sale of fixed assets	7,250		
Purchase of marketable securities	(355,000)		
Purchase of land	(500,000)		
Net cash increase (decrease) due to investing activities		(574,750)	
Cash flows from financing activities			
Proceeds from sale of treasury stock	150,000		
Payment of note	(100,000)		
Dividend payment	(450,000)		
Net cash increase (decrease) due to financing activities		(400,000)	
Net increase in cash		$263,250	
Beginning cash balance		57,000	
Ending cash balance		$320,250	

f.

Wallace Corporation
Balance Sheet
As of December 31, 1994

Assets			
Current Assets			
Cash		$ 320,250	
Marketable securities		450,000	
Accounts receivable	$275,000		
Less: Allowance for doubtful accounts	27,500	247,500	
Inventory		1,179,000	
Prepaid insurance		3,000	
Total current assets			$2,199,750
Equity investment in Lewis, Inc.			255,000
Property, plant, and equipment			
Land		899,000	
Building	125,000		
Less: Accumulated depreciation	43,000	82,000	
Plant & equipment	818,000		
Less: Accumulated depreciation	132,000	686,000	
Total property, plant, and equipment			1,667,000
Patent			10,000
Total assets			$4,131,750
Liabilities and Stockholders' Equity			
Current liabilities			
Accounts payable		$ 875,000	
Rent payable		20,000	
Unearned sales revenue		150,000	
Total current liabilities			$1,045,000
Bonds payable		500,000	
Less: Discount on bonds payable		45,880	454,120
Stockholders' equity			
Common stock		1,000,000	
Additional paid-in capital:			
Common stock		438,000	
Treasury stock		25,000	
Retained earnings		1,256,630	
Treasury stock		(87,000)	
Total stockholders' equity			2,632,630
Total liabilities and stockholders' equity			$4,131,750

C15–1

Airborne Express is using the indirect method for their statement of cash flows, which begins with net income, adds back expenses that do not use cash, and subtracts revenues that were accrued without cash collections. Depreciation and amortization are not a source of cash, they are adjustments that must be made to net income to reflect the fact that they are noncash expenses. It is not appropriate to consider depreciation and amortization a source of cash from operations.

C15–2

a. Cash borrowed from a bank represents funds derived from an outside source of capital. Accordingly, it would be included in the financing section of the cash flow statement. Cash paid for remodelling and cash paid to build a new restaurant are associated with the purchase of noncurrent assets. These would be included in the investing activities section of the cash flow statement.

b. The receipt of the cash from the sale of stock would appear in the financing section of the cash flow statement, because it reflects of a source of outside capital. The payment of cash for the expansion project (remodeling and the new restaurant) would appear in the investing activities section.

c. Cash payments associated with interest are included in the operating section of the cash flow statement. Dividend payments appear in the financing section. Although both dividends and interest represent compensation to the providers of capital, their payment appears in different sections of the cash flow statement. The FASB chose to include interest in the operating section to preserve the correspondence between the items on the income statement and those comprising the operating section of the statement of cash flows.

C15–3

a. Of the three types of activities, only operating activities have consistently generated cash. Consequently, it appears that Quaker Oats Company financed its expansion through cash provided by operating activities. An alternative source may have been the debt issued in 1986 and 1987.

b. In 1987, the company acquired some other companies, as indicated in the investing activities section. The primary source of these funds was probably the increase in debt in the same year, which is reflected in the financing activities section.

c. By examining the operating activities section, it can be seen that the company has been investing in receivables and inventories during the past three years, as each of these accounts have increased in each year. The total investment in these accounts are: receivables, $320.9 and inventories, $165.3.

d. Cash dividends ÷ Net income = Percent of net income paid in cash dividends.

1988: $79.9 ÷ $255.7 = 31.25%

1987: $63.2 ÷ $243.9 = 25.91%

1986: $57.5 ÷ $179.6 = 32.01%

e. The cash generated from operating activities, along with other cash accumulated over the years was used in 1988 to retire debt.

f. The company's strategy over the past three years has been one of expansion, which has been funded principally from cash provided by operations. Although some debt was issued in 1986 and 1987, a large portion of it was retired in 1988. The company has not issued any new common stock. The principal strategy for expansion has been the acquisition of new companies and the disposition of other businesses, which are reflected in the 1986 investing activities section.

C15–4

a. Cash provided by operating activities

Net income	$ 709	
Depreciation and amortization	491	
Other noncash charges to noncurrent accounts	213	
Increase in accounts receivable	(28)	
Increase in payables and accrue liabilities	216	
In creases in current assets (other items - net)	(91)	
Increase in inventories	(69)	
Decrease in short-term debt	(6)	
Cash provided by operating activities		$1,435

b. **The Procter & Gamble Company**
Statement of Cash Flows
For the Year ended December 31, 1986

Operating activities		
Net income	$ 709	
Depreciation and amortization	491	
Other noncash charges to noncurrent accounts	213	
Increase in accounts receivable	(28)	
Increase in payables and accrued liabilities	216	
Increases in current assets	(91)	
Increase in inventories	(69)	
Decrease in short-term debt	(6)	
Net increase (decrease) due to operating activities		$1,435
Investing Activities		
Captial expenditures	($1,069)	
Acquisitions of other companies	(1,532)	
Net increase (decrease) due to investing activities		($2,601)
Financing activities		
Net increase in long-term debt ($1,562 ≈ $114)	$1,448	
Issuance of preferred stock	250	
Dividends to shareholders	(445)	
Net increase (decrease) due to financing activities		$1,253
Net increase (decrease) in cash	87	
Beginning cash balance	100	
Ending cash balance		$ 187

c. The present format provides an improved format in that it clearly classifies the sources and uses of cash into operating, financing, and investing activities. These are mixed together in the statement of changes in financial position.

d. Procter & Gamble has used cash derived from operating activities, along with cash raised through the issuance of long-term debt and preferred stock to acquire other companies and undertake capital expenditures.

C15–5

a. Capitalizing costs creates the ability to match revenues and expenses because the periodic amortization and depreciation charges against a capitalized amount are matched with the revenues derived from the investment in future periods. For example, depreciating a piece of equipment over its useful life turns the equipment cost into an expense as it creates revenue. Periodic charges of a capitalized amount represent noncash expenses. The cash was paid out when the amount was originally capitalized. Thus, it appears harder to find the cash available in a company.

b. Earning power refers to a company's ability to generate net assets. Over time, the is necessary for the company to be considered a going concern. The earning power of a company is assessed by examining the income statement to determine profitability. Solvency refers to the company's ability to pay its current obligations in cash. This is assessed by examining the balance sheet, especially the cash flow statement. Both earning power and solvency are necessary for a company to operate as a long-term, viable concern.

c. Bankruptcy occurs when a company is unable to pay its present obligations. This generally results from the occurrence of a deficit in cash. Accordingly, a wave of bankruptcies would draw attention to the cash flow of a company.

CHAPTER 16 Consolidated Financial Statements and International Operations

E16–1

Purchase price = Net book value + Net market value in excess of book value + Goodwill

Transaction

(1) Purchase price = \$7,000 + \$1,000 + \$1,000

Purchase price = \$9,000

(2) \$6,000 = \$6,000 + Net market value in excess of book value + \$0

Net market value in excess of book value = \$0

(3) \$12,000 = Net book value + \$4,000 + \$3,000

Net book value = \$5,000

(4) \$15,000 = \$10,000 + \$3,000 + Goodwill

Goodwill = \$2,000

(5) Purchase price = \$2,000 + \$1,000 + \$3,000

Purchase price = \$6,000

(6) \$12,000 = \$4,000 + \$8,000 + Goodwill

Goodwill = \$0

E16–2

a. Book value per share = Net book value ÷ Number of common shares outstanding
\$12 = \$36,000 ÷ Number of common shares outstanding
Number of common shares outstanding = 3,000 shares

b. Market value per share = Net market value ÷ Number of common shares outstanding
= \$48,000 ÷ 3,000 shares
= \$16

c. Conglomerate would be willing to pay more than the market value per share due to goodwill. Mesley has generated goodwill, such as name recognition and employee and customer loyalty, that makes its net assets more valuable taken as a whole than taken as individual net assets. In other words, due to synergy, Mesley is worth more than the sum of its parts. Additionally, combining Mesley's assets with Conglomerate's assets may provide economies of scale, thereby making Mesley's assets more valuable than their fair market value to Conglomerate.

d. Investment in Subsidiary $60,000*
Cash 60,000
To record acquisition of subsidiary.

---

* $60,000 = $20 per share purchase price x 3,000 common shares outstanding

Cash	15,000	
Receivables	26,000	
Inventories	25,000	
Fixed Assets	42,000	
Goodwill	12,000	
Liabilities		60,000
Investment in Subsidiary		60,000
To consolidate financial statements.		

E16–3

Goodwill = Excess of purchase price over FMV of net assets purchased
= Purchase price – FMV of net assets purchased
= [(10,000 shares x 80%) x $18 per share] – [80% x ($140,000 + $75,000
– $70,000)]
= $144,000 – $116,000
= $28,000

Minority interest = FMV of net assets x Percentage of net assets not owned by parent
= ($140,000 + $75,000 – $70,000) x 20%
= $29,000

OR

Minority interest = (FMV of net assets + Goodwill) – Purchase price
= [($140,000 + $75,000 – $70,000) + $28,000] – $144,000
= $29,000

E16–4

Purchase 1

Investment in Subsidiary	7,000	
Cash		7,000
To record acquisition of subsidiary		
Assets	23,000	
Liabilities		16,000
Investment in Subsidiary		7,000
To consolidate financial statements.		

Purchase 2

Investment in Subsidiary	33,000	
Cash		33,000
To record acquisition of subsidiary		
Assets	43,000	
Goodwill	3,000	
Liabilities		13,000
Investment in Subsidiary		33,000
To consolidate financial statements.		

Purchase 3

Investment in Subsidiary	10,000	
Cash		10,000
To record acquisition of subsidiary.		
Assets	21,000	
Goodwill	5,000	
Liabilities		16,000
Investment in Subsidiary		10,000
To consolidate financial statements.		

E16–5

a. Investment in Subsidiary	45,000	
Cash		45,000
To record acquisition of subsidiary.		
b. Current Assets	24,000	
Noncurrent Assets	50,000	
Goodwill	11,000	
Current Liabilities		10,000
Long-Term Liabilities		30,000
Investment in Subsidiary		45,000
To consolidate financial statements.		

E16–6

Purchase 1

Investment in Subsidiary	6,300	
Cash		6,300
To record acquisition of controlling interest of investee.		
Assets	23,000	
Liabilities		16,000
Minority Interest		700*
Investment in Subsidiary		6,300
To consolidate financial statements.		

---

* $700 = FMV of net assets x Percentage of company not owned by parent
= ($23,000 – $16,000) x 10%

Purchase 2

Investment in Subsidiary	24,000	
Cash		24,000
To record acquisition of controlling interest of investee.		

Assets	43,000	
Liabilities		13,000
Minority Interest		6,000*
Investment in Subsidiary		24,000
To consolidate financial statements.		

* $6,000 = FMV of net assets x Percentage of company not owned by parent
= ($43,000 – $13,000) x 20%

Purchase 3

Investment in Subsidiary	3,500	
Cash		3,500
To record acquisition of controlling interest of investee.		

Assets	21,000	
Liabilities		16,000
Minority Interest		1,500*
Investment in Subsidiary		3,500
To consolidate financial statements.		

* $1,500 = FMV of net assets x Percentage of company not owned by parent
= ($21,000 – $16,000) x 30%

E16–7

a.

Investment in Subsidiary	21,000	
Cash		21,000
To record acquisition of controlling interest of investee.		

b.

Current Assets	25,000	
Noncurrent Assets	60,000	
Goodwill	6,000[a]	
Current Liabilities		10,000
Long-Term Liabilities		50,000
Minority Interest		10,000[b]
Investment in Subsidiary		21,000
To consolidate financial statements.		

[a] $6,000 = Purchase price – Portion of FMV of net assets purchased
= $21,000 – [60% x ($25,000 + $60,000 – $10,000 – $50,000)]

[b] $10,000 = FMV of net assets x Percentage of company not owned by parent
= ($25,000 + $60,000 – $10,000 – $50,000) x 40%

E16–8

a. Entry to eliminate intercompany note receivable/payable

Note Payable	100,000	
Note Receivable		100,000
To eliminate intercompany note receivable/payable.		

b. Entry to eliminate intercompany interest receivable/payable

Interest Payable	5,500	
Interest Receivable		5,500
To eliminate intercompany interest receivable/payable.		

c. Entry to eliminate intercompany revenue/expense

Interest Revenue	5,500	
Interest Expense		5,500
To eliminate intercompany revenue/expense.		

E16–9

			Adjustments and Eliminations		
Accounts	**Harrison**	**Watson**	**Debit**	**Credit**	**Consolidated Balance Sheet**
Cash	73,000	10,000			83,000
Accounts Receivable	110,000	40,000			150,000
Inventory	220,000	60,000	10,000*		290,000
Investment in Subsidiary	100,000	0		100,000*	0
Fixed Assets	615,000	120,000	5,000		740,000
Goodwill	30,000	0	5,000*		35,000
Total assets	1,148,000	230,000	20,000	110,000	1,298,000
Accounts Payable	80,000	70,000			150,000
Long-Term Notes	450,000	80,000			530,000
Common Stock	500,000	70,000	70,000*		500,000
Retained Earnings	118,000	10,000	10,000*		118,000
Total liabilities & stockholders' equity	1,148,000	230,000	80,000	0	1,298,000

* Entry to adjust assets to market value, to eliminate the investment account, to eliminate the stockholders' equity section of Watson, and to recognize goodwill.

E16–10

a. The following entry would be prepared on the date of acquisition.

Investment in Subsidiary	27,000*	
Common Stock		27,000
To record acquisition of subsidiary.		

* $27,000 = Book value of net assets acquired = $10,000 + $22,000 – $5,000

After the entry above, the Investment in Subsidiary account would increase from $0 to $27,000, while Common Stock would increase from $40,000 to $67,000.

The following entry would be prepared at year end as part of the consolidation process.

	Debit	Credit
Current Assets	10,000	
Fixed Assets	22,000	
Long-Term Liabilities		5,000
Investment in Subsidiary		27,000
To consolidate financial statements.		

b.

Account	Acquisition	Sub	Adjustments and Eliminations Debit	Adjustments and Eliminations Credit	Consolidated Balance Sheet
Current Assets	$ 80,000	$10,000			$ 90,000
Investment in Sub	27,000	0		27,000*	0
Fixed Assets	60,000	22,000			82,000
Total assets	$167,000	$32,000	$ 0	$27,000	$172,000
Long-Term Liabilities	$40,000	$5,000			$45,000
Common Stock	67,000	20,000	20,000*		67,000
APIC: Common Stock	10,000	0	7,000*		3,000
Retained Earnings	50,000	7,000			57,000
Total liabilities & stockholders' equity	$167,000	$32,000	$27,000	$ 0	$172,000

* Entry to eliminate investment in subsidiary account against stockholders' equity.

E16–11

Date	Account	Debit	Credit
1/1/88	Cash	200,000*	
	Notes payable		200,000
	To record borrowing of British pounds.		

* $200,000 = 100,000 British pounds x $2.00/pound

Date	Account	Debit	Credit
12/31/88	Exchange Loss	10,000*	
	Note Payable		10,000
	To record exchange loss on debt expressed in British pounds.		

* $10,000 = Adjusted value of borrowing – Carrying value of borrowing
= (100,000 British pounds x $2.10/pound) – $200,000

Date	Account	Debit	Credit
12/31/89	Note Payable	20,000*	
	Exchange Gain		20,000
	To record exchange gain on debt expressed in British pounds.		

* $20,000 = Adjusted value of borrowing – Carrying value of borrowing
= (100,000 British pounds x $1.90/pound) – $210,000

E16–12

1/1/88	Notes Receivable	4,000*	
	Sales		4,000
	To record sale for a note expressed in Canadian dollars.		

---

* $4,000 = Sales in Canadian dollars x Exchange rate
= 5,000 Canadian dollars x $0.80/Canadian dollar

12/31/88	Notes Receivable	250*	
	Exchange Gain		250
	To record exchange gain on receivable expressed in Canadian dollars.		

---

* $250 = Adjusted value of receivable – Carrying value of receivable
= (5,000 Canadian dollars x $0.85/Canadian dollar) – $4,000

12/31/89	Exchange Loss	500*	
	Notes Receivable		500
	To record exchange gain on receivable expressed in Canadian dollars.		

---

* $500 = Adjusted value of receivable – Carrying value of receivable
= (5,000 Canadian dollars x $0.75/Canadian dollar) – $4,250

E16–13

January 1, 1988

Notes Receivable	4,000*	
Sales		4,000
To record sale for a note expressed in Canadian dollars.		
Cash	4,000*	
Notes Payable		4,000
To record debt expressed in Canadian dollars.		

---

* $4,000 = Sales in Canadian dollars x Exchange rate
= 5,000 Canadian dollars x $0.80/Canadian dollar

December 31, 1988

Notes Receivable	250*	
Exchange Gain		250
To record exchange gain on receivable expressed in Canadian dollars.		
Exchange Loss	250*	
Note Payable		250
To record exchange loss on debt expressed in Canadian dollars		

---

* $250 = Adjusted value of receivable – carrying value of receivable
= (5,000 Canadian dollars x $0.85/Canadian dollar) – $4,000

December 31, 1989

Exchange Loss	500*	
Notes Receivable		500
To record exchange loss on receivable expressed in Canadian dollars.		
Notes Payable	500*	
Exchange Gain		500
To record exchange gain on debt expressed in Canadian dollars.		

---

* $500 = Adjusted value of receivable – Carrying value of receivable
= (5,000 Canadian dollars x $0.75/Canadian dollar) – $4,250

Exchange gains and losses on debt and receivables for the same amount and expressed in the same foreign currency always offset each other. When the exchange rate increases, both the receivable and the payable increase by the same amount. The increase in the receivable gives rise to a gain (i.e., the company will receive more U.S. dollars), while the increase in the liability gives rise to a loss (i.e., the company must pay out more U.S. dollars). When the exchange rate decreases, both the receivable and the payable decrease by the same amount. The decrease in the receivable gives rise to a loss while the decrease in the liability gives rise to a gain. Therefore, through hedging Outreach is able to avoid wide fluctuations in its net income from fluctuations in exchange rates.

E16–14

a. Carrying value of receivable = Receivable in British pounds x Exchange rate
= 40,000 British pounds x (1.60 dollar/1 British pound) = $64,000

b. The current ratio is calculated as current assets divided by current liabilities. If International Services is to maintain a current ratio of at least 1.5, its current assets after considering the effect of exchange-rate fluctuations must be 1.5 times its current liabilities. The company's current assets not affected by exchange-rate fluctuations are $16,000 (i.e., $80,000 – $64,000 from Part [a]). Therefore, the minimum acceptable exchange rate would be calculated as follows:

(Current assets not affected by exchange rates + Current assets affected by exchange rates) ÷ Current liabilities = 1.5
= ($16,000 + Current assets not affected by exchange rates) ÷ $50,000 = 1.5
= [$16,000 + (Receivable in British pounds x Exchange rate)] ÷ $50,000 = 1.5
= [$16,000 + (40,000 pounds x Exchange rate)] ÷ $50,000 = 1.5

Exchange rate = 1.475

c. For International Services to maintain a current ratio of at least 1.5, its current assets after considering the effect of exchange-rate fluctuations must be 1.5 times its current liabilities adjusted for the effects of exchange-rate fluctuations. The company's current liabilities not affected by exchange-rate fluctuations are $48,400 (i.e., $50,000 – $1,600 payable to British bank). Therefore, the minimum acceptable exchange rate would now be calculated as follows:

(Current assets not affected by exchange rates + Current assets affected by exchange rates) ÷ (Current liabilities not affected by exchange rates + Current assets affected by exchange rates) = 1.5

= ($16,000 + Current assets not affected by exchange rates)
÷ ($48,400 + Current assets affected by exchange rates) = 1.5
= [$16,000 + (Receivable in British pounds x Exchange rate)]
÷ {$48,400 + (Payable in British pounds x Exchange rate)] = 1.5
= [$16,000 + (40,000 pounds x Exchange rate)]
÷ {$48,400 + (1,000 pounds x Exchange rate)] = 1.5

Exchange rate = 1.47

d. Increases in the exchange rate cause exchange gains when holding receivables and exchange losses when holding payables. Decreases in the exchange rate cause exchange losses when holding receivables and exchange gains when holding payables. Therefore, changes in the exchange rate have opposite effects on receivables and payables. By holding a payable in the same amount as a receivable, exchange gains will perfectly offset exchange losses. In this way, a company can hedge against exchange rate-fluctuations. A company never enjoys an exchange gain, but also never incurs an exchange loss.

P16–1

a.

Investment in Subsidiary	180,000	
Cash		120,000
Bonds Payable		60,000
To record investment in subsidiary.		

After posting this entry, Burns' Cash account would decrease from $156,000 to $36,000, the Investment in Subsidiary account would increase from $0 to $180,000, and its Long-term Liabilities would increase from $300,000 to $360,000.

Cash	10,000	
Accounts Receivable	40,000	
Inventory	70,000	
Fixed Assets	120,000	
Goodwill	10,000*	
Accounts Payable		20,000
Long-Term Liabilities		50,000
Investment in Subsidiary		180,000
To consolidate financial statements.		

* $10,000 = Purchase price – FMV of net assets
= $180,000 – ($10,000 + $40,000 + $70,000 + $120,000 – $20,000 – $50,000)

b.

Accounts	Burns	Jordan	Adjustments and Eliminations Debit	Adjustments and Eliminations Credit	Consolidated Balance Sheet
Cash	36,000	10,000			46,000
Accounts Receivable	150,000	40,000			190,000
Inventory	300,000	40,000	30,000*		370,000
Investment in Subsidiary	180,000	0		180,000*	0
Fixed Assets	400,000	130,000		10,000*	520,000
Goodwill	0	0	10,000*		10,000
Total assets	1,066,000	220,000	40,000	190,000	1,136,000
Accounts Payable	80,000	20,000			100,000
Long-Term Liabilities	360,000	50,000			410,000
Common Stock	400,000	90,000	90,000*		400,000
APIC: Common Stock	100,000	10,000	10,000*		100,000
Retained Earnings	126,000	50,000	50,000*		126,000
Total liabilities & stockholders' equity	1,066,000	220,000	150,000	0	1,136,000

* Entry to adjust assets to market value, to eliminate the Investment account, to eliminate the stockholders' equity section of Watson, and to recognize goodwill.

P16–2

a. Investment in Subsidiary 136,000
Cash 136,000
To record investment in subsidiary.

After posting this entry, Burns' Cash account would decrease from $156,000 to $20,000, and the Investment in Subsidiary account would increase from $0 to $136,000.

	Debit	Credit
Cash	10,000	
Accounts Receivable	40,000	
Inventory	70,000	
Fixed Assets	120,000	
Accounts Payable		20,000
Long-Term Liabilities		50,000
Minority Interest		34,000*
Investment in Subsidiary		136,000
To consolidate financial statements.		

* $34,000 = FMV of net assets x Percentage of net assets not owned by parent
= ($10,000 + $40,000 + $70,000 + $120,000 – $20,000 – $50,000) x 20%

b.

Accounts	Burns	Jordan	Adjustments and Eliminations Debit	Adjustments and Eliminations Credit	Consolidated Balance Sheet
Cash	20,000	10,000			30,000
Accounts Receivable	150,000	40,000			190,000
Inventory	300,000	40,000	30,000*		370,000
Investment in Subsidiary	136,000	0		136,000*	0
Fixed Assets	400,000	130,000		10,000*	520,000
Total assets	1,006,000	220,000	30,000	146,000	1,110,000
Accounts Payable	80,000	20,000			100,000
Long-Term Liabilities	300,000	50,000			350,000
Minority Interest	0	0		34,000*	34,000
Common Stock	400,000	90,000	90,000*		400,000
APIC: Common Stock	100,000	10,000	10,000*		100,000
Retained Earnings	126,000	50,000	50,000*		126,000
Total liabilities & stockholders' equity	1,006,000	220,000	150,000	34,000	1,110,000

* Entry to adjust assets to market value, to eliminate the investment account, to eliminate the stockholders' equity section of Watson, and to recognize minority interest.

P16–3

a.

	Debit	Credit
Investment in Subsidiary	140,000	
Cash		140,000
To record investment in subsidiary.		

After posting this entry, Burns' Cash account would decrease from $156,000 to $16,000, and the Investment in Subsidiary Account would increase from $0 to $140,000.

	Debit	Credit
Cash	10,000	
Accounts Receivable	40,000	
Inventory	70,000	
Fixed Assets	120,000	
Goodwill	4,000[a]	
Accounts Payable		20,000
Long-Term Liabilities		50,000
Minority Interest		34,000[b]
Investment in Subsidiary		140,000
To consolidate financial statements.		

[a] $4,000 = Purchase price – FMV of net assets purchased
= $140,000 – [80% x ($10,000 + $40,000 + $70,000 + $120,000 – $20,000 – $50,000)]

[b] $34,000 = FMV of net assets x Percentage of net assets not owned by parent
= ($10,000 + $40,000 + $70,000 + $120,000 – $20,000 – $50,000) x 20%

b.

Accounts	Burns	Jordan	Adjustments and Eliminations Debit	Adjustments and Eliminations Credit	Consolidated Balance Sheet
Cash	16,000	10,000			26,000
Accounts Receivable	150,000	40,000			190,000
Inventory	300,000	40,000	30,000*		370,000
Investment in Subsidiary	140,000	0		140,000*	0
Fixed Assets	400,000	130,000		10,000*	520,000
Goodwill	0	0	4,000		4,000
Total assets	1,006,000	220,000	70,000	150,000	1,110,000
Accounts payable	80,000	20,000			100,000
Long-Term Liabilities	300,000	50,000			350,000
Minority Interest	0	0		34,000*	34,000
Common Stock	400,000	90,000	90,000*		400,000
APIC: Common Stock	100,000	10,000	10,000*		100,000
Retained Earnings	126,000	50,000	50,000		126,000
Total liabilities & stockholders' equity	1,006,000	220,000	150,000	0	1,110,000

* Entry to adjust assets to market value, to eliminate the investment account, to eliminate the stockholders' equity section of Watson, to recognize goodwill, and to recognize minority interest.

P16–4

a. Investment in Subsidiary 150,000*
Common Stock 150,000
To record investment in subsidiary.

* $150,000 = Book value of Jordan's net assets = Book value of total assets – Book value of total liabilities = $220,000 – $70,000

After posting this entry, the Investment in Subsidiary account would increase from $0 to $150,000, and Burns' Common Stock account would increase from $400,000 to $550,000.

	Debit	Credit
Cash	10,000	
Accounts Receivable	40,000	
Inventory	40,000	
Fixed Assets	130,000	
Accounts Payable		20,000
Long-Term Liabilities		50,000
Investment in Subsidiary		150,000
To consolidate financial statements.		

b.

Accounts	Burns	Jordan	Adjustments and Eliminations Debit	Adjustments and Eliminations Credit	Consolidated Balance Sheet
Cash	156,000	10,000			166,000
Accounts Receivable	150,000	40,000			190,000
Inventory	300,000	40,000			340,000
Investment in Subsidiary	150,000	0		150,000*	0
Fixed Assets	400,000	130,000			530,000
Total assets	1,156,000	220,000	0	150,000	1,226,000
Accounts Payable	80,000	20,000			100,000
Long-Term Liabilities	300,000	50,000			350,000
Common Stock	550,000	90,000	90,000*		550,000
APIC: Common Stock	100,000	10,000	60,000*		50,000
Retained Earnings	126,000	50,000			176,000
Total liabilities & stockholders' equity	1,156,000	220,000	150,000	0	1,226,000

* Entry to eliminate the Investment account by offsetting it against stockholders' equity.

P16–5

a. Cash 180,000
    Common Stock 180,000
  To record issue of common stock.

Investment in Subsidiary 180,000
    Cash 180,000
  To record investment in subsidiary.

After posting these two entries, Burns' Cash account would be unchanged, the Investment in Subsidiary account would increase from $0 to $180,000, and the Common Stock account would increase from $400,000 to $580,000.

	Debit	Credit
Cash	10,000	
Accounts Receivable	40,000	
Inventory	70,000	
Fixed Assets	120,000	
Goodwill	10,000*	
Accounts Payable		20,000
Long-Term Liabilities		50,000
Investment in Subsidiary		180,000

To consolidate financial statements.

* $10,000 = Purchase price – FMV of net assets purchased
= $180,000 – ($10,000 + $40,000 + $70,000 + $120,000 – $20,000 – $50,000)

b.

Accounts	Burns	Jordan	Adjustments and Eliminations Debit	Adjustments and Eliminations Credit	Consolidated Balance Sheet
Cash	156,000	10,000			166,000
Accounts Receivable	150,000	40,000			190,000
Inventory	300,000	40,000	30,000*		370,000
Investment in Subsidiary	180,000	0		180,000*	0
Fixed Assets	400,000	130,000		10,000*	520,000
Goodwill	0	0	10,000*		10,000
Total assets	1,186,000	220,000	40,000	190,000	1,256,000
Accounts payable	80,000	20,000			100,000
Long-Term Liabilities	300,000	50,000			350,000
Common Stock	580,000	90,000	90,000*		580,000
APIC: Common Stock	100,000	10,000	10,000*		100,000
Retained Earnings	126,000	50,000	50,000*		126,000
Total liabilities & stockholders' equity	1,186,000	220,000	150,000	0	1,256,000

* Adjustment of assets to market value, to eliminate the Investment account, to eliminate the stockholders' equity section of Watson, and to recognize goodwill.

c. Under a pooling-of-interests, two companies merge their resources. A pooling-of-interests usually arises when the parent company swaps some of its stock for the outstanding shares of the subsidiary. The stockholders of the subsidiary no longer own shares in the subsidiary. Instead, they possess ownership rights in the parent company which now controls the subsidiary. Therefore, all the stockholders now have an interest in the assets and liabilities of both companies.

Under a purchase, the parent purchases the outstanding common shares of the subsidiary. The stockholders of the subsidiary are "bought out" and no longer have an ownership interest in either the parent or the subsidiary.

In this particular case, the parent company issued additional shares of common stock. These shares were not issued to the stockholders of the subsidiary company in exchange for the common shares of the subsidiary company. Rather the parent company issued stock to various investors and used the proceeds from the stock issue to buy out the stockholders of the subsidiary company. Therefore, the stockholders of the subsidiary company no longer have any ownership interest in either the parent or the subsidiary. Thus, Burns' acquisition of Jordan should be accounted for using the purchase method.

P16–6

Company A

Investment in Subsidiary	84,800	
Cash		84,800
To record purchase of controlling interest in subsidiary.		

Cash	6,000	
Accounts Receivable	12,000	
Inventory	45,000	
Fixed Assets	75,000	
Current Liabilities		7,000
Long-Term Liabilities		25,000
Minority Interest		21,200*
Investment in Subsidiary		84,800
To consolidate financial statements.		

---

* $21,200 = Net assets x Percentage of company not owned by parent
= [($6,000 + $12,000 + $45,000 + $75,000) – $32,000] x 20%

Company B

Investment in Subsidiary	24,000	
Cash		24,000
To record purchase of controlling interest in subsidiary.		

Cash	4,000	
Accounts Receivable	9,000	
Inventory	18,000	
Fixed Assets	35,000	
Goodwill	3,600[a]	
Current Liabilities		12,000
Long-Term Liabilities		20,000
Minority Interest		13,600[b]
Investment in Subsidiary		24,000
To consolidate financial statements.		

---

[a] $3,600 = Purchase price – FMV of net assets purchased
= $24,000 – [60% x (FMV of total assets – FMV of total liabilities)]
= $24,000 – {60% x [($4,000 + $9,000 + $18,000 + $35,000) – $32,000]

[b] $13,600 = Net assets x Percentage of company not owned by parent
= (FMV of total assets – FMV of total liabilities) x 40%
= [($4,000 + $9,000 + $18,000 + $35,000) – $32,000] x 40%

Company C

Investment in Subsidiary	16,500	
Cash		16,500
To record purchase of controlling interest in subsidiary.		
Cash	2,000	
Accounts Receivable	7,000	
Inventory	18,000	
Fixed Assets	15,000	
Goodwill	2,250[a]	
Current Liabilities		5,000
Long-Term Liabilities		18,000
Minority Interest		4,750[b]
Investment in Subsidiary		16,500
To consolidate financial statements.		

---

[a] $2,250 = Purchase price – FMV of net assets purchased
= $16,500 – [75% x (FMV of total assets – FMV of total liabilities)]
= $16,500 – {75% x [($2,000 + $7,000 + $18,000 + $15,000) – $23,000]

[b] $4,750 = Net assets x Percentage of company not owned by parent
= (FMV of total assets – FMV of total liabilities) x 25%
= [($2,000 + $7,000 + $18,000 + $15,000) – $23,000] x 25%

P16–7

a.

	Amount of Transaction In Foreign Currency	Exchange Rate	Amount of Transaction In U.S. Dollars
(1)	240,000 pounds	1 dollar/.75 pound	$320,000
(2)	300,000 yen	1 dollar/100 yen	3,000
(3)	50,000,000 Lira	1 dollar/1,000 Lira	50,000
(4)	150,000 Canadian dollars	1 dollar/1.50 Canadian dollar	100,000

b.

(1)	Account Receivable	320,000	
	Sales		320,000
	To record sale on account expressed in British pounds.		
(2)	Notes Receivable	3,000	
	Sales		3,000
	To record sale for a note expressed in yen.		
(3)	Inventory	50,000	
	Notes payable		50,000
	To record purchase of inventory for a note expressed in Lira.		
(4)	Inventory	100,000	
	Accounts Payable		100,000
	To record purchase of inventory on account expressed in Canadian dollars.		

c.

12/31/90 Calculations		Adjusted Value	Carrying Value	Exchange Gain/Loss
(1) 240,000 pounds x (1 dollar/1.20 pound)	=	$200,000	$320,000	($120,000)
(2) 300,000 yen x (1 dollar/75 yen)	=	4,000	3,000	1,000
(3) 50,000,000 Lira x (1 dollar/1,600 Lira)	=	31,250	50,000	18,750
(4) 150,000 Canadian x (1 dollar/1.20 Canadian)	=	125,000	100,000	(25,000)

		Debit	Credit
(1)	Exchange Loss	120,000	
	Accounts Receivable		120,000
	To record exchange loss on receivable expressed in British pounds.		
(2)	Notes Receivable	1,000	
	Exchange Gain		1,000
	To record exchange gain on receivable expressed in yen.		
(3)	Notes Payable	18,750	
	Exchange Gain		18,750
	To record exchange gain on debt expressed in Lira.		
(4)	Exchange Loss	25,000	
	Accounts Payable		25,000
	To record exchange loss on debt expressed in Canadian dollars.		

d. Receivables and payables are stated in a particular currency; for example, in British pounds. Assume that money from the receivable/payable is to be converted into U.S. dollars. At a given point in time, one British pound can be converted into a certain number of dollars. These dollars can, in turn, be used to purchase items. At a different point in time, one British pound can be converted into a different number of dollars. Holding everything else constant, these dollars can now be used to purchase either more or less goods than before. This change in purchasing power affects a company's wealth. Changes in wealth are captured by gains and losses. Since these gains or losses arise due to fluctuations in exchange rates, they are aptly called exchange gains or exchange losses.

P16–8

		Debit	Credit
a.	Notes Receivable	80,000*	
	Sales		80,000
	To record sale in exchange for a note expressed in yen.		
	Cash	80,000*	
	Bonds Payable		80,000
	To record bond issue.		

* $80,000 = Amount in yen x Exchange rate = 10,000,000 yen x .008 dollars/yen

		Debit	Credit
b.	Exchange Loss	20,000*	
	Notes Receivable		20,000
	To record exchange loss on receivable expressed in yen.		
	Bonds Payable	20,000*	
	Exchange Gain		20,000
	To record exchange gain on debt expressed in yen.		

* $20,000 = Adjusted value of receivable/payable – Carrying value
= (10,000,000 yen x .006 dollars/yen) – $80,000

		Debit	Credit
c.	Notes Receivable	10,000*	
	Exchange Gain		10,000
	To record exchange gain on receivable expressed in yen.		
	Exchange Loss	10,000*	
	Bonds Payable		10,000
	To record exchange loss on debt expressed in yen.		

* $10,000 = Adjusted value of receivable/payable – Carrying value
= (1,000,000 yen x .007) – $60,000

P16–9

a. If Mammoth Enterprises accounts for the this investment using the purchase method, Mammoth would make the following entries.

		Debit	Credit
(1)	Investment in Subsidiary	60,000	
	Cash		60,000
	To record purchase of subsidiary.		
(2)	Assets	180,000	
	Goodwill	15,000[a]	
	Liabilities		90,000[b]
	Minority Interest		45,000[c]
	Investment in Subsidiary		60,000
	To record consolidation under the purchase method.		

[a] $15,000 = Purchase price – FMV of assets purchased
= $60,000 – [50% x ($180,000 – $90,000)]

[b] FMV of liabilities:
Book value of assets = FMV of assets – $20,000 = $180,000 – $20,000 = $160,000
FMV of liabilities = Book value of assets – Book value of net assets
= $160,000 – $70,000 = $90,000

[c] $45,000 = FMV of net assets x Percentage of company not owned by parent
= ($180,000 – $90,000) x 50%

The net effect of these two entries on Mammoth's books would be to
Increase assets by $135,000 (including the goodwill);
Increase liabilities by $135,000 (including the minority interest); and
Not affect stockholders' equity.

Debt/equity ratio = Total liabilities ÷ Total stockholders' equity

Prior to acquisition of Atom, Inc.
Debt/equity ratio = ($30,000 + $200,000) ÷ ($100,000 + $170,000)
= .85

Subsequent to acquisition of Atom, Inc.
Debt/equity ratio = ($30,000 + $200,000 + $135,000) ÷ ($100,000 + $170,000)
= 1.35

b. If Mammoth accounted for this investment using the equity method, it would make the following entry.

Long-Term Investment in Equity Securities	60,000	
Cash		60,000
To record investment in Atom, Inc.		

This entry does not affect any liability accounts or stockholders' equity accounts, so Mammoth's debt/equity ratio would be the same both before and after the investment. As shown in Part (a), Mammoth's debt/equity ratio would increase if it accounted for the investment using the purchase method. Buy using the equity method, Mammoth presents a more favorable debt/equity ratio. Therefore, using the equity method allows Mammoth to avoid moving closer to violating its debt covenant. Such a move gives the company more accounting flexibility and decreases the probability that it will eventually violate its debt covenant. For these reasons, Mammoth would probably prefer accounting for the investment in Atom, Inc. using the equity method rather than the purchase method.

P16–10

a. If Lampley uses the pooling-of-interest method to account for this investment, it would make the following entries.

Investment in Subsidiary	54,000*	
Common Stock		54,000
To record investment in subsidiary.		

* $55,000 = Net book value of Greystoke = ($20,000 + $44,000 – $10,000)

After this entry, the Investment in Subsidiary account would increase from $0 to $54,000, and Lampley's Common Stock account would increase from $80,000 to $134,000

Accounts	Lampley	Greystoke	Adjustments and Eliminations Debit	Adjustments and Eliminations Credit	Consolidated Balance Sheet
Current Assets	160,000	20,000			180,000
Investment in Subsidiary	54,000	0		54,000*	0
Fixed Assets	120,000	44,000		0	164,000
Total assets	334,000	64,000	0	54,000	344,000
Current Liabilities	80,000	10,000			90,000
Common Stock	134,000	40,000	40,000*		134,000
APIC: Common Stock	20,000	0	14,000*		6,000
Retained Earnings	100,000	14,000	0		114,000
Total liabilities & stockholders' equity	334,000	64,000	54,000	0	344,000

* Elimination of the investment against the stockholders' equity.

b. If Lampley uses the purchase method to account for this investment, it would make the following entries.

Cash	80,000	
Common Stock		80,000
To record issue of common stock.		
Investment in Subsidiary	80,000	
Cash		80,000
To record investment in subsidiary.		

After posting these entries, Cash would be unchanged, the Investment in Subsidiary account would increase from $0 to $80,000 and Lampley's Common Stock account would increase from $80,000 to $160,000.

Accounts	Lampley	Greystoke	Adjustments and Eliminations Debit	Adjustments and Eliminations Credit	Consolidated Balance Sheet
Current Assets	160,000	20,000	10,000*		190,000
Investment in Subsidiary	80,000	0		80,000*	0
Fixed Assets	120,000	44,000	6,000*	0	170,000
Goodwill	0	0	10,000*	0	10,000
Total assets	360,000	64,000	16,000	80,000	370,000
Current Liabilities	80,000	10,000			90,000
Common Stock	160,000	40,000	40,000*		160,000
APIC: Common Stock	20,000	0			20,000
Retained Earnings	100,000	14,000	14,000*		100,000
Total liabilities & stockholders' equity	360,000	64,000	54,000	0	370,000

* To adjust assets to fair market value, to recognize goodwill, to eliminate investment in subsidiary, and to eliminate subsidiary's stockholders' equity.

c. Current ratio = Current assets ÷ Current liabilities

Pooling-of-interests: $180,000 ÷ $90,000 = 2.00
Purchase: $190,000 ÷ $90,000 = 2.11

Debt/equity ratio = Total liabilities ÷ Total stockholders' equity

Pooling-of-interests: $90,000 ÷ $254,000 = .354
Purchase: $90,000 ÷ $280,000 = .321

Based on these two ratios, the purchase method makes Lampley appear to be more financially sound than the pooling-of-interests method. Under the purchase method, assets are reported at their fair market value. Since the current assets' fair market value exceeds their cost, the company's current ratio is higher under the purchase method. Further, under the purchase method, any stock issued as part of the investment (or as in this case, simply to raise money) is recorded at the market value of the shares issued. Under the pooling-of-interests method, any stock issued as part of the investment is only recorded at the book value of the net assets acquired. The difference in the value of the stock issued can give rise to economic consequences which, in turn, can cause a company to prefer one accounting treatment over another. An example of a potential economic consequence is a debt covenant that specifies a maximum debt/equity ratio; violating the debt covenant could require Lampley to either repay the debt immediately or enter into a costly renegotiation. By selecting the purchase method, Lampley can decrease the probability that it will violate the debt covenant.

Alternatively, the purchase method can adversely affect future income. Under the purchase method, goodwill is created. The goodwill will be amortized over future periods, thereby decreasing net income. Further, the fixed assets are recorded at their fair market value which, in this case, exceeds their cost. Therefore, future depreciation expense will be higher. Since goodwill is not created under the pooling approach, and assets are not adjusted to their fair market value, the pooling method will not affect future income.

P16–11

a.

	Debit	Credit
Investment in Subsidiary	100,000	
Common Stock		100,000
To record purchase of subsidiary.		

b. Due to the entry in Part (a), the Investment in Subsidiary account would increase from $0 to $100,000, and Lake Forest's Common Stock account would increase from $200,000 to $300,000.

Accounts	Lake Forest	Smallville	Adjustments and Eliminations Debit	Adjustments and Eliminations Credit	Consolidated Balance Sheet
Cash	170,000	10,000			180,000
Accounts Receivable	23,000	15,000			38,000
Interest Receivable	3,000	0		1,000[c]	2,000
Notes Receivable	12,000	0		12,000[b]	0
Inventory	100,000	30,000			130,000
Investment in Subsidiary	100,000	0		100,000[a]	0
Fixed Assets	300,000	80,000			380,000
Total assets	708,000	135,000	0	113,000	730,000
Short-Term Payables	6,000	13,000	$12,000[b]		7,000
Interest Payable	2,000	2,000	1,000[c]		3,000
Long-Term Notes	100,000	20,000			120,000
Common Stock	300,000	75,000	75,000[a]		300,000
Retained Earnings	300,000	25,000	25,000[a]		300,000
Total liabilities & stockholders' equity	708,000	135,000	113,000	0	730,000

Accounts	Lake Forest	Smallville	Adjustments and Eliminations Debit	Adjustments and Eliminations Credit	Consolidated Income Sheet
Sales	250,000	80,000	$20,000[d]		310,000
Interest Income	2,000	0	1,000[e]		1,000
Cost of Goods Sold	(140,000)	(40,000)			(180,000)
S & A Expenses	(50,000)	(10,000)		20,000[d]	(40,000)
Interest Expense	(10,000)	(2,000)		1,000[e]	(11,000)
Income Taxes	(15,000)	(7,000)			(22,000)
Net income	37,000	21,000	21,000	21,000	58,000

[a] Entry to offset the investment account against subsidiary's stockholders' equity.
[b] Entry to eliminate intercompany note receivable/payable.
[c] Entry to eliminate intercompany interest receivable/payable.
[d] Entry to eliminate intercompany revenues/expenses.
[e] Entry to eliminate intercompany interest income/expense.

c. Current ratio = Current assets ÷ Current liabilities
= ($180,000 + $38,000 + $2,000 + $130,000) ÷ ($7,000 + $3,000) = 35.00

Debt/equity ratio = Total liabilities ÷ Total stockholders' equity
= ($7,000 + $3,000 + $120,000) ÷ ($300,000 + $300,000) = .217

Earnings per share = Net income ÷ Common shares outstanding
= $58,000 ÷ (25,000 shares + 15,000 shares) = $1.45

P16–12

a. Cash 150,000
Common Stock 150,000
To record issue of common stock.

Investment in Subsidiary 150,000
Cash 150,000
To record acquisition of Smallville.

b. Due to the entry in Part (a), Lake Forest's Cash balance would be unchanged, its Investment in Subsidiary account would increase from $0 to $150,000, and its Common Stock account would increase from $200,000 to $350,000. The purchase of Smallville does not affect Smallville's books, since Lake Forest purchased the common shares from the stockholders of Smallville, not from Smallville.

Goodwill = Purchase price – FMV of net assets purchased.
= $150,000 – ($10,000 + $15,000 + $45,000 + $85,000 – $13,000 – $2,000 – $20,000)]
= $30,000

Minority Interest = FMV of net assets x Percentage of company not owned by parent
= ($10,000 + $15,000 + $45,000 + $85,000 – $13,000 – $2,000 – $20,000) x 0%
= $0

			Adjustments and Eliminations		
Accounts	**Lake Forest**	**Smallville**	**Debit**	**Credit**	**Consolidated Balance Sheet**
Cash	170,000	10,000			180,000
Accounts Receivable	23,000	15,000			38,000
Interest Receivable	3,000	0		1,000[c]	2,000
Notes Receivable	12,000	0		12,000[b]	0
Inventory	100,000	30,000	15,000[a]		145,000
Investment in Subsidiary	150,000	0		150,000[a]	0
Fixed Assets	300,000	80,000	5,000[a]		385,000
Goodwill	0	0	30,000[a]		30,000
Total assets	758,000	135,000	50,000	163,000	780,000
Short-Term Payables	6,000	13,000	$12,000[b]		7,000
Interest Payable	2,000	2,000	1,000[c]		3,000
Long-Term Notes	100,000	20,000			120,000
Common Stock	350,000	75,000	75,000[a]		350,000
Retained Earnings	300,000	25,000	25,000[a]		300,000
Total liabilities & stockholders' equity	758,000	135,000	113,000	0	780,000

[a] Entry to adjust assets to market value, to eliminate the Investment account, to recognize goodwill, and to eliminate subsidiary's stockholders' equity section.
[b] Entry to eliminate intercompany note receivable/payable.
[c] Entry to eliminate intercompany interest receivable/payable.

Sales	$250,000
Interest income	2,000
Less: Cost of goods sold	140,000
Selling & administrative expenses	50,000
Interest expense	10,000
Income taxes	15,000
Net income	$37,000

Note: Since Lake Forest Developers is using the purchase method to account for the consolidation, and since it acquired Smallville on December 31, Lake Forest should only report the income it generated. Under the purchase method, net incomes of the parent and subsidiary are not combined for the portion of the accounting period prior to the acquisition. The purchase price and, hence, the fair market value of the subsidiary's assets already reflect its results of operations prior to the acquisition. Therefore, for the current accounting period, Lake Forest's net income is the income it generated, not the combined net income of itself and Smallville.

c. Current ratio = Current assets ÷ Current liabilities
= ($180,000 + $38,000 + $2,000 + $145,000) ÷ ($7,000 + $3,000) = 36.50

Debt/equity ratio = Total liabilities ÷ Total stockholders' equity
= ($7,000 + $3,000 + $120,000) ÷ ($350,000 + $300,000) = .20

Earnings per share = Net income ÷ Common shares outstanding
= $37,000 ÷ (25,000 shares + 15,000 shares) = $0.925

P16–13

a. Investment in Subsidiary 120,000
Cash 120,000
To record purchase of subsidiary.

b. Due to the entry in Part (a), the Cash balance of Lake Forest would decrease from $170,000 to $50,000, and the Investment in Subsidiary account would increase from $0 to $120,000. The purchase of Smallville does not affect Smallville's books, since Lake Forest purchased the common shares from the stockholders of Smallville, not from Smallville.

Goodwill = Purchase price – FMV of net assets purchased.
= $120,000 x [80% x ($10,000 + $15,000 + $45,000 + $85,000 – $13,000 – $2,000 – $20,000)]
= $24,000

Minority Interest = FMV of net assets x Percentage of company not owned by parent
= ($10,000 + $15,000 + $45,000 + $85,000 – $13,000 – $2,000 – $20,000) x 20%
= $24,000

Accounts	Lake Forest	Smallville	Adjustments and Eliminations Debit	Adjustments and Eliminations Credit	Consolidated Balance Sheet
Cash	50,000	10,000			60,000
Accounts Receivable	23,000	15,000			38,000
Interest Receivable	3,000	0		1,000[c]	2,000
Notes Receivable	12,000	0		12,000[b]	0
Inventory	100,000	30,000	15,000[a]		145,000
Investment in Subsidiary	120,000	0		120,000[a]	0
Fixed Assets	300,000	80,000	5,000[a]		385,000
Goodwill	0	0	24,000[a]		24,000
Total assets	608,000	135,000	44,000	133,000	654,000
Short-Term Payables	6,000	13,000	12,000[b]		7,000
Interest Payable	2,000	2,000	1,000[c]		3,000
Long-Term Notes	100,000	20,000			120,000
Minority Interest	0	0		24,000[a]	24,000
Common Stock	200,000	75,000	75,000[a]		200,000
Retained Earnings	300,000	25,000	25,000[a]		300,000
Total liabilities & stockholders' equity	608,000	135,000	113,000	24,000	654,000

[a] Entry to adjust assets to market value, to eliminate the investment account, to eliminate subsidiary's stockholders' equity section, to recognize goodwill and to recognize minority interest.
[b] Entry to eliminate intercompany note receivable/payable.
[c] Entry to eliminate intercompany interest receivable/payable.

Sales	$250,000
Interest income	2,000
Less: Cost of goods sold	140,000
Selling & administrative expenses	50,000
Interest expense	10,000
Income taxes	15,000
Net income	$ 37,000

Note: Since Lake Forest Developers is using the purchase method to account for the consolidation, and since it acquired Smallville on December 31, Lake Forest should only report the income it generated. Under the purchase method, net incomes of the parent and subsidiary are not combined for the portion of the accounting period prior to the acquisition. The purchase price and, hence, the fair market value of the subsidiary's assets already reflect its results of operations prior to the acquisition. Therefore, for the current accounting period, Lake Forest's net income is the income it generated, not the combined net income of itself and Smallville.

C16–1

a. The pooling-of-interests method of accounting for business combinations permits the assets and liabilities of an acquired company to be added to those of a parent at their book value. No goodwill is recognized, and the retained earnings of the subsidiary and its income to date are added to those of the parent. Companies would favor the pooling-of-interests method because it offers a quick method of increasing their Retained Earnings balances; avoids carrying assets at the higher market values (which are required under the purchase method); avoids recording goodwill, which results in increased future amortization charges; and increases consolidated net income, because the entire year's income of the subsidiary is added to the parent, irrespective of when, during the year, the parent acquired them.

b. In 1970, the accounting profession significantly limited the conditions under which the pooling-of-interests method of accounting could be used. The restrictions imposed included requirements that at least 90% of the payment made by the parent be in the form of common stock, that the exchange must occur in a single transaction, and that the parent intend to hold the stock for a long period of time. Such restrictions would require companies to comply with provisions that may be unacceptable, just to be permitted to use pooling-of-interests accounting.

c. The practice of accounting was never intended to promote any type of specific policy or type of business transaction. Instead, it seeks to provide objective and fair reporting of business transactions, whatever their source and whatever their outcome. To depart from this motive removes objectivity, which lends credibility to accountant's reports.

C16–2

a. The equity method is used when a parent owns 20% to 50% of a subsidiary's outstanding stock. Under this method, a subsidiary's net income increases the Investment account; and dividend payments from the subsidiary decrease it. All the effects of the subsidiary relationship are reflected in the Investment account. Preparing consolidated statements is required when the level of ownership of a subsidiary exceeds 50%. In this case, the assets and liabilities of the subsidiary are added to those of the parent up to the extend of the partent's investment in the subsidiary. The companies are viewed as a single entity, even though they often operate as relatively independent companies.

Requiring consolidated financial statements could cause difficulties with bond indenture agreements because such statements combine the net assets of the parent with those of the subsidiary. If the subsidiary's financial statements includes a large portion of debt, the consolidated statements may show a higher debt/equity ratio that the parent had individually.

b. If users of financial statements are reasonable sophisticated, then the FASB faces a decreased responsibility for developing standards that encompass and account for every possible business situation that arises. Thus, the FASB would be able to promote broad standards, without a lessening of their responsibilities to users of financial statements.

C16–3

a. If a company holds receivables or payables denominated in a foreign currency, they must be converted to U.S. dollars when financial statements are prepared. This may give rise to exchange gains and losses, as the value of the U.S. dollar fluctuates significantly in relation to that of foreign currencies. Exchange gains and losses can cause income and other reported values to vary substantially from one period to the next. Further, economic consequences are associated with these gains and losses as they would affect stock prices, credit ratings, management compensation and debt covenants. Centralizing the treasure function permits a company the ability to monitor their overall exchange gains and losses, because different foreign currencies react differently to the U.S. dollar. Without a centralized treasury function, a company may not realize it is incurring losses in time to do something about it.

b. The main strategy used by U.S. companies to reduce the risks of holding receivables or payables denominated in non-U.S. currencies is hedging.

c. Hedging involves taking a position in a foreign currency in an equal and opposite amount to a particular receivable or payable expressed in that currency. When a company takes a hedged position, it is protecting itself from fluctuations in currency values. The gain or loss incurred in exchange-rate fluctuations is exactly offset by the loss or gain on the hedge. This strategy may be used to reduce the possibility of violating a covenant by protecting a company from experiencing an unexpected gain or loss. If a company is originally compliant with a debt covenant when it incurs a foreign denominated asset or lability, it can insulate itself against swings in exchange rates by hedging and prevent the debt covenant from being violated as a result of exchange-rate fluctuations.

C16–4

a. Accounting standards are developed within the environment and culture of a country and are intended to respond to the needs and customs that exist. Since different countries possess varying cultures, economic systems, and environments, accounting practices vary widely. Investors operating in an international environment are faced with differing accounting standards across countries, which decreases the comparability of financial statements. Accordingly, such investors must be well informed about each country's practices and make their own adjustments as they analyze foreign financial statements.

b. Several efforts have been undertaken to achieve greater international understanding and uniformity of accounting practices. The International Accounting Standards Committee was established in 1973 to develop worldwide accounting practices. Other groups have also been formed, including the International Federation of Accountants and the Organization for Economic Cooperation and DEvelopment. The United Nations also participates in such activities.

C16–5

a. U.S. generally accepted accounting principles require complete and fair presentation of all relevant financial information, which permits an informed investor to make decisions. This would include disclosure of reserves and other items which, in other countries may not be reflected in financial statements. Goerdeler's comments reflect the foreign practice of hiding reserves, which is contrary to the complete disclosure that is part of U.S. accounting standards.

b. Requiring German banks to apply U.S. disclosure rules seems appealing, especially when the foreign bank participates in business in the U.S. However, such a practice would require the bank to present two sets of financial statements, which doesn't make sense, because one may be regarded more credibly than the other. The role of financial statements in Germany is much different than in the U.S., and it may be inappropriate to force German banks to follow U.S. GAAP. The environments in the two countries differ, so the demand for financial statement information differs as well.

c. Uniformity in accounting practices may be slow in coming because extant accounting standards respond to the financial reporting needs in each country. The standardization of accounting across countries imposes costs upon all companies and may require a disclosure that was previously not required and may not be useful in all cases. Other influences, such as cultural pride and local environments, both political and economic, may further slow the progress of standardizing accounting practices.

d. There are ways that U.S. companies can establish certain kinds of 'hidden reserves.' It is possible for a company to have reserves by holding a less than 50% interest in a subsidiary when the only acceptable method of accounting for it is the equity method. When the company needs the reserves, which exist in the subsidiary, it can increase its ownership to over 50% and then consolidate the subsidiary into the parent's financial statements. Another method of hiding reserves would be to hold stock that was acquired at a low cost and is presently worth significantly more. The lower-of-cost-or-market rule provides that the investment be carried at a maximum of its original cost. If it has increased in value over time, this increase would not be reflected in the financial statements until the stock is sold. Thus, the company would be able to hide the reserves until the time it needs them. Other techniques of creating "hidden reserves" include overstating accounts receivable's bad debt estimate, using accelerated depreciation, and overstating expense estimates in end-of period accruals.

CHAPTER 17 Using Financial Statement Information

E17–1

	a. Formula	b. Classification
(1)	Income from continuing operations ÷ Net sales	Profitability ratio
(2)	(Cash + Marketable securities) ÷ Current liabilities	Solvency Ratio
(3)	Interest expense(1 – tax rate) ÷ Average interest–paying liabilities	Capitalization ratio
(4)	Total liabilities ÷ Total stockholders' equity	Capitalization ratio
(5)	Current assets ÷ Current liabilities	Solvency ratio
(6)	Dividends per share ÷ Market price per share	Market ratio
(7)	(Income from continuing operations + Interest expense) ÷ Average total assets	Profitability ratio
(8)	Pretax income from continuing operations ÷ Interest expense	Profitability ratio
(9)	Net credit sales ÷ Average accounts receivable	Activity ratio
(10)	Return on equity – Return on assets	Capitalization ratio
(11)	Income from continuing operations ÷ Average common shares outstanding	Profitability ratio
(12)	(Market price$_1$ – Market price$_0$ + Dividends per share) ÷ Market price$_0$	Market ratio
(13)	Cost of goods sold ÷ Average inventory	Activity ratio
(14)	Income from continuing operations ÷ Average stockholders' equity	Profitability ratio
(14)	Market price per share ÷ Earnings per share	Market ratio

E17–2

Profitability Ratios

Return on equity = Income from continuing operations ÷ Average stockholders' equity
= $16,500 ÷ [($29,000 + $36,500) ÷ 2] = .504

Return on assets = (Income from continuing operations + Interest expense) ÷ Average total assets
= $($16,500 + $5,000) ÷ [($81,000 + $99,000) ÷ 2] = .239

Earnings per share = Income from continuing operations ÷ Average common shares outstanding
= $16,500 ÷ [(2,000 shares + 2,000 shares) ÷ 2] = $8.25

Return on sales = Income from continuing operations ÷ Net sales
= $16,500 ÷ $72,000 = .229

Times interest earned = Pre–tax income from continuing operations ÷ Interest expense
= $25,000 ÷ $5,000 = 5.00

Solvency Ratios

Current ratio = Current assets ÷ Current liabilities
= ($9,000 + $12,000 + $18,000) ÷ $16,500 = 2.36

Quick ratio = (Cash + Marketable securities) ÷ Current liabilities
= ($9,000 + 0) ÷ $16,500 = .55

Activity Ratios

Receivable turnover = Net credit sales ÷ Average accounts receivable
= $72,000 ÷ [($9,000 + $12,000) ÷ 2] = 6.86

Inventory turnover = Cost of goods sold ÷ Average inventory
= $30,000 ÷ [($15,000 + $18,000) ÷ 2] = 1.82

Capitalization Ratios

Cost of debt = [Interest expense(1 – Tax rate)] ÷ Interest–paying liabilities
= [$5,000(1 – 34%)] ÷ [($40,000 + $46,000) ÷ 2] = .077

Financial leverage = Return on equity – Return on assets
= .504 – .239 = .265

Debt÷equity = Total liabilities ÷ Total stockholders' equity
= ($16,500 + $46,000) ÷ ($20,000 + $5,000 + $11,500) = 1.71

Market Ratios

Price/earnings ratio = Market price per share ÷ Earnings per share
= $36 ÷ $8.25 = 4.36

Dividend yield = Dividends per share ÷ Market price per share
= ($9,000 ÷ 2,000 shares) ÷ $36 = .125

Return on investment = Market price$_1$ – Market price$_0$ + Dividends per share) ÷ Market price$_0$
= ($36 – $30 + $4.50) ÷ $30 = .35

Balance Sheet	1990		1989	
Cash	$ 9,000	9%	$ 7,000	9%
Accounts receivable	12,000	12	9,000	11
Inventory	18,000	18	15,000	19
Long–lived assets (net)	60,000	61	50,000	62
Total assets	$99,000	100%	$81,000	100%
Accounts payable	16,500	17%	12,000	15%
Long–term liabilities	46,000	46	40,000	49
Common stock	20,000	20	20,000	25
Additional paid–in capital	5,000	5	5,000	6
Retained earnings	11,500	12	4,000	5
Total liabilities & stockholders' equity	$99,000	100%	$81,000	100%

Income Statement		
Sales	$72,000	100%
Less: Cost of goods sold	30,000	(42)
Gross profit	42,000	58%
Less: Operating expenses	12,000	(17)
Income from operations	30,000	41%
Less: Interest expense	5,000	(7)
Income from continuing operations (before taxes)	25,000	35%
Less: Income taxes	8,500	(12)
Net income	$16,500	23%

E17–3

a. Current ratio = Current assets ÷ Current liabilities

1987
$24,000 ÷ $10,000 = 2.40

1988
$25,000 ÷ $10,000 = 2.50

1989
$35,000 ÷ $12,000 = 2.92

1990
$42,000 ÷ $14,000 = 3.00

b. Gross margin = Gross profit ÷ Net sales

1987
$15,000 ÷ $35,000 = .43

1988
$18,000 ÷ $40,000 = .45

1989
$20,000 ÷ $45,000 = .44

1990
$22,000 ÷ $50,000 = .44

c. Inventory turnover = Cost of goods sold ÷ Average inventory

1987
$20,000 ÷ $12,000 = 1.67

1988
$22,000 ÷ [($12,000 + $12,000) ÷ 2] = 1.83

1989
$25,000 ÷ [($12,000 + $14,000) ÷ 2] = 1.92

1990
$28,000 ÷ [($14,000 + $15,000) ÷ 2] = 1.93

Average days supply of inventory = 365 ÷ Inventory turnover

1987
365 ÷ 1.67 = 218.56

1988
365 ÷ 1.83 = 199.45

1989
365 ÷ 1.92 = 190.10

1990
365 ÷ 1.93 = 189.12

d. Receivables turnover = Net credit sales ÷ Average accounts receivable

1987
$35,000 ÷ $7,000 = 5.00

1988
$40,000 ÷ [($7,000 + $8,000) ÷ 2] = 5.33

1989
$45,000 ÷ [($8,000 + $14,000) ÷ 2] = 4.09

1990
$50,000 ÷ [($14,000 + $20,000) ÷ 2] = 2.94

Average number of days outstanding = 365 ÷ Receivable turnover

1987
365 ÷ 5.00 = 73.00

1988
365 ÷ 5.33 = 68.48

1989
365 ÷ 4.09 = 89.24

1990
365 ÷ 2.94 = 124.15

e. Based upon its current ratio, Blanchard has more than sufficient current assets to meet its current liabilities. Given its relatively small cash balance, however, Blanchard will have to rely on its accounts receivables and its inventory to generate cash to meet its current liabilities. The trend in accounts receivable turnover is, therefore, quite disturbing. Fewer receivable turns implies that it is taking longer to collect the cash from credit customers. During 1987, customers paid their open accounts in slightly over two months, while during 1990, customers paid their open accounts in approximately four months! Consequently, Blanchard is generating less cash from its accounts receivable which, in turn, implies that the company may have insufficient cash to meet its current liabilities as they come due.

E17–4

a. Cash at end of the year = Cash at beginning of the year + Change in cash

Change in cash = Cash from operating activities + Cash from investing activities + Cash from financing activities

1988

Cash at end of the year = $0 + $78
Cash at end of the year = $78

$78 = Cash from operating activities + (–$400) + $800
Cash from operating activities = –$322

1989

$76 = Cash at beginning of the year + (–$2)
Cash at beginning of the year = $78

–$2 = –$252 + Cash from investing activities + $400
Cash from investing activities = –$150

1990

$156 = $76 + Change in cash
Change in cash = $80

$80 = Cash from operating activities + $150 + (–$200)
Cash from operating activities = $130

b. Other than at the beginning of 1988, the company always had a positive cash balance. From that standpoint the company was solvent throughout the three–year period. A more detailed analysis of Beecham's solvency, however, requires an analysis of the company's operating performance, financial flexibility, and liquidity. During 1988 and 1989, Beecham did not generate cash flows from operating activities. The company remained solvent by issuing additional debt or equity. Since the company was able to acquire additional debt or equity financing in 1988 and 1989 and was able to sell off assets during 1990, it appears that Beecham does have some financial flexibility. However, without having the associated balance sheets, it is not possible to adequately assess Beecham's financial flexibility and liquidity. Based upon the limited information provided, it appears that Beecham faced some potential solvency problems in 1988 and 1989, but was able to overcome these problems by issuing additional debt or equity.

E17–5

Transaction	Quick Ratio	Current Ratio	Debt ÷ Equity Ratio
(1)	–	–	+
(2)	NE	NE	+
(3)	NE	–	+[a]
(4)	+	+	–
(5)	NE	+	–[b]
(6)	–	NE	NE

[a] The Bad Debt Expense would be closed into Retained Earnings at the end of the accounting period as part of the closing process. Consequently, recording bad debt expense decreases total stockholders' equity.

[b] This transaction would increase both Sales and Cost of Goods Sold. Both of these accounts would be closed into Retained Earnings as part of the closing process. Since the sales price exceeds the cost of the inventory, the net effect of this transaction would be to increase Retained Earnings. Consequently, total stockholders' equity would increase.

E17–6

a. (1) Current ratio = Current assets ÷ Current liabilities

1989: $385,000 ÷ $170,000 = 2.26
1990: $400,000 ÷ $460,000 = .87

(2) Quick ratio = (Cash + Marketable securities) ÷ Current liabilities

1989: ($30,000 + $10,000) ÷ $170,000 = .235
1990: ($15,000 + $225,000) ÷ $460,000 = .522

b. Receivables turnover = Net credit sales ÷ Average accounts receivable

1989: $780,000 ÷ [($100,000 + $95,000) ÷ 2] = 8.00
1990: $800,000 ÷ [($95,000 + $90,000) ÷ 2] = 8.65

Number of days outstanding = 365 ÷ Receivables turnover

1989: 365 ÷ 8.00 = 45.625
1990: 365 ÷ 8.65 = 42.197

c. Solvency refers to a company's ability to meet its debts as they come due. Current liabilities represent the debts that are expected to come due first. Therefore, to be solvent, a company must have sufficient cash or near–cash assets to meet these current liabilities. Total current assets is one measure of near–cash assets. As indicated by the change in the company's current ratio, the company has insufficient current assets available to settle its current liabilities. On the other hand, the company's quick ratio improved during 1990, which indicates that it now has more near–cash assets (i.e., cash and marketable securities) to meet its obligations. Therefore, it is difficult to state whether the company's solvency position has actually improved or worsened. However, given that the company has insufficient cash and marketable securities to meet its debts, it can probably be concluded that the company's overall solvency position has worsened.

E17–7

a. Return on equity = Income from continuing operations ÷ Average stockholders' equity

1987: $510,000 ÷ [($100,000 + $100,000) ÷ 2] = 5.10
1988: $490,000 ÷ [($100,000 + $290,000) ÷ 2] = 2.51
1989: $515,000 ÷ [($290,000 + $315,000) ÷ 2] = 1.70
1990: $505,000 ÷ [($315,000 + $510,000) ÷ 2] = 1.22

It appears that the additional capital provided by the owners has not been used to generate net income. The company's net income has been relatively constant from 1987 to 1990. If the company had been effective at using the additional capital, the company's net income should have increased, and return on equity should have been relatively constant or increasing over time. However, if the company has used the additional capital for long–term projects, such as a new product, these projects may not generate any net income for several years. Once these projects begin generating income, the company's return on equity may increase to more appropriate levels. Therefore, the effectiveness of the company at using the owners' capital cannot be adequately evaluated without additional information.

b. It appears that the company has overinvested in inventory. The inventory turnover and the days' supply of inventory for each year are

	1987	**1988**	**1989**	**1990**
Inventory turnover	12.00	5.93	4.85	4.09
Days' supply	30.42	61.55	75.26	89.24

These ratios indicate that the company went from having one month's supply of inventory on hand to having almost three months of inventory on hand. It appears that the company has more inventory on hand than is warranted given demand for the inventory. The company could reduce inventory on hand and invest the proceeds in income–producing assets such as marketable securities. Such a move would make the company more profitable and provide owners a greater return on their investments. This change in investment policy would increase the company's return on equity.

E17–8

a. Debt/equity ratio = Total liabilities ÷ Total stockholders' equity
= ($130,000 + $150,000) ÷ $200,000
= 1.40

b. The maximum debt Montvale can have outstanding is 1.5 times total stockholders' equity. Therefore, the total debt it can have outstanding is $300,000 (i.e., 1.5 x $200,000). Since Montvale already has $280,000 in debt outstanding, it can incur an additional $20,000 in debt without violating its debt covenant.

c. The minimum level of stockholders' equity that Montvale can have is total debt divided by 1.5. Therefore, the total stockholders' equity it can have is $186,667 (i.e., $280,000 ÷ 1.5). Since Montvale's stockholders' equity is already $200,000, and since dividends decrease stockholders' equity, the maximum dividend that the company can declare is $13,333.

d. If Montvale had declared, but not paid, a $20,000 dividend prior to obtaining the loan, then the $20,000 is already included in the current liabilities reported on the balance sheet. Paying the dividend would decrease both current assets and current liabilities by $20,000. Therefore, the debt/equity ratio after the dividend has been paid would be 1.3 (i.e., [($130,000 – $20,000) + $150,000] ÷ $200,000). Since this ratio is less than the maximum debt/equity ratio allowed by the debt covenant, Montvale could pay the $20,000 dividend without violating its debt covenant.

E17–9

a. 1986: $12,000 ÷ $20,000 = 60.00% 1987: $10,000 ÷ $24,000 = 41.67%
1988: $16,000 ÷ $40,000 = 40.00% 1989: $15,000 ÷ $50,000 = 30.00%
1990: $24,000 ÷ $60,000 = 40.00%

b. Price earnings ratio = Market price per share ÷ Earnings per share
= Market price per share ÷ (Net income ÷ Average common shares outstanding)

1987: $35 ÷ {$24,000 ÷ [(10,000 + 10,000) ÷ 2]} = 14.58
1988: $30 ÷ {$40,000 ÷ [(20,000 + 20,000) ÷ 2]} = 15.00
1989: $37 ÷ {$50,000 ÷ [(20,000 + 20,000) ÷ 2]} = 14.80
1990: $42 ÷ {$60,000 ÷ [(18,000 + 18,000) ÷ 2]} = 12.60

Dividend yield = Dividends per share ÷ Market price per share

1987: ($10,000 ÷ 10,000 shares) ÷ $35 = .029
1988: ($16,000 ÷ 20,000 shares) ÷ $30 = .027
1989: ($15,000 ÷ 20,000 shares) ÷ $37 = .020
1990: ($24,000 ÷ 18,000 shares) ÷ $42 = .032

Return on investment = (Market price$_1$ – Market price$_0$ + Dividends per share) ÷ Market price$_0$

1987: ($35 – $30 + $1.00) ÷ $30 = .200
1988: ($30 – $35 + $0.80) ÷ $35 = –120
1989: ($37 – $30 + $0.75) ÷ $30 = .258
1990: ($42 – $37 + $1.33) ÷ $37 = .171

c. Based upon the dividend yield, dividends are not important in explaining the price of Morrissey Brothers' stock. On the other hand, the price of its stock is quite sensitive to changes in earnings. For example, in 1990 a $1 increase in earnings per share would cause a $12.60 increase in the stock price. Without knowing the performance of similar firms over this same period, it is difficult to determine whether the company's stock has performed well or not. However, Morrissey's stock does appear to have performed reasonably well. With the exception of 1988, it has provided an annual return greater than 17% in each year. The overall return for the four–year period is 52.93% (i.e., ($42 – $30 + $3.88) ÷ $30).

E17–10

a. To avoid violating the debt covenant, Mayberry must maintain a level of current assets twice its level of current liabilities. Therefore, the company must maintain current assets equal to $18,000 (i.e., 2 x $9,000 of current liabilities). Since prior to any investment the company has current assets totaling $52,000, the company can use $34,000 of current assets to invest in noncurrent assets.

b.

Account	1989
Current assets	$ 18,000
Land investment	89,000
Total assets	$107,000
Accounts payable	$ 9,000
Long–term liabilities	70,000
Stockholders' equity	28,000
Total liabilities & stockholders' equity	$107,000

Current ratio = Current assets ÷ Current liabilities
= $18,000 ÷ $9,000 = 2.00

Debt/equity ratio = Total liabilities ÷ Total stockholders' equity
= ($9,000 + $70,000) ÷ $28,000 = 2.82

c. 12/31/90 current assets = $18,000 from Part (b) + $150,000 cash revenues – $9,000 cash paid for accounts payable – $123,000 cash expenses
= $36,000

12/31/90 predividend current liabilities = $9,000 from Part (b) – $9,000 reduction of accounts payable + $7,000 for accrued expenses
= $7,000

12/31/90 long–term liabilities = $70,000 from Part (b)

12/31/90 predividend stockholders' equity = $28,000 + $20,000 in net income
= $48,000

Since Mayberry's total current assets are now $36,000, the minimum acceptable level of current liabilities (including any dividends payable) is half this amount, or $18,000. Therefore, Mayberry must maintain a level of current liabilities not greater than $18,000. Since Mayberry's December 31, 1990 current liabilities before declaring a dividend equals $7,000, the maximum dividend Mayberry can declare is $11,000 (i.e., $18,000 – $7,000). After declaring, but not paying, this dividend, Mayberry's current assets would be $36,000, and its current liabilities would be $18,000. Its current ratio would then be 2.00 (i.e., $36,000 ÷ $18,000).

If Mayberry declares, but does not pay, the $11,000 dividend, its debt/equity ratio would be:

($7,000 + $11,000 + $70,000) ÷ ($48,000 – $11,000) = 2.378

E17–11

a. Current ratio = Current liabilities ÷ Current liabilities

1987: $20,000 ÷ $ 8,000 = 2.500
1988: $24,000 ÷ $13,000 = 1.846
1989: $31,000 ÷ $25,000 = 1.240
1990: $35,000 ÷ $30,000 = 1.167

Debt/equity ratio = Total liabilities ÷ Total stockholders' equity

1987: $ 8,000 + $15,000) ÷ ($20,000 + $10,000) = .767
1988: ($13,000 + $35,000) ÷ ($20,000 + $20,000) = 1.200
1989: ($25,000 + $40,000) ÷ ($20,000 + $32,000) = 1.250
1990: ($30,000 + $40,000) ÷ ($20,000 + $38,000) = 1.207

Return on assets = (Income from continuing operations + Interest expense) ÷ Average total assets

1987: ($13,000 + $2,000) ÷ $53,000 = .283
1988: ($14,000 + $4,000) ÷ [($ 53,000 + $ 88,000) ÷ 2] = .255
1989: ($21,000 + $5,000) ÷ [($ 88,000 + $117,000) ÷ 2] = .254
1990: ($24,000 + $5,000) ÷ {($117,000 + $128,000) ÷ 2] = .237

b.

	1990	1989	1988	1987
Current assets	27.34%	26.50%	27.27%	37.74%
Noncurrent assets	72.66	73.50	72.73	62.26
Total assets	100.00	100.00	100.00	100.00
Current liabilities	23.44	21.37	14.77	15.09
Long–term liabilities	31.25	34.19	39.77	28.30
Capital stock	15.62	17.09	22.73	37.74
Retained earnings	29.69	27.35	22.73	18.87
Total liabilities and stockholders' equity	100.00	100.00	100.00	100.00

c. Solvency measures a company's ability to meet its debts as they come due. The current ratio provides one measure of a company's solvency. Based upon this ratio, Lotechnic has sufficient current assets to meet its current obligations. However, the trend in its current ratio indicates that the company's excess of current assets over current liabilities is decreasing. Therefore, the company has fewer current assets available to meet its current obligations. This trend indicates that Lotechnic Enterprises' solvency position may be worsening.

The debt/equity ratio provides an indication of a company's capitalization which, in turn, indicates how risky a company is. Lotechnic is relying increasingly on debt relative to stockholders' equity to finance operations. At some point in time, the company will have to repay this debt. The company will either have to repay this debt by (1) generating cash from operations, (2) selling assets, (3) borrowing additional cash, or (4) acquiring cash by issuing stock. From the statement of cash flows, the cash generated from operations has been decreasing and is now negative; therefore, it appears that the company cannot rely on operations to generate cash. The statement of cash flows also indicates that the company has been using cash for investment purposes every year; therefore, the company may have some assets that it could sell. But if these assets are used in operations, the company's operations may be adversely affected by selling them.

Since total assets equal total liabilities and stockholders' equity, the proportion of total liabilities to the sum of total liabilities and stockholders' equity reported on the common–size balance sheet equals the proportion of total liabilities to total assets. This measure indicates the proportion of total assets (based upon book value) that would have to be sold to satisfy all the company's obligations. To meet its obligations, Lotechnic Enterprises would have to sell approximately 55% of its total assets, which would virtually decimate its asset base.

Based upon the trend in the current ratio, the debt/equity ratio, cash flows from operations, and the proportion of total liabilities to total assets, it appears that Lotechnic Enterprises may face severe solvency problems as its long–term debt matures.

Earning power is defined as a company's ability to increase its wealth through operations and to generate cash from operations. Earning power and solvency are closely related. A company must have adequate resources to generate wealth. If a company experiences solvency problems, it will most likely have to divert its resources to paying its obligations. Therefore, due to its solvency problems, Lotechnic Enterprises may not have strong earning power. While Lotechnic's income from continuing operations has increased every year, the company's effectiveness at managing capital has decreased every year. This trend indicates that the company may have limited earning power. This conclusion is also supported by the trend in the company's cash flows from operations.

It must be remembered, however, that this analysis was based on very limited information. To adequately analyze a company, additional information would be needed. Complete financial statements, financial information for similar companies, and general economic information should all be considered when analyzing a company's earning power and solvency position.

P17–1

a. (1) Current ratio = Current assets ÷ Current liabilities
= ($15,000 + $100,000 + $150,000 + $100,000) ÷ ($95,000 + $50,000 + $50,000)
= $365,000 ÷ $195,000 = 1.872

(2) Quick ratio = (Cash + Marketable securities) ÷ Current liabilities
= ($15,000 + $150,000) ÷ $195,000 = .846

(3) Earnings per share = Income from continuing operations ÷ Common shares outstanding
= $500,000 ÷ 20,000 shares*
= $25

---

* 20,000 shares = Total common stock par value ÷ Par value per share = $200,000 ÷ $10

(4) Times interest earned = Pretax income from continuing operations ÷ Interest expense
= $757,575 ÷ $100,000 = 7.576

(5) Return on assets = (Income from continuing operations + Interest expense) ÷ Total assets
= ($500,000 + $100,000) ÷ $970,000 = .619

(6) Inventory turnover = Cost of goods sold ÷ Inventory
= $900,000 ÷ $100,000 = 9.00

(7) Return on equity = Income from continuing operations ÷ Stockholders' equity
= $500,000 ÷ ($200,000 + $125,000 + $200,000) = .952

b. (1) Current ratio = ($365,000 – $150,000 of securities at cost + $200,000 of securities at market value) ÷ $195,000
= $415,000 ÷ $195,000 = 2.128

(2) Quick ratio = ($165,000 – $150,000 of securities at cost + $200,000 of securities at market value) ÷ $195,000
= $215,000 ÷ $195,000 = 1.103

(3) Earnings per share = ($500,000 + $50,000) ÷ 20,000 shares = $27.50

(4) Times interest earned = ($757,575 + $50,000) ÷ $100,000 = 8.076

(5) Return on assets = ($500,000 + $50,000 + $100,000) ÷ ($970,000 + $50,000) = .637

(6) Inventory turnover: No change from Part (a)

(7) Return on equity = ($500,000 + $50,000) ÷ ($525,000 + $50,000) = .957

Market values would probably be more useful than historical cost for determining a company's earning power and solvency. Market values, in many cases, better reflect an asset's value to a company and, hence, the future cash flows that the assets can be expected to provide. However, remember that market values are often quite subjective. Overly subjective market values might prevent people from agreeing on a company's solvency position and earning power.

P17–2

a. (1) Earnings per share = Income from continuing operations ÷ Average common shares outstanding
= ($2,250,000 – $765,000) ÷ [($100,000 + $150,000) ÷ 2] = $11.88

(2) Cost of debt = Interest expense(1 – tax rate)] ÷ Interest–paying liabilities
= [$80,000(1 – 34%)] ÷ $800,000 = .066

Note: Tax rate = Income taxes ÷ Income from continuing operations (before taxes).

(3) Price ÷ earnings = Market price per share ÷ Earnings per share
= $35 per share ÷ $11.88 per share = 2.946

(4) Dividend yield = Dividends per share ÷ Market price per share
= $1,500,000 ÷ [(100,000 + 150,000) ÷ 2] = .343

(5) Return on investment = Market price$_1$ – Market price$_0$ + Dividends per share) ÷ Market price^0
= ($35 – $30 + $12) ÷ $30 = .567

b. Declaring and paying dividends would decrease stockholders' equity but would not affect income from continuing operations, thereby increasing return on equity.

A decrease in the market price of a company's stock does not affect its return on equity.

Interest on interest–bearing debt reduces income from continuing operations, which is part of net income. Since net income is closed into Retained Earnings, interest expense reduces stockholders' equity. The actual effect of interest expense on return on equity depends on the relative values of income from continuing operations and average stockholders' equity. In most cases, however, return on equity would decrease because the relative effect of interest expense is usually greater on income from continuing operations than on stockholders' equity.

Issuing additional common stock increases stockholders' equity, but does not affect income from continuing operations, thereby decreasing return on equity.

P17–3

a. Return on equity provides a measure of a company's effectiveness at managing the owners' capital. The formula for calculating return on equity is income from continuing operations divided by average stockholders' equity. The 1990 return on equity for Hathaway Toys and for Yakima Manufacturing would be:

Hathaway: $875,000 ÷ [($1,585,000 + $2,460,000) ÷ 2] = .433
Yakima: $755,000 ÷ [($30,000) + $725,000) ÷ 2] = 2.173

Note: Beginning stockholders' equity = Ending stockholders' equity – Net income.

Based upon return on equity, Yakima Manufacturing has been approximately five times more efficient than Hathaway Toys at managing owners' capital.

b. Return on assets provides a measure of a company's effectiveness at managing all investors' capital. The formula for calculating return on assets is the sum of income from continuing operations and interest expense divided by average total assets. The 1990 return on assets for Hathaway Toys and for Yakima Manufacturing would be:

Hathaway: ($875,000 + 0) ÷ [($1,825,000 + $2,700,000) ÷ 2] = .387
Yakima: ($755,000 + $195,000 ÷ [($1,945,000 + $2,700,000) ÷ 2] = .409

Note: Beginning total assets = Ending total assets – Net income
= Ending total liabilities and stockholders' equity – Net income

Based upon return on assets, Yakima Manufacturing and Hathaway Toys are essentially equally efficient at managing all investors' capital.

c. Earnings per share = Income from continuing operations ÷ Average common shares outstanding

Hathaway: $875,000 ÷ [(80,000 + 80,000) ÷ 2] = $10.94
Yakima: $755,000 ÷ [(35,000 + 35,000) ÷ 2] = $21.57

d. Yes. Stockholders are realizing a return on their investment of 217.3% (from Part [a]) while debtholders are only realizing a return on their investment of approximately 10% (i.e., Interest Expense ÷ Mortgage Payable). This differential return is due to the company using debt rather than equity to finance operations. Since the debtholders are only entitled to interest, any earnings from operations in excess of interest accrue to the stockholders. Therefore, Yakima Manufacturing has efficiently used debt to benefit its stockholders.

P17–4

a. Return on equity = Income from continuing operations ÷ Average stockholders' equity

Robotronics: $610,000 ÷ [($395,000 + $1,005,000) ÷ 2] = .87
Technology: $375,000 ÷ [($235,000) + $1,440,000) ÷ 2] = .62

Note: Beginning stockholders' equity = Ending stockholders' equity – Net income.

Robotronics appears to be slightly more efficient at managing stockholders' capital.

If extraordinary items are considered, then return on equity for each company would be:
Robotronics: $610,000 ÷ [($395,000 + $1,005,000) ÷ 2] = .87
Technology: $1,675,000 ÷ [(($235,000) + $1,440,000) ÷ 2] = 2.78

If extraordinary items are considered, Technology, Ltd. appears to be approximately three times more efficient than Robotronics, Inc. at managing its stockholders' capital. Considering extraordinary items in calculating return on equity does provide a more complete measure of how efficiently a company managed its stockholders' equity in the current year. However, since extraordinary items are, by definition, items that occur infrequently and are unusual, these items do not indicate that the company will continue to manage the stockholders' capital as efficiently in the future. Consequently, extraordinary items probably should not be used to calculate return on equity.

b. Financial leverage indicates how effectively a company uses debt for the stockholders. Financial leverage is calculated as return on equity less return on assets. Therefore, before calculating financial leverage, return on assets must be calculated.

Return on assets = (Income from continuing operations + Interest expense) ÷ Average total assets

Robotronics: ($610,000 + $100,000) ÷ ($3,360,000 ÷ 2) = .21
Technology: ($375,000 + $175,000) ÷ ($1,870,000 ÷ 2) = .29

Therefore, the financial leverage of the two companies would be:
Robotronics: .87 – .21 = .66
Technology: .62 – .29 = .33

From this analysis, Robotronics is approximately twice as effective as Technology at using debt to generate returns for its stockholders.

If extraordinary items are considered, the return on assets for each company would be:
Robotronics: ($610,000 + $100,000) ÷ ($3,360,000 ÷ 2) = .21
Technology: ($1,675,000 + $175,000) ÷ ($1,870,000 ÷ 2) = .99

Therefore, the financial leverage of the two companies would be:
Robotronics: .87 – .21 = .66
Technology: 2.78 – .99 = 1.79

If extraordinary items are considered, Technology, Ltd. is almost three times more effective than Robotronics, Inc. at using debt to generate returns for its stockholders. Therefore, extraordinary items affect the conclusions one draws when analyzing a company.

P17–5

a. Return on equity = Income from continuing operations ÷ Average stockholders' equity

	1989	1990
Williams	$17,000 ÷ [(0 + $55,000) ÷ 2] = .618	$23,000 ÷ [($55,000 + $63,000) ÷ 2] = .390
Warner	$ 7,000 ÷ [(0 + $45,000) ÷ 2] = .311	$17,000 ÷ [($45,000 + $47,000) ÷ 2] = .370

Return on sales = Income from continuing operations ÷ Net sales

	1989	1990
Williams	$17,000 ÷ $52,000 = .327	$23,000 ÷ $81,000 = .284
Warner	$ 7,000 ÷ $52,000 = .135	$17,000 ÷ $81,000 = .210

Current ratio = Current assets ÷ Current liabilities

	1989	1990
Williams	$8,000 ÷ $6,000 = 1.333	$15,000 ÷ $7,000 = 2.143
Warner	$8,000 ÷ $6,000 = 1.333	$15,000 ÷ $7,000 = 2.143

Debt ÷ equity ratio = Total liabilities ÷ Total stockholders' equity

	1989	1990
Williams	($6,000 + $37,000) ÷ $55,000 = .782	($7,000 + $25,000) ÷ $63,000 = .508
Warner	($6,000 + $37,000) ÷ $45,000 = .956	($7,000 + $25,000) ÷ $47,000 = .681

Based upon return on equity and return on sales, Williams appears to have the stronger profitability ratios. Williams, therefore, appears to have the greatest earning power. However, the differential between Williams and Warner decreased during 1990, so it is difficult to absolutely conclude that Williams has the greatest earning power.

b.

	Straight- line Depreciation	Double-Declining-Balance Depreciation	Cumulative Difference
1989	$10,000	$20,000	$10,000
1990	10,000	16,000	16,000

Return on equity

1989: ($ 7,000 + $10,000) ÷ {[(0 + ($45,000 + $10,000)] ÷ 2} = .618

1990: ($17,000 + $ 6,000) ÷ {[($45,000 + $10,000) + ($47,000 + $16,000)] ÷ 2} = .390

Return on sales

1989: ($ 7,000 + $10,000) ÷ $52,000 = .327

1990: ($17,000 + $ 6,000) ÷ $81,000 = .284

Current ratio

1989: $ 8,000 ÷ $6,000 = 1.333

1990: $15,000 ÷ $7,000 = 2.143

Debt/equity ratio

1989: ($6,000 + $37,000) ÷ ($45,000 + $10,000) = .782

1990: ($7,000 + $25,000) ÷ ($47,000 + $16,000) = .508

After adjusting for the different depreciation methods, the ratios for the two companies are identical. The earning power of the two companies, therefore, appears to be identical. The difference in earning power detected in Part (a) is due solely to the different depreciation methods selected by Williams Company and Warner Services. Therefore, it is important to consider the effect of different accounting methods when comparing the performance of different companies.

P17–6

a. Return on equity = Income from continuing operations ÷ Average stockholders' equity
1989: $14,000 ÷ [($34,000 + $38,000) ÷ 2] = .389
1990: $25,000 ÷ [($38,000 + $51,000) ÷ 2] = .562

Return on assets = (Income from continuing operations + Interest expense) ÷ Average total assets
1989: ($14,000 + $1,000) ÷ [($49,000 + $ 55,000) ÷ 2] = .288
1990: ($25,000 + $5,000) ÷ [($55,000 + $113,000) ÷ 2] = .357

Return on sales = Income from continuing operations ÷ Net sales
1989: $14,000 ÷ $45,000 = .311
1990: $25,000 ÷ $70,000 = .357

Times interest earned = Pretax income from continuing operations ÷ Interest expense
1989: ($14,000 + $ 6,000) ÷ $1,000 = 20.00
1990: ($25,000 + $13,000) ÷ $5,000 = 7.6

Financial leverage = Return on equity – Return on assets
1989: .389 – .288 = .101
1990: .562 – .357 = .205

Debt/equity ratio = Total liabilities ÷ Total stockholders' equity
1989: ($ 7,000 + $10,000) ÷ $38,000 = .447
1990: ($12,000 + $50,000) ÷ $51,000 = 1.216

b. Return on equity = Income from continuing operations ÷ Average stockholders' equity
= ($25,000 + $4,000 in interest saved) ÷ [($38,000 + $40,000) + ($51,000 + $40,000 + $4,000 in interest saved) ÷ 2] = .335

Return on assets = (Income from continuing operations + Interest expense) ÷ Average total assets
= [($25,000 + $4,000 in interest saved) + $1,000] ÷ {[$55,000 + ($113,000 + $4,000 cash saved on interest)] ÷ 2} = .349

Return on sales = Income from continuing operations ÷ Net sales
= ($25,000 + $4,000 in interest saved) ÷ $70,000 = .414

Times interest earned = Pretax income from continuing operations ÷ Interest expense
= ($25,000 + $4,000 in interest saved + $13,000) ÷ $1,000 = 42.00

Financial leverage = Return on equity – Return on assets
= .335 – .349 = –.014)

Debt/equity ratio = Total liabilities ÷ Total stockholders' equity
= ($62,000 – $40,000) ÷ ($51,000 + $40,000 + $4,000 in interest saved) = .232

c. The company appears stronger by issuing equity than issuing debt if one examines return on sales, times interest earned, and the debt/equity ratio. However, if one examines return on equity and financial leverage, the company appears much stronger by issuing debt than by issuing equity. The company can effectively manage additional debt capital to the benefit of its stockholders, but it does not effectively manage additional equity capital to the benefit of its stockholders. In fact, the company manages equity capital to the detriment of its stockholders. Therefore, based upon this limited ratio analysis, it appears that the company made the correct decision to issue debt rather than equity. Remember, though, that the company may want or need to consider other factors in deciding whether to issue debt or equity. It may want to consider the effect of the alternative financing arrangements on existing debt covenants, incentive compensation schemes, taxes, and so forth.

P17–7

a.

	1990	1989	Dollar Change	Percent Change
Assets				
Current assets				
Cash	$ 110,000	$ 115,000	–$ 5,000	– 4.35%
Short–term marketable securities	175,000	220,000	– 45,000	–20.45%
Accounts receivable	350,000	400,000	– 50,000	–12.50%
Inventory	290,000	240,000	50,000	20.83%
Prepaid expenses	50,000	35,000	20,000	57.14%
Total current assets	980,000	1,010,000	– 30,000	
Property, plant, and equipment	650,000	590,000	60,000	10.17%
Less: Accumulated depreciation	(165,000)	(130,000)	– 35,000	26.92%
Total assets	$1,465,000	$1,470,000	–$ 5,000	
Liabilities and stockholders' equity				
Current liabilities:				
Accounts payable	$ 60,000	$ 50,000	$10,000	20.00%
Wages payable	15,000	20,000	– 5,000	–25.00%
Unearned revenue	50,000	35,000	15,000	42.86%
Income taxes payable	55,000	35,000	20,000	57.14%
Current portion of long–term debt	110,000	135,000	– 25,000	–18.52%
Total current liabilities	290,000	275,000	15,000	
Bonds payable	380,000	440,000	– 60,000	–13.64%
Common stock ($10 par value)	220,000	170,000	50,000	29.41%
Additional paid–in capital	145,000	115,000	30,000	26.09%
Retained earnings	430,000	470,000	– 40,000	– 8.51%
Total liabilities & stockholders' equity	$1,465,000	$1,470,000	–$ 5,000	

b.

	1990		1989		Percentage
	Dollar	Percent	Dollar	Percent	Change
Assets					
Current assets					
Cash	$ 110,000	7.51%	$ 115,000	7.82%	– 3.96%
Short–term marketable securities	175,000	11.94%	220,000	14.97%	–20.17%
Accounts receivable	350,000	23.89%	400,000	27.21%	–12.20%
Inventory	290,000	19.80%	240,000	16.33%	21.25%
Prepaid expenses	55,000	3.75%	35,000	2.38%	57.56%
Total current assets	980,000	66.89%	1,010,000	68.71%	
Property, plant, and equipment	650,000	44.37%	590,000	40.14%	10.54%
Accumulated depreciation	(165,000)	(11.26%)	(130,000)	(8.85%)	27.23%
Total assets	$1,465,000	100.00%	$1,470,000	100.00%	
Liabilities and stockholders' equity					
Current liabilities:					
Accounts payable	60,000	4.10%	$ 50,000	3.41%	20.59%
Wages payable	15,000	1.02%	20,000	1.36%	–25.00%
Unearned revenue	50,000	3.41%	35,000	2.38%	43.28%
Income taxes payable	55,000	3.75%	35,000	2.38%	57.56%
Current portion of long–term debt	110,000	7.51%	135,000	9.18%	–18.20%
Total current liabilities	290,000	19.79%	275,000	18.71%	
Bonds payable	380,000	25.94%	440,000	29.93%	–13.33%
Common stock ($10 par value)	220,000	15.02%	170,000	11.57%	29.93%
Additional paid–in capital	145,000	9.90%	115,000	7.82%	26.60%
Retained earnings	430,000	29.35%	470,000	31.97%	– 8.20%
Total liabilities & stockholders' equity	$1,465,000	100.00%	$1,470,000	100.00%	

c. Common–size financial statements provide relative comparisons of account balances rather than absolute comparisons of account balances. Absolute comparisons only provide information about whether an account balance has increased or decreased. Alternatively, relative comparisons provide information about whether an account balance has increased or decreased relative to a benchmark measure. This relative comparison allows financial statement users to determine more easily if a company is altering the composition of its assets, liabilities, or stockholders' equity. Relative comparisons of account balances may also provide users with insights into why account balances are changing.

P17–8

(1) Cost of debt measures the average cost a company is paying for its debt. Cost of debt is calculated as the product of interest expense and 1 minus the tax rate divided by the sum of interest–paying liabilities. Gidley's cost of debt for 1989 and 1990 is

1989: [$165,000(1 – 40%)] ÷ [($440,000 + $135,000)] = .172
1990: [$150,000(1 – 40%)] ÷ [($440,000 + $135,000) + ($380,000 + $110,000) ÷ 2] = .169

Interest expense is deductible for tax purposes. Consequently, the government effectively pays a portion of a company's interest expense. Thus, the company incurs a smaller portion of its interest expense than it would otherwise incur. Therefore, income taxes decrease the effective cost of debt to the borrower.

(2) Return on equity measures a company's effectiveness at managing equity investments. Return on equity is calculated as income from continuing operations divided by average stockholders' equity.

1989: $515,000 ÷ [($755,000 + $450,000) ÷ 2] = .855
1990: $510,000 ÷ [($755,000 + $795,000) ÷ 2] = .658

The company generated returns on its owners' investments in excess of 65%, which appears to be rather substantial. However, without being able to compare Gidley Electronics' performance to industry averages, it is difficult to conclude whether the company is really effective in managing the owner's capital.

(3) Return on equity measures a company's effectiveness at managing owners' investments, while return on assets measures a company's effectiveness at managing all investments, both debt and equity. The excess of return on equity over return on assets indicates a company's effectiveness at using debt to generate returns for the owners. This measure is called financial leverage. Since financial leverage is calculated using return on assets, the first step is to calculate return on assets. Return on assets is calculated as the sum of income from continuing operations and interest expense divided by average total assets. Gidley's return on assets from 1989 and 1990 is

1989: ($515,000 + $165,000) ÷ [($1,450,000 + $1,470,000) ÷ 2] = .465
1990: ($510,000 + $150,000) ÷ [($1,470,000 + $1,465,000) ÷ 2] = .450

Gidley's financial leverage for 1989 and 1990 is

1988: .855 – .465 = .390
1990: .658 – .450 = .208

The company is using debt to the benefit of its equity owners. The positive leverage indicates that proceeds from debt are generating sufficient profits to provide a return for the equity owners. In other words, the return from using debt exceeds its cost.

(4) The current ratio measures whether a company has sufficient current assets to meet its current liabilities. The current ratio equals current assets divided by current liabilities. Gidley's current ratio for 1989 and 1990 is

1989: $1,010,000 ÷ $275,000 = 3.673
1990: $980,000 ÷ $290,000 = 3.379

Gidley Electronics' current assets are over three times greater than its current liabilities. The company, therefore, appears to have no solvency problems. However, the company may be unable to convert some of its current assets to cash quickly enough to meet some of its current liabilities. Another measure of solvency that compares near–cash assets to current liabilities is the quick ratio. The quick ratio equals the sum of cash and marketable securities divided by current liabilities.

1989: ($115,000 + $220,000) ÷ $275,000 = 1.218
1990: ($110,000 + $175,000) ÷ $290,000 = .983

Gidley Electronics appears to have sufficient cash and near–cash assets available to meet its current obligations. Therefore, the company should have no significant short–term solvency problems.

(5) The price/earnings ratio measures the sensitivity of stock prices to changes in earnings. This ratio is calculated by dividing the market price per share by earnings per share. Since this ratio uses earnings per share in the calculations, the first step is to calculate earnings per share. Earnings per share is calculated by dividing income from continuing operations by the average number of common shares outstanding during the year. Gidley's earnings per share for 1989 and 1990 are

1989: $515,000 ÷ [(17,000 + 17,000) ÷ 2] = $30.29
1990: $510,000 ÷ [(17,000 + 22,000) ÷ 2] = $26.15

Gidley's price ÷ earnings ratio for 1989 and 1990 is

1989: $69.00 ÷ $30.29 = 2.278
1990: $54.00 ÷ $26.15 = 2.065

It appears that the price of Gidley Electronic's stock is rather sensitive to changes in earnings. A change in earnings per share should cause the market price to change by approximately twice the change. To obtain a better idea of how sensitive the company's stock is to changes in earnings, the company's price/earnings ratio should also be compared to industry averages.

(6) The average number of days accounts receivable are outstanding is calculated as 365 days divided by accounts receivable turnover. The accounts receivable turnover is, in turn, calculated by dividing net credit sales by average accounts receivable. Gidley's accounts receivable turnover for 1989 and 1990 is

1989: $3,010,000 ÷ [($400,000 + $400,000) ÷ 2] =7.525
1990: $2,450,000 ÷ [($400,000 + $350,000) ÷ 2] = 6.533

The number of days outstanding for receivables during 1989 and 1990 is

1989: 365 ÷ 7.525 = 48.505 days
1990: 365 ÷ 6.533 = 55.870 days

The average number of days accounts receivable are outstanding slightly increased. Therefore, customers are not paying their open receivables as quickly as before. If this problem persists, Gidley may have to consider more stringent credit and/or collection policies.

P17–9

Return on sales = Income from continuing operations ÷ Net sales
.08 = $25,000 ÷ net sales
Net sales = $312,500

Cost of Goods Sold = Net sales x (1 – Gross margin percentage)
= $312,500 x (1 – 40%)
= $187,500

Income from continuing operations = Sales – Cost of goods sold – Expenses
$25,000 = $312,500 – $187,500 – Expenses
Expenses = $100,000

Tumwater Canyon Campsites
Income Statement
For the Year Ended December 31, 1990

Sales	$312,500
Less: Cost of goods sold	187,500
Gross profit	125,000
Less: Expenses	100,000
Net income	$ 25,000

Inventory turnover = Cost of goods sold ÷ Average inventory
5 = $187,500 ÷ [(0 + Ending inventory) ÷ 2]
Ending inventory = $75,000

Receivable turnover = Net credit sales ÷ Average accounts receivable
8 = $312,500 ÷ [(0 + Ending accounts receivable) ÷ 2]
Ending accounts receivable = $78,125

Quick ratio = (Ending cash + Marketable securities) ÷ Current liabilities
.5 = (Ending cash + $0) ÷ $150,000
Ending cash = $75,000

Current assets		Current liabilities	
Cash	$ 75,000	Accounts Payable	$150,000
Accounts Receivable	78,125		
Inventory	75,000		
Total Current Assets	$228,125		

P17–10

Mountain–Pacific Railroad
Balance Sheet
As of December 31, 1990 and 1989

	1990		1989	
	Dollar	Percentage	Dollar	Percentage
Current assets				
Cash	$ 10,000	0.68%	$ 312,000	20.36%
Short–term marketable securities	125,000	8.47%	120,000	7.83%
Accounts receivable	500,000	33.90%	150,000	9.79%
Inventory	200,000	13.56%	210,000	13.71%
Prepaid expenses	50,000	3.39%	75,000	4.90%
Total current assets	885,000	60.00%	867,000	56.59%
Long–term investments	225,000	15.25%	225,000	14.69%
Property, plant, and equipment	430,000	29.15%	540,000	35.25%
Accumulated depreciation	(65,000)	(4.40%)	(100,000)	(6.53%)
Total assets	$1,475,000	100.00%	$1,532,000	100.00%
Liabilities and stockholders' equity				
Current liabilities				
Accounts payable	$ 10,000	0.68%	$ 50,000	3.26%
Wages payable	5,000	0.34%	2,000	0.13%
Dividends payable	125,000	8.47%	5,000	0.33%
Income taxes payable	50,000	3.39%	35,000	2.29%
Current portion of long–term debt	100,000	6.78%	175,000	11.42%
Total current liabilities	290,000	19.66%	267,000	17.43%
Mortgage payable	350,000	23.73%	450,000	29.37%
Common stock ($10 par value)	200,000	13.56%	110,000	7.18%
Additional paid–in capital	135,000	9.15%	95,000	6.20%
Retained earnings	500,000	33.90%	610,000	39.82%
Total liabilities & Stockholders' equity	$1,475,000	100.00%	$1,532,000	100.00%

Mountain–Pacific Railroad
Income Statement
For the years ended December 31, 1990 and 1989

	1990		1989	
	Dollar	Percentage	Dollar	Percentage
Revenue				
Net cash sales	$1,955,000	32.02%	$2,775,000	66.31%
Net credit sales	4,150,000	67.98%	1,410,000	33.69%
Total revenue	6,105,000	100.00%	4,185,000	100.00%
Less: Cost of goods sold				
Beginning inventory	210,000	3.44%	300,000	7.17%
Net purchases	4,005,000	65.60%	2,475,000	59.14%
Cost of goods available for sale	4,215,000	69.04%	2,775,000	66.31%
Less: Ending inventory	200,000	3.28%	210,000	5.02%
Cost of goods sold	4,015,000	65.77%	2,565,000	61.29%
Gross profit	2,090,000	34.23%	1,620,000	38.71%
Selling & administrative expenses				
Depreciation expense	75,000	1.23%	90,000	2.15%
General selling expenses	575,000	9.42%	600,000	14.34%
General administrative expenses	480,000	7.86%	420,000	10.04%
Total selling & administrative expenses	1,130,000	18.51%	1,110,000	26.52%
Income from operations	960,000	15.72%	510,000	12.19%
Less: Interest expense	50,000	0.82%	65,000	1.55%
Income from continuing operations (before taxes)	910,000	14.91%	445,000	10.63%
Less: Income taxes	365,000	5.98%	175,000	4.18%
Income before extraordinary items	545,000	8.93%	270,000	6.45%
Extraordinary loss (net of tax benefit of $40,000)	60,000	0.98%	0	0.00%
Net income	485,000	7.94%	270,000	6.45%

b. The proportion of credit sales and cash sales to total sales changed dramatically from 1989 to 1990. The company made approximately twice as many sales on credit during 1990 as it made during 1989. This shift also flowed through to the balance sheet. Fewer cash sales caused the Cash balance to decrease and also caused a large increase in the Accounts Receivable balance during 1990.

c. Common–size financial statements allow comparisons to be made across time and across companies by providing a benchmark against which to make the comparisons. Standard financial statements only allow absolute comparisons. By providing a benchmark, common–size financial statements allow relative comparisons. Such comparisons allow financial statement users to focus on the relative importance of an account rather than whether the account has simply increased or decreased in absolute terms. Further, common–size financial statements can provide financial statement users with insights as to why an account balance changed or why a certain trend developed. For example, in the case of Mountain–Pacific Railroad, the shift in the relative importance of Cash and Accounts Receivable can be explained by examining the shift in the relative importance of cash and credit sales.

P17–11

Return on equity = Income from continuing operations ÷ Stockholders' equity

1989: $270,000 ÷ $815,000 = .331
1990: $545,000 ÷ [($815,000 + $835,000) ÷ 2] = .661

Current ratio = Current assets ÷ Current liabilities

1989: $867,000 ÷ $267,000 = 3.247
1990: $885,000 ÷ $290,000 = 3.052

Quick ratio = (Cash + Marketable securities) ÷ Current liabilities

1989: ($312,000 + $120,000) ÷ $267,000 = 1.618
1990: ($10,000 + $125,000) ÷ $290,000 = .466

Return on assets = (Income from continuing operations + Interest expense) ÷ Total assets

1989: ($270,000 + $65,000) ÷ $1,532,000 = .219
1990: ($545,000 + $50,000) ÷ [($1,532,000 + $1,475,000) ÷ 2] = .396

Cost of debt = [Interest expense(1 – tax rate)] ÷ Interest–paying liabilities

1989: [$65,000(1 – 40%)] ÷ ($450,000 + $175,000) = .0624
1990: [$50,000(1 – 40%)] ÷ {[($450,000 + $175,000) + ($350,000 + $100,000] ÷ 2} = .056

Receivables turnover = Net credit sales ÷ Accounts receivable

1989: $1,410,000 ÷ $150,000 = 9.400
1990: $4,150,000 ÷ [($150,000 + $500,000) ÷ 2] = 12.769

Earnings per share = Income from continuing operations ÷ Common shares outstanding

1989: $270,000 ÷ 11,000 shares = $24.55
1990: $545,000 ÷ [(11,000 + 20,000) ÷ 2] = $35.16

Price/earnings ratio = Market price per share ÷ Earnings per share

1989: $45.00 ÷ $24.55 = 1.833
1990: $70.00 ÷ $35.16 = 1.991

Debt/equity ratio = Total liabilities ÷ Total stockholders' equity

1989: ($267,000 + $450,000) ÷ $815,000 = .880
1990: ($290,000 + $350,000) ÷ $835,000 = .766

Return on sales = Income from continuing operations ÷ Net sales

1989: $270,000 ÷ $4,185,000 = .065
1990: $545,000 ÷ $6,105,000 = .089

Financial leverage = Return on equity – Return on assets

1989: .331 – .219 = .112
1990: .661 – .396 = .265

Dividend yield = Dividend per share ÷ Market price per share

1989: ($10,000 ÷ 11,000 shares) ÷ $45 = .020
1990: [$595,000 ÷ (11,000 + 20,000) ÷ 2] ÷ $70 = .548

Return on investment = (Market price$_1$ – Market price$_0$ + Dividends per share) ÷ Market price$_0$
1989: ($45 – $50 + $0.91) ÷ $50 = –.082
1990: ($70 – $45 + $38.39) ÷ $45 = 1.409

Times interest earned = Pretax income from continuing operations ÷ Interest expense

1989: $445,000 ÷ $65,000 = 6.846
1990: $910,000 ÷ $50,000 = 18.200

Inventory turnover = Cost of goods sold ÷ Inventory

1989: $2,565,000 ÷ $210,000 = 12.214
1990: $4,015,000 ÷ [($210,000 + $200,000) ÷ 2] = 19.585

It appears that during 1990 the company became more efficient at using capital provided by all investors and by equity owners. Both return on assets and return on equity increased by almost 100% during 1990. Further, as evidenced by the increase in financial leverage, the company was also more effective at using debt to benefit its equity owners.

The dramatic increase in inventory turnover is probably the primary reason the company became more efficient at using capital. The higher number of inventory turns allowed the company to generate more profits, thereby increasing return on equity, return on assets, financial leverage, and earnings per share. The company also became more efficient at managing its costs, as evidenced by the increase in return on sales.

The only troubling aspect of the company's financial health is its solvency position. The company has more than sufficient current assets to meet its current liabilities (as evidenced by the current ratio). However, the lower level of and the large drop in the company's quick ratio indicates that the company has insufficient cash and near–cash assets to meet its current liabilities as they come due. If the company is to be able to meet its debts as they come due, it will have to be able to convert its other current assets to cash. The company's receivable turnover increased dramatically during 1990, which indicates that it is doing a better job of collecting from its customers. However, upon closer inspection of the receivable turnover, it appears that Mountain–Pacific may actually be doing a worse job of collecting from its customers. If the 1990 receivable turnover is calculated using the December 31, 1990 Accounts Receivable balance rather than the average receivable balance, the receivable turnover falls to 8.3. This turnover rate indicates that the company was turning over its receivables during 1990 at the same rate as in 1989. Further, the increase in inventory turnover may indicate future solvency problems. As inventory turnover increases, the company will have to acquire inventory more often. The more often Mountain–Pacific acquires inventory, the more often it will have to pay for it. Therefore, increasing the number of inventory turns places added pressure on the company to have sufficient cash to meet its debts as they come due. If the company is unable to generate cash from its receivables on a timely basis, and if it continues to suffer a decline in cash sales, it could very well experience severe solvency problems.

b. Based on the average of the company's 1989 and 1990 ratios, return on equity, current ratio, return on assets, cost of debt, receivables turnover, debt/equity ratio, and return on sales are almost identical to the industry averages. While the absolute levels of these ratios are similar, the trend of Mountain–Pacific's ratios provides additional information on the company's performance. Based on return on equity, the company has become more efficient during 1990 at managing owners' investments, and based on return on assets, the company has also become more efficient during 1990 at managing all investments, both debt and equity. These trends imply that the Mountain–Pacific has also become more effective at using debt to benefit its stockholders. Further, the company is now more efficient then the average company in the industry. Several other ratios, such as cost of debt, receivables turnover, and times interest earned, indicate that Mountain–Pacific is also performing better than the industry average.

The only troubling aspect of the company is its solvency position relative to the rest of the industry. As noted in Part (a), the dramatic drop in Mountain–Pacific's quick ratio could indicate solvency problems. When its quick ratio is compared to the industry average, the company's solvency position becomes even more troubling. The average company in the industry has more cash and marketable securities than current liabilities while Mountain–Pacific has over twice as much in current liabilities as the sum of cash and marketable securities. It may be that Mountain–Pacific is investing in long–term projects rather than holding cash or near–cash assets. Such a strategy may explain why the company has become more efficient (and now outperforms the industry) at managing debt and equity.

Without having additional information about the causes of Mountain–Pacific's solvency position, it is difficult to conclude how the company is performing relative the rest of the industry.

P17–12

As a loan officer, I would be concerned with whether a potential borrower has the ability to meet its debts as they come due. Since both companies are only requesting nine–month loans, I would be interested in the potential borrowers' short–term solvency. Therefore, I would examine their current ratios and quick ratios. Further, I would consider the effect of the potential loan on these ratios. The current ratio is calculated as current assets divided by current liabilities.

Selig Equipment: $715,000 ÷ ($285,000 + $125,000) = 1.74
Mountain Bike: $835,000 ÷ ($325,000 + $125,000) = 1.86

It appears that both companies have more than sufficient current assets to meet their current obligations, including the new loan. However, some current assets, such as prepaid expenses, accounts receivable, and inventory, are not near–cash assets. Therefore, a better measure of potential borrowers' ability to meet their current obligations is the quick ratio. This ratio is calculated as the sum of cash and marketable securities divided by current liabilities. Again, the effect of the additional debt should be considered.

Selig Equipment: $15,000 ÷ ($285,000 + $125,000) =.037
Mountain Bike: $160,000 ÷ ($325,000 + $125,000) = .356

Based upon the quick ratio, Mountain Bike, Inc. appears to be a much better risk than Selig Equipment. Mountain Bike has approximately ten times more near–cash assets available than Selig Equipment to meet its current obligations. Therefore, Mountain Bike does not have to rely as heavily on converting other assets to cash as Selig Equipment does to meet its current obligations. However, neither company has sufficient near–cash assets to meet their current obligations. So the company that can most readily convert its inventory and accounts receivable to cash might be the better risk. Two possible measures of a company's ability to generate cash from its receivables and inventory are the turnover and number–of–days ratios. Receivable turnover is calculated as net credit sales divided by accounts receivable, while the numbers of days for receivables is calculated as 365 divided by the receivables turnover.

Receivables turnover

Selig Equipment: $1,005,000 ÷ $215,000 = 4.67
Mountain Bike: $1,625,000 ÷ $470,000 = 3.46

Number of days

Selig Equipment: 365 ÷ 4.67 = 78.16
Mountain Bike: 365 ÷ 3.46 = 105.49

These ratios indicate that Selig Equipment, on average, collects its receivables 27 days quicker than Mountain Bike. Therefore, Selig can more easily convert its receivables to cash than Mountain Bike can.

Inventory turnover is calculated as cost of goods sold divided by inventory, while number of days is calculated as 365 divided by inventory turnover.

Inventory turnover

Selig Equipment: $755,000 ÷ $305,000 = 2.48
Mountain Bike: $960,000 ÷ $195,000 = 4.92

Number of days

Selig Equipment: 365 ÷ 2.48 = 147.18
Mountain Bike: 365 ÷ 4.92 = 74.19

These ratios bode well for Mountain Bike. Mountain Bike sells its inventory, on average, 73 days sooner than Selig Equipment sells its inventory. This difference implies that Mountain Bike generates more sales which, in turn, implies that it generates more accounts receivable. Although Mountain Bike does not turn over its receivables as often as Selig, it has a larger amount of receivables to turn over. Therefore, Mountain Bike potentially has more assets that can easily be converted into cash than Selig Equipment.

Based upon Mountain Bike's superior quick ratio and potential ability to generate cash from its superior receivable base, I would recommend that the bank grant the loan to Mountain Bike.

P17–13

a. Watson Metal Products would report the following 1990 income statement amounts under each financing alternative.

	Alternative 1	Alternative 2	Alternative 3
Income from operations	$16,500,000	$16,500,000	$16,500,000
Interest expense	4,000,000	4,750,000	4,375,000
Income from continuing operations (before taxes)	12,500,000	11,750,000	12,125,000
Income taxes*	5,000,000	4,700,000	4,850,000
Income from continuing operations	$ 7,500,000	$ 7,050,000	$ 7,275,000

* Tax rate = Income taxes ÷ Income from continuing operations before taxes
= $4,400,000 ÷ $11,000,000

The formulas for the requested ratios follow:

Earnings per share = Income from continuing operations ÷ Average common shares outstanding
Return on equity = Income from continuing operations ÷ Average stockholders' equity
Return on assets = (Income from continuing operations + Interest expense) ÷ Average total assets
Financial leverage = Return on equity – Return on assets
Debt/equity ratio = Total liabilities ÷ Total stockholders' equity

Note: Although several of the ratios use averages, ending balances were used, as specified in the problem.

Alternative 1
Earnings per share: ($7,500,000) ÷ (2,000,000 shares* + 200,000 shares) = $3.41

---

* 2,000,000 shares = Income from continuing operations ÷ Earnings per share
= $6,600,000 ÷ $3.30 per share.

Return on equity: ($7,500,000) ÷ ($45,000,000 + $5,000,000[a] + $7,500,000[b]) = .1304

---

[a] $5,000,000 = 200,000 shares issued x $25 per share
[b] $7,500,000 = 1990 income from continuing operations

Return on assets: ($7,500,000 + $4,000,000) ÷ ($35,000,000 + $45,000,000 + $5,000,000 + $7,500,000) = .1243

Financial leverage: .1304 – .1243 = .0061

Debt/equity ratio: $35,000,000 ÷ ($45,000,000 + $5,000,000 + $7,500,000) = .609

Alternative 2
Earnings per share: $7,050,000 ÷ 2,000,000 shares = $3.53

Return on equity: $7,050,000 ÷ ($45,000,000 + $7,050,000) = .1354

Return on assets: ($7,050,000 + $4,750,000) ÷ ($35,000,000 + $45,000,000 + $5,000,000 + $7,050,000) = .1282

Financial leverage: .1354 – .1282 = .0072

Debt/equity ratio: ($35,000,000 + $5,000,000) ÷ ($45,000,000 + $7,050,000) = .768

Alternative 3
Earnings per share: $7,275,000 ÷ (2,000,000 + 100,000 shares) = $3.46

Return on equity: $7,275,000 ÷ ($45,000,000 + $2,500,000* + $7,275,000) = .1328

---

* $2,500,000 = 100,000 shares x $25 per share

Return on assets: ($7,275,000 + $4,375,000) ÷ ($35,000,000 + $45,000,000 + $5,000,000 + $7,275,000) = .1263

Financial leverage: .1328– .1263 = .0065

Debt/equity ratio: ($35,000,000 + $2,500,000) ÷ ($45,000,000 + $2,500,000 + $7,725,000) = .685

b. Alternative 2 prevents a dilution of the stockholders' position. Since this alternative did not require any additional shares of stock to be issued, it provides the largest earnings per share. Alternative 2 allows the company to most effectively manage its stockholders' investment, as evidenced by return on equity, and all investments, as evidenced by return on assets. The only potential serious drawback of this alternative is that it makes the company more risky, as evidenced by the largest debt/equity ratio. Further, Alternative 2 allows the company to use debt to benefit stockholders more effectively than allowed with either of the other alternatives. Under Alternative 3, stockholders earn a slightly smaller return on their investment, but incur fewer risks, since the company has issued less debt. Alternative 1 provides a marginally lower return to stockholders, but imposes even less risk on them. Stockholders must trade off the risk from issuing debt against the benefits of issuing debt. If the company is close to violating debt covenants or projects weak future cash flows, than Alternatives 1 or 3 would probably be preferable. But if the company is not close to violating debt covenants or projects strong future cash flows, then Alternatives 2 or 3 would probably be preferable.

c. **Alternative 1**
$3.30 = ($6,600,000 + Income from expansion project) ÷ (2,000,000 shares + 200,000 shares)

Income from expansion project = $660,000

Alternative 2
$3.30 = ($6,600,000 + Income from expansion project) ÷ 2,000,000 shares

Income from expansion project = $0

Alternative 3
$3.30 = ($6,600,000 + Income from expansion project) ÷ (2,000,000 shares + 100,000 shares)

Income from expansion project = $330,000

P17–14

a. Return on equity = Income from continuing operations ÷ Total stockholders' equity
.75 = $450,000 ÷ Total stockholders' equity
Total stockholders' equity = $600,000

b. Debt/equity ratio = Total liabilities ÷ Total stockholders' equity
.4 = total liabilities ÷ $600,000
Total liabilities = $240,000

c. Total assets = Total liabilities + Total stockholders' equity
Total assets = $240,000 + $600,000 = $840,000

d. Return on assets = (Income from continuing operations + Interest expense) ÷ Total assets
.65 = ($450,000 + Interest expense) ÷ $840,000
Interest expense = $96,000

e. Income from continuing operations after taxes = Income from continuing operations before taxes x (1 – tax rate)

$450,000 = Income from continuing operations before taxes x (1 – 34%)

Income from continuing operations before taxes = $681,818

f. Return on sales = Income from continuing operations ÷ Net sales

.2 = $450,000 ÷ Net sales

Net sales = $2,250,000

g. Credit sales = 80% x Net sales

= 80% x $2,250,000

= $1,800,000

h. Receivable turnover = Net credit sales ÷ Accounts receivable

25 = $1,800,000 ÷ Accounts receivable

Accounts receivable = $72,000

i. Cost of goods sold = 70% x Net sales

= 55% x $2,250,000

= $1,237,500

j. Average days' supply of inventory = 365 ÷ Inventory turnover

12.167 = 365 ÷ Inventory turnover

Inventory turnover = 30

k. Inventory turnover = Cost of goods sold ÷ Inventory

30 = $1,237,500 ÷ Inventory

Inventory = $41,250

l. Current liabilities = 35% x Total liabilities

= 35% x $240,000

= $84,000

m. Current ratio = Current assets ÷ Current liabilities

3.00 = Current assets ÷ $84,000

Current assets = $252,000

n. Quick ratio = (Cash + Marketable securities) ÷ Current liabilities

1.5 = ($68,000 + Marketable securities) ÷ $84,000

Marketable securities = $58,000

o. Noncurrent assets = Total assets – Current assets

= $840,000 – $252,000

= $588,000

p. Earnings per share = Income from continuing operations ÷ Number of common shares outstanding

$16.00 = $450,000 ÷ Common shares outstanding

Number of common shares outstanding = 28,125 shares

q. Total par value of common shares outstanding = Number of common shares outstanding x par value per share

= 28,125 shares x $10 per share

= $281,250

C17–1

a. Return on equity is computed by dividing income from continuing operations by average stockholders' equity. This ratio compares the profits generated by a company to the investment made by the company's stockholders. Quaker Oats expresses its financial objective in such terms to provide equity providers with a relevant and important measure of expected performance. The ratio is a measure of the efficiency with which the stockholders investment is being managed.

b. Without the inflation adjustment to convert to "real" earnings per share and "real" earnings growth, stockholders might get a false sense of these measures because inflation is included in the historical amounts. Over time, the dollar is not stable, even though, generally accepted accounting principles assume no inflation. Removing the effects of inflation provides investors with a 'constant-dollar' measure of these ratios.

c. Earning power refers to a company's ability to increase its wealth through operations and generate assets in the future. Solvency refers to a company's ability to meet its obligations as they come due. Accordingly, Objectives 1 through 3 refer to measures of earning power because they relate to wealth and growth. Objective 4 refers to solvency because it addresses Quakers' financial position and credit ratings.

C17–2

a. This excerpt implies that Allegheny International's status as a going concern is contingent upon its ability to consummate the reference merger and maintain adequate financing. Such information is useful to investors because it reveals that Allegheny may be a risky investment. The continued operation and profitability of a company is questionable when it receives a "going concern" exception in its audit opinion.

b. An investor, creditor or other interested party would be wise to collect other information about Allegheny, based on the message conveyed in the audit opinion. Because the continued existence of the company is contingent upon the merger, an interested party would want to followup on the progress of the merger and be attentive to Allegheny's progress in meeting its financing and operating goals. The auditor's letter provides this incentive, which would not be apparent in just a reading of the financial statement numbers.

C17–3

a. A company's choice of depreciation methods has no direct cash flow effects. It is observed only in reported earnings. Investors and creditors are able to make adjustments themselves when they interpret such financial statements. They are able to "see through" the cosmetic changes a company makes. An important effect of changing depreciation methods would be the implications for existing bond covenants. If a heightened depreciation charge makes a debt covenant "binding," this may be sending a signal to the company's creditors regarding future projects.

b. Because there is no direct cash flow effect of the depreciation method used, it would be unlikely that credit-rating agencies would give lower ratings to companies using conservative depreciation methods. The change in method may provide a signal to the credit-rating agency to probe into reasons for the change and may thus reveal some other relevant aspect, but the depreciation change, per se, is unlikely to affect a company's rating.

c. Switching to a less conservative depreciation method would decrease the company's depreciation expense and, therefore, increase its net income. If management was paid a bonus based on the level of net income, any device that increases net income would be viewed favorably. Further, higher net income increases stockholders' equity through the Retained Earnings account, thereby decreasing the company's debt/equity ratio. Since this ratio is often used in debt covenants, the change in depreciation methods would decrease the probability the company would violate the covenant.

d. Companies that use conservative deprecation methods may be viewed more favorable by investors because the company is viewed as being able to absorb the heightened charge to income of a higher depreciation expense. This implies that the quality of their earnings is higher than for companies that use other methods.

C17–4

a. Economists, who hold the concept of human capital in broad terms, are correct in their assessment that it is a component of the wealth of an organization. Accountants, however, lack an objective and verifiable method of valuing such capital. Accordingly, accountants believe it is best to not value it because such a valuation would be open to dispute.

b. The auditor would have a hard time stating that human capital is valued 'fairly." The methods and procedures used to record the value of fixes assets are not available for human capital valuations. The legal liability faced by auditors would preclude them from accepting any value of human capital as fair.

c. The financial statements of companies that use the most human resources would tend to be misstated the most. These would include principally service companies, which rely almost exclusively on human capital for their productive capabilities. Other companies (i.e., manufacturers) have a directly measurable sense of their productive resources in the form of machinery and inventory.

d. Some limitations of financial accounting information include no accrued goodwill, few market values, no inflation adjustments, and management biases and incentives. Goodwill represents the value of the company as a working unit. It is not recorded on the financial statements (unless purchased in an acquisition and therefore directly measurable), yet it represents a major component of a company's continued existence. Few market values are included on financial statements because historical costs are relied upon. Individuals interested in replacement-cost information must gather it elsewhere. Finally, the biases and incentives of management are directly reflected by the choice of accounting methods and the manner of presentation of accounting information. In a sense, investors are presented with only one alternative of reporting, which may favor management. Other points of view are not included.

C17–5

a. An efficient market implies that all publicly available information is reflected in the price of a security immediately. Therefore, it would be difficult to use financial accounting information to identify undervalued securities, because the information contained in the reports would already be reflected in the value of the stock.

b. Accounting information can be useful in assessing the risk and return associated with a particular stock, which are important components of an investor's decision to invest or not. Further, banks use financial statement analysis in their loan decisions. Also, the information contained in reports can be used to assess the probability of bankruptcy and provide some sense of the future cash flow of a company. Thus, while financial reports are not useful in identifying undervalued securities traded in an efficient market, they do provide other relevant information.

APPENDIX A The Time Value of Money

EA–1

a. Dollar amount = \$20,000 x Future value factor for i = 10% and n = 4
= \$20,000 x 1.46410 (from Table 1 in App. A)*
= \$29,282

* All references to table numbers are to the tables in Appendix A.

b. Dollar amount = \$29,282 (from Part [a]) x Future value factor for i = 12% and n = 3
= \$29,282 x 1.40493 (from Table 1)
= \$41,139.16

c. Dollar amount = \$41,139.16 (from Part [b]) x Future value factor for i = 15% and n = 5
= \$41,139.16 x 2.01136 (from Table 1)
= \$82,745.66

EA–2

a. Dollar amount = (\$500,000 x Present value factor for i = 12% and n = 10) + (\$50,000 x Present value of an ordinary annuity factor for i = 12% and n = 10)
= (\$500,000 x .32197 from Table 4 in App. A) + (\$50,000 x 5.65022 from Table 5)
= \$160,985 + \$282,511
= \$443,496

b. The dollar amount can be calculated in one of the following ways.

Dollar amount = (\$500,000 x Present value factor for i = 12% and n = 10) + (\$50,000 x Present value of an annuity due factor for i = 12% and n = 10)
= (\$500,000 x .32197 from Table 4) + (\$50,000 x 6.32825 from Table 6)
= \$160,985.00 + \$316,412.50
= \$477,397.50

Dollar amount = (\$500,000 x Present value factor for i = 12% and n = 10) + \$50,000 + (\$50,000 x Present value of an ordinary annuity factor for i = 12% and n = 9)
= (\$500,000 x .32197 from Table 4) + \$50,000 + (\$50,000 x 5.32825 from Table 5)
= \$160,985.00 + \$50,000.00 + \$266,412.50
= \$477,397.50

EA–3

Option 1

Present value = \$500,000 x Present value of an ordinary annuity factor for i = 10% and n = 20
= \$500,000 x 8.51356 (from Table 5)
= \$4,256,780

Option 2

Present value = \$4,500,000

Option 3

Present value = $1,000,000 + [($2,100,000 x Present value of an ordinary annuity factor for i = 10% and n = 3) x Present value factor for i = 10% and n = 4]
= $1,000,000 + [($2,100,000 x 2.48685 from Table 5) x .68301 from Table 4]
= $1,000,000 + $3,566,942
= $4,566,942

Option 3 has the highest present value.

EA–4

		Ordinary Annuity	Annuity Due
a.	$800 x 2.48685 (from Table 5)	$1,989.48	
	$800 x 2.73554 (from Table 6)		$2,188.43
b.	$800 + ($800 x 1.73554 from Table 5)	$2,188.43	
	($800 x 1.10000 from Table 1) + $800 + ($800 x .90909 from Table 4)		$2,407.27
c.	($800 x 1.10000 from Table 1) + $800 + ($800 x .90909 from Table 4)	$2,407.27	
	$800 x 3.31000 (from Table 3)		$2,648.00
d.	$800 x 3.31000 (from Table 2)	$2,648.00	
	$800 x 3.64100 (from Table 3)		$2,912.80

e. The present value is the value of future cash values at the current point in time. Therefore, the values in Part (a) represent the present value of the two different annuities.

f. The future value is the value of future cash flows at a future point in time. Since the ends of Periods 1, 2, and 3 are all in the future, the value of the cash flows at those points in time all qualify as future values.

EA–5

a. **Option 1**

Present value = $240,000

Option 2

Present value = $500,000 x Present value factor for i = 12% and n = 8
= $500,000 x .40388 (from Table 4)
= $201,940

Option 3

Present value = $600,000 x Present value factor for i = 12% and n = 10
= $600,000 x .32197 (from Table 4)
= $193,182

Option 4

Present value = \$50,000 x Present value of an annuity due factor for i = 12% and n = 6
= \$50,000 x 4.60478 (from Table 6)
= \$230,239

OR

Present value = \$50,000 + (\$50,000 x Present value of an ordinary annuity factor for i = 12% and n = 5)
= \$50,000 + (\$50,000 x 3.60478 from Table 5)
= \$230,239

b. By comparing the present value of the future cash flows of each option, the cost of each option is comparable. Since Option 3 gives rise to the lowest present value of future cash outflows, it appears to be the best possible deal for Dunn Drafting Company.

c. **Option 1**

Present value = \$240,000

Option 2

Present value = \$500,000 x Present value factor for i = 8% and n = 8
= \$500,000 x .54027 (from Table 4)
= \$270,135

Option 3

Present value = \$600,000 x Present value factor for i = 8% and n = 10
= \$600,000 x .46319 (from Table 4)
= \$277,914

Option 4

Present value = \$50,000 x Present value of an annuity due factor for i = 12% and n = 6
= \$50,000 x 4.99271 (from Table 6)
= \$249,635.50

Option 1 now minimizes the present value of future cash flows. Therefore, it appears to be the best possible deal for Dunn Drafting Company.

EA–6

a. Since the Croziers plan to invest a lump sum today and then withdraw money in the form of an annuity, two steps are required to determine how much the Croziers must invest today to pay for Ryan's college education. The first step is to calculate how much money they will need fifteen years from now when Ryan enters college to make the four payments at the end of each year Ryan is in college (i.e., the value of the annuity). The second step is to calculate how much they would have to invest so that it will grow to the value calculated in the first step over the next fifteen years. The calculations are shown below.

Present value of college expenses fifteen years in the future:

Value = \$35,000 x Present value of an ordinary annuity factor for i = 10% and n = 4
= \$35,000 x 3.16986 (from Table 5)
= \$110,945.10

Present value of college expenses today:

Value = \$110,945.10 x Present value factor for i = 10% and n = 15
= \$110,945.10 x .23939 (from Table 4)
= \$26,559.15

b. The present value of fifteen annual payments must equal the present value of $26,559.15 calculated in Part (a). Therefore, by using the following formula, the amount of the annual payments can be calculated.

Present value = Annuity payment x Present value of an ordinary annuity factor for $i = 10\%$ and $n = 15$
$26,559.15 = Annuity payment x 7.82371 (from Table 5)
Annuity payment = $3,491.83

c. **Current Investment**
Present value of college expenses fifteen years in the future
Value = $35,000 x Present value of an ordinary annuity factor for $i = 8\%$ and $n = 4$
= $35,000 x 3.31213 (from Table 5)
= $115,924.55

Present value of college expense today
Value = $115,924.55 x Present value factor for $i = 8\%$ and $n = 15$
= $115,924.55 x .31524 (from Table 4)
= $36,544.06

Annuity payment
$36,544.06 = Annuity payment x 8.55948 (from Table 5)
Annuity payment = $4,269.42

PA–1

The price that Christie is willing to pay for the stock is comprised of two components: the present value of the dividends received while holding the investment and the present value of the proceeds upon sale of the investment. The values of these two components are calculated below.

Present value of dividends
Present value = ($5 x .86957 from Table 4) + ($6 x .75614 from Table 4) + ($7 x .65752 from Table 4) + ($8 x .57175 from Table 4)
= $4.34785 + $4.53684 + $4.60264 + $4.574
= $18.06

Present value of proceeds from sale
Present value = $100 x .57175 from Table 4)
= $57.18

Total present value = $18.06 + $57.18
= $75.24

Therefore, Christie would be willing to pay up to $75.24 for one share of South Bend Iron Works.

PA–2

a. **Investment 1**
Present value = ($1,000 x Future value of an ordinary annuity factor for $i = 10\%$ and $n = 5$) x Future value factor for $i = 12\%$ and $n = 5$
= ($1,000 x 6.10510 from Table 2) x 1.76234 from Table 1)
= $10,759.26

Investment 2

Present value = \$3,000 x Future value of an ordinary annuity factor for $i = 15\%$ and $n = 7$
= \$3,000 x 11.06680 (from Table 2)
= \$33,200.40

Therefore, Wharton's total investment at the end of ten years will equal \$43,959.66.

b. Current investment = Future value x Present value factor for $i = 12\%$ and $n = 10$
= \$43,959.66 (from Part A) x .32197 (from Table 4)
= \$14,153.69

Therefore, Wharton would have to invest \$14,153.69 for ten years earning 12% compounded annually to have an amount equivalent to the two investments.

PA–3

a. **Contract 1**

Present value = \$8,000 x Present value of an annuity due factor for $i = 6\%$ and $n = 10$
= \$8,000 x 7.80169 (from Table 6)
= \$62,413.52

OR

Present value = \$8,000 + (\$8,000 x Present value of an ordinary annuity factor for $i = 6\%$ and $n = 9$
= \$8,000 + (\$8,000 x 6.80169 from Table 5)
= \$62,413.52

Contract 2

Present value = \$8,000 + (\$20,000 x Present value factor for $i = 12\%$ and $n = 10$)
= \$8,000 + (\$20,000 x .32197 from Table 4)
= \$14,439.40

Contract 3

Present value = (\$8,000 x Present value factor of an ordinary annuity factor for $i = 10\%$ and $n = 3$) x Present value factor for $i = 10\%$ and $n = 3$
= (\$8,000 x 2.48685 from Table 5) x .75132 from Table 4
= \$14,947.36

b. (1) Equivalent values at the end of Year 5:

Contract 1

Value = (\$8,000 x Future value of an annuity due factor for $i = 6\%$ and $n = 5$) + (\$8,000 x Present value of an annuity due factor for $i = 6\%$ and $n = 5$)
= (\$8,000 x 5.97532 from Table 3) + (\$8,000 x 4.46511 from Table 6)
= \$47,802.56 + \$35,720.88
= \$83,523.44

Proof: \$83,523.20 x .74726 = 62,413.54 = Present value of Contract 1 in Part (a)

Contract 2

Value = (\$8,000 x Future value factor for i = 12% and n = 5) + (\$20,000 x Present value factor for i = 12% and n = 5)
= (\$8,000 x 1.76234 from Table 1) + (\$20,000 x .56743 from Table 4)
= \$14,098.72 + \$11,348.60
= \$25,447.32

Proof: \$25,447.32 x .56743 = \$14,439.57 = Present value of Contract 2 in Part (a)

Contract 3

Value = (\$8,000 x Future value factor for i = 10% and n = 1) + \$8,000 + (\$8,000 x Present value factor for i = 10% and n = 1)
= (\$8,000 x 1.10000 from Table 1) + \$8,000 + (\$8,000 x .90909 from Table 4)
= \$24,072.72

Proof: \$24,072.72 x .62092 = \$14,947.23 = Present value of Contract 3 in Part (a)

(2) Equivalent values at the end of Year 10:

Contract 1

Value = (\$8,000 x Future value of an annuity due factor for i = 6% and n = 10)
= (\$8,000 x 13.97164 from Table 3)
= \$111,773.12

Proof: \$111,773.12 x .55839 = 62,412.99 = Present value of Contract 1 in Part (a)

Contract 2

Value = (\$8,000 x Future value factor for i = 12% and n = 10) + \$20,000
= (\$8,000 x 3.10585 from Table 1) + \$20,000
= \$24,846.80 + \$20,000
= \$44,846.80

Proof: \$44,846.80 x .32197 = \$14,439.32 = Present value of Contract 2 in Part (a)

Contract 3

Value = (\$8,000 x Future value of an ordinary annuity factor for i = 10% and n = 3) x Future value factor for i = 10% and n = 4
= (\$8,000 x 3.31000 from Table 2) x 1.46410 from Table 1
= \$38,769.37

Proof: \$38,769.37 x .38554 = \$14,947.14 = Present value of Contract 3 in Part (a)

PA–4

Option 1

Present value = \$25,000

Option 2

Present value = \$60,000 x Present value factor for i = 9% and n = 8
= \$60,000 x .50187 (from Table 4)
= \$30,112.20

Option 3

Present value = \$5,000 + (\$27,000 x Present value factor for i = 9% and n = 3) + (\$20,000 x Present value factor for i = 9% and n = 20)
= \$5,000 + (\$27,000 x .77218 from Table 4) + (\$20,000 x .17843 from Table 4)
= \$5,000 + \$20,848.86 + \$3,568.60
= \$29,417.46

Option 2 provides the highest present value.

PA–5

Equivalent value today

Value = \$5,000 + (\$10,000 x Present value of an ordinary annuity factor for i = 8% and n = 5) + (\$15,000 x Present value factor for i = 8% and n = 5)
= \$5,000 + (\$10,000 x 3.99271 from Table 5) + (\$15,000 x .68058 from Table 4)
= \$5,000 + \$39,927.10 + \$10,208.70
= \$55,135.80

Equivalent value at end of Year 2

Value = (\$5,000 x Future value factor for i = 8% and n = 2) + (\$10,000 x Future value factor for i = 8% and n = 1) + \$10,000 + (\$10,000 x Present value of an ordinary annuity factor for i = 8% and n = 3) + (\$15,000 x Present value factor for i = 8% and n = 3)
= (\$5,000 x 1.16640 from Table 1) + (\$10,000 x 1.08000 from Table 1) + \$10,000 + (\$10,000 x 2.57710 from Table 5) + (\$15,000 x .79383 from Table 4)
= \$5,832.00 + \$10,800.00 + \$10,000.00 + \$25,771.00 + 11,907.45
= \$64,310.45

Equivalent value at end of Year 4

Value = (\$5,000 x Future value factor for i = 8% and n = 4) + (\$10,000 x Future value of an ordinary annuity factor for i = 8% and n = 4) + [(\$10,000 + \$15,000) x Present value of an factor for i = 8% and n = 1)
= (\$5,000 x 1.36049 from Table 1) + (\$10,000 x 4.50611 from Table 2) + (\$25,000 x .92593 from Table 4)
= \$6,802.45 + \$45,061.10 + \$23,148.25
= \$75,011.80

Equivalent value at end of Year 5

Value = (\$5,000 x Future value factor for i = 8% and n = 5) + (\$10,000 x Future value of an ordinary annuity factor for i = 8% and n = 5 + \$15,000
= (\$5,000 x 1.46933 from Table 1) + (\$10,000 x 5.86660 from Table 2) + \$15,000
= \$7,346.65 + 58,666.00 + \$15,000.00
= \$81,012.65

Proof

Value of each equivalent value today

	Option 1	**Option 2**	**Option 3**	**Option 4**
1. \$55,135.80 x 1.00000	\$55,136			
2. \$64,310.45 x 0.85734		\$55,136		
3. \$75,011.80 x 0.73503			\$55,136	
4. \$81,012.65 x 0.68058				\$55,136

PA–6

Present Values

Case A

Value = $10,000

Case B

Value = $2,000 x Present value of an ordinary annuity factor for i = 12% and n = 8
= $2,000 x 4.96764 (from Table 5)
= $9,935.28

Case C

Value = $5,000 x Present value of an annuity due factor for i = 12% and n = 3
= $5,000 x 2.69005 (from Table 6)
= $13,450.25

Case D

Value = $3,000 x Present value of an ordinary annuity factor for i = 12% and n = 5
= $3,000 x 3.60478 (from Table 5)
= $10,814.34

Case E

Value = $25,000 x Present value factor for i = 12% and n = 7
= $25,000 x .45235 (from Table 4)
= $11,308.75

Case F

Value = $3,000 x Present value of an ordinary annuity factor for i = 12% and n = 2
= $3,000 x 1.69005 (from Table 5)
= $5,070.15

Case G

Value = $4,000 x Present value of an annuity due factor for i = 12% and n = 3
= $4,000 x 2.69005 (from Table 6)
= $10,760.20

Future Values

Case A

Value = $10,000 x Future value factor for i = 12% and n = 4
= $10,000 x 1.57352 (from Table 1)
= $15,735.20

Case B

Value = $2,000 x Future value of an ordinary annuity factor for i = 12% and n = 8
= $2,000 x 12.29969 (from Table 2)
= $24,599.38

Case C

Value = $5,000 x Future value or an annuity due factor for i = 12% and n = 3
= $5,000 x 3.77933 (from Table 3)
= $18,896.65

Case D

Value = (\$3,000 x Future value of an ordinary annuity factor for i = 12% and n = 5) x Future value factor for i = 12% and n = 5
= (\$3,000 x 6.35285 from Table 2) x 1.76234 from Table 1)
= \$33,587.65

Case E

Value = \$25,000.00

Case F

Value = \$3,000 x Future value of an ordinary annuity factor for i = 12% and n = 2
= \$3,000 x 2.12000 (from Table 2)
= \$6,360.00

Case G

Value = \$4,000 x Future value of an annuity due factor for i = 12% and n = 3
= \$4,000 x 3.77933 (from Table 3)
= \$15,117.32

PA–7

a. The contract specifies two types of future cash flows: annual receipts of \$2,000 for ten years and a lump–sum receipt of \$300,000 in ten years. To determine whether the offer of \$110,000 today is a good deal, the future cash flows must be converted into equivalent values in present dollars (i.e., present values). The present value of both types of future cash flows are calculated below.

(1) Present value of annual receipts

Present value = \$2,000 x Present value of an annuity due factor for i = 10% and n = 10
= \$2,000 x 6.75902 (from Table 6)
= \$13,518.04

(2) Present value of lump–sum receipt

Present value = \$300,000 x Present value factor for i = 10% and n = 10
= \$300,000 x .38554 (from Table 4)
= \$115,662.00

(3) Total present value

Present value = \$13,518.04 + \$115,662.00
= \$129,180.04

Since the present value of the future cash flows exceeds \$110,000, it would not be wise for JoyDon to accept the \$110,000 in place of the note.

b. As the discount rate increases, the present value of future cash flows decreases. Since the present value of the future cash flows discounted at 10% exceeds \$110,000, the discount rate at which JoyDon would be wise to accept \$110,000 instead of the note must be greater than 10%.

Try 12%

Present value = (\$2,000 x 6.32825 from Table 6) + (\$300,000 x .32197 from Table 4)
= \$12,656.50 + 96,591.00
= \$109,247.50

With a discount rate of 12%, the present value of the future cash flows is less than \$110,000. Therefore, JoyDon would be better off accepting \$110,000 rather than accepting the note.

APPENDIX B Error Corrections

EB–1

a.

	Rent Revenue per Company's Books	Correct Rent Revenue	Annual Difference	Cumulative Difference
1990	$450,000	$150,0000	$300,000	$300,000
1991	0	150,000	(150,000)	150,000
1992	0	150,000	(150,000)	0
Total	$450,000	$450,000	0	

b. Rent revenue will be understated by $150,000 in 1992.

c. The account balance of Collections of Rent in Advance will be understated by $150,000 as of December 31, 1991.

d. Retained Earnings will be overstated by $150,000 after closing entries on December 31, 1991.

e. Retained Earnings will be overstated by $300,000 prior to closing entries on December 31, 1991.

f. The balance sheet accounts will be correctly stated after closing entries on December 31, 1992. At that point in time, the company has fulfilled its obligation to the tenants and, consequently, has no further liabilities associated with the rent collected in advance. Further, the entire $450,000 should have been recognized as rent revenue by December 31, 1992, so the amount has correctly flowed into Retained Earnings.

EB–2

1. Error discovered prior to closing the books on December 31, 1988:

	Debit	Credit
Prepaid Insurance	8,000	
Insurance Expense		8,000
To adjust for insurance policy not yet expired.		

2. Error discovered prior to closing the books on December 31, 1989:

	Debit	Credit
Prepaid Insurance	4,000	
Insurance Expense	4,000	
Retained Earnings		8,000
To correct the books for a prior incorrect entry.		

3. Error discovered prior to closing the books on December 31, 1990:

	Debit	Credit
Insurance Expense	4,000	
Retained Earnings		4,000
To correct the books for a prior incorrect entry.		

4. Error discovered prior to closing the books on December 31, 1991. No correcting journal entry is necessary. Since the policy expired at the end of 1990, no policy exists that will provide a future benefit. (i.e., no asset) and no asset was consumed or no liability was created during 1991 associated with the policy (i.e., no expense). Consequently, the error has counterbalanced itself, and the books are now correctly stated.

EB–3

a. Accumulated Depreciation 60,000*
Retained Earnings 60,000
To correct for an error.

---

* $60,000 = $240,000 accumulated depreciation – {[$500,000 – $20,000) ÷ 8 years] x 3 years}

Depreciation Expense	48,000	
Accumulated Depreciation		48,000
To record depreciation for 1991.		

b.

Depreciation Expense	48,000*	
Accumulated Depreciation		48,000
To record depreciation for 1991.		

---

* $48,000 = [($500,000 – $240,000 of accumulated depreciation) – $20,000] ÷ 5 years

c. The latter accounting treatment is appropriate. The useful life estimated by the company on January 1, 1988 was correct given the information the company had at its disposal. During 1990 the company acquired new information that allowed it to make a better estimate. The company never made an error; it simply had insufficient information to make the appropriate estimate. Hence, the change in the estimated useful life should be accounted for as a revision of an estimate.

EB–4

a.

1986 Bad debt estimate*	$480		
1986 Write-offs	(700)		
12/31/86 Allowance balance		($220)	
1987 Bad debt estimate*		620	
1987 Write-offs		(500)	
12/31/87 Allowance balance			($100)
1988 Bad debt estimate*			700
1988 Write-offs			(750)
12/31/88 Allowance balance			($150)

---

* Bad debt estimate for 1986, 1987, and 1988 = Credit sales x 2%.

b.

Bad Debt Expense	1,175*	
Allowance for Doubtful Accounts		1,175
To record bad debt expense.		

---

* $1,175 = $47,000 in credit sales x 2.5%.

c.

1986 Bad debt estimate*	$600		
1986 Write-offs	(700)		
12/31/86 Allowance balance		($100)	
1987 Bad debt estimate*		775	
1987 Write-offs		(500)	
12/31/87 Allowance balance			$175
1988 Bad debt estimate*			875
1988 Write-offs			(750)
12/31/88 Allowance balance			$ 300

* Bad debt estimate for 1986, 1987, and 1988 = Credit Sales x 2.5%.

d.

Retained Earning	450*	
Allowance for Doubtful Accounts		450
To correct books for a prior error.		

* $450 = 12/31/88 allowance balance (Part [c]) – 12/31/88 allowance balance (Part [a])

e. The change to 2.5% should be considered a revision of an estimate. An estimate may not necessarily be accurate and will be subject to revision as better information becomes available. In 1986 when the company began, it used all available information and decided that 2% of credit sales would prove to be uncollectible. In 1989, the company acquired better information (i.e., the trend in accounts written off) and decided that 2.5% would be a better estimate of the portion of credit sales that would prove to be uncollectible. Since the company used the information available at the time of making both decisions, the change to 2.5% should be considered a revision of an estimate and not the correction of an error.

EB–5

a.

Clements, Inc.
Income Statement
For the Year Ended December 31, 1988

Revenues			
Sales		$ 760,000	
Less: Sales discounts		50,000	
Net sales			$710,000
Cost of goods sold			
Beginning inventory		900,000	
Purchases	$450,000		
Less: Purchase returns	40,000		
Net purchases		410,000	
Cost of goods available for sale		1,310,000	
Less: Ending inventory		795,000	
Cost of goods sold			515,000
Gross profit			195,000
Operating expenses			
Selling expenses		225,000	
Administrative expenses		110,000	
Depreciation expenses		96,000	
Total operating expenses			431,000
Income (Loss) from operations			(236,000)
Gain on sale of marketable securities			320,000
Income from continuing operations (before taxes)			84,000
Income taxes			28,560
Income from continuing operations			55,440
Extraordinary loss from flood (net of tax benefit of $192,100)			372,900
Net loss			–$317,460

b.

Clements, Inc.
Statement of Retained Earnings
For the Year Ended December 31, 1988

Beginning retained earnings balance: January 1, 1988	$895,000
Less: Net loss	317,460
Dividends	200,000
Ending retained earnings balance: December 31, 1988	$377,540

EB–6

a.

Retained Earnings	25,000	
Cost of Goods Sold		25,000
To correct inventory physical count error.		

b.

Inventory	40,000	
Cost of Goods Sold		40,000
To correct inventory physical count error.		

c. Retained Earnings		25,000

	Debit	Credit
c. Retained Earnings	25,000	
Inventory	40,000	
Cost of Goods Sold		65,000
To correct inventory physical count error.		

	1991	1990
d. Sales	$800,000	$700,000
Cost of goods sold	285,000	325,000
Gross profit	515,000	375,000
Operating expenses	300,000	275,000
Net income	$215,000	$100,000

PB–1

	Debit	Credit
Retained Earnings	12,000[a]	
Unearned Revenue	4,000	
Fees Earned		8,000[b]
To correct the books for an error in a prior period.		

[a] $12,000 = $16,000 x Percentage of collection not earned as of January 1, 1989
= $16,000 x (1 – 25%)

[b] $8,000 = $16,000 x Percentage of collection earned during 1989
= $16,000 x 50%

PB–2

a.

	Depreciation Expense per Company's Books	Correct Depreciation Expense	Annual Difference	Cumulative Difference
1990	$500,000	$ 85,000	($415,000)	($415,000)
1991	0	85,000	85,000	(330,000)
1992	0	85,000	85,000	(245,000)
1993	0	85,000	85,000	(160,000)
1994	0	85,000	85,000	(75,000)
Total	$500,000	$425,000	($ 75,000)	

b. Accumulated depreciation will be understated by $340,000 as of December 31, 1993. Fixed assets will also understated by $500,000 resulting in total assets being understated by $160,000.

c. Retained earnings will be understated by $245,000 prior to closing entries on December 31, 1993.

d. Retained earnings will be understated by $160,000 after closing entries on December 31, 1993.

e. The company's books will continue to be misstated until the remaining error is detected and corrected. Over the estimated five–year life, the books corrected themselves in the amount of $425,000, which represents the depreciation base of the computers. However, the books are still misstated for the salvage value. As of December 31, 1994, the salvage value represents the expected future benefit of the computers and, as such, should be recorded as an asset. There is no way in which this remaining error can correct itself, except possibly when the company disposes of the asset. Until that time, the books will remain incorrectly stated.

PB–3

a. 1984 Depreciation expense* $22,500
12/31/84 Accumulated depreciation $22,500

1985 Depreciation expense* 22,500
12/31/85 Accumulated depreciation $45,000

1986 Depreciation expense* 22,500
12/31/86 Accumulated depreciation $67,500

1987 Depreciation expense* 22,500
12/31/87 Accumulated depreciation $ 90,000

1988 Depreciation expense* 22,500
12/31/88 Accumulated depreciation $112,500

---

* Depreciation expense = ($500,000 – $50,000 Salvage value) ÷ 20 years.

b. Depreciation expense = [(Cost – Accumulated depreciation) – Estimated salvage value]
÷ Estimated remaining useful life
= [$500,000 – ($112,500 from Part [a]) – $50,000] ÷ 5 years
= $67,500

c. Depreciation expense = [(Cost – Accumulated depreciation) – Estimated salvage value]
÷ Estimated remaining useful life
= {[$500,000 – ($112,500 from Part a + $67,500 from Part b)]
– $50,000} ÷ 4 years
= $67,500

d. If the revised estimated useful life had been known when the asset was acquired, it would have been depreciated using a useful life of ten years (i.e., beginning of 1984 to end of 1993) instead of twenty years.

1984 Depreciation expense* $45,000
12/31/84 Accumulated depreciation $45,000

1985 Depreciation expense* 45,000
12/31/85 Accumulated depreciation $90,000

1986 Depreciation expense* 45,000
12/31/86 Accumulated depreciation $135,000

1987 Depreciation expense* 45,000
12/31/87 Accumulated depreciation $180,000

1988 Depreciation expense* 45,000
12/31/88 Accumulated depreciation $225,000

---

* Depreciation expense = ($500,000 – $50,000 salvage value) ÷ 10 years.

If the estmate revision is treated as an error, the appropriate correcting entry to restate the books for the errors from 1984 through 1988 would be

Retained Earnings	112,500*	
Accumulated Depreciation		112,500
To correct books for a prior error.		

* $112,500 = $225,000 from above – $112,500 from Part (a)

e. The change in the estimated useful life of fixed assets should be considered a revision of an estimate. An estimate is not necessarily accurate and will be subject to revision as better information becomes available. In 1984 when the company acquired the fixed assets, it used all available information and decided that the useful life of the assets was twenty years. However, because of technological developments learned of in 1989, the company acquired better information and decided that the assets would now only provide future benefits for the next five years. Since the company used the best information available at the time of making both decisions, the change in the estimated useful life should be considered a revision of an estimate and not the correction of an error.

Since revisions of estimates are not considered errors, the books are considered to be correctly stated at the time of the revision. If the books are correctly stated, then there is no need to make a prior period adjustment. Hence, revisions will only affect future periods and should, therefore, be accounted for prospectively.

PB–4

a. **1987**

	As Reported	Corrections	Correctly Stated
Sales	$35,000	$ 0	$35,000
Less: Cost of goods sold	21,000	(3,000)	18,000
Gross profit	14,000	3,000	17,000
Less: Operating expenses	8,000	(1,500)	9,500
Net income	$ 6,000	$1,500	$ 7,500

1988

	As Reported	Corrections	Correctly Stated
Sales	$38,000	($4,000)	$34,000
Less: Cost of goods sold	25,000	3,000	28,000
Gross profit	13,000	(7,000)	6,000
Less: Operating expenses	10,000	1,500	10,000
		(1,500)	
Net income	$ 3,000	($7,000)	($4,000)

1989

	As Reported	Corrections	Correctly Stated
Sales	$46,000	$ 4,000	$50,000
Less: Cost of goods sold	30,000	(3,000)	27,000
Gross profit	16,000	7,000	23,000
Less: Operating expenses	12,000	1,500	10,500
Net income	$ 4,000	$ 8,500	$12,500

b.

Retained Earnings	8,500	
Cost of Goods Sold		3,000
Fees Earned		4,000
Interest Expense		1,500
To correct for prior period errors.		

APPENDIX C Accounting for Changing Prices: Inflation and Market Values

EC–1

a.

Cash	Monetary
Accounts Receivable	Monetary
Office Equipment	Nonmonetary
Accumulated Depreciation: Office Equipment	Nonmonetary
Bonds Payable	Monetary
Inventory	Nonmonetary
Accounts Payable	Monetary
Discount on Bonds Payable	Monetary
Long–Term Marketable Equity Securities	Nonmonetary
Building	Nonmonetary
Land	Nonmonetary
Mortgage Payable	Monetary
Wages Payable	Monetary

b. Monetary accounts are accounts whose balances represent a fixed amount of cash inflow (in the case of assets) or a fixed cash outflow (in the case of liabilities) regardless of changes in price levels. For example, a customer who purchases an item on account for $10,000 is obligated to remit $10,000 to the company regardless of changes in price levels. The accounts classified above as monetary accounts are all accounts whose balances represent such fixed cash flows. The accounts classified above as nonmonetary accounts are all accounts whose balances do not represent fixed cash flows.

EC–2

a. Under conventional accounting practices, the president's statement is correct. Conventional accounting practices use nominal dollars, which ignore the effects of inflation. From an economic viewpoint, however, the president's statement is incorrect. To determine whether the company's sales doubled in real dollars from 1986 to 1988 or tripled in real dollars from 1986 to 1990, the effect of inflation must be considered.

b. **1986 to 1988**

Step 1: Convert 1986 sales to 1988 dollar sales.
$20,000 x (360 ÷ 320) = $22,500

Step 2: Compute percentage change in sales.
($40,000 – $22,500) ÷ $22,500 = 77.78%

1986 to 1990

Step 1: Convert 1986 sales to 1990 dollar sales.
$20,000 x (400 ÷ 320) = $25,000

Step 2: Compute percentage change in sales.
($60,000 – $25,000) ÷ $25,000 = 140%

EC–3

1989

Net monetary assets as of January 1, 1989
= Cash + Accounts receivable + Notes receivable – Accounts payable – Notes payable
= \$7,000 + \$9,000 + \$4,000 – \$10,000 – \$6,000 = \$4,000

Net decrease in monetary assets during 1989
= Decrease in cash + Decrease in accounts receivable
= \$3,000 + \$2,000 = \$5,000

Net increase in monetary liabilities during 1989
= Increase in accounts payable + Increase in notes payable
= \$2,000 + \$1,000 = \$3,000

Item	Balance	Conversion Ratio	Adjusted Balance	Purchasing Power Gain/(Loss)
Net monetary assets	\$4,000	(360÷340)	\$4,235	(\$235)
Net decrease in monetary assets	5,000	(360÷350)	5,143	143
Net increase in monetary liabilities	3,000	(360÷350)	3,086	86
Net purchasing power loss				(\$ 6)

1990

Net monetary liabilities as of January 1, 1990
= Cash + Accounts receivable + Notes receivable – Accounts payable – Notes payable
= \$4,000 + \$7,000 + \$4,000 – \$12,000 – \$7,000 = \$4,000

Net increase in monetary assets during 1989
= Increase in cash + Increase in accounts receivable – Decrease in notes receivable
= \$1,000 + \$1,000 – \$1,000 = \$1,000

Net decrease in monetary liabilities during 1989
= Decrease in accounts payable + Decrease in notes payable
= \$9,000 + \$2,000 = 11,000

Item	Balance	Conversion Ratio	Adjusted Balance	Purchasing Power Gain/(Loss)
Net monetary liabilities	\$ 4,000	(380÷360)	\$ 4,222	\$222
Net increase in monetary assets	1,000	(380÷370)	1,027	(27)
Net decrease in monetary liabilities	11,000	(380÷370)	11,297	(297)
Net purchasing power loss				(\$102)

EC–4

a. **Gain on sale under GAAP**
Total sales price – Total cost of rings
= (10 rings x \$15,000 per ring) – (10 rings x \$5,000 per ring)
= \$100,000

Portion of gain due to inflation
(1) Constant value of rings on 12/31/90
= (10 rings x $5,000 per ring) x (500 ÷ 400)
= $62,500

(2) Increase in value of rings due to inflation
= 12/31/90 adjusted value of rings – Cost of rings
= $62,500 – $50,000
= $12,500

Portion of gain due to changes in supply and demand
Total gain – Portion of gain due to inflation
= $100,000 – $12,500
= $87,500

b. The final measure, portion of gain due to changes in supply and demand, represents the company's increase in wealth. During the year, the inflation rate was 25%. Therefore, the value of diamond rings would be expected to increase 25%, and the relative purchasing power of the rings at the beginning of the year would be identical to their purchasing power at the end of the year. Thus, the company would be in the same economic position at the beginning and at the end of the year. Due to the changes in supply and demand, however, the diamond rings increased in value by more than 25%. This increase in value indicates that the economic position of the company actually improved during the year.

EC–5

a.

	Conventional		Current Cost	
	Year 1	Year 2	Year 1	Year 2
Sales	$850	$850	$850	$850
COGS	(500)	(500)	(600)	(700)
Realized holding gain	0	0	100	50
Unrealized holding gain	0	0	150	0
Profit	$350	$350	$500	$200

b. Both accounting methods give rise to total net income over the two–year period of $700; however, each method recognizes different amounts of income in each year. The basic difference between generally accepted accounting principles and current-cost accounting is the recognition of realized and unrealized holding gains. Under current–cost accounting, Cost of Goods Sold reflects the replacement cost of the inventory on the date of sale while under GAAP, Cost of Goods Sold only reflects the cost of the inventory. Further, the carrying value of inventory at the end of the accounting period is adjusted to replacement cost under current–cost accounting. Therefore, current–cost accounting allows a company to report changes in wealth simply from holding an asset, while GAAP does not allow a company to report increases in wealth until the increase is realized.

EC–6

	Conventional Accounting	Current–Cost Accounting
Sales	$210,000	$210,000
Cost of goods sold	(70,000)	(105,000)
Realized holding gain	0	35,000[a]
Unrealized holding gain	0	10,000[b]
Profit	$140,000	$150,000

[a] $35,000 = Number of units sold x (Current cost – Historical cost)
= 35,000 units x ($3 – $2)

[b] $10,000 = Number of units in ending inventory x (Current cost – Historical cost)
= 5,000 units x ($4 – $2)

	Exit–Value Accounting
Expenses	$ 0
Holding gain	160,000*
Net income	$160,000

* $160,000 = Number of units purchased x (Selling price – Historical cost)
= 40,000 units x ($6 – $2)

EC–7

1988

	Conventional Accounting	Constant Dollar Accounting	Exit Value Accounting
Revenues from sale of land	$0	$0	N/A
Cost of land	0	0	N/A
Holding gain	0	0	$10,000
Income	$0	$0	$10,000

1989

	Conventional Accounting	Constant Dollar Accounting	Exit Value Accounting
Revenues from sale of land	$30,000	$30,000	N/A
Cost of land	(15,000)	(18,000)*	N/A
Holding gain	0	0	$ 5,000
Income	$15,000	$12,000	$ 5,000

* $18,000 = $15,000 cost of land x (480÷400)

EC–8

a.	
Sales	$172,500
Less: Cost of goods sold	36,000
Less: Depreciation expense	29,000
Net income	$107,500

b.

Sales	$172,500
Less: Cost of goods sold	90,000
Less: Depreciation expense	26,500
Realized holding gain: Inventory	54,000[a]
Unrealized holding gain: Inventory	6,000[b]
Less: Realized holding loss: Building	2,500[c]
Less: Unrealized holding loss: Building	22,500[d]
Net income	$ 91,000

[a] $54,000 = Number of units sold x (Replacement cost on date of sale – Historical cost)
= 4,500 units x ($20 – $8)
[b] $ 6,000 = Number of units in ending inventory x (Replacement cost on 12/31 – Historical cost)
= 500 units x ($20 – $8)
[c] $ 2,500 = (Cost – Replacement cost) ÷ Useful life
[d] $22,500 = (Replacement cost – Salvage value) – Realized holding loss
= ($275,000 – $300,000) – $2,500

c.

Sales	$172,500
Less: Cost of goods sold	22,500
Less: Depreciation expense	36,500
Less: Realized holding loss: Inventory	13,500[a]
Less: Unrealized holding loss: Inventory	1,500[b]
Realized holding gain: Building	7,500[c]
Unrealized holding gain: Building	67,500[d]
Net income	$173,500

[a] $13,500 = 4,500 units x ($5 – $8)
[b] $ 1,500 = 500 units x ($5 – $8)
[c] $ 7,500 = ($375,000 – $300,000) ÷ 10 years
[d] $67,500 = ($375,000 – $300,000) – $7,500

EC–9

a. $504,000

b. The value of holding the equipment equals the present value of the future cash flows, which equals $380,304 (i.e., $50,000 x 7.60608).

c. The value of selling and replacing the equipment equals the present value of the future cash flows from the new machine plus the net proceeds from selling the equipment. The total value is $425,678 (i.e., $50,000 x 8.51356) – $371,000 (i.e., $504,000 – $875,000), or $54,678.

d. The option with the highest value is selling the equipment.

PC–1

Account	a. Classification	b. Effect
Accounts payable	Monetary	Unchanged
Plant equipment	Nonmonetary	Increased
Accounts receivable	Monetary	Unchanged
Bonds payable	Monetary	Unchanged
Investment in bonds	Monetary	Unchanged
Inventory	Nonmonetary	Decreased

There are two reasons why these accounts are treated differently for inflation. First, some items are monetary items and some are nonmonetary items. Monetary items represent future cash flows which are unaffected by inflation. Therefore, the purchasing power of these future cash flows depends upon the inflation rate. Changes in purchasing power result in gains or losses. On the other hand, nonmonetary items do not represent future cash flows. Therefore, holding supply and demand of nonmonetary items constant, the purchasing power of nonmonetary items is constant over time, implying no purchasing power gains or losses.

Second, the assets are acquired and liabilities incurred at different points in time. Therefore, the change in inflation from the date the asset or liability was first recorded and the end of the current accounting period is different for each account. Some accounts experienced inflation, while other accounts experienced deflation.

c.

Account	**Magnitude**
Accounts payable	N/A
Plant equipment	[1,000 x (400 ÷ 312)] – 1,000 = 282
Accounts receivable	N/A
Bonds payable	N/A
Investment in bonds	N/A
Inventory	[1,000 x (400 ÷ 438)] – 1,000 = –87

PC–2

a. (1) Plant Equipment 200,000
Cash 200,000
To record acquisition of plant equipment.

(2) Office Furniture and Equipment 150,000
Cash 150,000
To record acquisition of office furniture and equipment.

(3) Inventory 250,000
Cash 250,000
To record purchase of inventory.

b. All the assets acquired are nonmonetary assets.

c.

Account	**Balance**	**Conversion Ratio**	**Adjusted Balance**
Plant equipment	$ 200,000	(390÷300)	$ 260,000
Office furniture & equipment	150,000	(390÷300)	195,000
Inventory	250,000	(390÷300)	325,000

d.

Account	**Balance**	**Conversion Ratio**	**Adjusted Balance**
Plant equipment	$ 200,000	(450÷500)	$ 180,000
Office furniture & equipment	150,000	(450÷500)	135,000
Inventory	250,000	(450÷500)	225,000

e. The income statement measures changes in a company's wealth. Under constant–dollar accounting, changes in wealth represent changes in purchasing power. If a company can now purchase a bigger basket of goods with its assets, it has an increase in purchasing power and, consequently, an increase in wealth. Alternatively, if a company can now only purchase a smaller basket of goods with its assets, it has a decrease in its purchasing power and, consequently, a decrease in wealth. The nominal value of nonmonetary items varies with inflation. If the supply of and demand for these items are held constant, inflation should explain the entire change in the nominal value of a nonmonetary item. Therefore, the real value of nonmonetary items is unaffected by inflation. A nonmonetary item can be used to purchase the same size basket of goods, regardless of the inflation rate. Since nonmonetary items do not give rise to changes in purchasing power, they do not give rise to changes in wealth.

PC–3

Elliot Book Company
Income Statement
For the year ended December 31, 1994

	Historical Cost	Conversion Ratio	Constant–Dollar Amount
Sales	$1,550,000.00	450÷425	$1,641,176.50
Less: Cost of goods sold*	965,000.00		1,071,029.40
Gross profit	585,000.00		570,147.10
Less: Expenses			
Depreciation expense	50,000.00	450÷400	56,250.00
Selling & administrative expenses	305,000.00	450÷425	322,941.18
Interest Expense	100,000.00	450÷425	105,882.35
Total Expenses	455,000.00		$ 85,073.57
Purchasing power gain			450.00
Net income	$ 130,000.00		$ 85,523.57

* Cost of goods sold:

Beginning inventory	$ 380,000.00	450÷400	427,500.00
Net purchases	995,000.00	450÷425	1,053,529.40
Less: Ending inventory	410,000.00	450÷450	410,000.00
Cost of goods sold	965,000.00		1,071,029.40

PC–4

a. **No change in Consumer Price Index**
Total gain = Sales price – Cost of land
= $750,000 – $500,000 = $250,000

Portion of gain due to inflation
Inflation–adjusted cost of land as of 12/31/90 – Cost of land
= [$500,000 x (340 ÷ 340)] – $500,000 = 0

Portion of gain due to change in exit value
Total gain – Portion of gain due to inflation
= $250,000 – $0 = $250,000

Consumer Price Index Increases from 340 to 425

Total gain = Sales price – Cost of land
= $750,000 – $500,000 = $250,000

Portion of gain due to inflation
Inflation–adjusted cost of land as of 12/31/90 – Cost of land
= [$500,000 x (425 ÷ 340)] – $500,000 = $125,000

Portion of gain due to change in exit value
Total gain – Portion of gain due to inflation
= $250,000 – $125,000 = $125,000

Consumer Price Index Increases from 340 to 595

Total gain = Sales price – Cost of land
= $750,000 – $500,000 = $250,000

Portion of gain due to inflation
Inflation–adjusted cost of land as of 12/31/90 – Cost of land
= [$500,000 x (595 ÷ 340)] – $500,000 = $375,000

Portion of gain due to change in exit value
Total gain – Portion of gain due to inflation
= $250,000 – $375,000 = ($125,000)

b. Conventional accounting ignores the effects of inflation. Since in the first case (no change in the Consumer Price Index) inflation is not a factor, the first case is the most similar to conventional accounting under GAAP.

c. Inflation does not affect the purchasing power of nonmonetary assets such as inventory and fixed assets. Holding everything else constant except inflation, a tract of land could be traded for the same amount of inventory at the end of the year as at the beginning of the year. Therefore, changes in these assets' values due to inflation do not change a company's wealth. On the other hand, changes in exit values due to changes in supply and demand do represent changes in a company's purchasing power. If the demand for a tract of land increases, the land could now be traded for more inventory than previously. Such changes in purchasing power represent changes in a company's wealth. Since financial statement users are interested in changes in a company's wealth, they would prefer to have the effects of inflation separated from the effects of shifts in supply and demand.

PC–5

a.

Asset	Value of Holding Asset	Value of Selling Asset	Value of Selling and Replacing
A	$32,000	$28,000	$30,000*
B	26,000	30,000	31,000*
C	21,000	23,000	22,000*

* The value of selling and replacing the asset equals the value of selling the asset less the cost of replacing the asset plus the present value of the future cash flows arising from the new asset.

Steve should select the option that yields the highest values. Based on the above analysis, holding Asset A, selling and replacing Asset B, and selling Asset C yields the highest values.

b. Historical cost represents sunk costs and sunk costs are not relevant for decision making purposes. Hence, doubling the dollar amount of historical cost will not alter the conclusions reached in Part (a).

PC–6

a. Depreciation is simply the allocation of a fixed asset's cost. Consequently, depreciation does not directly provide or use cash. However, depreciation can provide an indirect source of cash in at least two ways. First, depreciation expense is deductible for tax purposes. So depreciation expense reduces a company's tax liability, thereby reducing the cash outflow for taxes. Depreciation, therefore, "provides" cash through reduced taxes. Second, depreciation can affect cash through a company's dividend policy. If a company maintains a policy of paying dividends equal to some percentage of net income, any item that reduces net income will, in turn, reduce dividend payments. Since depreciation expense reduces net income, depreciation reduces the cash outflow from dividends. Depreciation, therefore, "provides" cash through reduced dividend payments.

In this particular case, the company has generated cash flows from operating activities and net income over the five–year period of $94,000 and $44,000, respectively. The difference of $50,000 represents the allocation of the fixed asset cost over its useful life. The cost of the new machine represents replacement cost. Therefore, the reason that the company does not have sufficient cash to purchase the new asset is that it used historical cost rather than replacement cost to depreciate the fixed asset.

b.

	1989	1988	1987	1986	1985
Cash income	$25,000	$20,000	$17,000	$17,000	$15,000
Less: Depreciation	15,000	14,000	13,000	12,000	11,000
Net income	$10,000	$ 6,000	$ 4,000	$5,000	$4,000
Beginning cash	$50,000	$36,000	$23,000	$ 11,000	$ 0
Cash income	25,000	20,000	17,000	17,000	15,000
Less: Dividends	10,000	6,000	4,000	5,000	4,000
Ending cash	$65,000	$50,000	$36,000	$23,000	$11,000

If Buckingham Enterprises used replacement cost to depreciate its fixed asset, it would have $65,000 in cash at the end of 1989 as opposed to $50,000. Therefore, using replacement cost would "save" the company $15,000 in cash.

c. As discussed in Part (a), depreciation does not directly provide or use cash, but it can provide an indirect source of cash. Using replacement cost (assuming increasing prices) results in higher depreciation expense. High depreciation expense, in turn, gives rise to lower net income. Lower net income implies lower cash outflows for taxes and may also imply lower cash outflows for dividends. Therefore, compared to using historical cost, using current cost may "save" a company some cash.

PC–7

a.

Revenues	$40,000 x	(330÷300)	$44,000
Less: Expenses	30,000 x	(330÷300)	33,000
Less: Purchasing power loss*			5,378
Constant dollar income			$5,622

---

* Purchasing power loss:

Net monetary assets: January 1

[($15,000 + $10,000 – $8,000) x (330 ÷ 270)] – ($15,000 + $10,000 – $8,000) = – $3,778

Increase in monetary assets during the year

{[($20,000 – $15,000) + ($15,000 – $10,000)] x (330 ÷ 300)} – [($20,000 – $15,000) + ($15,000 – $10,000)] = – 1,000

Decrease in monetary liabilities during the year

[($8,000 – $2,000) x (330 ÷ 300)] – ($8,000 – $2,000) = – 600

Purchasing power loss – $5,378

b. Amandie Villages is not using inflation to its advantage. The purchasing power of monetary assets decreases over time. Therefore, by holding large amounts of cash and receivables, the company is losing wealth. The economic value of debt decreases during inflationary periods. The money used to repay debt is worth less than its value when borrowed. By delaying the repayment of debt, a company can use "cheaper" dollars to settle its obligations. Since Amandie Villages repays its debts as soon as they arise, the company is using more valuable dollars to repay debt than it would otherwise have to use. The company would be better off delaying repaying its debts and investing its monetary assets in a nonmonetary asset, such as land, that maintains its economic value during inflationary periods. As for the company's dividend policy, the policy ignores the true wealth of the company. During the current year, the company paid out $9,000 in dividends. However, the company only increased its wealth by $5,622 after considering the effects of inflation.

PC–8

a. Under conventional accounting, Temple Industries has a balance in Retained Earnings of $28,000. If the company must maintain a balance in this account of at least $10,000, it can declare a dividend of $18,000.

b. If Retained Earnings is measured under constant–dollar accounting, then the account balance must reflect both current net income calculated under constant dollar accounting and the beginning account balance adjusted to end–of–year dollars. The net income calculated under conventional accounting equals the increase in the Retained Earnings balance during the year, or $13,000. Net income under conventional accounting would be adjusted to constant–dollar accounting as follows:

Conventional net income:		
$13,000 x (425 ÷ 400)	=	$13,812
Purchasing power gain(Loss):		
Net monetary assets on January 1		
[($20,000 – $15,000) x (425 ÷ 375)] – ($20,000 – $15,000)	=	– 667
Increase in monetary assets during the year		
[$5,000 x (425 ÷ 400)] – $5,000	=	– 313
Decrease in monetary liabilities during the year		
[$10,000 x (425 ÷ 400)] – $10,000	=	– 625
Constant dollar net income		$12,208

The adjustment of the beginning balance to end–of–year dollars would be
$15,000 x (425 ÷ 375) = $17,000

Therefore, the ending balance in Retained Earnings under constant–dollar accounting would be $12,208 plus $17,000, or $29,208. To maintain a minimum account balance of $10,000, the maximum dividend that Temple could declare is $19,208.

c. Creditors demand debt covenants to limit a borrower's operating, investing, and financing actions, thereby increasing the probability that the borrower will have sufficient cash or other assets available to make interest and principal payments. Debt covenants often specify a maximum debt/equity ratio, a minimum current ratio, or a minimum Retained Earnings balance. Under conventional accounting, the effects of inflation are ignored, while constant–dollar accounting adjusts the financial statements for the effects of inflation. Since debt is usually a monetary item, total debt would not change during inflationary periods. On the other hand, the components of stockholders' equity are nonmonetary items. These items would increase during inflationary periods. Therefore, during inflationary periods, constant–dollar accounting, compared to conventional accounting practice, would tend to understate the debt/equity ratio and overstate Retained Earnings. The borrower would, therefore, have more freedom in making decisions and taking actions than under conventional accounting practice, the very thing the creditor was trying to avoid by requiring a debt covenant. Borrowers would, therefore, prefer that debt covenants be written in terms of constant–dollar accounting rather than in terms of conventional accounting.

The primary problem with using constant–dollar accounting is determining the appropriate inflation rate. Selecting an inflation rate is quite subjective,which decreases the objectiveness of the financial statements. Further, constant–dollar accounting allows companies to recognize gains simply from holding monetary assets or liabilities. Recognizing these gains violates conservatism.